Europe Contested

CH00922465

Europe Contested analyses the failures and achievements of an astonishing era of economic advance and political chaos, from the First World War up to the present day.

Beginning with the Great War, the book goes on to examine connections between the self-destruction of liberal democracy, market economics, and the international political and security framework in the interwar period. It then considers the mass politics that surrounded the glorification of new-style leaders Lenin, Stalin, Mussolini, and Hitler before moving on to explore the ways in which the interwar legacy was superseded post-1945. James examines the deceptive appearance of stability brought by a new convergence in European politics that focused around the market and the principle of liberal democracy, and demonstrates how the impact of globalization and openness to migration and to destabilizing financial capital flows has eroded traditional politics and ended the stable left–right polarization at the core of the postwar order. This new edition has been thoroughly updated throughout, demonstrating also how an era of crisis is challenging Europe and its values.

Supported by boxed case studies, illustrations, chronologies, and an annotated bibliography, and focusing on Europe as a whole, it is the perfect introduction for students of Modern European History.

Harold James is the Claude and Lore Kelly Professor in European Studies at Princeton University, USA. His books include *The German Slump* (1986), *The End of Globalization* (2001), and *Making the European Monetary Union* (2012).

Longman History of Modern Europe

In this series:

Europe 1850–1914
Progress, Participation and Apprehension
Jonathan Sperber

Revolutionary Europe 1780–1850
Jonathan Sperber

Europe Contested
From the Kaiser to Brexit
Harold James

For more information about this series, please visit: www.routledge.com/
Longman-History-of-Modern-Europe/book-series/PEAMODE.

Europe Contested

From the Kaiser to Brexit
2nd edition

Harold James

Routledge
Taylor & Francis Group

LONDON AND NEW YORK

Second edition published 2020
by Routledge
2 Park Square, Milton Park, Abingdon, Oxon, OX14 4RN

and by Routledge
52 Vanderbilt Avenue, New York, NY 10017

Routledge is an imprint of the Taylor & Francis Group, an informa business

© 2020 Harold James

First edition published by Pearson Education Limited 2003
Second edition published by Routledge 2020

British Library Cataloguing-in-Publication Data
A catalogue record for this book is available from the British Library

Library of Congress Cataloging-in-Publication Data
Names: James, Harold, 1956- author.
Title: Europe contested : from the kaiser to Brexit / Harold James.
    Other titles: Europe reborn
Description: Second edition. | London ; New York, NY : Routledge/
    Taylor & Francis Group, 2020. | Revised edition of: Europe reborn :
    a history, 1914-2000. | Includes bibliographical references and index.
Identifiers: LCCN 2019022922 (print) | LCCN 2019022923 (ebook)
    | ISBN 9781138303065 (hardback) | ISBN 9781138303072
    (paperback) | ISBN 9780429340680 (ebook)
Subjects: LCSH: Europe—History—20th century. | Europe—
    History—21st century.
Classification: LCC D424 .J27 2020 (print) | LCC D424 (ebook) |
    DDC 940.5—dc23
LC record available at https://lccn.loc.gov/2019022922
LC ebook record available at https://lccn.loc.gov/2019022923

ISBN: 978-1-138-30306-5 (hbk)
ISBN: 978-1-138-30307-2 (pbk)
ISBN: 978-0-429-34068-0 (ebk)

Typeset in Sabon
by Swales & Willis Ltd, Exeter, Devon, UK

Contents

Acknowledgments

I should like to thank the following for helping me with individual points of information, for reading parts of the manuscript, and for helpful suggestions: Michael Bordo, Cynthia Hooper, Molly Greene, Stephen Kotkin, and Arno Mayer. David Childs, Marzenna James, Philip Nord, Hamish Scott, and Richard Vinen gave insightful comments on the whole manuscript. Heather McCallum at Longmans was an inspiring and helpful editor. Judy Hanson of the Princeton History Department helped me enormously by organizing time and assistance, and Alicia Pittard did a wonderful job in researching individual questions and organizing biographical and chronological information. The usual caveat applies: none of my friends is responsible for remaining errors of fact or for problematical arguments.

The process of thinking about history is accompanied by numerous, indeed endless, discussions. I should like to record my gratitude to an exceptional and inspirational group of teachers in the Cambridge of the 1970s, who helped to shape my view of Europe: John Tanfield of the Perse School, and Christopher Andrew, the Rev. Owen Chadwick, the Rev. Dermot Fenlon, Neil McKendrick, Edward Shils, Jonathan Steinberg, and Norman Stone of Cambridge University. When I came to Princeton in the 1980s, Cyril Black and Arno Mayer were giving lucid and innovative accounts of Europe's twentieth century.

I would also like to thank friends and colleagues with whom I have discussed European affairs in a number of institutions at which I have stayed as a guest or worked over the past fifteen years: Claudio Borio, Piet Clement, and Hyun Song Shin, at the Bank for International Settlements; Hans Werner Sinn and Clemens Fuest at CES-ifo Munich and at the European Economic Advisory Group; Melanie Aspey, Hugo Bänziger, Catherine Schenk, Niels Viggo Haueter, at the European Association of Banking and Financial History; Sebastian Conrad, Giancarlo Corsetti, Giovanni Federico, Tony Molho, Emanuel Mourlon-Druol, Kiran Klaus Patel, and Bartolomé Yun Casalilla, at the European University Institute, Fiesole; Tam Bayoumi, Rex Ghosh, Martin Muhleisen, and Siddharth Tiwari, at the International Monetary Fund; Knut Sogner at the Oslo Business School (BI); Bridget Kendall and Brendan Simms at Peterhouse,

Cambridge; and Stephen Szabo of the Transatlantic Academy of the German Marshall Fund.

The book is dedicated to Marzenna James, to whom I am lucky enough to be married, and to Maximilian, Marie Louise, and Montagu James.

Harold James, Princeton University, September 2019

Illustrations

Plates

Figures

Tables

Boxes

Map

Habsburg empire

0   200 miles

Petsamo

Murmansk

Archangel

ATLANTIC OCEAN

FINLAND

NORWAY

SWEDEN

Viborg

Lake Ladoga

Aaland Islands

Helsinki

KARELIAN ISTHMUS

Petrograd

Christiania

Tallinn

ESTONIA

Stockholm

BALTIC SEA

Riga

LATVIA

DENMARK

Copenhagen

Memel

LITHUANIA

S O V I E T

U N I O N

Kiel Canal

EAST PRUSSIA

Danzig (Free City)

Kaunas

Vilna

Minsk

Bremen

Berlin

Warsaw

P O L A N D

Curzon Line

Brest-Litovsk

Kiev

Russian Frontier 1914

GERMANY

Prague

GALICIA

CZECHOSLOVAKIA

Bessarabia

Munich

Vienna

Budapest

AUSTRIA

HUNGARY

TRANSYLVANIA

R U M A N I A

Trieste

Fiume

YUGOSLAVIA

Bucharest

ITALY

Belgrade

Danube R

BLACK SEA

ADRIATIC SEA

Sofia

BULGARIA

Rome

ALB.

Europe in 1919.

Introduction

I was especially pleased when the editors of this series asked me to write this volume, as the first book written by a practicing historian I ever bought was that of John Roberts, *Europe 1880–1945*, published in 1967, which previously closed the Longman series on the history of Europe. Roberts began his book by remarking that "One big difference between ourselves and our predecessors centuries ago, is our acceptance of historical change" (p. 1). One of the reasons that I found writing this book to be a novel challenge is that this proposition is no longer self-evident. We are certainly as aware of change as the generation writing in 1967 was, but we are much more worried about it. We are painfully aware of the cost of change, but also of the cost of refusing to change. We are skeptical of simple ideologies of progress, which are now frequently cast off as outdated, or even demonized as "the Enlightenment master narrative". Anti-modern ideologies have fared even worse. The result of disenchantment with linear versions of history (either progressive betterment, or alternatively deterioration from a golden age) has led many intellectuals and academics to adopt a potpourri of disconnected snippets that subvert any coherent picture and call it postmodernism. Some recent attempts at an overall history of Europe, such as the illuminating book by Richard Vinen, *A History in Fragments* (2000), aim deliberately at showing that modernity produces division and fractionalization, and that there is no coherent master narrative. Mark Mazower's brilliant *Dark Continent: Europe's Twentieth Century* (1998) puts a needed spotlight on the underside of European existence.

This final volume in a series is also different from that of Roberts, who was aware that his dates were – just about – the last in which it made any sense to speak of "European history". He pointed out that after 1945 (in other words for the bulk of the chronological span of this book) "the decisions taken in Washington and Tokyo were as important as those taken in London, Moscow or Berlin (soon the decisions taken in Peking would be important too)" (p. 2). He may have been wrong about the date – 1941 seems a better time to choose for this shift than 1945 – but of course quite right about the impossibility of a European history of the last three-fifths of the twentieth century. It only makes sense to speak about a European history in a global context, in which European events are to a considerable extent shaped by big developments that operate largely outside the European continent, in particular the unfolding of "the American century", decolonization, and globalization.

These forces shape this book, which starts with the destructive trauma of the First World War, which brutalized politics, transformed society, and brought the United States into European politics. The aftermath of war included a twin crisis of democracy and global capitalism. The twentieth century, and the book, end not only with the almost complete ascendancy of democracy and capitalism (certainly in Europe), but also at the same time with a disenchantment about that ascendancy that makes many people actually long for a new crisis of global capitalism. The book begins with war and then a major and prolonged stock exchange crash, and a general economic crisis. It ends at a time when a new slump in stock prices (the greatest since the Great Depression) raised questions about the stability of the populist share-owning democracy that had been the outcome of a long period of global cultural, political, and economic integration; and when resort to military force became once more a part of global politics.

In the Great Depression, parliamentarism, democratic politics, and market economics looked old-fashioned and discredited. The modern ideas were those of communism, for in the Soviet Union the years of the depression were exactly the moment of a breakthrough in industrial performance and of an apparently unprecedented triumph of theory over reality; and of fascism, or its German variant of National Socialism, which also looked on society as requiring large collectivist organization.

In 1945 the fascist alternative to market society and democracy was completely defeated. It had argued its cause as that of historical necessity and of the right of the stronger. As a consequence, an unambiguous and overwhelming military defeat was enough to destroy the ideology that was at its core. The claims of communism remained attractive for much longer. But by the 1970s and 1980s it was clear that the communist claim to produce a more modern and efficient as well as a more just society through the application of scientific planning was seriously flawed. In communist societies, opportunists replaced true believers. The final collapse between 1989 (in central Europe) and 1991 (when the Union of Soviet Socialist Republics, which had always been both the standard bearer and the enforcer of the international movement, collapsed) came as a surprise to many observers. They were perhaps theoretically right in the sense that regimes founded on opportunism and pragmatism can last quite long. But they were obviously wrong about the practice of communism and its dependence on a particular ideology.

In a new century, the twenty-first, it is possible to take a different perspective. This book proposes a twenty-first-century view of the past century. The fundamental development that shaped the end of the century had actually been long developing: an international society, in which international law began to shape the interactions of states, and in which individual human rights played an increasingly important role. Such a vision was part of the post-Second World War peace settlement. The emphasis on human rights (in particular in the United Nations Universal Declaration on Human Rights) was a dramatic contrast with the world after the First World War, in which the international regime (the League of Nations) had regarded itself as the protector of a set of collective rights: of states, but also of defined minorities.

Something happened toward the end of the century to make this agenda more relevant. In particular, four completely unrelated and independent events over a quite brief span of time in 1978–79 fundamentally changed world politics. In October 1978, the Archbishop of Krakow, Karol Wojtyła, was elected as Pope John Paul II. On January 16, 1979, the Shah of Iran fled his country in the face of opposition from radical Islamicists. On May 3, 1979, a British general election produced a victory for the Conservative Party led by Margaret Thatcher, who took the election as a mandate to reverse a tradition of consensus politics based on Keynesian economic management. On October 6, 1979, the new Chairman of the Federal Reserve Board, Paul Volcker, instituted a tight money policy designed quickly to squeeze inflation out of the US economy.

No amount of historical interpretation will ever reduce these – or for that matter most other – events to a simple "meaning". But together, they changed the kind of issues that had previously lain at the center of politics: for the previous period, most conflicts had been about redistribution by states. How could government action promote greater welfare or justice? A political left wanted to redistribute wealth and income, and a political right resisted. These clashes were resolved through the use of domestic fiscal and monetary policy, in the seemingly magic formula of Keynesianism (there are many "isms" in the twentieth century: they are explained briefly in boxes in the text). In a globalized world after the 1970s, these domestic solutions did not work satisfactorily any longer. As a result, the level of debate shifted either to a more profound level, or to a more trivial one. The new conflicts were much harder to put on a simple left–right spectrum. They were conflicts about the moral and religious meaning of political action.

By contrast, the previous history of Europe since at least the French Revolution had revolved around the story of states and their actions, in a realm disconnected from moral judgment and discussion. States functioned in order to advance the interests of their citizens, or of powerful classes or groups of citizens. They conducted a realist foreign policy, based on perceptions and calculations about national interest. This view of what states did and why they existed reached a preliminary ascendancy with the triumph of Bismarck and his defense of realpolitik. But the role of statism and a state-centered view was initially strengthened by the great European wars of the twentieth century, before reflection on the experience and legacy of those wars worked to gradually undermine and subvert it.

When John Roberts was writing in the 1960s, historians largely felt uncomfortable about morality and the application of moral judgment to history. They saw themselves much more as technical analysts of important or knotty "problems". Publishers devoted their attention to "themes" and "issues" such as the standard of living during the Industrial Revolution, or the motivation behind imperialism, or the relationship of capitalism and fascism. The historians applied social science in a way that they claimed to be objective and indifferent. They rejected, above all, the view that history was an appropriate subject for moral verdicts, which they regarded as a hopelessly outdated view preached by figures of ridicule such as Lord Acton or G.M. Trevelyan. As political conflicts began to deal more and more with moral choices and less and less with the technical application of income and wealth redistribution, the older view, however, came back. By the 1990s it was no longer unfashionable to see some virtue in a statement such as: "It is a duty of a historian to display a bias for the moral law, impartially applied."[1]

One sign of the new shift was the outbreaks of new "debates", no longer about themes but about moral responsibility: such as the German discussion about responsibility for the Holocaust, the so-called "historians' debate" (*Historikerstreit*) of 1986, about the Vatican in the Second World War, or later about the crimes of communism as depicted in Stéphane Courtois's *Black Book of Communism*, originally published in France in 1997.[2] Many practicing historians felt very uncomfortable about these new issues, which they felt somehow did not belong in the professionalized domain of academic history. Others, however, detected a new shift in what mattered in history.

In an analogous way, much of twentieth-century discussion of international relations was shaped by "realism", a doctrine according to which inter-state relations were a process akin to physics shaped by the interaction of masses of "power" or "force" in the form of states. As set out by Hans Morgenthau or E.H. Carr, realism was also a way of discovering structures lying beneath the moral rhetoric of both sides in the Cold War, and uncovering a different, eternal, reality that was susceptible to scientific analysis. But this doctrine found it hard to explain the end of the Cold War, since masses of power do not simply give up. And the new forms of post-Cold War politics were largely alien to realists.

The shift of the world in the early 1980s, then, also coincided with alterations in the way in which the world was understood. Before, domestic politics was about the distribution and management of resources, and the clashes that arose over income and wealth in the setting of a clearly defined geographical entity, the nation-state. Before, international politics was about the interactions and conflicts of units of power. After, the scope for domestic redistribution was reduced and domestic politics looked more easily understood in terms of the manipulation of meaning. After, morality, and international instruments devised to enforce it, came back to the international stage.

As a result, the history of the last 70 years is a story, not only of the recreation of an international society, culture, and economy ("globalization"), but also of the rise and fall of ways of looking at historical processes: the waning of class-based sociological analysis, and the fading of realism.

I have tried to be even in the coverage of Europe, as traditionally conceived, from Ireland to the Urals, including Turkey, while excluding North Africa and the Middle East, although there is much to be said for a treatment that makes the Mediterranean a center of European life and of political and social innovation. Some countries at some point get an attention which some readers will feel to be excessive; but some specific situations embody (and are seen to embody) much more general issues. Hegel liked the idea of a world spirit that resided in a particular place for a time, before taking wing. Spain in the 1930s was in this way a focus of the European debate; so was Berlin between 1945 and 1968, Poland in the 1980s, and Bosnia in the 1990s. Auschwitz from 1940 to January 1945 was a center of death and destruction, and of the Nazi project to destroy the Jews in Europe; the still living in the camps built a peculiar, multilingual tower of Babel, a dark and deformed version of European integration. Auschwitz subsequently became a contested site of memory in which Jewish and Polish claims clashed. As for the other sites of the European experience, having passed their moment of fame – the Polish reformer of 1989 Leszek Balcerowicz spoke of a half hour of history – they reverted to normalcy if not necessarily stability. The task of a book like this clearly involves an attempt to follow the world spirit, and to pin down its wings for a moment of analysis.

History and historical writing can never be definitive, and of course this is especially true in the case of contemporary history. A volume that is revised and reprinted needs to be adjusted, and not just because there have in the meantime been more events, in other words more material for writing history. There inevitably will be differences of tone and mood. The pentimenti of the author will reflect the development of the surrounding world, and its worries and fears as well as its hopes and dreams. An important book that is in a sense a predecessor of this volume, the *History of Europe in the Nineteenth Century* (later *History of Europe in the Nineteenth and Twentieth Centuries*) by Arthur James Grant and Harold Temperley, the Master of Peterhouse, Cambridge, and published by Longman (which became part of Pearson and then of Taylor & Francis), first appeared in 1927. A final section examined international order through a point-by-point comparison of the Congress system after 1815 and the League of Nations, showing how in each point the Congress was doomed to fail, and that the League constituted a substantial improvement. The League

> is the natural development of strong tendencies that had been visible during the last century of European history. [. . .] As we balance hope against fears we may derive comfort from the study of history which shows that some such organisation as is given by the League is at once necessary, reasonable, and possible.

(pp. 557–8)

The 1939 edition understandably left out this section, but tried to look beyond the catastrophes of the present to a future that might hold up more hope: "It is most probable that the democratic governments, either of the Old or of the New World, will acquiesce ultimately in an international system from which law and morality are absent" (p. 686). When the volume was revised again in 1952, after the Second World War (and the death of Temperley) the new conclusion had the same point-by-point comparison, but this time contrasting the weakness of the League and the superiority of the United Nations ("an attempt was made to avoid the errors inherent in the constitution of the League"). After the experience of the recent past, understandably, "the hopes for the United Nations were more restrained and less optimistic" (pp. 584–5).

Revising a book that first appeared in 2003 raises a similar – but perhaps fortunately less dramatic – set of issues. The 2003 volume ended with the twentieth century, and thought of ways that European destinies were converging. The financial crisis that erupted after 2007 drove Europeans apart again, and the present volume is notably more pessimistic than its predecessor. The chapters which became more enthusiastic about Europe's great postwar stabilization turn into gloomier reflections. Nightmares come in place of dreams. Many ghosts from the European past are returning. There is here no boasting of the inherent superiority of European institutions, no great confidence in the ability of the nation-state to handle general and global issues such as industrial transformation, demographic developments, or climate change. There is still a hope that Europeans may find collective solutions, that international organization is necessary, reasonable, and possible, but the optimism must be tempered by a considerable amount of skepticism. In that sense, concluding this book in 2019, on the anniversary of the Paris Peace Conference and the Versailles Treaty, and in the world overshadowed by Trump, Xi Jinping, Putin, and Brexit, I can only echo the words of Grant and Temperley in 1939 and hope that the peoples of Europe and the world will not acquiesce ultimately in an international system from which law and morality are absent.

Notes

1 David Cannadine, *G.M. Trevelyan: A Life in History*, New York: Norton, 1993, p. 199.
2 Stéphane Courtois (ed.) (transl. Jonathan Murphy and Mark Kramer), *The Black Book of Communism: Crimes, Terror, Repression*, Cambridge, MA: Harvard University Press, 1999.

Chronology

1914

June 28: assassination of Archduke Franz Ferdinand in Sarajevo

July 23: Austrian ultimatum to Serbia

July 28: Austrian declaration of war on Serbia

August 1: German declaration of war on Russia

August 3: German declaration of war on France

August 4: German invasion of Belgium and British declaration of war on Germany

August 26–28: battle of Tannenberg

September 6–10: battle of the Marne

October 14: first battle of Ypres begins

1915

Friedrich Naumann, *Central Europe*

April: Turkish deportations and genocide of Armenians begins

April 23: Treaty of London (secret) between France, the United Kingdom, and Italy

May 23: Italy declares war on Austria–Hungary

1916

V.I. Lenin, *Imperialism: The Highest Stage of Capitalism*

February 21: German offensive against Verdun begins

April 24: Easter Sunday uprising in Dublin

May 9: Sykes–Picot (secret) agreement on dismemberment of Ottoman Empire

June 1: Russian attack in Galicia (Brusilov offensive)

July 1: British offensive on the Somme

August 27: Romania declares war on Austria–Hungary

1917

February 1: Germany begins unrestricted submarine warfare

March 14: formation of Provisional Government in Russia under Prince Lvov

March 15: abdication of Tsar Nicholas II

April 6: United States declares war on Germany

April 16: Lenin returns to Russia

July 19: German Reichstag votes Peace Resolution

July 20: Kerensky Prime Minister of Russia

November 6: Bolshevik seizure of public buildings in Petrograd

November 8: Russian People's Council of Commissars established (October revolution)

November 16: Georges Clemenceau Prime Minister of France

December 20: establishment of Cheka (Russian secret police)

1918

January 8: Woodrow Wilson presents the Fourteen Points

March 3: Treaty of Brest-Litovsk between Germany and Russia signed

March 21: "Ludendorff offensive" on Western Front

July 16: murder of Tsar Nicholas II and his family

August 8: "black day" of German army

August 27: Auxiliary Treaty of Brest-Litovsk

September 29: Bulgaria concludes armistice

October 4: abdication of King Ferdinand of Bulgaria

October 30: Turkey concludes armistice

November 3: Austria–Hungary conclude armistice

November 9: proclamation of German Republic and abdication of Kaiser Wilhelm II; Stinnes–Legien pact between employers and unions in Germany

November 11: Germany concludes armistice

December 14: British ("khaki" or "coupon") general election

1919

John Maynard Keynes, *The Economic Consequences of the Peace*

January 18: opening of Paris Peace Conference

January 19: elections to German Constituent Assembly

March 2: formation of Third (Communist) International

March 22: Bela Kun's revolution in Hungary

April 24: Italian Prime Minister Orlando leaves Paris conference

June 28: signature of Treaty of Versailles (Germany)

September 10: signature of Treaty of Saint-Germain (Austria)

November 27: signature of Treaty of Neuilly (Bulgaria)

1920

January 10: beginning of League of Nations

March 13–17: Kapp putsch

June 4: Treaty of Trianon signed (Hungary)

July 11: British proposal of Curzon line as eastern frontier of Poland

July 19 to August 7: Second Conference of Communist International; establishes Twenty-One Conditions August 6

August 10: Treaty of Sèvres signed (Turkey)

December 23: Government of Ireland Act

1921

Jaroslav Hašek, *The Good Soldier Švejk*

April 15: failure of British miners' strike

April 27: Reparation Commission fixes German reparations at 132 billion gold marks

May 15: Italian elections: first significant breakthrough of Mussolini's fascist party

August 26: assassination of German politician Matthias Erzberger

December 6: treaty establishes Irish Free State

1922

Oswald Spengler, *The Decline of the West*

April 16: Germany and Russia conclude Treaty of Rapallo, establishing diplomatic representation and renouncing financial claims

June 24: assassination of Walther Rathenau

September 22: Turkish troops capture Smyrna

October 30: Mussolini Prime Minister of Italy

1923

January 11: Belgian and French troops occupy Ruhr

June 14: Bulgarian leader Alexander Stamboliski killed

July 24: Treaty of Lausanne signed, establishing borders of Turkey

September 13: General Primo de Rivera seizes power (Spain)

September 26: abandonment of passive resistance in Ruhr

November 8–9: Ludendorff and Hitler's "beer hall putsch" in Munich

November: stabilization of German currency after hyper-inflation

December 6: UK general election and formation of first Labour government under Ramsay MacDonald

1924

Thomas Mann, *The Magic Mountain*

January 21: death of Lenin

April 6: election in Italy with single government list dominated by fascists

April 9: presentation of Dawes reparations plan

May 11: election victory of *cartel des gauches* in France

June 10: assassination of Italian socialist leader Matteotti

October 29: UK general election and formation of Baldwin government

1925

Adolf Hitler, *Mein Kampf* (My Struggle)

April 26: Von Hindenburg elected President of Germany

May 5: The United Kingdom returns to gold standard at the rate of $4.86 to the pound

October 2: Pact of Palazzo Vidoni (labor and employers) in Italy

October 5–16: Conference of Locarno: Germany accepts western frontier

1926

May 3–12: General Strike in UK

May 12–14: coup of General Piłsudski (Poland)

July 23: formation of Poincaré government in France

September 8: Germany admitted to League of Nations

1928

August 27: Pact of Paris signed (Briand–Kellogg Pact to abolish war as an instrument of policy)

1929

Erich Maria Remarque, *All Quiet on the Western Front*

February 11: Lateran Accords of Italy and Vatican

April 25: launch of first Soviet Five-Year Plan at Sixteenth Party Congress

June 7: presentation of Young reparations plan

October 3: death of Stresemann

October 24: New York stock market crash ("Black Thursday")

December 22: referendum on Young Plan in Germany

1930

Sigmund Freud, *Civilization and its Discontents*

José Ortega y Gasset, *The Revolt of the Masses*

March 2: Stalin's "dizzy with success" speech calls temporary halt to collectivization and dekulakization

June 17: US Congress approves Smoot–Hawley Tariff Act

June 30: Belgian and French troops leave Rhineland

August 17: Pact of San Sebastian (Spain) leads to Alfonso XIII's abdication and democratization

September 14: German elections, with large Nazi vote

1931

May 11: failure of Austrian Creditanstalt

June 20: Hoover moratorium of one year on reparation and war debt payments announced

July 13: failure of German Danat Bank

September 18: Mukden incident and beginning of Japanese occupation of Manchuria

September 20: United Kingdom abandons gold standard

October 27: UK general election returns "National Government" under MacDonald

1932

Charles de Gaulle, *The Edge of the Sword*

March 10: de Valera becomes President of Executive Council in Ireland

May 30: Brüning resigns as German Chancellor and is replaced by von Papen

June 16 to July 9: reparations conference in Lausanne, Switzerland

July 21 to August 21: Ottawa Imperial Conference establishes preferential tariffs in British Empire

October 4: Gyula Gömbös forms government in Hungary

December 2: Von Schleicher becomes German Chancellor

1933

January 30: Hitler becomes German Chancellor

February 27: Reichstag fire

March 5: Reichstag elections

March 23: Enabling Act in Germany

April 20: United States abandons gold standard parity

June 12 to July 27: World Economic Conference in London

1934

January 26: German–Polish Non-Aggression Treaty

February 6: demonstrations by fascist leagues in Paris

February 1–16: civil war in Vienna, and suppression of socialists

June 30: Nazi purge ("Night of the Long Knives")

July 25: assassination of Austrian Chancellor Dollfuss by Austrian Nazis

October 9: assassination of King Alexander of Yugoslavia and French Foreign Minister Barthou, followed by regency of Prince Paul

December 1: assassination of Kirov

1935

Beatrice and Sidney Webb, *The Soviet Union: A New Civilisation?*

January 5: Laval agrees to cession of Abyssinia to Italy

January 13: plebiscite in Saar

March 16: introduction of universal military service in Germany in breach of Versailles treaty

April 11–14: Stresa Conference of France, the UK, and Italy

May 2: Franco-Soviet Pact signed

May 12: death of Marshal Piłsudski

September 15: Nuremberg racial laws in Germany

October 11: League of Nations imposes sanctions on Italy

1936

John Maynard Keynes, *The General Theory of Employment, Interest and Money*

February 16: elections in Spain with victory of Popular Front and formation of Quiroga government

March 7: Germany sends troops into Rhineland

May 3: Popular Front elections in France

July 17: Spanish Civil War begins with army revolt in Morocco

August 5: proclamation of martial law in Greece and establishment of dictatorship of General Metaxas

September 26: dismissal of Yagoda and replacement by Ezhov as Soviet secret police chief; beginning of large-scale purges

October 1: devaluation of French franc

October 6: death of Gömbös

December 11: abdication of King Edward VIII of the United Kingdom after constitutional crisis

1937

November 6: Italy joins German–Japanese "Anti-Comintern Pact"

1938

History of the Communist Party of the Soviet Union (Bolsheviks), A Short Course

March 12–13: Germany seizes Austria (*Anschluss*)

April 26: German law requires registration of Jewish property

September 29: the UK, France, Germany, and Italy conclude Munich agreement on Czechoslovakia

November 9–11: anti-Semitic pogroms in Germany

November 12: decree excludes German Jews from economic life

1939

March 15: Germany invades Czechoslovakia

March 28: surrender of Madrid (end of Spanish Civil War)

May 3: Molotov replaces Litvinov as Soviet Foreign Minister

August 23: Nazi–Soviet Non-Aggression Pact

September 1: Germany invades Poland

September 3: France and the United Kingdom declare war on Germany

September 17: Soviet attack on Poland

September 21: Heydrich orders annexed areas of Poland to be "made free of Jews"

November 30: Soviet attack on Finland

December 14: Soviet Union expelled from League of Nations

1940

April 9: Germany invades Denmark and Norway

May 10: Germany invades Belgium, Luxembourg, the Netherlands; Churchill becomes UK Prime Minister

June 10: Italy declares war on France and the United Kingdom with effect on June 11

June 14: German troops enter Paris

June 17: Pétain asks for armistice

June 18: de Gaulle's first radio appeal from London for "Free France"

June 22: France signs armistice with Germany and Italy

July 10: new French constitutional law establishes *État français*

September 3: British–American agreement on destroyers

October 14: meeting of Pétain and Hitler at Montoire, France

October 23: meeting of Franco with Hitler at Hendaye, France

October 28: Italy invades Greece

1941

January 6: Roosevelt's Four Freedoms speech

March 25–27: coup against pro-German Regent in Yugoslavia

April 6: Germany invades Yugoslavia and Greece

June 22: German Operation Barbarossa: invasion of Soviet Union

July 3: radio address of Stalin

August 14: Anglo-American Atlantic Charter

September 6: German Jews forced to wear yellow star

October 14–16: beginning of systematic deportation of German Jews to eastern camps

December 3: Führer decree orders rationalization of German armaments production

December 7: Japanese attack on Pearl Harbor, Hawaii

December 11: Germany and Italy declare war on United States

December 13: Bulgaria declares war on United States

1942

Social Insurance and Allied Services (Beveridge Report)

January 18: military agreement between Germany, Italy, and Japan signed in Berlin

January 20: Wannsee Conference on planning details of murder of European Jews

July 1: German advance in North Africa halted at El Alamein

August 24: First Quebec Conference (Churchill and Roosevelt)

November 8: US soldiers in North Africa

November 11: Germany takes over unoccupied France

December 17: Allied joint declaration on German extermination of Jews

1943

Jean-Paul Sartre, *Being and Nothingness*

January 24: policy of unconditional surrender declared by Allies at Casablanca

February 2: German troops surrender at Stalingrad

July 10: Allied invasion of Sicily

July 25: Marshal Badoglio replaces Mussolini as head of Italian government

September 8: announcement of Italian armistice

September 10: German troops occupy Rome

September 15: German paratroopers rescue Mussolini

October 9: Churchill visits Moscow and concludes percentages agreement

November 28 to December 1: Teheran Conference of Churchill, Roosevelt, and Stalin

1944

Friedrich Hayek, *The Road to Serfdom*

Raphael Lemkin, *Axis Rule in Occupied Europe: Laws of Occupation, Analysis of Government, Proposals for Redress*

March 22: Germany takes over Hungarian government; deportation of Hungarian Jews begins

June 4: Americans and British capture Rome

June 6: Allied landings in Normandy

July 1–15: United Nations monetary conference at Bretton Woods, New Hampshire

July 20: bomb explodes in Hitler's headquarters, the Wolfschanze, near Rastenburg in the Masurian Lakes

August 1: Warsaw Rising begins (until October 2)

August 23: King Michael of Romania dismisses Antonescu and accepts Allied armistice

September 5: Soviet declaration of war on Bulgaria

October 17: German soldiers arrest Admiral Horthy

1945

January 11: Soviet capture of Warsaw

February 4–11: meeting of Stalin with Roosevelt and Churchill (the "Big Three") at Yalta

April 16: Russian offensive against Berlin begins

April 28: execution of Mussolini by Italian partisans

April 30: suicide of Hitler

May 7: Admiral Dönitz's government declares unconditional surrender

May 8: conclusion of European armistice

July 5: UK general election: the result (Labour victory) announced July 26

July 17 to August 2: Potsdam Conference of "Big Three"

August 6: US bombing of Hiroshima with atomic bomb

August 8: Soviet declaration of war on Japan

August 9: atomic bomb dropped by United States on Nagasaki

August 14: Japan announces unconditional surrender

November 20: Nuremberg trial of 20 Nazi leaders opens

1946

March 31: Greek elections supervised by western military protection

May 5: French referendum rejects constitutional proposal

May 9: abdication of King Vittorio Emanuele III of Italy

June 2–3: election to Italian Constituent Assembly

October 16: French approval of new constitution

1947

Maurice Merleau-Ponty, *Humanism and Terror*

January 7: adoption of French plan (Monnet plan)

January 19: elections in Poland produce 78.9 percent vote for government bloc after widespread intimidation

February 22: Secretary of State Marshall's speech at Princeton Alumni Day

May 4: communists ousted from French government

May 31: resignation of Ferenc Nagy in Hungary

June 5: Marshall announces European Recovery Program at Harvard commencement

August 15: end of British rule in India; establishment of Pakistan

August 31: in Hungarian elections, communist party the strongest party (22 percent of vote)

1948

George Orwell, *Nineteen Eighty-four*

February 25: communist seizure of power in Czechoslovakia

March 10: death of former Czech Foreign Minister Jan Masaryk

June 18: German currency reform in Berlin and western zones

June 19: Soviet blockade of West Berlin begins

June 28: Cominform (successor to Comintern) denounces Yugoslav "Trotskyism"

September 3: Polish communist leader Gomułka confesses "errors"

December 9: United Nations General Assembly adopts Convention on the Prevention and Punishment of the Crime of Genocide

December 9–10: United Nations Universal Declaration of Human Rights

1949

Simone de Beauvoir, *The Second Sex*

April 4: establishment of North Atlantic Treaty Organization (NATO) by Washington Treaty

May 23: establishment of the Federal Republic of Germany

August 29: first Soviet atomic bomb test, revealed to the world by US, British, and Canadian intelligence reports on September 22

September 16: trial of László Rajk (hanged October 15)

1951

April 18: signing of Treaty of Paris (European Coal and Steel Community, or ECSC)

October 25: UK general election produces Conservative victory and new prime ministership of Churchill

1952

February 18: Greece and Turkey join NATO

May 27: European Defence Community treaty signed in Paris

July 25: ECSC Treaty in force (realization of Schuman plan)

November 27: Slánsko trial in Prague

1953

March 5: death of Stalin

June 16–17: street protests in East Berlin

June 26: arrest of Beria

July 4: Imre Nagy becomes Prime Minister of Hungary

1954

May 7: defeat of France at Dien Bien Phu, Vietnam

August 30: French Assembly rejects European Defence Community treaty

November 1: attacks on French police and military in Algeria

1955

May 5: Federal Republic of Germany becomes a sovereign state, under terms of 1954 Paris Agreements

May 9: Federal Republic of Germany joins NATO

May 11–14: Warsaw security conference of eight east and central European states creates Warsaw Pact

June 1–2: discussions of six ECSC members at Messina, Sicily

July 18–23: France, United Kingdom, Soviet Union, and United States leaders meet in Geneva

1956

Anthony Crosland, *The Future of Socialism*

February 14: Khrushchev attacks Stalin at Twentieth Communist Party Congress

June 23: Nasser elected President of Egypt

June 28–30: riots in Poznań, Poland

July 26: Egyptian nationalization of Suez Canal

October 23: student and worker demonstrations in Budapest

October 30: end of one-party system in Hungary announced

November 4: Soviet tank attacks on Budapest begin

November 5: France and the UK capture Port Said, Egypt

1957

Milovan Djilas, *The New Class: An Analysis of the Communist System*

March 25: signature of Treaty of Rome establishing European Economic Community

October 4: Soviet launch of Sputnik 1

1958

January 1: beginning of European Economic Community

May 13: coup of French army and settlers in Algeria

June 1: de Gaulle becomes Prime Minister of France

October 28: election of Cardinal Roncalli as Pope John XXIII

1959

Günter Grass, *The Tin Drum*

November 13–15: German SPD party congress at Bad Godesberg accepts capitalism

1960

Daniel Bell, *The End of Ideology*

February 13: French atomic bomb test

May 27: Turkish military coup against government of Adnan Menderes, who is killed

1961

Frantz Fanon, *The Wretched of the Earth*

August 13: construction of Berlin Wall begins

1962

Rachel Carson, *Silent Spring*

Alexander Solzhenitsyn, *One Day in the Life of Ivan Denisovitch*

March 18: ceasefire and establishment of independent Algerian state, in Évian, France

October 11: opening of Second Vatican Council (until December 8, 1965)

October 22: Cuban missile crisis

1963

January 22: Franco-German treaty of reconciliation signed

1964

October 14–15: deposition of Khrushchev as Soviet leader, replaced by Brezhnev as Party Secretary and Kosygin as Prime Minister

October 15: UK general election won by Labour Party and Wilson becomes Prime Minister

1965

March 22: Ceauşescu becomes leader of Romanian communist party

November 11: White Rhodesians under Ian Smith make unilateral declaration of independence

1966

March to May: protests in Barcelona (Caputxinada)

December 1: formation of Great Coalition government in Germany under Kiesinger

1967

April 21: coup of Greek military ("the Colonels")

June 2: Berlin demonstration against Shah

December 13: unsuccessful attempted counter-coup of King of Greece

1968

January 5: Dubček becomes general secretary of Czechoslovak communist party

April 4: assassination of Martin Luther King Jr.

April 11: shooting of Rudi Dutschke

May 10–11: students build barricades in Paris, followed by mass strikes

May 19–20: elections in Italy

June 30: parliamentary elections in France produce victory for right

July 14–15: Warsaw Pact summit

July 29: Papal encyclical on birth control, *Humanae Vitae*

August 21: Soviet invasion of Czechoslovakia

September 25: Brezhnev doctrine about the irreversibility of communism published in *Pravda*

1969

Kate Millett, *Sexual Politics*

April 17: Dubček dismissed as general secretary of Czechoslovak communist party

June 16: presidential election in France won by Pompidou

September 28: election in West Germany produces social–liberal coalition under Brandt

1970

June 18: UK general election produces Conservative victory and Heath becomes Prime Minister

August 12: signature of Moscow Treaty (German–Soviet)

December 7: signature of Warsaw Treaty (German–Polish)

1971

August 15: end of gold convertibility of US dollar at $35 per ounce, and collapse of Bretton Woods monetary system

1972

Club of Rome, *The Limits to Growth*

January 30: massacre by British troops of 13 civilians during civil rights march in Londonderry, Northern Ireland, on "Bloody Sunday"

March 30: direct rule of Northern Ireland from Westminster

June 3: Four Power Agreement on Berlin

November 19: German elections in which Brandt's government is re-elected

1973

January 1: Denmark, the Republic of Ireland, and the United Kingdom join European Community

1974

February 28: Conservative defeat in UK general election and Wilson becomes Prime Minister

April 25: overthrow of Caetano government in Portugal and establishment of Junta of National Salvation headed by General de Spínola

May 6: resignation of Brandt as German Chancellor (succeeded by Schmidt)

May 19: Giscard d'Estaing elected President of France

1975

July 30 to August 1: Final Act of the Conference on Security and Cooperation in Europe signed in Helsinki

November 15–17: Rambouillet summit of leaders of major industrial countries

November 20: death of General Franco

1976

April 15: Callaghan succeeds Wilson as UK Prime Minister

June 7: Agreement of UK with International Monetary Fund (IMF)

June 20–21: Italian elections with strong communist vote

1977

October 13–18: hijacking of Lufthansa jet ended with storming at Mogadishu, Somalia

October 18: suicide of German Red Army Faction terrorist leaders Baader, Ensslin, and Raspe

1978

August 26: election of Cardinal Albino Luciani as Pope John Paul (I)

October 16: election of Cardinal Karol Wojtyła as Pope John Paul II

December 6: new Spanish constitution with substantial measure of devolution passes national referendum

1979

January 16: flight of Shah of Iran

May 3: UK general election and victory for Margaret Thatcher's Conservative Party

June 2–10: Pope's first visit to Poland

October 6: US Federal Reserve Bank increases interest rates

1980

Willy Brandt (Chairman of Independent Commission on International Development Issues), *North–South: A Program for Survival*

January 12: creation of Green Party in Germany

May 4: death of Tito

August 14–31: strikes in Gdańsk shipyards, Poland

1981

January 3: admission of Greece to European Community

March 10: Geoffrey Howe's UK budget raises taxes in a recession

May 10: election of Mitterrand as French President

May 13: assassination attempt against John Paul II

July 13: riots in Toxteth and Southall, England

December 13: imposition of martial law in Poland

1982

April 2: Argentina invades the Falkland Islands (Islas Malvinas), a British Dependent Territory

September 17: defeat of Schmidt government in motion of confidence and Kohl becomes Chancellor of a center-right coalition government in Germany

November 10: death of Leonid Brezhnev

1983

Jean-François Revel, *Why Democracies Perish*

March 25: French austerity plan in response to exchange rate crisis

1984

February 9: death of Yuri Andropov

March 12: coalminers start unofficial strike in the United Kingdom

October 19: kidnapping of Father Popiełuszko; body discovered October 30

1985

March 10: death of Konstantin Chernenko, followed by election of Mikhail Gorbachev as General Secretary of Soviet Communist Party

September 22: Group of Five Finance Ministers meet to discuss exchange rates at Plaza Hotel, New York

1986

January 1: Portugal and Spain join European Community

February 17 and 28: Single European Act providing for the creation of single internal market in Europe

February 26: Marshall ruling. The European Court of Justice sets out the principle of equality of treatment between women and men

March 16: victory of right in French parliamentary elections

April 26: nuclear accident at Chernobyl in Ukraine

December 17: Jakes replaces Husák as first secretary of Czechoslovak communist party

1987

February 21–22: finance ministers discuss exchange rates at Louvre meeting, Paris

1989

January 25: Soviet troops begin last stages of withdrawal from Afghanistan

April 5: Polish government legalizes Solidarność

May 7: local elections in German Democratic Republic (GDR)

June 3–4: crushing of pro-democracy movement in Tiananmen Square, Beijing

June 4 and 18: free elections in Poland

September 11: Hungary opens border with Austria

October 9: Monday demonstrations in Leipzig begin

October 18: Honecker replaced by Egon Krenz as First Secretary in East Germany

November 9: lifting of travel restrictions in East Germany, including across Berlin Wall

November 10: dismissal of Bulgarian communist leader Zhivkov

December 2–3: Bush and Gorbachev summit at Malta

December 10: non-communist government in Czechoslovakia after resignation of Husák

December 21–22: revolution against Ceauşescu in Romania

December 25: execution of Ceauşescu and his wife

December 29: Czech parliament elects Václav Havel President

1990

March 18: elections in GDR with victory for parties supporting unification

April 1: UK government introduces poll tax

July 1: currency union of two Germanies

July 16: Kohl visit to Gorbachev secures Soviet consent for NATO membership of united Germany

August 2: Iraq invades Kuwait

September 12: Two Plus Four Treaty (Treaty on Final Settlement with Respect to Germany) signed

October 3: East and West Germany unite

November 24: Thatcher announces resignation

November 28: John Major becomes UK Prime Minister

December 2: Kohl victory in elections in united Germany

December 9: Wałęsa elected President of Poland

December 23: Slovenia votes for independence in a referendum

1991

January 13: Soviet troops kill demonstrators in Vilnius, Lithuania

March 31: dissolution of military command of Warsaw Pact

June 12: Yeltsin elected as President of Russia

June 27: Yugoslav army begins to fight Slovenia

June 28: announcement of end of Council for Mutual Economic Assistance (Comecon)

July 1: end of Warsaw Pact

August 18–21: coup against Gorbachev in Soviet Union

August 24: President of Ukraine calls for independence

August 31: Kyrgyzstan declares independence from Soviet Union, followed by six other Soviet republics and Chechnya after referendum

December 1: declaration of Ukrainian independence

December 11: Treaty of Maastricht lays out concrete timetable for European Monetary Union

December 21: dismantling of Soviet Union as 11 Presidents of former Soviet Republics meet at Alma Ata

December 23: German recognition of Croatian and Slovenian independence

December 25: resignation of Gorbachev as President of Soviet Union

1992

Francis Fukuyama, *The End of History and the Last Man*

January 15: European Union (EU) recognition of Croatia and Slovenia

February 29: Bosnian referendum for independence

September 16: United Kingdom exchange rate crisis ends UK membership of European Monetary System Exchange Rate Mechanism

1993

January 1: breakup of Czechoslovakia into Czech Republic and Slovakia ("the velvet divorce")

August 2: agreement on wider bands of fluctuation in European Monetary System due to speculative attacks against French franc

September 21: Yeltsin's siege of Russian parliament

December 12: Russian parliamentary elections produce large vote for non-democratic parties

1994

September 2: first Chechen war (until August 31, 1996)

1995

January 1: Austria, Finland, and Sweden become members of the EU

March 26: Schengen agreement on internal movement between some EU countries in force

July 11: Serb massacre of Bosnian Moslems at Srebrenica

November 21: Dayton agreement on Bosnian "entities"

1996

Samuel Huntington, *The Clash of Civilizations and the Remaking of the World Order*

July 3: re-election of Yeltsin as President of Russia

1997

May 1: UK general election victory of Labour Party under Tony Blair

August 17: Russian financial crisis produces default and devaluation

1998

March: intensified Serb attacks on Albanians begin

1999

January 1: legal beginning of euro as common European currency

March 8: Czech Republic, Hungary, and Poland join NATO

March 24: NATO bombing of Serbian positions

August 7: Chechen war restarts

August 9: appointment of Putin as Russian Prime Minister

December 31: resignation of Yeltsin as President

2000

March 26: election of Putin as President of Russia

September 24: defeat of Milošević in election for Presidency of Yugoslavia

2001

April 1: Netherlands is first country to legalize same-sex marriage

September 11: Terrorist attacks on World Trade Center and Pentagon

2002

January 1: physical introduction of euro notes and coins

2003

March 14: German Chancellor Gerhard Schröder announces welfare and labor relations reforms ("*Agenda 2010*")

March 20: Outbreak of Iraq war as US forces start invasion of Iraq

October 4: Intergovernmental Conference in Rome to implement constitution as outcome of European Constitutional Convention

2004

May 1: expansion of EU to include Cyprus, the Czech Republic, Estonia, Hungary, Latvia, Lithuania, Malta, Poland, Slovakia, and Slovenia

2005

April 2: death of Pope John Paul I, followed by election of Cardinal Joseph Ratzinger as Benedict XVI

May 25: 55 percent of French voters reject European Constitution in referendum

June 1: 62 percent of Netherlands voters reject European Constitution in referendum

September 18: German election leads to Great Coalition government headed by Angela Merkel (CDU)

2007

January 1: Bulgaria and Romania join EU

April 22 and May 6: French presidential elections won by Nicolas Sarkozy

December 13: Lisbon Treaty on EU signed

2008

August 10: Russian armies move through South Ossetia into Georgia

September 15: failure of Lehman Brothers

September 30: Irish government announces a two-year blanket guarantee for deposits and debts at six financial institutions

2009

September 27: elections in Germany, with Angela Merkel remaining as Chancellor but a change of coalition to center-right (CDU-liberal)

October 4: George Papandreou leads Pasok party to victory in Greek elections

2010

March 25: euro area leaders announce their readiness to contribute to coordinated bilateral loans to Greece as part of a package with IMF financing

April 11 and 25: Fidesz, led by Viktor Orbán, wins Hungarian election with 53 percent of vote

May 6: UK election won by Conservatives led by David Cameron

October 18: German Chancellor Merkel and French President Sarkozy agree in Deauville to create a permanent crisis resolution mechanism that provides for the possibility of sovereign debt restructuring, and to relax fiscal criteria

2011

February 25: Irish elections, with ruling Fianna Fáil party defeated and Enda Kenny (Fine Gael) becomes Prime Minister

March 11: earthquake and tsunami lead to uncontrolled meltdown of Japanese nuclear reactor at Fukushima

March 23: Portugal's Prime Minister Jose Socrates resigns after opposition parties reject the fourth package of austerity measures in a year

June 30: German government decides to close down nuclear power generation on accelerated schedule (*"Atomausstieg"*)

November 3: Greek Prime Minister Papandreou resigns and is replaced by an interim coalition government, headed by a technocrat, Lucas Papademos

November 13: Italian Prime Minister Silvio Berlusconi resigns after losing majority in parliament and is succeeded by a technocratic government headed by Mario Monti

2012

March 2: EU adopts Fiscal Compact

April 22 and May 6: presidential election in France, with victory of François Hollande over Nicolas Sarkozy

July 26: European Central Bank (ECB) President Mario Draghi announces the ECB's willingness to do "whatever it takes to preserve the euro"

2013

February 24–25: election in Italy with victory of center-left coalition

March 13: election of Cardinal Jorge Mario Bergoglio as Pope Francis following retirement of Benedict XVI

July 1: Croatia joins EU

November 21: protesters gather at Kiev's Maidan Square

2014

February: revolution ousts Ukrainian president Viktor Yanukovych

February 26: Russian invasion and annexation of Crimea, and fighting in eastern Ukraine

2015

Michel Houellebecq publishes novel *Soumission* (Submission)

January 7: Islamicist terrorists attack office of *Charlie Hebdo* in Paris and kill 12 people

January 22: ECB announces quantitative easing

January 25: Syriza wins Greek elections

May 17: UK general elections won by Conservatives led by David Cameron, after a pledge to hold a referendum on EU membership

July 5: Greek referendum rejects bailout terms

July 16: Greek parliament supports new bailout package

August 31: at a press conference, discussing refugee crisis, Chancellor Merkel says, "We can do it."

September 4: Austria and Germany open borders to Syrian refugees passing through Hungary

October 25: Law and Justice (PiS) party wins Polish elections with 38 percent of vote

2016

June 23: UK referendum to leave the EU (Brexit)

November 8: presidential election in United States won by Donald Trump.

2017

April 23 and May 7: Presidential election in France with victory of Emmanuel Macron

June 8: election in UK with narrow victory for Conservatives led by Theresa May but without an overall parliamentary majority

1 The twentieth century in an iron cage
Modernization and rationalization

There is a way of telling the story of Europe's twentieth century that casts a particular and perhaps disconcerting light on politics, and on what politics can accomplish. The easiest way to summarize that view of development is "modernization". Modernization involves a transformation of society, a shift to urban existence, industrial and service sector employment, female emancipation, the individualization of existence, the questioning of traditional values, and frequently a waning of religion. There is in short a remaking of the idea of man and woman. By the early twenty-first century, this development had reached a point where many began to challenge the binary division of human society, instead favoring the notion that gender itself could be fluid.

Modernization

Modernization also usually produces new demands about what political institutions should do to help in the realization of the new vision of humanity. Should and does the political process play a part in the breaking down of traditions? Sometimes, indeed, the long-term developmental story is politicized, and commentators point out the modern aspects of brutal and repressive dictatorships. This path has been taken by a minority of scholars in the case of Mussolini's Italy (James Gregor), and by rather more for Hitler's Germany (David Schoenbaum, and most provocatively Rainer Zitelmann); but it has been the bedrock of much of the analysis of Stalin's Russia (beginning with the studies of Isaac Deutscher and Alec Nove, which explained that brutality was the price for advance).[1] The theory underlying this approach was that the new world could not emerge without a violent destruction of the old world, and that the old encrustations were stronger and more resistant on a gradient to the south and east of the European continent.

Tested against empirical evidence, these theories of the need for violent modernization actually fare surprisingly badly. The period of Mussolini's regime, far from representing a "developmental dictatorship", actually saw the poorest performance of the Italian economy in the twentieth century. Nazi Germany published some impressive statistics about growth, but recent investigations of infant mortality and nutrition (which are the most reliable guides to overall well-being) indicate that the rhetoric about generating a new general prosperity was essentially empty.[2] Stalin's Russia produced quick industrialization, by transferring resources out of the big agricultural sector and impoverishing it (so that it is wrong to talk about rising living standards), and set the stage for decades of dismal economic performance. Conversely, it was the country which was usually held up as a pioneer of modernity, the United Kingdom, that did its best to maintain and even invent odd traditions, and which preserved feudalism longest (until 2004, in Scotland).

Politics (even or indeed especially when based on a promise to "modernize") actually more easily obstructed modernization than promoted it. It may be true that political developments could hold up, and perhaps sometimes accelerate, the emergence of "modernity", but so many different elements went into Europe's modernization that it would be grossly overstating the case to say that politics in any country consciously made modernity in the old continent. The causation from politics to modernity is by no means clear. Again, to take the three examples mentioned, there was a substantial but chaotic modernization in Italy, Germany, and Russia during and immediately after the First World War. Indeed, it would be much more plausible to argue that this modernization on a broad front created a room for new politics, rather than the other way round.

After that initial demand for a new kind of political existence, spurred by economic change and reflecting the demands of new social groups (above all of a new and uncomfortable working class), a different relationship between the push to modernize and its political manifestation was established (that is the theme of Chapters 3 and 4). When modernization became controversial, and politics more violent, a vicious cycle developed in which poor growth and bad politics reinforced one another. That cycle could only, in general, be broken from the outside: by military defeat and political humiliation.

Greater wealth

Mostly, however, the modernization story seems to work rather independently of politics. Since the European political and social response to modern life is the subject of almost all of this book, this initial chapter discusses modernity in its simplest form, without politics. The elemental story is one of a relatively constant process of enrichment, and its consequences.[3] Modernization, in other words, simply means the greater control of resources by individuals. The misapprehension about modernization that gripped many people in the twentieth century (and which is analyzed in more detail in Chapters 5, 7, 8, and 9) is that it involved an entrapment, or a fundamentally inhuman dynamic of the greater control of individuals by the resources that they might want.

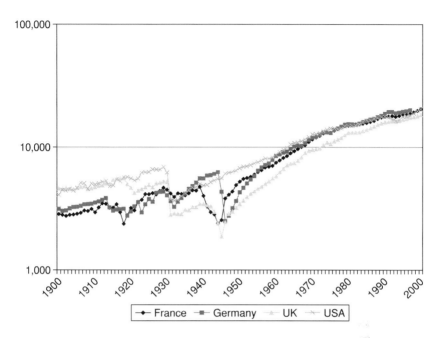

Figure 1.1 Gross Domestic Product (GDP) per capita, 1900–2000 (1990 US dollars).
(Source: Angus Maddison (2001), *The World Economy: A Millennial Perspective*, Paris: OECD Development Centre, updated from University of Groningen and the Conference Board, GGDC Total Economy Database, 2003, www.eco.rug.nl/ggdc).

Figure 1.1 shows one way of thinking about this process: it simply depicts the development of Gross Domestic Product (GDP; in other words, the sum of services and goods produced in the economy) per head of population. In this figure, the calculation is shown on a logarithmic axis, in order that a constant rate of growth should appear as a straight line (in a conventional figure, the line would appear to curve upwards). Unlike GDP charts, which show a falling-off of European performance toward the end of the century, this chart depicts an astonishing constancy of growth in most European societies, the exception being catch-up periods of faster growth in the aftermath of the interruptions produced by war. During the First, but even more in the Second World War, the US economy grew while that of Europe contracted, setting the stage for a large potential for Europeans to catch up by taking over American technological and managerial innovation.

There is broad agreement on what caused this amazing performance, unprecedented in previous centuries: even in the eighteenth century (in the United Kingdom) or in the nineteenth century (in continental Europe), in the age of the classical Industrial Revolution, growth rates were lower. The great riches of the modern world flowed from the adoption of modern technology. This concept in its broadest sense encompasses not only the process of applying the results of scientific discovery, but also organizational and managerial improvements. The two are interconnected, most obviously in the case of advances in information technology, from the typewriter, telephone, and cable before the First World War to the revolution of computing (see Chapter 9), and the new linkages created by the internet in the 1990s (Chapter 13).

Indeed, the effect of the technology is so profound that it is really hard to compare the living standards of Europeans at the end and the beginning of the century. To be sure, it is possible to calculate the great decline in the time of work needed to earn a loaf of bread or a pint or liter of beer. But such figures do not really measure adequately the change in people's lives. No one would now want to spend all their income on bread or beer, and it is the possibilities that exist for new sorts of spending that have transformed lives most. It was thus possible at the end of the century to see and hear a great opera or symphonic performance, or a popular singer, for a small price (by purchasing a video or DVD), or indeed even at no marginal cost at all (through the Internet); while at the beginning of the century such enjoyment would have required a long and expensive journey and hotel costs, as well as the price of a theater or concert ticket. Some of the goods that are now available, and readily taken for granted, represent major conveniences: the item most commonly missed by participants in experiments to recreate the way of life a century ago is hair shampoo, which simply did not exist. More significantly, at the beginning of the century an effective medical treatment of bacterial infections was impossible; but by the end of the century, antibiotic drugs had become quite cheap (though some drug-resistant forms of bacteria were beginning to emerge).

It is important to notice that the increase in prosperity does not necessarily mean more happiness. Weighing the happiness gain is a much harder exercise: to take one of the examples above, a large part of the world of house-made music disappeared under the pressure of aesthetically superior recorded and reproducible music. If the pleasure of participation is balanced against the enjoyment of passive listening, some will feel that "the world we have lost" had its own unique attractions.

Transformed demographics

Being richer – the major fact of the twentieth century in all of Europe – dramatically changed what people did with their lives. It changed, to start with the most basic level, the way they were born, lived, and died.

In demographic terms, both fertility and mortality declined more or less continuously in the course of the century. A "demographic transition" had begun in almost every northern and western European country in the 1890s, with reduced numbers of births. This long-term trend continued through the big political disturbances of the twentieth century, which had some impact, but only of a temporary character: births fell further in most countries during the world wars, and then bounced back in a recovery phase of "baby boom".

The lower rates of fertility reflected increasingly prevalent birth control, which was often described in the vocabulary of modernization and rationalization. In 1928, the Prussian Minister of Social Welfare described the new situation: "There is no doubt that the limitation of births is willful. Intercourse is rationalized, at least by the great part of the population. People simply do not want more than one or two children."[4]

Where contraception failed or was not used, abortion was frequent. In Russia, physicians had spoken about an epidemic of abortions before the First World War. In revolutionary Russia it became the standard method of birth control, and in 1920 doctors in hospitals (but not the traditional midwives of rural Russia) were permitted to perform abortions. In Leningrad the number of abortions per 1,000 people soared from 5.5 to 31.5 between 1924 and 1928. The Soviet state eventually retreated and reversed its abortion policy in 1936, because it was alarmed by the demographic consequences of too much abortion. Elsewhere in the 1920s, a large-scale demand for liberalization of abortion laws began. In Germany, it was estimated that in 1931 1 million women had abortions. After the Second World War came a new wave of abortions, justified in part as a pragmatic response to the mass raping of women. Abortion continued to be practiced as a widespread method of family planning in communist Europe, in the absence of readily available contraception, and in some cases (as in Romania) in secret defiance of natalist policies designed to increase national population and power.

Abortion, especially when it was conducted in the illegal circumstances of the back streets or was self-induced, often produced infections and high rates of mortality. Legalization, and the availability of better methods of contraception, was a key to the reduction of female mortality.

Improvements in hygiene also reduced mortality rates. The big innovations of the nineteenth century concerned public hygiene: the provision of clean water and separate sewage systems. In the twentieth century, hygiene was personalized. It took a long time for some basic elements of hygiene to become regularly established. Washrooms with baths and showers for students were installed in most Oxford and Cambridge colleges only in the interwar period, with often peculiar names ("the gate of necessity"). France's *Elle* magazine in 1951 reported that a quarter of the women surveyed never brushed their teeth. Flossing was unusual in Europe until the 1980s and 1990s.

Medical advances had a relatively late impact on mortality rates, and then they were mostly pharmaceutical. In the nineteenth century, immunization began to limit some types of epidemic (it was especially successful against smallpox). Only, however, in the mid-twentieth century did improved medicine, largely the result of the introduction of penicillin and then other antibiotics, dramatically alter the response of the human body to bacterial infection.

Individuals thus lived longer. Life expectancy at birth had risen very slowly in the nineteenth century, but much more dramatically in the twentieth. For a French person born in 1820, for instance, the average life expectancy was 40; in 1900 it was 47, and in 1992, 77. In the nineteenth century, female expectations were lower than those of males, because of the risks associated with childbirth; and in the twentieth century, they rose to higher levels than those of men.

After and before work

People also had a more constant expectation about how long they might live, and were less prone to meditate on the uncertainty of life. Nineteenth-century life had frequently been short and uncertain, and "retirement" rare. In 1881, three-quarters of men in the United Kingdom over 65 were still working. It was only in 1898 that the British civil service began to enforce a retirement age. By 1931, half of men in the United Kingdom over 65 were still in employment; by 1981 that ratio had fallen to a tenth. Retirement ages fell at the same time as life expectancy increased. At its most extreme, Italians by the end of the century had a retirement age of 55 for men and 50 for women. In the European Union as a whole, in 2000 only 31 percent of men and 15 percent of women aged between 60 and 65 were working.

In addition, more people spent longer in full-time education. Higher education grew enormously. At the beginning of the twentieth century, there were 35,000 university students in Germany, as well as another 17,000 in technical high schools (the equivalent of universities). In France, there were around 20,000, as there were in the United Kingdom; by 1939 these figures had risen to 80,000 and 50,000 respectively. The rapidity of growth continued after the Second World War. By the end of the century, there were over 2 million students in higher education in France (2,012,000), Germany (2,087,000), and the United Kingdom (2,081,000), and almost as many in Italy (1,797,000).[5]

Years spent by children in compulsory education expanded. Before the First World War, the school-leaving age was between 12 and 14 in most European countries; at the end of the century, it was 18 in Belgium and Germany, 17 in the Netherlands, and 16 in Denmark, France, and the UK. Before the First World War, the average time spent by a German in education was over eight years, in 1992 over 12. The result of longer schooling, the explosion of tertiary education, and increased longevity was a dramatic diminution of the proportion of men's and women's lives spent in paid employment, and correspondingly an increase in leisure, and in spending associated with leisure. It was this, again the effect of raised income levels, that made the century the century of the consumer.

The prospect of a sustained span of life in retirement also focused attention on pensions and savings. The majority of the population of nineteenth-century Europe had not saved, except for putting small amounts of money aside to cover their own funeral expenses. Bismarckian Germany, and then some Scandinavian countries, had introduced limited versions of old-age pension plans in the late nineteenth century. The United Kingdom in 1908 followed with a very small-scale plan, but in 1911 introduced a contribution-based national insurance scheme. In 1911, the reformist Italian Prime Minister Giolitti nationalized the life insurance business, hoping to cater for a newly enlarged demand for insurance products. Such schemes at first covered relatively few people. Instead, there was a greater dependence on private savings, and on privately financed pensions and annuity plans. Many concluded life insurance policies, which became the most popular form of saving in a period in which there were – at the beginning – no automatic state pensions.

In the interwar period, employers gradually began to introduce their own pension plans: for instance, in the United Kingdom in 1936 there were 0.2 million with occupational pensions, but 8.9 million with state pensions. By 1979 occupational pensions had grown to 3.7 million and state pensions to 8.9 million.

Governments made great efforts to induce their populations to save, with elaborate propaganda campaigns to celebrate the virtues of prudence and restraint. These campaigns reached their heights in the two world wars, when consumption would detract from the war effort and saving would be used to pay for armaments and national defense. The campaigns were deceptive, as their advocates must have realized. At the same time as the propensity to save increased, because of higher incomes and longer life, and as the demand for savings on the part of the state rose, because of higher public expenditure (in large part military), the currency and monetary uncertainties of the twentieth century devalued these savings often quite spectacularly and quickly. In this way, savers were disappointed; often they resigned themselves to their misfortunes, but in some societies such as post-inflation Germany in the 1920s their disappointment turned to embittered and militant radicalism.

Greater equality

Increased savings reflected the rising living standards, which character-ized the century as a whole, with interruptions during the wars; and also large reductions in inequality. Both world wars and their aftermaths also brought reduced inequalities in both income and wealth, in part as a result of increased tax rates which hit the rich, and in part because of the labor market effects which increased the demand for unskilled labor. Before the First World War, the top 1 percent of income earners had 19 percent of income in France and Germany, and 20 percent in the United Kingdom. Income distributions in fact were surprisingly similar over Europe, and are thus a testimony to the mobility of factors of production, and an essential similarity of European societies, that are both largely neglected by historians of national cultures (as well as in popular images of national stereotypes). The clichés considered the United Kingdom to be dominated by plutocrats, Germany to be the country of a prosperous bourgeoisie that traded political rights for more prosperity, and France to be the country of the small business and farm. In fact, they all had an astonishingly rich upper crust, of almost the same thickness.

In interwar Europe, and after the Second World War, the income disparities largely disappeared, in large part as the consequence of new tax regimes. The proportion of income earned by the top 1 percent in the United Kingdom fell to 18 percent in 1929 and 10 percent in 1940. In Germany it was 8 percent, and in France also 8 percent in 1945.[6]

The move toward greater equality also coincided with a rise of professional management, and a decline of wealth based on inherited position. The new elites, in politics and the media, as well as in economic life, were formed by education rather than by birth.

The long-term twentieth-century trend toward more equal income distribution was reversed (but not very dramatically) toward the end of the century: from the late 1970s in the UK; from the mid-1980s in France and West Germany, the Netherlands, and Sweden; and from the early 1990s in Finland and Italy. But there was no dramatic trend in favor of the very rich. The lowest share of income of the top 1 percent in France (7 percent) was reached in 1982, and after that the ratio rose slowly to 8 percent in the 1990s. Formerly communist societies also – and much more suddenly – became unequal in income and wealth with the introduction of market economics in the 1990s (while the system of political privilege was dismantled).

Mobility

When low-range wages for unskilled work were very low, there were big incentives to move and look for higher-paid work elsewhere. Before the First World War, there had been substantial labor mobility, including large amounts of transoceanic migration. Emigration had played a large part in reducing population pressure and increasing wages in poor areas of Europe, such as Ireland and Scandinavia. Some rich European countries also attracted large numbers of immigrants. Germany recruited Italian seasonal migrant workers in the south, and Poles in the north, as well as long-term Polish immigration into the industrial areas of the Rhine–Ruhr. After the First World War, France in the 1920s still recruited large numbers of workers in order to make up for what its policy makers considered to be a demographic deficit in comparison with Germany. But after the Great Depression, voluntary migration almost ceased. Instead, countries regarded themselves as over-populated, and rejected the involuntary flows of racial and political refugees produced by virulently racist and xenophobic regimes in Germany and elsewhere.

After the war, some migrations took place in special circumstances. Germans expelled from eastern Europe and fleeing from communist East Germany came to the Federal Republic. Ex-colonial settlers from North Africa returned to France. The United Kingdom imported cheap textile workers from the Indian sub-continent. Southern Italians, who had previously migrated abroad, went to the expanding cities of northern Italy. From the 1960s, migrant workers from Mediterranean countries (Portugal, Greece, Yugoslavia, and Turkey) came as "guest workers" to northern Europe. The implication of their special status was that they might be returned if circumstances on the labor market changed (as occurred in the slow growth phase of the 1970s). From the 1980s, general levels of movement increased, and rose even more rapidly after the break-down of communism in 1989–91. Migrants tended to move into low-paid unskilled jobs, often ones which locals no longer wished to perform. In 1999, 3.4 percent of the European Union population were nationals of third countries, a level which had doubled since 1985.

International migration thus was higher at the beginning and end of the century, in the eras that were more internationally open, but also more unequal (in terms of income). In part, immigration responded to income differentials; but it also helped to produce some of the increase in inequality that characterized the more "globalized" phases of European history.

Leisure

The reduced hours spent working generated new demands for leisure. The cinema developed quickly, until the late 1920s with silent movies. In Germany in 1914, there were some 2,500 cinemas (in 2000 there were 3,750). The press also expanded, with the numbers of newspapers surging during the world wars (where the demand for information increased). In the 1920s, radio broadcasting developed. The British Broadcasting Corporation (BBC) was created in 1927. After the Second World War came television, with the BBC resuming a television service after 1946. Attendance at cinemas reached its peak in the late 1940s and early 1950s; after that it was quickly reduced by the competition of television. The print media survived better, until the early twenty-first century, when traditional newspapers were challenged by electronic media. Television's dominance broke down too. Instead of nation-ally distributed news and television programs, social platforms like Facebook distributed information in a carefully targeted way. The fragmentation of the media then contributed to an increased fragmentation, and a political polarization, of society.

Women, work, and families

Great disruptions such as the two world wars accelerated developments that were occurring anyway. The largest employment of female labor at the beginning of the twentieth century was in domestic labor. The First World War gave a major but temporary push to female industrial employment, but after the war many women left the workforce again. The permanent gains were in the increased employment of women as workers in office jobs. Much of the twentieth century became the age of the female secretary, replacing the male clerk of the late-nineteenth-century world.

Both world wars produced assertive and emancipated "new women", whose demands for softer and more sensitive "new men" led to great clashes between the sexes in the aftermath of military conflicts in which many males had thought that they were asserting their virility. An initial period of liberalization after both wars was followed in the 1930s and in the 1950s by reactions. Politicians and the media, including the increasingly popular women's magazines, set out an ideal in which women's traditional roles as wife and mother were emphasized. They insisted on the incompatibility of a job and a family life, and the media gave advice on how to find a good husband (which was a problem, because of the losses of males in the wars). The reaction of the 1930s ended with the new war and the conscription of more women into the workforce; that of the 1950s ended with the cultural revolution of the 1960s (see Chapter 9). Women's magazines were reformulated, along the lines of new journalistic successes such as *Cosmopolitan* (from 1965), which succeeded by setting a new tone about liberated sexuality and about women's careers.

A wave of marriages had accompanied the world wars, and both wars were followed by a surge in divorce. It may be that the marriages had originally been rather rashly concluded, by soldiers departing for the front and anxious to cement some sort of precarious stability; or that soldiers were so traumatized by the war that they did not want to settle down upon return; or that their women met other men while their husbands were away at the front, or that men fell in love with attractive nurses in military hospitals (a constant phobia on the home front); or even that reduced rates of divorce during the war represented a pent-up demand to separate which was released with the end of military hostilities and a turn to marital hostilities. But in general, the war produced an attitude in which changeability predominated, and certainties were discounted. "Modern" had a distinct connotation when applied to values. In Germany there had been 16,657 divorces in 1913, but there were 36,107 in 1919; the number rose further during the Depression (40,722 in 1930) and during the Nazi dictatorship (49,497 in 1938, and 61,789 in 1939, including large numbers of non-Jewish spouses divorcing Jews). After another war, with similar effects on the perceptions women had of men, and on attitudes to the family, the new postwar peak was reached in 1948 (88,374, in the reduced territory of what became West Germany). Divorce fell in the 1950s, in a brief-lived reconstitution of the family idyll, but rose to new heights in the 1960s and 1970s.

Revolutionary Russia had the reputation as the country with the most "modern" attitude to divorce. Some revolutionaries, such as Aleksandra Kollontai, propagated the idea of free love, which they believed to be found in communities of workers, though Lenin himself rejected this as a fantasy of bourgeois intellectuals. Divorce had been legalized in 1918; and after that, the Bolshevik leadership considered what ways would be best to destroy the peasant family unit, which they considered the center of political reaction. The new code of 1926 recognized "free unions" as alternative forms of marriage, and divorce became very easy: from 1927, it could be carried out at the request of one partner, with the result that divorce by postcard became possible. It remained quite rare in rural Russia, but became common in the cities. In Leningrad in 1927, there were 9.8 divorces per 1,000 couples; more dramatically put, by the mid-1930s, there were 37 divorces for every 100 marriages. Periodically, as in 1926–7 and 1934, the party denounced libertinism and urged a return to more conventional morality, but without much success. In 1936 a law designed to end the "frivolous attitude to the family" illegalized abortion, and provided a larger measure of family assistance. One of the reasons to move back to a conservative attitude was the flood of homeless children, orphaned or abandoned by their parents, who roamed the streets and contributed greatly to prostitution and criminality: the *besprizorniki*. In the early 1920s, there may have been as many as 7.5 million of these "homeless waifs".

In John Galsworthy's novel of 1925, *The Silver Spoon*, the conflict of "modern morality" with that of the Victorian world was played out: the description of a society lady with the phrase "she hasn't a moral about her" was, for the "advanced" part of society, a compliment and not a rebuke. Even clergymen had to recognize that the tone of the age had changed. The Bishop of Durham told the House of Lords in 1922 that marriage laws needed to be changed in the light of "modern conditions, social and intellectual". He added: "We live in a time of revolutionary change, nowhere more far-reaching than in the region of social morality."[7]

The reform of divorce law followed the prevailing social practice. In the United Kingdom, new Acts of 1923 and 1937 made divorce easier, but it could still be blocked by the opposition of one reluctant spouse, and it was only in 1967 that the notion of divorce following simply and automatically from separation was introduced. France had its law reform in 1972 and 1975, making "no fault" divorce possible, and Germany in 1977. A new surge of divorces in those countries in the 1960s and 1970s anticipated, as well as followed, divorce law reform. Before 1970, on the other hand, divorce was almost impossible in Italy. In communist Europe, too, divorces soared in the 1960s and 1970s, though the shortages of housing meant that divorced couples were often obliged to live uncomfortably together in the same apartment.

Through this period, the average age of marriage was falling (more quickly in eastern than in western Europe). From the 1960s, marriage was often preceded by periods of cohabitation (and in some cases cohabitation continued without marriage). In France in 1968, 17 percent of couples marrying were already living together; one decade later that ratio had risen to 44 percent.

The combination of lower ages at first marriage, with cohabitation and easier and more socially tolerated divorce, meant that marriage was treated increasingly as an experiment that could easily be unwound if it proved unsatisfactory. Prominent figures in the arts and in the political world survived divorces that before the 1960s would have resulted in professional setbacks. Indeed, when the chairman of the British Conservative Party, Cecil Parkinson, had a pregnant mistress (1983) he was disgraced and forced to resign for *not* leaving his wife and marrying the mistress.

Individualism

Society was becoming more individualistic. This again can be traced back to the general rise in incomes. Poverty creates dependence, and requires mutuality in order to overcome hardship. Greater wealth and greater mobility (which it facilitates) allow people to liberate themselves from what they see as restrictive social relationships. They can now afford to escape from their kin, their spouses, their children, their churches, their classes, even their countries. Larger numbers of people now lived alone. Romantic myths in print and in film encouraged notions of personal and physical perfection in the search of partners that were unrealizable. A society of "singles" cultivated the search for the "perfect partner" which – human nature being as it is – could never be found.

As families became smaller, individual children became more particularized. The cost and horror of war from a family perspective thus increased. Most parents and siblings treated the losses of the First World War as unavoidable misfortunes that reflected the triumph of the patriotic call to duty. The schoolboy Anthony Eden's letter to his mother after the death in battle of his brother is characteristic of the age:

> Poor little Mummie. You are having a fearfully trying time just now. But we must all do our share & the greater the share the greater the sense of honour if it is nobly borne. Poor little Nicholas [younger brother] too! I fear it will be a sad blow to him but we must all take our share.[8]

By the Second World War, there was a greater sense of personal loss. By the end of the century, military losses were generally believed to be absolutely unsustainable in modern societies, and a relatively low level of casualties (at least in any historical comparison) in the Afghan war was enough to undermine the legitimacy of the Soviet Union for Russian parents.

Belief

Religious observance declined, in a much more dramatic way than in some otherwise equally or even more modern societies, such as the United States.

Again, the two wars accelerated this practice, as many were repelled by the sanctimonious patriotic piety of military chaplains and felt abandoned by God on the battlefields. Robert Graves, the British war poet and author, felt it to be natural that his children should not be baptized. His wife, Nancy Nicholson, concluded that "God is a man, so it must all be rot."[9] In the late 1940s and early 1950s, unlike after the First World War, there was a brief revival of church attendance and membership in most European countries, and a new political Christianity (Christian Democracy) was formulated. The American preacher Billy Graham conducted mass evangelization in worldwide "crusades", with almost 2 million participating in the London meetings of 1954.

The religious revival, like that of traditional family life, was quite short-lived. Even those who remained Catholics largely stopped traditional practices, in particular the regular sacrament of confession. Protestant churches lost regularly practicing members at even faster rates than the Catholics, and by the 1980s more people in traditionally Protestant England attended Catholic services than those of the state Church of England. By the end of the century, Christianity in Europe (but not in America) was a minority religion. Even the religious movement that was most universal in its aspirations, the Roman Catholic Church, began to reformulate its doctrine to fit an age in which believers formed only a small part of the population. The head of the Congregation of the Faith, Cardinal Joseph Ratzinger, explained that the modern Church was "less identified with the great societies, [and was] more of a minority church; she will live in small, vital circles of really convinced believers who live their faiths". He admitted that there was "a decay of Christianity in the midst of the Church", and saw a possibility that "while still present as a form, it is hardly lived as a reality any longer".[10]

The decline of rural life

These transitions were characteristic of a society that was becoming more urban. The shift toward greater wealth, leisure, and individualization was matched by a change in the occupation of most of the population. Most of Europe's population at the beginning of the twentieth century was still rural, and quite traditional. In 1907, 37.8 percent of the German labor force was still employed in agriculture; in France the ratio was 42.7 percent (1906), in Austria 53.1 percent, and in Hungary 62.5 percent (both 1910).

This transition to modernity took a long time. Strip agriculture continued for a long time in many parts of Europe: despite decades of efforts at land consolidation, at the end of the century many southern German farming areas were still broken into strips similar to those of pre-modern farming. Old non-market forms of land tenure survived. In 1912 there were still 1,277 entailed estates in Prussia, covering 7 percent of its territory. A similar proportion of

Hungarian land was entailed before the First World War. Feudalism ended in Europe, not with 1789 or 1848, but with the 2000 Abolition of Feudal Tenure (Scotland) Act, which abolished still-existing feudal obligations in the Scottish Highlands. The provisions of the Act came into force in 2004. Other countries had had radical land reform earlier. After the First World War, most central and eastern European countries had land reforms that limited the size of holdings: in Romania, the maximum was 100 to 500 hectares, depending on the location; in Czechoslovakia it was 150–250 hectares, in Bulgaria 30–50 hectares. In the new Yugoslavia, each peasant family was to have its own land. Interwar agriculture thus suffered from a proliferation of micro-holdings that stood in the way of "modernity": in this context, the rational economic management of land. After the Second World War, communism in eastern Europe imposed a more far-reaching land reform, but only temporarily. Instead of splintering holdings further, the communist governments soon imposed collectivization, and only in Poland was there a reversal and a decollectivization in the 1950s.

Modernity extended into the countryside in the form of credit and military mobilization. "Cattle usury", the lending against the security of individual cattle, with a lien on any calves that were born, died out in the late nineteenth century, as new credit institutions spread. In 1910 23,751 credit cooperatives existed in Germany. But the Great Depression shook credit relations, and pushed many farmers into bankruptcy.

Despite much of the ideology of the time, which praised the rural way of life as a healthy antidote to the ills of modern urbanism, that way of life went into decline with the agricultural depression. In 1931, 35.8 percent of the labor force in France and 46.8 percent in Italy, and in 1933 28.0 percent in Germany, worked in agriculture, forestry, and fishing. The United Kingdom alone had a very reduced rural sector (5.9 percent) and a population heavily concentrated in extractive industries (mining) and manufacturing. In the aftermath of the Second World War, agriculture continued its relative decline everywhere, and manufacturing began to lose out to the service sector. By 2000, only 1.3 percent of the British labor force, 2.5 percent of the German, 4.1 percent of the French, and 5.3 percent of the Italian were in agriculture, forestry, and fishing, while the service sector in all these large economies accounted for the overwhelming share of the workforce (the respective figures are 77.8 percent, 69.1 percent, 69.5 percent, and 62.6 percent). Modernity thus meant service industries, almost always with more changing employment patterns than in industry or agriculture, where workers had frequently remained in one place and often with one employer.

Designing urban life

Modernity meant urban existence, and the new freedoms that it offered. Late-nineteenth-century towns could grow very much larger because of the introduction of the electric streetcar or tram, of the suburban railroad, and – in some large conurbations – of underground railroads. The deep Piccadilly Line in London, a triumph of the Chicago financier Charles Tyson Yerkes, was opened in 1907. In the interwar period, the Metropolitan Line was extended out to Uxbridge (1925). A great deal of transportation within cities, however, was still horse-drawn, which led to big environmental problems.

The first continental European underground line was built in Budapest, a comparatively shallow under-the-street excavation (1896). In Paris, the Metro began with the new century (1900). In 1931 the Communist Party Central Committee voted to build a metro in Moscow, which became a prestige object of widespread admiration when it opened in 1935. The basic Berlin S-Bahn system (rapid suburban railroad) was constructed between 1924 and 1929, and electrified from 1927, with sturdy cars that were still in use in the 1990s.

At the end of the First World War, Prime Minister David Lloyd George described his task as making the United Kingdom a fit country for heroes to live in. Some response to this challenge came from private house building, with building societies encouraging saving for house construction and purchase. By 1939, one-third of housing in the United Kingdom had been built since the end of the First World War. But mostly incomes were not sufficiently high for the task of rehousing the people to be effectively managed by the private sector alone.

The greatest and most urgent task in almost all of Europe was the provision of public housing. In countries with high inflation or hyper-inflation, the destruction of the private capital market, coupled with rent controls, made private construction very rare: in Germany, for instance, over two-thirds of housing in the 1920s was publicly constructed. It produced some of the great architectural achievements of the interwar period: Bruno Taut's Hufeisen settlement in Berlin (1924–7); Ernst Mach's Siedlung Sinnheimer Hang in Frankfurt (1926); or Karl Ehn's massive and fortress-like Karl Marx Hof in Vienna (1930) (which was indeed subjected to a siege in Austria's civil war in 1934).

The results of the interwar building boom were controversial. As a result of the new construction, many people lived more comfortably than before. The Swiss-French architect Le Corbusier propagated the idea that a house was "a machine for living in"; and argued that architectural reform and large-scale city planning was a way of avoiding social and political breakdown ("Architecture or revolution: revolution can be avoided").[11] But aesthetes disliked the suburban sprawl, and sometimes put their opposition in a very radical way. The genteel John Betjeman in the United Kingdom even called for mass destruction: *Come friendly bombs and fall on Slough*.

In a similar but more radical vein, German Propaganda Minister Joseph Goebbels declared that he welcomed the bombing of total war, because it would make for a universal equality, and allow reconstruction on aesthetically superior terms.

Modernism

"Modernism" is an eclectic term which has different meanings in varied contexts, but where the meanings – as is often the case in such a plurality – shift over from one domain to the other. On one level, it means an embracing of modern life and ideas, of urbanization, industrialization and the industrial society, technology, and the application of Enlightenment ideas about human capacity for improvement.

As a cultural movement, the term is often used more specifically to mean the rejection of the legacy of nineteenth-century romanticism, which modernism derided as sentimental, inauthentic, and aesthetically exhausted. The social and political disintegration of the First World War led to an explosion of cultural creativity. Some modernists, such as Pablo Picasso (1881–1973), thought of themselves as being politically on the left, and saw their art as part of a process of reformist politics. But a large number of modernists were conservative in political matters, and thought of themselves as rescuing tradition from its Enlightenment and post-Enlightenment advocates. Artists as diverse as Igor Stravinsky (1882–1971) and Arnold Schoenberg (1874–1951), whose approach to musical composition was revolutionary, or the poet T.S. Eliot (1888–1965), or the painter Henri Matisse (1869–1954) (who became an icon of modernity) emphatically used tradition as a way of rescuing their art from what they saw as the danger of twentieth-century superficiality. Stravinsky emphasized Russian folk traditions, and Schoenberg insisted more and more intensely that great music could come only from deep religious faith, and wrote a prose drama on "the biblical path". The prevalence of anti-Semitic persecution only strengthened Schoenberg's resolve. Linked to this conception was that of an artistic elite, defined by the purity of its goals and opposed to a democratic and commercialized vulgarity. Eliot's anti-Semitism was for him a way of signaling his opposition to mass culture, whether commercialized or Bolshevik. Modernism thus did not need to be modern, and could frequently become what Jeffrey Herf has termed "Reactionary Modernism". The aftermath of the Second World War and the subsequent stabilization of European politics had the opposite effect of the previous conflict: cultural innovation became fragmented and the level of ferment died down.

Architecture introduced a modern aesthetic which sustained itself through much of the century. In 1919, an appeal of German architects, signed by the leading modernists, argued that "architecture was the leader and master" of the visual arts, since it provided a shape and form which guided human interactions. In the same year Walter Gropius formulated the program of the state building school (Bauhaus) in Weimar.

The Bauhaus self-consciously designed modern, functional buildings for a new type of person who would cast off the fussiness and ornamentation of the past. Buildings were intended clearly to reflect their use, nothing more nor less, along the lines of the slogan "form follows function". In this regard, new industrial materials could be openly used. Steel and concrete did not have to be concealed. Glass and light became central elements of the new design. In the immediate aftermath of the First World War, Gropius designed vast utopian and unrealizable projects for glass pyramids ("mountains for living").

In the later 1920s and 1930s, the push to modernism was in part offset by a new monumentalism. Its most political manifestations were in the totalitarian states, in the wedding-cake architecture of the Stalinist reconstruction of Moscow in the 1930s, and in the neo-classicism of Albert Speer's designs for Hitler. The Nazi government in Anhalt closed the Bauhaus in Dessau in 1932. But the new classicizing monumentalism was found equally in Republican France, as well as in the United Kingdom (the Giles Gilbert Scott design for the Cambridge University Library). And in the same way as parliamentary and democratic regimes moved to classicism (some of the most extreme examples are to be found in US New Deal work creation projects, such as Philadelphia's 30th Street Station), totalitarian regimes took up the modernist aesthetic. Nor was there a necessary contradiction between modernism and totalitarianism. In 1933 and 1934, Mies van der Rohe tried to convince Nazi ideologues such as Alfred Rosenberg that modernism was compatible with a new, scientifically focused and economically strong Germany, and he entered designs for government architectural competitions (such as for the new Berlin Reichsbank building). The totalitarian regimes in fact took up architectural modernism where it was judged appropriate: in Ernst Sagebiel's streamlined but massive 1935 Luftwaffe Ministry building, or in the Olympic Village to house athletes for the 1936 Berlin Olympic Games (Sagebiel was a pupil of the outstanding modernist architect Erich Mendelsohn).

After the war, however, classicism was linked in many architects' minds to fascism, and the modern style became fully ascendant as the "international style". It was at its most effective in buildings such as Hans Scharoun's Berlin Congress Hall, designed to celebrate American–German friendship.

Eventually international modernism became a platitude, and a reaction against it set in. It was the architecture of the new towns that spread in Europe from Cumbernauld and Glenrothes in Scotland, Harlow New Town and Milton Keynes in England, and Poissy and Mantes-la-Jolie in the suburbs of Paris, to Eisenhüttenstadt, Nowa Huta, and Magnitogorsk (the prototype) in Russia. In existing cities, whole new areas were constructed with high-rise architecture, termed *Plattenbau* in the German Democratic Republic, and tower architecture in the United Kingdom. Between 1964 and 1974 384 tower blocks were built in London, often linked with high-level (and vandal-prone) walkways.

In the last two decades of the twentieth century, something of a retreat from the extreme features of the modernist aesthetic occurred. There was a playful allusion to a wide variety of styles, but not in the historicist mode of the early twentieth century. Postmodernist architecture tried to avoid the obvious, including right angles and straightforward facades. It lived by being intriguing, rather than in forcibly organizing the viewer. Successful examples, such as James Stirling's Neue Staatsgalerie in Stuttgart, succeeded in recreating the idea of an aesthetic.

Architecture was following a trend that had been long identifiable in the rest of the visual arts: toward an avant-garde in which artists deliberately formulated visions to startle and shake assumptions. A large part of the phenomenon of artistic modernism involved the revolt of artists against society. During the First World War, Tristan Tzara had launched Dadaism in Zurich as a protest against the irrationality of war; but in the 1920s André Breton took it (as "surrealism") in a much more political direction. Dreams should be restated in order to transform reality. Surrealism was meant as a kind of revolution, and some of its disciples became involved in orthodox communism.

In the end artistic modernism, born of a revolt against bourgeois conventionality, became a central part of the new order. Companies embraced its abstraction, since the traditional themes of most great visual art, erotic or religious, seemed inappropriate in boardrooms; while patterns and shapes, even when they were intended to disturb or provoke, actually reassured. The corporate art market sent up the prices for modern art, which became another commodity for speculative investment. By the end of the century, many commentators seized on the analogies between the modernistic enterprise in the visual arts and a new knowledge-based economy. Modern art was supposed to challenge conventions, and modern entrepreneurs were continually discovering new ideas and new products and markets. Even more outrageously, both the modern artist and the modern businessman could depict their consumers as traditionalists and reactionaries, whose views could be treated with unconcealed contempt. As one pair of commentators wrote, "Gallery visitors did not tell Picasso to invent cubism, customers function as rearview mirrors. They are extremely conservative, boring, lack imagination, and don't know their own minds."[12]

The sociologist Max Weber described the modern rationality that followed from twentieth-century prosperity as an "iron cage". Writing about the ethic of capitalism in 1906, he explained that: "material goods have gained an increasing and finally an inexorable power over the lives of men as at no previous period in history".[13] Goods were at the same time liberating and enslaving. This was the world against which artistic modernism revolted; it was the world against which an increasingly narcissistic individualism of personal style reacted. But ultimately, as Weber had foreseen, it was hard to escape the trap. The revolt of individualism against mass society, stimulated by the cult of the consumer, was in practice one way of rationalizing mass society. It was modernization while protesting against it. These protests, often violent and destructive, and which created new social and political realities, form the subject of most of this book.

Notes

1 A. James Gregor, *Italian Fascism and Developmental Dictatorship*, Princeton, NJ: Princeton University Press, 1979; David Schoenbaum, *Hitler's Social Revolution; Class and Status in Nazi Germany, 1933–1939*, Garden City, NY: Doubleday, 1966; Ralf Dahrendorf, *Society and Democracy in Germany*, Garden City, NY: Doubleday, 1967; Rainer Zitelmann (transl. Helmut Bogler), *Hitler: the Policies of Seduction*, London: London House, 1999; Isaac Deutscher, *Stalin, a Political Biography*, London and New York: Oxford University Press, 1949; Alec Nove, *Economic Rationality and Soviet Politics; or, Was Stalin Really Necessary?*, New York: Praeger, 1964.
2 Jörg Baten and Andrea Wagner, "Health under National Socialism: the mortality and nutritional crisis in Germany 1933–38", *Economics and Human Biology*, 2003.
3 See J. Bradford Delong, *The Economic History of the Twentieth Century: Slouching Towards Utopia?*, University of California at Berkeley, draft available at www.j-bradford-delong.net/TCEH/Slouch_title.html.
4 Atina Grossman, *Reforming Sex: The German Movement for Birth Control and Abortion Reform 1920–1950*, New York: Oxford University Press, 1995, p. 4.
5 Eurostat figures for 1999.
6 From Thomas Piketty, *Les haut revenues en France au XXᵉ siècle. Inégalités et redistributions 1901–1998*, Paris: Bernard Grasset, 2001.
7 Lawrence Stone, *Road to Divorce: England 1530–1987*, Oxford: Oxford University Press, 1990, p. 395.
8 Robert Rhodes James, *Anthony Eden*, London: Weidenfeld, 1986, p. 30.
9 Robert Graves, *Goodbye to All That*, Harmondsworth: Penguin, 1960 (orig. 1929), p. 221.
10 Joseph Cardinal Ratzinger, *Salt of the Earth: The Church at the End of the Millennium – An Interview with Peter Seewald*, San Francisco: Ignatius Press, 1997, pp. 222–3.
11 Le Corbusier (transl. Frederick Etchells), *Towards a New Architecture*, New York: Praeger, 1960, pp. 89, 269.
12 Kjell Nordström and Jonas Riderstrale, *Funky Business: Talent Makes Capital Dance*, Harlow: Pearson, 2000, p. 158.
13 Max Weber (transl. Talcott Parsons), *The Protestant Ethic and the Spirit of Capitalism*, Los Angeles: Roxbury, 1995, p. 181.

2   War and peace
Lenin and Wilson

The first half of the twentieth century, and in particular the 30 years from 1914 to 1945, was an age of military, political, economic, social, and cultural conflict, a period of disenchantment, disillusion, discord, and despair, in which hatred flourished and the humanitarian impulse was scarce.

To an observer in 1900, this development would have looked surprising. There was plenty to be confident about at the beginning of the century: in the domestic politics of many European states, representative and responsible government was becoming more common. Internationally, conflicts were resolved by arrangements between the Great Powers. Economically, there was a substantial level of integration, with large flows of goods, capital, and labor that were largely unaffected by national control and regulation (modern historians speak about an initial period or first wave of "globalization"). Property rights were secure and widely understood as a basis of civilization. It is plausible to believe that the phenomena of better domestic government, international stability, and economic integration stand in a causally linked relationship. Certainly, that belief in progress was plausible at the time, and quite widespread. Some analysts, notably the British writer Norman Angell, in a book entitled *The Great Illusion*, even suggested that the extent of integration and interdependence made war impossible. These optimistic illusions were shattered by the First World War.

What were the problems that effectively destroyed the belief in secular human progress? Some might reply that it was the chance of the First World War. But historians who look at the origins of the disintegration actually see many causes for concern before 1914: the seeds of destruction were sown at the moment of greatest optimism. In particular, people suffered because they increasingly saw human problems in terms of the struggles of large collectives: the nation, the working class. The claims or supposed rights of such collectives were the center of large-scale political clashes. It was war that produced Europe's first modernization shock.

War and mobilization

The First World War started after a terrorist incident escalated into a conflict that sucked in the major European powers. They had locked themselves into a system of alliances that now entailed security commitments and preemptive strikes. On June 28, 1914, a Bosnian Serb nationalist, Gavrilo Princip, killed the Archduke and heir to the Austrian throne, Franz Ferdinand, and his wife, the Countess Chotek, as they drove in an open car through the streets of the Bosnian capital Sarajevo. Austria demanded to investigate the terrorist networks of the Black Hand (Crna Ruka) that had allegedly staged the attack, and that reached into the neighboring kingdom of Serbia. It believed that there was some involvement on the part of Serbian government agencies, and in particular of the intelligence service of Colonel Apis, and hence that Serbia could not be trusted with a police investigation. The ultimatum that Austria sent to Serbia on July 23, 1914, after having consulted its German ally, was incompatible with Serbian sovereignty. On July 28, Austria declared war on Serbia, and started to shell Belgrade (despite a last-minute attempt by the German Kaiser Wilhelm II to hold up the military action). Serbia appealed to Russia, which had seven years earlier been humiliated in the Balkans when the Austrian Empire had annexed Bosnia– Herzegovina. Russia ordered a partial mobilization of its armies on July 29, and a full mobilization the next day. On August 1, Germany declared war on Russia, and on August 3, on France, Russia's ally. In order to defeat France quickly, German troops were sent through Belgium (August 4), violating the international treaty guaranteeing the neutrality of that country, and bringing the United Kingdom into the war on the side of France and Russia.

Gavrilo Princip, a devotee of irrationalist thinkers such as Friedrich Nietzsche and Kropotkin, was incarcerated by the Austrians in the prison of Theresienstadt in Bohemia, where he died in April 1918. In interviews with an Austrian psychologist, Dr. Martin Pappenheim, he insisted that he "could not believe that a World War would break out as the result of an act like this".[1]

At the outset of the war, each side believed that it could win quickly via a short offensive. The Germans were insouciant about the violation of Belgium because they thought that in a short war, the United Kingdom (with a small army) could make little difference. Two Russian armies launched a pincer movement on the German position in East Prussia. German soldiers invaded France by marching through neutral Belgium in line with a plan developed by Count Schlieffen: as chief of the German general staff (1891–1905) he had calculated that Germany could fight a two-front war against France and Russia by destroying France first, because Russian mobilization could be expected to be slow. By the time it was complete, Russia would no longer have an ally, and Germany would then be able to concentrate resources on the Eastern Front. But in the reality of 1914, the Russian and German offensives both failed. The Russian army that had invaded East Prussia from the south was itself the victim of an encircling pincer movement under General von François (in the battle of Tannenberg).

The German attack on France was halted at the Marne, so close to Paris that the sound of artillery could be heard. The German chief of the general staff, Helmuth von Moltke, one of the major architects of Germany's push to war, had a nervous breakdown and was replaced by the Prussian Minister of War, von Falkenhayn. New German offensives, above all near the Channel coast at Ypres in Flanders, failed to produce any breakthrough, and the two sides in the west settled down to a war of trenches and barbed wire, in which for four years there was little movement in the fronts. There were still violent battles at Ypres in the late summer of 1918. After the war, a giant commemorative arch, the Menin Gate, 140 feet wide, 135 feet long, and 80 feet high, recorded in small lettering simply the 54,900 names of the "missing", those whose bodies had never been identified because they had been lost in the mud.

The war widened out from the two original fronts. Turkey joined Germany in November 1914, a vital partner for the Central Powers (Germany and Austria) in that the Turkish control of the Black Sea straits could be used to restrict Allied supplies to Russia. The Turkish alliance extended the war as far east as Persia. In October 1915 the Central Powers won an alliance with Bulgaria by promising territorial gains at the expense of Serbia. Meanwhile, in the secret Treaty of London (April 1915), France and the United Kingdom promised Italy Austrian territory in the Trentino (South Tyrol), and around Trieste and in Dalmatia.

Especially in the west, the war became a clash simply between soldiers much more than previous wars, largely (after the chaotic beginning) because civilians were kept away from the well-defined fronts. But in those initial stages there had been some considerable brutality against civilians, chiefly in Belgium and northern France: when the German armies seized Liège, they used civilians as human shields. In August 1914, German troops killed 4,421 Belgian civilians. They destroyed much of the city of Louvain, including the famous university library. Two thousand buildings were destroyed in this German attack. On the Eastern Front national and ethnic differences meant that combatants looked at some peoples as fifth columns for the other side, and atrocities took place on a much bigger scale. Russians suspected Jews of being in league with the Austrians and Germans. Since the Turkish defeat of 1877, Turkish nationalists had suspected the Christian Armenians of sympathizing with and supporting the Russians. From April 1915, Turkish officials deported first Armenian leaders and then men of military age, and engaged in a systematic killing that destroyed over half of the 2 million-strong Armenian population of the Ottoman Empire. By August 1915, the Turkish Interior Minister was saying that "the Armenian question no longer exists".

Most of the victims of this war, however, were soldiers. By November 1918, there were 2 million German military deaths, 1.8 million Russian deaths, 1.4 million in France, 1.1 million in the Austrian Empire, 1 million from the United Kingdom and its Empire, 800,000 Turks, 600,000 Italians, 300,000 Serbians, and 100,000 Americans.

Where the fronts were static and defended by barbed wire and earth entrenchments, the only hope for movement was to use explosives. Nobody had envisaged the gigantic quantity of munitions, especially shells, that would be required to fight the new kind of war. A Russian estimate was that in order to tear holes in a 50-meter stretch of three-strand barbed wire (a pretty light defense), 400 heavy shells or 25,000 light shells would be needed.[2] The United Kingdom in 1914 had produced 5,000 tons of explosive, and in 1917 was making 186,000 tons; Germany was better stocked in 1914 with 14,000 tons, and raised production in 1917 to 144,000 tons. Explosives required nitrates; until the First World War, the major demand had been for agricultural fertilizer, and the source imported guano from South America. This was obviously vulnerable to blockading, but the Germans quickly developed a synthetic alternative, through the Haber–Bosch chemical process that fixed nitrogen from the air.

As it became clear that the war would not be quickly won by any side, a reorientation of society and economy toward the production of war materiel was needed. The need to produce on such a large scale required a rethinking of how economies should be run. Economic liberalism no longer seemed adequate: there needed to be a coordinated, centralized process of planning. The First World War thus produced the economic plan.

Germany was the quickest to adapt in this way. Already in August 1914, it established a War Raw Materials Office (*Kriegsrohstoffamt*). The leading figures in the new organization were well-connected businessmen, Wichard von Moellendorff and Walther Rathenau. They saw the war as an opportunity to build a better society for the future, in which there would be more planning as a permanent fact of social organization.

What Moellendorff and Rathenau called "war socialism" (*Kriegssozialismus*) reached its culmination in 1916, after a new round of offensives had failed. On the Western Front, Germany engaged in a cynical and brutal attempt to knock out France by attacking a point so important both symbolically and strategically that France would defend it to the last man. Since France had a smaller population than Germany, and could thus sustain only a smaller army, France would be literally bled into the ground. The German offensive against the citadel of Verdun began on February 21, 1916. In order to relieve the pressure on Verdun, the British agreed to stage a large-scale offensive on the Somme (July 1). In the east, the Russian army under General Brusilov, in an offensive in Galicia beginning on June 1, 1916, virtually destroyed the Austrian war effort, and took 200,000 Austrian prisoners, but then ground to a halt.

After all these offensives, new increases in production were needed, but they required a greater degree of social cohesion at home. War was now presented as only part of a package of promised social reform. Before the war, Imperial Germany had rejected and demonized socialists. In 1914, the German government persuaded the socialist leadership that it was fighting a war against reactionary Russian autocracy. In 1916, socialist and union leaders were brought into political and economic decision-making.

The large increase in munitions output envisaged in the Hindenburg Program was accompanied by a state mobilization of labor through the

Patriotic Auxiliary Service Law. Workers were conscripted into war industries; they were not allowed to change their jobs without a certificate of release; but in return, workers as well as representatives of the employers and the military would set wages and conditions of work. Trade union membership, which had fallen sharply from 1914 to 1916 (from 2.5 million before the war in socialist unions to less than 1 million in 1916), now rose again (by 1919 it had risen to 5.5 million). The new degree of central control, and the element (admittedly small) of workers' involvement, looked to socialists everywhere (including Lenin in Switzerland) as a demonstration of the practical feasibility of socialism.

Other countries were also impressed by the example of German mobilization. In 1916, the British Liberal administration collapsed, and was replaced (in December) by the much more *dirigiste* vision of David Lloyd George. The new Prime Minister wanted to bring in business leaders in order to run the war economy on more efficient lines. Ulster Unionist and cabinet member E.H. Carson spoke of a "new collectivism".

In France, Etienne Clémentel, the Minister of Commerce and Industry from 1915, had long warned about "Germany's compact economic masses". He now encouraged employers to organize in order to produce more efficiently, and established "consortiums" to market each product. In November 1917, Georges Clemenceau became Prime Minister; he had made a reputation as a relentless critic of the war effort, who accused his predecessors of defeatism and compromising with the enemy. His politics were militantly anti-socialist, but he tried to bring union leaders into the government and to make concessions to the economic and social demands of the socialists.

The new politics also involved a greater role for parliamentary and democratic politics, but often with a plebiscitary and demagogic tone. The German generals Hindenburg and Ludendorff largely invented their roles in the initial 1914 victory on the Eastern Front (they had actually not been there when the crucial decisions were made); but they then quite skillfully used their victory as the basis of a political myth and a political movement. The name Tannenberg, although not geographically quite appropriate for the wide area of the battles in the Masurian Lakes area, deliberately recalled the battle of 1410, in which the Teutonic Knights had been defeated: the new Tannenberg was to mark the reassertion of German interests in the east. Hindenburg was idolized as a new Siegfried. Ludendorff explained: "Words are today battles: right words are battles won, and wrong words, battles lost."[3]

The German military leadership gradually undermined the Chancellorship of Theobald von Bethmann-Hollweg by mobilizing the political opposition in parliament, supplying it with information, and suggesting that Bethmann's conservatism stood in the way of a quick end to the war. They presented a new version of the short-war strategy. On the basis of calculations about the effects of a blockade, they believed that a submarine war in the Atlantic would cut off the supply to the United Kingdom and France, and produce a

German victory. Such a move might drive the United States into the conflict, but the war would be won before an American intervention could make any difference (a replication of the argument of 1914 that it did not make much difference whether or not the United Kingdom was in the war, because France would be defeated so soon). In April 1917, after Germany deployed unconditional submarine warfare, the United States indeed entered the war.

As the war went on, and as its costs mounted, the argument grew stronger in each belligerent that large territorial gains and financial payments were needed: the cost of the war would be imposed on the loser. Territorial gains might be used to buy allies, in the way that the United Kingdom and France had made concrete promises to Russia and Italy, and Germany to Bulgaria and Turkey.

The reality was that no country could either wish or afford to pay for such a costly conflict out of taxation or other current revenue. The United Kingdom raised income tax (to 25 percent), and also imposed a supertax on the rich. In other countries, governments feared that tax increases would undermine social consensus. There was no general income tax in France until 1917, although a partial tax of 2 percent came in 1914. Instead, war was paid by deficit finance: the government deficit as a proportion of government expenditure in 1917 amounted to 76 percent even in the United Kingdom, while in France it was 86 percent and in Germany 91 percent. Only the much fresher United States looked healthy, with 44 percent. Some of these deficits were funded by the sale of debt, but most were financed simply through the printing press. Even the sale of debt was in practice made into part of an inflationary mechanism, as citizens were allowed to buy debt and then take their bonds to the banking system and turn them into new cash. From 1913 to 1918 there was a 600 percent increase in the German money supply, 900 percent in Austria, and 1,000 percent in Russia; the western powers looked a little better, with 400 percent for France and less than 100 percent in the case of the United Kingdom.

Most government debt was raised on the domestic market, but governments also needed to borrow abroad in order to pay for necessary strategic imports. The main source of new money was ultimately the United States, which rose to the status of a financial superpower because of the war. But the United Kingdom played a major role too. The United Kingdom borrowed $6.5 billion, mostly from the United States, but lent more: $10.4 billion. France borrowed $7 billion, from the United Kingdom and America, but lent $3.5 billion. Half of the British loans and one-third of the French loans went to Russia, which was in an increasingly desperate position and was in effect being paid to fight by the western powers.

The internal and the external debt would need to be paid off in some way. But how? Large increases in taxes in an impoverished postwar world were unthinkable. An alternative lay in placing the costs of war on those outside the national community. The German Treasury Secretary, Karl Helfferich, talked about hanging the "lead weight of the billions" of war expenditure around the necks of the losers. Such a strategy required dramatic victory, rather than compromise peace. As more and more was invested in war, the chance of any compromise was thus reduced.

But by 1917, there was a growing demand for peace: it formed one of the major elements in the demands of Russian revolutionaries; and in Germany the opposition parties (left liberals, Catholics and socialists) in July 1917 voted a peace resolution in the Reichstag. In France, there were extensive mutinies after the French high command launched a new series of costly offensives, though the German generals never found out how near the opposing army was to complete collapse.

At an international level, on August 1, 1917, Pope Benedict XV presented a peace note, in which he called for a peace without annexations or indemnities. The initiative was taken most seriously in Austria, which by this stage was near to collapse: the Prime Minister had been assassinated in 1916, by the son of the leading socialist politician; the old Emperor Franz Joseph was dead and his successor, Charles, inexperienced and terrified. But peace initiatives had the potential politically to destroy anyone who dared to associate themselves with the cause of compromise. In 1917, Clemenceau blasted Joseph Caillaux, the former prime minister who pushed a peace initiative, for being willing to sacrifice some French demands. In 1918, the Austrian Foreign Minister Count Czernin said that France had made a peace proposal, and when Clemenceau showed that this was not true and that it was the Austrians who were asking for negotiations, Czernin was obliged to resign.

If compromise was impossible, and short offensives seemed to produce only failure, another alternative lay in the political subversion of the other side. Often this push to destabilize the political system of the other side was quite crude and amateurish. In early August 1914, just after the outbreak of the war, the German chief of the general staff spoke of inciting risings against British and Russian rule in India, Egypt, and the Caucasus, and argued that Germany would be able to use its alliance with Turkey to "excite the fanaticism of Islam". In North Africa, the Mannesmann company was instructed to set off Algerian and Moroccan revolts against France. Later Germany tried to persuade Mexico to attack the United States. Irish nationalists, such as Roger Casement, also had some German encouragement, and were allowed to recruit a nationalist army from German-held prisoners-of-war. Germany arranged to send a shipment of arms by Easter Sunday, 1916, and to bring Casement back to Ireland. But the arms ship was captured, and Casement was arrested after landing from a submarine. The rising went ahead, regardless, as an act of defiance which would create a martyrology. On Easter Monday, Irish nationalists seized central buildings in Dublin, including the Post Office. The Easter Rising was quickly and brutally suppressed, with heavy casualties (450 dead). The leaders of the rising were executed, with the exception of the half-Spanish Eamon de Valera, an American citizen, who was spared in order not to provoke anti-British feeling in the United States.

In 1917, Germany embarked on its biggest experiment in undermining the other side by the application of a revolutionary bacillus. It allowed the transit, in a sealed railroad car, of some of the leaders of the Russian Bolshevik revolutionary movement from Switzerland. Lenin proved to be a more effective revolutionary than Roger Casement.

The United Kingdom encouraged an Arab rising against the Ottoman Empire, which was allied with the Central Powers. Germany quickly found that its links with Turkey did it little good in the Arab world. The British High Commissioner in Egypt, Sir Henry McMahon, explained that the United Kingdom was "prepared to recognize and support the independence of the Arabs". A British and Indian offensive in Mesopotamia had initially been successful, but was surrounded and then surrendered to the Turkish army in April 1916. But then in June, Sharif Husayn declared the Arab revolt, and Arab forces formed one-half of a gigantic pincer movement that eventually in 1918 imposed a decisive defeat on the Turkish army.

The multi-national Habsburg Empire also seemed like a prime candidate for political undermining, but only after the Russian Empire had disintegrated. At the beginning of 1916, Lloyd George told the British Trades Union Congress that "a break-up of Austria–Hungary is no part of our war aims", but at the same time spoke of "genuine self-government on true democratic principles". President Wilson's Fourteen Points made a similar appeal. But Czech nationalists, and their supporters in Paris, London, and Washington, pressed for much bolder language; and in June 1918 the French government recognized Czech independence, and was followed by the British in August and the United States in September.

War and empire

Before the war, Charles Mangin, a French officer who had participated in France's Fashoda expedition of 1898, when French soldiers had clashed with a parallel British expedition, had argued that France's inadequate population relative to Germany needed to be augmented by the resources of empire. There was a need for a "plus grande France". The French government responded to the campaign, and in 1912 introduced forced recruitment in French West Africa. In 1914, Mangin published a new book with the title *The Black Force*, with a map of Africa on the front cover. In the course of the war, France mobilized and deployed almost half a million indigenous troops from Africa, including West Africans (Tirailleurs Sénégalais), Algerians (Turcos and Spahis), Tunisians, Moroccans, Malagasies, and Somalis; most of these soldiers fought in Europe. In addition, settlers of European origin from North Africa provided another 110,000 soldiers (Chasseurs d'Afrique and the terrifying Zouaves). The casualty rates were very high, but cannot be calculated with precision. Henri Barbusses's great anti-war novel, *Le feu*, describes Moroccan soldiers: "Of course they are heading for the front line. This is their place, and their arrival means we are about to attack. They are made for attacking."[4] Mangin, who was by now a general, argued that African and Asian soldiers felt less pain than white men.[5] In the most celebrated of the pointless attacks of the French army, General Nivelle's April 1917 offensive, half the African soldiers died. In the controversy that followed about whether Africans constituted "human cannon fodder", Mangin was relieved of his command.

For the British Empire, the First World War definitively turned the calculation away from colonies and empire as a source of pointless military commitment. At the end of the nineteenth century, the Secretary of State for India, Lord George Hamilton, had complained that "our Empire is in excess of our armaments, and even of our power to defend it in all parts of the world".[6] Now it was clear that empire hung together in a massive military–economic complex. Over 3 million soldiers and workers from the Empire were part of the British war effort. Some 10 percent of the 1 million soldiers were killed. There were 140,000 Indians fighting on the Western Front, and they played a crucial part in fighting in the Middle East, where the attacks on the Turkish army helped to promote Islamic nationalism among the Indian soldiers. More than 62,000 Indians were killed in the course of the conflict. The Canadian Expeditionary Force took part in the major battles of the Western Front, including Second Ypres, Vimy Ridge, and Passchendaele. The involvement of the Australian army in the abortive Gallipoli campaign and the British failure to give symbolic acknowledgement to the Australian contribution in the Syrian campaign (the Arab soldiers were allowed to enter Damascus in a dramatic staging on October 1, 1918) contributed to Australian resentment of the British system of continued control of the white dominions.

The German Empire did not use colonial troops in Europe, and indeed German propaganda depicted the French and British mobilizations as violations of international law. In 1915 the German Foreign Office issued a pamphlet with the title *The Illegal Use of Colored Troops on the European Battlefield by Britain and France*.

Revolution

The Russian Revolution grew out of increasing dissatisfaction with the government's handling of the war effort. In part, there was a nationalist resentment that there might be pro-German elements in the highest echelons of the state (especially around the German-born Tsarina Alexandra), or that businessmen were conspiring for peace while making money out of selling arms. The demand for reform existed at the elite level, among Russians who wanted to modernize and westernize.

It also had a very powerful grassroots component. Russian peasant farmers had initially appeared to be among the great beneficiaries of the war and of the increased food prices. Frequently they spent their new riches on luxury goods, but also on the acquisition of land, for which a substantial market developed. But as the inflation became more severe, sales of land dried up as owners did not want to surrender real assets. Farmers thus found themselves with large quantities of cash which seemed to promise an entitlement, but actually now meant little.

In the big industrial centers, employment had been expanded. There were vast ammunition factories, such as the Putilov works in Petrograd (as St Petersburg was renamed in deference to anti-German sentiment). But little attention had been given to either housing or feeding the new workers. Urban Russia was starving and bitter.

The revolution occurred at two levels. In local settings – in the big cities and in the countryside – Russians took justice into their own hands. The revolution began with urban protests. In January and February 1917 strikes occurred in Petrograd, Moscow, and Kharkov, called by socialist leaders to mark the anniversary of a massacre in 1905. But the political appeals to revolutionary memories do not appear to have been as persuasive as the miserable conditions of wartime Russia. There were much larger riots in Petrograd about inadequate food distribution, starting on March 8, 1917. The government tried to use the army to restore order, but the soldiers of the Pavlovsky Regiment mutinied. On March 12, workers and soldiers captured the Peter and Paul fortress and released its prisoners. Workers soon created committees (soviets) to allocate food, and began to requisition the houses and apartments of the rich and well-fed.

At the level of high politics, the parliament (Duma) and the liberal leaders believed that the Tsar no longer had the confidence of Russians, and on March 14 formed a provisional government. Nicholas II abdicated the next day, in favor of his brother Grand Duke Michael (and in violation of the law of succession, which required that the eldest son should succeed). His last act as monarch showed how little he understood either law or Russia, and how much he saw his throne as a simply private possession. The inheritance question proved irrelevant, since Michael declined this offer of the Russian throne. Russia was thus no longer a monarchy (this was the "February Revolution": the Russian calendar was 13 days behind the western one, until Lenin brought Russia onto the western system in February 1918). There was widespread rejoicing in rural as well as urban Russia.

Peasants began to seize land, cut down trees, and take equipment from the aristocratic estates, immediately after the fall of the Tsar. They quickly reconstituted the peasant commune, which had been the major fact of nineteenth-century life, supervising periodic redistributions of land, but which had been suppressed in the major agrarian reforms at the beginning of the twentieth century. With the revival of the commune came a sort of rural socialism, which found its clearest political expression in a party which drew on the Russian populist revolutionary tradition, the Socialist Revolutionaries or SRs (in particular the left SRs).

Between March and November, Russians experienced a "dual power" in which there was a central government which made foreign policy and gave orders to the army, but most practical political decisions affecting local issues were taken by the soviets in the cities and by peasant meetings on the land. Lenin interpreted the dualism as representing a gap between an old "bourgeois" power that was waning, and the new embryonic dictatorship of the proletariat and the peasantry, which was being built up more or less spontaneously. In practice, Russia was quickly disintegrating. One of the challenges for any government in the center now lay in establishing a new base for the exercise of power and authority.

The major figures in the Provisional Government were the Prime Minister Prince Lvov, a constitutional liberal, who had long pressed for a lightening of the autocracy, and Milyukov, the Foreign Minister. The new regime immediately promised reform: land reform, increased political liberty, and autonomy for Poles and Finns. The most immediately pressing issue was how to disengage from the war with Austria and Germany. On April 8, after long bargaining between the soviets, which wanted a peace without indemnities or annexations, and Milyukov, who wanted to maintain Russia's commitment to the western allies, the government announced that:

> The aim of free Russia is not the domination of other people, or the conquest of their national territories, nor the occupation by force of foreign lands, but the establishment of an enduring peace based on the people's right of self determination. Russia has no desire either to subjugate or humiliate anyone.[7]

But then came the "Milyukov note", in which the Foreign Minister appeared to disavow the revolutionary demand for a separate peace with Germany by reassuring the Allies that Russia still wanted a "decisive victory", and made no reference to "democratic Russia". After large-scale protests, Milyukov resigned, and a socialist, Kerensky, who was Vice-President of the Petrograd Soviet, became War Minister. In July Kerensky replaced Prince Lvov as Prime Minister. His major strength was his ability to make heart-tugging and histrionic appeals to the soviets: "if you do not trust me I am right here just before your eyes ready to die" and

> Ah comrades, it is too bad I didn't die two months ago . . . Then I would have died with the sweetest dreams. A new life had begun for my country, for ever. There would be no need for whips or sticks in order to make people respect one another.[8]

His major weakness also lay in that histrionic quality, which drove him to the edge of psychic collapse.

Lvov and Kerensky's government talked about reforms without really being able to change conditions on the ground. The soviets looked as if they were much more effective. Politically, different parts of the Russian Empire moved in quite varied directions. Most soviets were dominated by socialists, but not by the Bolsheviks: the major political stream in the council movement was that of the "mensheviks", so called because they had been in the (less extreme) minority of the Marxist Russian Social Democratic Workers' Party meeting in London in 1903. Only a few soviets, in Kransoyarsk and Ivanovo, and in some industrial cities in the Urals and the Donbas, had Bolshevik majorities in the spring of 1917. The most important soviet, because of its location, that of Petrograd, was not in Bolshevik control until September 1917. On June 16, a soviet congress met, with 1,090 deputies elected by some 20 million voters: 285 of the deputies were SRs, 248 mensheviks, and 105 Bolsheviks.

The Bolsheviks (who had been the radical majority in the London conference) played a comparatively small role in the opening stages of the 1917 revolution. They had been taken by surprise by the collapse of the autocracy. In April, Lenin arrived at Petrograd's Finland Station, and one month later the non-Bolshevik revolutionary Leon Trotsky arrived and then joined Lenin's party. In July, the Bolsheviks staged a coup, which quickly failed, and Lenin fled to Finland.

The radical position was rescued when General Kornilov feared that the soviets would take over the government, and marched on Petrograd. Kerensky had little alternative except to appeal to the soviets to defend him, and to release the Bolshevik leaders that he had imprisoned. Kornilov's offensive crumbled, and Trotsky was elected to head the Petrograd soviet. Kerensky was quite discredited: many in the soviets believed that he had actually invited Kornilov in order to build a dictatorship. On November 6, Bolshevik units took over the government buildings in Petrograd in a largely bloodless revolution. On November 7, a congress of soviets from different parts of Russia met. On the next day, November 8, a decree established the People's Council of Commissars as a "provisional workers' and peasants' government", under Lenin, which began to rule until the calling of a constituent assembly. Dual power had come to an end, though the problem of authority in the former empire remained acute.

Marxism

The theory set out by Karl Marx (1818–83) in *Das Kapital* (the first volume of which was published in 1867) identified historical laws in which the historical process moved through the dialectical conflicts of opposed classes, defined in terms of their different relationship with the means of production. Feudalism, which was based on landholding and dominated by an aristocratic order, produced a class of traders and manufacturers, the bourgeoisie, who resented their lack of privileges and knew that the political order worked to their disadvantage. Their discontent built up until a revolution swept away the feudal order, and created a bourgeois state, which protected their class interests. But

(continued)

(continued)

the development of industrial capitalism created a large working class or proletariat, which was excluded from political rights and which constituted an inherently revolutionary potential. Returns on capital fell, requiring the capitalist class to impose ever-harsher conditions on its workforce, which became immiserated. Its political movement, socialism, would in turn sweep away capitalism, and the socialist state would allow workers to control the means of production. Workers' control would eventually generate a classless society (communism), in which a state apparatus was no longer needed to enforce class rule. At this stage the "government of people" would be replaced by the "administration of things".

Marx drew on the tradition of German idealism, and in particular on Hegel, when he described the paradoxes of class relations, in which the superior and inferior classes depended on each other, because they were defined by their respective and unequal relations to property. Hegel had elaborated this issue in the famous passage of the *Philosophy of Right* on the dialectic of master and slave. By enslaving, the master made himself too a slave, and in order to emancipate himself the institution needed to be transcended by a new form of the relationship.

Marx had little skill in concrete political operations, and subjected the largest working-class socialist party, the one created in 1875 in Germany, the SPD, to a withering critique. Eventually the SPD, and most other European socialist parties, adopted his theory. But as developed by Marx's main collaborator, Friedrich Engels, and by his disciple Karl Kautsky, the historical development at the heart of the Marxian vision had an involuntary dynamic of its own, and was analogous to Darwinian evolution. This seemed to many followers to be the strength of their movement: they believed that history was on their side against the powerful and the oppressors. Some, however, believed that the involuntary character robbed humans of their agency, and that an excessive emphasis on the automatic quality of evolution robbed the essence of what was supposed to be an emancipatory and liberating movement. Much twentieth-century Marxism wrestled with the problem of keeping the overall vision while trying to restore some room for human action.

Later in the month, elections were held to the Constituent Assembly. The Bolsheviks received about 10 million votes (24 percent of the total), the mensheviks 3 percent, and the constitutional democrats 5 percent. The majority of the deputies elected were SRs, though it was not clear whether they were right or left SRs, the left SRs being at this time quite closely allied to the Bolshevik position. When the Assembly met on January 18, it rejected the Bolshevik-drafted Declaration of the Rights of Working People by 237 to 146 votes, and the Bolsheviks declared that the Assembly was in the hands of agents of the counter-revolution. They then argued that soviet power was a fact which obviated the need for a "bourgeois-democratic assembly"; then, as the debates went on long into the night, the Red Guards announced that the Assembly was being closed because the "guard was tired". It never met again. Instead, Lenin used the third congress of soviets as a way of implementing his program, and the soviet congresses would be the legislature of the new state.

Lenin and the Bolsheviks in November reduced their platform to a simple formula: Peace, Bread, and Land. Bread was essential for the urban revolutionaries. The promise of land reform would win over rural Russia, and meant the realization of the program of the left SRs. Lenin now spoke of a tactical alliance (*smychka*) with the peasants. And the army needed peace.

In practice, Lenin found reaching a peace with Germany hard. He was aware that the foreign policy of the new government would determine its chances of success: a revolutionary wave throughout the world would guarantee the success of the Russian Revolution. But Germany appeared in no mood to agree a lenient peace, and did not seem near to political collapse. Faced by German demands to break up the Russian Empire and institute a series of puppet satellite regimes, the Bolsheviks at first supported Trotsky (the new Foreign Minister), and first broke off negotiations and then said that Russia was withdrawing from the war without agreeing a peace. But the German armies pressed on, and eventually Lenin was obliged to conclude a peace at Brest-Litovsk (March 3, 1918). It ended Russian sovereignty over Finland, Courland, Lithuania, and Ukraine, and gave substantial areas of Transcaucasia to Turkey.

Even after Brest-Litovsk, the new government still had to fight a civil war, and a war against western troops. Ukraine had signed a separate peace with the Central Powers, and built up a new state under the Cossack Hetman (Chief) Skoropadsky. Siberia had a conservative military regime under General Kolchak. General Denikin operated a volunteer army in southern Russia and the Caucasus. Most threateningly, General Yudenich, with British support, launched an offensive from the Baltic against Petrograd. But the White armies found it had to recruit soldiers, and became ludicrous associations of decorated tsarist officers without the other ranks; and foreign intervention discredited their operations in the eyes of a Russia that had become fiercely nationalistic as a result of years of war propaganda.

Leninism

While Marxism had provided a clear guide to the process of historical evolution, it did not provide much guidance as to how to make a revolution, or how to interpret the concrete features of a particular political context. How should the proletariat make sense of conflicting interpretations of such issues as whether the time was "ripe" for revolution?

(continued)

(continued)

The main contribution of Vladimir Ilyich Lenin (1870–1924) to the development of Marxism was to devise a theory in which a revolutionary party acted as the "vanguard" of the working-class movement, and interpreted events and social and political phenomena in such a way as to constitute objective truth. The party thus logically constituted an equivalent of the Church in Christianity in being a community of believers but also an authority on doctrine and dogma.

Lenin's party would discuss issues until it arrived at a solution, and then impose that solution by authority: "democratic centralism". In a postrevolutionary situation, the party would, as the leading instrument of the working class, control the state apparatus in order to realize the principle of socialist control.

Lenin also aimed to deal with the problem that there had been no general crisis of capitalism in the second half of the nineteenth century, and in answering that problem explained why a revolution was more likely to occur in his backward country, Russia, rather than in the more advanced and industrialized countries. European capitalism had not collapsed because it had exported its misery. That required an extension of formal empire, as well as the control of informal colonies, such as the South American states, the weak Ottoman Empire, or the Russian Empire, which had been "colonized" by west European capital. Here capitalism could derive a new source of high profits. Lenin saw in empire the root of collapse of world capitalism. Clashes between imperial systems produced wars, and wars produced revolutionary upheaval, especially in the periphery. When the challenge undermined the grip of the imperialist powers on the exploited periphery, the logic of the system dictated that as imperialism collapsed, so too would capitalism.

After Lenin's death, "Marxism–Leninism" was coined as a term to describe the ideology of communist states, and a philosophy of personal life (lonely hearts columns in newspapers, for instance, carried the abbreviation "m.l." to indicate belief).

In December 1917, the United Kingdom and France had reached an agreement to divide Russia into spheres of influence: the British would take the Caucasus, with its petroleum reserves, and France the industrial areas of Ukraine and the Crimea, where prewar French investments had been concentrated. The two west European powers sent troops to the south after the collapse of Germany in November 1918; but already in April 1918 a British expedition had landed in Murmansk. It did not take skillful Red propaganda to make this seem like imperialist aggression.

The White leader in the south, General Denikin, also appealed in 1919 to the new Polish state and its leader, Marshal Piłsudski, but Piłsudski was reluctant to do anything that might restore Imperial Russia. After the collapse of the White armies, however, the situation was different, and in April 1920 Piłsudski launched an offensive to rescue Ukrainian independence. Within weeks Polish troops entered Kiev. But they then faced a dramatically effective counter-offensive of the Red cavalry, with another soviet army in the north embarking on a giant pincer maneuver. By July 1920, it looked as if the Red Army was about to capture Warsaw, and the Russian leadership offered peace terms under which Poland would be substantially disarmed (with a limit of 50,000 on the army). On August 16, however, the Poles began a successful counter-strike, cutting off and capturing large numbers of Russian soldiers. With the battle of Warsaw came the end of the first great Russian effort to export the revolutionary principle.

Trotskyism

Leon Trotsky (1879–1940), originally Lev Bronstein, was the most charismatic and brilliant of the Russian revolutionaries. He was politically handicapped by both his Jewish origins and the fact that he had been a menshevik (non-Leninist Marxist) before 1917. In 1917 he became Commissar for Foreign Affairs, having declined the post of Commissar of Home Affairs because he feared that such an appointment would allow the Whites to use anti-Semitism against the Bolsheviks (which they did anyway). Subsequently, in March 1918, he was made Commissar of War and President of the Supreme War Council, and in effect became the creator of the Red Army and its leader in victory in the Civil War. In 1928 he was banished to Alma-Ata (by coincidence the place where in 1991 the disintegration of the Soviet Union was agreed). In 1929 he was expelled from the Soviet Union and moved first to Turkey, then to France, Norway, and Mexico. He was assassinated by a Spanish communist, who attacked him with an ice axe. The phrase "Trotskyism" was used at an early stage – 1924 – by Stalin to denote a "specific ideological current" that deviated from *Marxism–Leninism*.

Trotsky was closest to Lenin when the revolution seemed to be spreading over the whole of Europe: this corresponded to the theory of "permanent revolution". He was bitterly opposed to the idea, developed by Stalin, that socialism in one country was possible.

Having lost his struggle with Stalin, he escaped into exile, and there drew up a critique of Russian developments that blamed the bureaucratization of party and state for the loss of revolutionary *élan*. In Lenin's vision, he argued, the party was supposed to be the corrective and the counter-balance to the power of state bureaucrats, but under Stalin the party had itself become a bureaucracy that replicated that of

(continued)

(continued)

the state. In his final reckoning with Stalin's Russia, *The Revolution Betrayed* (1937), Trotsky wrote (p. 235):

> In its intermediary and regulating function, its concern to maintain social ranks, and its exploitation of the State apparatus for personal goals, the Soviet bureaucracy is similar to every other bureaucracy, especially the fascist. But it is also in a vast way different . . . it is something more than a bureaucracy. It is in the full sense of the word the sole privileged and commanding stratum in the Soviet society.

Through its control of the means of production, it had become a new ruling class.

Trotskyism could be developed into a theory that subjected the Soviet Union, and states shaped on its model, to a Marxist analysis. When, for instance, the Yugoslav communist Milovan Djilas claimed to have identified the communist elite as a "new class", orthodox Marxist–Leninists could reply with the accusation of Trotskyite deviationism. As a practical model of revolution, Trotskyism emphasized the use of subversive tactics and infiltration of existing institutions. It also claimed to be, and was, less organized than Soviet-style Marxism, with the result that the movement usually divided into small but endlessly bickering sects.

With the Civil War practically over, some elements of the original revolutionary grouping revolted. The Kronstadt sailors, who were more sympathetic to an anarchist vision than to Lenin and Trotsky's militarized and centralized revolution, were brutally suppressed by Trotsky in March 1921.

After this, Lenin could reassemble the Russian Empire. The July 1918 constitution for the Russian Socialist Federated Soviet Republic provided a basis for rule in Russia. In December 1922 the Russian Federation made an agreement with Ukraine, Belarus, Armenia, Azerbaijan, and Georgia, and established the Union of Soviet Socialist Republics.

The formal constitution of a state required – if it were to be effective – a consolidation of rule, after years in which power had been localized and fragmented. One of the first creations of the successful revolution was a secret police. The Cheka was established on December 20, 1917, under the leadership of the Polish revolutionary Feliks Dzerzhinsky, ostensibly as an instrument against counter-revolution and sabotage. It was also intended as a revolutionary instrument: not just a means of punishing opponents of the revolution, but also a way of raising everybody's revolutionary consciousness by attacking the innocent as well. In the theory of revolutionary terror, the Russian revolutionaries drew directly from the French model. Trotsky eulogized "the example of the great French revolutionaries. The guillotine will be ready for our enemies and not merely the jail." After an assassination attempt on Lenin by Fanny Kaplan (August 30, 1918), the Cheka launched a wide-scale purge of the bourgeoisie, mensheviks and SRs (Plate 1). The date of the government's declaration of war on the counter-revolution was deliberately chosen as September 2, 1918, the anniversary of the Paris terror of 1793: "To the White Terror of the enemies of the Workers' and People's Government the workers and peasants will reply by a mass red terror against the bourgeoisie and its agents."[9]

After a period of radical socialist expropriation, which he labeled "war communism", Lenin ordered a "strategic retreat", the New Economic Policy, in March 1921. In order to feed cities and the revolutionary armies, it was necessary to allow the independent peasant farms to operate, and to allow the armies of small traders and peddlers to function as a market. This looked like the kind of deflationary retreat that other European governments were also embarking on in the early 1920s; like them, the Russian government was obliged to cut back its public sector employment. The number of railroad workers was reduced from 1,240,000 in the summer of 1921 to 720,000 in the summer of 1922.

By this time, Lenin was rapidly declining. Physically, he was undermined by a series of strokes, the first of which came in May 1922, with a second in December. By the spring of 1923 he could no longer speak. Mentally, he was paralyzed by indecision about which of his comrades he held in least contempt. His political testament contained (subsequently famous)

Plate 1 Fanny Kaplan's attempted assassination of Lenin as he addressed Russian peasants and workers in 1918. © Bettman/Corbis.

warnings about every one of his likely successors – perhaps on the grounds that it would in the manner of a fortune-cookie slip ensure that, whatever happened, Lenin would be prophetic. In particular, "Comrade Stalin, having become General Secretary, has accumulated quite enormous power in his hands, and I am not quite sure whether he will always be able to use this power carefully enough." On Trotsky: "Personally, he is to be sure the most capable man in the Current Central Committee, but is much too much possessed by self-confidence and given too much to the administrative side of things." Bukharin was the most valuable theoretician, but had not "mastered dialectics" (the arcane pseudotheology of the party; see Chapter 5). The fact that Kamenev and Zinoviev had been against the October rising was "not accidental". As a general point, he also stated that "I would strongly advise that this Congress should adopt several changes in our political system" (though the only concrete one he proposed involved the doubling or quadrupling of the Party's Central Committee).[10] In Lenin's final memorandum (March 1923, with the title "Better Fewer, but Better", which provided the line for Comrade Ninotchka's opening salvo in an Ernst Lubitsch comedy film of 1939: "Soon there will be fewer but better Russians"), he appealed for world revolution, and based his hope on the fact that Russia, India, and China constituted the overwhelming majority of the population of the world.

Lenin's model had proved instantly attractive all over war-torn Europe. He thought that it would prove irresistible. In January 1918, the Declaration of Rights of the Toiling and Exploited People had announced that a fundamental task of the Soviet order lay in "the socialist organization of society and the victory of socialism in all countries". Lenin had spent much of his life as a revolutionary intellectual explaining why capitalism and its "highest stage", imperialism, formed a world system. This view fitted well with the powerful conviction of the Russian streets and factories that the war was in the interest of the foreigner and the bourgeois (*burzhui*), not of the Russian.

The Third (or Communist) International was summoned by the Bolshevik leaders at the end of 1918, and organized in 1919 under the presidency of Zinoviev. It embraced fully Lenin's theory of a worldwide revolution, and indeed at its first congress a quarter of the delegates came from Asia. Its second congress (July 1920) was held at the moment when the Red Army was at the height of its triumph over the Polish army. At this meeting, the Comintern imposed a list of 21 conditions, targeted against reformist socialist compromisers, with which member parties had to comply. These conditions included the denunciation of both socialist nationalists ("social patriots") and the extreme anti-war left ("social pacifists"), a call to form communist cells in trade unions and cooperatives, and to fill positions in the workers' council movement with party members. Parties would be obliged to publish the decisions of the Comintern. Anyone who would vote against acceptance of the conditions should be expelled from the party. Debates about whether or not to accept the 21 conditions split the west European socialist movements and created a vulnerability of European labor in the face of a rapidly resurgent right. Thus, by the time of Lenin's decline, the chances of a generalized European revolution looked slight.

The vision of the Russian revolutionaries, in which blood and violence were the necessary midwives of a new and better social order, drew much from Russian populist and revolutionary traditions of the nineteenth century. But such visions of revolution and its potential were not confined to Russia, and other countries too drew from native wellsprings. The Irish nationalists also had an almost theological view of sacrifice. Patrick Pearse stated that: "We may make mistakes at the beginning and shoot the wrong people, but bloodshed is a cleansing and sanctifying thing."[11]

In April 1917, widespread strikes occurred in Germany, which explicitly referred to the Russian "February Revolution". The final days of the German monarchy in November 1918 were accompanied by rumors that the German High Seas Fleet would be used in a last suicidal act of defiance, and the German sailors mutinied. They soon formed councils or soviets on the Russian model – *Räte* in German. After the Kaiser abdicated, there was for a time a dual government as in Russia, with a council of people's commissars in parallel to the workers' and soldiers' council movement. In January 1919, the leaders of the newly formed German Communist Party, Rosa Luxemburg and Karl Liebknecht, reluctantly consented to a revolutionary seizure of power designed to replicate Lenin's October. They were killed by counter-revolutionary paramilitaries. Soviet republics were formed in Bremen and Munich.

In Hungary, Bela Kun launched a soviet republic with a strongly nationalist theme. It attacked the western vision of a peace settlement with independent Slavic states, and launched attacks against Slovakia and Romania. Apart from defying the western powers, Kun aimed at establishing a land connection with revolutionary Russia.

In Italy, socialist workers formed councils and occupied factories. In Scotland, workers hoisted the Red Flag over Glasgow's city hall.

Outside Russia, however, none of the soviet movements succeeded in attracting sustained support from the countryside. Farmers had been worried during the war about urban attempts to use political influence and price controls to hold down food prices and thus rural incomes. They saw town-dwellers as unscrupulous thieves who left the cities during the "hunger winters" in order to steal potatoes and other crops. Faced with urban revolution, they took up arms. Bavarian farmers in traditional dress marched into Munich to fight against the soviet republic.

Soon, the revolutionary wave gave place to a generalized fear of revolution, which rapidly shifted European politics to the right. In an election speech in November 1918, Winston Churchill said: "Civilization is being completely extinguished over gigantic areas, while Bolsheviks hop and caper like ferocious baboons amid the ruins of cities and the corpses of their victims."[12] Lenin's vision of the rapidly spreading international revolution came to haunt the traditional politicians of Europe (but also North and South America, and Asia) assembled at the peace conference in Paris in 1919. They had a double task: providing some alternative to Lenin, and at the same time negotiating the territorial and financial details of a contested peace that followed a war of hatred.

Oil

A fossil or carbon fuel revolution began with the Industrial Revolution, when energy from coal could be substituted for human and animal labor. It changed productive capacity, and it also changed the course of human conflict. The economist William Stanley Jevons in the 1860s had depicted British power based on coal: "Of a total produce of 136 ½ millions of tons, 103 millions are produced by nations of British origin and language, and 80 millions are produced in Great Britain itself."[13] But there was increasing fear that coal would be exhausted, and so scientists and politicians began to focus on other potential sources of energy. While nineteenth-century conflicts had centered around coal, petroleum would be the focus of the twentieth century grand strategy. Just before the outbreak of war, in 1911, the British First Lord of the Admiralty, Winston Churchill, made the decision to base "naval superiority upon oil". Oil-powered ships would be quicker, and Churchill was persuaded that Germany was close to adopting an oil-driven navy. From 1913, the British navy was converted to coal. There were big doubts about the amount of petroleum that might be produced – and the United Kingdom had almost no oil but a great deal of coal – but oil gave greater flexibility and speed. It was a dramatic reorientation that changed the balance of advantage and made Persia (modern Iran) and then the Middle East central to world politics. Control of oil was vital to the outcome of both world wars of the twentieth century.

For the United Kingdom, the initial key to the global conflict thus became Persia. The United Kingdom included Persia in its sphere of influence, using its financial leverage over Russia to extend its zone and equipping an army known as the South Persia Rifles. Germany tried to penetrate the area, largely unsuccessfully. A central aim in British postwar policy was to preserve control, and to ensure that Russian or Soviet influence was excluded from the region.

In the First World War, the Western Front remained more or less stationary, and Germany seemed triumphant in the east. But Germany depended up to 90 percent on imported oil, most of which came from Romania. It took a long time for the western powers to realize this vulnerability. Lloyd George in his memoirs argued that had the United Kingdom assured control of Romanian oil in 1915, "as we ought to have done [. . .] the failure of oil supplies would have shortened the war by at least two years". In August 1916, after the massive Russian onslaught of the

Brusilov offensive, the Allies persuaded Romania to enter the war on their side by promising the addition of Transylvania, in the Hungarian monarchy but with a large Romanian peasant population. When it was clear that the disorganized and ineffective Romanian armies were being pushed back, a British officer, John Norton-Griffiths, directed the wrecking of the Ploesti oilfields. By the spring of 1918, Romania gave up, and in May 1918 surrendered to the Central Powers with the Treaty of Bucharest. In the last months of the war, as the new Soviet authorities signed a peace with Germany, the Germans tried to push to take control of Russian oil in Baku – but that attempt also was frustrated.

Peace-making

When the Russian armies collapsed in early 1918, German units pushed forward. The German high command had also staged a last great offensive in the west, on March 21, 1918 (the Ludendorff offensive). The signs of German victory seemed clear. In addition to the humiliating peace imposed on Russia at Brest-Litovsk, Germany added a supplementary treaty in August 1918 which imposed a financial burden (reparation): Russia pledged to pay 6 billion gold marks, as well as one-third of the oil revenues from the Baku fields.

But Germany actually derived little benefit from the end of the war on the Eastern Front. One of the many illusory German hopes of the summer of 1918 was that Baltic troops might fight with Germans on the Western Front. They were never used; on the contrary, many of the German soldiers were demoralized and also radicalized by their contacts with the Bolshevik soldiers on the other side. Transferring them to the Western Front would have been a costly gamble.

In August 1918, the German position in the west began to crumble, and within a few weeks it was clear that the war was lost. Ludendorff had a nervous breakdown. On September 25, the western powers launched the first really successful offensive on the Western Front. On September 29, Bulgaria concluded an armistice, and on October 30, Turkey.

At this point, Germany tried to transform its political structure by drawing representatives of the major parties into the government: less because democracy was an inherently superior mode of organization than because the establishment of Imperial Germany embarked on a new gamble. It hoped that democratization would incline the American leadership, which it viewed as immature and naïve, to agree to more favorable peace terms. President Woodrow Wilson's second note of October 15 had demanded an end to Prussian "militarism".

The demand was the outcome of a vision that Wilson had already formulated at the beginning of 1918, and which he regarded as the only possible basis of a lasting peace. Indeed, he carried these "Fourteen Points" with him through the peace negotiations. They were the democratic alternative to Lenin's vision.

I   Open covenants of peace, openly arrived at, after which there shall be no private international understandings of any kind but diplomacy shall proceed always frankly and in the public view.

II   Absolute freedom of navigation upon the seas, outside territorial waters, alike in peace and in war, except as the seas may be closed in whole or in part by international action for the enforcement of international covenants.

III The removal, so far as possible, of all economic barriers and the establishment of an equality of trade conditions among all the nations consenting to the peace and associating themselves for its maintenance.

IV   Adequate guarantees given and taken that national armaments will be reduced to the lowest point consistent with domestic safety.

Wilsonianism

Woodrow Wilson was an academic political scientist and university president (of Princeton University) before he entered politics. As President of the United States, he opposed the involvement of his country in the European War of 1914, but then declared war. He was the first President to leave the American continent while in office, and he came to the Paris Peace Conference of 1919 with a brilliantly formulated vision that he had elaborated over the course of 1918.

He castigated the ills of the old European world, and in particular its autocracy, its secret diplomacy, and its belief that alliances prompted by balance-of-power considerations were stabilizing. On the contrary, he held, it was these three flaws that had produced the catastrophe of 1914. This analysis prompted a remedy. First, if all countries were democratic, and their peoples could really influence policy, they would not go to war. In this regard, Wilson was developing an idea of the German philosopher Immanuel Kant that would become very influential again at the end of the twentieth century, when the political scientist Michael Doyle reformulated the proposition that wars between democracies are an impossibility. Second, if countries would agree to public commitments ("open covenants of peace openly arrived at") these would be controlled by the domestic political participants, and therefore would be non-aggressive. Third, the check to bad behavior lay not in balancing actions, which could be radically unstable, but in the overall control of an international public opinion, which could be expressed in an institutional way. The League of Nations he intended to "operate as the organized moral force of men throughout the world, and that whenever wrong or aggression are planned or contemplated, this searching light of conscience shall be turned upon them". There should not be alliances in advance to deter possible aggression, but a system of "collective security" in which the international conscience would respond to violations. In the "Covenant", a quasi-religious agreement, members of the League "undertake to respect and preserve as against external aggression the territorial integrity and existing political independence of all Members of the League".

In formulating this radically new approach, Wilson encountered a tragic paradox. World public opinion would need institutions with which to enforce the controls needed to ensure democratization, and such institutions would amount to at least the beginnings of a world government. Kant, in eighteenth-century Germany, where there was no clear or well-defined concept of sovereignty, found this possible. But Wilson's own democratic country, the United States, found and continued to find it impossible to agree to such an abdication of its own sovereignty. The result was that Wilsonian internationalism could not be applied by an international, overriding institution, but only by the United States itself, which was only one among several players in the international game. Immediately, in 1919, the US Congress rejected Wilson and refused to ratify the Covenant; the main opponent of the Covenant, Senator Henry Cabot Lodge, proposed an amendment under which the "United States assumes no obligation to preserve the territorial integrity or political independence of any other country", which ran counter to the purpose of the action.

American realists, such as Henry Kissinger, think that the objection that Wilsonian internationalism compromises American sovereignty is so devastating that the whole idea must necessarily be an illusion. In the middle of the twentieth century, Presidents Roosevelt and Truman applied a version of Wilsonianism, limited to part of the world (and part of the European continent) by the realities of Soviet countervailing power. At the end of the twentieth century, with no countervailing power, under both Republican and Democratic Presidents, Wilsonianism resurfaced. Its acceptance by the American political process and American public opinion is uncertain and hesitant, as it was in 1919 and 1920. But it is, as it was then, the best hope for the world.

V   A free, open-minded, and absolutely impartial adjustment of all colonial claims, based upon a strict observance of the principle that in determining all such questions of sovereignty the interests of the populations concerned must have equal weight with the equitable claims of the government whose title is to be determined.

VI The evacuation of all Russian territory and such a settlement of all questions affecting Russia as will secure the best and freest cooperation of the other nations of the world in obtaining for her an unhampered and unembarrassed opportunity for the independent determination of her own political development and national policy and assure her of a sincere welcome into the society of free nations under institutions of her own choosing; and, more than a welcome, assistance also of every kind that she may need and may herself desire. The treatment accorded Russia by her sister nations in the months to come will be the acid test of their good will, of their comprehension of her needs as distinguished from their own interests, and of their intelligent and unselfish sympathy.

VII   Belgium, the whole world will agree, must be evacuated and restored, without any attempt to limit the sovereignty which she enjoys in common with all other free nations. No other single act will serve as this will serve to restore confidence among the nations in the laws which they have themselves set and determined for the government of their relations with one another. Without this healing act the whole structure and validity of international law is forever impaired.

VIII   All French territory should be freed and the invaded portions restored, and the wrong done to France by Prussia in 1871 in the matter of Alsace–Lorraine, which has unsettled the peace of the world for nearly fifty years, should be righted, in order that peace may once more be made secure in the interest of all.

IX   A readjustment of the frontiers of Italy should be effected along clearly recognizable lines of nationality.

X   The peoples of Austria–Hungary, whose place among the nations we wish to see safeguarded and assured, should be accorded the freest opportunity to autonomous development.

XI   Romania, Serbia, and Montenegro should be evacuated; occupied territories restored; Serbia accorded free and secure access to the sea; and the relations of the several Balkan states to one another determined by friendly counsel along historically established lines of allegiance and nationality; and international guarantees of the political and economic independence and territorial integrity of the several Balkan states should be entered into.

XII   The Turkish portion of the present Ottoman Empire should be assured a secure sovereignty, but the other nationalities which are now under Turkish rule should be assured an undoubted security of life and an absolutely unmolested opportunity of autonomous development, and the Dardanelles should be permanently opened as a free passage to the ships and commerce of all nations under international guarantees.

XIII   An independent Polish state should be erected which should include the territories inhabited by indisputably Polish populations, which should be assured a free and secure access to the sea, and whose political and economic independence and territorial integrity should be guaranteed by international covenant.

XIV   A general association of nations must be formed under specific covenants for the purpose of affording mutual guarantees of political independence and territorial integrity to great and small states alike.

The end of the German Empire came on November 9, 1918, when the military leadership instructed the Kaiser to resign. At this point the fronts were still in foreign territory. The German headquarters were in Spa in Belgium. Hindenburg himself was too cowardly to present the disloyal message. He sent his new quartermaster general, Ludendorff's replacement, Wilhelm Groener. At midnight, the imperial train was pushed across the border into the neutral Netherlands, where ex-Kaiser Wilhelm II lived out the rest of his life. The Dutch government, whose extradition treaties did not include political offenses, refused to consider British and French demands to hand the Kaiser over to a court that would consider war crimes charges.

On November 11, 1918, an armistice was signed and at 11 a.m. the guns on the Western Front at last stopped firing.

President Wilson set sail from New York in December 1918, the first US President to travel to Europe while in office. He would have preferred to have held the peace conference in a neutral country, and recommended the charms of Geneva. But France was keen to use Paris and to make every event associated with the peace as symbolically potent as could be. For France it was the undoing of the Franco-Prussian war of 1870–71 and its legacy. The conference was thus opened on January 18, the anniversary of the proclamation of the German Empire, in the Hall of Mirrors in Louis XIV's palace of Versailles. The peace treaty would be imposed on Germany and signed by an official German delegation in that hall of mirrors, on June 28, 1919, the fifth anniversary of the Archduke's assassination.

The five allied Great Powers (the United States, the United Kingdom, France, Italy, and Japan) each sent two representatives to the Council of Ten that would direct the proceedings of the conference. In practice, Japan played a limited role in the European settlement, but was deeply concerned about the future of China; and on April 24, 1919, the Italian Prime Minister Orlando left the conference in a pique of temper. Most pictures of the conference thus show the Big Three, in the persons of Wilson, Lloyd George, and Clemenceau, the host of the conference (see Plate 2).

Versailles and the Paris treaties have come to represent (in the popular mind) the most striking example of a pointlessly vindictive peace settlement. The British economist John Maynard Keynes, who was part of the British delegation to the conference before he resigned, in his famous polemic against the treaty used an ancient analogy when he called this a "Carthaginian peace" (victorious Rome had destroyed the city of Carthage and strewn salt over the fields to make them infertile). Most recent historians have a milder view of the peace, and rightly point out that the real problem was the legacy of the war that was so painful and costly that any settlement would be a disillusion.

The peace treaties, however, included not only punishment of the defeated but also the idealism of Wilson. Nations would commit themselves to a higher order of international law in the Covenant. The League of Nations

Plate 2 The initial meeting of the peace conference in Paris in the French
Foreign Ministry with Wilson, Clemenceau, and Lloyd George. Wilson
intended to create a new and more moral international order. Painting
by G. William Orpen: Peace Conference at the Quai d'Orsay, 1919 (oil
on canvas). ©Imperial War Museum, London, UK/Bridgeman Images.

would be an international institution of a new type. The International
Labour Organization would supervise economic justice (and limit Japanese
competition by insisting on high standards of safety and pay in factories).

Clemenceau, and many Frenchmen, saw the logic of dismantling 1870–71
as requiring also a breaking up of the fruit of the Franco-Prussian war,
German unity. From the point of view of military logic, a frontier at the
Rhine with a separate Rhineland buffer state seemed attractive. From the
point of view of economic logic, French industry required the coal base of
the Ruhr in order to expand.

At the same time, France also demanded a large payment of reparation, in
order to pay for the cost of the reconstruction of the devastated areas, and
in order to address the precarious state of public finance.

The United Kingdom, which had paid a large human and financial price,
also wanted reparation, and eventually successfully set the terms of the

reparation claim so as to include the payment of pensions to war widows and orphans. (The United Kingdom, unlike Belgium and France, would receive almost nothing from a claim simply based on material destruction.) On the other hand, some British business and industrial leaders worried that a high payment by Germany would require it to run large export surpluses and that German competition would destroy Britain's industrial position.

The United States was not directly interested in the reparation issue, except in so far as reparation might be important to allow France and the United Kingdom to repay the war debt due mostly to private American lenders.

Wilson thus quickly found that his grand program had little to do with the intricate financial issues that formed the heart of the Franco-British discussions. And as regards territories, much of the settlement regarding the old and defeated empires (Habsburg, Romanov, Ottoman, and Hohenzollern) was being fought out on the ground, rather than being settled by politicians drawing lines on the large maps laid out in the French Foreign Ministry at the Quai d'Orsay. Wilson's influence was also restricted politically, because the Democratic President had failed to bring any members of the Republican Party with him, and his basis of domestic support was thus precarious. In addition, he was sick, and suffered a stroke that increased his temper and reduced his capacity.

For Germany, the terms of the treaty included no specific reparations claim (that was to be determined later). The American lawyers insisted that reparation could not be demanded without a cause, a wrong or tort that had been inflicted, and the treaty thus included Article 231:

> The Allied and Associated Governments affirm and Germany accepts the responsibility of Germany and her allies for causing all the loss and damage to which the Allied and Associated Governments and their nationals have been subjected as a consequence of the war imposed upon them by the aggression of Germany and her allies.

Alsace–Lorraine was returned to France (as had been stipulated in the Fourteen Points); the Saar area (a rich coal basin) was to be administered by a commission directed by the League of Nations, but the mines were to be controlled by France; small pieces of territory (including some valuable zinc mines) were handed to Belgium; plebiscites would determine which areas of Schleswig should go to Denmark, and were also to be held in some parts of Upper Silesia. East Prussia was to remain German, but with referenda in some areas (which voted by large majorities to stay in Germany, even where there were substantial Polish populations); but it was physically separated from the rest of Germany by a strip of territory that was needed to give the new Polish state access to the sea ("the Polish corridor"). The largely German-speaking city of Danzig was to be self-governing, but its status would be supervised by the League of Nations.

Germany's colonies were divided between the Allies on the basis of a system of "mandates" proposed by a member of the British delegation, the

South African leader Jan Smuts. A different type of mandate ("A" mandate) was to be used for territories from the former Ottoman Empire, which were judged to be almost capable of self-government. Germany's African and Pacific island colonies, however, were subjected to much more wide-ranging ("B" and "C") mandates, but still with an obligation to provide reports to the League. The Cameroon territory was transferred directly to France; a small part of German East Africa, the Kionga triangle, went to Portugal; and Japan was given the former German rights in Shantung, to the dismay and fury of the Chinese delegation.

Germany was to be disarmed: the navy was limited to six battleships, six light cruisers, 12 destroyers, and 12 torpedo boats. The army was to be no more than 100,000 men, who would serve on a long-term basis (the treaty aimed to avoid a draft system that might be used to train much larger numbers of Germans). It was not allowed to enter a demilitarized zone marked by a line 50 kilometers east of the river Rhine.

Parallel treaties to Versailles were signed at other old French royal palaces near Paris. At Saint-Germain (September 10, 1919), a small rump of Austria, with 250,000 German speakers in Tyrol south of the Brenner, was transferred to Italy, and the German part of Bohemia and Moravia left in the new Czechoslovakia. Austria was forbidden to merge with Germany (or to call itself Deutsch-Österreich, the name its political leaders wanted). It gained one piece of territory relative to the old boundaries within the Habsburg Empire, a part of western Hungary that spoke German and had close links with Vienna, which became Burgenland; its major city, Sopron/Odenburg, however, voted to stay Hungarian. Hungary was brutally treated at Trianon (signed June 4, 1920), which left about 3.5 million Hungarians out of the new state, in Romania, Yugoslavia, and Czechoslovakia. The Allies did add a covering letter in which they established a complicated and in practice unworkable mechanism for altering the frontier through reports by a frontier delimitation commission to the League of Nations. Bulgaria gave back southern Dobruja to Romania (in the Treaty of Neuilly).

The practical violations of the self-determination principles need not by themselves have been fatal, if the new governments had followed better and more tolerant policies. A model which shows how the treaties might have worked is Czechoslovakia, which was multi-ethnic and quite stable. No historical or any other kind of law states that the only viable state is one that is culturally homogeneous. However, with that exception, the small states created by the Paris treaties, with new elites that adopted nationalistic and autarkic policies, were politically and economically dysfunctional.

The problematical character of the Paris vision became most quickly apparent with the Turkish treaty (Treaty of Sèvres). The secret treaties between the United Kingdom and France to partition Turkey had been revealed by the Bolsheviks: the promised cession of Constantinople and the Black Sea straits to Russia, and the promise of areas in Armenia and northeastern Anatolia. In the Sykes–Picot Agreement, the United Kingdom and

France carved out their own spheres of influence. In the actual peace treaty, part of western Anatolia around Smyrna was to be controlled by Greece for five years, after which a plebiscite would be held (as for the Saar); Armenia was to be independent, and Kurdistan to have an autonomous government. Although a representative of the Turkish government signed the treaty at Sèvres on August 10, 1920, it was never implemented and only fanned the strong nationalist movement led by a senior general, who in 1919 had been Inspector of the Turkish Army in Anatolia. Mustafa Kemal called a parliament, negotiated with Russia to receive military supplies, and reformed the Turkish army. He halted the Greek advance in Anatolia, made an agreement with Italy and France to withdraw their troops, and then pushed back the Greek armies until in September 1922 Turkish troops retook Smyrna. Several thousand Armenians were killed in the Turkish onslaught.

A new treaty was worked out in 1923 at Lausanne (which was, with Geneva, the city in which Woodrow Wilson had originally wished to hold the peace conference). It guaranteed free passage of ships through the Black Sea straits (unless Turkey were at war, when this right would apply only to neutral ships). It restored eastern Thrace from Greece to Turkey, as well as two largely Greek-speaking islands near Turkey. It also provided for a systematic exchange of populations: 400,000 Turks in areas that Greece had gained since 1912 against 1.3 million Greeks. No other post-First World War treaty had such a stipulation. Lausanne seemed to indicate that the European diplomats felt that in one case, where there had been a conflict of such ferocity as that between Greeks and Turks, there could be no expectation that the two peoples would in the near future be capable of living together in harmony in the same political unit. But for Armenians and Kurds, distributed between several states (Armenians in Turkey, the Soviet Union, and Iran; Kurds in Turkey, Iran, Iraq, and Syria), the Lausanne Treaty did nothing.

The First World War had a long and chaotic aftermath as large numbers of individuals were expelled or fled from states that opposed their ethnic, cultural, or social values. Aristocratic and bourgeois Russians fleeing from the revolution, Hungarians, Germans, Armenians, Greeks, and Turks usually had no means and often no identification. Constantinople was swamped with defeated remnants of General Wrangel's Crimean army. In 1924, the League of Nations believed that there were well over 1 million refugees from Russia, with 500,000 in Germany and 400,000 in France. Other refugees from the Russian Revolution went throughout the Middle East and to China, where Shanghai and Harbin developed as major centers of the Russian emigration.

The refugee issue became a permanent twentieth-century problem. The Norwegian scientist and Arctic explorer Fridtjof Nansen built up a private organization (Nansen Help) whose original function was to negotiate the return of prisoners-of-war in Russia. In 1921 the League of Nations placed him in charge of a new refugee agency: he was appointed as High Commissioner on Behalf of the League in Connection with the Problem of Russian Refugees in

Europe. He issued documents ("Nansen certificates" or "Nansen passports") to the stateless, and financed further relief operations through the fees for a "Nansen stamp" on documents. In 1924, the use of these documents was extended to Armenian refugees; and in 1928 to a diversity of peoples from the former Ottoman Empire (described as "Assyrian, Assyro-Chaldean and assimilated refugees"). When Nansen died in 1930, the League general secretariat took over the functions of political and legal protection, and left a separate office dealing with material assistance.

The politics of the twentieth century globally were shaped by a series of protests that occurred all over the world at the conclusion of the war. The years 1918 and 1919 constituted a defining moment in world history. Even though most of them were brutally suppressed, the experience and its memory cemented a new anti-imperial vision. China had been a participant in the First World War, declaring war in 1917 and sending a labor corps to Europe. As a reward, the indemnity payments for the attacks on westerners in the authorized Settlements during the Boxer Rebellion were suspended. When they were reimposed at the Paris Peace Conference, the May Fourth Movement burst out as a mass protest against foreign "meddling" in China. It had its origins in a student movement aimed at generating a new national literature written not in the classical language but in the vernacular, or living "national language" (*guoyu*), and at the same time using western ideas of rights and democracy to break down stultifying Chinese Confucian traditionalism. The historiography of Communist China would see the May Fourth demonstrations as an anticipation of the Chinese Revolution. It led to a reorganization of the Nationalist Party (Kuomintang), but also was central to the launching of the Chinese Communist Party.

The Chinese movement appeared analogous to other ethnic nationalist upsurges in the aftermath of the disruption of the war and the disintegration of the old empires. In Iraq, in 1920, Sheikh Mehdi Al-Khalissi led a military movement against the British mandate, which was suppressed with around 10,000 deaths. Emir Faisal, the third son of Hussein bin Ali, the Grand Sharif of Mecca, who had proclaimed himself King of the Arab lands in October 1916, and had tried to play off both the Turkish and the British armies in trying to establish independent Arab principalities, was eventually installed as King of Iraq (Faisal I). In Egypt after the armistice, a movement led by Saad Zaghlul's Wafd party staged a campaign of civil disobedience and demanded independence. After a report by Lord Milner, the British government agreed to abandon the protectorate and institute self-rule with a monarchy in 1922. The sultan, Fuad, became King Fuad I, and Saad Zaghlul was allowed to return and to introduce a western-style constitution (1923). The best way of containing protest from the British perspective appeared to be through the engagement of compliant local rulers.

An analogous campaign of civil unrest in India failed. There too protests were met with extreme force, notably in the Amritsar massacre (Jallianwala Bagh massacre) on April 13, 1919. Around 1,000 were killed when the British army fired at a peaceful Sikh assembly for the day of Baisakhi, one of the largest festivals of the Sikh community, that was also the occasion of protests against the arrest of two leaders after a *hartal* (strike), called by Mahatma Gandhi. The British commander, Colonel Reginald Dyer, claimed he was responding to the deaths of three British bank employees and to a gang attack on Marcella Sherwood, the supervisor of a Mission Day School for Girls. But he reacted with a disproportionate use of force that constituted a violation of the army's rules. The initial surge of patriotic support for Dyer turned Amritsar into a test case of British rule in India (Plate 3). Salman Rushdie's 1981 novel *Midnight's Children* provides a lightly fictionalized version of this iconic moment. Dyer wrote an article in the newspaper *Globe* of January 21, 1921, under the title "The Peril to the Empire". He began by claiming that "India does not want self-government. She does not understand it." The Anglo-Indian writer Rudyard Kipling depicted Dyer as "the man who saved India", and he started a campaign for financial support. In the short run, however, the British government pushed back against Dyer and tried to push on with what it saw as an experiment in liberal empire. The Montagu–Chelmsford report of 1918 had laid the basis for the Government of India Act of 1919. Edwin Samuel Montagu, the Secretary of State for India, told the British parliament that there would be "increasing association of Indians in every branch of the administration, with a view to the progressive realization of responsible government in India as an integral part of the empire". Self-determination was the "inevitable result of education in the history and thought of Europe".[14]

Plate 3 The Jallianwala Bagh or Amritsar massacre, April 1919. © Chronicle/Alamy Stock Photo.

In fact, empire and domestic politics were closely woven together by assumptions about difference. They depended on privilege in the old as well as the new sense of the term, particular advantages resulting from a chance of birth. Some of the shrewdest children of empire saw the point very clearly already in the 1920s. The young British Conservative R.A. Butler, the son of a member of the Indian Civil Service, noted that "Caste is the bane of India and the luxury of England – India must learn from Burma to lessen this bane and England to indulge less freely in this luxury."[15]

The quest for security

Paris and Versailles thus left a large variety of visions of how European security might be established, and could not be held to be a coherent alternative to the vision of Lenin. The treaties themselves contained an idealistic vision that seemed at odds with most of the concrete clauses. In some areas "security vision" is too complex a notion for what was simply a demand for revenge and the payment of impossibly high costs. Some countries, like Russia, had been excluded from the peace-making process altogether. Germany, Austria, Hungary, and Turkey were humiliated, resentful, and infuriated.

Japan's efforts to include a clause in the Covenant about racial equality were frustrated, and the principle was contradicted by the differentiation between different types of mandate. China and Italy were both indignant that they were not adequately rewarded for their participation in the war against Germany. China, mortified by the adoption of the Japanese Shantung solution, refused to sign the treaty. The Italian delegation withdrew when its claims to wide-ranging Dalmatia were not accepted.

The United Kingdom in its age of imperial greatness had never been interested in continental European rule. After the First World War it could not afford it, even if it had desired it. The League of Nations was Britain's answer to the need to provide security on the cheap. In its broadest outline, it came from the Wilsonian vision. The details were largely worked out by the British delegates, in particular Smuts and Robert Cecil, the scion of Britain's most distinguished political family.

Wilson was committed to the League, but was unable to convince the American public or the American political system that European affairs could really have an impact on American security. He returned to Washington already worn out. The US Congress then refused to ratify the peace treaties.

France distrusted the "Anglo-Saxon" idea of a security organization, and thought it better to contain Germany by making a new pattern of alliances with Germany's (and Austria's) eastern neighbors. In 1919, it had also tried, without success, to negotiate supplementary treaties with the United Kingdom and the United States for assistance in the case of new German aggression. In 1921, however, France concluded an alliance with Poland, and later treaties followed with Czechoslovakia (1924), Romania (1926), and Yugoslavia (1927). Czechoslovakia, Romania, and Yugoslavia, the major beneficiaries of the break-up of the Austro-Hungarian Empire, had already concluded their own "Little Entente" (1920–21). France believed that the new international institutions could only generate a misleading sense of security. Instead, French policy-makers set out to formulate a doctrine of "realism" as an alternative to Wilsonian liberal internationalism.

Realism

The Wilsonian revolution in foreign policy made many Europeans (and American critics of *Wilsonianism*) rethink and restate their opposed position. International politics is solely concerned with the interplay of power. Self-determination can be dangerous and destabilizing: for this reason, for instance, nineteenth-century Europeans wanted to keep the decaying Ottoman Empire (whose fragility they fully realized) in place. Small states, such as those generated in 1919 at the Paris Peace Conference, intrinsically do not have enough power of their own to protect themselves (in the absence of the Wilsonian concept of collective security, which realists held to be absurd).

Realism largely rejects the value of international institutions, concepts, and laws: they have value and meaning only in so far as they are expressions of national interest. As a theory of international relations, as expounded by its leading practitioners in the twentieth century, E.H. Carr (British) and Hans Morgenthau (American), it sounded academically sharp but humanly unappealing and even immoral. As a practice of international politics, it worked extremely well in the hands of skilled practitioners who coated the politically unattractive core with the sugar of national sentiment. The foremost exponent, who almost single-handedly revived the idea of a European style of politics as it had been practiced by the realists of the nineteenth century, was Charles de Gaulle (see Chapter 7: *Gaullism*).

Doctrines in international politics depend not only on their inherent logical appeal, but also, crucially, on the strength of the powers that wish to enunciate them. France was increasingly vulnerable as its political and parliamentary system came under strain, and because of its economic and demographic weakness. It found itself in the paradoxical position that its appeal to political realism was undermined by a reality of power that did not allow France to develop and realize what was, in its way, the only coherent alternative to revolutionary Leninism or Wilsonian internationalism.

Notes

1 Vladimer Dedijer, *The Road to Sarajevo*, New York, NY: Simon and Schuster, 1966, p. 357.
2 Norman Stone, *The Eastern Front 1914–1917*, London: Hodder and Stoughton, 1975, p. 237.
3 Cited in George G. Bruwitz, *Allied Propaganda and the Collapse of the German Empire in 1918*, Stanford, CA: Stanford University Press, 1938, p. 3.
4 Henri Barbusse, *Le feu. Journal d'une escouade*, Paris, 1916, pp. 48–9.
5 See the picture in the magazine *Le rire*, 17 February 1917, *Le general Mangin et ses exécutants*. http://etudescoloniales.canalblog.com/archives/2014/07/16/30243155.html.
6 Jennifer Siegel, *Endgame: Britain, Russia and the Final Struggle for Central Asia*, New York, NY: I.B. Tauris, 2002, p. 14.
7 Cited in Marc Ferro, *The Russian Revolution of February 1917*, London: Routledge, 1972, p. 192 (March 27, 1917, by the Russian calendar).
8 Ferro, February, p. 255.
9 E.H. Carr, *The Bolshevik Revolution*, Vol. 1, Harmondsworth: Penguin, 1966, pp. 166, 176.
10 Adam Ulam, *Lenin and the Bolsheviks: The Intellectual and Political History of the Triumph of Communism in Russia*, Glasgow: Fontana, 1969, pp. 740–1.
11 Roy Foster, *Modern Ireland 1600–1972*, Harmondsworth: Allen Lane, 1988, p. 477.
12 Margaret Macmillan, *Paris 1919: Six Months that Changed the World*, New York, NY: Random House, 2002, p. 67.
13 William Stanley Jevons, *The Coal Question; An Inquiry Concerning the Progress of the Nation, and the Probable Exhaustion of Our Coal Mines*, London: Macmillan, 1865, p. 349.
14 Adam Tooze, *The Deluge: The Great War and the Remaking of Global Order 1916–1931*, New York, NY: Viking, 2014, p. 189.
15 Quoted in Anthony Howard, *RAB: The Life of R.A. Butler*, London: Jonathan Cape, 1987, p. 366.

3 The 1920s

Precarious democracy

"Self-determination" had been a key part of many peace demands, from the February revolutionaries in Russia to Woodrow Wilson's Fourteen Points. The Wilsonian vision included a trio that the President believed would play harmoniously together: a stable and secure international order; prosperity, inevitably built on secure property rights; and political democracy. The weakness of the arrangement was that, if one part went badly out of tune, there would be discord and the music would stop. In 1919, as the peacemakers met in Paris, all of these elements seemed precarious. Versailles had been a disappointment to the Wilsonian faith. But – almost by a miracle – the musicians gradually fell into tune in the 1920s, and by the middle of the decade the President's vision was surprisingly close to being realized.

The League of Nations was functioning as a very new type of international regime. The leading British history textbook of the interwar years, by Harold Temperley and A.J. Grant, concluded with a point-by-point comparison between the League and the nineteenth-century Concert of Europe as devised by Metternich and Castlereagh, and pointed out how in each respect the League was superior. (Later editions produced after 1945 made similar comparisons between the United Nations and the League, showing how the UN was a great advance.)[1]

Leaving economic reconstruction to private business and the market was the only course open in the post-Wilsonian mood of the United States. American (and to some extent British) investors persuaded themselves that there would be an economic miracle producing large returns, and poured large sums of money into continental Europe. To a great extent, they set the commercial and mercenary tone of the decade. The German caricaturist George Grosz depicted the dollar as a sun lighting up the corruption of *ancien régime* Germany.

Subsequent chapters examine the problems that the economic and international parts of the Wilsonian vision soon encountered, after the brief honeymoon of the mid-1920s went sour. This chapter examines the problematic issue of democracy. In most countries, there was a significant push to democratize. The franchise was extended, and in some cases also now included women (the United Kingdom with restrictions until 1928; Austria, Belgium,

Estonia, Germany, Latvia, the Netherlands, Poland, and revolutionary Russia after 1918–19; Sweden after 1921; Portugal and Spain after 1931; and Turkey after 1934). In Denmark, Finland, and Norway, women had already voted before the First World War.

At the same time, large-scale organization had developed in the war, and the new corporatism, rather than supporting, threatened – and in the Italian case overwhelmed – the initiative to democratize.

Weimar democracy

The Weimar Republic was both perfect and very unstable. It was the world's most sophisticated experiment in externally induced democratization. Its godfathers were Woodrow Wilson and the Hindenburg–Ludendorff team. The parliamentarians who in the war had been most responsive to the military leadership, Matthias Erzberger of the Catholic Center Party, and Gustav Stresemann of the Liberal People's Party, after 1919 turned (at least on the surface) into model and even courageous democrats.

The new constitutional order was produced not in Berlin, but in the quiet artistic and cultural town of Weimar in Saxony, the home of Goethe and Schiller and of German classicism. Berlin was too revolutionary, but modern technology allowed the new law and constitution makers to keep in contact with all of Germany: Germany's first airmail service was instituted in 1919 to link Weimar and Berlin.

The new constitution was devised by a commission which included some of Germany's finest legal and political minds: Hugo Preuss, a public law professor in Berlin, who had emerged as a powerful critic of the Prussian authoritarian state, had been asked by the provisional government on November 15, 1918, to produce a new draft constitution. He worked with socialists as well as with the distinguished sociologist and economist Max Weber. Even after its demise, Weimar was still regarded as a model of democratic perfection, and important features of its constitution were later replicated in other states, notably Israel, which have preserved democratic practices in militarily, politically, and economically turbulent times.

It introduced a perfect system of proportional representation, by electoral circles, but in which surplus votes could be pooled nationally. The number of seats in parliament depended on the number of votes. Women as well as men over 21 could vote.

A president was directly elected, for a different term (seven years) than that of parliament (the Reichstag), which sat for four-year periods. The President was entitled to dissolve parliament, and could appoint and dismiss prime ministers (chancellors). The great power of the President under the constitution was in part intended to restrain a parliamentary majority from imposing controversial measures. Max Weber saw the charismatic qualities of an elected president as an important counterweight to "parliamentary absolutism". In addition, foreseeing that there might be circumstances in which a government supported by a majority of parliament might find it hard to take unpopular measures needed to protect security, the constitution under Article 48 provided for the President to use emergency powers to maintain public order.

The constitution included a wide range of social as well as political rights – an innovation in European politics. It spoke of a right to employment, without specifying what that meant. More importantly, it created an economic council which would be at the top of a pyramid of district and factory workers' councils, and would be consulted on economic policy issues and on possible nationalizations.

Its most immediately obvious unsatisfactory aspect was its failure to reorganize the system of states in Germany (*Länder*) so as to provide a basis for a working federalism. Prussia was left, as under the Empire, as by far the largest German state, because to dismantle Prussia would have been to invite France to take parts of it (in particular, the industrially tempting Rhineland).

The major political parties at the beginning of Weimar democracy were the three parties of the "Weimar coalition", the opposition parties of Imperial Germany which in 1917 had proposed a peace resolution in the Reichstag: the socialists (SPD), the Catholic Center Party, and the liberal Democratic Party (DDP). Each of these parties faced big difficulties. The socialist movement had been split by wartime debates over support for the war: a threefold division emerged, which corresponded less to divisions over social and economic policies than to the date at which the group had originally opposed war. The Communist Party developed out of the group around Karl Liebknecht, who in 1914 had already opposed war. Then there was the independent socialist party (USPD), whose leaders had opposed the war in 1915 and 1916. Finally, the mainstream SPD had supported the peace resolution, but only in the coalition of 1917. In the elections of January 1919 the SPD had a massive 37.9 percent of the vote, but the share fell to 21.7 percent in 1920, with 17.9 percent choosing the USPD. The Center, which had 15.9 percent in 1919, was a confessional party of the Catholic minority in Germany, whose vote remained quite stable (much more so than the other Weimar parties), but which could not hope for much of an increase in its votes and was largely unable to attract Protestant voters. Finally the Democratic Party had a relatively large vote in 1919 (18.6 percent), but few of these voters seem to have had any long-standing attraction to left liberalism, and had voted in the circumstances of 1919 for a bourgeois party which could work with the dominant socialists. These voters would inevitably soon abandon the Democrats, whose vote in 1920 fell to 8.3 percent and in 1924 to 5.7 percent.

The actual, as opposed to the theoretical, construction of Weimar democracy occurred on the basis of two compromises: one between industry and labor, and the other between the mainstream socialist party and the military leadership. Both foundations were laid on the day that Imperial Germany ended: November 9, 1918. A major German business figure, Hugo Stinnes, made a pact with the secretary-general of the labor unions, Carl Legien. It included the continuation of wartime corporatism in the postwar period, the eight-hour day, and the creation of a central corporate association (*Zentralarbeitsgemeinschaft*).

On the same day, General Groener, who had forced the Kaiser's abdication, spoke by telephone with the socialist leader, Friedrich Ebert, and put the army at the disposal of the socialist leadership (for use against the radical left of the council movement). Ebert welcomed the returning troops back to Berlin in December 1919, with words that would provide the basis for one of the political myths that would undermine the Republic. He spoke to the soldiers as heroes who "were undefeated on the field of battle"; the implication was clear: that it was a domestic enemy or a stab in the back (*Dolchstoss*) that had produced the German defeat. The myth drew on old Germanic stories, and Richard Wagner's musical version of them, in which the invulnerable hero Siegfried was stabbed from behind by the sinister Hagen.

The army (still known as the Imperial Army or *Reichswehr*), was unenthusiastic about democracy under the leadership of General Hans von Seeckt, but developed a precarious loyalty to the Republic. The most threatening moment came early. In 1920 Wolfgang Kapp seized power in Berlin in a military-supported putsch with substantial additional assistance from large landowners and from big business; the army refused to protect the government on the grounds that it believed a major left-wing insurrection was imminent. Most of the army, however, hedged its bets and simply waited out the crisis. The putsch collapsed after a general strike. The *Zentralarbeitsgemeinschaft* denounced Kapp only very late in the day. In 1923, the army fought against a communist insurrection in Saxony, and put down another putsch in Munich carried out by the radical and racist National Socialist Party under Adolf Hitler as well as by Erich Ludendorff. On November 9, 1923, when the insurrectionaries marched on the center of Munich, they were confronted in the Odeonsplatz by the Bavarian police, who opened fire and killed 16 National Socialists. The rebels dispersed and fled without fighting.

This episode, the so-called "beer hall putsch", was the most dramatic incident produced by a spread of extreme right-wing nationalist and racist movements. They had easy access to arms, because the demobilization of the Imperial Army had never been properly supervised, and – especially in country areas – it was easy to find farms and barns in which weapons could be hidden.

Corporatism

Corporatism requires a different form of political organization than that of democracy, which corporatists criticize as being too mechanical, and too unreflective of the reality of social existence. It looks for a way of reconciling class conflicts by a range of institutional mechanisms. Different social groups should have their own interest associations, such as trade unions or employers' organizations or farming organizations: these were then ways of articulating a specific interest that could be brought together and harmonized. In some versions of corporatism, notably the *fascist* kind, the state is required as an external arbiter representing a notion of the general interest. Other versions of corporatism envisage agreement and reconciliation through bargaining between the interest groups.

As a doctrine of politics, corporatism was most influential in the interwar period, especially among Catholic social thinkers who opposed both classical liberalism as atomizing and atomistic, and *Marxism* or socialism as promoting conflict. The most authoritative expression of Catholic corporatism was in the papal encyclical of 1931, *Quadragesimo Anno*, which declared the aim of social policy to be the re-establishment of vocational groups, and associations as a building bloc of order. "Order, as St. Thomas well defines, is unity arising from the proper arrangement of a number of objects." Politically, this doctrine was most clearly reflected in Austrian politics between 1934 and the German invasion of 1938, and in the politics of Éire after full Irish independence was established through the 1937 constitution.

As a social and economic doctrine, corporatism continued to be influential after the war, especially in attitudes to corporate governance and the representation of employees on boards of directors in Germany and in Scandinavian countries, and in the German and Italian patterns of labor bargaining.

The key to democratic stabilization was the corporatism that linked business and labor. In an environment in which many prices were controlled, businesses paid higher wages, and labor representatives agreed to higher prices for products. Some commentators called the result a cartel of producers against consumers.

The government did its best to support this system by producing new public sector jobs, and by subsidizing big deficits in the public post and railroad administration. It needed to pay reparations, and found it politically unpopular to raise taxes. The central bank (*Reichsbank*) printed money to deal with what it interpreted as the demand for money. Its leadership was proud of its organizational achievement not only in its own printing works, but in its conscription of 30 paper factories, 29 printing plate factories, and 132 printing works.

Matthias Erzberger, who had signed the Versailles Treaty, and had tried to introduce some sort of financial reform, was assassinated by the radical right in August 1921 (after five previous murder plots had failed). The Republic was dealt an even more serious blow in June 1922 by the assassination of Walther Rathenau, the brilliant Foreign Minister of the cabinet.

The judiciary, still a largely conservative body which thought of itself as continuing the legacy of Imperial Germany, treated right-wing political terror with amazing leniency. Only after the June 1922 outrage did parliament pass a law for the protection of the Republic.

With the Rathenau murder, most foreigners lost hope that Germany would stabilize itself. The pace of inflation increased, and the government blamed reparations for the new financial and economic collapse. In December 1922, it stopped a reparations shipment, in the hope that this would produce a revision of the settlement. Instead, the new right-wing nationalist government in France, under Raymond Poincaré, sent troops into the Rhineland in order to extract reparations coal. The German government meanwhile instructed the businesses and workers of the Ruhr not to work for the French, and promised to pay them for not working. Such a move immediately and obviously destroyed any chance that Germany might have had of stabilizing its budget. The German government in 1923 produced the most severe hyper-inflation that the world had yet seen (the record was, however, broken by the Hungarian government after the Second World War). By November 1923, the exchange rate to the dollar (which had been 4.2 marks before the war) was 4,200,000,000,000.

Germany disintegrated into anarchy, as different extreme movements tried to seize power on a local basis, and as the feeling that Berlin was controlling the money and disadvantaging the provinces led to movements for separatism in the Rhineland (where there was a bait of working with the French and thus obtaining more favorable terms for the occupation), in Saxony, and in Bavaria.

In November 1923, a new government was formed by Gustav Stresemann. Unlike Rathenau, he did not look for brilliant coups in foreign relations but saw that for the moment the only realistic course was for Germany to work with the western powers. Rathenau, by contrast, had been intrigued by the geopolitical opportunities offered by an alliance of the discontented: while attending the Genoa Economic and Financial Conference at Easter 1922, he had slipped away to talk with representatives of the Soviet government at Rapallo, as a way of showing the Allies that Germany might also consider an eastern alliance. Stresemann remained as Foreign Minister in subsequent governments, until his death in 1929. President Ebert used the emergency authorization of Article 48 to authorize the *Reichswehr* to act against coups, and in order to implement a program of budgetary stabilization.

The legacy of the inflation was terrible and long-term. Many savers had been completely expropriated by the collapse in the value of money. A complicated package of different revaluation levels for different categories of public and private debt in 1924 brought only small relief. Many felt cheated by the powerful organizations or big business and the big union bosses, and that there was a "system" that was working against the "ordinary man". Many also felt humiliated by having to participate in all kinds of grey-market and speculative activities. Joseph Goebbels, an intelligent

Rhineland Catholic, became a violent anti-Semite as a result of working as a clerk in the Dresdner Bank, and saw anti-Semitism as a way of protesting against materialism and the money culture. At its most profound the monetary uncertainty destroyed any remaining standards of values. The scientist and author Elias Canetti later concluded that it was the irrational numbers and zeroes of the inflation years that made Germans later see human lives as simply another version of absurd numbers.

In the short term, economic stabilization looked as though it worked, and a new inflow of American money buoyed up Weimar democracy. Governments at all levels – national, state, and particularly municipal – could restart their spending and their work-creation measures. New housing projects sprang up, especially in socialist-controlled towns, aimed at satisfying the skilled, working-class socialist voting base. The less skilled and the unemployed were less well taken care of, and tended to vote for the Communist Party. Cities had green parks, tram and railroad systems (the magnificent Berlin and Hamburg S-Bahn), and swimming pools. For a time it was possible to think that happiness and democracy could be bought. One socialist leader, Rudolf Hilferding, developed a theory of the "political wage": that workers could get higher pay settlements not by violent conflict, but by voting for governments that would arbitrate in labor disputes to the benefit of the working class. The legacy of the war and the inflation era was that collective action was the best way to better income and status. Labor organized in unions, the employers formed powerful and influential organizations, and businesses created cartels to fix prices. This worked reasonably well while the economy was growing, when there was indeed a direct link between the flow of funds and an incentive structure that encouraged responsible and democratic behavior.

In 1924, the Allies produced a new reparations plan (the Dawes Plan), which was to be accompanied by a hard currency loan to stabilize the German budget. Some of the measures in the London Treaty (which implemented the Dawes Plan) changed the governance of the publicly owned *Reichsbank* and the railway system, and constitutionally required a two-thirds majority to pass through the Reichstag. The parties of the right could have defeated these measures, but they realized that that would produce new economic chaos, and sufficient right-wingers abstained to let the Dawes legislation pass. This could be read as a sign that German parliamentarians were learning that democracy required responsible behavior.

In 1925 at Locarno Stresemann agreed with the French Foreign Minister, Aristide Briand, a security pact for the western frontiers. For the first time since the war, Germany was treated as an equal power; and Stresemann at the same time skillfully undermined the French effort to build up a system of containment alliances in central Europe. As with the Dawes Plan, the German nationalist right bitterly criticized Locarno, and the Nationalist Party members left the cabinet – but without voting against the government. As with the Dawes debate, the right realized that an international crisis would spark a profound collapse in Germany.

An even more striking sign of a new political maturity came in 1925, when President Ebert died. He was by then widely credited as having saved Germany and the Republic. But the republican parties were divided, and unwisely supported Wilhelm Marx, under whose regime as Chancellor many of the painful post-1923 austerity measures had been taken. The candidate of the nationalist right, the veteran hero of Tannenberg, Paul von Hindenburg, was elected as President. But – again this was a sign of how responsible Germany was becoming – for his first presidential term (which expired in 1932) Hindenburg behaved with great constitutional propriety. Both Hindenburg and Stresemann (who during the war had worked with the military leadership) had less than perfectly democratic credentials, but German democracy first produced them as major political figures and then depended on them.

The United Kingdom

The United Kingdom after the First World War was much less democratic in a formal sense than Germany, and it too experienced a deep crisis of its political institutions. In part the British problem stemmed from a rather technically institutional feature: the way that political divisions mapped onto a single-member first-past-the-post electoral system (the election of Members of Parliament by the largest vote in individual constituencies, with no requirement of an absolute majority or possibility of transferring votes among candidates). With two parties, as for much of the nineteenth century, this could be a stable system of representation. With three parties, as in the 1920s, it produced odd results (gaining over 40 percent could establish a landslide dominance, while less than 30 percent meant oblivion); and the instability of the political order led to constant political intrigue.

The three competing British parties were the nineteenth-century ones, the Liberals and the Conservatives, and now additionally Labour, which had emerged as a real force with the economic and labor mobilization of the First World War. Each party reflected rather different assumptions about British society and its place in the world; and their visions could be combined only in ways that meant splitting other parties and creating new political issues.

The Liberals were committed to the nineteenth-century classical vision of free trade and balanced budgets, but one wing, led by the charismatic wartime Prime Minister David Lloyd George, had moved much further in the direction of social reformism. Lloyd George's great prewar achievement had been the "People's Budget" of 1909, which had been the first British peacetime budget to raise the income tax (from 5 to 6 percent), and which placed a supertax on the very rich. But Lloyd George divided the party, and a large grouping preferred the classically patrician Whig liberalism of Herbert Asquith. This wing despised Lloyd George, and hoped to work with internationalist Conservatives.

The Conservatives grouped Anglican traditionalists and old-style Tory peers such as Lords Curzon and Derby, who had a mindset from the open world of the nineteenth century, with a business lobby that was increasingly worried by the competitive threats to Britain's international position, and which wanted a higher measure of trade protection. The latter influence was increasing. Conservatives were becoming an inward-looking party that saw Britain's road to prosperity turning away from international markets and toward a protected imperial sphere.

The Labour Party was strongly influenced by the trade union movement. Its leadership included some wartime pacifists, above all Ramsay MacDonald, who were committed to a search for a more peaceful international order. There was a potential for collaboration with the Liberals of a Lloyd George cast of mind, and indeed "Lib–Lab" alliances had been one of the prewar themes of the Lloyd Georgians. The only problem was that Labour regarded Prime Minister Lloyd George with great suspicion, because of his gifts for intrigue and mischief (and also because his loose personal life did not fit well with Labour's rather austere concept of political dignity).

At first, Lloyd George's wartime national coalition continued to rule in peace, with a heavily patriotic and quite Conservative House of Commons elected in the "khaki election" of December 14, 1918, so-called because many of the MPs returned wore officers' uniforms. Its other epithet, the "coupon election", is more telling: the election was fought and won, not so much on a party basis, as following the endorsement of individual Liberal or Conservative candidates with a "coupon" from Lloyd George. The national coalition received 53.2 percent of the vote. Lloyd George's government then presided over a brief postwar boom, followed in 1920 and 1921 by a sharp collapse. It tried to deal with the postwar world by fiscal retrenchment, although the Prime Minister, who remained a committed social reformer, would have preferred more public works.

Labor radicalism rose during the postwar boom, as the scope for pressing claims increased (for a brief moment it seemed as if there was a shortage, not a surplus of labor); and also in immediate response to the postwar slump as employers began pay cuts and layoffs. In part the motivation that united the labor movement was political: the wish to avoid another war that might result from the government's interventions against the Russian Revolution. In May 1920 London dockers refused to load munitions onto ships that would supply the Polish army in its struggle with the Red Army.

On April 15, 1921, the powerful triple alliance of coalminers, transport workers, and railroadmen, the legacy of wartime corporatism in the United Kingdom, broke down when the railroad and transport workers refused to support the miners' strike.

In 1922 Conservative Members of Parliament met at the Carlton Club, revolted against the coalition, and brought down the government. They had been told (by Austen Chamberlain, the Conservative leader) that the coalition was needed to keep out Labour, which posed a fundamental threat to the essential principles "of both great parties" (Liberals and Conservatives) "upon which our national, industrial, and commercial greatness is based". Stanley Baldwin could not conceal his distaste for the morally and financially corrupt Prime Minister, and explained that he was a "dynamic force" who was also a danger, who had destroyed the Liberal Party and would destroy the Conservatives.[2] Lloyd George's government was not corrupt by the standards of late-twentieth-century European politics, or nineteenth-century politics, but he was particularly candid about the prices that were demanded for political favors and honors. The return to party politics was enthusiastically welcomed by Labour and the Asquithians.

In the November 1922 general election, the Conservatives and their allies had 38.5 percent of the vote, but dominated the House of Commons with an absolute majority (they had 344 seats). The Liberals, with 28.3 percent of the vote, had 115 Members of Parliament, and the only slightly higher-polling (but more geographically concentrated) Labour Party had 142 members. The Conservatives under the leadership of David Bonar Law formed a government, but it was soon clear that he was mortally ill. He had always been an uncomfortable leader, and in his short spell in office took the unusual step of writing an anonymous article in *The Times* denouncing his government's handling of the American war debt issue. The choice of his successor as Prime Minister was made by the King, George V, as the (undemocratic) British constitutional practice dictated. He picked as the new Prime Minister the relatively inexperienced Midlands ironmaster, Stanley Baldwin. Bonar Law had promised not to engage in a discussion of the controversial issue of tariffs for the life of parliament, but Baldwin effectively reopened the question in October 1923 by saying the promise should indeed end with the life of the parliament, and that tariffs would be useful in confronting the ills of unemployment.

In the general election which rapidly followed (December 1923) the Conservative vote remained almost the same as in 1922 in proportional terms (38 percent), as did that of Labour (30.7) and the Liberals (29.7), but the Labour Party was greatly strengthened (191 seats) as it consolidated a hold on working-class areas. With support from the Liberals, Ramsay MacDonald became Britain's first Labour Prime Minister.

MacDonald engaged energetically and enthusiastically in foreign policy making. The illegitimate son of a Scottish servant girl, he was the finest British political orator of his day, in a highly Gladstonian manner, and cut an aristocratic dash. He brilliantly outmaneuvered France at the London Reparations Conference of 1924, and he tried hard to bring the Soviet Union into European politics (on the sensible grounds that otherwise it would be pushed into an alliance of discontent with Germany). The latter position gave the Conservatives a political opportunity to run "red scare" stories, and they used a forged letter allegedly from the President of the Comintern,

Zinoviev, to the British Communist Party, in the election campaign of 1924. That election in October 1924, the third in a two-year span, came when the Liberals turned against MacDonald in a vote over the government's refusal to prosecute a communist agitator who had published an appeal to soldiers not to use force.

The Labour vote rose to 33 percent, but the Liberals collapsed, and the Conservatives with 48.3 percent of the popular vote had a massive majority in the House of Commons. Baldwin thus came back to power, and lasted an almost full five-year term.

He actually then did little on the tariff reform that had been so explosive a few years earlier: he had promised already before the election not to raise this specter. The critical economic measure was the 1925 return to the gold standard at the prewar rate of $4.86. This was carried out largely at the insistence of the financial community and with pressure from the Bank of England. Its Governor, a mysteriously enigmatic depressive, Montagu Norman, convinced the politically astute but economically illiterate Chancellor of the Exchequer (Finance Minister), Winston Churchill, of the importance of showing Britain's strength and credibility by taking the tough course of resuming gold convertibility in line with the promise written on all the Bank of England's notes ("I promise to pay the bearer . . ."). Keynes launched a furious polemic against the choice of what he saw as a wrong, deflationary exchange rate. The irony is that in the longer run, Norman may have been right in the sense that a relatively small overvaluation is not economically crippling provided industries and labor movements adjust. However, prices and wages did not adjust smoothly. In 1926 the unions launched a general strike to protest against a planned reorganization of coalmining that would involve some improvement in working conditions, but also lower wages and longer working hours. The government declared the strike illegal. There was little violence. Churchill fought against the strikers, but was quite aware of the political cost, and never forgave Norman.

By the end of its term of office, the Baldwin government looked complacent and ineffective. In 1929 a new election produced a second Labour government, again under Ramsay MacDonald.

Like German voters, British voters were turning against office-holders and were disillusioned by the political conventions of the 1920s. Britain's form of economic and financial stabilization had destroyed corporatism. On the labor side, the trade union coalition had been destroyed in 1920, and its broken power was underlined by the failure of the 1926 general strike. Employers' associations had been ineffective in pushing for an extension of temporary wartime tariff protection measures. By the late 1920s a non-corporatist political dynamic had asserted itself, in which Labour and the Conservatives competed in a new two-party system. This generated some political stability at last, but the turbulent political experience of the 1920s and of the experiments in reshaping old parties to address the new economic and social issues made British politicians and British thinkers skeptical about democracy, in the United Kingdom and elsewhere.

France

Measured in terms of numbers of governments, France was even more unstable than Germany or the United Kingdom. From the end of the war to the beginning of 1933, there were 27 French cabinets, but only 14 in Germany and seven in the United Kingdom. Like those of the United Kingdom, French electors chose an overwhelmingly conservative and patriotic legislature in the immediate aftermath of the war. Like the United Kingdom, France was ruled by center-right governments that responded with fiscal austerity to the 1920–21 collapse of the postwar boom. As in the United Kingdom, a failed general strike in 1920 ended the wartime corporatism of the left. And as in the United Kingdom, the major figures of the political elite hated each other and engaged in constant intrigue. The moments which turned politics also, as in the United Kingdom, hinged on foreign policy events.

France had introduced a new electoral system in 1919, in which voters had a choice between departmental party lists. It immediately offered an advantage to the national bloc (essentially the Clemenceau coalition). Clemenceau had wanted to round off his political career with the largely ceremonial office of President of the Republic, but his supporters feared that he might actually try to use the presidency, and instead elected a candidate who soon deteriorated into insanity. He was succeeded by a one-time socialist who had made his political way to full-fledged and conservative nationalism. French lawmakers also debated the question of women's votes, and the measure was passed in the Chamber of Deputies, but was rejected by the left in the Senate on the grounds that women were likely to be too clerically influenced. The moderate center-right government of Aristide Briand, which tried to build better relations with the Vatican (traditionally the enemy of the French Republic), eventually fell. Its leader seemed to have moved too close to Lloyd George and to have believed too much in empty British promises as a way of dealing with the threat of German aggression. The symbolic presentation of this French sell-out came when Briand played golf with the British Prime Minister at Cannes. He resigned in January 1922 without even waiting for a parliamentary vote of no confidence. Instead, the hard-line nationalist, Raymond Poincaré, came back to politics, and precipitated the German economic and political collapse of 1923 with his decision to occupy the Ruhr.

The labor movement had been weakened by the failure of a general strike in 1920, and membership in the labor unions fell by a half in that year. A split between the communists, who remained in political isolation until 1936, while attracting a substantial vote, further undermined the political strength of the left.

In 1924, the center-left finally came to power in a *cartel des gauches* under Edouard Herriot. Herriot, a radical, was supported by the socialists, but not by the French Communist Party. He, and his Foreign Minister Briand, who was much more influential in that role than he had been as Prime Minister, were much more amenable to compromise with Weimar Germany. But the government was torn apart by a financial crisis, for which it blamed not its own tax program but rather sinister vested interests. "Two hundred families", represented on the Board of Regents of the Banque de France, were pulling France toward a new war. France's industrialists were interested in conflict with Germany because it meant more orders for weapons and steel – thus went the conspiracy theory of the left.

In July 1926 Poincaré returned to power yet again in the face of a monetary and financial crisis, with wide support from the right to the center. He announced his task as "saving the franc", and appealed largely to an audience of rentiers and *petits bourgeois* scared of a repetition of Weimar-style hyperinflation. On the other hand, some of the business associates who had pressed for an end to the cartel were worried by the possibility that the franc might rise too high. Eventually, Poincaré managed a stabilization which left the franc at one-fifth of its old gold value, but secured relatively favorable competitive terms for French exports.

For a few years, France regained a precarious economic strength, but its international influence had been terribly eroded in the period of political and currency instability between 1924 and 1926. The legacy of war and inflation, as in Germany, left France divided along class lines, and France's enemies could play on these divisions to undermine France's international standing.

Italy

Italy had begun a rapid process of political democratization before the war. The extension of the franchise (from 3 million voters in 1912) had produced 8.6 million electors, at least 3 million of whom were estimated to be illiterate. The war had added a new element of economic modernization. The combination produced profound uncertainty: was Italy modern? Did modernity involve a reassertion of Italy's role as a great European power? How stable was modernity?

At the 1919 peace conference, Italy was the most marginal of the Great Powers, and the Italian Prime Minister Orlando walked out of the conference when it was clear that Italy would not be awarded the city of Fiume, which it regarded as its reward for its support of the Allies. This Habsburg port city was to be part of the new Yugoslav state. Postwar Italian democracy thus developed in the context of a painful national humiliation.

After a clash in Fiume in which some French soldiers were killed, the Paris Peace Conference Council ordered a recall of much of the Italian garrison. Some units then mutinied and called on the nationalist poet Gabriele d'Annunzio to support their revolt. He promised not to leave until the annexation of Fiume by Italy was complete. More and more soldiers and veterans joined d'Annunzio's "dictatorship" in Fiume. Italian diplomacy achieved a major success at the Treaty of Rapallo (April 16, 1920), which gave the whole of the Istrian peninsula (with a largely Slav-speaking population) to Italy, while Fiume was supposed to become a "Free City". D'Annunzio refused to accept even this very favorable solution, and declared war on an Italy whose leadership he despised. The Italian army fought for four days in late 1920 to recapture the city, so that the Rapallo solution could be implemented. But then, in February 1922, a coup staged by the Italian fascists overthrew the Free City government, and Italian troops moved in again. In January 1924, finally, with Mussolini in power in Italy, Yugoslavia formally ceded Fiume.

The old style of a shifting coalition among a liberal elite was threatened by the emergence of two popular and populist parties: the Catholic Popolari Party, and the socialist movement. Before the First World War, the Church forbade Catholics to take part in the politics of the Italian monarchical state, or even to vote in elections. In late 1918, as the rest of the old European political order was crumbling, the Cardinal Secretary of State, Cardinal Gasparri, gave permission to a Catholic Action priest (Don) Luigi Sturzo to found a new political movement. It was intended to be independent of the Church and non-confessional; it would not concern itself with the thorny question of the relationship between the Holy See and the Italian state, and instead it looked for social and economic reform, including land and tax reform. Like the Center Party in Germany, it had a quite miscellaneous social base: some farmers, some businessmen, some workers.

On the left, the socialist movement had been strengthened by the war and the example of the Russian Revolution. Italian cities had been radically and quickly transformed during the war, with a large and ill-housed new working class forming as a product of a rapid industrialization: in Turin, the Fiat works expanded from 4,000 to 40,000 workers. After the war, workers organized to protect their position. At the end of the war, the trade union federation CGL had fewer than 250,000 members, while by late 1920 it had over 2 million. In the factories, workers' committees looked as if they could provide an analogy with the Russian revolutionary movement.

In some areas of Italy – the Roman Campagna, and in Sicily – peasants seized land. In other areas, notably the lower Po valley, landless workers organized and tried to obtain improvements in wages and living conditions, on an analogy to factory workers.

At a quite different level, groups of demobilized soldiers formed paramilitary organizations (*arditi*). Benito Mussolini, a former socialist journalist and editor of the party newspaper *Avanti*, who had split with his party over his support for Italian intervention in the First World War, founded a party designed to appeal to the radical veterans of the War: the Fasci Italiani di Combattimento (fascists). One of his co-founders was the futurist theorist Marinetti, who had developed the theme of violence as a social and artistic force.

Orlando had resigned after his mishandling of the Paris Peace Conference. His successor Francesco Nitti, frustrated at the upsurge in violence and the embarrassment of d'Annunzio's Fiume adventure, dissolved parliament.

The election (1919) was held on the basis of proportional representation, in which voters would choose between party lists in 54 constituencies. The socialists gained 156 seats out of the total of 508, and the Popolari 100. The old parties of liberal Italy were thus (slightly) outnumbered; and they were bitterly divided. On the other hand, the radical right had had no substantial electoral support.

Fascism

Benito Mussolini chose the name "fascism" on the basis of the classical Roman "fasces", the symbol of consular authority. The consuls, who carried this emblem, ruled in the name of the Roman people, and the bound bundle of twigs was a powerful symbol of the binding of individuals into a community.

Before Mussolini's seizure of power in October 1922, fascism was rather ill-defined, and was heavily modified in order to suit particular and pragmatic political circumstances. Sometimes Mussolini interpreted its collectivism in a socialist way; while at other times he appeared to be militantly in favor of capitalism. He consistently opposed communism, although the modification of *Marxian* socialism in order to provide greater room for the individual will seems quite analogous to the *Leninist* transformation.

In 1932, Mussolini produced a definition of "The Doctrine of Fascism" for the *Enciclopedia Italiana*. In it he stated that: "Fascism is a religious conception in which man is seen in his immanent relationship with a superior law and with an objective Will that transcends the particular individual and raises him to conscious membership of a spiritual society." Within a nation, there were classes and interest associations ("syndicates"), but they were subordinated to the state. Mussolini also reflected on democracy, which he rejected in its form of rule by the majority. Instead he argued that fascism was "the purest form of democracy", if democracy was thought of not as the most popular but as the "most powerful" idea "which acts within the nation as the conscience and the will of a few, even of One". (This is presumably a reference to himself as Duce, or leader.)

The doctrine emphasized power; it did this even more emphatically in the field of foreign relations:

> Above all, Fascism, in so far as it considers and observes the future and the development of humanity quite apart from the political considerations of the moment, believes neither in the possibility nor in the utility of perpetual peace. [. . .] War alone brings up

(continued)

(continued)
to their highest tension all human energies and puts the stamp of
nobility upon the peoples who have the courage to meet it.

This was probably (together with the related German version of
fascism, *National Socialism*) the most radically anti-liberal doctrine
of the twentieth century, and found a quite wide international reception that went well beyond Europe. Almost every European country
developed a fascist movement, often identified by the wearing of shirts
of a particular color as a way of creating a cheap uniform. Mussolini
had his followers wear black shirts. The Chinese Blue Shirts developed
when cadets at the Whampoa military academy asked the nationalist
leader Chiang Kai-shek to appoint a leader: he did this in a traditionally Chinese way by demanding that the cadets each write an essay on
how Bismarck had unified Germany.

After the military defeat of Italy, fascism (which had asserted the
primacy of force) was largely discredited. The term became widely
used not only as a means of historical analysis, with competing schools
of interpretation seeing fascism as an extreme form of imperialism
(i.e. the highest form of capitalism in Leninist thought), or alternately as
a protest movement of the marginalized lower-middle classes (Trotsky's
interpretation), or as a form of an anti-modern rejection of liberal
values (the mainstream liberal interpretation). But the term "fascism"
was also used to make analogies to the present and define some aspect
of the behavior of political opponents as irrational, violent, or undemocratic. Thus at different moments, populist and nationalist leaders
such as General de Gaulle, conservative politicians such as Margaret
Thatcher, whole governments (especially that of the United States), but
also student revolutionary leaders in 1968, were all termed "fascist"
by their political opponents. Neo-fascist parties rarely used the term,
but tried to rescue some of the rather inchoate ideology.

Nitti continued to rule, with inflation soaring, but the Popolari turned
against him. The veteran radical liberal of prewar Italy, Giolitti, returned
as Prime Minister in June 1920. Almost immediately he faced an apparent
repetition of Russian circumstances: simultaneous military, peasant or land
laborer, and urban working-class unrest. There was a military mutiny, when
mountain troops who were to be dispatched to Albania refused orders. The
socialist land laborers' organization in Bologna went on strike, and won
major concessions from the landowners in October. In August 1920, Turin
metalworkers responded to an employer lockout with factory occupations,
which then were imitated in Milan and Genoa. In a settlement, pay was
increased and the factory councils were recognized by the employers.

The left quickly became rather demoralized, despite the apparent successes. In part the disenchantment emanated from the international scene, which was turning against the export of revolution (the Poles had won the battle of Warsaw in the late summer of 1920). In part it reflected the socialists' fear that they had missed an opportunity to turn the dynamic of social protest, once as fierce as that of 1917 Russia, in the political direction that Lenin's leadership had taken.

By late 1920, local elections showed more support for Giolitti's regime, but he now faced a severe economic downturn. Violence began to come more from the right than from the left. In the countryside, in Venezia and Emilia-Romagna, fascist *squadre* attacked socialist unions; and by 1921 they were strong and bold enough to take counter-revolutionary war to the big northern industrial centers. Mussolini, who in 1919 still seemed to have a great deal of admiration for the Russian Revolution, of course in an Italianized form, now started to court business leaders and speak in favor of private property.

While fascism advanced and got stronger, the socialist movement split over the Comintern's conditions for allegiance. Mussolini began to see a link between the new strength of his movement and the collapse of Italian communism. He also looked for reconciliation with Giolitti, and when the Prime Minister called new elections to demonstrate the return of order to Italy, Mussolini contested the election as part of a pro-government and anti-socialist national bloc (May 1921). The elections did not change the parliamentary scene greatly: the socialists were reduced to 123, but there were now 15 communists; and there were 35 fascist deputies.

Giolitti was soon defeated in a foreign policy debate, and replaced by Ivanoe Bonomi, who included some Popolari ministers in the cabinet. Bonomi also began to take some measures against the violence of the fascists. It looked much like Giolitti without the great man himself.

Mussolini decided at this stage that he would turn fascism into a respectable movement, and he opened his parliamentary career with a speech applauding "Manchesterite capitalism" (the raw early capitalism of the British Industrial Revolution) as an alternative to the "collectivist state" produced by the war. He then made what appeared to be another about-turn when he approved negotiations for a truce between the fascists and the socialists.

For the next year, there were major tensions between Mussolini and his very radical and violent followers. He relied on this conflict to present himself to the Italian political and business elite as the only figure who could control the new culture of violence. Many liberals and Popolari thought that Mussolini, unlike his wild followers, could be trusted to strike political bargains. The Italian elite disintegrated under the impact of depression, deflation, and financial crisis. Anti-clerical liberals withdrew from the Bonomi government, and a new government was created under an aide of Giolitti's, Luigi Facta. The Church's position also shifted to the right. The Pope elected in 1922 after the death of Benedict XV, Achille Ratti, had been papal nuncio in Warsaw during the battle with the Red Army, and was profoundly anti-communist. He ordered a replica of the Black Madonna of Czestochowa for the papal chapel at Castelgandolfo.

Mussolini depended on a balance between political compromise at the level of high politics and terror and intimidation at the basis of local life. In Cremona, fascists led by the anti-clerical Roberto Farinacci started to attack and break up Catholic land laborer unions, in the same brutal manner as they had treated the socialist unions. In Milan, Genoa, Ancona, and Livorno, socialist municipal councils were broken up (August 1922).

By early October 1922, Mussolini made it clear that he intended to seize power at a national level also. A last chance for democracy might have been a new Giolitti coalition government, but for this to work the socialists and Popolari pointed out (logically enough) that Giolitti would need to exclude fascists from his government, while at the same time Mussolini told intermediaries that he would be part of a Giolitti government. Giolitti hesitated, while Mussolini began intense discussions with Italian business leaders.

Facta tried to summon the King and Giolitti to Rome, to confront Mussolini's challenge, and the military command began to prepare for a fascist siege. During October 27–28, fascist *squadre* took over most of central and northern Italy, and began to move on Rome. But on October 28, King Vittorio Emanuele refused to sign the laws prepared by Facta imposing a state of siege, and Facta had no alternative but to resign. Mussolini went on a night train to Rome, secure in the knowledge that he would be asked to form a government.

Once in office, Mussolini gradually built up a reserve of political power. From July 1923, the government was authorized to issue decree laws. Then a fascist administrator, Giacomo Acerbo, drafted a law which revised proportional representation so as to make the whole of Italy a single constituency and then to award two-thirds of the parliamentary seats to the largest party (if it won over a quarter of the vote). King Victor Emmanuel refused to sign this as a decree law, and it passed parliament after great fascist intimidation. It was passed by 235 votes, with most socialists and communists voting against and the Popolari abstaining.

The corporate state was based on a monopoly employer's organization (Confindustria) and the newly created fascist labor unions. They concluded a pact in October 1925 at the Palazzo Vidoni, in which they pledged themselves to recognize each other as the only legitimate representatives of capital and labor. At a local level, fascist violence continued; communist and socialist leaders were arrested and maltreated.

The election under the new law was held on April 6, 1924, with a single government list, dominated by fascists but including some Catholics, liberals, and conservatives. One prominent liberal, Salandra, who was on the list, said that Mussolini was "the banner of the liberal idea".[3] As a result of the election, non-government Popolari, socialists, and communists still had some seats. The secretary-general of the Socialist Party, Giacomo Matteotti, made a long speech in the first meeting of the new parliament denouncing the intimidation and fraud of the fascist victory. He was shouted at in parliament, and 12 days later disappeared. He had been kidnapped and killed by a fascist terror squad. Mussolini promised that there would be a fair investigation. In the wake of the assassination, the remnants of the socialists and the Popolari tried a rapprochement, but it was too late.

A number of assassination attempts gave Mussolini the pretext to close every party except the fascists; there was a tight censorship, and from 1927 a secret police. Mussolini had effectively destroyed democracy and its institutions, and also political liberty (Plate 4).

Democracy, community, and hatred

Any close examination of the political life of the 1920s is dispiriting. Parties in the liberal center, in the United Kingdom but more spectacularly in France, Germany, and Italy, broke into fragmented grouplets. The centrist parties were loosely defined, and dependent on grand or not-so-grand personalities who engaged in continual internecine disputes. Democracy failed to articulate itself in stable party structures.

Plate 4 Benito Mussolini at the height of his success, addressing a crowd in Rome.
© Keystone/Getty Images.

There were two reasons for this, one organizational and the other concerned with the language of politics. The push to democratization occurred at the same time as an enhanced organization of interests that was a product of the wartime mobilization of society and its aftermath. Sectional interests locked themselves into conflicts over the distribution of resources in a world impoverished by the war. They largely frustrated the process of discussion at a political level.

The move to democratization also occurred with a new and radicalized vocabulary that transformed political conduct. The war had seen a search for and definition of enemies, not just externally but also internally. The nationalist poet Ernst Lissauer had offered Germans a "hymn of hate". Defeat and humiliation made the search for internal enemies even more passionate and desperate. The duration and inhumanity of the war had prompted some to search for peace while others denounced them as pacifist traitors. Clemenceau had built his political career on the denunciation of French betrayals, and was propelled into power in the wake of a series of espionage scandals (such as the activity of the exotic dancer Mata Hari). Even on the side of the anti-war position, socialists were divided by the memories of how late they had declared their opposition to imperialist war.

Parties now addressed each other in absurd exaggerations. Even in the polite United Kingdom, Austen Chamberlain, a man usually admired for his moderation and courtesy, in 1922 said that Labour was a direct challenge to the fundamental principles of British life; he was talking irresponsible nonsense. When the Nationalist deputies in the Reichstag denounced Erzberger's tax plans as a betrayal, and criticized the author as the signatory of Versailles, they were using the inflammatory language of the radical right.

The best practitioners of interwar politics treated it as a game, in which attitude and cleverness paid off: Stanley Baldwin, when he was half-way through his cynical gamble to first raise and then drop the trade protection issue, told his party at a dinner meeting:

> What I want to impress upon you is that, with this enormous new and young electorate, a knowledge of which no party can yet be said to possess, the tendency will be for them to go to the party which offers them an attractive case, put with great persuasion and with great enthusiasm – to the party which, as far as possible, can save them the trouble of thinking.[4]

The outcome of the new political language was a search for differentiation that went hand-in-hand with the building of new sorts of (often unexpected) alliances. An Italian liberal in 1922 argued that "Democracy has no other purpose than that of tying together liberalism and its natural enemy socialism." Another concluded that fascism was "the principle that unites us".[5]

The believers in democracy came mostly at this time from a very beleaguered political center, but it was exactly this group that, driven by the logic of electoral systems, looked most desperately for allies in the oddest of quarters. But they appeared more and more helpless and ridiculous as a result. The witty left-wing intellectuals of the Weimar Republic – the great satirists Carl von Ossietzky, the editor of the *Weltbühne*, and Kurt Tucholsky – did their best to make the SPD leadership look timid and silly: in the vegetable garden of German politics, the socialist leaders were like "little modest radishes: red on the outside and white within".[6]

The German novelist Thomas Mann, as a contribution to First World War propaganda, had written *Reflections of an Unpolitical Man*, in which he had attacked western-style liberalism as superficial "civilization" which contrasted with a deeper German *Kultur*. In 1922 in a speech on the sixtieth birthday of the socialist writer Gerhart Hauptmann, Mann recanted and appealed for the Republic, "for what is called democracy and I call humanity". He also tried to work out what underlay the European war of ideas.

The high point of his novel *The Magic Mountain* (*Der Zauberberg*, 1924) as a political fable (which is in part what Mann intended it to be) is the conflict between two inmates of the sanatorium, an optimistic Italian liberal progressive (Settembrini) and a dark irrationalist (Naphta). Naphta's conclusion is that

> it is an unloving miscomprehension of youth to believe that it finds its pleasure in freedom: its deepest pleasure lies in obedience . . . Liberation and development of the individual are not the key to our age, they are not what our age demands. What it needs, what it wrestles after, what it will create – is Terror.[7]

Mann also intended the novel to be a depiction about the death-instinct of European culture. The protagonist arrives in the Alpine sanatorium for a short stay (to visit his cousin), but stays for seven years. When he returns, he goes back to a Europe at war.

In the interwar period, Sigmund Freud, whose prewar writings had been ostensibly non-political, set out to give a political diagnosis. In *Civilization and its Discontents* (*Das Unbehagen in der Kultur*, 1930), Freud made an analogy between the development of a society and the emergence of an individual personality. The repression of instinctual violence occurs on an individual level in conscience and at the level of political society in law. It provoked a violent reaction:

> besides the instinct to preserve living substance and to join it into ever larger units, there must exist another contrary instinct seeking to dissolve those units and to bring them back to their primaeval, inorganic, state. That is to say, as well as Eros there was an instinct of death.[8]

In particular, individuals tried to differentiate themselves from others by "small differences" and then to make these differences the basis of a negative bonding defined by violence.

The German legal and political philosopher Carl Schmitt developed the analysis of *The Concept of the Political* (the title of a 1927 book), and arrived at a pessimistic conclusion quite close to that of Freud: "The political is the most intense and extreme antagonism, and every concrete antagonism becomes much more political the closer it approaches the most extreme point, that of the friend–enemy grouping."[9] Such a politicization ran against, and destroyed, the electoral logic of coalition-building.

The most telling and pathetic of the confessions of the failure of the democratic idea came from the Italian socialist leader, Filippo Turati. Shortly after the seizure of power, in November 1922, Mussolini told parliament: "I could have made this grey and gloomy hall into a bivouac for my legions . . . I could have barred up parliament and formed an exclusively fascist government. I could have: but at least for the moment, I did not will it." Turati replied: "Democracy will win, because it must win, because it is history; yes, for that simple reason." To which Mussolini gave the retort: "History does not have fixed rails like a railway."[10] Few advocates of democracy in the 1920s were able to explain precisely by what process of historical inevitability democracy should win in the clash of European ideals.

A British textbook – the standard one on European history of the time – published by Longman in 1931, and in a sense the predecessor of this volume, commented on political decay. Parliamentary corruption was the result of "the parliamentary system, with its irresponsible finance committee, its never-ending 'group' adjustments and petty political intrigues". Its conclusions seem very cynical and very wrong to a modern reader:

> The destruction or suspension of the representative system has, in neither country [Italy or Spain] been greeted with that panic or horror which one would have expected. Such dictators seem, in fact, to be considered by the democracy as more truly their representatives than the corrupt or inefficient deputies in parliament.[11]

It needed the full force of the crisis of the 1930s to reveal how brutally destructive was the non-democratic option.

Notes

1 A.J. Grant and Harold Temperley, *Europe in the Nineteenth Century (1789–1914)*, London: Longmans, Green, 1931.
2 Maurice Cowling, *The Impact of Labour 1920–1924*, Cambridge: Cambridge University Press, 1971, p. 210.
3 Christopher Seton-Watson, *Italy from Liberalism to Fascism*, London: Methuen, 1967, p. 647.
4 Cowling, *Labour*, p. 413.
5 Quoted in Charles S. Maier, *Recasting Bourgeois Europe: Stabilization in France, Germany, and Italy in the Decade after World War I*, Princeton, NJ: Princeton University Press, 1975, p. 342.
6 Kurt Tucholsky, "Feldfrüchte", orig. publ. in *Die Weltbühne*, 1926; repr. in *Gesammelte Werke*, Hamburg: Rowohlt, 1960, Vol. I, p. 508.

7 Thomas Mann (transl. H.T. Lowe-Porter), *The Magic Mountain*, New York, NY: Knopf, 1927, p. 507.
8 Sigmund Freud (transl. James Strachey), *Civilization and its Discontents*, New York, NY: Norton, 1961, pp. 65–6.
9 Carl Schmitt (transl. George Schwab), *The Concept of the Political*, New Brunswick, NJ: Rutgers University Press, 1976, p. 19.
10 Adrian Lyttelton, *The Seizure of Power: Fascism in Italy 1919–1929*, London: Weidenfeld, 1973, pp. 100, 367.
11 Grant and Temperley, *Europe*, p. 517.

4 Europe and the world of the Depression

The year 1929 marked the realization that all was not well in European politics. "Crisis" rapidly became the most over-used word in the political vocabulary, and the idea of "crisis" was intertwined with the memory of conflict and war. The Soviet newspaper *Izvestia* marked June 28, the fifteenth anniversary of the assassination of the Austrian archduke in Sarajevo, by stating that the new era was an "interwar period" (a phrase which is now of course a common characterization).[1]

The New York Stock Exchange crash of October 24, 1929, is conventionally taken as the beginning of the Great Depression, and the end of the illusion of prosperity. Another October date that marked the end of an illusion of peace had occurred three weeks before: on October 3, the Foreign Minister of Germany, Gustav Stresemann, who had rebuilt German relations with the western powers, died of a heart attack. Another architect of the postwar order, Georges Clemenceau, died on November 24.

The Great Depression, the crisis of democracy, and the crisis of the international system, are all closely linked. The economic crisis put great, and frequently intolerable, strains on democracy. The price collapse of agricultural products destroyed the precarious livelihoods of peasant producers, and turned them against the state. In the industrial areas of Europe, unemployed workers were alienated; they often included in the objects of their attack traditional labor organizations that seemed blind to their plight. On a global level, the malfunctioning of the international economic order, and in particular the drying up of the world's capital markets, reduced the rewards for good behavior internationally, and made defiance of the international political order much more attractive. As a beginning of what would prove to be a long slide to international anarchy and lawlessness, Japan soon defied the League of Nations in Manchuria, and Benito Mussolini's Italy flexed its muscles in the Mediterranean.

The failure of markets, the failure of conventional politics, the failure of the international system: these three failures made up the crisis of the late 1920s. It was frequently diagnosed as the crisis of modernity and of mass culture. In the 1930s, Spain became the field on which disputes about the past were fought out. A cult book in the early 1930s, José Ortega y Gasset's

The Revolt of the Masses, published first in Spain in 1930 at the moment when that country was embarking on its tragically doomed experiment with democratization, started with the description of the "mass" phenomenon:

> Towns are full of people, houses full of tenants, hotels full of guests, trains full of travellers, cafés full of customers, parks full of promenaders, consulting rooms of famous doctors full of patients, theatres full of spectators, and beaches full of bathers. What previously was, in general, no problem, now begins to be an everyday one, namely, to find room.

The outcome of this pressure was a crisis of expectations and a crisis of the state: "Statism is the higher form taken by violence and direct action when these are set up as standards. Through and by means of the State, the anonymous machine, the masses act for themselves."[2]

Society and depression

There were plenty of economic problems in the world before the dramatic collapse of Wall Street in October 1929. Australia, highly dependent on wool exports, and Brazil, almost exclusively reliant on coffee exports, were deeply depressed. In Germany cyclical production indicators already turned around in the autumn of 1927 (the stock market weakness appeared even earlier). The story of what produced 1929 in the United States is still slightly mysterious, at least for believers in the rationality of markets. What did stock market investors know on "Black Thursday", October 24, 1929, that they had not known on Tuesday or Wednesday? There had been "bad news" since early September, and the weight of evidence had accumulated to such an extent that there was a panic in the face of the likelihood of the future decline of stock prices. The only plausible answer for those who wish for a rational account of the stock market collapse is that American investors were contemplating the likelihood of the implementation of a new piece of legislation, which went under the names of Smoot and Hawley. This tariff bill had begun as a promise in the presidential campaign of 1929 by Herbert Hoover to improve the situation of the American farmer (with the agricultural price collapse, the farmer was the major loser of Jazz Age prosperity). In the course of congressional debate, however, each representative tried to add on new items (there were 1,253 Senate amendments alone). The result – a tariff with 21,000 tariff positions – was extreme protectionism; but worse, until the final narrow voting in June 1930, there was constant uncertainty about the future of trade policy.

If the story of the Depression does not begin with the stock market crash and Smoot–Hawley, neither does it end there. There were some signs of recovery in 1930: stock prices in the US rebounded, and the lower level of the market made foreign issues appear attractive again.

What made the Depression the *Great* Depression rather than a brief-lived stock market problem or a depression for commodity producers was a chain of linkages that operated through the financial markets. The desperate state of the commodity producers along with the reparations-induced problems of Germany set off a chain of domino reactions. In this sense the Depression was a product of disorderly financial markets.

In the events of 1931, which made the Depression "Great", financial contagion brought the continent into crisis. At the beginning of *Anna Karenina*, Leo Tolstoy famously describes how happy families resemble each other, but each unhappy family is unhappy in its own peculiar way. At the beginning of 1931, all the central European economies had problems, but they were quite special ones.

Hungary was above all a victim of the worldwide collapse of agricultural prices, which declined at first gently between 1925 and 1928 and then plummeted. It had a budget crisis because of two highly costly and ultimately ineffective schemes to stabilize the price of wheat (a buffer stock and a direct price subsidy). As the wheat price continued to fall, these operations required increased subsidies. Domestic and foreign creditors – who in November 1930 had still been willing to buy Hungarian short-term debt at a good price – now worried about the ability of the government to service its debt, and began to anticipate a default. They thus withdrew money from Hungarian banks, and Hungary had a banking problem. The withdrawals took place across the exchanges (creditors converted *pengö* into foreign exchange) and the crisis thus threatened the maintenance of the gold-standard attachment. What started out as a budget issue transformed itself into a banking and foreign exchange crisis.

In Austria, the causation ran the other way round: the largest bank, the Creditanstalt, was unable to produce its accounts on time, and its depositors panicked. It was clear that the government could not allow such a big institution to fail, and the cost of the bank bailout would have to be borne by the state. With every week that passed, the calculation of that cost became ever higher. Depositors, in the Creditanstalt but also in other Austrian banks, also withdrew money across the exchange, and the National Bank lost its reserves. Here a banking crisis became a budget crisis.

The gold standard

The gold standard had been the central feature of the international monetary order before the First World War. Its major feature lay in the automaticity of adjustment, in a mechanism which had been described in the eighteenth century by David Hume: if a country had a deficit in its trade balance and thus lost gold (to pay for the trade deficit), its monetary stock would be reduced. This would reduce prices, making its goods more attractive on international markets, and the goods of other countries more expensive. Exports would rise and imports fall, and the trade deficit would thus be corrected automatically.

In reality, the gold standard was more managed than this, and most gold-standard countries had central banks, which had some power to control money markets. They were expected to react quickly to stop the adverse consequences of a gold outflow by raising rates, and thus attracting inward flows of funds seeking a higher return. The central bank held reserves of gold, against which it was entitled to issue banknotes.

Before the First World War, some countries already held their reserves not in the form of gold, but in foreign exchange of other countries (mostly British securities). After the war, when the gold standard was restored, the use of foreign exchange (dollars and pounds) became more prevalent, so that the system was usually now described as a "gold exchange standard".

Compared to the prewar system, the interwar system was much more fragile. In part this lay in the substitution of foreign exchange for gold: what would happen if too many claims built up against the British, as the issuers of the major reserve currency? In part it lay in another measure used to economize on the use of physical gold: the prevalence of so-called fractional reserve systems, in which the central bank issued banknotes that were covered by a specific ratio (say 40 percent) of gold or foreign reserves. In this example, a trade deficit and gold outflow would require a far sharper contraction of the domestic money stock (by 100/40 or 2.5 times) than under the Hume model. But there was a more basic flaw in the system, in that the greater rigidity of prices and wages (because of cartels and trade unions) meant that prices did not easily fall, and adjustment occurred more in output and job losses than in price falls. Since, in the aftermath of the Russian Revolution and the First World War, unemployment had become politically more sensitive, markets could calculate that some levels of unemployment would be politically intolerable, and that the monetary authorities would be unable to withstand speculative attacks. This made speculative attacks more likely to be successful, and they thus became more common. The result was that many commentators increasingly saw the gold standard as an invitation to speculation and a cause of politically dangerous unemployment. Keynes described the system as "golden fetters" which stood in the way of rational economic policy management, i.e. *Keynesianism*.

In Germany, few people had any idea how bad the loans of institutions such as the Darmstädter Bank in reality were. But there was a widespread fear that the reparations debate might lead to an exchange crisis. Withdrawals weakened the banks and brought out the latent problems in their portfolios that might otherwise have remained unexposed. The weakness of the exchange position weakened the capital market, so that the government could no longer finance even relatively small short-term deficits. Previously it had depended on the banks, but as these lost their deposits they withdrew from such financing. Here a foreign exchange crisis, measurable in terms of the *Reichsbank*'s reserve losses, set off the banking and budget crises.

The sequence of the different aspects of crisis was different in each of the central European crisis economies, but the outcomes were surprisingly similar. In each case, capital movements across frontiers destroyed a banking system that had already been weakened by the effects of war and postwar inflations. And in each case, the concatenation of problems produced a policy paralysis. Some years ago, the German economic historian Knut Borchardt analyzed the limited room for maneuver, and warned against a retrospective optimism about the solubility of problems.[3] The astonishing feature of the world depression was how rapidly this paralysis was transferred across national frontiers. A similar contagion mechanism operated in Latin America.

A crisis in the creditor countries followed the problems of the debtors. In the United Kingdom, there were no fundamental problems with banks. But many investment houses suffered from the freezing of their credits in central Europe, and their depositors feared possible insolvencies. The German bank closures of July 1931 set off a run on sterling: rumors of an impending Latin American default provided the final straw that broke the back of the UK's gold standard. The Bank of England refused to use all the instruments at its disposal – interest rate increases, or the use of its reserves – in defense of the parity, as it feared that allowing further transfers over the exchange would bring down at least some of the weaker London banks. The devaluation stabilized the British financial system because of the skill with which it was managed. The pound fell sharply on the exchange, creating expectations that the next movement would be up rather than down, and thus discouraging depositors from realizing their losses. It is important to note – particularly for those who suggest that this British-style solution might have been appropriate for central Europe or South America – that in these cases it would have been impossible to find an exchange rate which would have given rise to the expectation of recovery.

The British panic, in common with the preceding debtor crises, had an abrupt reversal of expectations. Depositors and investors saw a danger of being trapped in a particular engagement, and – as they saw the door closing – rushed to get out. Once this mechanism had operated in one creditor country, it might apply to others. The United States was vulnerable, not because it had an external current account problem, but because it was apparent that US banks were vulnerable to losses elsewhere. The resulting capital movements, which set on quite suddenly after the sterling devaluation of September 1931, changed the possibilities for anti-cyclical measures. Before September 1931, President Hoover had been contemplating quite extensive measures to stimulate the economy through government expenditure. After the panic, in which as a result of experience elsewhere government deficits were synonymous with failures of confidence, the President started to assert the necessity of balanced budgets. But so, remarkably, did his Democratic opponent in the 1932 presidential race, Franklin Delano Roosevelt, who made criticism of Hoover's deficits a focal point of his campaign. The withdrawals and the shocks to confidence only ended when Roosevelt, seeing every other alternative fail, took the dollar off the gold standard on April 20, 1933, and then announced (July 3) that he had no intention of stabilizing its external value since all that concerned Americans was the internal value or purchasing power of their currency. Again the dollar fell sharply, encouraging belief that it might be stabilized or even recover. Then the crises continued in the remaining gold-standard countries – Belgium, France, the Netherlands, and Switzerland – until in the end they too saw an abandonment of the parity regime as the only way of ending continual budget strain and bank panics.

Unemployment became the scourge of the age, with 3.5 million unemployed in the United Kingdom, over 6 million registered as out of work in Germany, and over 12 million in the United States at the height of the crisis in 1932. Throughout the world, around 30 million people were estimated as being out of work. The crisis of production and of employment was especially pronounced in the classic sectors of the Industrial Revolution, in producer goods such as iron and steel, and mechanical engineering. Thus, in Germany, while unemployment in all manufacturing doubled from 1929 to 1931, in mining it increased six-fold, in the chemical industry four times, and in metallurgy three times.

History and progress looked as if they were going into reverse. Indeed, when an occupational census was carried out in June 1933 in Germany, for the first time since 1882, there were more persons actively employed in agriculture and forestry (9 million) than in industry and manufacturing (8.86 million).

A fine contemporary study by Marie Jahoda, Paul Lazarsfeld, and Hans Zeisel depicted the Austrian textile town of Marienthal, where the major factory had been closed down in 1929. Petty criminality increased. Most families (the study estimated 69 percent) were best characterized by the word "resignation": "the renunciation of a future, which no longer even plays a role as a plan of phantasy". The workers "lost the material and moral possibilities of using time". A British study of the chronically unemployed argued in a similar way: "It cannot be reiterated too often that unemployment is not an active state; its keynote is boredom – a continuous sense of boredom. This boredom was inevitably accompanied by a disbelief which gave rise to cynicism."[4] Men in particular, used to a position as the earning head of a household, were humiliated by unemployment. Some photographs of the time show the neatly clad unemployed, sometimes wearing collars and ties, going out on the streets in order to maintain the illusion that they were going to work. Female employment, usually in less skilled occupations, fell less violently, and this added to the resentment of males and to campaigns to stop "dual income earners".

Youth criminality, including violent crimes, rose during the Depression years in most countries. There were street gangs, some of which were connected with political movements: Berlin had around 600 gangs with 14,000 members. Hitler later estimated that between 300,000 and 400,000 members of the paramilitary SA and SS had been unemployed. The suicide rate increased.

The working class was also fragmented and polarized by the experience of prolonged depression. Despite wage cuts, the number of strikes fell away dramatically as workers feared for their jobs. Especially where unions had some negotiating power, young and strong workers who lost their positions blamed the labor movement's insistence on saving the livelihoods of older family fathers. Ruhrort-Meiderich, where unions rejected a plan to save an iron and steel plant by big wage cuts in early 1931, voted heavily Nazi in 1932, as a gesture of defiance to the labor leadership.

Farming had its crisis, too: indeed, outside northern and western Europe, the problems caused by the collapse of prices since the middle of the 1920s were as immediately striking as the malaise of the industrial world. Even in the United States, the classic Depression-era novel is John Steinbeck's *The Grapes of Wrath*, about displaced Oklahoma farmers looking in vain for a new existence in California. Over-indebtedness, inability to service debt, foreclosure, proletarianization: these were the dangers that affected the world of small peasant farmers, and drove them to despair and to radical political movements.

Workers and farmers were most directly hit by the effects of depression and the collapse of demand. Their work was devalued by the economic blizzard. So were the assets of those who owned securities, as stock markets fell, and many foreign loans were defaulted. The fundamental economic trauma of the 1920s lay in a series of monetary disorders: first, at the beginning of the decade, widespread inflation which produced a great fear of possible repetition; then the legacy of inflation set the political and economic stage for the deflation (falling prices) of the end of the decade and the early 1930s. In central Europe, Poland, Hungary, Austria, and Germany, large parts of the middle classes had already been expropriated by inflations in the immediate postwar years. In the Depression, while tenant farmers and workers complained about high rents, landlords also saw their income shrinking. What survived of the great aristocratic families cut back expenditure and economized. In short, every kind of activity and enterprise was devalued too, with the exception of money (cash) holding. Deflation increased the value of assets of those who held only cash – but who were these people? Always, the answer went, someone else. In western Europe, resentment against money-holders was usually expressed in class terms, as resentment against the bankers (in England), or the "two hundred families" who were supposed to monopolize bourgeois France. In central Europe, such resentment almost always turned in an anti-Semitic direction.

Deflation thus destroyed social cohesion and society. Some ingenious schemes were proposed to deal with the ill of deflation: to devalue money more quickly than money devalued people. The small west Austrian town of Wörgl introduced a moderately successful experiment in disappearing money (*Schvundgeld*), notes that needed a new stamp attached each month in order to keep their value. The hope was that this might make people spend more and break the cycle of deflation. But, in general, most people and most politicians felt quite hopeless, that deflation was something that came from the big outside world. They were right, in that it emanated from a combination of the international monetary system of the time (the international gold exchange standard) and the inadequate management provided by the central bankers.

There are some general lessons that might be drawn from the experience of the Depression. First, countries with high foreign debts and weak banking structures are vulnerable to deflationary shocks. Second, the mechanisms of financial contagion transfer the weakness to creditor countries with sound banking systems. Third, the most obvious transmission mechanism was the fixed exchange rate commitment. As soon as the United Kingdom or the United States – or Belgium or Switzerland – abandoned the gold-standard link, while preserving fiscal orthodoxy, the banking threat that had been a prime mechanism for the transmission of depression disappeared.

Most contemporaries, however, drew a much simpler and much more ideological lesson: first, that the international order had failed; and second, that the market mechanism had produced internationalization of depression, and needed to be replaced by a healthier concentration on domestic ordering and planning.

Germany's slide into dictatorship

Germany was the initial focus of the economic and political crisis in Europe. It was the largest European economy, the greatest debtor country of the world, and, above all, the defeated Great Power of the First World War. The economic crisis was bound up with the unsolved problems of postwar reparations.

The Paris peace treaties in 1919 had not specified an amount that Germany should pay: the gap between what the Allies (and in particular France) hoped and what Germany might realistically be expected to pay was simply too wide. It was only in 1921 that a figure was set; but the reparations schedule had to be revised after the German hyper-inflation, a fiscal and monetary collapse in the early 1920s. Under the 1924 Dawes Plan, reparations payments would rise as the German economy recovered. In addition, "prosperity clauses" linked specific indicators – such as the number of automobiles sold in Germany – to higher payments. After 1924, Germany borrowed extensively. Some members of the German government, notably the central bank president, Hjalmar Schacht, saw the borrowing as a way of forcing a new and much lower reparations settlement, in that as the loans (mostly from the United States) built up, they would constitute a rival claim on Germany to the political payments of reparation, largely for Belgian and French reconstruction. In 1929 Foreign Minister Gustav Stresemann was successful in persuading the western powers that Germany was a good neighbor, and that Germany would accept the western frontiers with the loss of Alsace and Lorraine as imposed in the Paris treaties. The reward was a downward revision (and a final figure) for reparations, as well as an earlier than planned withdrawal of French troops from the Rhineland. Stresemann's strategy was directly at odds with that of Schacht, who needed a major financial crisis in which the foreign lenders would press the French to lower their claim. Schacht did his best to sabotage and disrupt the reparations negotiations, and when he failed to stop the new settlement (the Young Plan) he resigned from the central bank.

The government, a so-called "great coalition" under the leadership of a socialist, Hermann Müller, was severely tested. It was already suffering the fiscal effects of the economic downturn (which had begun in Germany in 1928, well before the Wall Street crash). The left wing of the coalition, the Socialist Party, wanted to deal with the problems by imposing an additional 3 percent levy on wages; while the right, a pro-business liberal party (the German People's Party, which had been Stresemann's party) saw the solution as lying in a cut in benefit levels (which would also reduce resistance to wage cuts). While the Young Plan was being debated and ratified, the bad consequences of a collapse of the government were clear to all the coalition partners, and they swallowed their differences. Once the Young Plan had been ratified, however, this external bracket no longer held German politics together, and the SPD left the government because of a proposed increase in the rate of contributions for the unemployment insurance system.

The Young Plan provided a catalyst for German politics. At the same time as it held the moderate parties together in the government, it also alienated many people from the "system" which seemed to demand unpalatable and even impossible concessions from Germans: under the terms of the settlement, they (or their descendants) were to continue to pay reparations until 1984. Adolf Hitler's National Socialist Workers' Party had been one of a large number of extremist and racist parties that had flourished in the early 1920s in the hothouse atmosphere created by defeat and inflation. With the stabilization of the currency and the arrest of the Nazi leaders for their part in the beer hall putsch in Munich of November 1923, the threat seemed to have passed away. Indeed, the British ambassador in Berlin from that period, who published his memoirs of those troubled times in 1929, thought that he needed to add a biographical footnote to his account of radical nationalism in postwar Germany:

HITLER, Adolf. Son of a petty Austrian official living near the Bavarian border [. . .] In the autumn of 1923 he joined with General von Ludendorff in leading the insurrection in Bavaria, but after a temporary escape, was arrested and subsequently tried for high treason, receiving a sentence of five years' fortress. He was finally released after six months and bound over for the rest of his sentence, thereafter fading into oblivion.[5]

When the Müller great coalition government collapsed, the right implemented a solution which had been prepared some time in advance: a presidential cabinet, without the backing of a majority of the parliament (Reichstag). The new Chancellor, the Catholic politician Heinrich Brüning, thought that he could increase his support by calling elections. The result of the September 1930 Reichstag elections was a great surprise, and an enormous blow to Brüning. The radical parties were strengthened, with the communists getting 13.1 percent of the vote, and the Nazis 18.3 percent. With 107 seats, they became the second largest party in the Reichstag, after the SPD (which had 24.3 percent of the vote, and 143 seats).

At this point, Brüning decided on a strategy that fundamentally depended on the notion that very little could be done to combat the Depression. Monetary policy was tied as a result of the commitment to the gold standard, imposed on Germany by international treaties. Fiscal policy was tied by the memory of the irresponsible inflationism of the early 1920s, and by the justified belief that new public sector deficits would lead to a crisis of confidence and an outflow of foreign investments from Germany. Given the absence of real economic policy choice, politically the best option would be to include opposition parties in the government, and let them bear some of the responsibility for a handicapped and fundamentally hopeless policy. Thus, he started negotiations with Hitler in October 1930, but Hitler had a good sense of the trap that was being laid out and declined to participate in the government of Depression austerity. Brüning thus continued with a minority government, whose unpopular decrees increased taxes and cut government expenditure and had to be passed by presidential authority, under emergency provisions provided by Article 48 of the Weimar Republic's constitution.

In the spring of 1931 there were some signs of a business recovery, but those were quickly blown away by a massive financial and banking crisis that originated with the collapse of the largest Austrian bank, the Creditanstalt, in May 1931, and then spread to the German banks. In an effort to stop the financial panic, US President Herbert Hoover announced a one-year moratorium on war debt and reparation payments (on June 20, 1931); but the crisis continued, and on July 13 the German banks were closed by government decree. German creditors were obliged to negotiate their own moratorium on the extensive foreign debt built up by Germany in the later 1920s (the standstill agreement).

The spread of the financial crisis to the United Kingdom in August and September, and the UK's abandonment of the gold standard (September 20), required a new round of austerity in Germany, with a dramatically deflationary decree of December 1931. There is no reason, however, why Brüning could not have continued to operate his minority government, which was tacitly supported by the Social Democrats in the largest German *Land*, Prussia, until the next Reichstag elections (required only every four years; i.e. in 1934). By this time, there was every reason to believe that the Depression would be over, and normal politics could resume.

Brüning was undermined by a political cabal, in part sustained by an ambitious army general, Kurt von Schleicher, and in part by large land-owners in eastern Germany, who called his plan to break up over-indebted estates and settle unemployed workers on them "agrarian bolshevism". This high political opposition managed to bring down first Brüning's Interior Minister, General Wilhelm Groener, and then Brüning himself (May 1932).

Brüning was replaced by Franz von Papen, another member of the Catholic Center Party (whose party rapidly disavowed him for destroying Brüning). Von Papen was a rather amateur politician, whose first love was horses and whose major contact with world politics had been during the First World War, when he arranged a campaign of sabotage in the (at first) neutral United States. He was hardly a statesman commanding international respect, yet he pulled off a major diplomatic coup. At the reparations conference in Lausanne in July 1932, all the powers (including France) agreed to what amounted in practice to a cancellation of reparations. With that, the great problem that had disturbed international politics through the 1920s was removed at a stroke.

Von Papen's talents for domestic politics were much lower than his skill in reparations diplomacy. At the same time as his diplomatic success, he also staged a true coup or putsch, when he dismissed the socialist coalition government in Prussia and ran the largest German state through a "Reich commissar". He also dissolved the Reichstag, hoping that a new major-ity might be found to support his new politics. Instead he was completely humiliated, and tried to dissolve the parliament before it could vote on a motion of no confidence in the government – under the direction of the new Reichstag President, Hermann Göring, a former air ace from the First World War who had become a charismatic Nazi politician. A new round of parliamentary elections, in November, while it produced no majority for the government, had a much reduced Nazi vote. In consequence, many people (including many Nazis) believed that the Nazi momentum had been stopped, and that the movement would now collapse as a result of internal disputes. Hitler had been consulted about participating in government, but as in October 1930, when he had discussed the same issue with Brüning, refused to be drawn in on terms other than those that he would set himself.

Von Papen was largely discredited by his failures in government, and was replaced by von Schleicher, who envisaged a radical new form of government in which the Socialist Party, the Catholic workers' movement, and some parts of the Nazi Party would support a large anti-depression and work creation program. This coalition never materialized, and Hitler expelled his principal lieutenant, Gregor Strasser, who had supported it.

At the beginning of January 1933, the high political intrigue contin-ued as Hitler and von Papen met, and negotiated for a new government in which Hitler would take the Chancellorship, and von Papen the Vice-chancellorship, and in which the most sensitive positions (the Army Ministry, Foreign Affairs, and the Interior) would not be in Nazi hands, but be controlled by safe Weimar conservatives. Von Papen thought that he had at last succeeded where Brüning had failed, that Hitler was being drawn into responsibility (and with it political failure), and that the major beneficiary would be the conventional right, boosted by a new populism. At the time, he boasted that he had boxed Hitler in. Von Papen might even have been right, had it not been for *two* circumstances, neither of which on their own would have been enough to turn Hitler into a political success, and the second of which might not have been predictable. First, the Nazis were exceptionally ruthless; second, the Great Depression was coming to an end in a natural recovery process.

The Nazis celebrated Hitler's accession to the Chancellorship on January 30, 1933, with a gigantic torchlight parade in Berlin. But it is actually rather hard to say what these supporters imagined that they wanted, or what they thought the new government could provide. Hitler had developed into an orator of great passion and persuasion. He denounced his enemies – the Weimar political parties, the international system with its reparations and the League of Nations – with great brilliance. But his program was quite unclear. The most long-standing theme of Nazi agitation in the first half of the 1920s, the denunciation of Jews as responsible for Germany's misfortunes, had been deliberately played down in the election campaigns of the early 1930s. The only consistent promise was that Hitler's movement would overcome the splintered and fragmented German political system, which had been a cause of Germany's malaise. How could this be achieved? He had no detailed plan for economic recovery, and Nazi economic policy veered backwards and forward between inconsistent plans and ideas.

There was one circumstance, besides the pettiness and fractiousness of the Weimar political elite, that favored Hitler. The international system set in place at the end of the First World War with the goal of controlling Germany had collapsed in the early 1930s. Germany now had much more room in which to assert national power. France and the United Kingdom had been weakened, and largely disengaged from European affairs as they sought consolation for their weakness in their overseas colonial possessions. The League of Nations had been discredited by the Japanese defiance of its admonitions in Manchuria.

To realize how important this international circumstance was for the establishment of Hitler's government, it is enough to conduct a simple thought experiment. Before 1930, Germany was held down by treaty obligations, and there were foreign troops on German soil (in the Rhineland). If a radical German populist had seized power before the evacuation of the Rhineland, French troops would have reacted to any attempt at military self-assertion or rearmament, and they could have dealt easily with any challenge to their authority. Even after 1930, the treaty limitations (in particular reparations) remained. Had a populist dictator come to power at any point before the Lausanne conference of July 1932, he would have had a choice about whether to continue to pay reparations or not. If he had paid, he would have looked foolish and discredited to supporters who believed that German national reassertion involved casting off the fetters of the Versailles Treaty. But had he not paid, French troops would have had the justification for marching on Berlin.

The magnitude of the subsequent catastrophe makes most observers – at the time and since – cast their explanation in terms of some demonic and diabolical power of Hitler's. The truth is that he was quite ordinary, and that this was the primary ingredient in his political success. Saul Friedländer writes:

> Of the four men who directed the destiny of the world between the great economic depression and the end of World War II, none but Hitler cultivated the image of the petty bourgeois Mr. Everyman, the middle class common denominator throughout the West. Churchill remained an aristocrat and Roosevelt a patrician, and Stalin, the little father of the people, cloaked himself in steadily increasing mystery, avoiding great public events and direct contact with the masses.[6]

In 1940, the most prominent American diplomatic historian of his age, William Langer, who was deeply troubled by why he had not comprehended the Hitler phenomenon until 1938, told his Harvard students: "At first no one could recognize him for what he was any more than they could recognize Napoleon."[7]

Hitler was good at persuading people in very small, intimate conversations; and he could produce emotional and dramatic simplifications, shouted in a hoarse voice, for mass audiences when he sought that communion with the masses. In conventional meetings, however, he was largely ineffective. The basis of his appeal was that he was "one of us", not a part of a discredited elite. An astute observer in the German civil service, Ernst Trendelenburg, in the early 1930s noted that whereas Lenin and Mussolini as orators gave the appearance of being great men, Hitler had "the empty face of a waiter" (in that age waiters were trained to put on an impassive facial expression).[8] But on that empty face, his audience could project their own concerns, hopes, wishes, and illusions.

Hitler himself learnt many quick lessons in politics from his experience of a meteoric rise in the early 1930s. He learnt above all that the governing elite in Germany was both profoundly scared and insecure and at the same time desperately complacent about its own superiority. This was a devastating combination that made for great vulnerability. Hitler assumed that the governing elites of the other European powers were composed of the same mettle. That belief drove his foreign policy calculations. The tragedy was that to a substantial extent he was correct in his assessment.

First, he managed the transformation of a coalition government into a dictatorship with startling rapidity and brutality. The opportunity was presented by the fire that destroyed the Reichstag on February 27, 1933, which seemed to fit so conveniently into the Nazi plan that the arson was immediately (and for a long time after) assumed to be the work of the Nazis. In reality, the fire had almost certainly been laid by just one man, a deranged Dutch citizen called Marinus van der Lubbe. Hitler used the fire as the opportunity to attack and ban the Communist Party, which made it almost certain that the Nazi Party could win a majority of seats in the Reichstag election scheduled for March 5. There was in addition a substantial amount of intimidation. But the Nazis won only 43 percent of the vote: it was only because of the ban on the communists that they controlled a majority in the new Reichstag. Hitler then asked that new body to pass an enabling act that would give government decisions the force of law. The liberal parties were weakened by the Depression, and capitulated easily. The Catholic Center Party, at the instigation of its leader Monsignor Kaas, and to Brüning's disgust, voted to accept the government bill. Thus, only the SPD opposed, and the SPD leader Otto Wels delivered a courageous defense of constitutionalism. But the votes of the SPD alone were insufficient to block the law, and the Reichstag thus in effect voted itself into insignificance on March 23.

The political situation was still quite unstable, and in particular it was unclear whether there were major differences between Hitler and his party. At first, Hitler seemed to be turning himself into an orthodox nationalist statesman. When he appeared at the "day of Potsdam" (a celebration of Prussian history and militarism) alongside President von Hindenburg, he wore a tailcoat. When he managed to shake off the troublesome Nationalist leader Alfred Hugenberg as Economics Minister, he appointed a fairly orthodox businessman in his place (Kurt Schmidt, the director of the Munich Allianz insurance company). When Schmidt's health broke down, he replaced Schmidt with Schacht. He called off an anti-Semitic boycott of Jewish stores as it might damage business confidence. Most spectacularly, on June 30, 1934, he attacked the leadership of the party paramilitary organization, the SA, along with other political opponents (General von Schleicher, as well as the young conservative intellectual who had written a speech critical of Hitler that had been delivered by von Papen). The army leadership, which had been very anxious about the threat posed by the SA as an alternative to a conventional army, was reassured, despite the murder of von Schleicher (along with his wife). A few months later, after the death of von Hindenburg, it was agreed that German soldiers would swear an unconditional personal oath of loyalty to the Führer. With that the German dictatorship was consolidated, and a quite new regime of a terrifying brutality emerged.

British crisis management

How did other countries deal with the twin crises of capitalism and democracy? The postwar peace had been built around the power of the United Kingdom and France, and both these great imperial countries looked particularly vulnerable, and experienced some kind of fascist challenge. In the United Kingdom, it was a Labour government, under Prime Minister Ramsay MacDonald, that faced the threat of the Depression. At Christmas 1929, MacDonald noted:

> Unemployment is baffling us. The simple fact is that our population is too great for our trade . . . I sit in my room in Downing Street alone and in silence. The cup has been put to my lips – and it is empty.[9]

Philip Snowden, the Chancellor of the Exchequer (Finance Minister), was deeply orthodox, and embarked on a series of austerity budgets.

After the German financial crisis of July 1931, the pressure on the United Kingdom increased, the country's gold reserves drained away, and the Bank of England along with the international financial community (in what the Labour Party activists called "the bankers' ramp") pressed for further deflation. In August 1931, the cabinet was deeply divided, and nine ministers said they would rather resign than accept cuts in unemployment benefit. MacDonald then formed a version of a great coalition government, with Conservative and Liberal ministers, as well as those Labour ministers who were still willing to follow the orthodox path. He was shocked when the majority of the Labour Party moved into opposition. The new cabinet was called the "National Government", and MacDonald claimed that it would continue only for the "limited period" of the financial emergency, with the task of balancing the budget and staving off the attack on the pound. But the financial attack continued. When naval ratings at Invergordon in Scotland mutinied in response to pay cuts, the financial markets panicked, remembering how the Russian and German revolutions had begun with sailors' mutinies. The Bank of England then advised ending the gold link of the pound (on September 20), to which the veteran socialist intellectual Sidney Webb (ennobled as Lord Passfield) is supposed to have responded: "Nobody told us we could do this."

MacDonald dissolved parliament, and called an election for October 27, which he fought on the basis of fiscal rectitude (he often waved banknotes from the German hyper-inflation in order to demonstrate what would happen if unorthodox remedies were adopted). The government won with a great landslide, which was magnified by the British "first past the post" electoral system. The Conservatives and their allies won 67 percent of the vote, and 521 seats in the House of Commons, while the Labour Party won a third of the vote but only 52 seats. Fringe parties had little chance of success. The old Liberal leader of the Great War, David Lloyd George, had broken with the rest of the Liberals because he wanted a more activist government policy against depression (on the lines advocated by the Cambridge economist John Maynard Keynes), and came back to the Commons as a family party of four (his son, daughter, and son-in-law were also elected as MPs). An equally charismatic but much more sinister figure, Oswald Mosley, who had been a Labour MP, revolted against Snowden's austerity, and founded in early 1931 a "New Party", which included four other MPs (one of them his wife) and won no seats. Mosley, whose New Party was supported by a wide range of intellectuals, including Keynes, was so disillusioned that he moved much further to right-wing populism, and founded the British Union of Fascists in 1932. Keynes no longer supported him.

British democracy survived, for three reasons. MacDonald, and above all his successor as Prime Minister, the Conservative iron manufacturer Stanley Baldwin, were much more skillful than their German counterparts, and more appealing. They projected religious concern and decency, rather than a defense of the narrowly defined material interests of an elite.

On its own, though, decency was not enough. The new government had much better luck than most continental governments in its economic policy. In particular, the end of the gold standard (not the government's doing, but that of the Bank of England) ended constraints on monetary policy. Cheap money meant an end to the threat of banking collapse (which hovered over the United Kingdom, as over other countries, in 1931), but also in the longer run a sustained economic recovery in the 1930s, with readily available loans for house construction and for the purchase of consumer durables, such as radios, refrigerators, and even automobiles. Baldwin was brilliant in addressing the newly prosperous citizens of English suburbia.

Third, the political structure mattered, and the two-party system (which was encouraged by the first-past-the-post constituency election system) greatly helped the United Kingdom to escape the continental collapse of democracy. The system that had generated great instability in the first half of the 1920s now produced a political simplicity and a clear choice for voters. It was a blessing that the Labour Party in the great crisis of August and September 1931 rebelled against MacDonald. In the elections of the 1930s, those who did not participate in the prosperity of recovery – and there were many still unemployed throughout the decade – could vote for an opposition that was democratic. They did not need to reject the "system" altogether and vote for radical parties such as that of Mosley (as their equivalents in Germany did if they wished to enter a protest vote).

The fragility of British politics was revealed by the abdication crisis of 1936. King George V had died on January 20. His eldest son, who would become King as Edward VIII, disliked the "old men" who ran the government, and had strong views that unemployment and slums were blights on the modern United Kingdom. In 1920, he had written to his mistress that

> the more I think of it all the more certain I am that really the day for Kings and princes is past, monarchies are out of date, though I know it is a rotten thing for me to say and sounds Bolshevik.[10]

He was also a society figure, who lived a fast life of cocktail parties, emancipated women, and casual sex. A bachelor, he now proposed to marry an American divorcee, Wallis Simpson, who would need a divorce from her second husband were she to marry the King. She was older than Edward (slightly) and appeared to have an extraordinary hold over him. Baldwin told the King that he could either forgo marrying Mrs Simpson or abdicate. The King tried to propose compromises, such as a "morganatic marriage" (in which there would be marriage, but the wife would not become Queen and her children would not stand in the line of succession to the throne: the ill-fated Archduke of Austria, Franz Ferdinand, had made such an arrangement with Countess Sophie Chotek, whose only disadvantage was that she was not of royal blood). Baldwin refused this, and he refused to let the King speak to the British people on the radio in defense of his position. Only very late in the day did the affair become a matter of public knowledge or discussion (after a bishop had preached a sermon in which he said, rather obliquely, that the King needed "God's grace"). Some people, including both the fascists and the communists, demonstrated for the King and against the ministers. Edward gave in, abdicated on December 11, and his much less glamorous brother became King George VI. Removed from power and exiled to France (where he married Mrs Simpson), Edward became increasingly bitter and resentful of the British establishment. He made a tour of Germany, and did nothing to conceal his admiration of Hitler and National Socialism. It is hard, on the basis of this subsequent behavior, to reach the counter-factual conclusion that if he had remained King, if he had won the conflict with Baldwin, he would have also taken his revenge by realizing his political views, fighting unemployment with work creation on a fascist model. But such an outcome was certainly possible, and it is difficult not to conclude that the United Kingdom was lucky that Stanley Baldwin made such a striking defense of conventional morality.

That the United Kingdom escaped dictatorship was fortunate; but the escape had its darker side. The new National Government took up the cause of trade protection as a way of responding to the Depression. This owed much to ideology: Snowden's successor as Chancellor of the Exchequer, Neville Chamberlain, was the son of the great and charismatic Victorian scourge of the free trade school, Joseph Chamberlain. But in the circumstances of the world depression, protectionism no longer split the Conservative Party. At first, the government adopted emergency tariffs; in 1932, these were regularized and built into a scheme of imperial preference at the Ottawa conference. The United Kingdom turned economically away from Europe and toward empire, in exactly the way that Joseph Chamberlain had always (but unsuccessfully) advocated. The United Kingdom virtually stopped buying wheat, and other agricultural products, from south-central Europe, which in consequence had little alternative except to cultivate the German market. The adoption of protectionist trade policies thus contributed to the growing lopsidedness of the European balance of power.

The Depression convinced many politicians in the metropol that empire was more necessary, both for the economy and for defense. Only the empire could provide the markets and also supply the soldiers that would be needed in the increasingly likely event of a new conflict.

But for the subjects of empire, precisely those arguments provided a dramatic demonstration of the costs, and the wickedness, of empire. The logic was particularly apparent in India, where the British experiment in liberal empire was intended to appear in the most benign and humanitarian light. Initially the main problems appeared to be for wheat farmers, who suffered from Australian competition. The collapse of the rice price between November 1930 and 1933 led to severe and widespread rural over-indebtedness. The currency, the rupee, was fixed against the British pound. Indians pointed to the example of Australia, where a devaluation produced substantial benefits to exporters. Meanwhile, the September 1931 devaluation of the pound against gold made Indian holders of gold see an advantage to selling gold for rupees. The resulting gold flows were used to pay the "home charges" that the United Kingdom imposed as the price of colonial rule and order.

In Burma, under British control, and in Vietnam, under French rule, high taxes and falling prices produced widespread riots and protests. The Vietnamese situation, with a currency, the piastre, linked to the French franc, was even graver than in India, in that the French franc still remained on the gold standard at the old rate. A poll tax in Nigeria caused unrest in 1931. Some analysts contrast the experience of the British and French empires with that of the Philippines, controlled by the United States, where there was much more forbearance in tax collection, and much less anti-colonial protest in consequence.[11]

The Depression also prompted a search for new sources of income. Imperial territories complained because their trade policy was tied, and they could not engage in the import substitution industrialization that helped to spur Latin American recovery in the 1930s. In other parts of the world, there was also a search for new activities to respond to changing global opportunities. The Hejaz region had been dependent on a stream of pilgrims for the Hajj to Mecca, mostly from southern and southeast Asia. The consequence of the economic plight was that the number of pilgrims sank dramatically, from an annual 100,000 to 40,000. Ibn Saud, who in 1925 had captured Mecca from Sharif Hussein, now started to think that the geological similarity to Persia might produce riches out of the ground. A subsidiary of Standard Oil of California (SOCAL) found oil in Bahrain in 1932, the same year that Ibn Saud united his territories as the Kingdom of Saudi Arabia. The explorations continued, with a 1933 concession for SOCAL. There is a further aspect to British stabilization and recovery policies which is worth noting, also because of its effect on European power politics. The key to Snowden's and Chamberlain's vision of how to fight the Depression was fiscal balance: any large deficit would invite speculative attacks. In this, they were reading, probably correctly, the psychology of financial markets in the 1930s. But this policy made additional spending controversial, and in particular limited the ability of the United Kingdom to expand its military budget in response to the increasingly obvious threat of German rearmament.

For both these reasons, British political priorities in the 1930s required disengagement from the concerns of continental Europe. In the end, the affairs of the continent came back with great force, and threatened the political equilibrium that the British had been able to reach.

French crises

The Depression affected France later than most other European countries; but, in large part because France stayed on the gold standard for such a long time, it lasted longer than elsewhere. It divided and demoralized France, and sowed the seeds for military defeat in 1940.

France went into the Depression with a center-right government. Stresemann's French opposite number, Aristide Briand, was Foreign Minister from 1926 until his death (1932). In the Depression elections of 1932, right and left were quite balanced, but the French system of two stages of an election meant that the outcome was shaped by deals between the parties, in which they might agree to mutual declarations of support between the two election rounds. In 1932, the centrist "Radicals" joined the Socialists for a center-left coalition under Edouard Herriot. Herriot had already presided over a similar center-left government in 1924, and had been defeated by financial speculation, a run on the franc, which he and his supporters believed was the result of a conspiracy of the French financial elites: a "wall of money" (*mur d'argent*) put up by the "two hundred families" (*deux cent familles*) which controlled the Banque de France. This time, in consequence, he thought that only tight fiscal discipline could avoid a new catastrophe for the left. But such discipline alienated supporters, who looked to government patronage. Government after government collapsed in 1933 under the fiscal pressure: the most long-lived government, that of Edouard Daladier, survived simply by not making budget proposals. When its plans were eventually drawn up and included a cut in civil service pay, the Socialists voted against the government. At the same time, the financial system was shaken by bank collapses; and one financial scandal, in which there were widespread political connections and ramifications (the Stavisky affair), seemed to discredit the Republic. On February 6, 1934, in the wake of Stavisky's suicide, a variety of fascist leagues organized demonstrations and tried to mount a revolution. Fourteen Frenchmen were killed in street fighting.

Some of the Radicals began to look for other coalition partners on the right; and after more government collapses, Pierre Laval formed a cabinet which pushed through deflationary and unpopular fiscal policy on the basis of decree-laws (so that parliament did not need to vote on the budget). The sequence of events looked like a parallel to events in Germany some years earlier: with the Jacobin republican strong-man Daladier playing the part of Hermann Müller and the swarthy sweating peasant figure of Laval as a reincarnation of the austere Heinrich Brüning, all against a background of fascist violence and threats. The threats were sufficient, and the German model frightening enough, to convince the left to unite in a way that had been impossible in Germany itself. The response to February 6, and to Laval, was the creation of a "Popular Front" alliance that went well beyond Herriot's old center-left coalition, in that it included communists. The radicals, socialists, and communists celebrated Bastille Day, July 14, 1935, as a festival of republican defense and solidarity, and began to evolve a common political program. In the elections of 1936, they achieved a majority of seats: again, not because of a fundamental shift in voting behavior, but because of the way that the outcome of the second balloting round was shaped by the political deal that the parties had done.

The Socialist leader, Léon Blum, then formed a government; and a massive wave of labor unrest broke out that took the organized political left by surprise. A number of large factories were occupied, in particular the large armament and aircraft plants near Paris. It was part of the doctrine of the labor movement that the worst and most ruthless capitalist profiteers were the arms barons, who made their fortunes by selling death. Blum tried to negotiate a solution, and held talks at his official residence, the Hotel Matignon, which eventually produced an agreement (the Matignon Accord). Wages were raised (by an average 12 percent), and employers recognized the right of trade unions to represent workers in wage bargaining, while the unions in reciprocation renounced the idea of direct action (i.e. factory occupation). The arms industry was taken into state control. Blum's social program involved a restriction of the hours of work (the 40-hour week had long been a socialist demand), and paid holidays.

Speculative pressure forced a devaluation of the franc (on October 1, 1936), against Blum's original design; but unlike in the United Kingdom, the abandonment of gold did not end the crisis. The Popular Front's reform program also cost a substantial amount, so that – again unlike in the United Kingdom – the move to a floating exchange rate occurred with a very vulnerable fiscal position. In consequence, capital flight continued, particularly when the Popular Front tried to raise taxes and clamp down on the traditional French practice of tax evasion. Increased control, the use of intense police methods to track down tax evaders and exchange rate speculators, and the nationalization of the Banque de France did little to stabilize the French economy. Speculative pressure built up, and new devaluations brought a fresh round of government crises and collapses.

Domestically, the experience of the Popular Front polarized and radicalized France yet further. Some dissident leftists complained that Blum and his communist allies had sold out on a truly radical or transformative program. Marcel Déat, a socialist, and Jacques Doriot, a communist, left their parties and formed their own, rival, fascist leagues. The radicals, Blum's allies from the political center, and a group with quite disparate political and economic ideas, were also quite divided. At the party congress at Biarritz, in October 1936, one group of deputies stood up, sang the *Internationale*, and gave the clenched-fist salute of the communists, while another group countered by singing the *Marseillaise* and making the fascist salute of the raised right arm.[12]

The permanent fiscal difficulties also weakened France's ability to project power. Few resources could be devoted to defense against the threat posed by German rearmament. The available resources were poured into concrete in the massive fortifications of the Maginot Line. When Daladier was Prime Minister once again, he agreed at Munich in September 1938 to a devastating agreement that allowed Germany to partition Czechoslovakia, and thus greatly increased German power. Deflation and its legacy undermined both the internal stability and the external security of France.

Successful corporatism

When Léon Blum organized the Matignon negotiations and brought workers and employers together, he intended to end the factory occupations and create a new social peace as a basis for French economic and political recovery. The most successful of such attempts to build a political corporatism occurred in small states in western and northern Europe. In Sweden, the Social Democrats came to power in 1932 under Per Albin Hansson in a coalition with the Farmers' Party. The socialist economist Eric Wigforss presented work creation programs as a way of raising farm prices and thus benefiting farmers. The Social Democrats also proposed to restrict agricultural imports. After 1935, they dominated the government, and in 1938 the employers' organization and the general trade union federation concluded the Saltsjöbaden Agreement, which limited employers' abilities to fire workers and provided for collective bargaining agreements.

Switzerland had had a history of conflictual labor relations, with a traumatic general strike in November 1918, that embittered and polarized politics for a generation. In the 1930s, trade unions put forward a "crisis initiative" modeled on President's Roosevelt's New Deal, including work creation and expansionary fiscal measures, but it was defeated in a referendum held in 1935. After the devaluation of the Swiss franc in 1936, which accompanied the devaluation of the French franc, the deflationary pressure eased, and it was easier for farmers, workers, and employers to conclude agreements. The background to this was *geistige Landesverteidigung*, or "spiritual defense", in the face of an increasingly threatening Germany. The fascist movements in German-speaking Switzerland, the Bündische Bewegung, had a small amount of middle-class support, but remained on the fringes of mainstream politics.

In the Netherlands, a system of social "pillars" – the socialist movement, the liberals, and the Catholics – developed in the 1930s, which laid a basis for political stability. The smaller countries thus evolved a potential for solidarity in place of the bitter social conflict of the immediate postwar era, but that solidarity became fully galvanized only in the later 1930s and 1940s in the face of a threat of war and occupation.

Ireland was born out of a bitter civil war, which was not fought on class lines – unlike the other clashes in Europe in the aftermath of the First World War.

The British 1920 Government of Ireland Act had provided for a devolution of power, with separate parliaments in the six largely Protestant counties of the North, and in the overwhelmingly Catholic South. This did not end the conflict, and in December 1921 a treaty gave southern Ireland the status of a dominion (analogous to Canada and Australia) as the Irish Free State. A second civil war broke out in 1922–23, between a part of the Irish nationalist movement the IRA (Irish Republican Army) that was prepared to accept the treaty and organized itself as the army of the Free State, and the irregulars who continued the IRA tradition as Sinn Féin. There were some resemblances to the emergence of a right-wing populism in continental Europe, with farm unions organizing against "socialism, Labour and bolshevism". In 1926 the Sinn Féin leader, Éamon de Valera, founded a political party, Fianna Fáil, which in 1927 won 44 seats in the parliament (Dáil) as compared with the government's 47 seats. De Valera pressed for full independence with only an "external association" with the United Kingdom, and no oath to the King. This became constitutionally easier as a result of the British Statute of Westminster in 1932. De Valera in the same year was elected President by the Dáil, and assumed a fundamental control over Irish politics. In 1937, he succeeded in obtaining full independence for Éire (which replaced the "Irish Free State"). De Valera concluded an agreement with the United Kingdom, which he defended by a reference to the worsening international situation of Europe:

> because we see that a strong Britain would be our defence against attack from the Continent once we were free and independent, we would be anxious to see that Britain was strong and was not attacked through us as through a back door.[13]

But the Ireland of the 1930s rapidly became complacent, clerical, and corporatist. One disenchanted republican complained that "smoked salmon became the symbol of the risen people".[14] The constitution of 1937 gave a special status to the Catholic Church, and forbade divorce. The constitution consigned women to the home. Semi-state corporations were created to run the major economic activities, foremost among them the Agricultural Credit Corporation. It had its own fascist movement, the Blueshirts, led by a former police commissioner, Eoin O'Duffy, who later led volunteers to Spain to fight for Franco; but they hardly provided any threat in a society held together in part by backwardness and in part by the hated memory of the long period of British domination. The British presence took some of the role that the German threat played in creating Danish, Dutch, Swedish, or Swiss solidarity.

Turkey: the strong man of Europe?

Interwar Turkey, whose government was trying to modernize and westernize quickly, consequently adopted the strong-man and single-party formula as practiced in contemporary Italy or in the Soviet Union. National existence was an essential part of modern development, in the eyes of the new elite; the universal, non-national, and non-Turkish vision of the Ottoman Empire belonged to a medieval world of incompetence and inefficiency. In the wake of Mustafa Kemal's revolution, power was exercised through a state party, the Republican People's Party. The strong commitment to secularization came almost by accident. In 1920, the party's Grand National Committee had still begun its activities by praying for the Sultan, who was also caliph of the faithful. But the caliph dealt with the opposition by issuing a *fatwa*, or religious head price, calling for the killing of any and all nationalists as a deed pleasing to God. In 1924, Mustafa Kemal abolished the caliphate, and moved on to prohibit the use of Arabic script and the wearing by men of the small religious cap (*fez*), as well as restricting the veiling of women. But this was not an irreligious movement; it was merely one of Turkish particularity. One of the most important reforms was that the call to prayer should be made in Turkish, and not in Arabic.

Most of the program of secularization was presented as modernization, or an adoption of the western normality that the Ottoman Empire had rejected – to the cost of its subjects, in the view of the nationalist movement. The new Turkey took over a civil code wholescale from a small western country (Switzerland); introduced last names in a law of 1934 (so that Mustafa Kemal could become Atatürk); and allowed women to vote (also in 1934). It embarked on a program which mixed education with indoctrination: from 1931 "People's Houses" or *Halkevleri* (and in the countryside, "People's Rooms" or *Halkodarlan*) were established as culture and propaganda centers. In its management of the economy, the government unsurprisingly rejected laissez-faire, and announced that its goal was *étatisme* (*devletgilik*). With republicanism, nationalism, populism, secularism and revolutionism, *étatisme* was one of the "six arrows" incorporated in the constitution as a definition of the new Turkish state. In the 1930s, the government tried to implement this through Soviet-style five-year plans, in 1934 and 1939, which mostly lacked all the planning apparatus of the Soviet model and remained rather a piece of modernistic window-dressing.

President Atatürk died in November 1938, but his first Prime Minister, Ismet Inönü, took over as President and continued the program of authoritarian modernization. The original act of nation-building had been quite successful, but it was also unique. Unlike Italian fascism or Russian communism, Turkish nationalism was hardly an item for export. The Ottoman legacy, which remained a powerful force for a bureaucracy with a profoundly state-centered approach, could hardly make it an attractive guide for Balkan countries which had revolted against Ottoman hegemony. On the other hand, the other great multinational empire of southeastern Europe, the Habsburg Empire, did present a powerful legacy which affected many of its successor states. An idealized past came to haunt a deeply unsatisfactory present in the lands that had once been ruled by Emperor Francis Joseph.

Failed solidarity

Small states were not always successful in setting up complex systems of transfer payments designed to create social solidarity to deal with domestic challenges, and summoning up the spirit of national community to resist external challenges. Especially in central and eastern Europe, there was an almost general fragmentation of politics – analogous to that of Germany but often more extreme – that made democracy hard to practice; and then there were powerful neighbors who were frequently seen not as threats to sovereignty but as valuable allies in a fierce domestic political struggle.

Three elements made such tensions acute: demographic, historical, and geographical. First, central and eastern Europe was on the whole a region of very rapid population growth, unlike in western Europe, where commentators were predicting demographic decline.

Second, there was the inheritance of the past, which was distinctly not democratic. In particular, the Habsburg Empire left a striking myth as a legacy. From the revolution of 1848 until the First World War, the Habsburg lands had been ruled by the increasingly patriarchal Emperor Francis Joseph. He stood for a certain ideal – driven by duty, hard-working, and above politics – that became increasingly attractive in the aftermath of war and defeat. There was a wave of nostalgic literature, the most distinguished products of which were Joseph Roth's Habsburg novels, *Radetzkymarsch* and *Kapuzinergruft*, and some engaging children's stories with political themes by Felix Salten, whose other writings were middlebrow pornography in a distinctly Viennese tradition (*Josephine Mutzenbacher*). In *Florian the Emperor's Horse*, he set out a view of the monarchy from the perspective of the famous Spanish Riding School and the Kaiser's carriage horses. In *Bambi* (better known through its adaptation as a Walt Disney movie), the wise old stag is an animal version of the wise old emperor.

But Francis Joseph had also tried to preserve monarchical power by extending democracy, in the belief that it would produce chaos. In the Austrian part of the monarchy, the parliament (*Reichsrat*) of 1911 included five prime ministers or presidents of five different states: Tomáš Masaryk (Czechoslovakia), Karl Renner (Austria), Alcide de Gasperi (Italy), Wincenty Witos (repeatedly Prime Minister of Poland in the 1920s), and Anton Korosec (Prime Minister of Yugoslavia).

Third, the new politics took place in new states constructed as a result of the postwar peace treaties. Just building the state involved complex negotiations and compromises, often between different ethnic groups and in societies riven by class tensions. The clashes were inevitably not fully resolved, and they left bitter scars.

The one partial exception to the otherwise quite gloomy story is interwar Czechoslovakia, where democracy survived until the two great western powers, the United Kingdom and France, agreed with Italy and Germany at the Munich Conference in September 1938 to strip away the defensive and well-defended border areas of the Sudetenland, a ring circling the Czech state on the north, west, and south. Despite considerable ethnic diversity (23.4 percent of the population in 1921 was German-speaking, and 5.6 percent Hungarian), some sort of stable politics was established in the aftermath of the First World War. Most of the German speakers were loyal to the Czech state, and (mostly through the Agrarian Party) were brought into the patronage arrangements of the state. Unlike Austria, Hungary, Germany, or Poland, there was no traumatic postwar inflation to leave a bitter legacy of social cleavages.

But the Czech lands (Bohemia and Moravia) were also industrially developed, and showed a "modern", post-demographic transition pattern of low birth rates. By contrast, the Slovak part of the new state had the highest birth rates of anywhere in Europe, and was mired in hopeless backwardness, for which the Czechs did little to compensate. Along with the puppet Sudeten German party of Konrad Henlein, Slovak resentments provided the instrument for Hitler to prize apart the Czech state. In the 1935 elections, Henlein's party gained the largest share of the popular vote of any party. In 1939, after Munich, Slovak demands for autonomy precipitated the final crisis, and were coordinated with Hitler's application of intense diplomatic pressure and military threat.

Poland had been created out of territories that had been part of three different imperial systems in the wake of the late-eighteenth-century partitions: Austrian, German, and Russian. Norman Davies points out that the Second Polish Republic began life with six currencies, four languages of command in the army, three legal codes, two railway gauges, and 15 political parties.[15] The population was ethnically, linguistically, and religiously divided. In the early 1920s, 15 percent of the population of Poland was Ukrainian, 4.7 percent White Russian, and 2.2 percent German. Almost 3 million, or 8.5 percent, of Poles were Jewish.

In 1926, General Józef Piłsudski launched a coup in which he effectively controlled subsequent governments, which could thus largely ignore parliament (the *sejm*). He called the principle of his government *Sanacja* (cleansing). In June 1930, the major parties drafted a critical Convention of People's Rights, which called for the abolition of the "dictatorship" and a return to governments supported by the *sejm*. Numerous opposition parties remained active in politics, although their leaders were harassed and elections were manipulated. With the Depression, farmers in Poland – as elsewhere – became increasingly angry, and there was a new agrarianism. Both the peasant leaders – Wincenty Witos and Maciej Rataj – and the socialist leader Ignacy Daszyński came from the old Habsburg territories. The government introduced anti-Semitic measures.

Piłsudski died in 1935, and his successors failed to manage the pressing foreign policy issues. The Foreign Minister, Colonel Józef Beck, in particular believed that he might leverage growing Nazi power, and the apparently implacable opposition of Poland's two big neighbors, Nazi Germany and

Soviet Russia, in order to extract small gains for Poland. This policy achieved its dubious triumph when Poland annexed an area of the Sudetenland with a large Polish population, Teschen, during the Sudeten crisis. Its nemesis came when on August 23, 1939, Hitler and Stalin concluded a pact that implied the destruction of the Polish state.

Some parts of Polish policy were much more innovative: there was a systematic attempt at economic planning after 1936, supervised by Eugeniusz Kwiatkowski, which laid the foundation for postwar planning. Some Polish industries were modernized quite effectively: there was, for instance, a considerable and sophisticated aircraft industry, though its most advanced products were sold exclusively for export (including to the German Luftwaffe).

Though the Polish fascist movement was very small and marginal (the closest resemblance to a fascist party was a group of thugs organized by Bolesław Piasecki, called the Falanga), anti-Semitism as a social movement was on the rise in the 1930s, and Poland was becoming much less tolerant.

The quest for the strong man was equally dramatic in Hungary, a country not pieced together by the 1919 peace treaties but dismembered by the Treaty of Trianon. In addition, Hungary was ravaged by a bitter class-based civil war in 1919, which pitted right-wing peasants against a radical proletariat that tried to imitate Lenin's revolution. The new autocrat, Admiral Miklós Horthy, ruled as Regent (for the Habsburg dynasty, which was disbarred from the throne), and thought of himself as embodying the virtues of Francis Joseph. The delicate farm–town balance was kept first through inflation, which removed the debt burden of rural Hungary and created employment for Hungarian workers; and then, after inflation turned into hyper-inflation, by borrowing on foreign capital markets. The chance of prosperity was destroyed by the collapse of wheat prices; in order to save farmers, the government set up an expensive price support system, which eventually bankrupted it and caused the foreign creditors to panic (in the crisis year 1931). The moderate Prime Minister, István Bethlen, resigned in the wake of the crisis, and was replaced by a really political strong man, Gyula Gömbös, who found a new way of trying to bring farmers and workers together. A 95-point "national unity" plan introduced Italian-style corporations as a way of overcoming class conflict (see Mussolini's model). The aim of the plan was to restrict the "harmful growth of capitalism". It included strict measures against capital flight, which were applied increasingly in a one-sided way against Hungary's Jewish population, strongly associated with capitalism in the popular mind. As an explicitly fascist and anti-Semitic party, Ferenc Szálasi's Arrow Cross, started a campaign of political violence, Jews began to try to transfer more of their assets out of Hungary. Even before the introduction of explicitly anti-Semitic legislation in 1936, the majority of currency offenses tried in Budapest were committed by Jews – and such knowledge inevitably fanned the anti-Semitic flames.

Gömbös based much of his doctrine on the Italian model, and also tried to develop closer political ties with Italy, which he saw as a useful bulwark against the threat of increased German power. But such a calculation of political equilibrium became impossible when Hitler and Mussolini drew closer to each other. Gömbös, and his successor as Prime Minister Kálmán Darányi, at the same time banned Arrow Cross and tried to achieve a rapprochement with Germany. The government aimed at controlling independent social movements, and wanted to implement its own home-grown anti-Semitic program, in part as a defense against a more radical German influence. A *numerus clausus* in 1938 limited the number of Jews in professions. When Darányi was attacked for being too pro-German and was obliged to resign, his successor Béla Imrédy continued exactly the same course: rapprochement with Germany, accompanied by increased "native" anti-Semitism. But he also added a small dose of land reform. His hold on politics lapsed when it became known that he had a Jewish grandfather.

Yugoslavia (or rather its key component, Serbia) was the first and greatest victim of the First World War, which killed an estimated one-third of its population. The losses were compensated at the peace settlement by the creation of the Kingdom of Serbs, Croats and Slovenes as a de facto greater Serbia; in 1929 the state was named South-Slavia (Yugoslavia). The major Croat leader of the 1920s, Stjepan Radić, had opposed the idea of union with Serbia in 1919, and the Croats embarked on a long and violent struggle against Serb centralization. For a brief time he became a minister, then resigned and was shot dead. In the chaos that followed, King Alexander suspended the constitution, and imposed personal rule supported by the army – and by France, which Alexander viewed as the only steadfast guarantor of the Serb position. Croat terrorists assassinated him, and the French Foreign Minister Paul Barthou, in Marseilles in 1934. The new King, Peter II, was a boy, and a relative (Prince Paul) ruled as Regent, trying to come to better terms with Hitler as a way of defusing Croat demands (which were stoked by every revisionist success in eroding the peace treaties, and especially by the German seizures of Austria, the Sudetenland, and the Czech territories).

The world depression hit Greek exports of tobacco products very badly, and resentment directed against the Greek Republic increased. In 1935, a military revolt brought back the monarchy and reinstalled King George II, who quickly found a right-wing politician, Metaxas, who would act as his strong man. Metaxas managed trade, and intensified trade relations with Germany.

Romania was a beneficiary of the peace treaties, which added a substantial territory in Transylvania to the historic core of Moldavia and Wallachia. This meant the presence of large numbers of non-Romanian speakers, largely Germans and Hungarians, against whom Romanian nationalist pressure was easily mobilized. In a Depression-era coup (in this case in 1930) the Prime Minister, the Agrarian leader Iuliu Maniu, replaced the King. The former monarch, King Michael, had become King as a result of his father's love life: his father had been married to a Greek princess, but preferred to live with his mistress (Magda "Duduia" Lupescu) and renounce the throne. In 1930 he came back as King Carol I, ignored the promise to discard the mistress, removed the Prime Minister who had resurrected him politically, and proceeded to an absolute rule with some fascist tinges. He subsidized Corneliu Zelea Codreanu's militant and anti-Semitic Iron Guard ("League of the Archangel Michael"). Codreanu, much more than his Italian model, used a heavy Christian symbolism. By 1938 the government passed laws that imitated the German racial laws, barring Jews from the professions and from Romanian citizenship. Then Carol changed his mind about the Iron Guard, introduced a parliamentary constitution, and claimed that he was saving Romania from fascism and from international ostracism. At the same time, he increased his own power, and banned the Iron Guard. Codreanu was shot.

Bulgaria, a German ally in the First World War (and consequently a loser of the peace treaties), had an exceptionally violent 1920s – even by the standards of south-eastern Europe. In the 1920s, a common end to a prime minister's term of office was assassination, rather than dismissal or resignation. The most charismatic Bulgarian interwar politician, the Agrarian leader Aleksandr Stamboliski, was killed in 1923. He was the only eastern European leader who successfully built a democratic governing party on the basis of peasant support. In 1925 a bomb exploded in a Sofia cathedral and killed 123 people. King Boris III, who survived a large number of assassination attempts himself, managed to stabilize his regime by marrying the daughter of the Italian King, and thus buying a link with Italy which offered a pole of some stability. Trade with Germany expanded, but Boris also borrowed from the United Kingdom and France to pay for a rearmament program. He made no secret of the fact that he detested most of his own country's politicians, and he tried to present himself as a simple man of the people, making much of the fact that his favorite recreation was driving railroad locomotives. In May 1934 he staged a coup, dismissed parliament, and only slowly in the late 1930s began a slow reconstitutionalization, when the fascist leagues were dissolved or controlled.

Albania had become independent of the Ottoman Empire just before the First World War. Ahmet Zogu became Prime Minister in 1922 at the age of 31; in 1925 he became President and in 1928 declared himself King as Zog I. He managed this through a wide-ranging dependence on Italy, with which he signed a friendship treaty in 1926. Italy developed Albanian oil resources, and Italian officers reorganized the army. When Zog tried to restrict Italian activity in 1934, Italy made military threats; eventually, after Hitler had taken Prague, Mussolini tried to produce his own success by sending Italian troops to invade Albania.

Austria was at the epicenter of the 1931 financial crisis, since the failure of the Creditanstalt touched off the wave of European financial contagion. Austria had previously been a model of central European stabilization: hyperinflation had been ended through the imposition of a humiliating external control, under the supervision of the League of Nations, whose commissioner, the Dutchman Dr Alfred Zimmermann, directly controlled public funds and insisted on the dismissal of 100,000 civil servants (who then provided a strong base for nationalist radicalism). At this stage, Austrian democracy survived only by laying the blame for unpopular policies at the door of the League. The same solution was repeated after 1931, when another Dutchman appointed by the League, Rost van Tonningen, supervised Austrian financial restructuring. The Creditanstalt failure, which involved an enormous public cost in the rescue operation, also discredited many of the leading figures in the Austrian Republic, who had had close ties with the management of the Creditanstalt and were implicated in the scandal. In May 1932, a diminutive political leader, called Engelbert Dollfuss and caricatured as Milli-Metternich, headed a new version of a Christian Socialist and farmers' coalition. Dollfuss – one of the few men whom Mussolini could physically look down on – derived more and more support from Italy. In March 1933 he suspended parliament. At the urging of Italy, he conducted a brutal but short civil war against the socialist government of "Red Vienna" (February 1934). He also brutally repressed the Austrian National Socialist movement, which aimed at following a German path, and reorganized and unified the paramilitary movement of the non-Nazi right, the *Heimwehr*. In place of a divided democracy, he instituted a regime of clerical corporatism, or clerical fascism, based on a new clerical party (the Fatherland party) and modeled closely on the theories of the papal encyclical *Quadragesimo Anno*.

On July 25, 1934, he was assassinated by Austrian Nazis. Italy immediately moved army units to the Austrian border at the Brenner Pass in order to stop a German annexation, and Austrian politics were briefly stabilized under another, but much less effective, Catholic politician, Kurt von Schuschnigg.

A brief survey of the politics of eastern and south-eastern Europe is sufficient to generate a sense of the profound instability of interwar politics. Small states appeared to be brutal, inhumane, corrupt, petty, and second-rate. They provided a terrible and at the same time ridiculous contrast with the Wilsonian idealism of the First World War and the peace treaties. National self-determination had been achieved, and it turned out to be a bitter farce. Wilson's vision applied in reality was the love life of Magda Lupescu.

A new school of analysts ("realists") looking at the international system concluded that small states were disturbing and had little right to exist. In his famous polemic of 1919, the British economist John Maynard Keynes had already made clear his doubts about independent Poland: "an economic impossibility with no industry but Jew-baiting".[16] The feeble states depended on external protection, and it is striking how frequently and how importantly that role of external protector was taken on by Benito Mussolini.

Dictatorship

The prototype of the "new" European political leader was Benito Mussolini. His party, the Fascists, aimed, Mussolini said, at creating a "totalitarian" state. On May 26, 1927, he declared that he had accomplished his goals:

"We have created the Corporate State . . . Today we solemnly bury the lie of universal democratic suffrage." One of his supporters explained: "Religious dogmas are never discussed, because they are verities revealed by God. Fascist principles are not to be discussed, because they issue from the mind of a Genius: Benito Mussolini."

In practice, Mussolini's power base was less than stable, and depended on a series of tactical alliances. He managed to orchestrate agreements between labor and business interests; indeed, Italy provided a model not just for totalitarianism but also for the social corporatism that was used in the 1930s to reinforce democracy in France, Sweden, and Switzerland. The 1926 Law on Corporations instituted a system of nominally elected workers' and employers' syndicates. In 1934, these were organized into 22 "corporations", in which representatives of workers, employers, suppliers, and consumers of different economic sectors would be grouped together to regulate markets and modernize the Italian economy. They instituted campaigns for self-sufficiency, such as the "battle for grain", that would isolate Italy from destructive trends on world markets. Mussolini also hoped to reduce emigration, which the Fascists regarded as a drain of Italian skill, and to promote natality. But in the year – 1929 – in which he wanted Italian women to begin their contribution to Italy's drive to produce more, the Italian birth rate began to dip dramatically. This was not so much a protest against the Duce's exhortations as a facet of modernization: above a certain moderate level of income, every society experienced a "demographic transition" to lower birth rates.

Corporatist organization was set up as an alternative to unregulated capitalism (decried as profit-seeking "Manchesterism") and socialist control of the ownership of the means of production. It appeared to be the perfect embodiment of a "third way" of social organization, the establishment of a truce between labor and capital. This was, in fact, a concept that appeared at the time: it found one of its most systematic expositions in the papal encyclical of 1931, *Quadragesimo Anno*, published on the fortieth anniversary of Leo XIII's social encyclical *Rerum Novarum*. Mussolini envisaged corporatism as the answer to the dilemma of politics: how to organize people so as to produce collective opinion formation, and the balancing of interests, rather than opinion fragmentation and an embittered clash of interests. But this still left the problem of the Church and the Pope.

A second crucial truce was with the Catholic Church, which had been opposed to the secular liberal state since the unification of Italy, and in 1868 imposed a ban on political participation, including voting (the so-called *non expedit*), on Catholics. After the First World War, the emergence of a Catholic political party (the Popolari), together with the strength of the socialist movement, had shattered the liberal hold on Italian politics, and made the formation of stable governments almost impossible.

In 1929, Mussolini concluded three agreements (the Lateran Accords) with the Church. They defined the Pope's territorial and sovereign powers over a small part of Rome, the Vatican City, and compensated the Church for property that had been confiscated by the state. A concordat accepted Catholicism as the religion of the state, recognized canon law (which had an important effect on the view of marriage, and later played a significant role in the Vatican's policy toward the Italian racial laws of 1938), paid clergy from state funds, and exempted the Church from taxation. This was a new solution to the issue of the Church's relation with the modern state. Similar arrangements had already been made in Latvia, Bavaria, Poland, Lithuania, and Czechoslovakia. But the Italian concordat, because of the novel character of the Italian state, was the most striking agreement until an even more catastrophic compromise of the Church with a particular kind of modern state was reached with Nazi Germany in 1933.

Domestic stabilization was only one part of Mussolini's program. After 1929, and especially after 1931, backed by the new domestic agreements, Mussolini began to reach out for a much bolder and conflictual course in international politics. His foreign policy changed dramatically with the Great Depression. In 1928, Mussolini had explained in a speech replying to a worried Austrian political leader that fascism was an Italian product, and not for export. In 1930, he began a large naval program, since Italians "should not remain prisoners in the Roman Sea" (the Fascist term for the Mediterranean: they also called it *Mare nostro*). And he revised his previous stance:

> The phrase that Fascism is not an article of export is not mine: it is too banal. Today I affirm that Fascism, as regards idea, doctrine, realization, is universal. . . . One can foresee a Fascist Europe, a Europe which draws inspiration for its institutions from the doctrines and practice of Fascism – a Europe which solves in a Fascist sense the problem of the modern State, of the twentieth century, very different from the States which existed before 1789 or were formed afterwards.

By 1932, he predicted that: "The twentieth century will be the century of Fascism, of Italian power, the century during which Italy will for the third time direct human civilization." The Italian state radically increased its military spending: in the mid-1920s, it had been 2.6 percent of national income, in 1927 3.4 percent, and in 1931 it was 5.4 percent; by 1936 it rose to 18.4 percent.[17]

In 1930, the Italian Foreign Minister Dino Grandi formulated a classical doctrine of realpolitik. Italy should play the game of the European balance of power, and then "sell itself dearly in the great future crisis". By 1931, that crisis was near. Before 1931, Italy had needed international capital and the support of J.P. Morgan and the financial community of New York and London. The Italian leader consequently had little choice except to present himself as a moderate. When he had slipped in May 1930 and disparaged his own logophilia ("words are beautiful things, but rifles, machine guns, ships, aircraft, and cannon are still more beautiful"), the Italian bond markets plummeted, and the government needed to conduct an expensive support operation.[18] With 1931 and the failure of the international capital markets, there was no longer any need to keep up a mask. When the 1933 World Economic Conference failed, he explained that "the system of conferences is finished". In January 1935, the French Foreign Minister Pierre Laval tried to win over Mussolini by promising him that France would not oppose Italian expansion in Africa. In October 1935, the Italian army invaded Abyssinia (Ethiopia) and quickly captured the town of Adowa, the site of the most embarrassing of nineteenth-century Italy's colonial defeats. The next year, Mussolini extended his Mediterranean ambitions at the prompting of his son-in-law, Foreign Minister Count Galeazzo Ciano, with an extensive military intervention in the Spanish Civil War.

On January 10, 1938, the Duce received 60 bishops and over 200 priests who had played some part in Italy's "battle of grain". Father Menossi read out a text prepared by the clergy, in which they stated that they

> confirm their desire to collaborate – as they have already done in the victory of the grain, in the fight against sanctions and in the conquest of the Empire – in all the Duce's noble plans . . . so that Italy may be prepared – spiritually, economically and militarily – to defend her peace against the foes of her imperial greatness and her civilization, as also against the hostile designs of her godless and inhuman enemies.

In 1936 the Archbishop of Milan explained Mussolini's invasion of Abyssinia:

> In this national and Catholic work . . . on the plains of Ethiopia, the Italian standard carries forward in triumph the Cross of Christ, smashes the chains of slavery, and opens the way for the missionaries of the gospel.[19]

Ethiopia and Spain cemented a new vision of the harmony of Catholic interests with those of the Italian state, and against the international system. The clergy in Italy, and in many other European countries, was becoming "nationalized" (like other social groups), much to the dismay of Pope Pius XI, who still had a powerful vision of the Catholic Church as an international and a moral force.

Spain as the European hotspot

In the 1930s, the Europe-wide struggle over democracy focused on the problems of the Spanish Republic. This was where a great war of ideas was fought out, and where the powers that embodied the most strikingly new ideas – Germany, Italy, and the Soviet Union – fought a proxy war.

At the beginning of the war, each side approached the conflict with what was frequently described on both sides by sympathetic analysts as "fervent purity". On one side was the ideal of revolutionary purity. George Orwell recorded the revolution in Barcelona:

There was a belief in the revolution and the future, a feeling of having suddenly emerged into an era of equality and freedom. Human beings were trying to behave as human beings and not as cogs in the capitalist machine . . . To anyone from the hard-boiled, sneering civilization of the English-speaking races there was something rather pathetic in the literalness with which these idealistic Spaniards took the hackneyed phrases of revolution.[20]

On the other side, young soldiers participated in Mass daily before they went into battle.

Every European political tendency – anarchism, anarcho-syndicalism, communism, socialism, reformist socialism, left-wing republicanism, Catholic reformism, clericalism, monarchism, fascism – was represented in Spain in some form, but usually in an extreme one. This was one of the reasons why other Europeans could project their own political fantasies in apocalyptic terms onto the Spanish screen. When these ideals were distorted, and their holders disillusioned, Orwell came to the conclusion that history came to an end in 1936.

Democracy and the international economy in the form of the gold standard both came late to Spain. Economically, the country was exhausted by the deflationary sacrifices made in order to return the Spanish currency to the gold standard, and by the time Spain was ready the world had already collapsed in the contagious international financial crisis of 1931. From 1923 to 1930, Spain was ruled by a military dictator, General Miguel Primo de Rivera, who had seized power in a coup (*pronunciamento*) following the humiliation of the Spanish army in North Africa. He made his slogan "Country, Religion, and Monarchy", but gradually lost his grip on power. In August 1930, Republicans and socialists set out a reformist program in the Pact of San Sebastian, and eventually forced the abdication of the King, Alfonso XIII.

Politics in the Second Spanish Republic were marked by many divisions between regions, which were highly conscious of long-established historical claims to rights and privileges (*fueros*). The industrial areas, in particular in Catalonia and the Basque lands, formulated quite different demands from those of agrarian Spain. Major divisions also plagued the political parties, where different traditions regarded each other with suspicion. Communists, socialists, and anarcho-syndicalists all had contrasting approaches to how left-wing parties should conduct themselves with regard to political power. Monarchists were divided between intransigents (known as Carlists) and compromisers. Some Catholics thought that they should work with democracy and the new social forces, while other Catholics looked back to the blindly authoritarian past of the Spanish golden age.

Probably the greatest peculiarity of Spain was the quite exceptional extent of the tyranny of history, the extent to which the glories of past history overshadowed the present. In particular the right found it hard to accept that

Spain was no longer the Spain of the golden age, of the Catholic monarchs Ferdinand and Isabella, and Philip II. On the other hand, the left believed that Spain should modernize quickly and adapt itself to European modernity.

The major issue for the left-wing coalition produced by the elections of June 1931 was thus a double modernization: an economic modernization, which envisaged the prime task as the introduction of modern agriculture by breaking up large estates and distributing them to previously landless and largely impoverished peasants; and a social or intellectual modernization, whose major element was an attack on the Church which had previously dominated (and, the left argued, stunted) education.

The world depression, with its collapse in raw material and agricultural prices, was a bad time to undertake a large-scale reform of farming. Most unemployment was rural (70 percent in 1930). The government program intended to resettle peasants and farm workers was starved of funds because fiscal revenues fell during the Depression. It consequently literally dried up, and the government increasingly replaced genuine reform with symbolic action against the Church, which was also a great landlord, and whose leadership worked hand-in-hand with the aristocracy.

At the beginning of May 1931, a pastoral letter of Cardinal Segura, the Archbishop of Toledo, was published, attacking and threatening the Republic:

> If we remain 'quiet and idle', if we allow ourselves to give way to 'apathy and timidity', if we leave open the way to those who are attempting to destroy religion or if we expect the benevolence of our enemies to secure the triumph of our ideals, we shall have no right to lament when bitter reality shows that we had victory in our hands, yet knew not how to fight like intrepid warriors prepared to succumb gloriously.[21]

A church in Madrid which had been the site of a monarchist meeting was attacked by anti-clericals and burned. The provisional republican government refused to intervene. The liberal Prime Minister Manuel Azaña y Diaz (of the small Accíon Republicana party) told his cabinet that "all the convents of Madrid are not worth the life of a single republican". Article 26 of the 1931 constitution subjected the religious orders to state control, allowed the state to confiscate the property of those orders, and prohibited them from teaching and economic activity. Subsequently the Jesuit order was expelled from Spain.

The result of the new and highly militant anti-clericalism shaped a new right under José Maria Gil Robles. The commitment of his party, the CEDA, to the Republic was always ambiguous. Robles developed the theory that Catholics could live under any form of government that did not harm their faith. But the anti-clerical attacks continued, and the Republic indeed seemed to threaten the Catholic way of life. Meanwhile army officers, under General Sanjurjo, attempted, unsuccessfully, to stage a *pronunciamento*.

In November 1933, the socialists and left Republicans failed to agree on a common front, while the anarcho-syndicalist CNT, with its power base in

Catalonia, denounced left participation in a non-revolutionary government, and urged its supporters to abstain in the elections. In consequence, politics shifted to the right, with a government under an elderly former radical, Alejandro Garcia Lerroux, who had been a hero in a previous era of labor struggles but now looked like a defender of a moderate traditionalism.

The socialists shifted to the left, and began to look to the new leader of an alternative socialist party, the PSOA, Francisco Largo Caballero, who imagined himself as the "Spanish Lenin". In October 1934, workers' committees in the mining areas of Asturias created a Soviet-style regime, which the right-wing government attacked with considerable brutality. The War Ministry placed the conduct of operations against the strikers under the command of the youngest Major General of the Spanish army, a veteran of the Moroccan fighting, Francisco Franco.

In a new set of elections in February 1936 a Popular Front of the left parties defeated the CEDA. Azaña now became President, and appointed a rather weak Prime Minister, Santiago Casares Quiroga. Peasant unrest increased, and a massive wave of church burnings swept rural Spain. On July 13, 1936, the pro-business leader of the right-wing Bloque Nacional, José Calvo Sotelo (who had been Primo de Rivera's Finance Minister), was kidnapped and killed. Calvo Sotelo had been regarded as a political model of a new type of rule: in neighboring Portugal, General Carmona had mounted a military coup in 1926. His Finance Minister, Antonio de Oliveira Salazar, went on to create an oppressive and authoritarian regime.

The assassination provoked a new military revolt – which had already been planned well before the death of Calvo Sotelo. It began in Morocco on July 17. Two days later, General Franco took over its command and, using Italian aircraft, began to transport Spanish soldiers in Morocco to the Spanish mainland. Later, Hitler sent German aircraft, the Condor Legion of 100 planes, and Mussolini added as many as 47,000 ground troops, as well as aircraft and tanks.

In Germany, the left had been largely quiescent as the Nazis seized power. In Spain, there was a massive mobilization and radicalization, with a revolutionary and murderous terror applied by both sides. Madrid successfully resisted Franco's advance; and in Barcelona, the CNT effectively took over power.

A substantial amount of international assistance arrived for the Republic: at first from the French government, and later from the Soviet Union, but also in the form of many individuals who saw the Spanish Civil War as a final showdown between the left and the right, or between good and evil, between communism and fascism. Many prominent intellectuals joined the International Brigades – André Malraux, W.H. Auden, George Orwell – although the bulk of the recruits were French and Belgian workers (often immigrants from eastern Europe). There were also 2,800 American volunteers.

The Republic's fight for survival was handicapped by its divisions. The communists, under orders from Moscow, urged the "Popular Front" strategy that the Soviet Union had adopted. This required collaboration with "bourgeois reformists", who in Spain were strikingly ineffective, and at the same time war against the fiery radicals of the CNT and the dissident Marxist POUM (which the orthodox communists accused of "Trotskyist deviationism"). The communists had initially helped to propagate the idea of Largo Caballero as the "Spanish Lenin", but by 1937 they turned against him (he was now described as a "Trotskyist–fascist–anarchist") and wanted a more pliable figure.[22] In May 1937 Juan Negrín formed a new form of Popular Front and in 1938 proposed a single-party organization, which would have been dominated by the communists and controlled by Moscow.

The International Brigades soon lost their naïve idealism. In July 1937, a confidential report stated that

> The great majority of officers, noncommissioned officers and volunteers in the International Brigades are militants or political men who know how to see, judge, and understand. Whether they be Communist or Socialist, Republican or antifascist with no defined political party, today all are consumed by the idea that the International Brigades are considered to be a foreign body, a band of intruders – I will not say by the Spanish people as a whole, but by the vast majority of political leaders, soldiers, civil servants, and political parties in Republican Spain.[23]

The most famous non-Spanish account of disillusionment was George Orwell's *Homage to Catalonia*, in which he described the communist attack in Barcelona on the POUM militia (of which he was a part):

> In Barcelona, during all those last weeks I spent there, there was a peculiar evil feeling in the air – an atmosphere of suspicion, fear, uncertainty, and veiled hatred. . . . It is not easy to convey the nightmare atmosphere of that time – the peculiar uneasiness produced by rumours that were always changing, by censored newspapers, and the constant presence of armed men. It is not easy to convey it because, at the moment, the thing essential to such an atmosphere does not exist in England. In England political intolerance is not yet taken for granted.[24]

On the nationalist side, the military developments also seemed to many of the nationalists' supporters, both in Spain and in Rome and Berlin, to be intolerably slow. In the early weeks of the war, Franco had stood a good chance of capturing Madrid, but instead diverted his offensive to relieve the siege of some 2,000 nationalist supporters, surrounded by Republican forces in the Alcazar (a fortress from the age of Charles V) of Toledo. But Franco's military planning had a systematic logic: he disliked lightning attacks and always held onto territory that he had captured. Systematic conquest – and the ruthless elimination of opposition – was more important than quick victory. In February 1939, Barcelona was captured by Franco's troops, and in March Madrid was taken. The final victory of Franco occurred only in part because of the Generalissimo's initiatives: the Republican army, in an act of final self-destruction, had revolted against the leadership of Negrín.

One of the new regime's intellectual prophets in 1939 interpreted the victory:

> Spanish fascism will be the fascism of religion. . . . German and Italian fascism have invented nothing as far as we are concerned, Spain was fascist four centuries before them. It was one, great and free, and truly Spain in the sixteenth century when state and nation were identified with the eternal Catholic idea, when Spain was the model nation and alma mater of western Christian civilization.[25]

There was an alternative Spanish fascism, organized in the Falange Española by José Antonio Primo de Rivera, the son of the 1920s dictator, which was much closer to Mussolini. But José Antonio was killed by the Republicans, and his movement forcibly merged with the Carlist royalists. In April 1937 Franco imposed a decree of unification which recognized both movements as "the two authentic exponents of the spirit of the national rising initiated by our Glorious Army on July 17". The single party tolerated in Franco's Spain, whose chief was the Generalissimo, now had the title of Falange Española Tradicionalista y de las Juntas de Ofensiva Nacional-Sindicalistas. Most people just called it The Movement.

Franco celebrated his triumph with an order for the construction in the Sierra de Guadarrama of a vast monument, an underground church, topped with a gigantic cross, with a longer nave than that of St Peter's. The Valle de los Caídos was a tomb for the dead of the war, constructed by the defeated of the war. Franco realized that he needed some sort of external endorsement for his attempted recreation of himself as a golden-age monarch, a new Philip II. He had his coins stamped "Caudillo by the Grace of God".[26] But Cardinal Segura, whose attacks on the Republic in 1931 had begun the war of Church and state, and who had been expelled from Spain by the Republican governments, denounced Franco too and his compromises with the Falange and fascism.

Franco's regime has much closer analogies to that of Admiral Horthy in Hungary: a monarchy without a monarch, since Franco deeply distrusted the man who would have been King, Alfonso XIII's son, Don Juan, and made a promise to restore the monarchy only in the vaguest possible fashion. In fact, in the long run, after Franco's death it was Don Juan's son, Juan Carlos, who as King successfully managed the real democratization and modernization of Spain.

Spain in the 1930s brought a general perversion of ideals. The control of the state – power – became the central idea to which any ideal was ruthlessly sacrificed. As a response to the Spanish experience, the most idealistic figures of the non-communist left, such as George Orwell, developed an intense anti-communism. They refused to compromise. On the right, the Church and the Vatican hesitated before endorsing Franco – for all the

Masses that the Generalissimo had said – and issued a stern warning about state worship. But eventually they compromised.

Pius XI's encyclical *Mit brennender Sorge* stated:

> Whoever detaches the race or the nation, or the State, or the form of the State, or the Government from the temporal scale and raises them to be the supreme model, deifying them with idolatrous worship, falsifies the divinely instituted order of things.

The encyclical was directed specifically to Germany, which offered a new political model. But the new idolatry of the state was a common European phenomenon. In the 1930s, the most effective states seemed to be those that derived their legitimacy from the combination of a new ideology of government (government on old lines was discredited), and a defiance of the international order. Politically, Hitler finished the step-by-step demolition of the Versailles Treaty which was already well under way by 1933. Economically, the Soviet Union offered the most striking challenge to liberal capitalistic internationalism. These new states are the subject of the next chapter.

Notes

1 Klaus Hildebrand, *Das vergangene Reich: deutsche Aussenpolitik von Bismarck his Hitler, 1871–1945*, Stuttgart: Deutsche Verlags-Anstalt, 1995, p. 505.
2 José Ortega y Gasset, *The Revolt of the Masses*, New York, NY: Norton, 1932, pp. 11– 12, 123.
3 See Knut Borchardt (transl. Peter Lambert), *Perspectives on Modern German Economic History and Policy*, Cambridge: Cambridge University Press, 1991.
4 Marie Jahoda, Paul Lazarsfeld, and Hans Zeisel, *Die Arbeitslosen von Marienthal. Ein soziographischer Versuch über die Auswirkungen langandauernder Arbeitslosigkeit*, orig. 1933, Leipzig: Herzel. Heinrich August Winkler, *Der Weg in die Katastrophe: Arbeiter und Arbeiterbewegung in der Weimarer Republik*, Berlin and Bonn: J.H.W. Dietz, 1987, p. 21. Dick Geary, "Unemployment and working class solidarity: the German experience 1929–33", in Richard J. Evans and Dick Geary (eds), *The German Unemployed*, London: Croom Helm, 1987, p. 261.
5 Viscount d'Abernon, *An Ambassador of Peace: Lord d'Abernon's Diary, Vol. II: The Years of Crisis, June 1922–December 1923*, London: Hodder and Stoughton, 1929, pp. 51–2.
6 Saul Friedländer, *Reflections on Nazism: An Essay on Kitsch and Death*, New York, NY: Harper & Row, 1984, p. 66.
7 Peter Loewenberg, *Decoding the Past: The Psychological Approach*, Berkeley, CA: University of California Press, 1984, p. 86.
8 Arnold Brecht, *Mit der Kraft des Geistes: Lebenserinnerungen, Zweite Hälfte 1927– 1967*, Stuttgart: Deutsche Verlags-Anstalt, 1967, p. 272.
9 David Marquand, *Ramsay MacDonald*, London: Jonathan Cape, 1977, p. 537.
10 Letter to Mrs Dudley Ward, auctioned by Bonhams and Brooks, 2000: *Daily Telegraph*, June 6, 2001.
11 Dietmar Rothermund, *The Global Impact of the Great Depression 1929–1939*, London and New York, NY: Routledge, 1996.

12 Philip J. Larmour, *The French Radical Party in the 1930s*, Stanford, CA: Stanford University Press, 1964, p. 225.
13 Keesings Contemporary Archives (hereafter Keesings) 3061 (April 29, 1938).
14 Quoted in Roy Foster, *Modern Ireland 1600–1972*, London: Penguin, 1988, p. 533.
15 Norman Davies, *God's Playground: A History of Poland*, Volume II, Oxford: Oxford University Press, 1981, p. 402.
16 John Maynard Keynes, *The Economic Consequences of the Peace*, London: Macmillan, 1919, p. 273.
17 MacGregor Knox, *Common Destiny: Dictatorship, Foreign Policy, and War in Fascist Italy and Nazi Germany*, Cambridge: Cambridge University Press, 2000, p. 120.
18 Knox, *Common Destiny*, pp. 116, 129–130.
19 D.A. Binchy, *Church and State in Fascist Italy*, London: Oxford University Press, 1941, pp. 676, 679.
20 George Orwell, *Homage to Catalonia*, Harmondsworth: Penguin, 1966, p. 10.
21 Quoted in Hugh Thomas, *The Spanish Civil War*, Harmondsworth: Penguin, 1965, p. 50.
22 Ronald Radosh, Mary R. Habeck, and Grigory Sevostianov, *Spain Betrayed: The Soviet Union in the Spanish Civil War*, New Haven, CT: Yale University Press, 2001, p. 225.
23 Radosh et al., p. 241.
24 Orwell, *Homage*, pp. 186, 189.
25 José Maria Pemán, cited in Raymond Carr, *The Civil War in Spain*, London: Weidenfeld and Nicolson, 1986, p. 210.
26 Paul Preston, *Franco: a Biography*, London: HarperCollins, 1993, p. 622.

5 Peace and war
The failure of the international order in the 1930s

The catastrophe of the First World War hung over the succeeding decades. The hope for peace was increasingly expressed as a forlorn lament that war had become too terrible to contemplate. Extrapolating from the experience of soldiers in the trenches of the Western Front during the First World War, and realizing that a new war would entail aerial bombardment and the involvement of civilians, many observers believed that a new conflict would lead to large-scale psychological and social disintegration. The leader of the British Labour Party, Clement Attlee, stated: "We believe another world war would mean the end of civilisation." The British Home Office calculated that 20 million square feet of timber would be needed monthly for coffins, and the Ministry of Health thought that 2.8 million hospital beds would be required, and that air war would produce 4 million psychological casualties within six months.[1]

The view that modern war was too horrible to be a political choice was expressed by none as powerfully, as eloquently, and as tragically as by the British Prime Minister, Neville Chamberlain, on the eve of his trip to Munich where he was to cave in to Hitler's demands:

> How horrible, fantastic, incredible it is that we should be digging trenches and trying on gas-masks here because of a quarrel in a far-away country between people of whom we know nothing. ... I am myself a man of peace to the depths of my soul. Armed conflict between nations is a nightmare to me; but if I were convinced that any nation had made up its mind to dominate the world by fear of force, I should feel it must be resisted.[2]

The hypothetical character of the last part of this statement indicated how much he believed, and wanted to believe, that a need for resistance was a most unlikely eventuality.

In the 1920s, there had been high hopes that a new kind of state organization, both domestically and internationally, might avoid the problems of the past. This was the view of President Woodrow Wilson at Versailles: if representative or democratic and liberal governments were established, if minorities were adequately protected, then the world would be at peace. The Wilsonian analysis had blamed war on the vice of "secret diplomacy" and assumed that "open covenants, openly arrived at" would prevent a repetition of disaster. The League of Nations was designed to enforce a system of "collective security" by guaranteeing the rights of small states and prohibiting aggression. Article X of the League's Charter specified:

> The Members of the League undertake to respect and preserve as against external aggression the territorial integrity and existing political independence of all Members of the League. In case of any such aggression or in case of any threat or danger of such aggression the Council shall advise upon the means by which this obligation shall be fulfilled.

A Permanent Court of International Justice would arbitrate disputes. Idealistic visions of harmony in international relations reached a high point in August 1928, when the Pact of Paris (usually known as the Briand–Kellogg Pact) pledged its signatories to "condemn recourse to war for the solution of international controversies and renounce it as an instrument of national policy in their relations with one another".

At the same time, the peacemakers knew that there was a great deal of national and ethnic diversity that might shake the stability of the new states, and so inserted provisions that would defend the rights of "minorities". Poland was obliged under the terms of the Versailles Treaty to "adopt such provisions as may be necessary . . . to protect the interests of inhabitants of Poland who differ from the majority of the population in race, language, or religion." Czechoslovakia, Greece, Romania, and Yugoslavia, all multi-ethnic states, were obliged to take on similar treaty-imposed obligations. (Germany, and postwar Austria and Hungary, which no one thought of as multi-ethnic, had no such internationally imposed requirements.) None of the articles of the Covenant that created the League of Nations, however, dealt with individual rights.

Such a system faced a number of problems. What was meant by "aggression"? What would happen if a minority in one country appealed to a neighbor for support? How could a "minority" protect its rights? They were supposed to appeal to the Council of the League, and a Minorities Commission would first investigate whether there was any substance in a complaint; if there was, then the Council might work out a solution. What were the obligations of the Great Powers? They were committed to take measures – largely economic sanctions – against aggressors; but there was no mechanism for intervention.

After the Great Depression, the attractions of the League faded. The League itself provided the perfect illustration for one of C. Northcote Parkinson's laws: that institutions achieve the perfection of planned layout only at the moment of their obsolescence. The building of the enormous complex of the Palais des Nations in Geneva began in 1929, just as the Depression hit and Stresemann died; it was completed in 1936, when Italian troops were in Abyssinia, and German troops unilaterally reoccupied the demilitarized Rhineland; and it opened in 1937. Parkinson wrote: "Deep thought had gone into the design of secretariat and council rooms, committee rooms and cafeteria. Everything was there which ingenuity could devise – except, indeed, the League itself."[3]

By the end of the 1930s, the Great Powers looked upon smaller states with contempt. Stalin explained that: "in our days it is not the custom to reckon with the weak". Hitler spoke contemptuously of "the mess of small states" (*Kleinstaatengerümpel*), which he proposed to clean up. The British Prime Minister, Neville Chamberlain, more moderately commented that "in the world as we find it today an unarmed nation has little chance of making its voice heard".[4]

From the beginning, the League had had a dubious relationship with large states. The US Congress refused to ratify the Covenant, and the United States was consequently not a member. The Soviet Union was admitted in 1934, and eventually was expelled in 1939, following its attack on Finland (it was the only state to be expelled from the League). Defeated Germany was admitted only in 1926, and in 1933 Hitler noisily and contemptuously left. France had been consistently skeptical of the League system, and had tried to build up its own system of security (little "ententes" with the eastern European neighbors of Germany) as a protection against the dangers presented by a strengthened Germany. British politicians until the 1930s were more enthusiastic about the League: but that was, the UK's critics said, only because the League was a way for a financially and morally exhausted great power to continue to assert its internationalist pretensions.

French nationalists at the time, in the 1920s and 1930s, refused to distinguish between a "good" (republican, democratic) Germany and a "bad" (monarchical, nationalist, fascist or Nazi) Germany, and saw German *interests* as necessarily threatened by Versailles, antagonistic to France, and reflected in revanchism. There was a complete and relentless logic to this argument. With each loosening of the shackles of the Versailles treaty, Germany had more room to express those interests. The evacuation of the Rhineland in 1930 and the end of reparations in July 1932 at the Lausanne conference in this sense were necessary preliminaries to the reassertion of power after January 1933 by Nazi Germany.

Such a history of a progressive loosening of the chains constraining Germany raised the question of continuity of German political behavior before and after 1933, and of how far Germany could be thought of as a new type of state.

The dynamic states of the 1930s, largely excluded from the world political order, Nazi Germany and communist Russia, had some features in common, which might make their policy based more on ideology and less on interest. They both thought about the way in which human nature could be molded or transformed. A Soviet propaganda poster of 1934 by Konstantin Zotov shows a smiling clean-shaven man, a laughing mother, and a fair-haired child with his hands clasped, listening to a gramophone record. It bears the slogan: "Every Collective Farm Peasant or Individual Farmer Now has the Opportunity to Live Like a Human Being". The picture in presenting modernity draws on a very traditional iconography, of the Holy Family, with the child's hands clasped as in prayer. At first sight, no one would wish to disagree with the message about decent living. But the slogan implies that something needs to be done before peasants (often regarded as animals in Russian tradition) could become human, and that some remodeling by authority is required. Farmers are not intrinsically human: new human beings need to be made.

Both the Nazi and Soviet states had belief systems which claimed to explain in the broadest possible way how the world worked, and of course also how international relations functioned. The German view saw the historical process as a fight of racially based nations for dominance in a sort of pseudo-Darwinian evolutionary process. In the Soviet philosophy, all history was the history of class struggle, which transposed itself to interstate relationships and meant a permanent war between different forms of social organization, between capitalist and socialist states. For a large part of the 1930s, the Soviet Union and its international organization, the Comintern, disastrously treated fascism as simply an extreme form of imperialism, which was in Lenin's formulation the highest (and thus final) phase of capitalism.

The German and Soviet states had common features, sometimes described by political scientists (following a classic work by Carl Friedrich and Zbigniew Brzezinski[5]) in a rather static way as "totalitarianism". It should be no surprise that neither state actually corresponded completely to this model, which is best understood in Max Weber's terms as an "ideal type". The parties were quite fractious and fractured, and the leader who announced a leadership principle (*Führerprinzip* in German, *edinonachalie* in Russian) built his rule on the bitter rivalry and murderous mutual suspicions of his subordinates. Neither, of course, could the state really control what people thought, and the leaderships realized that they needed to woo and persuade as well as to coerce, punish, and terrify. Economic processes obeyed their own logic – that of millions of independent decision-makers, who reacted sometimes badly to perverse incentives created by a planning *apparat*. The nearest that the new states got to being total was in their control of force, and in their ability to project power on the international stage. At first it looked as if the Nazi regime was much better at doing this than the Russian regime. When it came to a proof of arms, however, the Soviet machine soon demonstrated an indisputable superiority.

Peace and war   155

Totalitarianism

The term "total" in connection with *fascism* originated in the movement's own claim to be introducing a new and all-embracing philosophy that would replace the partial and limited state of classical liberalism. Some Nazi constitutional lawyers also used the term "total state" to describe the new sort of state being created.

After the Second World War, totalitarianism was used exclusively as a hostile term, mostly by anti-communists who tried to identify common elements of right and left extremism, and of fascism and National Socialism with communism. The two major theoretical expositions of such a theory differ greatly in their emphasis: Carl Friedrich and Zbigniew Brzezinski, in *Totalitarian Dictatorship and Autocracy* (1956), created a typology to identify this sort of regime. "Totalitarianism" involved not only an ideology of politics, but also a means of enforcing it: through rule by a relatively monolithic party; through the control of the media, of press, radio, and thus of public opinion; through a monopoly of the means of force and violence in the police and the military; and through the organization and subordination of the economy to the state. Once in place there was little change or development, since the ideology was constant and unchanging. One variant of this school of interpretation, which was briefly influential in US policy-making in the 1980s and was associated with Jeanne Kirkpatrick, argued that the internal repressive force of totalitarian regimes meant that they could not be expected to reform themselves from the inside, but could only (like Hitler's Germany) be defeated by military force or at least by external power.

Hannah Arendt, on the other hand, in *The Origins of Totalitarianism* (1951) identified the desire to create a party that had an ideology and an inner coherence (and ever narrower circles of elites within the party, getting closer and closer to a mystical core) as the response of people uprooted by modernity and the breakdown of traditional communal societies. Looking for parties as the mediators of a new truth was a way of giving meaning to an otherwise meaningless world of anonymous modernity.

The new Germany

On the surface, the French view of Germany as driven by revanchist interests, whether under the Republic or under the Nazis, was highly plausible. It was indeed initially quite hard to see any shift in German foreign policy in the wake of the clear domestic political caesura of 1933. The personnel of foreign policy-making in fact remained unchanged through the Nazi revolution. Hitler's first foreign minister, Konstantin von Neurath, had had the same position in the previous chancellorships of von Papen and von Schleicher, as had the senior official in the Auswärtiges Amt (German Foreign Office), Bernard von Bülow. German politicians behaved badly at the World Economic Conference in London in June and July 1933, and on October 14, 1933, Hitler left the League (but on the same day announced his ambition to "pursue a policy of peace and reconciliation").[6] In fact, noisy nationalism had been practiced by all foreign ministers since Stresemann's death in 1929.

The only initial sign that German priorities had changed was in fact an act of peace and reconciliation, in that the Nazis ended the long-standing political and economic tensions between the Weimar Republic and Poland, and in January 1934 concluded a non-aggression pact. Here it looked as if Hitler had abandoned the traditional German right's demand for a revision of Germany's eastern frontier, in favor of an ideological solidarity between Germany and Poland as two countries opposed to Russian communism. Von Neurath, for instance, had consistently opposed such a pact with Poland.

Hitler deeply disliked the conventional German foreign policy establishment, which he thought of as a product and an extension of the intellectually limited politicians of the Weimar Republic. He called the Foreign Office the "garbage dump of the intelligentsia".[7] In particular, he believed that a new style of foreign policy, made by a new type of state, would disorientate the conventional bourgeois politicians of the old Great Powers, in the same way as he had managed to make a new politics in Germany in the early 1930s.

In fact, other European politicians found the signals that came from the new Germany quite confusing. When the world of European diplomacy looked at Hitler, it saw precisely what it wanted to observe, namely a real-politik that could reach compromises. Throughout the later 1930s, foreign politicians consistently tried to distinguish German "doves" (such as Hjalmar Schacht or Hermann Göring) from "hawks", believing that accommodation would strengthen the hands of the moderates and weaken the radicals.

After the death in 1934 of Reich President Paul von Hindenburg, at the same time both the hero of Imperial Germany and the last constitutional vestige of the Weimar Republic, Hitler set about finalizing the new German political vision. Explaining the plebiscite that he held to confirm the new constitutional arrangements, and that made him not Chancellor or President but *Leader* (Führer), Hitler told a British journalist that "we wild Germans are better democrats than other nations". Democracy did not live up to the Führer's high expectations. He obtained a "yes" vote of 84.6 percent, though support fell below 70 percent in some regions, including parts of Berlin. After this, Hitler explained, the "nervous age" of the nineteenth century was over, and there would be "no revolution in Germany for a thousand years".[8]

In the new Germany, traditional concepts such as "state" or "nation" lost their meaning. The regime's leading figures promoted a sort of pseudo-Hegelian blur: in the Nuremberg party congress of 1935, Hitler explained that "the Führer is the party and the party is the Führer". His deputy, Rudolf Hess, had gone further and had closed the 1934 congress with the phrase: "Hitler is the party; but Hitler is Germany as Germany is Hitler." In 1935, in a speech in Berlin, Hitler offered the following interpretation of identity in the new Germany: "What does state mean? Comrade, you are the state!"[9]

The old idea of the state and government simply faded away. The German cabinet met infrequently after 1934, only 12 times in 1935, six times in 1937, and not at all after February 1938.[10] The division of responsibilities between ministries and new agencies created by Hitler to tackle specific problems was never clear, and in reality became more and more obscure. Was the supervision of the economy the responsibility of the finance or economics ministries, or the Four-Year Plan authorities, or the Munitions ministry? What was the role of the National Socialist Party and its institutions, some of which were arranged on a functional or vertical basis (on the model of Italian fascist corporatism), and some geographically or horizontally? Looking at the bureaucratic confusion and infighting of the Nazi state, which produced tremendous amounts of paper documents, many historians have concluded that it was this chaotic and competing power structure which made for both increased policy radicalization and incompetent policy execution. Richard Overy, for instance, pointed out how frequent changes in the orders given for aircraft production led to a multiplicity of types, long delays as factories retooled for new products, and an inferior state of military preparedness. The term often used to describe this policy incoherence is "polycracy", which was actually first devised by the conservative (and briefly Nazi-supporting) political theorist, Carl Schmitt, as a critique of ministerial and bureaucratic incompetence in the Weimar Republic. Some of this incoherence was a deliberate strategy of divide and rule on Hitler's part, stemming from the logic of trying to impose a personalized charismatic concept of rule onto the bureaucratic complexity of decision-making in a modern industrialized society. It is not surprising that the finest historical analysts of Hitler's ruling methods originally were trained as medieval historians (Ian Kershaw, Michael Burleigh) or as early modernists (Hugh Trevor-Roper), who were used to the dynamics of a ruler and his court.

National Socialism

National Socialism was the doctrine of the National Socialist German Workers' Party, which developed out of the radical racist German Workers' Party founded in 1919 by Anton Drexler, but was soon taken over and renamed by Adolf Hitler. Although the party established a 25-point program in 1920, which was subsequently declared to be immutable, in practice the party was radical but highly opportunistic.

(continued)

(continued)

Many of the 25 points were anti-capitalist (and specifically directed against finance capital), but the party had a large following among small business leaders, and eventually also attracted the interest of some large businesses, which saw it as a bulwark against Bolshevism. The main direction of its program was fiercely anti-communist, but Nazis cooperated with communists in opposition to the Weimar Republic (notably in the November 1932 Berlin transport strike); and the Second World War was preceded and made possible by a Nazi–Soviet Pact that was the culmination of a period of secret intelligence cooperation. The Nazis claimed to be militantly nationalist, but Hitler both in opposition (and thus unconstrained by political realities) and in power had no sympathy for the German-speaking population of formerly Habsburg South Tyrol, which since 1919 was Italian, and regarded the Germans in Danzig as useful only when they fitted in with his foreign policy concept. It was racist, especially in regard to the "peoples of the east", but in practice treated some Slavs (Czechs, and especially Slovaks and Croats) quite favorably, while conducting genocidal policies toward others (Poles and Serbs). The only absolutely consistent part of National Socialism was its ferocious and radically genocidal anti-Semitism, but since Hitler and the party were so flexible about their "doctrine" many German Jews before 1933 refused to take this part of the program seriously and simply saw the movement as being about national awakening.

The philosophy of the movement rested on a popularized social Darwinism, in which evolution worked by a series of clashes in which the strongest and most racially fit group emerged victorious. Like *fascism*, it therefore glorified war and violence.

Unlike fascism it was not easily exportable from its country of origin, although it tried to form ideological alliances on the basis of anti-Bolshevism: the Anti-Comintern Pact, at first with Japan (which had a rather different and less populist form of government in the 1930s) and then with fascist Italy; later a substantial number of satellite states also joined.

The modern state, as it had evolved in the tradition begun by the French Revolution, treats all its citizens equally. Nazi Germany believed that this was unrealistic, and not in conformity with the needs and logic of modern science, which created hierarchies of capacity and fitness.

If the state was a concept of the past, so too was the nation. Nation, like state, had in Hitler's view come from the French Revolution: "With the idea of nation, France exported its great revolution beyond its own frontiers. With the idea of race, National Socialism will create a revolution that will reorder the world."[11] Race meant a hierarchy of different races, and a struggle to purify the higher types of impure or lower features. In this, National Socialism took up a great deal of eugenic thinking. During the 1920s, and especially during the Depression, many analysts, commentators and scientists had tried to work out who were the "asocial" or anti-social personalities, who represented a burden to the welfare state and its support of the community.

The concept of race also gave an answer to the question that perplexed many Germans, and indeed many Europeans, at the beginning of the twentieth century. What would give meaning in the modern world? Race gave a measure of individualization, and at the same time group coherence and superiority, in an otherwise anonymous and atomized environment.

The idea of the party was not to resemble traditional political parties, but rather to overcome them, and provide a new elite for Germany (which some members compared to the function of elite universities such as Cambridge or Harvard in the Anglo-Saxon world). Hitler at Nuremberg in 1934 referred to the party as a select group, whose duty was to do more than simply confess: *I believe* (the whole occasion of party congresses was permeated by pseudoreligiosity). The party was to be an "order", like religious orders, and especially like the militarized religious orders of the past, such as the Teutonic Knights (*der Deutsche Orden*). But within the party, there would be more and more narrowly defined and exclusive elites: the SS (*Schutzstaffel*), originally conceived as a protection unit in the rowdy street politics of the 1920s, was redefined as the elite of the new party after its role in the so-called Röhm-Putsch or Night of the Long Knives of 1934, in which the SA (paramilitary wing) leadership was purged. At the same time the SS was given police functions: in April 1934, its leader Heinrich Himmler became Inspector of the "Secret State Police" (Gestapo: *Geheime Staats-Polizei*); in 1936 he was confirmed as head of the entire German police force. Within the SS there were elites too.

The linking of a large popular movement, mobilized by mass rituals and striking dramaturgy such as Albert Speer's "cathedrals of light" at the Nuremberg party rallies, with a concept of elites within elites, was novel; but it had existing models, of which the two most important were the Catholic Church, with its extended rituals and the mystery of the Mass, and the Soviet-style Communist Party, with its notion of the party as the vanguard of the proletariat. Institutionally, Hitler borrowed greatly from both institutions; and psychologically, it seems, many communists and Catholics managed to make themselves at home in the National Socialist movement. But ideologically, these two models offered the greatest threat to National Socialism, a threat which appeared much greater than that presented by traditional liberalism, which many in the 1920s and 1930s viewed as tired and discredited.

Hitler's first moves in power involved the banning of the Communist Party and organization in the wake of the Reichstag fire (February 27, 1933). A number of leading communists were arrested and put on trial; many party members were simply interned. The party had to move into illegality.

The anti-Bolshevik parts of the National Socialist appeal held a powerful attraction for Catholics, especially after the concordat negotiated in 1933, which ended more than half a century of very strained relations between the Church and the German state. In 1936, as the regime became more radical ideologically, it started to attack the Church. Nazi newspapers campaigned against homosexuality and sexual perversion in the clergy, and the party demanded the removal of crucifixes from schools. This caused the most sustained popular protest in the whole story of the Nazi dictatorship, a fact which is both a demonstration of the degree of consensus that the regime was capable of creating, and of the strength of the ideology that drove the regime to attack a rival way of thinking. Joseph Goebbels later explained: "Only the church stands in our way now. The church has not abandoned its claim to domination over the secular world; it has merely dressed it up in religious clothing."[12]

The Nazis also tried to create a new culture of nationalist mobilization, using all the most advanced instruments held out by modern technology. Cinema in the 1920s was a highly internationalized business, for the obvious reason that silent movies could easily be shown in many countries. In 1929, revenue from film exports had paid for a third of the cost of producing films in Germany. The advent of the talking movie limited demand, although at the beginning films were made with multi-lingual casts in several languages. *The Blue Angel*, for instance, in which Marlene Dietrich gave a sensational performance as the nightclub dancer Lola, was made in both English and German in 1930 by Josef von Sternberg.

Film had already been a subject of intense political discussion in the 1920s. The Nazis had protested against the pacifist implications of *All Quiet on the Western Front*, and had disrupted performances. Joseph Goebbels, the Gauleiter of Berlin appointed as "Minister for Propaganda and Popular Enlightenment", summoned Germany's leading film-makers to a meeting in the Berlin Hotel Kaiserhof to discuss his ideas for a reorganization of the film industry. The most immediate effect was the exclusion of Jewish actors and film directors. It was much harder to do effective propaganda, and at the beginning Goebbels objected to many efforts at ideological films, such as a film with a perfectly Nazi title, *Blood and Soil* (*Blut und Scholle*). His newspaper, *Der Angriff*, gave a devastatingly negative review to a film that glorified the fallen heroes of the party, *SA-Mann Brand* (1933). For a sophisticated film audience, which Germany had in the early 1930s, bad or even simply sentimental propaganda would be ridiculous and would encourage people to laugh at the new political movement.

In the end Germany produced some stunningly effective cinematic embodiments of the totalizing ethos of the regime: above all Leni Riefenstahl's *Triumph of the Will*, the filmed version of the Nuremberg party rally of 1934, and *Olympia*, showing the 1936 Olympic Games.

For the peacetime years, much more effort went into harmless films that would be a diversion and not raise serious issues. Even here, the choice was problematic, and a planned treatment of *The Intoxication of Love* was rejected on the grounds that marital conflict should not be shown on the screen, even if there was no adultery. Some of the most ambitious ventures turned out to be highly orchestrated dance routines, such as *Hallo Janine* with Marika Rökk in 1939. Some stars of these lighter movies were still, in the old style, international celebrities: two of the highest-paid actresses in German films, the Swedish Zarah Leander and the English Lilian Harvey, were chosen because they could also speak English scripts. So could the best-paid male film star, the German Hans Albers.

As war approached, there were more films celebrating military virtues (*Pour le Mérite*, 1938), and after the outbreak of war, a series of vicious anti-Semitic propaganda films, most notoriously *Jud Süss* and *The Eternal Jew* (*Der ewige Jude*), both from 1940. Ideology really came to the fore, and films justified war against the United Kingdom (*Ohm Krüger*, about the Boer War, in 1941) and euthanasia (*I accuse, Ich klage an*, 1941). Even in 1944–45, the color film *Kolberg* was made justifying resistance to the end, and calling on civilian militias to resist the narrow-minded defeatism of the military establishment. Based on a real event during the Napoleonic Wars, it used 187,000 soldiers as extras at a moment when the German military was clearly desperate for every resource.

In foreign policy, Hitler was pushed back and forth between realpolitik calculations about what was possible on the international stage and the wish to demonstrate to his supporters, to the German people, and to the world, the radical energy of his new movement. In January 1935, a referendum or plebiscite in the Saar, as provided for in the Versailles treaty, produced a 91 percent vote in favor of a return to Germany, despite the large working-class and Catholic population that might have been expected to be suspicious and hostile to the Nazi regime. As the Saar became part of Germany again, Hitler announced: "Following the completion of your return, the German Reich had no further territorial demands to make of France."[13]

In practice, however, Hitler continued the military build-up, and almost immediately started to test the limits of the peace treaty. On March 10, 1935, Göring announced that a German air force existed: it had been built up using the personnel and resources of the civilian airline, Luft Hansa. On March 13, after a discussion with the Wehrmacht adjutant, Lt-Col. Hossbach, Hitler privately decided on a 36-division peacetime army, of 550,000 men: five and a half times as large as the limited force permitted by the Versailles treaty. The French National Assembly lengthened military service from one to two years on March 15, with the consequence that Hitler was able to present his move (which had already been decided on) as a response to France. On March 16 Germany thus celebrated what the newspapers called "the first great measures to liquidate Versailles".[14] It was a carefully timed moment of political opportunism, and Hitler began to construct a doctrine about the necessity of seizing chances. He explained to his cronies: "In political life you must believe in the Goddess of Fortune.

She passes by only once, and that's when to grasp her. She will never pass that way again."[15]

The response to German rearmament of the other European powers (the United Kingdom, France, Italy) was to state their intention of guaranteeing Germany's western frontier, and the separate existence of Austria, at Stresa in northern Italy (April 1935). Hitler sounded reassuringly pacific when he explained that Germany neither wished nor intended to incorporate Austria. Was he appearing to be too peaceful, and did the German public expect more vigor?

In the late summer of 1935, he responded to signs of popular discontent about price increases and labor conditions with a desire for some striking new foreign policy initiative. An obvious initiative would be the sending of German troops into the demilitarized Rhineland. But at this moment such an act, which would constitute a striking repudiation of the Versailles treaty, looked too dangerous and likely to provoke a response by the far stronger French army. So he settled for a new measure of radical anti-Semitism, the hastily drafted Nuremberg Laws, which created a new category of Reich citizenship based on racial descent and excluding non-Aryans (Jews, Roma, and Sinti). The foreign policy initiative had to wait until the next spring, when French political chaos offered a favorable opportunity and lessened the chance of a French military response. Alarmed by its increasing vulnerability, France had just concluded a pact with Russia (negotiated by Pierre Laval). Hitler saw another favorable moment, and summoned the Reichstag to meet on March 7, 1936. There he explained that the French action was in his eyes a breach of the Locarno treaty, and told his audience that German soldiers were at that moment crossing the Rhine bridges into the zone demilitarized under the Versailles treaty. Later, he admitted that if there had been any armed French resistance, the German troops would have been forced to withdraw.

In the following years, Hitler laid the basis of a more radical policy. Germany in 1936 was obviously still quite weak militarily. In economic terms, the Four-Year Plan of 1936 was designed to enable Germany successfully to fight a defensive war by 1940 and an offensive one by 1944. Hitler would be able to realize the old German hopes of fighting a short war, or Blitzkrieg ("lightning war"), to achieve ascendancy in western Europe. In November 1937, this timetable was shortened, and war seemed imminent.

Hitler consistently saw economic recovery in terms of providing the capacity to fight wars. Almost immediately after he became Chancellor, he told his cabinet that rearmament would cure unemployment, and that every work-creation measure should be judged on whether it was necessary from the standpoint of the reconstitution of German military might.

Recovery from the Depression was at first quite slow. For business, revival simply meant the restoration of production from unused capacity.

Unlike in the 1920s, when increased business had been accompanied by high wage demands and settlements, wages were more or less held in place by government controls. Trade unions were banned after May 2, 1933. As a proportion of German national income, wages fell from 57 percent in 1932 to 53.5 percent in 1936 and 51.8 percent in 1939. This relative decline in the position of labor followed the demoralization of workers in the Depression era, and there was relatively little working-class protest. There were many complaints where the Labor Service forced unemployed workers to build dams and highways in remote parts of Germany, but the factories were largely quiet. Only in the late 1930s, when full employment meant that workers were more or less undismissable, did absenteeism, lateness, and misbehavior (drinking) at work increase. But even then, it was hardly a sign of political resistance, and the Nazi state succeeded quite well in incorporating the working class in a new national consensus.

But as the German economy recovered, it sucked in more imports, and the consequent trade deficit pushed the government to a more rigorous system of trade control than that applied initially as an emergency measure in the financial and currency crisis of 1931. In 1934 Economics Minister Schacht moved to a bilateralization of trade with the "New Plan". With this, German trade also shifted away from western Europe, and toward South America and southeast Europe. Particularly in regard to the latter, trade was instrumentalized for foreign policy: Germans bought goods at above world-market prices from the primarily agricultural producers of central and southern Europe, and in return created a dependence. The simultaneous closing of the French and British markets to these producers, as the imperial countries adopted trade preferences for their empires, also helped to push many small states politically into the German orbit.

By 1936, Germany had reached nearly full employment, and industrial capacity was fully utilized. This was the period in which war preparation was increasing, but in which a policy simply oriented to Keynesian economic recovery should have applied brakes. Businesses were now hesitant about making new investments, especially if restrictive and protectionist trade policies were shutting off export markets. In consequence, the state took more of an initiative. It controlled prices more intensely and thoroughly; it regulated the credit markets and set up its own banks to finance rearmament; and a gigantic state heavy industrial and armaments holding company, the Reichswerke Hermann Göring, was established to end any state dependence on private business interests.

Many of the traditional iron and steel barons disliked the plans to create an autarkic steel industry via the Reichswerke, but they dared not risk any open confrontation. Fritz Thyssen, one of the few heavy industrialists who had financed Hitler before 1933, fled abroad (where he helped in the production of a revelatory but ghost-written book, *I Paid Hitler*).

Schachtianism

Hjalmar Schacht was President of the German central bank (*Reichsbank*) from 1923 to 1930 and again from 1933 to 1939, and Acting Minister of Economics under Hitler (1934–37). In his first period as *Reichsbank* President he had warned about the build-up of foreign debt, and in his second phase he presided over a continuing debt default. He used this skillfully to play off various creditor types (banks, bondholders, holders of public and private sector debts) and creditor countries (the United Kingdom, the United States, Switzerland, the Netherlands) against each other, and to get better terms for German exporters and debtors.

After 1934, he instituted a system of trade control (the New Plan) in which there were different exchange rates for different countries and products. The trade plan aimed to increase trade with some areas (Latin America and southeast Europe), and could also be used to establish increased political control over weak southeast European countries.

During and after the Second World War, "Schachtianism" became a term of condemnation for managed trade and currency regimes. It was the opposite of the vision of an open international economy. Schacht, who was discredited in Germany by his association with Hitler, had no significant role in postwar German economic or political life, but gave advice to countries which found managed trade attractive: Algeria, Egypt, India, Iran, the Philippines, and Syria. None of them did very well economically as a result of his advice.

Schacht also felt marginalized by the move to a war economy under Göring, who in 1936 had been appointed as Plenipotentiary for the Four-Year Plan. In 1937 he was dismissed as Acting Economics Minister, and in early 1939, after a conflict with Hitler over the large budget deficit resulting from rearmament, from the central bank (*Reichsbank*) as well.

The Four-Year Plan never succeeded in establishing autarky, despite costly investments in the development of low-grade German iron ores, synthetic rubber, and synthetic fuels. It was still much cheaper – as Schacht continued to point out – to buy petroleum from Romania and iron ore from Sweden, and in exchange sell goods on the export market. From the standpoint of the Nazis, however, such a policy looked like the discredited liberal capitalistic internationalism of the 1920s.

The result of the different policy requirements – maintenance of employment, high levels of consumption, and preparations for war – was an economy that was not fully planned in the Soviet sense, despite the obvious verbal acknowledgment in the Four-Year Plan of the successful Soviet model of the Five-Year Plan. Private ownership (except by Jews) was left largely untouched. But it was an economy that was increasingly state-directed, in which the major investor and the major consumer was the public sector.

The redirection of resources into government investment, and the priorities in trade policy which restricted the import of raw materials needed for the consumer economy (wool, cotton, bananas), produced consumer goods of ever poorer quality. Textiles were largely synthetic; shoes fell apart more quickly. One of the most popular hit songs mocked the unavailability of bananas.

If there had been no war (an improbable calculation since mobilization for war lay at the heart of the economic strategy), Germany would have looked rather like the postwar regime of the German Democratic Republic: increasingly impoverished and with an increasingly inadequate consumer sector. Indeed, in the 1980s the shortage of bananas became a symbol of the economic failure of the GDR.

Did these failures apply in the military–economic sector too? The ambitious goals of the Four-Year Plan were not met; and that meant that in order to engage in a large-scale war, Germany needed to acquire more industrial capacity before the outbreak of conflict. The industrial resources of Austria, and especially of Czechoslovakia, were a way out of this problem. The Reichswerke Hermann Göring used blackmail against leading Jewish-Austrian industrialists, notably Baron Louis Rothschild, in order to acquire control of the giant Czech Vitkovice steel works even before German troops occupied the Czech territories.

At the same time as economic policy geared up for war, the government's anti-Semitic campaign was stepped up; in part because of the perceived need to grab more resources for rearmament, but also because of an inherent logic of radicalization within the Nazi movement, in which subordinate officials calculated moves that went ever further in the direction of realizing a racial ideology. The historian Ian Kershaw encapsulated this dynamic by quoting the State Secretary in the Prussian Agricultural Ministry, who in 1934 announced the duty of Germans to "work toward the Führer".[16] Some of the Nazi leaders, such as Joseph Goebbels, saw the anti-Semitic movement primarily in terms of Nazi ideology, and realized how it might be used in internal power struggles: Goebbels set off the major pogrom of November 9–10, 1938, which he cynically termed the "Reich night of broken glass" (*Reichskristallnacht*) in part to rehabilitate himself after the socially respectable and conventional Hitler disapproved of his extra-marital liaison with a Czech film star, Lida Baarova. At least 91 Jews were killed in two nights of terror and destruction, and around 30,000 were interned in concentration camps. Other leaders, notably Hermann Göring, at this point indisputably the most powerful man after Hitler in Germany, made little of the ideology and saw the war on the Jews mainly as an opportunity to realize gains, personal and political, and in particular to finance the increasingly ambitious and fiscally problematical rearmament program. For him, greed and looting were indispensable elements of war, both in preparation and in execution.

Before 1938, there had been party-sponsored attacks on Jewish business, beginning with a boycott of Jewish businesses. Many Jewish businessmen could see the signs of danger, and many gave up their businesses. But until 1938, the state (as opposed to party) authorities had always denied that there was an anti-Semitic economic policy, and had protested against the party boycotts. Reich Economics Minister Schacht had in 1935 defined one of the tasks that "the economy must solve itself", namely "how to finance the transfer of Jewish businesses into Aryan hands". At the end of 1937, Jewish business activity was restricted at Göring's initiative by a discriminatory tightening of raw-material supplies. On January 4, 1938, a decree defined a Jewish enterprise as one owned or dominated by Jews, meaning that either one member of the executive board or one personally liable manager was Jewish in the sense of the Nuremberg Laws, or that one-quarter of the supervisory board was Jewish. On June 14, 1938, the Third Ordinance on Reich Citizenship reaffirmed and partly redefined the specific criteria for the assessment of what was a "Jewish" enterprise. On April 26, 1938, an "Ordinance on the Registration of Jewish Assets" required the registration of Jewish property exceeding 5000 RM in value; Section 7 allowed the Commissary for the Four-Year Plan to take measures "that are necessary in order to ensure that the notifiable property is deployed in accordance with the interests of the German economy". A few days earlier, the "Ordinance against the Support of Camouflage by Jewish Businesses" provided harsh prison penalties for German citizens who "through selfish motives help in this connection deliberately to obscure the Jewish nature of a commercial operation with a view to deceiving the authorities". The pogrom of November 1938 was followed by an immediate push to confiscate Jewish business, driven by Göring rather than Goebbels. On November 12, he introduced an "Ordinance on the Exclusion of Jews from German Economic Life", and the imposition of a 25 percent tax on assets (*Sühneleistung*). At the same time, Jewish enterprises were threatened with prosecution under existing legislation for actual or alleged "capital flight" – attempting to bring their assets to safety beyond Germany's frontiers. Göring announced that "The Jew will be eliminated from the economy, ceding his economic property to the state. He will be compensated for it. . . . The government trustee will value the business and decide what sum the Jew is paid." On November 12, a decree forbade Jews from engaging in the retail trade and craft manufacturing, and on November 23 a further decree required the liquidation of such businesses. In practice, the compensation was taken away by the fine on Jews, and by exchange controls which took up to 98 percent of the value when Jews wanted to convert their assets into foreign currency.

In 1938, Germany came close to war, in two successive crises. The first was in March, when Hitler orchestrated a political crisis in Austria and then launched an entirely peaceful (unresisted) invasion. Austria was annexed to Germany, which now referred to itself as the *Grossdeutsches Reich*, the realization of the nineteenth-century nationalism which had viewed Bismarck's Germany with contempt because it excluded the German-speaking populations of the Habsburg Empire. Unlike the remilitarization of the Rhineland, in the case of the *Anschluss* of Austria there was no realistic chance of any serious fighting.

The second political crisis of 1938 was different. Hitler had plans for the invasion of Czechoslovakia, code-named "Operation Green", developed already in 1937, which would undoubtedly have been resisted fiercely by a well-equipped Czech army from powerful defenses in the Czech border territories. However, these – usually referred to as the Sudetenland – had a largely German-speaking population, surrounding the Czech core to the north, west, and south; and Hitler's method of undermining the Czechoslovak state was to work closely with a Nazi agent: the leader of a radical nationalist Sudeten party, Konrad Henlein. Nationalism worked as a powerful solvent for the Czech state: Czechs and Slovaks saw Germans, but also German-speaking Jews, as their enemies; Slovaks saw a chance to get even with the Czechs who had dominated the Republic's history.

In May, the German army carried out intimidating troop movements near the Czech border. Neither the Austrian nor the Czech crisis would have been turned so signally to Hitler's advantage had the state of European international relations been different. When Austrian Nazis assassinated Chancellor Dollfuss in 1934, Mussolini had warned Hitler against intervening in Austria, and had mobilized the Italian army on the Brenner Pass into Austrian Tyrol; subsequently, he participated with the United Kingdom and France in the "Stresa Front" to contain Hitler. But after Mussolini had been isolated by the British and French response to the Italian invasion of Abyssinia, he sought Hitler's assistance. In 1937 the two leaders concluded a "pact of steel": Hitler could now invade Austria; and Mussolini in the diplomatic crisis of September 1938 brokered in the Nazi Party building in Munich a package in which France and the United Kingdom agreed – without consulting the Czech government – to the separation of the Sudetenland from Czechoslovakia. Despite Hitler's claim to be upholding the rights of mistreated minorities, the new frontier was created with a military rather than an ethnic or national logic. It provided for no plebiscite, and in fact around 800,000 Czechs lived in the districts that were ceded to Germany. Czechoslovakia's northern neighbor, Poland, then participated in the plunder, and took an area of the Sudetenland with a large Polish-speaking population (Teschen). Joseph Goebbels concluded: "We are really a world power again"[17] (Plate 5).

After the German army moved (ahead of time) into the areas which had been unilaterally redistributed in the Munich agreement, the rest of Czechoslovakia (which now changed its name in deference to Slovak nationalists to Czecho-Slovakia) was quite defenseless, and it was predictable that Germany would make further demands. On October 31, Hitler ordered the army to prepare for the occupation of the territory of Memel on the Baltic, and the seizure of the "Czech rump" (*Resttschechei*). German business

Plate 5 The illusory success of September: Neville Chamberlain returns from Munich with a message of peace as agreed by Adolf Hitler, September 1938. © Hulton-Deutsch Collection/CORBIS/Corbis via Getty Images.

prepared for the dismemberment of the Czech state; the heavy industrial centers of production (all located in the interior of the country) looked like a promising solution to an economy overheating as a result of armaments orders. On March 14, 1939, Hitler summoned the Czech President Hácha to Berlin, where he explained repeatedly that he wanted to avoid blood-shed and then fainted when Göring threatened an immediate air raid on Prague. The next day, after days of German diplomatic pressure and mili-tary mobilization, nationalist riots in major cities, and Slovak pressure for separation, the German armies moved into the Czech territories, encounter-ing little resistance. Germany created an occupied area (the "Protectorate of Bohemia and Moravia") and a separate Slovak state, under the nationalist cleric Father Tiso.

The Czech territories rapidly became a key part of the Germany economic– military preparations for large-scale war. The Reichswerke Hermann Göring took over key parts of Czech heavy industry, and 40,000 Czech workers were conscripted to work in Germany. The logic created by the choice of a strategy of autarky required the seizure of more territory in order to be able to prepare for war on the basis of self-sufficiency.

Humiliated by the way in which Hitler had broken all the promises of 1938, the British government proceeded to give a "guarantee" of Polish independence. The Germans in Poland, and especially in the City of Danzig (Gdańsk), separate from Poland and under the trusteeship of the League of Nations, looked as if they would be used in the same way as Hitler had instrumentalized the Sudeten Germans. But a British or French guarantee could not offer much help if Poland were attacked; and – as in the Czech situation – London and Paris refrained from any negotiation with the Soviet Union on how Germany might be contained.

Appeasement

"Appeasement" has changed its meaning and use as a result of the experience of the 1930s. As practiced by British and French politicians, in particular by Neville Chamberlain as UK Prime Minister, it literally meant pacification. The policy rested on a primitive intuition about an unfamiliar foreign regime with a strong measure of ideology: that there existed "hawks" and "doves" in the political establishment, who were in competition with each other. Concessions (often in the economic realm, but also in regard to Hitler's claim to speak for Germans in other countries) and favorable treatment would strengthen the doves: in the German case these were identified as either the Economics Minister Hjalmar Schacht (who became marginal politically in the late 1930s) or the Minister-President of Prussia Hermann Göring. On the other hand, harsh rhetoric or public condemnation, and the absence of any concessions, would strengthen hawks such as Foreign Minister Ribbentrop or Propaganda Minister Goebbels.

The Munich agreement of September 1938 represents the high-water mark of the appeasement argument. Hitler's advocacy of the allegedly violated minority rights of the Sudeten Germans was accepted by the western powers without any consultation with Czech leaders. The appeasers were largely discredited by the German invasion of the rest of Czechoslovakia in March 1939, but by then it was hard to begin with a new political strategy. Even then, some remnants of the appeasement lobby continued to urge Poland to make concessions over the Danzig issue. If Hitler had been rational, he could have derived major benefits from the willingness of the appeasers to make concessions; but had Hitler been rational, appeasement would not have been so urgent or attractive.

After the war, appeasement was used solely in a negative sense, as making concessions to dictators (rather than prompting regime change). Detente in the 1970s, as a strategy pursued from Washington and Bonn, but also from Moscow, had much of the logic of the original appeasement

(continued)

(continued)

strategy of the 1930s: the de-escalation of tensions, so that the other side might concentrate on internal reforms. The West believed that the Soviet Union would become more dependent on consumer goods and trade, and less inclined to military expenditure; and the East believed that the West might develop nearer in the direction of a socialist society. Neither of these calculations, plausible and even seductive though they might have been, came off. If detente had a long legacy, it was because part of the process involved the establishment of categories of human rights that might play an important part in the internal evolution of Soviet society (see the discussion of the Helsinki process in Chapter 10). It is this, rather than the offering of concessions in areas such as trade policy, that really made change possible. But in talking about rights and norms, the new vision of detente went beyond the *Realist* underlay of 1930s appeasement policies.

The consequence of such political marginalization was that Stalin changed tack. On May 3, 1939, Foreign Minister Maxim Litvinov, who had been the major exponent of working with the west European powers against fascism, was dismissed and replaced by Vyacheslav Molotov, who disliked the West. On August 23, Germany and Russia concluded a non-aggression pact, with secret clauses dividing up the Polish territories. After that, war became inevitable. Hitler, who believed that he had been cheated of war in 1938, ignored Polish efforts to negotiate about Danzig or the Polish corridor. On September 1, 1939, a beautiful, clear, late summer day, German police units staged a border incident, and the German army invaded Poland.

In the aftermath of the tragedy of a new world war, the western policy of "appeasement", and in particular the Munich agreement, looked like a foolish and weak response to the Nazi threat. But it had followed logically from the previous approach to foreign policy in the United Kingdom and France, from a combination of three errors: the stage-by-stage dismantling of the Versailles treaty; the moralistic and counter-productive "anti-fascist" reaction to Abyssinia (which did nothing for the victims of Italian aggression); and the moralistic and counter-productive "anti-communist" neglect of the Soviet Union. As a consequence, the western powers had driven together three states – Germany, Italy, and the Soviet Union, each of which was unhappy about some aspect of the postwar settlement – in an alliance of treaty revisionism. In practice, they thus made the Soviet dictator Joseph Stalin the arbiter of the European balance of power. For two years after the Nazi–Soviet pact, Hitler celebrated his "masterly" alliance with Russia; and then for three years the western powers were charmed by the sustenance of a benign "Uncle Joe" (the epithet became so widely used that official British documents referred to him as U.J.).

Soviet civilization?

In December 1929, Stalin was 50 years old, and there was widespread and ostentatious celebration. It was at this point, in the middle of a drive to collectivize agriculture and to promote a new industrial plan, that the "cult of personality" began – a cult which was later severely criticized as a deformation by two of Stalin's successors as first or general secretary of the Communist Party of the Soviet Union, Nikita Khrushchev and Mikhail Gorbachev. In 1940, the film *The Shining Path* contained a new hit song: "We were born to make fairy tales reality."

Stalinism

Joseph Stalin was Lenin's successor as leader of the Soviet Communist Party. After a period of hesitation, he adopted a policy of rapid and very brutal industrialization and of attacking private agriculture, and implemented a terror against his opponents. Stalin fostered a cult of his leadership, but consistently refused to use the word "Stalinism" or to label a doctrine as *Marxism–Leninism–Stalinism*. When Kaganovich suggested this term in the 1920s, Stalin (according to Khrushchev) responded: "How can you compare a dick to a watchtower?" On the other hand, many Russians by the 1930s used the adjective "*stalinskii*" and the noun "*stalinist*".

"Stalinism" as a term was used after Stalin's death, and then negatively, as a criticism of the Soviet Union under his leadership. It evoked hyper-industrialization, the use of terror, mass purges, and show trials, the bureaucratization of the revolution (especially in the *Trotskyist* critique), and the subordination of the international communist movement to Soviet interests. In particular, Khrushchev's secret speech at the Twentieth Party Congress (1956) was interpreted as a denunciation of Stalinism; although Khrushchev did not use this word, and instead referred to the "cult of personality", an expression already used by Malenkov soon after Stalin's death. The main use of a concept of Stalinism politically was to suggest that it was an utterly different phenomenon from Leninism: a distortion and a perversion. This view became increasingly both less plausible and less popular, both in and outside Russia, where by the late 1980s and 1990s most analysts believed that the Stalin phenomenon represented simply an evolutionary development from the basis of Leninism. The newer view of the role of Stalinism as a phase of socialist development is neatly embodied in the *matrosbka* (nestling) dolls for sale everywhere on the streets of Russia where tourists were likely to venture, in which Stalin nestled inside Lenin, who was inside Marx.

In 1935, the British socialists Beatrice and Sidney Webb published a study with the title, *The Soviet Union: A New Civilization?* When the book was reissued two years later, the Webbs omitted the question mark. The Soviet Union exercised an enormous fascination over the workers and intellectuals of Europe in the interwar years, and an even greater one in the aftermath of the Second World War. A Hungarian countess, who worked for the Comintern, later wrote about her first visit to the ancient university of Cambridge:

> I remember the trip to Cambridge in the rickety car of a young communist undergraduate who, on the way, explained to me dolefully that it was imperative though most regrettable, that the beautiful ancient universities of Oxford and Cambridge should be razed to the ground when the Proletarian Dictatorship was proclaimed. For centuries, he said, they had been the symbols of bourgeois privilege. . . . It was odd to see the students of such a famous university, obviously upper-class, with well-bred accents, speak about Soviet Russia as the land of promise.[18]

Internally as well as externally, the Soviet Union projected a vision of a new world, in which the problems and sins of the old one had been overcome. The Soviet order created modernity out of backwardness, and claimed to be the realization of a set of historical and philosophical principles derived from the writings of Marx, Engels, and Lenin: historical materialism and dialectical materialism (often abbreviated to "histmat" and "diamat").[19] This philosophy was supposed to offer an answer to the existential uncertainties of modern existence: it proclaimed a doctrine that was true, because it rested on authority, and was in accordance with the deep necessity of a historical law of development. Dialectics involved four fundamental laws, derived from Hegelian analysis: that all phenomena are interconnected; that the universe is in constant change; that qualitative changes come from a build-up of quantitative changes (water cools, until it suddenly at one temperature changes its substance and becomes ice); and finally all phenomena contain contradictions, and development comes out of the clash of contradictions. At the most fundamental, being required its opposite (not being); and the clash of the two could be resolved in the process of becoming. Historical materialism assumed that the basis for reality lay in "objective phenomena", such as goods, and the particular ways of producing them; ideas were "ideology", i.e. a reflection of the underlying reality. The most complete exposition of the Soviet doctrine occurred in a book largely written by Stalin, the *History of the Communist Party of the Soviet Union (Bolsheviks), A Short Course*, published in 1938, which explained that there had been a "dangerous cleavage in the sphere of propaganda between Marxism and Leninism which has appeared in recent years".[20]

Clashes of ideas, as they emerged in the Marxist movement with great frequency (and great bitterness), presented a problem: all the ideas, except one set, must be wrong, and a reflection of a false political stance. The imposition of the party's (and the leader's) authority was justified as "the unity of theory and practice", and was extended to cover art and aesthetics, scientific discussion, and economic thought. In all these directions, the Soviet Union was establishing a new reality and a new modernity.

The most impressive immediate claim in the world of 1929 was that of having discovered a new type of economics, as an alternative to the anarchy of the market and the self-destruction of "bourgeois economics". At the time of the Great Depression, Stalin used "scientific planning" or "socialist planning" to embark on a long-term process of industrialization. The theorists of the plan candidly acknowledged that their concentration on producer or investment goods would in the short term reduce the amount of goods available for consumption; in the longer run, however, the superiority of Soviet productive capacity would ensure a greater supply of consumer goods.

The turn to planning in the late 1920s followed almost a decade of experimentation with a mixed economy, in which the state controlled the "commanding heights" of heavy industry, but small-scale business agriculture was left in private hands and to market mechanisms. The major theorist of the so-called New Economic Policy (NEP), Nikolai Bukharin, had once told Russia's peasants to "get rich", in the belief that this would solve the problem of food supply. But in fact, NEP gradually lost steam, investment levels were very low, and the economy looked highly vulnerable.

In 1927, the Fifteenth Communist Party Congress discussed ideas about planning, and for two years the economists engaged in an ever more frenetic struggle to produce a basis for a plan. The political momentum at this time worked to make ever more ambitious plan targets "better" than conservative or hesitant ones, which could easily be denounced as anti-socialist. In 1928, the leading Soviet economist, Nikolai Kondratiev, was expelled from the Finance Commissariat's economics institute. The planners in Gosplan were slowly marginalized. By the end of 1928, the proposals were extraordinarily ambitious: an increase in industrial production over five years by 180 percent, and of agricultural production by 50 percent. In 1928 the USSR had produced 32.5 million tons of hard coal, 3 million tons of lignite, and 3.3 million tons of pig iron. After five years, the planners now proposed 75 million tons of coal and 10 million tons of pig iron. The Politburo's proposals in 1929 were quite deliberately confrontational, and spoke of all the difficulties in the way of the plan's realization: "These difficulties are made much more profound by the sharpening of the class struggle and the resistance of the capitalist elements."[21] The first Five-Year Plan was formally launched in April 1929 at the Sixteenth Party Congress. It was accompanied by a detailed three-volume plan proposal, with 1,700 large pages. (At almost the same time in the United States, a similarly detailed and even more voluminous economic blueprint was being drawn up, in an analogous process of cumulative radicalization as the more extreme proposal seemed the better one, with 21,000 separate tariff positions: the Smoot–Hawley Tariff Act.)

The Soviet plan was accompanied by detailed plans for the republics in the USSR. In 1932, it was declared to have been successfully completed, and was followed by a second and then a third Five-Year Plan. From the beginning, the plans aimed to shift production away from the traditional industrial areas, so that the benefits of modernity could be dispersed as widely as possible. Also, from the mid-1930s there were powerful military security arguments to move as much production as possible to the Urals, Siberia, and Central Asia.

The Five-Year Plans of the 1930s were indeed successful in producing large quantities of basic industrial goods – coal and steel. The failure to move into consumer goods could, at least for the time, be explained by the new priorities of the international situation, and the focus on armaments in the Third Five-Year Plan. The number employed in industrial production increased from 4.4 million in 1928 to 9.4 million in 1932 and 11.6 million by 1937. By 1940, 16 percent of industrial production took place in the east of the USSR, as compared to 11–12 percent in 1928.[22] The ambitious targets for coal and iron were not met (the actual production of coal was 57 million tons of hard coal in 1932, and 6.16 million tons of pig iron).

The plans of the 1930s became increasingly oriented toward military preparation. The concentration on metallurgy provided a base for a quick increase in armament production. As a proportion of the Soviet state budget, military spending constituted 3.6 percent in 1929, but 18.7 percent in 1933 and 25.6 percent in 1939. Official figures show a threefold increase in the output of the Soviet defense industry between 1933 and 1938.

The practice of planning was considerably less scientific than the theory of the rationalized development of an investment goods sector as discussed by the economic planners of the late 1920s. The plan in reality worked only by the constant management of crises and bottlenecks, which were then allocated the highest priority and were to be tackled by "storming" methods. In order to justify their methods, the planners even evolved a theory of "hortatory planning": that the eventual result was likely to be higher with blatantly unrealistic targets than if the targets reflected what might realistically be achieved. Overall priorities reflected big political considerations, with the result that prestige projects such as the beautifully elaborate Moscow underground system were built while the millions of new urban workers were forced into inadequate and overcrowded barracks.

The first Five-Year Plan was also accompanied by a reorganization of agriculture, "collectivization". Four-fifths of the population of the Soviet Union was "peasant". The coarsely bearded *muzhiks* were regarded with contempt by workers and intellectuals, who themselves of course had mostly peasant roots. The writer Maxim Gorky complained of their "animal-like individualism".[23] Like Peter the Great, Stalin strove for clean-shaven modernity. In 1917, Lenin had made what he termed a "tactical alliance" with the peasant population of Russia, but by the late 1920s, with towns (and their communist parties) complaining about the difficulties in getting food supplies, that alliance was under great strain. Collectivization was supposed to deal with the problem: by organizing the peasants in a non-market way, or by controlling them.

The traditional communal-based agriculture of Russia, which had only briefly been interrupted by attempts to introduce individual concepts of property in land reforms in the early twentieth century, was to be replaced by very large collectives (one collective would replace as many as 10 peasant villages). In practice, the implementation went literally at breakneck speed, as urban communists saw an opportunity of putting into acts their long-standing resentment of greedy peasant profiteers. In September 1929, 7 percent of farm households had been collectivized, and by March 1930, the figure was 59 percent. Stalin then declared a temporary halt, with a newspaper article which spoke about the collectivizers being "dizzy with success".

Agriculture was where the greatest shortfalls in meeting the planners' targets occurred, because of the brutal inefficiency of collectivization. By 1932 there was widespread famine. Even by the late 1930s, production in agriculture was barely above the levels of the late 1920s.

In the first half of the 1930s, as collectivization was implemented more systematically, the key lay in outside control of the peasant economy. The *kolkhoz* (collective farm) did not have its own equipment, but was to be supplied by new Machine Tractor Stations, of which there existed 3,500 by late 1934.

Such modernization required the support of a new science, which would be explicitly harnessed to the real needs of humanity. Soviet science embarked on its most precarious endeavors at the moment when the philosophy of Marxism appeared to be central to the scientific debate: thus – in probably the most bizarre and destructive episode – Stalin promoted T.D. Lysenko, who explicitly revived Lamarckian evolutionary theories in place of Darwinism. Since Darwinism applied to human conditions was un-Leninist (it implied that progress did not need an effort of the will), the truth of Leninism necessarily meant the falsity of Darwinian principles. If human societies could adapt by an effort of the revolutionary will, why not animals and plants? Lysenkoism reached heights of absurdity when it was used to justify a large-scale experiment in planting wheat in the inhospitable circumstances of the Arctic Circle.

The anti-Lysenkoist geneticist, Nikolai Dubinin, in his autobiography in the 1970s was still justifying the social argument on which Lysenko made his appeal:

> Let us remember the story of the emigration from Russia of many representatives of the bourgeois artistic, scientific and technological elite after the October Revolution. Some eugenicists considered this exodus as an irretrievable loss of valuable genes. But this was nonsense. New talents from the grass roots through the Revolution found their way to lead the country, the Party, to create new science, new art, to create

the Great Soviet Union! . . . This fact illustrates that the creation of personality does not depend on genes, but is induced by the information of social environment.[24]

These transformations of society in the name of a new truth required the creation and then the demonization of enemy figures. As in Mussolini's Italy or Hitler's Germany, the vocabulary of progress was militarized with slogans such as the "industrial front", the "agricultural front", and "shock brigades". For the industrialization drive, the enemy was the "capitalist" and the "bourgeois", Russianized as *burzhui*;[25] for collectivization, the peasant usurer or petty capitalist, the *kulak*. None of these enemies could be defined with any kind of scientific precision: the flexibility of the category was its chief advantage. In 1927, Molotov told the Fifteenth Party Congress that 3.7 percent of the farm population were kulaks; the Gosplan economists thought 3.9 percent; the Commissariat of Agriculture calculated that 2.1 percent of farms hired labor (but only 1 percent had more than one laborer); and Stalin in 1930 put the proportion of kulaks at 5 percent. But the ill-defined "kulak" was a pretext for a general onslaught on the rural way of life. As the historian Moshe Lewin puts it: "For propaganda purposes the kulak was singled out as the scapegoat but behind him lay the serednyak [middling peasant], who was the real obstacle."[26]

Within the Communist Party of the Soviet Union, which managed this gigantic social transformation, the result was also continuous uncertainty. The party attracted large numbers of recruits; then some of its members decided it had become too big, and that it required a purge. In 1929, at the outset of the industrialization and collectivization drive, 116,000 members were expelled and another 14,000 left voluntarily; in 1933 the party staged another purge, and 800,000 were expelled. Industrialization was also accompanied by a purge of the civil service. From 1928 to 1931, 138,000 civil servants were dismissed, and 23,000 classed as "enemies of the people".[27] After December 1934, when the leader of the Leningrad (St Petersburg) party, Kirov, was assassinated, the turmoil boiled over into a long period of denunciations, purges, and three spectacular show trials, staged for a national and international audience. Immediately after the assassination, a secret party directive ordered the rapid execution of all those accused of "terrorism". This was the beginning of the witch hunt: Khrushchev in 1956 described the decree as the "basis of mass acts of abuse against socialist legality". Many Russians, in particular many communist officials and leaders, simply disappeared. Guessing the numbers involved remains problematical: Stalin gave some indication of the scope when he explained in 1939 that 500,000 party members had been promoted to leading positions between 1934 and 1939. When parents were deported and killed, they frequently left their children orphaned and homeless. These children were then complete outcasts from Soviet society, and developed a wild street culture of their own. Eventually, in the last decades of the Soviet Union's existence, this evolved into networks of organized criminality whose existence was ignored by the Soviet establishment.

At the height of the terror, in 1937–38, 1,575,000 people were arrested by the NKVD, of whom 1,345,000 were sentenced and 681,692 executed. In all, 7 million people were sent to penal and labor camps between 1934 and 1941, though some remained there only for short periods. The largest extent of the camp population was reached on the eve of the war with Germany: at the beginning of 1941, there were 1,930,000 inhabitants of the Gulag system. A recent estimate of the number of deaths in the camps is 300,000 for the period 1934–40, with another 600,000 deaths reported among deportees, internal refugees, and the "specially displaced".[28]

While the number of victims remained obscure, the struggle of Stalinism to find and destroy its enemies was conducted with great publicity. The most striking feature of the time were the show trials, in which Stalin's former associates denounced themselves for counter-revolutionary activities. In January 1935, the chief prosecutor, Vishinsky, announced the trial of Zinoviev and Kamenev, critics of Stalin from the 1920s who were now accused of having been behind the Kirov assassination. In 1936 the secret police chief Yagoda was dismissed and replaced by Ezhov; both in the end were victims of the purges. Yagoda was accused of having poisoned Maxim Gorky and Kuibyshev. Many of the victims confessed to amazingly specific counter-revolutionary crimes. Bukharin, the most prominent of all the victims, and one of the few who had not been subject to physical torture, bravely avoided specifics and instead simply explained that: "We rebelled by criminal methods against the joyfulness of the new life." He also angered the prosecutor, Vishinsky, when he explained that "the confession of the accused is a medieval principle of jurisprudence".[29]

Why the victims confessed has been the subject of much discussion. Arthur Koestler's fictionalized account of the purges in *Darkness at Noon* (published in 1941) shows party members demonstrating the depth of their psychological commitment to the party and its scientific truth in the act of confession. There are obvious analogies to the victims of the Catholic Inquisition affirming the faith so that their souls could be free before their bodies were condemned. But – as with the Inquisition – it is most likely that the overwhelming majority of victims confessed because they were subject to unendurable torture, and because they were afraid.

The trials and purges destroyed the party and the intelligentsia, and decimated the leadership of the Red Army. Three out of five marshals, 13 out of 15 army generals, 50 out of 57 corps commanders, and all 11 Vice Commissars of War were purged. The evidence against Marshal Tukhachevski, in which he was accused of working with Germany, seems to have been manufactured by the Soviet secret police working together with its German opposite number – the NKVD with the Gestapo. Foreign communists, in exile in the Soviet Union from political repression, were purged as well.

Since their start in 1929, a large part of the attacks involved the denunciations of "experts"; the Soviet technical and scientific elite suffered as well.

Some, including A.N. Tupolev, continued to work on the development of aircraft in prison. The most famous artillery product of the Second World War, the multi-shell gun called the *katiusha* or "Stalin organ", was developed by Georgy Lanngemak, who had been arrested and sentenced to death along with his whole engineering group in 1937. One assistant who escaped death organized the production and developed the gun, which was delivered for military use at the beginning of the war.

At the height of the purges, in 1936, the Soviet Union adopted a new constitution. Stalin announced that it was "the only thoroughly democratic constitution in the world"; and on paper, this was certainly the most liberal constitution in the history of the Soviet Union. It provided for secret voting; it replaced a previously restrictive franchise with a universal one; and it contained guarantees of individual liberties. It also recognized the role of the Communist Party for the first time: Article 141 presented the party as one of the organizations with the right to present candidates for election.

By 1939, the party seemed to have been renewed. Ezhov was discredited by the end of 1938, and was replaced by Lavrenti Beria. Seventy percent of members had joined since 1929. Stalin now soberly told the Eighteenth Party Congress that "there is no doubt that we will not use again the method of the mass purge".

It is striking that in order to describe this "time of troubles", Russians could only take analogies from the past. The author Mikhail Bulgakov, whose novel about the revolution in Ukraine provided the basis of one of Stalin's favorite plays, used the stories of Pontius Pilate and Faust in *The Master and Margarita* to explain how the devil suddenly arrived in Moscow, caused people to disappear, manufactured money, reallocated apartments, and induced weirdly colorful confessions. The highpoint of the novel, Satan's ball, was inspired by the grand reception given by US Ambassador Bullitt at his residence in spring 1935, at the beginning of the terror; many of the prominent guests from Moscow's political, intellectual, and artistic elites disappeared soon after. But such macabre events were replicated all over Russia: in the new industrial city of Magnitogorsk, built from scratch in the Urals, on May Day 1936, the party instituted a new tradition of masked balls, with invitation lists and tickets that were designed to exclude "undesirable elements". In the prison and death camp of Magadan, where prisoners were forced to extract gold from the frozen ground, in 1944 the security guards organized a bizarre theater and concert performance for the benefit of a party headed by the visiting Vice-President of the United States, Henry Wallace. One naïvely sympathetic American gushed that this "high grade entertainment" "naturally seems to go with gold and so does high-powered executive ability". Another commented on the beautiful clothes of the prisoners, and asked why there were so many members of the intelligentsia.[30]

The film-maker Sergei Eisenstein, whose *October* and *Battleship Potemkin* had been milestones of successful propaganda for the cause of the revolution, now depicted Stalin in the guise of heroic figures from the Russian past: first,

Alexander Nevsky (1938), who resisted the invasion of the Teutonic Knights; but then, during the war, as the sinister and paranoid Ivan the Terrible, faced by continual conspiracies from the old Russian elites. Stalin himself, who liked to talk directly with the cultural elite (especially on the phone: he would call men such as Bulgakov, Ilya Ehrenburg, or the composer Dmitri Shostakovich), in February 1947 invited Eisenstein and his main actor, Nikolai Cherkasov (who had also played Alexander Nevsky), and told them that he liked Ivan, but believed his major weakness had been that he had not liquidated enough people. In fact, the second part of Eisenstein's film, in which Ivan's paranoia was clear and the analogy to the purges unmistakable, was quickly banned.

Eisenstein's new patriotism at the end of the 1930s hit precisely the right note. What enabled the Soviet experiment to survive – and what added to its luster internationally – was its pivotal role in the fight against Nazi Germany.

Initially, Stalin was shaken by the attack on June 22, 1941: he had long dismissed the repeated intelligence warnings about a forthcoming German offensive as British attempts to lure him into a war with Hitler. After June 22, he disappeared for almost two weeks, and seems to have had a psychic breakdown. On July 3, he returned with a radio address, in which he sounded deeply strained, breathed heavily, and could be heard drinking water. But what was remarkable was the new tone of his speech: "Brothers, sisters, I turn to you, my friends." There was no longer any reference to "comrades".

In general, the tone of propaganda changed dramatically. The attacks of the 1930s had focused on religion: of 20,000 Soviet churches and mosques in 1936, only 1,000 were still operating in early 1941. The campaign for atheism was now halted and reversed. In 1943 the Orthodox patriarchate was restored. The cult of leadership was cut back, Stalin hardly appeared in political posters between 1941 and 1945, and the regime emphasized women, peasants, and other social groups besides the idealized cleanly shaven workers who had been at the center of 1930s campaigns to make a new "Soviet man". Women were massively recruited to industrial labor, and by 1943 composed half of the industrial labor force.[31] The most widely circulated poster at the end of the war included the phrase "Glory to the Russian people."[32] By 1945, Stalin was celebrating Russianness:

> I want to offer a toast to the health of our Soviet people and, above all, to the Russian people. I drink, above all, to the Russian people because it is the outstanding nation of all the nations belonging to the Soviet Union.[33]

Stalin controlled the army directly (after August 7, 1941, he was "commander in chief", and later took the title "Generalissimo"). Unlike Tsar Nicholas II and Hitler, who both assumed the same function, he remained at the political center in Moscow, rather than directing operations in the field.

The economic and military potential of Soviet planning was fully realized during the war. From July to December 1941 alone, 1,523 enterprises were moved from threatened areas to the east of the Soviet Union. This was the industrial capacity that laid the basis of a gigantic and heroic military effort that would win the war.

Terrors compared

Both the new types of party-state of the 1930s were clearly brutal and inhumane, and outside observers whose eyes were not blinded by ideological sympathies could see this. The dictatorships justified their brutality by the necessities of a harsh new modern, industrial, and scientific world, and they soothed the alienated with occasional (in the Soviet case) or repeated (in that of the Nazis) reminders about national traditions and cultures.

Among modern historians and commentators, a long and futile debate has tried to resolve the question of which was "worse". The terror applied by communism (which lasted much longer) killed more people throughout the world, and functioned in a system-supporting way by being arbitrary, unpredictable, and indiscriminate. Nazi terror was applied in a more focused way to specific groups, racially and biologically defined as outside the community of the normal: the disabled, homosexuals, criminals, all of whom were branded by a common term as "asocial"; Roma and Sinti; Slavic peoples in some but not all circumstances; and above all the Jews. Whether the fact that people classed according to conventional stereotypes as "normal" had little to fear, and that by retreating into passivity and acquiescence they made themselves accomplices to evil, makes this regime more evil than any other may be open to debate. But in the eyes of most civilized people it was the murderous specificity of the Nazi terror that made it so appalling.

Domestically, while the Soviet system was bizarrely unpredictable, the Nazi regime looked as if it followed a clearly defined racial logic. In international politics, however, the relationship of unpredictable and predictable was the other way round. Hitler's choice of international enemies had no basis in the racial doctrine: why, for instance, should Poles be regarded as inferior to Czechs? Stalin's Russia, on the other hand, could be seen as a calculable force in international politics.

Nazi Germany was a clearer and a greater threat to the international order, in part because it was driven by a logic of expansion that followed not only from its ideology but also from its wish to get autarky (in theory) and its inability to get it in practice. By contrast, Stalin's revolution had been built quite firmly on an idea of "socialism in one country" and definitively subordinated the interests and ideas of the international communist movement to those of the Soviet Union. Its rich resource endowment meant that a pursuit of autarky was not an international threat. It might have an expansionist logic, but – if blocked by a clearly articulated opposing strategy – would not undertake reckless gambles on the destabilization of its opponents.

Finally, the specific character of Soviet Marxism gave the regime a strongly economistic and even deterministic flavor: a transformation in economics would transform the social and political order. Such an approach privileged the idea of "interest", with the result that Soviet policy appeared as clear and comprehensible to interest-oriented analysts and to politicians who assumed the rationality of the regimes with which they dealt. The Nazis on the other hand believed very firmly that interests could be reshaped by the power of ideas (such as those of Hitler). For international relations, this was more destabilizing and threatening as a philosophy of state.

Other countries and their leaders at the time felt that they were vulnerable and were threatened by Hitler not because he was uniquely evil (that appreciation came generally only rather later), but because he was much more unpredictable. Only in retrospect did they explain their actions by the moral impetus of a revulsion against profound evil.

Notes

1　Tom Harrisson, *Living through the Blitz*, London: Collins, 1976, pp. 23, 24, 39.
2　Keith Feiling, *The Life of Neville Chamberlain*, London: Macmillan, 1946, p. 372.
3　C. Northcote Parkinson, *Parkinson's Law and Other Studies in Administration*, Boston, MA: Houghton Mifflin, 1957, p. 63.
4　E.H. Carr, *The Twenty Years Crisis 1919–1939*, London: Macmillan, 1939, p. 133. Joachim Fest, *Hitler: eine Biographie*, Berlin: Propyläen-Verlag, 1973, p. 939.
5　Carl J. Friedrich and Zbigniew K. Brzezinski, *Totalitarian Dictatorship and Autocracy*, Cambridge, MA: Harvard University Press, 1956.
6　Klaus Hildebrand, *Das vergangene Reich: deutsche Aussenpolitik von Bismarck bis Hitler, 1871–1945*, Stuttgart: Deutsche Verlags-Anstalt, 1995, p. 585.
7　Hildebrand, *Das vergangene Reich*, p. 583.
8　Fest, *Hitler*, p. 652.
9　Ian Kershaw, *Hitler: 1889–1936 – Hubris*, London: Allen Lane, 1998, p. 574. Max Domarus, *Hitler: Reden und Proklamationen 1932–1945*, Vol. 1/2, Wiesbaden: Löwit, 1973, p. 545 (October 8, 1935, speech).
10　Kershaw, *Hubris*, p. 533.
11　Fest, *Hitler*, pp. 939–40.
12　Fred Taylor (ed.), *The Goebbels Diary 1939–1941*, London: Hamish Hamilton, 1982, p. 114 (diary entry of February 6, 1940).
13　Kershaw, *Hubris*, p. 547.
14　Kershaw, *Hubris*, p. 551.
15　Alan Bullock, *Hitler and Stalin: Parallel Lives*, London: HarperCollins, 1991, p. 577.
16　Kershaw, *Hubris*, pp. 527, 529.
17　Kershaw, *Hubris*, p. 122.
18　Catherine Karolyi, *A Life Together*, London: Allen & Unwin, 1961, pp. 298–9.
19　The best short account is to be found in Leszek Kołakowski, *Main Currents of Marxism: Its Origin, Growth and Dissolution. Volume III, Breakdown*, Oxford: Clarendon Press, 1978.
20　Leonard Schapiro, *The Communist Party of the Soviet Union*, London: Eyre & Spottiswoode, 1970, p. 476.
21　E.H. Carr, with R.W. Davies, *Foundations of the Planned Economy, Volume I: 1928– 1929*, Harmondsworth: Penguin, 1974, pp. 943, 947.
22　R.W. Davies, in *Cambridge Economic History of Europe, Vol. VIII*, Cambridge: Cambridge University Press, 1989, pp. 1029–32.
23　Moshe Lewin (transl. Irene Nove with John Biggart), *Russian Peasants and Soviet Power: a Study of Collectivization*, London: Allen & Unwin, 1968, p. 27.

24 N.P. Dubinin, *Perpetual Motion*, Moscow: Politizidat 1973; cited in Zhores A. Medvedev, *Soviet Science*, New York, NY: Norton, 1978, p. 227.

25 See the work of Victoria Bonnell, *Iconography of Power: Soviet Political Posters under Lenin and Stalin*, Berkeley, CA: University of California Press, 1997.

26 Lewin, *Russian Peasants*, p. 77. The preceding pages discuss the problems of defining the kulak with any degree of meaningfulness.

27 Nicholas Werth, "A state against its people", in Stéphane Courtois (ed.) (transl. Jonathan Murphy and Mark Kramer), *The Black Book of Communism: Crimes, Terror, Repression*, Cambridge, MA: Harvard University Press, 1999, p. 171.

28 Werth, "A state", pp. 190, 206–7, 213.

29 Kołakowski, *Main Currents*, p. 82. Robert Conquest, *The Great Terror: Stalin's Purge of the Thirties*, London and New York, NY: Macmillan, 1968, p. 423.

30 Conquest, *Great Terror*, p. 354. John N. Hazard, *Recollections of a Pioneering Sovietologist*, New York, NY: Oceana, 1984, p. 67. Stephen Kotkin, *Magnetic Mountain: Stalinism as a Civilization*, Berkeley, CA: University of California Press, 1995, p. 123.

31 Richard Overy, *Why the Allies Won*, New York, NY: Norton, 1996, pp. 181–2.

32 Bonnell, *Iconography*, p. 257.

33 Cited in Ernest B. Haas, *Nationalism, Liberalism and Progress*, Vol. II, Ithaca, NY: Cornell University Press, 2000, p. 361.

6   The Second World War

The Second World War was a continuation of the First, and marked the end of a long episode of a Thirty Years' War of the twentieth century. In this extension of conflict, Hitler was simply a more extreme version of the radical and destructive populist army command of von Hindenburg and Ludendorff in Imperial Germany. German war aims from 1914 had aimed at extensive annexations and a *Mitteleuropa* dominated by Germany; in the Second World War the demands were much more extensive. The First World War, which had begun as a confrontation of the Great Powers, became in the end also a war of ideas, in which Wilsonian internationalism fought and destroyed autocracy and militarism; and the Second World War too ended with a clash of universal principles and human rights against the brutal view that might was right.

And like the First World War, the Second clearly originated from the calculations of a relatively small number of men about how they could preserve and extend their personal power by foreign policy adventurism. Almost all historians have rightly emphasized how the Nazi regime's murderous anti-Semitism would have been impossible without widespread public participation (and even wider passivity). On the other hand, the decision to go to war followed very much from the vision of a small number of Nazi leaders, and historians have not generally tried to argue that they were captives of public opinion or popular pressure. Interrogated in prison, Hermann Göring said:

> Why of course the people don't want war. Why should some poor slob on a farm want to risk his life in a war when the best he can get out of it is to come back to his farm in one piece? Naturally the common people don't want war; neither in Russia, nor in England, nor in America, nor for that matter in Germany. That is understood. But after all it is the leaders of a country who determine the policy, and it is always a simple matter to drag the people along, whether it is a democracy or a fascist dictatorship.[1]

The immediate origin of the war lay in Hitler's plans and the way the other powers tried to deal with them through the secret diplomacy of the Munich agreement and of the Nazi–Soviet pact.

Blitzkrieg

At the beginning, however, the actual course of the conflict looked quite different from the earlier war. In 1914, the major European armies had mobilized, met in conflict, and suffered horrendous casualties in the first weeks of battle. The war did not remain contained as a conflict between Austria and Serbia. But in 1939 the only fighting was in the localized war over Poland. In September 1939, the German army, supported by airborne attacks, quickly moved into Poland (Plate 6). France and the United Kingdom declared war on September 3, but did not engage in any fighting and remained in a "phony war" (*drôle de guerre*); the Soviet Union invaded eastern Poland on September 17 (and on November 30, also invaded Finland). Germany annexed parts of Poland into Germany as the Warthegau and eastern Upper Silesia; and established a vicious occupation regime in the remainder of the country, the so-called *Generalgouvernement*, run with extraordinary brutality by Gauleiter Hans Frank from the Wawel castle in Krakow.

This was a war in which Hitler aimed to eat the surrounding European states one by one, like leaves of an artichoke. It took some time for the German armed forces to regroup and rearm – the Polish campaign, modest as it was by comparison with the rest of the war, had largely depleted their supplies of munitions. In the spring of 1940, the German armies were

Plate 6 A Polish cavalry charge in 1939: an action widely interpreted as highlighting the hopeless chivalry of the Old World. © Popperfoto/Getty Images.

prepared for new lightning campaigns: on April 9, 1940, German troops invaded Denmark and Norway, with the aim above all of securing continued access to the militarily indispensable Swedish iron ore. They rapidly occupied Copenhagen, and resisted a British counter-attack on Narvik.

In May it was the turn of western Europe: on May 10, the German armies crossed into Belgium, Luxembourg, and the Netherlands. After a tank thrust through the Ardennes, the Germans broke down French resistance, took almost 2 million men prisoner, and entered Paris on June 14. On June 17, a new French government headed by the hero of the First World War, Marshall Philippe Pétain, asked for an armistice. Hitler presented the armistice terms to the French commanders on June 21, in the same railway carriage at Compiègne in which Marshall Foch had received the Germans in November 1918. Hitler even sat in Foch's seat in order to demonstrate how the Versailles treaty was being undone.

The northern part of France was occupied by Germany, and three southern departments by Italy, which had joined the war at the last minute (from June 11). Pétain moved his government to the unoccupied zone, at Vichy. On July 3, in a pre-emptive move to stop Germany from taking France's Mediterranean fleet, British ships sank most of the French fleet in port at Oran and Mers el Kébir.

On July 6, 1940, Hitler staged a grand ceremonial parade on his return from France to Berlin which, in retrospect, marked the height of the German triumph. Field Marshal Keitel proclaimed him "the greatest warlord of all time". Economics Minister Walther Funk sketched out the basis of a new European economic order, in which the European currencies would be finally released from the shackles of the gold standard, but would be fixed in relation to each other. "By concluding long-term agreements with European countries, it is intended that the European economic systems shall adapt themselves to the German market by a system of production planned for the future."[2] The Funk proposals were not intended simply to be blueprints for German economic hegemony over Europe, however; they were intended as an attraction that would tie Europe firmly to the German cause. They were rapidly translated into at least eight languages (including English), and distributed as widely as possible.

At this stage, many people in Berlin thought that the United Kingdom would play a part in the Nazi reordering of Europe, and that the United Kingdom either might be invaded or – more probably – would sue for peace. The next victim of German military action was thus the United Kingdom. An extended aerial conflict from July to October (the Battle of Britain) failed to establish the German air superiority without which a full invasion would have been doomed to fail. When the Chamberlain government was replaced by Winston Churchill (rather than the more orthodox Lord Halifax), and when consequently it became clear that the United Kingdom would not negotiate an armistice, Hitler turned his attention to a new lightning war. He was also disturbed that Stalin seemed to have taken advantage of Germany's western engagements, and had occupied parts of Lithuania and the southern part of Bukovina (from Romania), in contravention of the secret protocols of August 23, 1939. On July 31, 1940, he summoned the military leadership to his mountain retreat at Berchtesgaden and announced: "England's hope is Russia and America. If the hope of Russia disappears, so does that of America. When Russia is defeated, England's last hope will be destroyed." At this stage, he contemplated a lightning strike against Russia in the spring of 1941, after a new pause in which the German military could restock. On December 18, he made a definite decision to launch an attack on the Soviet Union. In March 1941 in a speech in Berlin, he announced that Germany would win the war that year.

The decision on an exact date was delayed by other considerations. In October 1940, Mussolini had expected to be able to score a quick victory against Greece via Albania, but the Italian army met determined opposition and General Papagos pushed it back far into Albania. Hitler, feeling that he could not leave the Balkan question unresolved, extended an already existing pact with Hungary, Romania, and Slovakia to include Bulgaria, and then tried to persuade Yugoslavia to join. The Yugoslav Prince Regent signed the German pact, but was deposed by anti-German politicians and soldiers who installed King Peter as head of state. Attacking with very powerful forces on April 6, 1941, Germany quickly overran Yugoslavia, and by the end of May had subdued mainland Greece and a substantial number of islands, including Crete.

Less important distractions came from the German home front. On August 25, 1940, the British Royal Air Force staged a bombing raid on Berlin as a retaliation for attacks on the East End of London – a raid which the German air force had assured Hitler was impossible.

Germany also worried about the position of the United States, which had effectively isolated itself from European conflicts through the 1937 Neutrality Act, which embargoed arms sales to any belligerents. In November 1939 a revised Act allowed such sales, as long as they were paid for by the belligerents ("cash and carry"), a proviso which in effect still excluded the financially drained combatants from accessing the American market. After the fall of France showed how immediate was the threat to democracy, President Roosevelt moved closer to supplying the British needs for weapons. He now agreed a deal in which old destroyers were sold in exchange for British permission to use some naval bases. Once Roosevelt was re-elected in the November 1940 elections (to an unprecedented third term of office) he could move with more ease, and in January 1941 spoke about the "Four Freedoms". He now promised to supply arms to the democracies (at this point, in effect, only the United Kingdom was fighting in Europe). But the position of the United States and the United Kingdom was increasingly irrelevant to Hitler, who now concentrated on the eastern goals that he had written about in the 1920s, in his published autobiography, *Mein Kampf*, as well as in an unpublished manuscript (later known as the Second Book).

Operation Barbarossa, the attack on the Soviet Union eventually launched on June 22, 1941, was a Blitzkrieg operation. Hitler's advisers had assured him that the demoralized Soviet army would be quickly destroyed. He believed that the war would be "more or less over" in six weeks, and the Chief of the General Staff noted in his diary in early July that he expected only another fortnight of fighting.

Racial war

Barbarossa was also the culmination of Hitler's ideological obsessions: with the acquisition of large territorial expanses in the east, with the danger of international communism, and with racial wars to be waged against Jews, Slavs, and inferior peoples. On the anniversary of his seizure of power, on January 30, 1939, Hitler had told the Reichstag:

> If international finance Jewry in and outside Europe succeeds in plunging the peoples in a world war again, the consequence will not be the Bolshevization of the world and thus the triumph of Jewry, but on the contrary the annihilation of the Jewish race in Europe.

The historian Lucy Dawidowicz has appropriately called this speech "Hitler's declaration of war against the Jews".[3] The speech made a clear association between international finance (the West) and the Soviet Union, and described both as dominated by, or working for the interests of, Jews. On September 1, 1939, Hitler said that "a November 1918 [the collapse that he ascribed to Judeo-Bolshevist revolution on the home front] shall not be repeated in German history". These "prophecies" were frequently repeated by other German leaders, and used as the basis for more specific and murderous action. In November 1939, for instance, Göring said that there would need to be a big "reckoning" (*Abrechnung*) with the Jews.

Immediately after September 1939, German soldiers had begun a large-scale resettlement of eastern Europe, which involved the moving of Poles, the ghettoization of Jews, and the transfer to the new territories of German settlers, including Germans from the Soviet Union (the Volga and Volhynia Germans). They had also been given instructions to destroy the Polish elite, which involved a great deal of murder, in which there were many Jewish victims. On September 21, 1939, Reinhard Heydrich, the head of the *SS-Reichssicherheitshauptamt* (literally Reich Security Main Office), ordered the annexed areas of Poland "to be made free of Jews".[4]

On the other hand, the new *Generalgouverneur* of Poland, Hans Frank, tried to resist the resettlement of Jews in the *Generalgouvernement*, which, he explained, he did not want to see turned into a "human trash can". Jews had already been marginalized, deliberately. In humiliating and expropriating Jews immediately after the annexation of Austria in March 1938, Reich

Commissar Joseph Bürckel, one of the major instigators of a new method of "dealing with" Jews, quite explicitly declared:

> One should never forget that if one decides to 'aryanize' and take the natural basis of existence away from Jews, that one should then solve the Jewish question totally. It is impossible to think that the Jew should be a rentier of the state.[5]

A systematic dehumanization was the preliminary to mass murder.

One other strand of racist thinking went into the eventual systematic genocide of the European Jews. Eugenic theory had long suggested that some sorts of people were "unfit". In July 1933, Germany began the compulsory sterilization of disabled people, as did other European countries: the Swiss canton of Vaud from 1928, Denmark from 1929, Sweden from 1935 (and continuing until 1975), and Finland from 1935. These policies were heavily driven by fear that the mentally ill should be an increasing burden on welfare state systems. Germany went further and redescribed the mentally ill as "life unworthy of life". In the summer of 1939, as Germany prepared for war, there were calculations about the number of hospital beds that might be required to treat the wounded. Killing "life unworthy of life" might open hospital places and free scarce resources. This "euthanasia" or mercy killing was begun under the direction of an SS office on the Tiergartenstrasse 4 in Berlin-Charlottenburg (and was referred to by the code of T4). Hitler authorized it in a letter he signed in October 1939, but which was backdated to September 1, the day of the outbreak of war. According to this letter, which was not widely known and whose legal status was quite unclear, "patients who, on the basis of human judgment, are considered incurable, can be granted mercy death after a discerning diagnosis".[6] The Ministry of Justice found out about the Hitler letter only when it had to deal with complaints by relatives of killed patients, in the summer of 1940. Only on August 27, 1940, did Justice Minister Franz Gürtner abandon his investigation of the killing, on the grounds that he could not oppose the will of the Führer. Under the SS program, some 70,000 to 80,000 victims were killed before August 1941. Then the T4 "action" was suddenly halted, after a public denunciation of euthanasia by Bishop Clemens von Galen in Münster. Von Galen had said that the killing was openly discussed in the Reich Interior Ministry. Von Galen himself was threatened, but not punished. The provost of St Hedwig's cathedral in Berlin, Bernhard Lichtenberg, who wrote to support von Galen and also to protest against the persecution of the Jews, was arrested.

In addition to the attacks on the mentally and physically disabled, the theorists of racial purity also turned on the small population of mixed race (what was termed "colored") Germans, usually the offspring of black French occupation soldiers in the Ruhr: they were sterilized from 1937. Roma and Sinti ("gypsies"), who formed a tiny part of the German population (0.05 percent in 1933), and were accused of lawlessness and criminality, were interned in camps from 1933, and from 1940 transported from the annexed parts of Poland to the *Generalgouvernement* in an analogous manner to the deportation of Jews. In 1941, systematic deportations began.

The occupation of Poland and the shift of populations between occupied Poland and the *Generalgouvernement* were in practice a preparation for policies that would ultimately be applied on a much more generalized basis. In the course of resettlement (*Umsiedlung*), around 10,000 mentally ill people were killed in the areas annexed by Germany. The mobile gas-truck killings in the Warthegau, supervised by the personnel of the T4 program, represented a preliminary action to the eventual onslaught against the Jews.

Hitler himself talked to high German military officers in March 1941 of a brutal "war of racial annihilation". At the same time, orders were given to establish four *Einsatzgruppen* which would operate "independently" of military operations. These contained around 3,000 men, but were supplemented by a substantial number of police units (initially 11, later 26), as well as local non-German security forces, which would be recruited into the German killing effort. They would, their orders went, attack communist functionaries and Jews in leading party and state positions, and support what Reinhard Heydrich termed "the self-cleansing initiatives of anti-communist and anti-Jewish groups in the areas to be newly occupied".[7] Already by August 4, 30,000 persons had been killed; but then there was a dramatic increase in the pace of killing, and about 500,000 people, mostly Jews, were killed by the *Einsatzgruppen* before the spring of 1942: in other words, before the fully worked-out plan for the systematic "Final Solution of the Jewish Question" was bureaucratically prepared. At the same time, there were also systematic killings of Soviet prisoners-of-war (PoWs). The best-known case of a massacre by non-Germans is that at Jedwabne in eastern Poland on July 10, 1941, where at least 250–300 Jews were killed by Poles. But there were also dozens of similar actions in the neighborhood of Jedwabne.[8] In the Baltic states, local police forces rounded up and killed Jews.

Behind the front, one part of the SS worked out a plan to destroy Jewish lives in gigantic construction projects (above all, road building); in Galicia around 20,000 died in this way, in the Lublin district between 50,000 and 70,000. A conflict developed between one part of the SS, which wanted to extract the maximum labor potential from slave populations, and those who thought that the racial war of extermination (often dressed up as the "mercy killing" of unfortunate victims who had no humanity) had an unquestionable priority.

In September 1941, German Jews were obliged to wear a Star of David visibly sewn on their clothing (Polish Jews had faced a similar regulation since 1939), apparently at the insistence of Joseph Goebbels, who viewed the measure as a prelude to worse treatment. From October 1941, Jews from Germany were deported to overcrowded ghettoes. In the summer of 1942 Jews were deported from Belgium, France, and the Netherlands. In two of Germany's allies, Bulgaria and Hungary, Jews remained for the most part relatively safe – until the alliance collapsed, and Germans occupied

Hungary. Other allies – Slovakia under Father Tiso, and Croatia – deported and killed their Jews with enthusiasm.

The conference held in an SS villa in the Berlin suburb of Wannsee on January 20, 1942, was a high-level meeting of all the leading civil servants involved in the planning of deportation and murder. It had originally been scheduled for December 9, 1941, but had been delayed because of the upheaval in the aftermath of Pearl Harbor. Some historians, notably Christian Gerlach,[9] have argued that Hitler made a decision on December 12, and that there was a link between the full-scale implementation of the Judeocide and Germany's declaration of war on the United States. This thesis is unlikely, but the new globalization of the war made a difference to one group of Jewish victims: those from wealthier backgrounds, held in western Europe (the majority in the camp in Bergen-Belsen) with the idea of ransoming them for the hard currency that Germany needed for its war effort. Even some east European Jews, judged to be more prosperous, were sent to these western ransom camps. Some 20,000 Polish Jews were interned in Belsen and an analogous camp at Vittel. Though the idea of "Jews for sale" was never given up, and was revived in the last stages of the war, the intensified economic war of the United Kingdom and the United States meant that such ransoms stood little chance of becoming a widespread practice.[10] Indeed, even many of the Jews who were ransomed were actually tricked, and were killed.

The Wannsee Conference also assured Göring's representative that Jews working in munitions factories would not be deported.

Most of the Polish ghettoes were cleared entirely between July and December 1942, and the occupants dispatched to annihilation camps. The Warsaw ghetto was left to last, and in April and May 1943 staged a heroic but desperate rising against the German occupation forces. When the killing camps were overstrained, there were mass executions through shooting.

The move to a systematic or industrialized killing was pushed by Himmler, who had been disturbed in August 1941 when he actually witnessed the shooting of around a hundred partisans. At this point, T4 euthanasia specialists were sent to the eastern areas, and on October 13, 1941, Himmler authorized the construction of a site whose only purpose was killing: Bełzec. Subsequently, there were similar killing sites in Treblinka, Sobibór, Majdanek, and Chełmno.

The largest number of Jews, however, died at Auschwitz, where all elements of the murderous Nazi plans came together: the exploitation of Jewish labor, with disregard for massive loss of life, in a big factory of the chemical firm IG Farben; the killing of those unfit to work; at times, also, the immediate killing of strong and healthy adult men; and Josef Mengele's purportedly scientific experiments, supported by research grants from the German Scientific Research Corporation (*Deutsche Forschungsgemeinschaft*). Survival in the dehumanized environment of Auschwitz depended in large part on the chance of an arrival date: coming when there was a shortage of workers lengthened lives; arriving at the height of deportations was an almost certain death sentence. The enormity of the crimes, and the diversity of the countries from which the victims came, made Auschwitz into the perverse realization of the Nazi vision (Plate 7).

Oświęcim was a small town with a population of some 12,000 (of which a substantial proportion were Jews) and an old barracks complex, created originally by the Austrian army at the time of Maria Theresa. It was conveniently placed at the intersection of major railroad routes, and was just inside the Polish territory annexed to Germany as the Warthegau. The Germans renamed the settlement Auschwitz. In early 1940, Heinrich Himmler ordered the SS to inspect possible sites for a concentration camp, and in April the SS agreed to lease the barracks and to create a camp capable of holding 10,000 prisoners. In May 1940 a small group of German criminal prisoners from the camp in Sachsenhausen near Berlin was sent to Auschwitz (and given numbers from 1 to 30) to work on preparing the site for its new function. The first large group of prisoners in June 1940 was composed of 728 Polish prisoners, including many Jews, who were transferred from the prison in Tarnów. In May 1941, when the attack on the Soviet Union was being prepared, Himmler visited Auschwitz for the first time and ordered its extension to a capacity of 30,000 prisoners, with a new camp in nearby Birkenau for 100,000 PoWs. He proposed to invite

Plate 7 Children as the victims of genocide: Jewish children in Auschwitz. © Alexander Vorontsov/Galerie Bilderwelt/Getty Images.

IG Farben to construct a factory, which would be constructed largely by slave labor; and to bring in a large range of other industries, concerned above all with the supply of armaments. In 1942 a ramp was built for the unloading of prisoners at the goods station in Auschwitz, and in May 1944, at the moment when the mass deportations from Hungary were beginning, Birkenau was directly linked to the rail system.

At first prisoners in Auschwitz were carefully registered, photographed, and numbered. When large numbers of Soviet PoWs arrived in the autumn of 1941, the registration system became overstretched, and numbers were stamped on their chest by a machine with one-centimeter pins. This also was too time-consuming, and later a simpler tattoo, usually on the lower left arm, was used by the SS to identify prisoners. The photography was stopped because of a shortage of material.

Even at the beginning, there was an abnormally high rate of mortality. Between May 1940 and January 1942, the carefully kept records show 4,271 as "diminution" (*Abgang*) through release or death, but another 20,000 prisoners were unaccounted for and were no longer registered as inmates. Apart from beatings, shootings, and mistreatment, the SS also experimented with lethal injections with phenol, and (from August 1941) with poison gas, at first in a basement of Block 11 in the old camp and then in the crematorium in that camp. By the beginning of March only 945 Soviet prisoners were still alive, and from March gas chambers near the Birkenau camp (Auschwitz II) were systematically used to kill prisoners, sometimes on arrival in the camp. In the summer of 1942, the construction of four large crematoria was ordered, and they were operational by the spring of 1943 and were directly connected with newly constructed gas chambers. From July 1942, regular selections began, including selections of newly arrived prisoners. At this stage, 80 percent of the arriving deportees were condemned to immediate death.

Those who survived the selection slowly died of malnutrition, overwork, and epidemic disease. Once starved into a skeletal condition (which the camp vocabulary termed *Muselmann*), they would be condemned in new selections. Prisoners in Auschwitz were carefully classified by ethnicity or race, or as "asocial". Jehovah's Witnesses wore a violet triangle, Catholic priests a red one, homosexuals a pink one, criminals a green one, and Jews yellow. From the summer of 1942, the overwhelming majority of the prisoners were Jewish.

Though resistance was almost hopeless, there were underground organizations, revolts, and even escapes. In October 1944, the Jewish members of a special task force killed several guards and destroyed Crematorium IV. Some of the escapees brought out details of the camp life and above all the scale of camp death. In April 1944 Rudolf Vrba and Alfred Wetzler escaped, and then compiled a report in which they estimated that 1,765,000 Jews had been killed in Auschwitz since April 1942.

It is actually hard to be precise about the number of victims of Auschwitz. More than 400,000 camp inmates were registered, but the registration system soon broke down; and there is no doubt that Jews constituted the overwhelming majority of the unregistered victims, most of whom were killed immediately upon arrival. The most recent estimate is that 1.1 million Jews were deported to Auschwitz, and that around 200,000 were registered as prisoners. The rest were immediately killed.

The killings went on until the evacuation of the camp, in lethal forced marches and sometimes in open coal trucks, in January 1945 because of the approach of the Red Army.

As with the deaths at Auschwitz, the overall number of victims of the Nazi genocide is impossible to establish with complete precision, in large part because of uncertainty about the extent (and ethnic composition) of the Soviet victims. The overall number of Jewish victims of Nazism was over 6 million (over 3 million of whom were Polish citizens, with 270,000 Romanians, 200,000 Hungarians, and 160,000 Germans). At least 250,000 Roma and Sinti were murdered.

Auschwitz soon became a synonym for absolute evil: the evil both of the speedy killing following the selection process, and of the progressive deliberate degradation and dehumanization of those who survived the selections. It is only relatively recently that it has become clear how deeply and directly involved German society and German business were in the concrete implementation of genocide. IG Farben's Monowitz works was situated near Auschwitz in part because of geographic considerations: the new synthetic rubber plant should be built out of range of British bombers. But it was also clear that the SS and its supply of slave labor was a major inducement in an economy that was increasingly starved of labor. Many other businesses besides IG Farben worked in or near Auschwitz. The largest German insurance firm insured the SS barracks. The big Swiss banks provided trade credit for the import of timber for the barracks. The largest Austrian bank managed the transfer of funds from relatives to individual inmates (though in practice, they could buy little that was useful with such funds). The local branch of the largest German bank financed building companies that constructed the extended camps. Bombed-out Germans were given clothing, shoes, and watches that had been taken from arriving deportees. Gold from Auschwitz and the death camps, including dental gold taken from the mouths of living or dead prisoners, was used first in the dental treatment of SS members, and then – when the dental service reported that its stocks were very high – was melted down and refined, sold to the *Reichsbank*, and then resold to German commercial banks as well as to the Swiss National Bank. The links of terror and despoliation reached far and wide.

In part this involvement may reflect a deliberate decision by the SS to try to bring more people in Germany into contact with its criminal behavior. Himmler had been trying to interest business in his captive labor force from the early beginnings, in 1935, at that time without any success. He wanted to make his institution a central part of the new postwar Germany, and extending its influence meant extending its web of criminality.

Reports of what was happening in the eastern killing fields also came to the neutral countries and to the western allies. Apart from winning the war quickly, however, there was little that could be done in London and Washington to stop the killing. Precision bombing of any target in the camps or on railroad lines (which could anyway be quite easily repaired) was at that time an impossibility, and had such capacity existed it would presumably have been better expended in attacking the control centers of the regime in Rastenburg, Berchtesgaden, and Berlin. The negotiations that the SS from time to time proposed about ransoming Jews were deeply duplicitous and insincere. Jews in the United Kingdom and the United States were paralyzed. In August 1942 Gerhart Riegner of the World Jewish Congress in Geneva sent a cable to a prominent American and a British Jewish leader referring to a

> plan discussed and under consideration according to which all Jews in countries occupied or controlled by Germany numbering 3½–4 million should after deportation and concentration in east be exterminated at one blow to resolve once and for all the Jewish question in Europe.

After Riegner's cable, Nahum Goldmann told the Zionist Organization of America: "One half of the generation is being slaughtered before our eyes, and the other half has to sit down and cannot prevent this catastrophe."[11]

World war

With the war against the Soviet Union, the war became an ideological war, and a world war. In occupied Europe, the Germans announced that this was a war against Bolshevism. This provided the rationale for continued collaboration. Pierre Laval announced that he "wished for the victory of Germany, because without her, Bolshevism will install itself everywhere in Europe".

Hitler himself dismissed this rationale. He was outraged in July 1941 when a Vichy French newspaper suggested that a "European war" against Bolshevism was being fought.[12] The highpoint of German ideas about a New Order had come earlier, in the summer of 1940, when the concept was used to try to lure Europe into a German-dominated peace, and later, in 1944, when its readoption was a gesture of Germany's hopelessness. Economics Minister Walther Funk in 1944 repeated his European economic schemes of 1940 in an address, again in Königsberg, but no one could take such proposals seriously any longer.

In 1941 and 1942, Hitler was no longer thinking in European terms, but in a strategy operating at a global level. In mid-July 1941, he suggested that Germany had the same fundamental enemies as Japan, namely the United States and the Soviet Union, and that Japan should occupy the eastern territories of the Soviet Union.

On August 14, 1941, the Atlantic Charter set out some Anglo-American "common principles in the national policies of their respective countries on which they base their hopes for a better future for the world", which included "no aggrandizement, territorial or other"; "no territorial changes that do not accord with the freely expressed wishes of the peoples concerned"; "the right of all peoples to choose the form of government under which they will live"; and a postwar world in which people "in all lands may live out their lives in freedom from fear and want".

It was not clear when Hitler believed that Germany would fight the United States. In October 1941, he told the Italian Foreign Minister Count Ciano that a solution of "the Europe–America problem" would need to be left to a future generation.[13] But in the same way as the failure to make a decisive breakthrough in the Battle of Britain produced the resolution to resolve the war in a bigger context by invading the Soviet Union, so the fact that there was no quick end to Operation Barbarossa led Hitler to globalize the war.

When Japan reacted to the US oil embargo with an air attack on the Pacific Fleet in Pearl Harbor (December 7), two days after a large Soviet counter-offensive had started in Moscow, Hitler declared war on the United States (December 11). On January 18, 1942, a military agreement between Germany, Italy, and Japan was signed in Berlin.

At this point, Germany needed to completely change the basis of the war economy. Previously, the German economic preparation for war had focused on what the planners termed "armament in breadth", the stockpiling of a gigantic arsenal that could be unleashed, but that would need replenishing before a new wave of military onslaughts. The strategy suited the German economic situation, in which raw material supplies were constrained by the naval power of the United Kingdom and then the United States, and there were labor shortages already in the militarized peacetime economy of the late 1930s. But when the Blitzkrieg against Russia failed, a new approach to economic management became an urgent priority. A shift to "armament in depth", in which there could be steady new supplies, required a reorganization of the war economy, and in addition ran counter to the German tradition of flexible production, using adjustable machine tools. The United States, which historically had concentrated on specialized machine tools, found it much easier to engage in standardized production on a very large scale. Thus, the constraints on the German war economy remained, and Germany was short of both the raw materials and the labor required for intensive skill-based production.

The first attempt to reform the German war economy in order to be able to provide the continual resupply of armaments came with a Führer decree of December 3, 1941, ordering a rationalization and standardization of weapons production. In February 1942 the Munitions Minister Fritz Todt was killed in a plane crash, and was immediately succeeded by the young architect Albert Speer. Speer abandoned some of the earlier notions of a centralized command economy, reorganized the war economy in production rings, left much more to industrial self-management, and halted the sporadic dismantling of plants in occupied Europe.

It was harder to deal with the shortage of raw materials. Germany found petroleum scarce (since the German armies never securely controlled the oil-fields of the Caucasus in the Soviet Union), and Romania extracted a heavy price for its petroleum supply. The decisive constraint of the First World War reappeared. As German fortunes worsened, the Romanian government insisted on payment in convertible currency or gold. Another bottleneck lay in the supply of metal ores required in precision steelmaking, in particular wolfram, which Germany imported from Spain, Portugal, and South America. Again, in order to pay, Germany required hard currency. The military and economic need for hard currency to buy military supplies and strategic goods prompted another wave of looting. From the beginning of the war, Germany had applied harsh currency regulations in occupied areas. *Devisenschutzkommandos* of the SS moved in to seize precious metals, foreign exchange, and jewelry, in defiance of prevailing international law. Germany also seized the gold reserves of central banks in occupied countries, getting large amounts from the Netherlands and Belgium.

The other constraint on German war mobilization, the shortage of manpower, was solved with equally brutal methods. Foreign workers, designated differently and treated differently according to nationality, were conscripted into the German workforce. At the beginning of the war, most of the foreign labor (at that time mostly Polish) was employed in agricultural work. Together with Speer's reordering of the war economy in 1942, Gauleiter Fritz Sauckel of Thuringia was appointed as Plenipotentiary for Labor. At first he tried to recruit volunteers, but in August 1942 he issued a decree imposing compulsory labor service in the occupied territories. Soviet PoWs, treated differently from western prisoners on the pretext that the USSR had not signed the Geneva Convention of 1926 on the treatment of PoWs, were conscripted and treated despicably. Concentration camp labor was also used in the war economy as slave labor. In August 1944, a total of 7.6 million compulsory foreign workers and PoWs were employed. Most were civilians (5.7 million). Of the total, 2.8 million were Russians, 1.7 million Poles, 1.3 million French, and 600,000 Italians. Foreign forced labor constituted 46 percent of agricultural workers in Germany, 34 percent of miners, 32 percent of building workers, 30 percent of metalworkers, and even 6 percent of employment in banking.[14]

At the same time as Germany moved to total mobilization, the German attitude to anti-Soviet propaganda shifted: it suddenly looked as if it would be useful to Germany to encourage Ukrainians and Poles to be wary of Stalin. On April 13, 1943, Berlin radio announced that at Katyń near Smoleńsk, German soldiers had found a pit containing 12 layers of bodies of Polish officers, many with their hands tied behind their backs; some 3,000 bodies in all. But such attempts to win over east Europeans were mostly stymied by the clear brutality of the occupation regime.

It took rather a long time for the US economy to gear up for war production. 1942 might indeed easily have been a year of triumph for the Axis powers, but the military offensives were too uncoordinated. Japan pushed forward in the first half of the year with some dramatic successes, but was halted by the battle of Midway in June; while the German offensive in Russia resumed only in late June, and a large German offensive in North Africa began. In 1941 and 1942 German submarine attacks had made the Atlantic supply route from the United States to the United Kingdom dangerous. The interception of coded messages, and the use of radar by the western allies, gradually limited German operations. On July 5, 1942, the first German U-boat (submarine) to be detected by air-to-surface radar was sunk in the Bay of Biscay. But the real breakthrough in the war of the Atlantic did not come until the summer of 1943.

Pressed hard by Stalin to open a second front, the United States sent soldiers to North Africa on November 8, 1942. The French government's Head of Armed Forces, Admiral Darlan, quickly announced that France would not defend North Africa. Though he was disavowed by Pétain, on November 11, 1942, the German army moved into the southern half of France, the previously unoccupied zone run by Pétain's government in Vichy.

At this stage, the Allies raised the issue of the German treatment of Jews, and on December 17, 1942, a joint Allied declaration referred to reliable reports that the German authorities "are now carrying into effect Hitler's oft repeated intention to exterminate the Jewish people in Europe". It added that the Allied governments reaffirmed "their solemn resolution to ensure that those responsible for these crimes shall not escape retribution, and to press on with the necessary practical measures to this end".[15] At Casablanca on January 24, 1943, the western allies agreed a policy of unconditional surrender, in large part in order to assuage Soviet doubts that they were adequately committed to the anti-Hitler coalition. The decision ruled out any kind of peace negotiation with Germany, though the statement issued by the United Nations (the wartime coalition) specified: "In our uncompromising policy we mean no harm to the common people of the Axis nations. But we do mean to impose punishment and retribution in full upon their guilty, barbaric leaders."

At the beginning of February 1943, the German army, encircled and cut off at Stalingrad, surrendered. This was a first decisive defeat. But it was not – yet – the moment at which it became clear to many in Europe and Germany that Hitler could not win the war. Hitler himself went into a rapid physical decline, and kept going with an endless mixture of pills and potions; he developed a visible shake in his hand, and complained that he always tended to fall toward the right; when he went outside, he needed an abnormally broad peak on his military cap to shade him from the light. He refused to visit bombed cities, insisted that the shades on his car were drawn when he went through the streets of Berlin, and remained for Germany as an invisible but ever threatening presence.

On February 18, 1943, Goebbels in a speech in the Berlin Sportpalast asked his audience "Do you want total war?" It roared its approval: "Führer command, we will obey."

In practice, however, the very detailed intelligence reports collected by the *Sicherbeitsdienst* reveal growing apathy, cynicism, and a conviction that Germany would be defeated. More and more soldiers were shot for disciplinary offenses; civilians were taken to a savage People's Court (*Volksgerichtsbof*). The decisive moment of demoralization followed the great tank battle of Kursk in the summer of 1943, where Hitler had ordered the German Panzers to attack a Soviet salient, and 4,000 Soviet tanks engaged with 3,000 German tanks. By October 1943, the intelligence chief on the Eastern Front, General Gehlen, reported that "in the future the Soviet-Russian enemy will surpass Germany in terms of manpower, equipment, and in the field of propaganda".[16]

German businesses started planning for peace, which they recognized would be a peace imposed by the Allies. Through Swiss newspapers and other reports, they followed with great attention the discussion of the United Nations monetary and economic conference at Bretton Woods. At the same time, they continued to treat forced and slave laborers with brutality and inhumanity. That behavior seems to contradict the enthusiastic planning for peace; it can be explained rationally only by a conviction that it was essential for German business to build up as much wartime capacity as possible in order to be well situated to take advantage of the coming peacetime boom. This is not the only possible explanation. Much of the brutality was driven by lower- and middle-level employees, who had become brutally ideological and identified with the Nazi Party and its efforts to radically transform the German economy.

Conventional power structures in general disintegrated: in the civil service, in business life, and in the army. Especially on the Eastern Front, the rate of casualties was so high that a new leadership style emerged. German officers did not have to ask their superiors' permission to marry any more, and they no longer needed a high school graduation (*Abitur*).

Hitler and a few faithful reverted to a sort of dreamland, in which they asserted that willpower alone could win the war for Germany. They consoled themselves by reading Thomas Carlyle's history of Frederick the Great and its story of triumph over adversity. Joseph Goebbels engaged in some of his greatest propaganda exercises, such as the making of the (color) historical movie *Kolberg*, with thousands of soldiers working as extras, to extol the heroism of German resistance in the Napoleonic Wars. The film was airlifted into the surrounded German positions in La Rochelle in order to encourage continued resistance.

Faced with continued military setbacks, and in part also revolted by the brutality and inhumanity of the regime, a part of the officer corps staged an astonishingly far-ranging conspiracy to assassinate Hitler and replace him with a government that would represent a "different Germany", and that might also conclude a peace with the Allies on better terms. The bomb placed by Count Claus Schenk von Stauffenberg in Hitler's eastern field headquarters, the *Wolfschanze* near Rastenburg in the Masurian Lakes, on July 20,

1944, exploded; but it had been moved slightly after von Stauffenberg left the room, and failed to kill Hitler. Within hours, the Nazi leadership had reasserted itself, and loyalist officers arrested the military conspirators.

A month before the bomb plot, the western allies had at last opened up the "second front", with landings in Normandy. Hitler responded to the attack by removing resources from Army Group Center on the Eastern Front.

Along with the fighting against Germany in the east, there was fighting about the shape of postwar society. In Poland, the Soviet-backed Armia Ludowa or AL (Workers' Army) fought the Nazis, but also the non-communist Armia Krajowa or AK (Home Army), which it tried to incorporate. The Polish government in London pressed Churchill and Roosevelt against making concessions to Stalin over the postwar frontier of Poland. In order to strengthen their position, they wanted a dramatic gesture on the part of the AK: a demonstration that the Soviet army was not needed to liberate Poland. By July 1944, the London government thought that Warsaw could rise against the German occupation. The Soviets apparently supported this idea: the first radio appeal to the citizens of Warsaw to take to arms was made on the Soviet-run Radio Komciuszko on July 29. On August 1, the rising began. Hitler immediately appointed a brutal SS-*Obergruppenführer*, Erich von dem Bach-Zelewski, to suppress the revolt. Stalin did nothing to help the Poles of Warsaw, though the Red Army artillery could be heard in Warsaw. When Poles, Americans, and British leaders appealed to Stalin to let Soviet airfields be used by western aircraft in support of the uprising, he refused. He told the London leader Stanisław Mikołajczyk in mid-August that after careful consideration he believed the revolt to be a "reckless adventure causing useless victims among the inhabitants".[17] By October 2, when the last resistance was over, 15,000 members of the AK and 150,000–200,000 civilians had been killed; 10,000 German soldiers were dead. Hitler ordered the leveling of what remained of Warsaw.

An almost exactly parallel operation occurred in Slovakia, where a quarter of the Slovakian army joined a "free Slovakia" resistance movement, which was suppressed in October by German soldiers and SS units, including the Dirlewanger Brigade, which had just arrived from its butchery in the suppression of the Warsaw uprising.

In the autumn of 1944, the western advance came to a halt, as a parachute attack on the Dutch city of Arnhem, with its bridges over the River Rhine, failed ("a bridge too far"); and as Hitler personally dictated the last great German offensive of the war, in the Ardennes. In January 1945, as the Red Army again advanced on the River Vistula, Hitler again removed troops, this time to send to Hungary and the Baltic. In February the Soviet army reached the River Oder, and in March the United States army captured the first intact bridge over the Rhine, at Remagen. On April 1, 1945, the Soviet commander Marshal Ivan Konev told the Allied supreme commander, General Eisenhower, that Berlin was not an immediate target, and that Soviet troops would not fight for Berlin until the middle of May. It was a nice way to mark

April Fools' Day, because on the same day he ordered the Soviet offensive on the German capital to begin on April 16; on April 27, Russian and American troops met up at Torgau on the River Elbe.

Himmler made peace feelers through Swedish intermediaries in February and April, and released a small number of Jews as a sign of goodwill: of his intention, as he put it, "to bury the hatchet" between Jews and Germans. The news of these negotiations provoked an explosion of rage from Hitler, and cost the life of Himmler's liaison officer with the Führer's headquarters.

In the night of April 29/30, shortly after Hitler had heard on the radio how Mussolini's corpse had been hung upside down in Milan, Hitler and his wife of 24 hours, Eva Braun, killed themselves. Apart from the Irish government, which delivered its condolence to the German Embassy in Dublin, and that of Portugal, which ordered flags to be flown at half mast, few felt any sadness or surprise. The German high command in the west signed an armistice on May 8, and the fighting in Europe was over (Plate 8).

The Nazi New Order in Europe

Germany had set about reorganizing a new Europe, in large part because it had needed economic support for its war effort: both production and labor resources. In Poland and in the areas captured from the Soviet Union, the

Plate 8 The romance of resistance: partisans in Milan, 1945. © Keystone/Getty Images.

new regime was built around the German military and the SS. This was a regime of terror, with massive exploitation, but on the whole little economic benefit for the exploiter. The paradox of domination was that any effective extraction of resources required subtlety rather than just simple brutality. It needed the creation of collaboration, or collaborationism, but this was a hopeless proposition where the local population was treated with inhumanity and brutality. Elsewhere, however, even in occupied Europe, the Nazi regime depended on the establishment of a collaboration with existing elites: a collaboration which inevitably, as the tide of war turned, did much to discredit those elites.

The most valuable parts of Hitler's empire in quantitative terms were in northern and western Europe. Of the total resources extracted from occupied Europe – around 85–90 billion Reichsmarks, which amounted to about a quarter of the total military expenditure – 35.1 billion came from France, 12 billion from the Netherlands, 9.3 billion from Belgium, 4.9 million from Norway, and 2.5 million from Denmark. Considered relative to population, this extraction amounted to the lowest level in Denmark (771 Reichsmarks per head), and the most in Norway (1,956); the Netherlands (1,600), Belgium (1,281), and partly-occupied France (966) lay in-between. Occupied France, Belgium, and the Netherlands were run by the German military.

In Denmark the monarchy remained, and there was substantial latitude for domestic policy, in part because the country was so close to Germany and so easily dominated. As a result, a quite courageous government stopped the deportation of Jews, sent the majority abroad to safety in Sweden, and insisted on official visits to the relatively small number of Jews who had been taken to Theresienstadt. No Danish Jews took the route on which most German and west European Jews in Theresienstadt were forced by the Germans, to death in Auschwitz. Norway, on the other hand, with a much stricter occupation regime, and a much more fascist local government (under the former Minister of War, Vidkun Quisling), deported almost all of its very small Jewish population to Germany.

Parts of the new Europe were allied to Hitler, rather than directly dominated. Italy had entered the war quite late, in June 1940, at the moment of the German victory in France. Mussolini had consciously decided to delay fighting as long as possible. But he had moved into Hitler's foreign policy and ideological orbit much earlier: by the time of Munich, he was fundamentally an ally of the Führer. In 1938, Italy adopted racial and anti-Semitic laws (before that, Mussolini had been quite contemptuous of anti-Semitism, and there were some Jewish members of the Fascist Party).

In late 1940, the Italian armies were defeated in Greece and North Africa, and the navy badly damaged by a British attack. At this point, Mussolini was obliged to humiliate himself by begging Hitler for assistance. By 1943, as the Italian armies retreated from Libya into Tunisia, he lost his nerve. He sacked his Foreign Minister, his son-in-law Count Ciano, and seemed to be running the Italian government single-handedly although he was by now almost constantly sick, had difficulty speaking, and did a great deal of business by telephone from his bed. In July, the Allies began their landings in Sicily. On July 19, Rome was bombed. On July 24–25, a long meeting of the fascist Grand Council exhausted Mussolini physically and ended by voting a resolution that asked King Vittorio Emanuele to save Italy from destruction. When Mussolini saw the King the next day, he was told that Marshal Badoglio had been appointed as Prime Minister, and he was arrested on leaving the Villa Savoia.

Badoglio eventually negotiated an armistice (September 1943), to which the German army responded by seizing north and central Italy. Mussolini, who had been rescued from Italian captivity by a German SS commando raid, set up a puppet state which was to return to "real fascism": a much more radical, brutal, and socialist version of the corporatist doctrine his state had implemented while Italy had been at peace. The figure who was now closest to him was Nicola Bombacci, one of the original leaders of the Italian Communist Party; and he chose a socialist journalist, Carlo Silvestri, to produce an authorized interpretation of his new-old thinking. He executed five Fascist leaders who had voted against him at the Grand Council meeting (one of the five was Ciano, whom the Nazis hated). Mussolini as the ruler of the "Republic of Salò" in effect was out of power, and could only live in the past. On April 26, 1945, he was captured by partisans at Dongo on Lake Como as he tried to flee across the Swiss border, and was executed on April 28.

The formation of the Badoglio government had a major effect on support for the Nazi project elsewhere in Europe. Cooperation and collaboration now appeared to carry as many dangers as benefits. Even in Germany, people clearly saw the lessons of a fall of a dictator. One German bank director exclaimed that "fascism had disappeared without a murmur; the same would happen with us in Germany; National Socialism was in any case nothing more than a fart".[18] He was unwise enough to state this case on a train ride, and was arrested after being denounced by an informant. For Hitler's allies, as well, it was dangerous to contemplate the lessons to be learnt from the Duce's fall if German soldiers were nearby.

Admiral Horthy was ferociously anti-communist, and Hungarian units fought alongside the Germans in Operation Barbarossa. In January 1943, the Soviet offensive on the Don destroyed the Hungarian army, and Horthy then tried to extricate his country from the conflict. In late 1943, his Prime Minister, Miklós Kállay, reached a secret agreement with the western allies that the Hungarian forces would surrender unconditionally. As the Soviet army got nearer, however, Nazi German forces invaded Hungary (March 19, 1944) and Horthy replaced Kállay and appointed a pro-Nazi government. It was this government that supervised the deportation of Hungarian Jews.

Soon after fighting with the Red Army had begun in September 1944, the Germans arrested Horthy and appointed the Arrow Cross leader, Ferenc Szálasi, in his place. Szálasi was a genuine fascist, and his squads conducted a campaign of terror that kept Hungary in the war.

The first of the real Nazi satellite states had been Slovakia, under the dominance of a clerical militia and a Catholic priest, Jozef Tiso, who became President in October 1939. It introduced anti-Semitic laws (based on religious definitions of who was a Jew) in April 1939, and Jewish property was seized through the state-run post office and banking system. In October 1940, an SS officer, Dieter Wisliceny, came to Bratislava and reorganized the Hlinka Guard on the model of the SS. In September 1941 racial criteria of Jewishness were applied, and in March 1942 the deportation of the overwhelming majority of Slovakian Jewry began.

Yugoslavia had at first been important for Germany because of the strategic need to prepare the German support for Mussolini's ill-judged invasion of Greece. As a major producer of bauxite (aluminum ore), which became increasingly important as the air war developed, it also had a major economic significance.

The Regent, Prince Paul, gave in to German pressure to join the Axis alliance, but was quickly deposed by a military coup in which the young King Peter was installed on the throne and General Dusan Simović became Prime Minister (March 25–27, 1941). Simović tried to reassure Hitler that the coup was only a product of domestic Yugoslav disputes, and that it had no international significance. But on April 6, 1941, Germany launched a full-scale invasion and the dismemberment of the Yugoslav state.

Slovenia was divided between Germany and Italy, Hungary was compensated with some territory, and western Macedonia and Kosovo went to Italy. In Croatia, a secessionist movement, the Ustaša, led by Ante Pavelić, set up an independent state, which the Germans allowed to control Bosnia–Herzegovina. This was a viciously nationalistic regime, which attacked Jews and Serbs who would not convert to Catholicism. In all, at least 100,000 Serbs were killed by the Ustaša.

Serbia was run by a puppet government under General Milan Nedić. Two rival partisan movements emerged: Draža Mihajlović (who was appointed Minister of War by the royal government-in-exile in London), and the communist movement of Tito. After a large-scale German massacre at Kragujevac, in retaliation for partisan activities, Mihajlović started to reach a practical accommodation with the German forces, and instead concentrated on resisting Ustaša attacks. This quiescence gave Tito the chance to establish at Jajce in Bosnia in November 1943 (at the time of the Teheran meeting of Stalin with Roosevelt and Churchill) a provisional government for all of Yugoslavia that would be the basis for postwar rule.

Romania had initially tried to keep out of the war, but in June 1940 was so isolated after the fall of France that King Carol tried to establish a totalitarian constitution and build better relations with Germany. The price of this was massive territorial loss: first of Bessarabia and the southern Bukovina to the Soviet Union, and then of the contested area of northern Transylvania to Hungary and southern Dobruja to Bulgaria. General Antonescu, who had been appointed Prime Minister as a potential strong man, deposed the King and replaced him with a new king (Michael), who agreed to give absolute power to the Prime Minister. The leader of the fascist Iron Guard movement became deputy Prime Minister, and the fascists carried out extensive anti-Jewish pogroms. In September 1940, the government introduced anti-Semitic legislation based on the Nuremberg Laws. But at the beginning of 1941, Antonescu, backed by German troops, successfully crushed the Iron Guard and then agreed to take part in the invasion of Russia.

Antonescu was extremely sensitive to the overall development of the war. As mentioned above, as the German military position weakened in 1943, he began to demand hard currency payments for the valuable petroleum exports. The fall of Mussolini galvanized him, and he proposed a pact with Hungary and Bulgaria that would provide sufficient strength to protect southeast Europe against German anger. But the new toughness in dealing with Berlin was not enough to allow him to deal with a much more vocal opposition at home. On August 23, 1944, the fifth anniversary of the Nazi–Soviet pact, King Michael changed sides, built a broad national coalition of Liberals, Agrarians, Socialists, and Communists, and ordered his soldiers to arrest the remaining German forces.

Bulgaria had been drawn into the German orbit in the 1930s, and was bought over by territorial ambitions: the prospect of seizing Dobruja. Like Romania, it put tough anti-communist and anti-Semitic laws in place (in January 1941, in the so-called Law for the Defense of the Nation). In March 1941, it became the last state to join the Axis, and German troops immediately moved into the country. On December 13, 1941, King Boris III needlessly declared war on the United States and the United Kingdom, though Bulgaria kept diplomatic relations with the Soviet Union. He calculated that this act of war might be a gesture of compliance with Nazi Germany, without requiring any engagement on the Eastern Front. In August 1942, the Germans established quotas for the deportation of Jews from Bulgaria, and on February 22, 1943, the government verbally agreed to the deportation of 20,000 Jews, 14,000 of whom would be taken from Thrace (annexed from Greece as another prize for working with Germany). But the deportation was stopped at the last moment, after the news leaked out and Jewish leaders protested vociferously. Some Jews were deported in the end – 7,144 from Macedonia and 4,058 from Thrace – but Bulgaria's Jewish population was in part saved by a regime which did not hesitate to enact anti-Semitic legislation but regarded the handover of people as an affront to its integrity and to the terms of the Berlin Treaty of 1878 which had set up the state and guaranteed the rights of the Jewish population. In May 1943, the Metropolitan (Archbishop) of Sofia publicly condemned anti-Semitism. But as late as December 1943, the Jews of Sofia were ordered to leave the capital, and were dispersed to other towns and villages. Three thousand were sent to labor camps.

King Boris died suddenly in August 1943, prompting rumors that he had been poisoned by the Germans. His six-year-old son, Simeon, became King, and the Regency started to contact the United Kingdom and the United States about a peace settlement. Boris had tried similar feelers before his death, but had been deterred by the insistence of the western allies on unconditional surrender. The government tried to move to unconditional neutrality on the Swiss model, but the military situation did not really allow this attractive luxury. With the change of sides of Romania in August 1944, only a relatively small German military presence stood between Bulgaria and the Red Army. On September 2, 1944, a "democratic" government under Konstantin Muraviev, an Agrarian politician who had been the secretary of Bulgaria's most charismatic interwar political leader, Stambolisky, restored the constitution, canceled the anti-Semitic laws, and tried to make peace. On September 5, Stalin declared war on Bulgaria, and the government responded by declaring war on Germany. Since this was intended mainly to impress the western allies, the news was spread first through embassies, and the Germans at first did not know that another country had declared war on them and denied the rumors. The Bulgarian quest for Swiss-style neutrality had thus led the country to be at war with the United Kingdom, Germany, the Soviet Union, and the United States. In this not-very-hopeful situation, a communist-backed "Fatherland Front" (*Otechestven*) staged a coup and the government was arrested. In the new government, communists controlled three key ministries: justice, the interior, and public health. And in practice, the Soviet Red Army, under Marshal Tolbukhin, could secure the enforcement of the new ideology.

In general, in southeast Europe, the stronger the local strong man – Antonescu, Horthy, or even King Boris – the greater the room for policy maneuver, and the smaller the room for German influence, ideology, and German-inspired genocide. The links between the overall European situation and domestic political shifts between democracy, authoritarianism, corporatism, and fascism that characterized south-central Europe had a similar dynamic in the only major west European state to retain some notional independence. But in France, the strong man was weak.

On June 10, 1940, the French commander-in-chief, General Weygand, had announced that further resistance against Germany was futile; on June 16, Prime Minister Paul Reynaud turned down the British offer of a Franco-British Union, and declared Marshal Henri Philippe Pétain his successor. The armistice was concluded on June 22, and on July 10 the Chamber of Deputies and the Senate voted a new constitutional law, by the largest majority ever in the history of the Third Republic. Pétain used it to end the French presidency, and declared himself Chief of the French State. According to the terms of the armistice, the northern half of France was occupied; Italy later occupied three southern departments. A relatively young officer, who had once been under Pétain's immediate command, offered an alternative. In a radio address from London on June 18, General Charles de Gaulle announced the establishment of "Free France".

Many French citizens treated the sudden defeat of May and June 1940 as a verdict of history on the Third Republic and on democracy. In the 1930s, the fascist leagues had demanded an alternative to republican corruption: as one league leader put it, "the France of camping, of sports, of dances, of voyages, of collective hiking, will sweep away the France of aperitifs, of tobacco dens, of party congresses, and long digestions".[19] Marshal Pétain was a war hero of the First World War, who had skillfully defused the widespread mutinies of 1917, and was a vague, reassuringly non-dogmatic and non-practicing Catholic. Whereas some leading generals had close ties with the fascist right, Pétain looked like a more centrist figure, who could protect France in the hour of need, and had been accepted by the republican mainstream for that reason.

In reality, he soon set about using the defeat and the creation of the *État français*, which replaced the Third Republic, as an opportunity to remake French politics in a traditionalist style that had many similarities to Franco's Spain. The new France, unlike Nazi Germany, was unabashedly anti-modern. On September 15, 1940, Pétain explained in an article in the *Revue des Deux Mondes* that liberalism, capitalism, and collectivism – in short, all the doctrines of the modern world – were "foreign products" and that "France, returning to herself, naturally rejects them". He established his government in the fading spa town of Vichy, in the Hotel du Parc.

In practice, Vichy France was a strange coalition of diverse interests. There were Catholics, reactionary fascists such as Charles Maurras, and traditional conservatives, but also technocratic modernizers. Much of the Third Republic's civil service remained in place: only a few bureaucrats had been purged. The government immediately set about improving morality by prohibiting the sale of strong (over 32 proof) aperitifs, keeping children out of bars, and making divorce more difficult. A new law of 1941 forbade divorce during the first three years of marriage. Pétain would have liked to see the birthrate rise: one measure aimed at this was the overthrow of the Napoleonic law on partible inheritance, which many observers blamed for French demographic weakness. Critics derided such measures, which had already been suggested under the Third Republic, as "*lapinisme*" (rabbitry).

Industrial and commercial structures were organized into committees, which distributed the scarce raw material resources and administered orders. Some industrialists, such as Louis Renault, enthusiastically saw in German demand a way out of the stagnation of the Depression decade. Renault's nephew, François Lehideux, became Minister for Industrial Production, and set about rationalizing France's industrial structure. Wartime conditions gave an ideal opportunity. In December 1941 a rationalization law allowed the government to close down enterprises deemed inefficient or unproductive. In 1943, when Albert Speer reorganized European production to meet increased German demands, a new stage of rationalization was applied. The most important enterprises were specially denominated (*"S"-Betriebe*) and given access to scarce raw material and labor supplies.

Pétain consistently portrayed his rule as a defense of France: the sword had failed in 1940, and he was now the shield. He repeatedly emphasized in a pseudoreligious way how he had made the "gift of his person" for the cause of France. At his only meeting with Hitler, at Montoire on October 14, 1940, he was quite unsuccessful in getting Germany to offer improved conditions in France. Immediately afterwards, both Pétain and his Prime Minister, Pierre Laval, explained the purpose of "collaboration". Laval said: "In all domains, and especially in the economic and colonial spheres, we have discussed and we will continue to examine in what practical form our collaboration can serve the interests of France, Germany, and Europe."[20]

Irritated at not being able to move back into the German zone, if not to Paris then perhaps to Versailles, Pétain sacked Laval on December 13, 1940. Pétain, who felt disgusted by Laval's personal mannerisms, uncouth behavior, and porcine appearance, as much as by his pro-German proclivities, replaced Laval with an anti-British admiral, Darlan. Laval returned to his old office in April 1942, with a clear German protection.

At the same time as Pétain was trying to court Hitler into making Frenchmen happier, he imposed a series of anti-Semitic laws. Pétain con- sistently tried to explain that his measures were directed primarily against foreigners: against the Jewish immigration from Russia and Eastern Europe; against the refugees from racial persecution by the Nazis in Germany, Austria, and Czechoslovakia; and against the political refugees who came north after the end of the Spanish Civil War. After 1940, German Jews who were expelled from Baden and the Palatinate added to France's refugee population. The October 1940 laws required the re-examination of all naturalizations since 1927, and as a result of the enquiries, 15,154 French people (among them 6,307 Jews) lost their citizenship. On October 18, Jewish property was also confiscated, producing an economic and social marginalization similar to that imposed by the Nazis in Germany and Austria: 38,000 apartments were seized and 80,000 bank accounts paid into the state-owned Caisse des Dépôts et Consignations. The total in liquid assets seized amounted to 2.3 bil- lion French francs. The Germans meanwhile instituted a large-scale looting of art: a total of 96,812 works of art were stolen. Suspicious aliens had already been interned under the Republic, and after the end of the Spanish Civil War in very large numbers. In May 1941, mass internments of Jews began in the occupied zone. One year later, deportations began, and Jews in the occupied zone were obliged to wear a yellow star. In June 1942, Himmler specified quotas for the deportation of Jews from France, and on July 16 the French security forces organized a large round-up in the Vélodrome d'Hiver, where 13,000 Jews from the Paris area were herded together to be taken to a transit camp at Drancy and then to Auschwitz. In all, 76,000 Jews were arrested and deported; only 2,800 of these returned. Policy in the unoccupied zone was less ferocious, and Laval resisted the deportation of French Jews. But in both the Vichy zone and the occupied zone, the implementation of policy depended on French enforcement agencies.

Occupied France was run by the German military, by a military com- mander (*Militärbefehlshaber Frankreich*) based in the Hotel Majestic in Paris.

The headquarters worked with around 150 officials, and their commands were enforced by German soldiers: some 100,000 in December 1941, though their numbers decreased to 40,000 in March 1942 and rose again when Germany decided in November 1942 to occupy the whole of France. A considerable number of the German soldiers in France were invalids from the Eastern Front.

Clearly an apparatus of this kind and size could not have controlled all of France had it not been for a substantial collaboration of the French administrative service, in part out of fear of what the Germans might do, and in part out of ideological solidarity with Germany against the United Kingdom, which was presented as a "perfidious" betrayer, and against Bolshevik Russia. Such collaboration reached its height when Laval proclaimed: "I wish for the victory of Germany, because otherwise Bolshevism will install itself everywhere in Europe."[21]

At a private level, many Frenchmen tried to maintain a "patriotic" attitude and ignore the Germans. Guidebooks on manners explained how Germans should be not spoken with and not looked at. Shortly after the war, the film *Le Silence de la Mer* (1947, by Jean-Pierre Melville, based on a novel published clandestinely in 1941 by "Vercors" – Jean Bruller) gave an accurate impression of this: an old man and his niece simply ignore the humane and cultivated (and anti-Nazi) German officer billeted on them.

But large numbers did business of some sort; many bought the confiscated assets of persecuted Jews. The collaboration that touched the French national psyche most deeply was "horizontal collaboration": liaisons between French women and German soldiers. The Germans established their own brothels, but there were also 5,000–6,000 street girls equipped with bilingual cards to facilitate mutual comprehension and intercourse. There were many more "friendships". At the end of the war, an estimated 10,000–20,000 women were punished for such forbidden relations.

A more curious phenomenon was the extent to which intellectual and cultural activities went on as normal during the occupation. Edith Piaf and Maurice Chevalier made tours to Germany. A wide range of intellectuals, not simply fascist sympathizers such as Henri de Montherlant, Robert Brasillach, Drieu la Rochelle, or Louis Fernand Céline, hoped for the best. The director Jean Cocteau explained his belief that Hitler wanted a peaceful and integrated Europe, and that Hitler had been sadly led astray by his generals: "he has been dragged into a war which he detests". Jean Giono, the elegiacal celebrator of the romance of rural life, *La France Profonde*, who in 1939 had been arrested as a pacifist and communist sympathizer, celebrated Vichy values in *Triomphe de la Vie* (1941), but also the person of the Führer: "What is Hitler, if not poetry in action."

After the liberation, most French people wanted to forget about the wartime interlude. After the defeat of the Nazis, about 1,200 collaborators were killed (around five times that number had been executed by the resistance before the liberation). The big symbolic figures – Pétain, Laval, Robert Brasillach – were now put on trial. Pétain, whom the Germans had taken to a castle (Sigmaringen) in southern Germany in August 1945, was sentenced to death, but his opponent (and one-time subordinate) General de Gaulle as Prime Minister of France commuted this to lifetime penal servitude. Laval and the brilliant fascist intellectual Brasillach were executed. Some of the French officials responsible for the worst crimes against humanity had bought themselves insurance tickets by joining the resistance at a late stage. Maurice Papon, who in the 1990s became a symbol of France's reluctance to deal with its past, was a collaborating official who deported Jews but at the last moment joined the resistance. Later, in postwar France, he became Prefect of Police for Paris and then Minister of Finance of the Republic. For the moment of 1944–45, France tried to unite behind the myth of a general resistance to German occupation and the charisma of General de Gaulle.

The neutrals

Geopolitics, much more than ideology, shaped the behavior of the neutrals in the Second World War. The two neutral countries that might have appeared to be closest to Germany ideologically, Spain and Portugal, avoided any security commitment, while Sweden and Switzerland with strong democratic traditions made numerous concessions to appease or pacify Germany. Hitler's visit to Hendaye in October 1940 to meet Franco was an attempt to involve Spain in the war, and in particular to make Spain let Germany attack the important British base in Gibraltar, at the entrance to the Mediterranean. From the point of view of Spain, a country exhausted and depleted by the long and bloody civil war, a new conflict could hold no large attractions. But both Spain and Portugal traded extensively with Germany, providing in particular valuable metal ores which were needed for quality steel for armaments.

Spain and Portugal were generous in their refugee policies, kept their frontiers open, and let refugees pass through before crossing the Atlantic. They hoped that the passage would be as quiet and unremarked as possible: as the Spanish Foreign Minister poetically put it, like light passing through a glass, leaving no trace. There was even a kind of nationalism to their assistance: Spain, in particular, made substantial efforts to assist Sephardic (i.e. originally Iberian or North African) Jews fleeing from the Nazis.

Turkey had a key geographical position in regard to the German attempt to link up with the Arab world and cut off western supplies of petroleum; while for Russia, Turkey controlled access to the Mediterranean. The Inönü government followed a policy of strict neutrality, since it was convinced that any move toward one power, Germany or the Soviet Union, would lead to invasion by the other.

Sweden kept up a trade with Germany in high-grade iron ore, needed by the German armaments economy, and accepted gold from the *Reichsbank* in payment. It also let German troops cross Sweden en route to Finland. On the other hand, while in the 1930s it had vigorously tried to turn back refugees from Nazism, during the war it accepted 32,000 Norwegian refugees, including around 800 Jews, and the entire Jewish population of Denmark (around 7,500).

Shortly before the war, in 1938, Switzerland had adopted unconditional neutrality (in contrast to its previous stance, when as a member of the League of Nations it accepted a responsibility to enforce economic sanctions). At the same time, the Swiss army began to make secret arrangements for a coordination of responses in the event of a German attack. When the speed of the German attack in 1940 meant that French military records were not destroyed before being captured, the Swiss authorities felt that their position of strict neutrality had been badly compromised and that they would be more vulnerable to pressure from Hitler.

The defeat of France and the entry of Italy into the war left Switzerland in a unique position, completely surrounded by a potential aggressor. At the start of the war in 1939, there had been a general mobilization, and a supreme commander was elected: General Henri Guisan. After the French defeat, most of the army was demobilized and the Swiss command prepared for a retreat to a *réduit* in the Alps in the case of invasion. Guisan gave a powerful address on the Rütli meadow, the traditional site where the oath to resist foreign domination had been sworn in 1291. An agricultural program was devised to make Switzerland less dependent on imported foods, but Swiss industry needed employment, and the country still required food and energy (coal) imports. The result was a large expansion in trade with Germany, which in itself did not constitute any violation of neutrality (though the way the government supported German purchases of arms and other goods through a credit on the Swiss–German clearing account did). The Swiss National Bank bought gold from the *Reichsbank*, although it knew that this had been illegally seized from other central banks, and also that gold was being taken from persecuted individuals.

A substantial part of the Swiss elite and the Swiss government felt that a more tightly controlled and authoritarian regime would both be in accord with the spirit of the age and help to protect Switzerland from attack. In the 1930s, Guisan had expressed his admiration for Mussolini, and during the war he maintained good relations with Marshal Pétain. Both Guisan and Pétain saw their patriotic duty in quite similar terms. The Swiss Foreign Minister, Marcel Pilet-Golaz, went further when he wrote to the General in September 1940 about the lessons of the fall of France:

> Personally, I am convinced that we should be able to improve our relations with our northern neighbor if we could free ourselves from an irritatingly ideological way of seeing things, and from a certain demagogic ultra-democratism inspired by that French-style parliamentarism which has proved so deadly for France.[22]

Switzerland was very proud of its unique humanitarian tradition. It was the base for the International Red Cross, which badly compromised its humanitarian mission in not publicizing details of Nazi inhumanities, justifying its actions to itself by the argument that it wished to retain access to all belligerents.

Because of its geographic proximity, Switzerland had been a major recipient of emigrants and refugees in the 1930s. In 1938, the Swiss police authorities discussed with Germany the idea of marking the passports of German Jews with a stamped "J", and in August 1938 began refusing admission to all refugees without a visa. From October 1938, it insisted that "non-Aryan" Germans had a visa. Refugees were subsequently repatriated. In August 1942, as a response to the illegal frontier crossings which had increased after the beginning of the large-scale deportation of west European Jews, the government (without a debate in the full council of ministers) closed the frontier to all non-political refugees (i.e. Jews). Though there were undisclosed humanitarian exceptions, though not all frontier guards followed the instructions, and though there was a wave of public and press indignation at these measures, refugees were turned back at the frontier and many of these were captured by German and French authorities, deported, and killed. In 1943 and 1944, as the tide of war began to turn, Switzerland practiced a more generous refugee policy, although the damage had largely been done already: it was in 1942 that the Jewish population of western Europe was deported. In all, during the war some 10,000 refugees whose names were recorded were turned back by Switzerland, along with another 14,500 whose names were not recorded (though, of course, a proportion of these may well have been turned back more than once). At the same time, the country took 60,000 civilian refugees, about half of whom were Jewish. In addition, there were a substantial number of military refugees, including a division of 12,000 Poles in the 45th Corps of the French army, which had fled into Switzerland in June 1940.

The position of Switzerland and its diplomatic role in providing "good offices" also meant that this was the country where details of Nazi atrocities permeated most quickly. In February 1942, the intelligence services had detailed reports of mass shootings from the interrogation of German military defectors, and Swiss doctors on medical missions to the Eastern Front came back with witness accounts of the shooting of hostages. In May 1942, the Swiss consul in Cologne sent photographs of asphyxiated Jews unloaded from German cattle trucks. The International Red Cross also had details of the Nazi genocide.

The combination of a high level of knowledge of the extent of Nazi atrocities, Swiss humanitarian traditions, the Swiss belief that such traditions required neutrality, and Swiss political and economic interests in building and preserving good relations with Germany created an institutionalized hypocrisy. The British economist John Maynard Keynes put the point neatly, in reference not to Switzerland but to the United States, when he wrote to the American commentator Walter Lippmann on January 6, 1940: "There is a lot to be said for neutrality but moral beauty, no."[23]

The Pope and the war

The ferocious historical debates around the behavior of Germans – of the German elites, civil servants, businessmen, intellectuals, of German soldiers, of "ordinary Germans" – apply in slightly modified form to non-Germans who came in contact with Hitler's power. What did they know of evil, and how did they use their knowledge? Why, if they acquiesced or collaborated in some form, did they do this? Were they driven by simple opportunism? Institutions which have a special claim to "moral beauty" should carry a special duty to refrain from such opportunism. The discussion applies in a particular way to people or states that claimed a particular moral standing. Both during the war, in the quiet tones of diplomatic correspondence, and in a very open debate since the first performance of Rolf Hochhuth's play *The Deputy* in 1963, the morality of the Vatican's wartime policy has been questioned.

Eugenio Pacelli became Pope Pius XII in 1939. He had long been familiar with the Nazis: as papal nuncio in Bavaria during and after the First World War, just as the Nazi movement was beginning in Munich, and then as the nuncio to Berlin. He negotiated first a concordat with the Bavarian government, and then in 1933 the very controversial concordat with the German government: never agreed to under the Weimar Republic, but concluded once German political Catholicism in the form of the Center Party had been destroyed. He was Pius XI's Cardinal Secretary of State. Though he despised National Socialism and its godless inhumanity, he had a deep admiration for German culture that induced him to think that conditions in Germany might change in the near future.

He also contemplated recent history. During the First World War, the Vatican had been at the center of a major peace initiative. Pius XII rightly saw war as intrinsically evil, and believed it his duty to avoid it. The problem inherent in this position almost immediately became apparent, even before 1939: political intervention looked like partiality, and might get in the way of peacemaking. In May 1939, the Pope tried to solve the increasingly obvious tensions between Hitler and Poland by a Munich-style solution of a conference, or individual discussions, with British, French, German, Italian, and Polish leaders (the Poles were to be included, while in Munich the Czech government had of course been excluded). He spoke about injustices in the Versailles system, an attitude which indicated that he was expecting Poland to do the compromising and surrendering. He saw himself as a peacemaker. His first official homily as Pope, on Easter Sunday 1939, took as its text "Glory to God in the highest, and on earth peace, goodwill toward men" (*Luke* 2: xiv).

After the outbreak of war, in the encyclical *Summi Pontificatus* he condemned the German invasion of Poland quite explicitly:

The blood of countless human beings, even noncombatants, raises a piteous dirge over a nation such as Our dear Poland, which, for its fidelity to the Church, for its services in the defense of Christian civilization, written in indelible characters in the annals of history, has a right to the generous and brotherly sympathy of the whole world, while it awaits, relying on the powerful intercession of Mary, Help of Christians, the hour of a resurrection in harmony with the principles of justice and true peace.

The encyclical also speaks of the "unity of the human race", of "men as brothers in one great family". It cited St Paul on having

put on the new man, which is renewed in knowledge after the image of him that created him; where there is neither Greek nor Jew, circumcision nor uncircumcision, Barbarian, Scythian, bond nor free; but Christ is all, and in all" (*Colossians* 3: x–xi).

The encyclical also boldly asserted the existence of a universal morality that had been violated:

Before all else, it is certain that the radical and ultimate cause of the evils which We deplore in modern society is the denial and rejection of a universal norm of morality as well for individual and social life as for international relations.

The language of the encyclical is characteristic of the Pope's public utterances during the war: it unambiguously condemned the practice of brutality and evil, but would not say specifically who were the violators of divine law.

But the encyclical also included an unusually fulsome tribute to Italy, which was not then at war, as a "friendly power": "Our dear Italy, fruitful garden of the Faith". And the specific reference to Poland in a papal statement about the war was not to be repeated. The statement had indeed been widely used in the course of the conflict: the French air force dropped 88,000 copies over Germany, while in Poland the German occupation authorities distributed a version in which the word "Poland" was replaced by "Germany".

Pius XII allowed the Vatican diplomatic channels to be used for approaches by anti-Nazi German Catholics – in particular the Bavarian Josef Müller – who wanted to negotiate on what terms the Allies might make peace with a Germany that had deposed Hitler. The British ambassador to the Vatican reported that the German conspirators were planning to replace Hitler by a short-term military regime which would hand over power to a government that would be "democratic", "conservative", and "moderate". Such a government could negotiate a peace.[24] The Vatican's involvement was inherently high-risk, since Hitler would probably have severely punished not simply any conspirators, but also the Catholic Church in Germany. Many critics have pointed out that this was a higher risk than any that the Pope undertook on behalf of the Jews.

In reacting to the news of deportations and mass murder of Jews, Pius XII was extremely cautious, even when in 1942 the unambiguous evidence of the extent of murder came to him from several different and reliable sources. In March 1942, the World Jewish Congress's Geneva office and the Swiss Israelite Community sent to Rome an extensive documentation of persecutions in western Europe, and also in Croatia, Hungary, and Slovakia, where the papacy had a considerable leverage. The head of the Slovak state, Father Tiso, was indeed even a Catholic priest; and Slovakia was the only case in which Pius XII allowed the Vatican to intervene with a protest (which had no effect). The British ambassador, who also regularly conveyed BBC reports to the Pope, presented a letter with more details about the situation of the Jews, but the Pope never referred to the contents of the letter. In March 1943, Bishop Konrad von Preysing in Berlin asked the Pope to appeal for the Berlin Jews who were in immediate danger of deportation; when the Pope responded, on April 30, he did not commit himself but applauded the efforts of Catholics who had helped:

> it was a consolation for Us to learn that Catholics, notably in Berlin, had manifested great Christian charity toward the sufferings of 'non-Aryans' . . . Unhappily in the present circumstances, We cannot offer them effective help other than through Our prayers.[25]

Even more extraordinary was Pius XII's behavior during the internment and then the deportation of many Roman Jews in October 1943. The German Ambassador, Ernst von Weizsäcker, was pressing the Pope to make an official protest, and it was actually the German embassy staff who dictated a letter of protest signed by the German Bishop in Rome, Bishop Alois Hudal. The Pope himself was inactive. He did not visit the detained Jews: a contrast with his striking immediate response to visit the church of San Lorenzo when it was damaged in an Allied bombing raid. When Jews were saved in Rome, it was more due to the actions of individual priests and lay people, and less to any central directive from the Vatican.

In this episode, it is clear that the German Foreign Office, which feared mass protests in Rome, wanted a halt to the deportations and welcomed Vatican private protests but wanted no public condemnation from the Holy See. Von Weizsäcker had said to a friend at the time: "Any protest on the part of the Pope would have as a consequence that the deportations would be carried out in a truly complete fashion. I know how our people act on these occasions."[26] Pacelli consistently seems to have convinced himself that behind-the-scenes diplomacy could work better results than open confrontation. It was the policy that might be expected from a Vatican Secretary of State sitting on St Peter's chair. The time when such an intervention was most successful was in 1944, when most of the Jews in Hitler's power had already been killed, and when a Vatican intervention in Hungary temporarily suspended the deportations. At this stage around 230,000 Jews remained alive in Budapest, and 120,000 survived the war.

The most obvious flaw in the Vatican's policy lay in its inaction at an early stage, when discriminatory laws were created that singled out Jews and limited their rights. Measures such as the Nuremberg Laws, which were imitated in other countries under German influence, prepared the way for genocide, but the logic of that connection is much clearer in retrospect than it was at the time. In the face of rising anti-Semitism in the 1920s, Pius XI in 1928 considered but then rejected a proposal to delete references to the "perfidious Jews" from the Good Friday liturgy. Such a change was eventually undertaken only by Pope John XXIII, in 1959 at the beginning of his pontificate. In 1937 the Vatican also blocked proposals for a new encyclical condemning racism as a dangerous error, probably because of the increasingly close rapprochement of Mussolini's Italy with Nazi Germany. In Italy, however, the Vatican made it clear that it considered the racial laws not only immoral but illegal in that they were a breach of the 1929 concordat, which obliged the state to recognize Catholic marriages (including those of converted Jews, which were not accepted under the 1938 law).[27] Pius XII based a refusal to meet Mussolini in January 1940 on the grounds that the Duce had signed the racial laws.[28] During the war itself, it is obviously quite doubtful that even a really determined and public approach would have actually helped to save many Jewish, or other, victims of Nazi terror. It would, however, have strengthened the moral foundation of Pius XII's papacy.

In 1939, before the outbreak of war, a British Foreign Office official had commented:

> Personally, I feel that he would be able to influence events far more effectively as champion of certain moral principles in the world of today than he is likely to be able to act as a possible but improbable candidate for the post of mediator between the Axis and the Democracies.[29]

During the war, the British ambassador to the Vatican concluded:

> The fact is that the moral authority of the Holy See, which Pius XI and his predecessors had built up into a world power, is now sadly reduced. I suspect that H.H. [His Holiness] hopes to play a great role as a peacemaker and that it is partly at least for this reason that he tries to preserve a position of neutrality between the belligerents.[30]

The reason for the Pope's public silence in the face of almost certain proof of the extent of the Nazi killings of Jews will never be entirely clear, and indeed it is unlikely that there is one single reason. The argument that he was personally anti-Semitic is unconvincing and is not sustained by serious evidence, but there is no doubt about the anti-Semitism that the Church and its liturgy at that time encouraged. The majority of the most problematic decisions regarding the Church's response to the new anti-Semitism had been formulated in the pontificate of Pius XI. Pope Pius XII may have been frightened by the possibility of reprisals against Catholics and against his city of Rome. Most likely, as a man who had spent his lifetime in papal diplomacy, he thought like a diplomat more than like a spiritual leader. Diplomats always want to build bridges, and often build them across the abyss that separates humanity from inhumanity. He was under heavy pressure from the western allies to denounce the atrocities against Jews (especially after December 17, 1942), and under heavy pressure from the Axis powers to protest about Allied air attacks. The Italian fascist ideologue Roberto Farinacci attacked the "silence of the Pope".[31] Above all, Pius XII held to a notion of neutrality as a way of making peace, but as in the Swiss case, that neutrality ended up not seeming particularly moral.

For other states, a calculated neutrality may be acceptable (but it is now questionable): the realist tradition does not recognize any interest but self-interest in the behavior of states. But the Vatican should clearly not have thought of itself as yet another state in a big power game. The British envoy, d'Arcy Osborne, at the time asked, "is there not a moral issue at stake which does not admit of neutrality?"[32] Pope Pius, the successor to St Peter in the See of Rome, shared both the piety and dignity and the flawed humanity of the first bishop, who also chose to turn away from the persecuted: "Peter said: Man, I know not what thou sayest. And immediately, while he yet spake the cock crew. And the Lord turned and looked upon Peter." (*Luke* 22: lx–lxi).

In 1963, before the public discussion of the Vatican's role began, the sculptor Francesco Messina produced a bronze statue of Pius XII for St Peter's in which a strained and agonized visage was turned away, looking to the side. In 1998, in the interest of what it termed "the purification of history", the Vatican published a document entitled *We Remember: A Reflection on the Shoah*, in which Pius's role in rescuing Jews was praised, at the same time as the problem was stated. "For Christians, this heavy burden of conscience of their brothers and sisters during the Second World War must be a call for penitence."

The Anglo-American vision

Both Winston Churchill and Franklin Roosevelt had a large moral as well as a geo-political vision of the conflict to which they subordinated all the details of political or economic interaction after the war. Indeed, in striking contrast to the other wartime leaders, they had little time for or interest in general discussions about the future of capitalism, socialism, or collectivism. That is one of the reasons why they were so successful as strategic thinkers. They also formed a close personal relationship, and brought about a substantial level of Anglo-American cooperation.

Churchill became Prime Minister in May 1940 after the House of Commons, and in particular many Conservative MPs, turned on his predecessor Neville Chamberlain in the wake of the debacle of the United Kingdom's failed attempt to seize the Norwegian port of Narvik. There was a double irony, in that Churchill as First Lord of the Admiralty might have been held to be responsible for Narvik; and secondly, that Chamberlain's foremost enemies were the Tory imperialists who saw the defense of empire as a foremost priority. One of them, Leo Amery, shouted out to Chamberlain, "In the name of God, go." (This was the phrase that Oliver Cromwell had used to expel parliament in the seventeenth century.) Churchill, unlike the alternative politician who might have succeeded Chamberlain, Lord Halifax, was unambiguously committed to a vigorous prosecution of the war, and to a refusal to hold talks with Germany about an armistice. But it soon became clear that the end of empire would be the price to be paid for such a war, and that the Tory imperialists were relics of a past era.

The one "ism" that appeared to darken Anglo-American relations was imperialism, and Churchill seemed uniquely attached to the idea of a British Empire. Roosevelt occasionally lectured Churchill:

> You have four hundred years of acquisitive instinct in your blood and you just don't understand how a country might not want to acquire land somewhere if they can get it. A new period has opened in the world's history, and you will have to adjust to it.[33]

The problem for the British leaders was that empire was the only concept in international relations that had any appeal for them. Foreign Secretary Anthony Eden in May 1944 put the case very neatly in the major foreign policy debate in the House of Commons on the eve of the Allied landings in Normandy: "the British Commonwealth and Empire is the one really successful experiment in international cooperation there has ever been".[34] But while the two western wartime leaders were mapping out the future course of the conflict in Casablanca (January 1943), Roosevelt's emissary Wendell Philipps was in India trying to maneuver a British agreement on Indian independence.

The United Kingdom was vulnerable to pressure because of its economic and financial fragility. Through Lend-Lease, it became apparent how dependent the United Kingdom was on continued American support. The longer the war went on, the more industrial output mattered. US armaments production reached the British level only in the summer of 1942, but by 1944 it was six times as great. In particular, the US war economy concentrated on gigantic production runs of models which changed only little: in the most spectacular example, the Ford works at Willow Run, on a 65-acre site with a half-mile-long assembly line, produced one B-24 "Liberator" bomber every 63 minutes. At the Teheran conference, Stalin's final toast to Roosevelt was to the United States as the "country of machines". And he said, "the most important things in this war are machines".[35]

The massive power of the United States, and its capacity to use revolutionary technology, was demonstrated in its most terrifying fashion only after the end of the European war. On July 16, 1945, an atomic bomb was tested in the desert of New Mexico, on July 27 leaflets were dropped over Japanese cities warning of "destruction from the air", and on August 6 and 9 the US air force dropped single bombs on Hiroshima and Nagasaki. The use of atomic weapons made the end of the war speedier, and forestalled a Soviet attack on Japan (the Soviet Union had declared war on August 8).

The stunning US technical and economic performance won the war but also raised many questions about the postwar world. Both the United Kingdom and the United States saw in economic well-being a key to future stability. The United Kingdom had recovered well in general from the Depression, but there were still bitter memories of the painful economic aftermath of the First World War. Instead, a common and collectivized security – such as that envisaged by the Beveridge Plan (*Social Insurance and Allied Services*, a tract which sold over 600,000 copies) – would build up a new type of cross-class solidarity. The United States had struggled much longer with the Depression. The power of the US production machine during the war gave rise to a hope that a new and prosperous international economy, built upon increased civilian consumption once military orders fell away, could generate a social stability that might provide a model for the world.

The general outlines of postwar goals might be clear, but the specifics of how growth and stability would be reconciled could be established only after a long debate. The United States insisted on the opening of trade, as it had been more and more impatient with the trade policies of the 1930s, and its leaders were convinced that the Depression played a large part in the deterioration of international relations in the 1930s. Trade liberalization was written into the Lend-Lease Agreement with the United Kingdom (as Article VII). But such liberalization would create immediate problems for every country except the United States, and the idea that prosperity was indivisible of course meant that that would indeed also be an American problem. Such difficulties could only be avoided by some monetary mechanism which allowed countries access to financial resources while their economies adjusted to the postwar world. The search for such a mechanism was the major task of the United Nations monetary conference at Bretton Woods, New Hampshire, in July 1944. The new Bretton Woods "system" established a fixed but adjustable system of exchange rates, and created the International Monetary Fund (IMF) and the World Bank as institutions providing balance-of-payments assistance and development funding. This was assumed to be a universal arrangement: there was a Soviet delegation among the 45 countries represented at the conference, and much of the peculiarity of the agreement was the result of the need to include a state-run command economy. The Bretton Woods regime did not depend on the existence of capitalism or a market economy, and could as easily be understood as a way of protecting the international economic viability of state socialism.

The grand geo-political vision of the British–American leadership, and its dependence on good relations with Moscow, also meant a necessary lack of interest in the issue around which a great deal of post-First World War peacemaking had revolved, national self-determination. This hesitance to deal with the claims of self-determination in Europe is quite comprehensible in that it was nationalities disputes which had given rise to much of the instability and the fractured international system of the 1930s.

On July 1, 1940, the editorial of the London *Times* (written by E.H. Carr) discussed the institutional basis of "the new Europe": "The conception of the small national unit, not strong enough for an active role in international politics, but enjoying all the prerogatives and responsibilities of sovereignty, has been rendered obsolete by modern armaments and the scope of modern warfare."

The logic of a debate about national self-determination (which was still very much evident in the drafting of the Atlantic Charter in August 1941) gave way to a view that the international system and individual rights needed to be connected in the postwar world in a more satisfactory way. This would occur through institutions such as the IMF and the World Bank in the economic sphere, and through the United Nations in regard to security issues. Otherwise, many on the Allied side believed, a Third World War would be inevitable, as the same logic and dynamics of inter-state relations that had led to the First World War had, it seemed, also produced the Second.

Notes

1 Quoted in G.M. Gilbert, *The Psychology of Dictatorship*, New York, NY: Ronald Press, 1950, p. 117.
2 Walther Funk, *The Economic Future of Europe*, Berlin: Terramare Office, 1940, p. 11.
3 Lucy Dawidowicz, *The War against the Jews, 1933–1945*, New York, NY: Free Press, 1986.
4 Hans Mommsen, *Auschwitz, 17. Juli 1942: der Weg zur europäischen "Endlösung der Judenfrage"*, Munich: Deutscher Taschenbuch Verlag, 2002, p. 98.
5 Quoted in Hans Safrian, *Die Eichmann-Männer*, Vienna: Europa Verlag, 1993, p. 36.
6 See Henry Friedlander, *The Origins of Nazi Genocide: from Euthanasia to the Final Solution*, Chapel Hill, NC: University of North Carolina Press, 1995, p. 67.
7 Mommsen, *Auschwitz*, p. 119.
8 See Jan Gross, *Neighbors: the Destruction of the Jewish Community in Jedwabne, Poland*, Princeton, NJ: Princeton University Press, 2001. Gross gives the figure of 1,600 killed, which is disputed by the detailed findings of a Polish investigation triggered by the controversy over Gross's book: see Pawla Machcewicza and Krzysztofa Persaka (eds), *Wokół Jedwabnego*, Warsaw: Instytut Pamięci Narodowej, 2002.
9 Christian Gerlach, *Krieg, Ernährung, Völkermord: Forschungen zur deutschen Vernichtungspolitik im Zweiten Weltkrieg*, Hamburg: Hamburger Edition, 1998.
10 See on these transactions Yehuda Bauer, *Jews for Sale? Nazi–Jewish Negotiations, 1933–1945*, New Haven, CT: Yale University Press, 1994.

11 Riegner cable in Israel Gutman (ed.), *Encyclopedia of the Holocaust*, Vol. 3, New York, NY: Macmillan, 1990, p. 1275; Goldmann quoted in Peter Novick, *The Holocaust in American Life*, New York, NY: Houghton Mifflin, 1999, p. 44.

12 Michael Burleigh, *The Third Reich: A New History*, Basingstoke: Macmillan, 2000, p. 532.

13 Klaus Hildebrand, *Das vergangene Reich: deutsche Aussenpolitik von Bismarck bis Hitler, 1871–1945*, Stuttgart: Deutsche Verlags-Anstalt, 1995, p. 747.

14 Figures from Ulrich Herbert, *Fremdarbeiter: Politik und Praxis des "Ausländer-Einsatzes" in der Kriegswirtschaft des Dritten Reiches*, Bonn: J.H.W. Dietz, 1985, pp. 270–1.

15 Keesings 5506.

16 John Erickson, *The Road to Berlin: Continuing the History of Stalin's War with Germany*, Boulder, CO: Westview Press, 1983, p. 135.

17 Erickson, *Road to Berlin*, p. 283.

18 Hermann Köhler, quoted in Harold James, "The Deutsche Bank 1933–1945", in Lothar Gall et al., *The Deutsche Bank 1870–1945*, London: Weidenfeld, 1995, p. 350.

19 Robert O. Paxton, *Vichy France: Old Guard and New Order 1940–1944*, London: Barrie and Jenkins, 1972, p. 33.

20 Paxton, *Vichy*, p. 77.

21 Radio speech of June 22, 1942, https://www.youtube.com/watch?v=sHAwGQoAN3A.

22 Independent Commission of Experts, *Switzerland, National Socialism and the Second World War*, Zurich: Pendo, 2002, p. 79.

23 Robert Skidelsky, *John Maynard Keynes, Vol. III: Fighting for Britain, 1937–1946*, London: Macmillan, 2001, p. 93.

24 Owen Chadwick, *Britain and the Vatican during the Second World War*, Cambridge: Cambridge University Press, 1986, p. 92. See also John Cornwell, *Hitler's Pope: The Secret History of Pius XII*, London: Penguin, 1999, p. 238.

25 José M. Sánchez, *Pius XII and the Holocaust: Understanding the Controversy*, Washington DC: Catholic University of America Press, 2002, pp. 166–7.

26 Susan Zuccotti, *Under His Very Windows: The Vatican and the Holocaust in Italy*, New Haven, CT: Yale University Press, 2000, p. 161.

27 Chadwick, *Britain*, p. 71.

28 Sánchez, *Pius XII*, p. 73.

29 Cornwell, *Hitler's Pope*, p. 229.

30 Cornwell, *Hitler's Pope*, p. 284 (citing letter of Francis d'Arcy Osborne to Mrs McEwan).

31 Chadwick, *Britain*, p. 307.

32 Chadwick, *Britain*, p. 199.

33 Quoted in Warren Kimball, *The Juggler: Franklin Roosevelt as Wartime Statesman*, Princeton, NJ: Princeton University Press, 1991, p. 66.

34 Keesings 6468.

35 W. Averell Harriman and Elie Abel, *Special Envoy to Churchill and Stalin 1941–1946*, New York, NY: Random House, 1975, p. 277.

7   The reconstruction of Europe, Western style

Making the 1950s

In 1945, the future of Europe, wracked by war and civil war, appeared quite bleak. Large parts were physically devastated. Institutionally, the nation-state was discredited. Every continental country except the Soviet Union bore the scars of defeat, betrayal, and compromise, and even in the Soviet Union accusations of Ukrainian and Baltic collaborationism fueled Russian nationalism and chauvinism. The continental countries that had fought wars had been defeated and humiliated. The legacy of collaboration in economics and politics scarred even the neutral countries. The United Kingdom, though not militarily defeated, was financially exhausted. Realism, the tradition of foreign policy linked with the nation-state, was also at an end. A.J.P. Taylor quite correctly noted that "A realist foreign policy must always end at Vichy – cautious collaboration with the aggressor."[1] But in 1945, no one wanted to end at Vichy, and the world after Vichy and after Hitler needed morality as a guide to the behavior of states. The major new domestic political forces that emerged to face the new challenge were all oriented toward non-national politics and international ideals: communism, socialism, or Christian democracy.

Ideals and realpolitik

It was inevitable that the models for a management of the European crisis would come from the United States or the Soviet Union: in both, a staggeringly successful wartime economic performance had been the basis for a military predominance and for the international projection of power. They were also countries driven by powerful ideas and idealisms, as much as by interests. In the subsequent postwar period, dealing with economic issues seemed a prerequisite for tackling the big security and political problems of the European continent. It was also inevitable that the extent of preponderance of the two new superpowers would excite gradual European unease, discontent, and even resistance in the halves of Europe that they dominated. De Gaulle in the 1960s believed that France's defiance of US hegemony was an equivalent to the Chinese break with the Soviet Union.

This is not to suggest an equivalence of western and eastern Europe, which soon developed in markedly different directions. But at the beginning, each of the two parts saw themselves under new hegemonies with ties that rested on a security relationship, on economics, and on a common cultural outlook. In the longer run, for the East, the economic and ideological ties weakened, with the result that hegemony rested increasingly obviously on military force. In the West, on the other hand, the economics and politics of Europe and the United States became progressively closer. As they did, however, they provoked resentments and a deep questioning of the cultural and intellectual relationship.

Two big considerations drove superpower politics in the making of a new world: the first was the legacy of the joint struggle against National Socialism or fascism, which had required the application of new universal principles; and the second, countervailing, dynamic was that of the rising tensions between the superpowers, in terms of interests but also ideas. These two dynamics interacted with each other in an alarming and destabilizing fashion. The first, the search for universal principles, sometimes found expression in common words such as "rights" and "democracy", but they were interpreted in different ways. The American version, for example, took rights to be individual, while the Soviet Union saw them as a collective property (the rights of the working class). Moreover, since the concepts embodied in each ideology were inherently general rather than particular, they carried an implicit imperative to expand: if a principle was to be validated as true, it should be true for the whole world. Universal ideas thus brought conflict. An abdication or at least a sidelining of the grand principle, however, meant a return to competition between powers and realpolitik. As long as there existed a balance of power, this could produce stabilization. Stalin at first had affected to ignore US atomic power, and put on a convincing display of indifference when Truman told him about the bomb during the Potsdam conference. When the Soviet Union acquired atomic weapons in August 1949, the world tilted more to a balance of terror, in that even when (as at the beginning) the balance was overwhelmingly in favor of the US side, there still existed a chance of total destruction. The chance was significant enough for the risk of war not to be worth taking.

Postwar politics thus produced a paradox on a grand scale: that universal ideas about peace implied conflict and risked war; while conflictual definitions of interest and adversity begat peace. In consequence, at the level of superpower relations, but no longer for the nation-state, realism in politics crept in through the back door.

The clearest indication of the new internationalist principles came with the trials of the International Military Tribunal in Nuremberg. They offered a completely radical and new approach to international law, and made clear that national sovereignty could and should be subordinated to a broader consideration of international justice. Old-style thinking in power political terms was unsympathetic to the Nuremberg approach: Churchill, for instance, would have preferred simply to kill the Nazi leaders when they were captured. The Nazis themselves appear to have been perplexed by the legalism of the Allies. Hermann Göring expressed his surprise to one of his interrogators:

> You don't do this right. If we'd won, we wouldn't have done it this way – you'd be standing up, and you wouldn't have your uniform on, you'd have a black-and-white prisoner's suit, and there would be two SS men standing behind you, sticking you in the butt with bayonets. . . . That's the way you ought to treat us.[2]

The idea of a tribunal was a product of the Soviet tradition of public trials (which in the 1930s had culminated in the infamous show trials), and the new US President Harry S. Truman's strong dislike of the British preference for summary justice. The US prosecutor, Robert Jackson, opened the American case with a very striking declaration:

> That four Great Nations, flushed with victory and stung with injury, stay the hand of vengeance and voluntarily submit their captive enemies to the judgment of the law is one of the most significant tributes that Power has ever paid to Reason.[3]

The trials before the International Military Tribunal brought charges against individuals, but also against institutions (such as the SS and the National Socialist Party and its agencies). The first trial against the individuals identified as major war criminals involved four charges: crimes against peace (i.e. a preparation for aggressive war); crimes against humanity (such as the genocide the Nazis had perpetrated); war crimes; and conspiracy to engage in these crimes. The last was necessary in the eyes of the prosecutors because of the complexity of decision-making in the modern state. Without its inclusion, many of those who had been heavily involved in complicated bureaucratic processes that led to immoral and criminal acts could have denied their responsibility for specific crimes. But particularly in regard to the conspiracy to commit crimes against peace (to prepare for war in the 1930s), it was difficult to make charges stick. That charge looked problematical and indeed hypocritical in the light of the fact that one of the judging states had invaded Poland on September 17, 1939. As Jackson recognized, though, it was intellectually central to the case for a better international order; and, in Jackson's view, it also had a perfect legal justification in the fact that Germany had violated a treaty it had signed, the (rather idealistic) Briand–Kellogg Pact of 1928, which had outlawed war as an instrument of policy.

Judges from each of the four powers voted on each charge, and on the sentencing. Of the accused, Hjalmar Schacht, who had managed the financing of rearmament until his dismissal as Reichsbank President in January 1939, was acquitted. Some other verdicts looked curious: Gauleiter Sauckel, who had directly overseen the slave labor program, was sentenced to death;

while his superior, Albert Speer, who had needed the labor for his economic mobilization plans but who in the dock appeared to be the most sympathetic of the defendants, was sentenced to 20 years' imprisonment.

The trials produced a massive documentation of the extent of the Nazi butchery, on the murder of Jews and others, and on the brutal and inhumane treatment of PoWs. The openness of the proceedings, and the fact that the sentences were not automatic and some defendants were acquitted on some or all charges, left a powerful impression of justice, which could serve as the basis for the development of a new humanitarian law. In December 1946, the United Nations passed a resolution which endorsed the Nuremberg Charter, and in 1948 the United Nations adopted the Genocide Convention.

Human rights

The most far-reaching statement of the new order came in the United Nations Universal Declaration of Human Rights (1948). It began with a very general preamble:

> Disregard and contempt for human rights have resulted in barbarous acts which have outraged the conscience of mankind, and the advent of a world in which human beings shall enjoy freedom of speech and belief and freedom from fear and want has been proclaimed as the highest aspiration of the common people.

It had been drafted by a wide range of personalities, with Charles Malik of Lebanon and P.C. Chang of the Republic of China playing an important role in formulating a universal or global vision. Most of its articles must have seemed (they still do) hopelessly utopian aspirations that had little to do with everyday reality in most countries. In fact, at the time, every country was in violation of some aspect of this ambitious program for democratization and the guarantee of personal rights. To name only the two most obvious: color bars made Article 2 problematical for the United States, while the principle of free voting (Article 21) was grotesquely violated in Soviet-occupied Europe. It is worth recalling some of the most striking articles of the declaration:

1: All human beings are born free and equal in dignity and rights. They are endowed with reason and conscience and should act towards one another in a spirit of brotherhood.
2: Everyone is entitled to all the rights and freedoms set forth in this Declaration, without distinction of any kind, such as race, colour, sex, language, religion, political or other opinion, national or social origin, property, birth or other status. Furthermore, no distinction shall be made on the basis of the political, jurisdictional or international status of the country or territory to which a person belongs,

whether it be independent, trust, non-self-governing or under any other limitation of sovereignty.

13: Everyone has the right to freedom of movement and residence within the borders of each State. Everyone has the right to leave any country, including his own, and to return to his country.

17: Everyone has the right to own property alone as well as in association with others. No one shall be arbitrarily deprived of his property.

20: Everyone has the right to freedom of peaceful assembly and association. No one may be compelled to belong to an association.

21: Everyone has the right to take part in the government of his country, directly or through freely chosen representatives. Everyone has the right to equal access to public service in his country. The will of the people shall be the basis of the authority of government; this will shall be expressed in periodic and genuine elections which shall be by universal and equal suffrage and shall be held by secret vote or by equivalent free voting procedures.

22: Everyone, as a member of society, has the right to social security and is entitled to realization, through national effort and international co-operation and in accordance with the organization and resources of each State, of the economic, social and cultural rights indispensable for his dignity and the free development of his personality.

23: Everyone has the right to work, to free choice of employment, to just and favourable conditions of work and to protection against unemployment. Everyone, without any discrimination, has the right to equal pay for equal work. Everyone who works has the right to just and favourable remuneration ensuring for himself and his family an existence worthy of human dignity, and supplemented, if necessary, by other means of social protection. Everyone has the right to form and to join trade unions for the protection of his interests.

24: Everyone has the right to rest and leisure, including reasonable limitation of working hours and periodic holidays with pay.

Later in 1948, the United Nations augmented the Universal Declaration of Human Rights with the definition of a new international crime. In a study on the German occupation regime in various European countries, Raphael Lemkin in 1944 had proposed a new concept of "genocide", which did not necessarily mean immediate physical destruction, but rather "a coordinated plan of different actions aiming at the destruction of essential foundations of the life of national groups, with the aim of annihilating the groups themselves". In the circumstances of 1944, he saw it as a "new technique of occupation, aimed at winning the peace even though the war itself is lost". Lemkin, a Polish-Jewish lawyer, had experienced directly and intellectually the horrors of the twentieth century. His home had been directly on the German–Russian front in the First World War; after the war he had studied the massacres of the Ottoman empire, of Armenians and Syriacs; and in

1939 he had narrowly escaped from Poland to North America via Sweden. He now called for an international multilateral treaty to provide measures in the criminal code protecting minorities from persecution because of "their nationhood, religion, or race".[4] On December 9, 1948, the United Nations General Assembly indeed adopted the Convention on the Prevention and Punishment of the Crime of Genocide, based largely on Lemkin's definition, and accepting that preliminary measures designed to marginalize particular groups could be a preliminary stage to mass destruction:

> In the present Convention, genocide means any of the following acts committed with intent to destroy, in whole or in part, a national, ethnical, racial or religious group, as such:
>
> (a) Killing members of the group;
> (b) Causing serious bodily or mental harm to members of the group;
> (c) Deliberately inflicting on the group conditions of life calculated to bring about its physical destruction in whole or in part;
> (d) Imposing measures intended to prevent births within the group;
> (e) Forcibly transferring children of the group to another group.

The general principles articulated in the Universal Declaration of Human Rights and in the Genocide Convention were augmented by two quite firm beliefs that stood distinctly at odds with the bold philosophy of the Declaration: first, that ethnic mixing had been responsible for many of the problems of interwar Europe and that the history of the 1919 settlement showed that only a settlement containing some measure of unmixing could bring relief; and secondly, that economic recovery was central to the stability of the peace settlement, and therefore that a quick program of recovery should be built on the basis of existing institutions.

In forming their attitude, the wartime victors naturally drew on the experience of the previous, failed, effort at a postwar remolding of Europe. The initial treaty settlement of the Ottoman Empire in 1919, the Treaty of Sèvres, had quickly disintegrated as Turkish armies pushed forward into Greece. The Treaty of Lausanne, which more or less restored the prewar Turkish frontier, was accompanied by a separate agreement in which 400,000 Turks in territories acquired by Greece after 1912 were exchanged in return for 1.3 million Greeks. There was widespread agreement among politicians and experts that Lausanne was easily the most satisfactory and stable of the post-First World War settlements. By contrast, the defense of minority rights by the League had been difficult and the process had become hostage to potentially quite aggressive claims. Most obviously, Hitler had used minority rights in Czechoslovakia and Danzig as a way of advancing German claims, and built this into a claim that German policy was based on a strong fundamental morality. In 1935, for instance, he had told the Reichstag that Germany could not make an agreement with Lithuania, "because we cannot enter into political treaties with a state which disregards the most primitive laws of human society".[5]

The Americans, the British, and the Soviets thus now fully agreed that the ethnic and national tensions, heightened during the war, could best be resolved through the physical transfer of populations. The 1919 peace had been based on the principle of self-determination, and had left many ethnically diverse states. In 1945, the worst problem cases in central–eastern Europe were resolved by the expulsion of Germans: from Poland, the borders of which were shifted to the west in accordance with Stalin's demands for greater security, and from Czechoslovakia. The decrees issued by Czech President Edvard Beneš deprived persons of German and Hungarian nationality of their citizenship (August 1945), and then confiscated their movable and immovable assets without compensation, and imposed labor obligations. Forty thousand Hungarians were brought from Slovakia to the Czech territories for this purpose. In total, 2.4 million Germans were expelled, and at least 19,000 died, 6,000 by violence. Clearly, the Czechs felt that the overwhelming majority of Germans in Bohemia had supported Nazi rule, and deserved punishment. Indeed, even rabid Nazis such as Joseph Goebbels had been appalled by the extreme hatred of the Czech Germans for their former compatriots. But it is equally clear that substantial numbers of Germans had worked loyally in the interwar Czech Republic, and did not share the beliefs of the Nazis or participate in their actions, and in no sense could be held to deserve the punishment of the Beneš decrees in 1945. There were fewer expulsions from southeastern Europe, and some Germans remained in Romania.

The Allies had also agreed to the principle of the expulsion of Germans from Poland, both from the old Polish territories, where expulsions were made on the basis of the *Volksliste* compiled by the German wartime administration, and in the new territories of the west. As in Czechoslovakia, the expulsions were often carried out with great brutality, and there were many deaths. Around 100,000 Germans classed by the *Volksliste* as *Reichsdeutsche* (from Germany) or *Volksdeutsche* (local Germans) were sent to work in Russia. Just over 2 million Poles were moved from territories in the east that now belonged to the Soviet Union to western Poland. In addition, Ukrainians from Poland were rounded up and sent to the Soviet Union, with around 5,500 deaths. German figures show almost 7 million German expellees from Polish and Soviet territory, and in 1950 around a fifth of the population of West Germany were the victims of forcible eviction.

Economic prosperity

International justice and a reduced potential for ethnic conflict would mean nothing, however, if there were no economic stability or prosperity. Many American policy-makers believed that the terrible depression had in the final instance been the basic cause of the world war, and that international peace required international prosperity.

Such a position required a Europe-wide approach. Older alternative schemes, in which Germany was to be largely deindustrialized, would not in any sober reckoning produce sufficient resources to re-equip Europe and make it politically stable. The US share of world manufacturing, which in 1938 had been 31.4 percent, by 1953 was 44.7 percent; immediately after the war it was much higher still. In February 1947, the new Secretary of State of the United States, George Marshall, spoke at the alumni day of Princeton University about the lessons of history:

> Most of the other countries of the world [beside the United States] find themselves exhausted economically, financially and physically. If the world is to get on its feet, if the productive facilities of the world are to be restored, if the democratic processes in many countries are to resume their functioning, a strong lead and definite assistance from the United States will be necessary.[6]

He repeated the same message more elaborately in June in a more widely reported commencement speech at Harvard. The idea became the basis for the European Recovery Program. In 1948, Congress passed the Economic Cooperation Act, establishing a European Cooperation Administration, which would administer aid through an Organization for European Economic Cooperation (OEEC). The Act envisaged an extensive economic and political unification of Europe, on the grounds that economic problems such as European reconstruction could no longer be adequately managed on a national level. US State Department economic advisers, so-called Friendly Aid Boys, fanned out over Europe. From 1948 to 1951 "Marshall Aid" involved $12.4 billion, or about 2 percent of the GNP of the recipient countries.

Two percent is in itself obviously not enough to produce an economic miracle, as many subsequent would-be debunkers of the powerful myth that grew up around the Marshall Plan have pointed out. Europe in 1948 had already reached levels of industrial production only slightly below those of 1938 (96 percent). There was a substantial, but not a crippling, loss of capital: West Germany is estimated to have lost 13 percent of its prewar capital, France 8 percent, and Italy 7 percent.[7] What in particular made a difference, especially at the early stages, was the availability of capital equipment, above all machine tools, that in practice could come only from the United States (the other great machine tool maker, Germany, could not produce easily at this time). Such goods would have to be paid for in dollars, and in the face of a dollar scarcity that many Europeans feared to be permanent, could not be paid for without aid. Cotton for the production of textiles, and food (especially cereals) – basic necessities without which European workers would be physically incapable of work – were other imports necessary for recovery that could at this time be bought only from the dollar zone. Another important product of the Marshall program was the way governments could employ the so-called counterpart funds (the European importers paid not the exporter, who was paid by the US government, but their own governments). These could be and were used for infrastructure investments, although of course such investments might also have been financed in a less satisfactory way, through higher taxation or inflation. In general, then, as the American historian Charles Maier has pointed out, the Marshall program was part of a larger stabilization strategy in which European labor and political dissent was bought off, support for the communist left declined, and consensual solutions became easier.

Both the old right and the old left consequently disliked it. Sometimes it was hard to see from what political direction a critique came. In General Franco's Spain, Luis Garcia Berlanga made a film, *Bienvenido Mister Marshall* (1952). It offered biting satire of the way in which a new greed transformed Spain, and a condemnation of US economic imperialism. Was this a leftist or a traditionalist critique of the American way of life?

The European Recovery Program clearly had international effects. The institution it created, the OEEC, was supposed to supervise a political and economic integration of Europe. The grander parts of a plan for a United States of Europe were quickly abandoned, but one OEEC institution, the European Payments Union (EPU), provided a useful mechanism through which intra-European payments were gradually multi-lateralized and liberalized already in the early 1950s. The EPU thus facilitated a large expansion of intra-European trade.

A central part of the Marshall Plan was the economic rehabilitation of Germany. Throughout 1946 and 1947, the British and American zones had been working together more closely in a Bizone, and the United States gradually abandoned its program of dismantling and its commitment to the Potsdam goal of German reparations payments to those countries damaged by war. In June 1948, the Allies introduced a new currency (the Deutschemark) for the three western zones of Germany, and the western sectors of Berlin, but excluding the Soviet-occupied zone. The Soviet Union replied with a blockade of West Berlin, although its representatives still insisted that their overall goal was a unified Germany.

During the early postwar years, the strongest demand for a partition of Germany came from France. The French insistence reflected a vision of what constituted the most fundamental European problem. An essential part of Great Power rivalry since the nineteenth century had been the heavy industrial capacity required to put armies in the field and keep them supplied with arms and munitions. The easiest proxy for effective military might was steel-making capacity. On the eve of the First World War, Germany was making 17.6 million tons of crude steel annually and France only 4.7 million tons. This was in large part a consequence of Germany's seizure in 1871, at the end of the Franco-Prussian war, of the ore fields of Lorraine (though not all of Lorraine was controlled by Germany, and the Germans wanted the basin of Longwy–Briey as a war goal in the First World War). At Versailles, Lorraine with Alsace had been returned to France, but the Lorraine producers still had the problem that the best coking coal was not from Lorraine (whose coal was almost unusable for coking) but from the Ruhr valley. Correspondingly, after the First World War, and again after the Second, many French leaders believed that the coalfields and the metallurgical industries of the Ruhr valley were essential components of German militarism and that a solution to the German problem required the separation from Germany, or the internationalization, of the Ruhr.

The failure of such demands by 1948 meant that a solution of European management of the coal and steel industry became a political priority. The first institutional realization of European integration was thus the European Coal and Steel Community (ECSC; 1951), launched on the basis of Foreign Minister Robert Schuman's 1950 plan. The six members – France, Germany, Italy, Belgium, Luxembourg, and the Netherlands – agreed to create a supranational authority (the "High Authority") supervising a single market in coal and steel. The Authority would guide investment programs, give loans or guarantees, prohibit some sorts of subsidies from national funds, equalize prices, establish production quotas in periods of exceptionally low demand, and determine the allocation of steel and coal in cases of shortages. It would end discrimination in transport charges, which had long been a subject of contention between France and Germany.

The ECSC dealt with great success with what was indeed a central fissure in European history since 1871, and contributed greatly to European stabilization. Its preamble spoke of how "world peace may be safeguarded only by creative efforts equal to the dangers that menace it". The historian Alan Milward wrote that the ECSC treaty "ended eighty years of bitter and deadly dispute and made the reconstruction of western Europe possible. It did so by avoiding all major questions of war and peace and creating instead a formalized network of institutional economic interdependence".[8] Schuman's guru, the economist and diplomat Jean Monnet, later loved to explain how he overheard a conversation between two soldiers in a café: "With the Schuman Plan, one thing is certain: we shall not have to go to war."[9] The cooperation between its members formed the basis for the more extensive economic and political integration provided for in the 1957 Treaty of Rome. Monnet knew that the system he was constructing was incomplete and imperfect, but saw precisely the imperfections as a spur to further integration. He repeatedly reflected on a particular method of developing an institutional foundation for politics. Europe, he said would be "built on crises", and would be "the sum of their solutions".[10]

Security risks

The Schuman Plan came at a moment when its basic premise, that steel provided the fundamental basis of military power, was becoming antiquated. After August 1949, when the Soviet Union tested its first atomic bomb, atomic energy rather than steel-making capacity seemed to constitute the ultimate definition of a nation's capacity to defend itself, and hence, in a way, of national sovereignty.

In the immediate aftermath of the Soviet atomic test of 1949, the world looked very unstable. It was of course not possible to predict who would win an atomic war, if it were to be fought. General Omar Bradley, chairman of the US Joint Chiefs of Staff, told the National Security Council that if war did occur, "we might be in danger of losing it".[11] And war might break out over a wide range of problems and causes: in Berlin, in Yugoslavia (whose relations with the USSR were unclear, and which was claiming Trieste and threatening Italy), in Greece or Turkey, or Iran, or Korea. In turned out that war came in Korea, and it was extremely costly but non-atomic. As it was engaged in the Korean conflict, the United States feared that a Third World War might develop as a global multi-front war, like the Second, and that Europe could be vulnerable. So it urged the Europeans to do more to defend themselves. German Chancellor Konrad Adenauer told the US High Commissioner in Germany: "I am convinced that Stalin has the same plan for Europe as for Korea. What is happening there is a dress rehearsal for what is in store for us here."[12]

The first answer was the European Defence Community, on the basis of a plan drawn up by the French Defence Minister (and subsequent Prime Minister) René Pleven. It provided for a supranational authority, like that of the contemporaneous ECSC, to supervise European troops, including Germans. It was regarded with suspicion by the Anglo-Saxons: the US Secretary of Defense, George Marshall, called it a "miasmic cloud", and Winston Churchill a "sludgy amalgam".[13]

The French Assembly narrowly failed to ratify the plan, and instead the United States now pushed for the inclusion of Germany in the North Atlantic Treaty Organization (NATO). This had been created in 1949 in response to the Berlin crisis and the heightened tension of early Cold War, as a way of linking US and Canadian with west European security interests. In 1955, the Paris Treaty admitted the Federal Republic, and Germany once more had an army.

The Soviet response to this was the creation of its own security and treaty framework, the Warsaw Pact, in 1955. But the USSR also tried to destabilize the Western system by suggesting schemes which would detach West Germany and its industrial potential. On March 10, 1952, the Soviet government presented identical notes (the "Stalin note") to the British, French, and US ambassadors in Moscow, pointing out that seven years after the end of the war, there had still not been a German peace treaty, and sketching out the possible basis for such a treaty. The treaty would need to "ensure the elimination of the possibility of a revival of German militarism and aggression": Germany would have to be neutral. On this basis it would be possible to promote "the development of Germany as a united, independent, democratic, and peace-loving state". The suggestion horrified the West German government, which did its best to block it by pointing out the problem of the eastern frontier, the Oder–Neisse line; by demanding the inclusion of pre-1938 German areas; and by saying that Germany had carried out so much military "research" that disarmament proposals were not practicable. The idea of a united and neutral Germany surfaced again on Stalin's death, when Lavrenti Beria tried to shake up the diplomatic and political scene. In 1957 and 1958 the Polish Foreign Minister Adam Rapacki developed plans for an "atom-free zone" in central Europe, which would include Germany, in order to "relax tension" and "reduce the danger of war". Again, West Germany reacted with great nervousness, and emphasized the importance of its NATO commitments.

Another way for the Soviet Union to destabilize Germany was to raise the Berlin question. In 1958, the Soviet leader Nikita Khrushchev announced that he intended to sign a peace treaty with the German Democratic Republic (GDR; East Germany), and that the treaty would end the rights of the western Allies in Berlin. Adenauer urged Washington to take a hard line in the interest of West German stability, but he also insisted that no atomic weapons be used.

In August 1961, the GDR built a wall between East and West Berlin. Again, it was a moment of high crisis, but this time it was clear to all participants that there was no chance that atomic weapons would be used in a Berlin or German dispute. The most threatening moment was non-European in origin, when in October 1962 the United States discovered that Soviet missiles were being stationed in Cuba, only 90 miles off the Florida coast. The Berlin fault line already seemed to have calmed down.

By 1963 a Cambridge professor, Harry Hinsley, could write with great calm in an authoritative textbook that

> Since 1946 war by design and war by miscalculation have both been ruled out because the Great Powers have become acutely aware of the fatal consequences for themselves of using the weapons, and – except in retaliation against their use – have determined not to use them.[14]

The United Kingdom and France may have shared the logic of this calculation, and both acquired their own atomic weapons, which became a sort of badge of Great Power status for the "would-be's". On the other hand, no one took the Hinsley argument that atomic power creates restraint on the exercise of military force (which was put in a more widely circulated form by the American political scientist Kenneth Waltz) to its logical conclusion and urged the equipment of West Germany with nuclear weapons in order to stabilize it. Germany was still a very peculiar country.

Germany: a new kind of state

The Federal Republic of Germany was established in October 1949, not with a constitution but with a Basic Law – in order to underline the provisional character of the new state – worked out by a parliamentary council, which had begun its work in September 1948. The capital was in Bonn, as Berlin was not legally part of the new country (it sent deputies to the Bundestag, but they were not entitled to vote), and the obvious large city in the center of the new state, Frankfurt, seemed ruled out by its association with the failed liberal movements of 1848.

At the beginning, the Bonn Republic appeared to replicate Weimar. There were many small parties. In the first Bundestag, or parliament, of 402 seats, the two largest parties – the Christian Democrats (CDU) and the Social Democrats (SPD) – had only 139 and 131 seats respectively. There were 17 parliamentarians from the nationalist German party, and 15 communists, as well as 48 others. The smaller parties were excluded after 1953 by a law which stipulated a minimum of 5 percent. Like Weimar, the new German government in Bonn was initially very unpopular because of the compromises it made with the international order. Konrad Adenauer's enemies castigated him as the "Chancellor of the Allies" who had surrendered German statehood.

In practice, however, Adenauer's Germany created a new sort of political stability with surprising speed. Some of the causes for the new and unprecedented success of German political institutions lay in constitutional provisions. The President's power was limited and mostly symbolic. More importantly, the parliamentary parties had the clear responsibility to form governments, with a prohibition of negative votes of no confidence (governments could only be toppled by a vote in which a successor government was named, thus avoiding Weimar situations in which the incompatible far left and right combined to vote against a government). The federal character of the country and the rights of the states (*Länder*) were firmly anchored in the Basic Law. The legal restraints probably would not have meant much, however, if the new polity had run into bad trouble.

Stability was most obviously a product of economic success. At first, many Germans had been skeptical about the currency reform, especially when prices began to rise. Although more goods were now available, they appeared to be too expensive. Soon, however, Adenauer and Ludwig Erhard's party, the CDU, was reaping the electoral benefits of the liberal economic reform.

Erhard, the chief architect of that reform, consistently explained his policy as a "Third Way" between nineteenth-century individualistic liberalism, which he labeled "Manchesterism", and socialist (or Nazi) collectivism. Part of the Allied strategy had hinged on the breaking-up of cartels and trusts, and though some of the large corporations reformed in the 1950s, cartels were controlled through strong anti-cartel legislation.

Germany also built a consensus society, in which as many social groups as possible were included in a new consensus. Previously poor industrial relations were improved by workers' representation on the supervisory boards of companies (*Mitbestimmung*). The elderly population, in voting terms an increasingly powerful political constituency, was won over by provisions for automatically increasing pensions to reflect the increased prosperity of the Federal Republic. The law on pension reform was passed on the eve of the 1957 Bundestag election, the only election in the history of the Federal Republic in which one party achieved an absolute majority. The civil service was brought over with a decision in 1951 which acknowledged the rights and privileges of civil servants (*Beamte*), including the right of tenure, as constitutionally secured under Article 131 of the Basic Law. The 58,000 *Beamte* who had lost their jobs in the course of denazification were thus entitled to have their jobs returned to them.

The incorporation or reincorporation of former Nazi civil servants (including the very prominent case of Hans Globke, a Catholic who was one of the authors of the 1935 Nuremberg racial laws, and in the 1950s became one of Adenauer's closest advisers) into the new political establishment of the Federal Republic raises a question that was little discussed at the time. What was the relationship of the new Germany to the German past? Some historians and political scientists, notably Hermann Lübbe, have argued that the genius of Adenauer's Germany lay in suppressing discussion of a topic that at the time would only have divided Germans hopelessly. There was more to it than this: Adenauer and his political allies, in search of the consensus society, aimed at an explicit "de-moralization" of politics. One of the first acts of the West German parliament had been to declare an amnesty for anyone accused of offenses committed before September 15, 1949, for which the penalty was less than six months' imprisonment. Most of the 800,000 Germans relieved in this way had committed petty crimes in the immediate postwar period, but former Nazis benefited as well.

Politics would be about the present, the practical, and the pragmatic, and not about the past and its pain and penalties. This was also the vein of thinking that made Adenauer eager to conclude a quick settlement with the new state of Israel, based purely on a financial reckoning of reparation, that would "normalize" relations with the Jews.

All this could only take place in a more general European setting. Adenauer consistently emphasized his connections with France and the West, which he had maintained (to great controversy) in the 1920s as Mayor of Cologne. He explained that "a Federal Chancellor must be at once a good German and a good European". He even made outrageously impractical suggestions, such as the idea he launched in a newspaper interview in 1950 that France and Germany might merge in a complete union, with a common citizenship and joint political institutions.[15]

By the late 1950s, Adenauer was well on the way to the successful creation of a new West German consensus. He won the 1957 election on a campaign with the slogan "No Experiments". After the triumph of 1957, Adenauer's hold gradually weakened, as he appeared increasingly aged and out of touch with a modernizing society. He also engaged in an undignified speculation about whether he might sometime promote himself out of power to the largely ceremonial presidency of the republic. But one of the reasons why the Christian Democrats began to lose support to a younger and more dynamic-looking SPD was that the SPD had taken over key aspects of the Adenauerian consensus.

In particular, the SPD, in the first half of the 1950s, had been a vocal opponent of German rearmament, partly on moral grounds as a reaction against Nazi militarism, and partly on the apparently electorally appealing thesis that war in Europe would be a disaster for Germany, and that it would be Germans rather than Americans who would die as cannon fodder for the United States. By the late 1950s, the defense expert of the party, Helmut Schmidt, and the Mayor of West Berlin, Willy Brandt, appealed for an acceptance of Germany's commitments to NATO.

Moreover, the SPD, like parts of the CDU, had initially been highly critical of capitalism. In the immediate aftermath of the liberalization and currency reform of 1948, such opposition had produced electoral payoffs. By the mid-1950s, however, it was very clear that German capitalism was now working very effectively. The party therefore finally shed its semi-Marxist inheritance (it had been formed in 1875 at a congress at Gotha which fused a non-Marxist and rather nationally oriented party with Karl Marx's own movement). In 1959 at the party congress in Bad Godesberg, the SPD formally renounced and denounced Marxism, and proposed instead that it would guide itself by "Christian ethics, humanism, and classical philosophy". The most obvious sign of this volte-face was the acceptance of the market, with the formula "as much competition as possible, as much planning as necessary".

The post-national and post-imperial state created as the Federal Republic of Germany also looked new. Large parts of historic cities had been destroyed or damaged in the war, but there was little sympathy with any ideas of simple historical reconstructions, such as were carried out in Ypres and Rheims after the First World War. Some German architects explained their preference for demolishing even buildings whose façades had remained standing and which were evidently salvageable. Friedrich Spengelin, for example, claimed that "for us, an acknowledgment of guilt blocked access to a compromised past and forbade the reconstruction of the bourgeois city".[16] In practice, however, such views were not prevalent, and much of 1950s and even 1960s construction was hurried and undignified, but unabashedly commercial. In Munich, for instance, the old town square was completed with a brutally cubic department store. A department store skyscraper (later demolished) ended the Leopoldstrasse in a square at Münchener Freiheit (renamed from the Nazi Danziger Freiheit). Postwar cities emerged as a reflection of the Federal Republic: some restoration, little overall planning, and a sacrifice of aesthetics to commercialism.

The princess in the fairy stories: France

Postwar France at first sight looks like the exact opposite of the German experience. Whereas Germany sought to put aside its past, France clung firmly to its history and empire. While Germany was ruled by a stable coalition, with only one Chancellor until the 1960s, France returned quickly to the governmental instability that had dominated the Third Republic. From de Gaulle's first government in September 1944 to his return as Prime Minister in a dramatic political crisis in June 1958, France had 26 governments, of which the shortest lasted three days (the Queuille cabinet in July 1950) and the longest (that of the socialist politician Guy Mollet) only a year and a quarter.

There was no consensus about a suitable constitution. The first constitution, drawn up by a constituent assembly, which gave almost unchecked power to a single chamber, was rejected in a referendum in May 1946. A new assembly worked out a constitution which closely resembled that of the despised Third Republic, and in October 1946 it was accepted in a new referendum, in which, however, large numbers abstained. There were almost 9.3 million yes votes, but 8.1 million no votes and 8.5 million abstentions.

At first it looked as if there might be stable political parties. In the Constituent Assembly (October 1945), there were three big parties: the MRP (Mouvement Républicain Populaire), a new Catholic social movement, with 4.5 million votes; the communists and affiliated parties, with 4.3 million votes; and the Socialist Party, with 3.4 million votes. The first constitution had been the result of a communist–socialist alliance, and had been designed to perpetuate that alliance, through the provisions of the electoral law and through a preamble to the constitution which refused to allow Catholic schools. In the immediate aftermath of the war, the MRP had seemed the best protection for conservative voters, but those constituents rapidly drifted away, as could be seen in the October 1946 referendum, when the proposal had the endorsement of all three large parties but scraped through in such an embarrassing way.

Until May 1947, communists were included in broad coalition governments; from then until the parliamentary elections of 1951, there were center-left coalitions; from 1951 until new elections in January 1956 there were center-right coalitions. In the last two years of the Fourth Republic, 1956–58, the socialists returned to power. These big shifts were partly concealed by continual shifts and reshuffles in government, with ministers changing and swapping office. The communists had been marginalized after 1947, and were widely (and it turned out correctly, when Soviet archives began to open after 1991) suspected of being dependent on a foreign power. The socialists had a notionally revolutionary theory as Marxist as that of the Communist Party, but agreed to ignore it. Most observers saw them as the successor to the "radicals" of the Third Republic, committed to a political ideology that only masked a wish to get control of every kind of office. They became the party of civil servants, teachers, municipal employees, and policemen. When socialist ministers returned to power in 1956, the party experienced a massive new invasion of office-seekers. The MRP, in contrast, had at first looked like an austerely incorrupt party, dedicated to the principles of left-wing Catholicism as propagated by Marc Sangnier's *Sillon* movement (and as condemned by Vatican orthodoxy). But its conservative voters soon abandoned the party, and some of the deputies went with them to the much more conservative Catholicism of de Gaulle. And the MRP's leading politicians soon began to play the game of republican patronage.

Existentialism

The term goes back to the work of the Danish philosopher Søren Kierkegaard (1813–55), but its use became current to describe the philosophies of Martin Heidegger (1889–1976) and Jean-Paul Sartre (1905–80). Heidegger was preoccupied by the question of self-conscious and self-critical existence (*Dasein*), which he wanted to distinguish from simple being (*Sein*). It represented a decision in the face of nothingness (one of Heidegger's most famous wordplays was on the capacity of nothing to "noth": *das Nichts nichtet*). In this decision the critical element was an authenticity that followed from deep philosophical questioning.

Sartre too emphasized the need for an authentic act in the face of an existential void, of which he gave probably the most lucid description when he set out his thoughts on contemplating the root of a tree (in *La Nausée*). He was obsessed by the way in which man and woman were trapped by physical attributes of sex, and by the definition given to them by others. Sartre made this into a more political philosophy (of the radical left) than did Heidegger, who seemed for most of his life largely apolitical. His endorsement of National Socialism and his willingness as Rector of Heidelberg University to carry out anti-Semitic purges can scarcely be seen as an essential part of Heideggerian choices.

The contrast made by the term "existence" is with "essence", the existence of which the existentialists denied. There was in consequence no such thing as a human essence, with the rights and obligations that the Natural Law tradition ascribed to the human being. It is at this level that there exists a connection of existentialism with extreme forms of politics which eulogized the human will and human capacity for action and had no room for discussions of human dignity.

The most striking figures, however, were not the politicians in power but the rebels. Indeed, to be political after the defeat of 1940 and after Vichy was to rebel. The most prominent rebels were initially the intellectuals, who for the most part had played a discreetly clever cat-and-mouse game between 1940 and 1944 with the occupation authorities. Plays such as Jean Anouilh's reworking of Sophocles's *Antigone* (written in 1942, in response to the wounding of the collaborationist leaders Déat and Laval by a member of the resistance, and produced in 1944) or Jean-Paul Sartre's *The Flies* (*Les Mouches*, 1943) were ways of addressing immediately the wartime choices of resistance and compliance. Sartre's greatest philosophical work, *Being and Nothingness* (*L'Être et le Néant*, 1943), was also in part a reworking of the implications of Heidegger's thought in the context of a political situation in which categories externally applied became of vital importance.

> For myself I am not a professor or a waiter in a café, nor am I handsome or ugly, Jew or Aryan, spiritual, vulgar, or distinguished. We shall call all of these categories *unrealizables*. We must be careful not to confuse them with the imaginary. We have to do with perfectly real existences; but those for which these characteristics are really given *are not* these characteristics, and I who *am* can not realize them.

These categories, imposed from the outside, created an existence, which implied a responsibility (since existence could be avoided by suicide: a popular theme in Sartre's literary works). Again, these predicaments were particularly real in the context of wartime Paris.

> Thus there are no *accidents* in a life; a community event which suddenly bursts forth and involves me in it does not come from the outside. If I am mobilized in a war, this war is *my* war; it is in my image and I deserve it. I deserve it because I could always get out of it by suicide or desertion [. . .] But in addition this war is *mine* because by the sole fact that it arises in a situation which I cause to be and that I can discover it there only by engaging myself for or against it, I can no longer distinguish at present the choice which I make of myself from the choice I make of the war.[17]

After the war, many French intellectuals worked out the lessons of Vichy and the occupation as an endorsement of the need for resistance, violence, and revolution in the face of evil. The most elaborate statement of the case was Maurice Merleau-Ponty's *Humanism and Terror* (1947), whose title neatly outlined the major thesis. If the premises of Marxism or Stalinism were correct, if there was a historical meaning, and if the Communist Party embodied the force of history, then the great trials and the terror of the 1930s were also justified. He explained: "To be a Marxist is to believe that economic problems and cultural or human problems are a single problem and that the proletariat as history has shaped it holds the solution to that problem." While perfectly aware of the brutality of socialism in practice, Merleau-Ponty nevertheless concluded that it made humans better. "Within the USSR violence and deception have official status while humanity is to be found in daily life. On the contrary, in democracies the principles are humane but deception and violence rule daily life."[18] On the surface, it is difficult to see how Sartre's existentialism (in which meaning was produced by reflection in the actions of others) could easily be married to a hard version of the Marxism with which he associated, and indeed, Sartre supported but remained suspicious of the French Communist Party.

For the French leftist intellectuals, the attraction of communism lay as much in its promise of violence (which fascinated them) as of justice (which seemed rather too abstract). Some were disenchanted after the Soviet invasion of Hungary in 1956, but this violent intervention actually occasioned Sartre's greatest and most passionate defense of communism. "Its analyses are just: the errors, ignorance, and weakness of the moment do not affect that."[19] Other west European (but not Scandinavian) countries also had distinguished Marxist intellectuals, but nowhere, with the possible exception of Italy, were they as obsessed with the communist movement's violence as a means to create and perpetuate personal legitimacy. The British Marxist intellectuals, by contrast, were mostly historians rather than philosophers, and failed to really develop an engagement with the present. Like much else in the British establishment, they were essentially backward-looking, taking as their guiding light the radical experience of the seventeenth century.

In the late 1940s, however, French critical intellectual rebels were acutely aware of themselves as a pan-European phenomenon, a reaction to the divided world of the Cold War. In late 1947 Sartre associated himself with Georges Altman and David Rosset's attempt to launch a pan-European Rally for Revolutionary Democracy (Rassemblement Démocratique Révolutionnaire). Sartre, who hated the nation-state and compared de Gaulle not merely to Pétain but also to Hitler, explained:

> By creating Europe, this new generation will create democracy. With the constitution of a federation and the implementation of a movement that transcends all frontiers, European youth will finally be able to have its future, its peace, its true freedom.[20]

Sartre and his associates were not the only rebels against the restoration of capitalism in a western setting. In the mid-1950s, Pierre Poujade achieved a considerable success with an anti-modern, anti-American, anti-technocratic campaign, that urged Frenchmen to abandon Coca-Cola and drink wine. It appealed above all to farmers and to small business *patrons*.

The most strikingly effective French rebel, however, was France's great wartime leader, Charles de Gaulle, who had denounced the constitutional plans of 1946, and in 1947 launched his own political movement, the Rassemblement du Peuple Français (RPF). The RPF was not a very coherent movement: many of its leading figures felt themselves to be on the left, and disliked de Gaulle's more conservative clericalism. In political opposition in the 1950s, it shifted more and more to an anti-European and anti-American nationalistic stance. What saved it as a political force was the "purity" of de Gaulle's opposition: unlike many of his lieutenants, he did not want to make compromises or deals with the republican leadership, and remained in a sort of internal exile at his home in Colombey-les-Deux-Églises, waiting for the call to assume power.

Gaullism

General de Gaulle founded a political movement that remained vigorous long after his death. But he also enunciated a doctrine whose influence reached much more widely, with politicians in other European countries (notably Germany and the United Kingdom) identifying themselves as Gaullist. In the 1990s, President Yeltsin found elements of the Gaullist legacy an inspiring guide to building a new Russian state. Subsequent Presidents of France, in particular François Mitterrand (a socialist) and Jacques Chirac (a Gaullist), continued large elements of Gaullism as a philosophy of foreign policy.

Gaullism is a form of *Realism*, which casts a romantic aura around the nation whose interests are being championed. The most famous exposition of this is at the opening of de Gaulle's war memoirs, in which he greatly advanced the Gaullist legend:

> The emotional side of me tends to imagine France, like the princess in the fairy stories or the Madonna in the frescoes, as dedicated to an exalted and exceptional destiny. Instinctively I have the feeling that Providence has created her either for complete successes or for exemplary misfortunes.[21]

The nation ultimately rests on its power (as in realism). This is a doctrine that grew out of his theory of military leadership, which he set out in *Le Fil de l'Épée* (*The Edge of the Sword*, 1932, p. 9):

> Is it possible to conceive of life without force? Only if children cease to be born, only if minds are sterilized, feelings frozen, men's need anaesthetized, only if the world is reduced to immobility, can it be banished. . . . Force has watched over civilizations in the cradle; force has ruled empires, and dug the grave of decadence; force gives laws to the peoples and controls their destinies.

This doctrine made de Gaulle highly suspicious of institutions and legal processes that claimed to transcend the nation. He accepted European integration only if it remained based on a *Europe des patries*: otherwise it would simply produce a talking shop (areopagus). In practice, he also liked the small Europe of the original European Economic Community Six, because it could easily be dominated by France.

An increasingly important part of Gaullism was its anti-Americanism. Though it would be possible to trace the development of this biographically, especially to President Roosevelt's wartime neglect of and contempt for de Gaulle, and the consequent American preference for other French leaders (and its dealings with the Vichy regime), this hardly explains its longevity and its significance as an element in the Gaullist appeal. This part of Gaullist doctrine had a theoretical consistency, in that what de Gaulle disliked most was American cloaking of national interest in the language of universalism in politics and economics. Gaullism as anti-Americanism had a security and an economic element. As President of France in the 1960s de Gaulle attacked universalist US security ambitions, and the war in Vietnam, which he described as deserving French "reprobation". At the same time, in 1965, de Gaulle launched an onslaught against American control of the international monetary and financial system.

De Gaulle provided for many Europeans the most coherent rationalization of anti-American resentments, but the legacy was problematical to the extent that it was so clearly based on suspicion of principles of universal morality in politics.

Politics looked as if France had returned to business as usual, namely the corrupt instability of the Third Republic; but French society was changing quite rapidly. The political scientist Stanley Hoffmann described the "stalemate society" of the Third Republic: this was ended by war, economic mobilization during the war and occupation, and above all by the expansionary international economic environment of the 1950s. Elements of the welfare state had been put in place before the war: family allowances in 1932, paid holidays by the Popular Front in 1936. But welfare principles were now extended and systematized.

Politically, a group of technocratic planners – a class that would establish itself as the true elite of modern French politics – took credit for the strength of French economic performance. In 1947, the government adopted an overall plan for the economy. The head of the Plan Commission, Jean Monnet, explained repeatedly: "The only alternative to modernization is decadence." He envisaged not a static plan, but a series of flexible responses to new challenges. "The Plan, like life, is continuous creation."[22]

Investment took place more and more not with the resources of a private capital market, but with state funds. A National Credit Council, composed of representatives of the government and of large borrowers, would direct the allocation of investment in a rational manner: borrowers would have to make their pitch to the Council, which then set broad priorities for national development. Some heavy industries (coal and electricity), as well as companies that had collaborated ostentatiously with the German occupiers (such as the automobile producer Renault), and the four largest deposit banks, were nationalized. The railroads and the aircraft industry had already been placed under state control before the war. Those that remained in private hands were still subject to a substantial state "guidance" or control. The newly created École Nationale d'Administration (ENA), whose graduates, the *énarques*, would soon form the elite of French decision-making, was highly critical of conventional French business existence. French business-men in the past had been largely, the new technocrats argued, put in place by their families. French industry had been ruled by "bourgeois dynasties" such as the Schneiders and the de Wendels. Because business was limited by the family firm, which would lose its *raison d'être* if it expanded too much and borrowed on the capital market, it was inherently "Malthusian". It had limited growth, and thus had been responsible for France's economic and political debacle in the 1930s. It could not be expected to commit itself to a large-scale investment program. A new and rational business style would rely on credit – if necessary, force-fed by the state, which would need to play the role of a farmer rearing geese for their foie gras.

Although France grew rapidly during the 1950s, there was a substantial amount of macro-economic instability. High levels of inflation followed from large budget deficits, as the state tried to buy off new claims, and also as France tried to live up to its claim to be a world power.

In practice, being a world power meant the exercise of colonial control. During the 1930s, as the world political and economic scene disintegrated, both the United Kingdom and France fell back on colonies as the backbone of national existence. But maintaining the colonial tradition proved to be more and more expensive. For France, defeated in 1940, maintaining colonies became ever more of a national obsession, and a very painful one.

The most obvious legacy of defeat was in Asia, where Japan in the spring of 1945 had taken over French Indochina at the moment when metropolitan France was being liberated. After the Japanese defeat, France found it hard to reimpose the authority of the mother country. In 1954, French forces were humiliatingly defeated at Dien Bien Phu. France was clearly so over-extended militarily that it threatened to destroy the security system of western Europe by withdrawing from NATO. In order to keep a central part of the European security order stable, the United States agreed to assume France's military commitments in southeast Asia.

But while Indochina touched the French sense of national honor, there were few French settlers, and the practical results for France of French with-drawal were small. The struggle that tore apart the Fourth Republic was the Algerian revolution, where Arab nationalists struggled against a large settler presence. The French military had learned to take a very harsh line in Vietnam; many of the paratroop commanders referred to the Algerians as *les viets*.

On November 1, 1954, All Saints Day, a series of attacks on French military and police positions in Algeria began. The government's immediate reaction was to increase the military presence. The socialist Interior Minister, François Mitterrand, told the National Assembly: "Algeria is France. And who among you, Mesdames, Messieurs, would hesitate to employ every means to preserve France?"[23] But the Paris government was increasingly distrusted by those it wanted to protect. When the socialist Prime Minister

Guy Mollet visited Algiers in January 1956 he was first booed and then attacked by the French settlers (the so-called *pieds noirs*), and forced to ask his nominee for the post of Governor-General to withdraw.

At first it looked as if France might defeat Arab nationalism by tackling its international source. In July 1956, the Egyptian President Gamal Abdul Nasser nationalized the Suez Canal. By August, France was already preparing, with the United Kingdom and Israel, forces for a surprise attack on the canal. British politicians, above all Prime Minister Anthony Eden, viewed Nasser as a reincarnation of the 1930s threats of Hitler and Mussolini, and wanted to apply the lesson of the 1930s, namely that pre-emptive action was better than appeasement. French determination to attack Egypt increased when in October the French navy stopped and boarded a ship, the *Athos*, loaded in Alexandria and carrying weapons and munitions for the Algerian rising. By this time, Mollet had convinced himself that the destruction of Nasser would end the Algerian insurrection. On November 5, British and French paratroops landed near Port Said; one day later, and after immense US pressure, the United Kingdom agreed a ceasefire. The incident, a new humiliation for France, fanned resentment against the "Anglo-Saxon" world, which had frustrated the apparently successful French action. The paratroop commander, General Massu, went to Algiers determined to stamp out the Arab nationalist threat.

The French colonial ethos since the nineteenth century had based itself on a concept of the *mission civilisatrice* that France embodied in a unique way because of the legacy of 1789. The civilizing mission, however, hardly corresponded to the methods used in Algeria by the French army, the paratroop regiments, and the Foreign Legion (which had a particular historical commitment to North Africa). The Foreign Legion looked particularly sinister in that in the mid-1950s it was almost half-German, composed of recruits eager to escape the consequences of crimes they had committed in Hitler's armies (although it is hard to be sure of nationalities in the Foreign Legion, since it is safe to assume that most applicants had good motives to conceal their precise backgrounds). As metropolitan France heard more and more accounts of torture used in the war against Algerian terror, Catholic and left-wing intellectuals (but not the socialist or communist parties) were horrified. French soldiers were now committing Nazi crimes. Jean-Paul Sartre, by this time idolized as France's leading thinker and the conscience of the nation, explained:

> We are sick, very sick. Feverish and prostrate, obsessed by old dreams of glory and the foreboding of its shame, France is struggling in the grip of a nightmare it is unable either to flee or decipher. Either we'll see things as they are or we will die.[24]

The settlers and the military became increasingly hostile to the French governments, which they believed to be too complacent about the Algerian uprising, too much swayed by the Parisian intellectuals, and too eager to negotiate about cease-fires with "rebels" and "assassins". In May 1958, during a memorial service for three French soldiers executed by the Algerian resistance movement FLN (Front de Libération Nationale), the army and the *pieds noirs* formed a "Committee of Public Safety", which sent an ultimatum to Paris and then proceeded to seize power in Corsica.

Parisians thought a military coup increasingly likely, and the Gaullists – who had in part been behind the radicalization of opinion in Algiers – skillfully presented de Gaulle as the only figure who could save France, a view which the socialist leaders came to accept. De Gaulle himself came to Paris, and had long negotiations with the Prime Minister, Pierre Pflimlin, and with the President, René Coty, which hinged on de Gaulle's refusal to issue a condemnation of the violence used by the French army. By the evening and night of May 28/29, de Gaulle seemed to give up. He told the President of the Senate:

> Is the return of de Gaulle possible? Is it not possible? After all, you know, France will bury us all. We pass. She alone is eternal. If my return is not possible, I shall go back to my village with my chagrin.[25]

As it was, France looked closer to civil war even than it had been in the 1930s. In Paris, there were massive demonstrations by the unions and the left against "fascism".

Almost immediately, de Gaulle went to Algiers, where he opened his address from the balcony of the Gouvernement-Générale with the memorably ambiguous phrase "*je vous ai compris!*" (I have understood you). In this and subsequent speeches, he promised "renewal", urged "reconciliation" to those who had joined the FLN ("Never more than here, nor more than this evening, have I felt how beautiful, how great, how generous, is France"), but never – in Algiers or in his subsequent tour of the country – used the *pied noir* phrase "*Algérie française*".

De Gaulle presided over a constitutional revision, in which the President's powers were greatly increased (he could form and dismiss governments, and call new parliamentary elections), and he purged the army leadership. The Debré law of 1959 gave state aid to Catholic schools and thus ended the long-standing tensions between Catholics and the Republic. As President of the Republic (now generally known as the "Fifth Republic"), de Gaulle negotiated the Évian agreement, which provided for Algerian independence. When the military and the settlers again revolted, and there occurred a new military putsch, de Gaulle did not hesitate to stamp it down.

In 1962, the constitutional changes were completed when in place of a large nominated assembly voting for the President, the presidency of the republic was to be determined by popular election. De Gaulle undoubtedly stabilized France with the magic of the past, his authority, and his language. France to him, in the famous opening of his war memoirs, was the Madonna in the frescoes and the princess in the fairy stories. Juxtaposed with the modernistic technocracy of the Plan, however, his vision was creakily out of date.

The price of the UK's goodbye to empire

Unlike in the case of the continental countries, there appeared to be no need in the United Kingdom to redraw the (unwritten) constitution. But the United Kingdom had as much difficulty as any country in redefining its position in the new world. In particular, the legacy of Great Power status and empire, and the costs required for defense of those traditions, stood starkly at odds with the material condition of a country exhausted by war. The tensions between claims and reality brought a long and weary lament about "decline".

The chief problems of the United Kingdom were immediately economic and financial: they were the legacy of the cost of war, and of the selling-off of overseas assets. The competitive position of British industry had deteriorated, as no funds had been available for investment and modernization. In 1945, unlike in 1918, the United Kingdom was a net debtor, with foreign liabilities of £3.5 billion and assets of only £3 billion. With the end of the European war (even before the war in Asia ended), on August 21, 1945, the US government halted Lend-Lease. Eventually, it substituted a $3.75 billion loan, which came with a heavy condition attached, the return to currency convertibility by 1947. Given the gigantic increases in US production and productivity during the war, this seemed an almost impossible requirement, destined to force the United Kingdom into a speedy bankruptcy. In practice, convertibility in July 1947 was followed by an almost immediate reimposition of exchange controls, and a devaluation of sterling (September 1949) failed to be sufficiently effective and convincing to allow a return to convertibility. The outstanding economist of the time, John Maynard Keynes, who had led the British in their debt negotiations with Washington, commented on the English "inner reluctance to accept a situation so utterly reversed from what she is used to and to find herself asking for financial aid instead of giving it".[26]

In these circumstances, the economic resources of empire appeared to be an attractive substitute for the American diktat. Already a large part of war expenditure had been financed by running up British debts ("clearing balances") with many countries in the British Empire (notably India and Egypt), and also with other British trade partners. But maintaining empire required immediately more expense, not less, and defense budgets would have to rise. Keynes spoke dismissively about the choice of "squandering" the American loan in order "to cut a dash in the world".

The United States was broadly hostile to the idea of empire, at least as practiced by the Europeans and Japanese. One sign of the new climate was how quickly the United States compelled the Netherlands to recognize the independence of its former colony of Indonesia, which had been seized by

Japan in the war. Suspicion of empire also influenced relations with the United Kingdom. In the course of the prolonged debt negotiations, several Americans simply advised the United Kingdom to sell off the empire in order to pay off the war debts. British officials responded with the contemptuous view that "these people will never be able to run an Empire".[27]

British leaders were worried about the dominance of the United States. The (very costly) decision to build nuclear capability and an atomic bomb, which was made secretly and without any cabinet discussion, had its background in the perception that the United States (and in particular Secretary of State James Byrnes) did not take the United Kingdom seriously. The British Foreign Secretary Ernest Bevin said:

> That won't do at all, we've got to have this [bomb] [. . .] I don't mind for myself, but I don't want any other Foreign Secretary of this country to be talked at or by a Secretary of State in the United States as I just had [*sic*] in my discussion with Mr. Byrnes. We have got to have this thing over here whatever it costs. [. . .] We've got to have the bloody Union Jack flying on top of it.[28]

The most immediate British problem concerned India. The eventual independence of India had been a topic of serious debate since before the First World War. There had been an Indian parliament since 1919, and the Government of India Act of 1935 established some further elements of self-rule in the provinces, though central power was still firmly in the hands of a British Governor General. In 1942, at the height of the Japanese threat, the British government had offered the Indian nationalist leaders some kind of "autonomy", which most Indians rejected. The decision to move to complete independence and to create two states, one predominantly Moslem and one multi-ethnic but Hindu-dominated, was made astonishingly in a matter of weeks. In February 1947, Prime Minister Clement Attlee announced that the United Kingdom would hand over India to a government that could maintain peace by the end of June 1948. This looked like a rushed timetable. The Moslem leader, Jinnah, quickly told the newly appointed Viceroy, Lord Mountbatten, that June 1948 was much too early, and asked whether it was Mountbatten's "intention to turn this country over to chaos and bloodshed and civil war"?[29] Mountbatten promptly concluded that the transfer would have to be much quicker, and announced that it would be complete by August 14, *1947*. A Boundary Commission chaired by Sir Cyril Radcliffe drew up partition lines between Hindu and Moslem India in Bengal and Punjab. The lines were acknowledged at the time to be quite crude. In some cases within the disputed Punjab territories in Ferozepur and Zira, areas originally awarded to Moslem Pakistan were revised because they contained important military bases and equipment. The division of the Sikh population by the new boundary also posed problems. The United Kingdom therefore gave up any idea of policing the frontiers its bureaucrats had established, and on August 29, two weeks after partition and independence, the Punjab Boundary Force was dissolved and its tasks handed over to the new Indian and Pakistani governments. In all, some 8 million refugees fled in a few weeks, and Calcutta and Delhi were swamped with Hindu and Sikh refugees. The expulsions were as violent and brutal as anything that occurred in the postwar European population exchanges, and the estimates for the number of victims of communal violence range between 500,000 and 1 million people.

With the quick development of the automobile after the war, petroleum looked as if it would be the key resource of the rest of the century, and the UK's remaining interests in the Middle East acquired a new importance. In Iran, Prime Minister Mussadeq dissolved parliament in July 1953 and started to work closely with the Soviet Union. A joint British–American operation overthrew him and restored the Shah to the throne. The next threat to British petroleum supplies came from Arab nationalism, and directly from Nasser's nationalization of the Suez Canal. This was the British background to the Suez fiasco in which the United Kingdom was rapidly forced to back down.

In domestic terms, the postwar Labour government under Clement Attlee continued wartime collectivism. Churchill had already spoken of "national compulsory insurance from the cradle to the grave". The Beveridge Report of 1942 had laid out a plan of how social insurance could be used to eliminate poverty. The most important measures were National Insurance (old-age pensions and unemployment support, which were extended as universal benefits rather than being restricted to manual and low-income workers, as were the prewar equivalents); family allowances; National Assistance (to give additional assistance to those ineligible for the insurance schemes); and a National Health Service, which rapidly became the pride of the whole welfare state regime. As in France, the government nationalized the Bank of England and some key industries (coal, gas, railroads) in accordance with Clause IV of the Labour Party program – printed on every membership card – which called for the nationalization of "the means of production, distribution and exchange". The British steel industry, too, was nationalized. The leading Yugoslav communist Milovan Djilas later wrote of how Stalin approved of the British transformation. Anthony Crosland, a leading British socialist thinker, concluded that on [using] a historical definition "it is manifestly inaccurate to call contemporary Britain a capitalist society".[30]

From 1947, the finance minister ("Chancellor of the Exchequer" in the *ancien régime* parlance preserved in the United Kingdom) Sir Stafford Cripps tried a British version of planning. Annual Economic Surveys provided specific figures for output, export, and manpower targets. Manpower control was aimed at overcoming the scarcity of labor in key bottleneck industries: coalmining, agriculture, and textiles.

The opposition Conservatives, still under the veteran wartime leader Sir Winston Churchill, came back into power in 1951 with a campaign directed against the continuance of wartime austerity, embodied in the skeletal features of Cripps himself. The Conservative slogan in 1951 of "Set the people free" was just enough to win a narrow majority of parliamentary seats (though not of the popular vote). Public expenditure fell quite sharply between 1951 and 1957 (mostly due to falling expenditure on defense), but then began to rise again. The standard rate of income tax was cut from 47.5 percent to 42.5 percent in 1955. The Conservative governments, though, did not want to undo the social achievements of the Labour government. Indeed, at this time something approaching a consensus on social and economic issues developed between the two major parties: a reformism, based on the principles of economic management as set out by Keynes. It was termed "Butskellism" after the Labour leader Hugh Gaitskell and the leading Conservative social thinker R.A. ("Rab") Butler.

Keynesianism

John Maynard Keynes's *The General Theory of Employment, Interest and Money*, published in 1936, was the most influential book on economics published in the twentieth century. At the height of Keynes's posthumous reputation, in the 1960s, it was widely credited as being the book that saved western democracy. Immediately after its publication, it was rapidly translated into many languages, and totalitarian policy-makers in Japan and Germany also saw themselves as realizing parts of Keynes's vision on how to achieve economic and political stabilization. Some of Keynes's disciples at this time were bitterly frustrated that totalitarian rulers were learning Keynesianism more quickly than democrats.

Keynes's particular economic contribution was to identify a large range of economic equilibria, in some of which economies could remain for long periods of time with unemployment and an under-utilization of capacity. There was no single optimal equilibrium to which the economy must necessarily revert, as some economists of the classical school had believed. The major concern of the book is how investment decisions drive savings (while much of the "orthodox" vision that Keynes was rebelling against emphasized the need for saving and frugality). In terms of monetary theory, Keynes showed how the preference for holding money (for security or speculative reasons) could produce what became known as the liquidity trap, in which interest rates would continue at low levels without prompting new investment. In the 1920s and early 1930s, the United Kingdom and much of the industrial world was in such a trap.

Other economists in other countries were reaching similar conclusions at the same time: the Swede Knut Wicksell and his disciples in the Stockholm School, whose views were put into political practice by the socialist politician Eric Wigforss, and Michał Kalecki in Poland. In the United States, Keynesianism was popularized by Alvin Hansen.

The Keynesian remedy in practice usually involved fiscal policy: in the case of less than full employment equilibria, additional state spending would raise incomes. Keynes also applied his theory to the management of the wartime economy after 1939, in which the problem was quite the opposite of that of the interwar United Kingdom. Military expenditure created excessive demand, and inflationary dangers, that could be reduced by raised levels of taxation. In order to be useful as a theory of economic management, Keynesianism required the availability of national accounting data: it could be operationalized only by calculations of levels of national income, saving, and investment.

In practice, there was near full employment for two decades in the postwar world, although this is largely due to a rather uniquely favorable set of circumstances, rather than simply the transformative impact of a great idea. But the idea, and the vision behind it of more widespread economic prosperity, certainly helped to establish favorable political conditions for sustained economic growth.

Keynes also spent a great deal of his life thinking about international economics. His criticism of the Versailles Treaty in 1919 was mainly based on the ways in which it disrupted the integrated international economy of the nineteenth century. In the 1920s he was consistently against increases in trade protectionism. In the 1930s he liked to present himself as an economic nationalist, who believed in "national self-sufficiency", and argued that the volume of international trade was inevitably declining. But in the war, he became an internationalist again, and played (with his American opposite number, Harry Dexter White) the central role in the devising of a postwar monetary system, which was realized in July 1944 through the Bretton Woods agreements.

Butler never became leader of the Conservative Party: after Churchill's retirement as Prime Minister in 1954, the long-time crown prince, Sir Anthony Eden, took over. When Eden stumbled over Suez, Harold Macmillan, who had first urged the Prime Minister on and then exaggerated the threat of a run on the currency in order to force a retreat, successfully ensured that he rather than Butler was summoned by the young Queen Elizabeth to form a new government. Butler, who now became Deputy Prime Minister, was said to "lack the killer instinct".

Macmillan's greatest achievement was to end almost all of what was left of the British Empire in a manner that uniquely combined a grand Edwardian patrician style with a fundamental flippancy. His colleagues believed he was an "actor–manager". He regarded African leaders as jokes rather than threats, and this helped him to deal with them. The Sardauna of Sokoto in northern Nigeria was "a great character, a local swell, not unlike Trollope's Duke of Omnium". Ghana was "corrupt – reasonably corrupt, but I don't think it was badly corrupt. Not more corrupt than absolutely necessary." He memorably explained in a speech at Cape Town in February 1960 that "the wind of change is blowing through this continent, and, whether we like it or not, this growth of national consciousness is a political fact".[31]

Ghana was the first sub-Saharan African country to be "given" (as the British liked to say) its independence: it was handed over to Kwame Nkrumah on March 6, 1957. Then came Nigeria, Sierra Leone, Uganda, and Kenya. At the same time, the Central African Federation, an association of Nyasaland and Northern and Southern Rhodesia, and the outcome of a failed British attempt to create a multi-racial state, was broken up: Nyasaland became independent as Malawi and Northern Rhodesia as Zambia. The two largest British colonies in east Africa, Kenya and Southern Rhodesia, were the largest settler colonies, and the most likely to produce Algerian circumstances. But Kenya, after a brutal war against the so-called Mau-Mau in the early 1950s, was handed over astonishingly peacefully to Jomo Kenyatta. The Rhodesian problem was postponed, until in 1965 the white settlers under Ian Smith issued a unilateral declaration of independence. Attempts by the British government to negotiate with Smith collapsed, and the United Nations imposed sanctions on Rhodesia. The transition to majority rule was only made when after lengthy negotiations in Lancaster House, London, in 1979, the country became independent as Zimbabwe (March 1980).

Macmillan's major principle of government was that it should be "fun". The leading institutional historian of the British Prime Ministership, Peter Hennessy, concludes that "Of all our postwar PMs, the laughter rang loudest and longest through the Cabinet Room doors when 'Uncle Harold' was in the chair."[32] It was government by charm, charm as memorably described by Evelyn Waugh's Anthony Blanche in *Brideshead Revisited* (1945), the greatest of the novels of English decline: "Charm is the great English blight. It does not exist outside these damp islands. It spots and kills anything it touches."

In the 1959 general election, Macmillan ran on the slogan "Life's better with the Conservatives", which was widely interpreted as "You've never had it so good." (This derived from a speech he made in 1957 which included the widely reported assertion, "Let us be frank about it: most of our people have never had it so good.") He fell after a series of resignations, cabinet quarrels and sex scandals, in which his style looked increasingly antiquated. In 1960, he had been elected as Chancellor of Oxford University in a fiercely contested election, in which his leading supporter, the historian Hugh Trevor-Roper (whom he had appointed to the Regius Chair of History), explained: "We are going flat out for the young and the gay, to whom, I think, the Prime Minister has a greater appeal than to the staid and the respectable." But by 1963, in the middle of the Profumo scandal, in which his Defence Minister lied about an affair with a call-girl who was simultaneously "seeing" a Soviet military attaché, Macmillan was moved to say that "I do not live among young people much myself."[33] This was the "swinging sixties", and it rejected "Supermac".

Macmillan managed to engineer his own replacement by someone who was not R.A. Butler: a colorless member of the House of Lords who had to resign his peerage in order to become Prime Minister as Sir Alec Douglas-Home. He was defeated in the next general election, in 1964, by a Labour Party which could now paint itself in a very different guise than the austere frugality of Stafford Cripps's planning experiments. The party's leading intellectual, Anthony Crosland, argued that socialism was less about planning than about raising general living standards. Planning had "a lower priority than a decade ago", while "higher personal consumption must form part of any statement of the socialist goal on fundamental egalitarian grounds".[34]

The Labour Party in the 1960s, and especially its leader, Harold Wilson, looked largely to the United States for a model of how to build a new society with high levels of consumption. It argued that the new egalitarianism would require no great struggle and no great sacrifice, since after all the upper classes of society were close to consuming as much as they could. Economic growth could pull everyone up: it was simply that the United Kingdom had missed the chance to grow as quickly as continental Europe during the "12 wasted years" of Conservative rule. Crosland based his case about the new objective of higher living standards on the diminishing marginal utility of consumption: how many goods could an individual possess?

> Even more luxurious items also have a limit. The *Tailor and Cutter* asserts that the well-dressed man-about-town needs 30 suits; and although this sets the physical frontier further back than most of us would have supposed, it does at least concede that some saturation point exists.[35]

An affluent society could thus be achieved without any substantial social pain. In power, then, the Labour Party could follow simply a rejuvenated version of the Butskellite consensus. It was only a different style of presentation, with Harold Wilson as an ordinary, cloth-cap-clad "cheeky chappy". "Cheek" had simply replaced "charm" as a mode of political operation.

Italy and one-party politics

Italian postwar politics began in a very similar vein to those of France: these were two countries deeply divided by a past which had largely discredited the political right and its institutions. When the fascist Grand Council voted to overthrow Mussolini, King Vittorio Emanuele III chose to replace the Duce with a close associate, the fascist Marshall Badoglio. Fascism was in the end destroyed only by the British and American armies. The King abdicated in favor of his son in May 1946, but too late to save the monarchy, which was rejected by a quite narrow vote in a referendum.

As in France, the major parties in the immediate postwar era were those with no association with fascism or the old right: the Christian Democrats (Democrazia Cristiana or DC), who in June 1946 had 35 percent of the vote for the Constituent Assembly, the socialists (20 percent), and the communists (19 percent). The communists, at this stage loyal to instructions from Moscow, both stressed their commitment to legality and parliamentarism, and acted so as to keep the DC leader, Alcide de Gasperi, in power. The constitution continued the 1929 concordat, and at the same time added the characteristic elements of the historical moment of 1945: the right to employment, health care, and education, as well as the right of workers to participate in management. The first postwar governments in addition introduced rent controls, a partial indexation of wages (which later evolved into a rather rigid *scale mobile*), and a dramatic land reform, in which 2 million acres of uncultivated land on the great estates (*latifundia*) were distributed to small farmers.

In the elections of April 1948, soon after the communist coup in Czechoslovakia, the DC won 48 percent of the vote and a majority of seats in the Chamber of Deputies (306 out of 574); the second largest group, the communists, had 131; and the socialists were divided into a moderate wing (33 seats) and a Marxist wing under the leadership of Pietro Nenni.

De Gasperi was the longest serving of postwar Italian prime ministers, presiding in the Palazzo Chigi from December 1945 to August 1953. At first, he included even communists in his coalition governments, but as in France, they were squeezed out in 1947 with the hardening of Cold War antagonisms. From the perspective of the potentially fissiparous DC, however, it was useful to have so clearly defined and so threatening an enemy on the left, and the DC remained in power for as long as – and no longer than – the existence of a communist alternative. DC rule thus continued until the collapse of the communist regimes in eastern Europe in 1989–90.

The introduction of proportional representation meant that it was unlikely that any party would ever secure complete control of the Chamber. In 1953 the DC had 262 out of 590 seats, in 1958 273 out of 596, and in 1963 only 260 out of 630. Coalitions thus became the rule, and the DC became heavily factionalized (like the Japanese Liberal Democrats) and notoriously corrupt. There were big scandals about the agency for local tax collection, about the regulation of savings banks and social security, and of course about large public projects such as the new Fiumicino Airport in Rome. In February 1960, the Speaker of the Senate denounced "the atmosphere of corruption that weighs heavily on our public life".[36]

Even so, until the government of Giovanni Spadolini (1981–82), every government was headed by a member of the DC party. The party gradually sought to build broader coalitions. In particular the weak performance of the DC in 1963, when the Communist Party greatly increased its vote, led to an "opening to the left", in which the Nenni socialists agreed to join the cabinet.

Economic rehabilitation of Italy began with a dramatic stabilization program presided over by Luigi Einaudi, first as Governor of the Bank of Italy, and then as Finance Minister and Deputy Prime Minister. Einaudi had attacked the morality (or rather immorality) that he detected behind Keynes's writings, which in his view "inculcate into people's heads the wrong sort of idea that over any other is dear to him: that the responsibility for the evils which afflict men can be pinned on 'somebody' [else]".[37] For this reason, he refused to use the counterpart funds of the Marshall Plan for public investment projects, but rather thought that they should be used to build up Italian reserves: "the gift, like all gifts, is corrupting and damaging. In what consists the damage? In inducing us to believe that life is easier than it is, hampering our effort to be independent."[38]

Stabilization involved the responsibility for taking harsh decisions oneself. The 1947 stabilization imposed controls on bank credits, and limited the power of the Bank of Italy to monetize public debt. Einaudi thought that a harsh stabilization (it would now be called "shock therapy") would raise savings and exports, which it eventually did (in the 1950s). In the short term, however, such therapies are painful, and between October 1947 and January 1948 a sharp fall in industrial output occurred. As in the case of the slightly later liberalization and stabilization of Ludwig Erhard in Germany, the US experts from the European Recovery Program were worried and shocked by the drastic nature of the program, which they feared might undermine a highly precarious political stability. They criticized Italy for not engaging in enough public investment. Further dramatic liberalization took place in 1951, when Italy built up a large creditor balance in the EPU, and the Treasury Minister, Udo La Malfa, decided to liberalize almost completely imports from the EPU area, and to reduce average import duties by 10 percent. He took this action in complete defiance of Italy's industrial elite, which feared losses for Italian business. The measure was justified by external constraints, La Malfa claimed; and his gamble was quickly and brilliantly vindicated. The postwar era of liberalization provided the basis for the most rapid period of growth in Italy's history: between 1953 and 1961 real GDP grew at an annual rate of 5.8 percent.

The government did in fact soon begin large-scale housing projects. It also began to address the problem of the backwardness of the Italian south, the *Mezzogiorno*, with largely counter-productive effects. Publicly owned firms were told that 60 percent of their investments were to go to the *Mezzogiorno*. Increased spending channeled through the state budget produced a culture of clientelism.

De Gasperi, who as a young man had been a deputy in the multinational Reichsrat of Franz Joseph's Vienna, was also the major driving force into making Italy a European country: first through participation in the ECSC, and then in the European Economic Community (EEC; created by a treaty signed in Rome in 1957). Europe was the best setting for economic modernization and advance.

Internationalism was also the main claim of an alternative elite that emerged in post-fascist Italy. In its view, Italy's political elite was narrow, old-fashioned, provincial, and obviously Catholic. In contrast, the cultural leaders believed themselves to be the cosmopolitan products of a polity that had been divided from the fall of the Roman Empire until 1870. The main theorist of the idea of an intellectual class with its own mission was the dissident Marxist philosopher Antonio Gramsci. Gramsci's views had been formulated in part during the intense political conflicts of the early 1920s, but above all during his incarceration under Mussolini (repeating, it seemed, the pattern in which the key texts of nineteenth-century national revival had been produced in Habsburg prisons). Gramsci envisaged two sorts of influence, and contrasted "hegemony", which could be produced through intellectual activity, with political rule, oppression, or economic domination. Thus, the prisons could formulate a theory of opposition to the Habsburgs, or the fascists. Logically, intellectual culture – the novel, the cinema – should then produce its own alternative to the world of the DC. The critical vision was best embodied in the neorealist films of Federico Fellini, which documented the development of Italy's postwar economic "miracle": from the turbulence of *Roma Città Aperta* (1945, with Roberto Rossellini), through the marginalized poverty depicted in *La Strada* (1954), before reaching *La Dolce Vita* (1960). The cinematic depiction of Italy ran on parallel and politically opposed lines to the world of "economic–corporative" dominance, the world which managed and benefited from the stunning economic miracle.

Small (social) democracies

In the four big western European countries, despite the convergence of views about economic and social management, there were sharp political contrasts between right and left. Adenauer and the German SPD agreed by the early 1960s on the big principles of a mixed-market economy and integration in the western alliance; de Gaulle and the politicians of the Fourth Republic did not differ about the national management of the economy, the welfare state, or the importance of the French plans; Labour and the Conservatives apparently embraced each in "Butskellism"; and the Italian DC wanted to manage the market as much as did their opponents. But each of these political groupings thought of themselves as having sharp differences from their opponents, despite the amazing and unprecedented degree of consensus on every major conventional policy issue.

One way of explaining the phenomenon is by group solidarity: each of the political movements had what the Germans liked to call its own *Stallgeruch* (stable smell), by which it could recognize friends and enemies. The most obvious of these in continental Europe was provided by religion, where despite an increased dechristianization of society, clericalism and anticlericalism remained major issues. In the postwar era, progressive Catholicism was on the ascendant on the right, and pragmatic but secular reformism on the left. They looked similar in their outcomes, but felt quite different to their adherents. Despite the strong Christian Socialist, non-conformist traditions of the British Labour Party, such divisions also characterized the United Kingdom, where Labour was supported by some prominent leftist Catholics (such as Frank Pakenham, Lord Longford), and the state Church of England could still claim to be the Conservative Party at prayer.

The other dividing mark in continental Europe was the legacy of the recent past. The left viewed itself as anti-fascist (even where, as in the case of François Mitterrand, there was a Pétainist background); while the Church was tarnished by the concordats and compromises of the 1930s. Left-wing parties could thus present themselves as the "true" nationalists, even while the left embraced general or universal ideas.

The politics of smaller countries were different. Here there was also a *Stallgeruch*, and the legacy of occupation and collaboration. The wish to preserve the autonomy of a small country, however, justified and required compromises. In two of the most successful cases, Sweden and Switzerland, these had originated in the threatened environment of the 1930s.

Postwar Switzerland was ruled by governments in which all the major parties – Liberals, Christian Democrats, and Social Democrats – were represented, roughly in accordance with their share of the popular vote, through what was called the "magic formula". They were held together by a belief in the unique virtues of Swiss neutrality, which they thought had preserved the country in the midst of wartorn Europe. The Swiss conjured up a mythic vision of their past, which obliterated all the wartime compromises, trade links with the Axis powers, and inhumane aspects of their refugee policy.

Austria similarly built consensus around an amnesia about the Nazi role in the 1930s and the eagerness with which most Austrians had joined Hitler's Reich. The two major parties, the People's Party (what had been the Christian Social Party in prewar Austria) and the Social Democrats, ruled in a coalition until 1966. As in Switzerland, there was a magic formula, the *Proporz*, but in Austria the formula related less to the composition of the government than to the distribution of every kind of patronage job between the two political movements.

The Netherlands, in which there had been probably the most far-reaching purge of collaborators of any European country in the immediate aftermath of 1945, was also ruled by a coalition of the socialists with a Catholic People's Party until 1958; from 1958 to 1965 right-wing parties replaced the socialists, but then the latter returned. As in Austria, the major political task any government faced was the construction of an equilibrium between what the Dutch called the different "pillars" of Netherlands society: Catholic, reformed, and socialist.

Belgium provided probably the greatest success story of an external environment inducing political stabilization. The war left a very bitter legacy, with substantial Flemish collaboration (as in the First World War) and Walloon (French) resistance. The linguistic split was heavily reflected in political affiliation, with the Flemish voters largely supporting a Christian Democratic Party and the Walloons the socialists. There were some coalitions: an initial one lasted until 1949, and a new one formed in 1961. In between, however, the socialists were first out of power, and then returned with a language law that the Flemish population felt to be highly discriminatory. In the 1960s, the new coalition tried to federalize Belgium. The strategy worked largely because of the importance of the EEC for Belgium's international standing.

In Sweden, the Socialist Party dominated every government until 1976. In Denmark, socialists were in most coalitions until 1982, although they were briefly out of power between 1950 and 1953, and again from 1973 to 1975. In Norway, the socialists were voted out in 1965, but returned in 1971. In each case, socialism in power meant the use of the welfare state to create large constituencies among middle-class and previously anti-socialist voters. A central part of this strategy involved attracting women into the workforce and looking after children through the extension of education, kindergarten, and pre-school facilities (whereas traditionalists in Germany, Switzerland, and Italy ensured that schools were organized in such a way as to make it extremely hard for mothers to take full-time work). Scandinavian countries became very wealthy as a result of their stability, and by the 1960s regularly headed league tables of national prosperity. Some of this was illusory, in that paying large numbers of kindergarten teachers is statistically a remuneration for a service (and hence enters the GNP and other national accounts beloved by the propagandists of postwar "growthmanship"), while mothers who stay at home undoubtedly work but are not measured in GNP as they are not paid. Hence arose the caustic characterization of the Scandinavian model of the welfare state as paying women to look after other women's children.

Dictatorships

The Scandinavian states and the Benelux countries looked like the best advertisement for consensus politics embedded in a secure external environment for a Europe that had fully and safely emerged from the economic scarcities and the security predicaments of the 1930s. Other European countries, on the other hand, looked as if little had changed from the world of the 1930s and the wartime years.

Greece had a strong wartime resistance movement (EAM, or National Liberation Front), in which communist partisans played a leading role. By the time of the German evacuation of Greece, EAM had a powerful army. When the British troops arrived with a "government of national unity" under the socialist Papandreou, it contained EAM representatives. The government tried to disarm EAM, and in protest in December 1944 the EAM ministers resigned from the government. In February 1945, a truce was concluded, but EAM continued to build up its forces in northern Greece, Albania, and Yugoslavia (which supplied the communist forces).

In March 1946, the western military forces supervised elections, which were boycotted by EAM, and which produced a majority for conservative parties (Populists, equivalent to Christian Democrats in other countries). A Populist government was formed by Constantine Tsaldaris, and the monarchy was restored. The United Kingdom and the United States devoted very large amounts of money and arms to fight the rival communist structures, and Greece (with Turkey and Iran) became one of the first flashpoints of the Cold War.

The civil war against the EAM forces lasted until 1949, when the Yugoslav borders were closed and the communist forces were cut off from their major supplies. The center-right parties continued to rule until the 1960s, when the continent-wide leftward shift touched Greece and the center-left party of Papandreou won. In April 1967 the army carried out a coup, Franco-style, frustrated an attempt at a royal countercoup, and exiled the King.

Franco himself was getting old. Spain (and Portugal) remained very repressive, private societies, with an extensive police apparatus. The only significant movement was in the area of economic liberalization. In the immediate aftermath of the Civil War, Franco had followed a rigid policy of autarky, very much in line with the prevailing world view of the 1930s. In the 1950s, though, the price was economic stagnation. As in France, technocrats wanted a more modern policy. In Spain, the struggle was translated into a struggle about Catholicism. The modernizers in the Bank of Spain and in the Ministry of Commerce worked with the Catholic lay (and quite anti-clerical) movement, Opus Dei, while the traditionalists appealed to the Church hierarchy and the Falange. The modernizers won, with help from the outside. In 1959, Spain appealed to the OEEC and the International Monetary Fund (IMF) and set out a stabilization program:

> The time has come to redirect economic policy in order to place the Spanish economy in line with the countries of the Western world, and so free it from the interventions inherited from the past which do not correspond to the needs of the present situation.[39]

With this reform package, imposed by external international institutions, Spain reshaped its economy, and in the 1960s industrialized with remarkable speed. Manufacturing output in 1970 was almost six times that of 1950. Industrialization also brought a measure of domestic political relaxation, and Spanish society began to be more modern.

In neighboring Portugal, there was a similar development, and the pace of economic change was only slightly slower: manufacturing grew fourfold between 1950 and 1970. A social shift began as excess labor no longer emigrated permanently (previously Brazil had been a major center of Portuguese immigration), but went to temporary employment in western Europe, at first mostly in France, but later in Germany and Switzerland as well. They brought back not only cash, but also a new experience of "modernity".

That modernity contrasted dramatically with the conservative clericalism of Salazar's regime. The dictator's rule depended in part on the secret police; in part on the fostering of a conservative kind of Catholicism. There was a flourishing cult of Our Lady of Fátima, who had appeared to children with a secret message, generally believed to be anti-communist.

At the level of national politics, the country turned away from Europe and toward empire. This had been a logical response to the disintegration of the world market in the 1930s, but it was taken to an extreme in attempts to produce largely unsuitable cash crops in Africa, which produced widespread famine. In 1951, the colonies (the largest being Angola and Mozambique in Africa; they also included the enclave of Goa in India, and Timor and Macao) were renamed as "overseas territories" of Portugal. Of all the fossilized versions of the 1930s, Salazar's was the most durable, and disintegrated only in the 1970s.

The modernization of Turkey

In the aftermath of the Second World War, and confronted by a substantial communist challenge, the Kemalist movement started to allow a democratization. The immediate beneficiary of this was a secular, center-right party, the Democratic Party developed by Celal Bayar, who had been a loyal follower of Atatürk. This won a substantial election victory in 1950, and Bayar became President and Adnan Menderes Prime Minister. The new government at first followed a liberal economic course, deregulated some of the economic inheritance of the 1930s, introduced a liberal press law, and joined the NATO alliance (in 1951). At first it looked as if a stable two-party system would establish itself, with the center-right Democratic Party competing with the center-left Republican People's Party (RPP), the official Kemalist party; and these parties consistently dominated the voting in the more developed parts of Turkey.

In the late 1950s, however, the impulse to reform slowed down, and the handling of the economy and of the press became increasingly restrictive. On May 27, 1960, the army seized power, declaring that it was removing a "corrupt and inefficient system", and promising to revive the ideals of Atatürk. Menderes was killed. A military figure, General Cemal Gürsel, was appointed as Prime Minister by the army, but he promised to return quickly to democracy. In 1961, after new elections, he became President and the veteran Ismet Inönü, Atatürk's successor as President, became Prime Minister at the age of 78. The Labor Minister was Bülent Ecevit, who eventually replaced Inönü as leader of the RPP. The Democratic Party was disbanded, but a number of other parties (Justice Party, New Turkey Party) presented themselves as its successor. From then on, the Turkish party system became increasingly fragmented and fissiparous, and new parties were formed around powerful personalities, almost of all of whom saw themselves as defenders and interpreters of the legacy of Atatürk: Ecevit and later Deniz Baykal on the left,

Süleyman Demirel and later Turguz Özal on the right. The splintering of the party landscape occurred on the basis of personalized clan politics around these leaders, who would dominate Turkish politics for decades.

The modernization of the Church

In 1958, Pope Pius XII died. His successor, John XXIII, quickly announced that he intended to call an ecumenical council, with a pastoral and evangelical purpose. Previous councils had been concerned with the definition of Church doctrine; this was to be a council that would bring the Church in closer contact with the modern world. The Council met in St Peter's in sessions between 1962 and December 1965. Its most immediately visible effect was the reform and modernization of the Mass, which was now said in the vernacular, and of the liturgy. Churches were rearranged and new altars created in order to allow a more interactive Mass, in which the priest would face rather than turn away from the congregation. Lay people were to become more involved in Church affairs. Before and during the course of the Council, a number of papal encyclicals also spelled out new social and political philosophies that would have looked very strange during the highly conservative papacy of Pius XII. *Mater et Magistra* (1961) laid out a new demand for social justice; *Pacem in Terris* (1963) asked for international reconciliation and dialogue between faiths; and *Gaudium et Spes* (1965), partly drafted by Karol Wojtyła, the Archbishop of Krakow, set out a new sort of Christian humanism that put human experience at the center of the Church's mission: "Man can fully discover his true self only in a sincere giving of himself."

The dynamics of growth

Part of the gloom of interwar Europe had concerned population decline, in societies which – in a way the French termed "Malthusian" – were refusing to replicate themselves. For France, the economist Alfred Sauvy in 1930 predicted that the population would decline from around 42 million to between 30 and 39 million in 1975, with the upper figure depending on no further reductions in fertility. For Germany, in 1930 economist and statistician Ernst Kahn thought that the 65 million population would decline to under 50 million by 1975. In England and Wales, demographer Enid Charles foresaw a fall from 40 million to between 31.5 and 38.5 million by 1975.[40] On the other hand, the same forecasts showed rapid rises in the population of Russia and eastern Europe.

In the 1940s, the declining fertility of northern and western Europe, which had seemed an inexorable trend since the 1890s, was abruptly reversed (as it was also in the United States). The "baby boom" started in some countries even during the war. France showed signs of an upturn in 1943, which was inevitably interpreted in political terms. The Vichyites believed that it showed the success of the slogans of *"Travail, Famille, Patrie"*, and of a reform of inheritance law which ended the partible inheritance often blamed for the exceptionally poor French demographic experience. General de Gaulle thought it was the new hope that he gave to France that inspired mothers to have babies. But whatever else it might have been, it was difficult not to see the boom as a triumph of life over death, especially when it occurred in the camps of "Displaced Persons" all over Germany, where Hitler's surviving victims still stayed.

The economies of continental Europe were also boosted by high levels of immigration, which provided a marked contrast with interwar Europe, when immigration had been disparaged and obstructed after the depression. For Germany, the immigrants came from the East: *Vertriebene* (expellees) from Poland and Czechoslovakia, *Flüchtlinge* (refugees) from East Germany. From 1945 to 1950, some 9 million came to the Federal Republic, mostly expellees, and from then until the construction of the Berlin Wall in 1961, another 3 million, largely refugees. In Italy, high levels of internal migration replaced the international emigration that had characterized previous eras. From 1958 to 1963, at the high point of the Italian movement, around 1 million southerners left for the north. French settlers moved from North Africa back to the *métropole* in large numbers in the early 1960s. Of around 1 million *pieds noirs*, 850,000 returned to France. Native Algerians also started to emigrate to France after 1959. Part of the growth of the French labor force came from internal movement, as small independent farmers and artisans in the countryside gave up their former lifestyles (and left rural France increasingly depopulated, with abandoned and half-abandoned villages). From 1954 to 1962, the number of independent workers in France fell by 1.25 million.

The European economic miracle was clearly producing a substantial demand for labor, and foreign immigration looked a more and more attractive solution to the shortage of low-skilled laborers. In the 1950s, British textile factories systematically recruited a new workforce from the Indian subcontinent (mostly from Pakistan). In Switzerland in 1961, almost half of clothing workers and over two-fifths of textile workers were foreigners. Germany, from the mid-1960s experiencing an acute labor shortage, also began to recruit foreign workers (*Gastarbeiter*) from Italy and Greece, and later from Portugal, Turkey, and Yugoslavia.

The new supplies of labor allowed the European miracle to be sustained for longer than simply a period of catch-up after the setbacks of the depression era and the war. Investment was at very high levels in comparison with the prewar period. One of the starkest contrasts was in Germany, where investment ran at 17.7 percent of GDP between 1950 and 1970, while the average rate between 1928 and 1938 had been 11.8 percent. The equivalent figures for France are a postwar 15.6 percent, compared with a prewar 11.8 percent.

The new growth looked to consumer markets: for radios, household appliances, televisions, and above all, automobiles. It was the automobile, along with the scooter for the young, which quickly became the most effective symbol of Europe's postwar miracle, and of a new personal independence and mobility. It allowed cities to sprawl out into suburbia, and it made much of life much less dependent on the official public provision of transportation services. The car thus privatized living styles. It briefly gave a new lease of life to the ideal of the (small) nuclear family, which could pack itself into the confined space of the car for day trips and vacations.

European growth was not just resuming after the destructive interludes of wars and depressions; growth was also easier because it could be imported through productivity gains from the tremendous advances of the American economy. Catching up meant growing to be like the United States. The best way of depicting this development is to state European productivity per man-hour as a proportion of that of the United States: Germany in 1938 had been 56 percent; after the war, and the surge in American industrial output, this had declined to 33 percent. There was plenty of room for imitation, and in 1960 the German figure had reached 50 percent of the American and in 1970 66 percent. Italy is equally dramatic, starting from a lower level of 49 percent in 1938, with 32 (1950) rising to 39 (1960) and 59 (1970). In more traditional terms, Germany was the best performer of a talented 1950s cast: its growth of real GDP annually for the period 1953–61 was 7.2 percent, while Italy (5.8), France (4.7), and Spain (4.7) were also stunning testimonies to the European capacity for sustained growth in very different political and social circumstances. Only the United Kingdom, at 2.9 percent, looked rather dismal. The statistics alone suggest that at this time, the United Kingdom was developing in a different manner from that of the rest of Europe.

Most of continental Europe had one great advantage over the United Kingdom and France, and the United States, in the Cold War era: a significantly lower level of defense spending, which reduced the strain on the government budget and freed resources for productive investment. Europeans could thus look for alternatives to the world of steel and heavy industrial production that had long been regarded as the prime source of military strength. Above all, the very militarized societies of the interwar period now had substantially lower levels of military commitment: in 1960, Germany spent 4.0 percent of GNP in this way, while it had been 9.6 percent in 1937. Italy in 1960 was at 2.7 percent (and had been 9.9 percent in 1937); for Spain the comparable figures are 2.9 percent and 3.8 percent. France and the United Kingdom both spent more than in the interwar period as a result of the expense of their disengagement with empire. They continued to have substantial military ambitions, and were prepared to pay for this luxury. For France the 1960 figure is 6.3 percent (1937 5.5 percent); and for the United Kingdom 6.4 percent (5.3 percent). The contrast with low continental European defense spending is even more striking in the United States, which in 1960 spent 8.8 percent of GNP in this way, while in the isolationist 1930s it had paid out just 1.1 percent.[41] For non-imperial Europe, swords became ploughshares.

Security was provided by other powers (primarily the United States), and by a commitment to cooperation and integration.

European integration

In 1955 discussions began about a new attempt to build closer cooperation between the six members of the ECSC. Their attempt to create a supranational European Defence Community had failed in 1954 in the French Chamber. The new initiative involved more progress in economic integration, which the successful establishment of the ECSC had shown was probably easier. A customs union, with common external tariffs and a common agricultural and transport policy, would increase trade within the Six and create more political support for further and deeper integration. Already within the postwar system as run by the OEEC, which provided for a progressive liberalization of payments as managed through the EPU, intra-European trade had increased from $10 billion in 1950 to $23 billion in 1959, while over the same period, imports from the United States had only risen from $4 billion to $6 billion. The global framework of the General Agreement on Tariffs and Trade (GATT) promoted general trade liberalization.

Two issues framed the discussions about a customs union. The first looked forward: exports had been the key to growth in the most dynamic European economies of the 1950s, Germany, Italy, and the Netherlands. By 1958, the volume of exports per capita in those countries was almost 2.5 times that of 1936. The customs union would offer a way of continuing the export boom.

The second issue, however, was concerned with one of the major political problems of the European past: the position of agriculture, and especially of small agricultural producers. As in the First World War, European agriculture had been starved of resources from 1939 to 1945, and in the immediate postwar years Europe had consequently been heavily dependent on food imported from overseas. Prewar production had been reached in 1950, but the west European population was now 12 percent greater. Cereals in particular were urgently needed, but in the 1950s European imports still largely came from the dollar area. The point of the initial discussions in the first half of the 1950s was to promote European production and European trade as a way of saving dollars. But even at this time, there was the specter of the agricultural crisis of the 1920s: food prices had risen sharply after the First World War, but then had begun a long and destructive decline after 1925, eight years after the end of that War.

France, with the greatest political muscle of any of the original Six, was worried that any systematic tariff reduction would undermine its industrial structure. Its policy-makers still liked to think of a tradition of Colbertism and explained their conviction that "France has never been a free-trade country, and it believes more in organization".[42] The major attraction of an EEC, such as was established by the Treaty of Rome, was that it provided a good institutional mechanism for dealing with the problems of French agriculture. Farming still employed a quarter of the French labor force in 1959. Between the wars, farmers had been a continual source of political instability as farm prices fell. Many French farms by the 1950s were quite modern. The proportion of micro-holdings, contrary to the popular image of France, was much smaller than in Italy or even Germany: farms of between half a hectare and five hectares constituted 85 percent of Italian and 55 percent of German, but only 35 percent of French farms. French farmers wanted export markets, but were acutely aware that they could not produce as cheaply as the extensive agriculture of North and South America, or of Australia and New Zealand.

Germany, on the other hand, wanted to ensure a wider market for its rapidly reviving and highly competitive export industries; its machine tool industry could profit from the extent of French and Italian industrial modernization. German farmers, in the more efficient north and west at least, did not need so much agricultural protection; but agriculture was an important constituency of the CDU and also of its Bavarian sister party, the CSU. A great deal of European integration was thus driven by a Franco-German double act, in which both countries balanced their manufacturing and agricultural interests; and indeed, this pattern remained later as an almost permanent feature of European politics. De Gaulle developed a complex, semi-historical, and semi-theological account in which nations needed to use Europe in order to atone for their past. France had been the west European country that suffered most in the Second World War, de Gaulle argued, because only in France had a legitimate government remained and collaborated with Germany (he neglected to consider the Danish case). Vichy was the betrayal of France by her leaders. Germany had first triumphed and then been humiliated. Only France as the bearer of suffering and at the same time France as liberated under de Gaulle could "lift Germany up from her decadence".[43] European links presented a means of overcoming the legacy of a profound political but also moral and psychological defeat. Europe was, in short, a national psychotherapy.

At first, French policy-makers had also given themselves powerful security and geopolitical goals. In 1955–56, France was working on acquiring atomic weapons, and a most important part of the negotiations centered on atomic energy and nuclear fuel. This eventually produced a parallel community to the ECSC, Euratom. For a time, under Guy Mollet, France was even thinking about developing an atomic bomb as a joint Franco-German project, with German finance and French technology.[44] The humiliation of France by the United States and also its abandonment by the United Kingdom over the Suez crisis in November 1956 pushed the French demand for continental integration further.

In June 1955 the Six decided to explore "unity in Europe", and also invited the United Kingdom to join the discussions. In these negotiations, the UK's preferences to non-European agricultural producers in the former

Empire (now Commonwealth) looked like an obstacle, particularly to the important French farming lobby. Through all of this process, the British remained apart: bored, as they said, by the tedium of concentrating on the economics of customs unions. Rab Butler later said: "[Prime Minister] Anthony Eden was bored with this. Frankly he was even more bored than I was." He tempered this harsh judgment in a characteristically wry way: "To do Anthony justice, of course, he had a certain amount of, not exactly genius, but he had a certain amount of flair in foreign affairs. I think he thought the French were a bit difficult." Macmillan was convinced that the EEC would not emerge.[45] The reality was that the United Kingdom looked too different from the rest of Europe, as it supplied a large part of its food deficit from countries within the old imperial system, above all Australia and New Zealand, which were given preferred access to the British market.

When de Gaulle came to power in the Algerian crisis of May 1958, most observers believed that he would quickly sabotage the EEC. But actually, the new institutions provided a valuable back-up to the urgent necessity of stabilizing the French economy. The managing director of the IMF had given de Gaulle a long lesson on how France since Napoleon required a stable currency, and loved the man who had the power to create monetary order. He set out clearly his view, which he made that of his organization too: "I do not think that there will ever be esteem for a country that has a bad currency."[46]

De Gaulle's explanation of his European project was partly cast in terms of the prestige and grandeur to which his rhetorical gifts inclined him. "The purpose of Europe", he said, "is to avoid domination by the Americans or Russians [. . .] Europe is the means by which France can once again become what she has not been since Waterloo: first in the world." But, as Andrew Moravcsik has pointed out, this eloquence in fact covered a profound devotion to the cause of agricultural modernization. De Gaulle explained that if an adequate solution were not found to the farm problem, "we will have another Algeria on our own soil".[47]

At the beginning, the average tariff on all EEC imports was 7.4 percent, with a relatively high level on foodstuffs (14.2 percent), and a promise laid down in the Treaty of Rome (Article 40) that there would be a common agricultural policy. This could be used as an instrument of French governments to stabilize French society by promoting effective modernization.

In 1962 at last the specifics of the Common Agricultural Policy were agreed and implemented. The core was a price support mechanism that held prices stable at well above world market levels. The result was to encourage large increases in agricultural output. French wheat production, for instance, rose from 9.6 million tons in 1958 to 15 million in 1968; sugar beet from 12.9 million tons to 17.6 million, and wine from 47.7 million hectoliters to 66.5 million over the same time frame. In the 1970s, when the very efficient British and Danish producers were also in the EEC, the issue of surpluses, with wine lakes and butter mountains, became acute. Some could then be exported to the Soviet Union, and other east European countries.

The EEC generated a new level of economic integration between countries. After 1958, the EEC share of trade of all the EEC countries increased dramatically: most of all for France, where EEC trade had been 30 percent of the total in 1958 and was 57 percent by 1970. Italy's share rose from 30 to 50 percent, and Germany's from 37 to 52 percent.

In the 1960s, de Gaulle largely achieved what he wanted. When the central institutions of the EEC talked about more integration, and qualified majority voting on the Council of Ministers threatened French positions, France objected: de Gaulle ordered his representative to come back to Paris and blocked any further moves in agricultural policy and GATT negotiations. The crisis was only solved by the January 1966 "Luxembourg compromise", allowing national vetoes rather than majority voting when "vital interests" were at stake. The compromise effectively stopped the development of the EEC as a true supranational institution (which by its nature must on occasion be capable of overriding national sovereignty) for two decades, until the mid-1980s.

Rather late, in 1961, the United Kingdom under Harold Macmillan did apply to join the EEC. At Rambouillet on December 15–16, 1962, when Macmillan visited de Gaulle to finalize the membership terms, he referred insistently and unwisely to the importance the United Kingdom attached to an independent nuclear deterrent. De Gaulle told Macmillan: "France could say 'no', even against the Germans; she could stop policies with which she disagreed, because of the strength of her position. Once the United Kingdom and all the rest joined the organization things would be different."[48] Faced with this assertion of French strength and implied British weakness, Macmillan became sad, and almost broke down. Later, de Gaulle in a meeting of the French cabinet (December 17, 1962) satirized Macmillan with a line from a famous song of Edith Piaf's, "*Ne pleurez pas, Milord*" (Don't cry, my lord) (actually a rather inappropriate song, since Piaf invites Milord to come into her room and out of the cold: *Allez venez, Milord / Vous asseoir à ma table / Il fait si froid dehors / Ici c'est confortable*), and allowed the news to leak at the same time as the press conference in January which made public the General's "*Non*".

Europe and the United States

The United States profoundly shaped Europe's modernization and growth. It provided in the first place a security umbrella, which allowed most of continental Europe to cut back on military expenditure. After the government payments of the Marshall Plan era fell away, there followed the investments of large US firms, on their way to becoming transnational corporations. These investments involved not only monetary inflows, but also transfers of technologies and management skills that modernized European firms, transformed their industrial relations, and made them think much more of marketing issues and of the cultivation of consumer demand.

For the European elites, both political and intellectual, the American predominance, so heavily asserted in the economic sphere, was hard to bear. The immediate postwar years had been marked by the struggle over economics, and (for the United Kingdom and France) battles about empire. The Korean War, and the threat of war in Europe, made some Europeans scared by American military adventurism. France rejected a US offer to defend Dien Bien Phu in 1954 with atomic weapons. But in fact, as the 1956 Suez episode would show, the British and the French had even stronger adventurist impulses. Harold Macmillan, who thought that he could patch up political relations with the United States after the Suez fiasco, complained of every American: there was firstly "the colonial sort of American, which has to hate England out of snobbishness – to prove that their ancestors were at the tea party"; and then the new, "immigrant" Irish, sort of American like President Kennedy, disposed to stew in Gaelic resentments. In the course of decolonization, both France and the United Kingdom were infuriated by the US position and its naked and unsentimental realism. De Gaulle complained already in 1960 that "the Atlantic Alliance, as it exists, seems to France inadequate to realities and incompatible with her world responsibilities".[49] He remembered how he had been humiliated by Roosevelt during the war, and believed that the United States could tolerate no government in other countries, only American "marionettes".[50] In the 1960s, he developed a wide-ranging critique of the US economic role, of the position of the dollar in the international monetary system, and of American ersatz imperialism in southeast Asia (Vietnam).

For the United Kingdom and France it was the trauma – more psychological than a real hurt to concrete interests – of decolonization that drove a wedge between the national myth and the power of the United States. For Germany, the equivalent role was played by the Berlin crisis. In August 1961, East Germany had built a wall around West Berlin, primarily in order to halt the increasing outflow of its citizens to the West. The first days of the Wall, after August 13, were very tense, and a minor incident could have started a war escalating to a nuclear confrontation. The United States was cautious. US soldiers were forbidden to help Germans injured by border guards on the eastern side of the frontier. For the German political elite, the attitude of the United States appeared to be sharply at odds with previous rhetorical commitments to "freedom". The very pro-American Mayor of West Berlin, the SPD leader Willy Brandt, concluded that Germans could in reality expect little from the "West" and its military strength.[51]

For Italy, the major complaint about US influence related to its cultural preponderance. The interwar Italian Marxist theorist Antonio Gramsci had seen America as producing a new culture and a new way of life. In his *Prison Notebooks*, he quoted a 1929 interview by Luigi Pirandello: "Americanism is swamping us [. . .] The money that runs through the world is American."[52] Economics and military power were both American. But there could be a cultural "resistance", a term dear to the anti-fascist left because it drew legitimacy from the memory of the struggle against tyranny. Because he had shown how culture was at the center of hegemony, Gramsci became a cult figure of the postwar left.

In the 1960s, in response to a powerful movement for enhanced mass consumption that originated in the United States, the subdued elite anti-Americanism erupted into a much more widely diffused mass movement of protest. At this stage, the European protesters tried to turn their critique of the new form of power into a new "hegemony" that might overthrow the American danger to the European spirit. They thought of themselves as Greece revolting against Rome.

Notes

1 A.J.P. Taylor, *Europe: Grandeur and Decline*, Harmondsworth: Penguin, 1967, p. 357.
2 Richard J. Overy, *Interrogations: The Nazi Elite in Allied Hands 1945*, London: Allen Lane, 2001, pp. 148–9.
3 Statement of November 21, 1945, www.roberthjackson.org/speech-and-writing/opening-statement-before-the-international-military-tribunal/.
4 Raphael Lemkin, *Axis Rule in Occupied Europe: Laws of Occupation, Analysis of Government, Proposals for Reform*, Washington, DC: Carnegie Endowment for International Peace, 1944, pp. 79, 81, 93.
5 Quoted in E.H. Carr, *The Twenty Years Crisis 1919–1939*, London: Macmillan, 1939, p. 196.
6 *Princeton Alumni Weekly*, February 28, 1947, p. 13.
7 Lucrezia Reichlin, "The Marshall Plan", in Barry Eichengreen (ed.), *Europe's Postwar Recovery*, Cambridge: Cambridge University Press, 1995, p. 41.
8 Alan S. Milward, *The Reconstruction of Western Europe 1945–1951*, London: Methuen, 1984, p. 418.
9 Jean Monnet (transl. Richard Mayne), *Memoirs*, London: Collins, 1978, p. 339.
10 Ibid., p. 417.
11 Marc Trachtenberg, *A Constructed Peace: The Making of the European Settlement, 1945–1963*, Princeton, NJ: Princeton University Press, 1999, p. 98.
12 Monnet, *Memoirs*, p. 338.
13 Trachtenberg, *Constructed Peace*, p. 110.
14 F.H. Hinsley, *Power and the Pursuit of Peace: Theory and Practice in the History of Relations between States*, Cambridge: Cambridge University Press, 1963, p. 348.
15 Monnet, *Memoirs*, p. 285.
16 Jeffrey M. Diefendorf, *In the Wake of War: The Reconstruction of German Cities after World War II*, New York, NY: Oxford University Press, 1993, p. 106.
17 Jean-Paul Sartre (transl. Hazel E. Barnes), *Being and Nothingness: A Phenomenological Essay on Ontology*, New York, NY: Washington Square, 1992, pp. 675, 708–9.
18 Maurice Merleau-Ponty (transl. John O'Neill), *Humanism and Terror: An Essay on the Communist Problem*, Boston, MA: Beacon Press, 1969, pp. 130, 180.
19 Quoted in Tony Judt, *Past Imperfect: French Intellectuals 1944–1956*, Berkeley, CA: University of California Press, 1992, p. 122.
20 Annie Cohen-Solal, *Sartre: A Life*, New York, NY: Pantheon, 1987, p. 303.
21 Charles de Gaulle, *War Memoirs I: Call to Honor 1940–42*, London: Collins, 1955, p. 1.
22 Monnet, *Memoirs*, 1979, p. 259.

23 Alastair Horne, *A Savage War of Peace: Algeria 1954–1962*, Harmondsworth: Penguin, 1979, p. 99.

24 Cohen-Solal, *Sartre*, p. 364.

25 Horne, *Savage War*, p. 298.

26 Robert Skidelsky, *John Maynard Keynes, Vol. III: Fighting for Britain, 1937–1946*, London: Macmillan, 2001, p. 461.

27 Skidelsky, *Keynes*, p. 414.

28 Quoted in Alan Bullock, *Ernest Bevin: Foreign Secretary 1945–1951*, New York, NY: Norton, 1983, p. 352.

29 Andrew Roberts, *Eminent Churchillians*, London: Weidenfeld & Nicolson, 1994, p. 82.

30 Milovan Djilas, *Conversations with Stalin*, London: Hart-Davis, 1962, p. 104: "Yes, socialism is possible even under an English king." C.A.R. Crosland, *The Future of Socialism*, New York, NY: Schocken, 1963 (original version 1956), p. 29.

31 Alastair Horne, *Harold Macmillan II: 1957–1986*, London: Penguin, 1989, pp. 189, 192.

32 Peter Hennessy, *The Prime Minister: The Office and its Holders since 1945*, London: Penguin, 2000, p. 250.

33 Horne, *Macmillan*, pp. 270, 481.

34 Crosland, *Future*, pp. 214, 340.

35 Ibid., p. 210.

36 Denis Mack Smith, *Modern Italy*, Ann Arbor, MI: University of Michigan Press, 1997, p. 442.

37 Quoted in Marcello de Cecco, "Keynes and Italian economics", in Peter A. Hall (ed.), *The Political Power of Economic Ideas: Keynesianism across Nations*, Princeton, NJ: Princeton University Press, 1989, p. 210.

38 Quoted in Juan Carlos Martinez Oliva, *Italy and the Political Economy of International Cooperation*, Banca d'Italia Working Paper, 2002.

39 Quoted in Harold James, International Monetary Cooperation Since Bretton Woods, New York: Oxford University Press, 1996, pp. 109-110.

40 From A.M. Carr-Saunders, *World Population: Past Growth and Future Trends*, Oxford: Clarendon Press, 1936, Figure 26 (opposite p. 129).

41 Vito Tanzi and Ludger Schuknecht, *Public Spending in the 20th Century: a Global Perspective*, Cambridge: Cambridge University Press, 2000, p. 28. These shares remained similar in 1980, although the French share of GNP was then substantially reduced to a non-imperial continental European norm (3.3 percent).

42 Charlton, *Victory*, p. 226.

43 Alain Peyrefitte, *C'était de Gaulle*, Paris: Gallimard, 2002, p. 77.

44 Andre Moravcsik, *The Choice for Europe: Social Purpose and State Power from Messina to Maastricht*, Ithaca, NY: Cornell University Press, 1998, p. 149.

45 Charlton, *Victory*, pp. 195–6. See also Moravcsik, *Choice*, p. 129.

46 Erin E. Jacobsson, *A Life for Sound Money: Per Jacobsson – His Biography*, Oxford: Oxford University Press, 1979, p. 296.

47 Both quotations from Andrew Moravcsik, "De Gaulle: between grain and grandeur: the political economy of French EC policy 1958–1970", *Journal of Cold War Studies*, 2/2, spring 2000, pp. 11, 18–19.

48 Horne, *Macmillan*, p. 431.

49 Both quotations from Horne, *Macmillan*, p. 208.

50 Peyrefitte, *de Gaulle*, p. 643.

51 Willy Brandt, *Erinnerungen*, Frankfurt: Ullstein Propyläen, 1989, pp. 58–9.

52 Antonio Gramsci, *Selections from the Prison Notebooks*, London: Lawrence and Wishart, 1971, p. 316.

8 Yalta and communism

The reconstruction of Europe, Eastern style, from the 1940s to the 1970s

In eastern Europe, the Soviet Union created a world based on a utopian anti-fascist vision of making an entirely new type of human. The other aspects of its rule – a military presence to thwart the counter-attack of the imperialist powers, and the economic planning to provide a material basis for Soviet man – followed from the utopian vision. The vision eventually disintegrated, at the same time as the military strength of the Soviet system faltered, and its economic base crumbled. Many analysts in consequence take the hard "reality" of military matters, tanks, planes, and submarines, or of economics, steelworks, and space satellites, as central to the story of the Soviet collapse. But the flaws in the vision actually appeared long before anyone could really detect any strain in the Soviet army or the planned economy.

The result has been the widespread misinterpretation in the 1980s and later of both the reason for the establishment of a relatively long-lived Soviet rule, and for its eventual decay. Both were interpreted much more – almost exclusively – in terms of the Great Power interests that also indeed played some part in the story. The shift in interpretation can be judged from a quite simple test about the self-description of those who lived through the great political and social transformations of eastern Europe. In the 1940s and 1950s, when East Europeans thought about what marked them out they gave the visionary answer: "communism". By the 1970s and 1980s, however, that appeared either problematical or downright unattractive, and so there was an alternative answer in terms of Great Power realism. The East Europeans then claimed that they were, in one word, defined by "Yalta". Thus, the more the actual meeting of Stalin with Roosevelt and Churchill in February 1945 receded into the past, the more important and epochal seemed the event.

Yalta

The problem lay in the curious fact that the division of Europe was the product of wartime discussions between the Allied leaders, although it is not at all clear that they knew that they were doing this. In October 1944

Churchill in Moscow had initialed a paper which was sometimes called the "percentages" agreement, in that it allocated different degrees of influence to the United Kingdom and the Soviet Union in southeast Europe (Bulgaria, Greece, Hungary, Romania, and Yugoslavia). But it was not in any sense a binding document, and President Roosevelt's highly idealistic Secretary of State, Cordell Hull, had rejected this preposterous revival of old-style diplomacy.

At the Yalta Conference in February 1945, Churchill, Roosevelt, and Stalin may have thought in terms of spheres of interest, but they voiced their intentions in a quite different fashion. There is no reference to Soviet political control over the development of Poland or Germany. At Yalta, the "Big Three" explicitly declared

> their mutual agreement to concert during the temporary period of instability in liberated Europe the policies of their three Governments in assisting the peoples liberated from the domination of Nazi Germany and the peoples of the former Axis satellite states of Europe to solve by democratic means their pressing political and economic problems.[1]

Germany would be divided into zones of occupation, with a French zone being taken out of the areas previously allocated to the United Kingdom and the United States. A Control Council would ensure uniformity of Allied action between the various zones, and also direct the administration of Berlin. But it was not clear how much of a single Germany would be left. Article 12 of the Surrender Instrument would state: "In the exercise of such authority they [the Allies] will take such steps including the complete disarmament, demilitarization and the dismemberment of Germany as they deem requisite for future peace and security." Germany would pay reparations to those countries most heavily damaged by the war. The Moscow Reparations Commission suggested that $20 billion would be an appropriate figure, of which half would go to the Soviet Union; and that the German reparations should include "the use of German labor". Stalin and Foreign Minister Molotov explained that this would mean using German war criminals and the German unemployed for a period of ten years.

Poland should be established with a frontier in the East following the "Curzon line" (the line established by the British government in July 1920 as the "legitimate frontier" of Poland, running through Grodno, Brest-Litovsk, Krilov, and east of Przemyśl to the Carpathians), and would be compensated with substantial German territory in the north and west: east of the line of the rivers Oder and Neisse to the Czech border. Molotov initially hesitated about this shift of Poland to the west, which he described as "stuffing the Polish goose so full of German food that it got indigestion".[2] The Yalta agreements also provided for a guarantee of Polish democracy: the new

Polish Provisional Government of National Unity shall be pledged to the holding of free and unfettered elections as soon as possible on the basis of universal suffrage and secret ballot. In these elections all democratic and anti-Nazi parties shall have the right to take part and to put forward candidates.

Despite these pledges, the non-communist Polish leadership felt increasingly uncomfortable. The leader of the Polish government in London, Stanisław Mikołajczyk, later recalled: "We were becoming increasingly isolated. The Big Three regarded us either openly or privately as saboteurs of their unity."[3]

After the end of the European fighting, there was no peace conference or treaty analogous to the Paris conference and the Versailles treaty. In legal terms, indeed, the treaty that ended the Second World War is the one signed by the two Germanies, France, the United Kingdom, the Soviet Union, and the United States in 1990 (the so-called Two Plus Four Treaty, setting the conditions for German unity).

At Potsdam in July 1945, the Big Three reached a provisional agreement, in which Germany was divided into occupation zones, and the German–Polish frontier set at the rivers Oder and Neisse. The agreement called for central administrative agencies, but in practice the zonal divisions between the United Kingdom, France, the Soviet Union, and the United States constituted a separation into spheres of influence.

Ideals and violence

The division of Europe was in part a matter of geo-politics, but it was also a question of ideals. The critical Yugoslav communist leader, Milovan Djilas, described the contrast between the two great political movements of inter-war Europe: "Fascism is nightmare and madness; communism is force and taboo. Fascism is temporary, communism is an enduring way of life."[4] The new post-1945 communism was built on a legacy of anti-fascism. The communist leaders, many of whom had been in Moscow during the later 1930s and the war, looked to the Soviet Union as the model for anti-fascist social organization. The USSR wanted to create a single style, but at the same time it wrestled with the obvious fact that local political conditions varied greatly between the countries that its armies had liberated from fascism. Everywhere, the Communist Party became the party of power, which it exercised through drawing up lists of people who were suitable for appointment to positions of responsibility (*nomenklatura*). In this way, the party self-consciously fashioned a new elite, or what Milovan Djilas termed a "new class" (drawing, without saying so, on Leon Trotsky's critique of Stalinism).

The communist imposition of power was dramatically brutal after the Second World War, but it was precisely then that it exercised its greatest fascination and appeal for its worker and intellectual adherents. A great part of the attraction lay precisely in the violence that was thought to be required.

Many who later would be implacable critics of Marxism were convinced, at this stage, of an overwhelming historical logic or historical necessity that drove in the direction of communism. Leszek Kołakowski, for instance, as a young philosophy lecturer in Warsaw in the 1940s, liked to let his jacket fall open to reveal the revolver which signaled his commitment to the "unity of theory and praxis". One of the earliest critical thinkers to see the precise hold of Marxist theory was the Polish diplomat and poet Czesław Miłosz, who left his position as Polish cultural attaché in Paris in 1951 to write an account with the title *The Captive Mind*. In it he explained how it was an idea as much as compulsion that made for the communist hold over the imagination of the intelligentsia: "The pressure of the state machine is nothing compared with the pressure of a convincing argument."[5]

One part of the intellectual argument was about historical necessity and the logic of the development from capitalism to communism. Another, at that time equally attractive, idea was about the end of nationalism, and the nation-state, which appeared to have brought so much harm to Europe. Miłosz saw this too, and he was quite unusually nostalgic about the loss:

> Each people's democracy becomes a province of the Empire, ruled by edicts from the Center . . . Perhaps the era of independent states is over, perhaps they are no more than museum pieces. Yet it is saddening to say goodbye to one's dreams of a federation of equal nations, of a United States of Europe in which differing languages and differing cultures would have equal status. It isn't pleasant to surrender to the hegemony of a nation which is still wild and primitive, and to concede the absolute superiority of its customs and institutions, science and technology, literature and art. Must one sacrifice so much in the name of the unity of mankind? The nations of Western Europe will pass through this phase of integration later, and perhaps more gently.[6]

Marxism was a way of replacing the discredited idea of the nation-state. As Miłosz implied, the European Union did the same task in an infinitely better way.

Coalition rule

The countries occupied and politically reorganized by the Soviet Union were initially ruled by coalitions, as in western Europe, which tried to embrace all political shades of anti-Nazi resistance movements. In most countries, the coalitions followed a common course: beginning with an initial agreement to make social reforms, they quarreled about the implementation, and the communists then used their Soviet links to secure supremacy. The initial social reforms usually included the redistribution of large rural estates in favor of poorer peasants and landless laborers, and the property of Germans and their collaborators, but otherwise preserved intact the notion of private property. In 1944 the Czech National Front at Košice, the Hungarian Front of Independence, and the Polish National Liberation Committee, had all promised some land reform, and these promises were quite quickly fulfilled. In Poland, almost all the new farms were established on captured German territories. There was less of a need for dramatic redistribution in other east European states, where (as in Romania and Yugoslavia) more property was already in the hands of small peasant farmers, and there the confiscations were largely limited to collaborators. In Bulgaria, only 2 percent of land was reallocated.

In Poland, the Polish National Liberation Committee had arrived with the Soviet army in July 1944, and in December 1944 changed its name to the Provisional Government of the Polish Republic. After the defeat of Germany, it merged with a group of non-communist "London" Poles around the leader of the prewar Peasants' Party, Mikołajczyk. Mikołajczyk had already been engaged in a long and increasingly acrimonious confrontation with both Stalin and the western leaders about the appropriate postwar boundaries of Poland. The Polish Communist Party had been purged by Stalin, and some 5,000 members killed. It was after that quite loyal.

The interim government set the stage for socialism with a series of social reforms that went beyond simply the creation of more peasant farms. Already in 1945, instead of restituting factories confiscated by the Germans after 1939, it nationalized them (thus saving any need to compensate the legitimate owners or their heirs); and in 1946, the government nationalized any factory employing more than 50 workers.

In preparation for the first postwar elections, four pro-government parties announced that they would form a single bloc: the Communist and Socialist parties, the Democratic Party and a peasant party (with the same name as Mikołajczyk's movement, but opposed to him, which of course misled some voters). The elections (January 1947) were preceded by large-scale arrests of Mikołajczyk's supporters (because they were supposed to be connected with "illegal underground organizations"). On the eve of the elections, the Security Ministry announced that an underground army of 15,000 men had killed over 500 members of the security police. At the time of the elections, 2,110 members of Mikołajczyk's party, including 22 candidates, were in prison. At the elections, the government bloc obtained just over 9 million votes (78.9 percent), with only about 1 million going to Mikołajczyk. He announced that he would appeal to the Supreme Court to declare the election void. The US government took the position that though the Polish elections had not fulfilled the provisions of the Potsdam agreement, it would not break off diplomatic relations with Poland. The US ambassador in Warsaw resigned in protest and published his letter to President Truman in which he said that the elections were "a farce" in "cynical disregard of [the Polish government's] international obligations".[7] The communists denounced Mikołajczyk and he fled Poland once again to return to London.

At the same time as the parliament passed a new constitution, it also endorsed a "charter of freedom" which contained a list of human rights principles (freedom of conscience and religion, inviolability of the home, secrecy of correspondence) and remained in practice meaningless. In March 1948, the socialist leader and Prime Minister, Józef Cyrankiewicz, was summoned to Moscow and told to merge his Socialist Party with the Communist Party, to create the United Polish Workers' Party. The "loyal" peasant party and the notionally independent liberal Democratic Movement were allowed to survive as "bloc" parties.

In Hungary, a provisional government formed in December 1944 at Debrecen included the Communist Party, the Independent Smallholders' Party, the Social Democrats, the National Peasants' Party (which was in practice little more than a front organization for the communists, who were bitterly disliked in the countryside), and a liberal party. These parties were loosely associated in the National Independence Front. In elections in 1945, the smallholders established an apparent predominance: they had over half the vote in municipal elections even in urban Budapest, and then in November 1945 they won 57 percent of the vote, while the communists and socialists had 17 percent each. The most important figure in the government formed by Zoltan Tildy was the Interior Minister, a communist, Imre Nagy, who quickly established tight control over the police force and created a gigantic State Security Office (AVO).

In 1946, tensions between the smallholders and the communists increased over the form of the new constitution, the boundaries of Hungary (the smallholders wanted to include ethnic Hungarians in Romania and Slovakia, while the communists and the Soviet Union insisted on the interwar frontier), and the obvious packing of the civil service with communists. When Tildy was elected President, the new government (headed by Ferenc Nagy) continued the coalition. The communist leader, Matyas Rákosi, replaced Imre Nagy as Interior Minister with another communist, László Rajk (who was later vilified as a cosmopolitan Jew). Rajk had not been in Moscow in the 1930s, which made Stalin suspicious, but had fought in Spain, been captured by the Germans in France, and then escaped to join the Hungarian underground. Rákosi attacked the right wing of the smallholders, and large-scale communist demonstrations in Budapest forced the smallholders to expel 22 deputies. Rajk continued to find smallholders' conspiracies against the republic, and in spring 1947 began to attack Ferenc Nagy. He resigned in June 1947, and in new elections, conducted under heavy Soviet pressure, the Communist Party became the largest party with 22 percent of the vote. The National Peasants had another 7 percent.

Rákosi formed a government, forcibly merged the Socialist Party with his own party, and took over direct control of the AVO. In 1948, he attacked the Catholic Church, and organized an alternative hierarchy of so-called "peace priests".

In Czechoslovakia, some prewar politicians returned to power: notably the new President, Edvard Beneš, and Jan Masaryk, the son of the founder of the first republic, who became Foreign Minister. The basis for the postwar regime was laid down by the Košice Government Program. The all-party anti-Nazi coalition included the Communist Party, the National Socialist Party, Czech Social Democrats, the Czechoslovak People's Party, and the Slovak Democratic Party.

In the 1946 elections, the communists had the largest vote (37.9 percent). The new Prime Minister was Klement Gottwald, a communist, and his party colleague Vaclav Nosek was Interior Minister. Nosek reorganized the police, so as to be sure of its loyalty. In February 1948, the non-communist ministers resigned in protest after an agreement to stop the dismissal of non-communist police officers had been ignored. Gottwald detected a plot to replace the government, and on February 22 the police arrested opponents of Gottwald's regime. Beneš agreed to a purely communist government, and on March 10, Masaryk was "suicided" from a window of the Foreign Ministry. In June Beneš resigned, and was replaced by Gottwald.

In Romania, King Michael tried to sack his Prime Minister Sanatescu, who had accused him of acting as a tool for the communists (in the same way as he had been used in the Antonescu period as a tool by the Nazis). The Communist Party then pressed hard for a more rigorous "anti-fascist" course, which meant in practice a thorough purge of the old elites. Their leaders were called to Moscow and told to press for a monopoly of power for the communist-dominated National Democratic Front. Once back in Romania, their maneuver was supported by the Russian member of the Allied Control Commission, General Vinogradov, who issued his orders without any consultation with the western Allies. The National Democratic Front then deposed King Michael. A similar operation was used in Bulgaria to remove the infant King Simeon.

Stalinism and the Zhdanov line

Economic reconstruction should logically have been a continent-wide business, since the fundamental aim of those who wanted economic recovery was to overcome the fragmentation and nationalism of interwar Europe. The Marshall Plan was initially open to the countries of eastern Europe. It had been preceded by a substantial flow of funds administered multilaterally, by the United Nations Relief and Reconstruction Administration. In 1946, Poland had also obtained a moderately sized ($90 million) credit from the US government to buy steel and other goods needed for reconstruction, although the US ambassador in Warsaw had bombarded the State Department with memoranda imploring the administration not to give money to "the Polish ruling clique" which was running the "terroristic activities of the Security Police".[8] That the eastern European states rejected the Marshall Plan was a consequence above all of the changing political line emanating from the USSR, and a much more conflictual ideology.

The dominant figure in shaping Stalin's and Soviet thinking in the immediate aftermath of the war was Andrei Zhdanov, who provided the clearest definition of the new Cold War mentality. The world was divided into "two hostile camps", marked by different politics, different economics, and different cultures. Zhdanov reshaped cultural policy, formulating the 1946 Central Committee resolution condemning the works of the modernist Soviet writers Anna Akhmatova and Mikhail Zoshchenko, and refocusing Soviet aesthetics around socialist realism and anti-modernism. The new policy was part of a much broader attack on "cosmopolitanism", which had strong anti-Semitic elements. Zhdanov also founded a new organization to replace the disbanded Comintern: the Cominform. He died suddenly in 1948, a few months after the Cominform had denounced the policies and philosophy of one of the most apparently successful cases of communist government, that established in Yugoslavia by Tito.

At this time, Czechoslovakia, Hungary, and Romania moved to a much greater degree of state control over the economy. Domestic and international trade was nationalized, as trading seemed to give too many opportunities for unplanned private initiatives. One country, Yugoslavia, had already moved in this direction in the immediate aftermath of the war, in 1945–46.

Yugoslavia had always been in a peculiar position relative to Moscow, largely because it was the only east European country not liberated from the Germans by the Red Army. The military success of Josip Broz Tito's partisans created a unique legitimacy for Tito. Tito was a Croat, who had fought in the Austro-Hungarian armies (i.e. against Serbia) in the First World War. He had spent seven years in the Soviet Union.

In November 1943, Tito had headed a National Committee appointed by the Anti-Fascist Council of National Liberation. In May 1944 he had reached an agreement with the government-in-exile in London, and the result was endorsed at Yalta. In government Tito at first replicated Stalinism as a domestic model more completely than in any east European state, where coalition constraints limited the room for maneuver for some time. The Soviet model looked particularly attractive as it "solved" the issue of federalism: an all-state Communist Party could provide a link between notionally quite autonomous republics. The 1946 Yugoslav constitution thus took over the 1936 Soviet constitution mostly unaltered; and in 1947 Yugoslavia launched a four-year plan.

Tito provoked Stalin not because of anything he did in domestic policy, but because of his ambitious approach to foreign policy – he demanded control over Trieste, he supported the communists in the Greek civil war, and he criticized west European communist parties which were missing revolutionary opportunities. Stalin, at this time, was eager not to provoke large-scale conflict against a western alliance equipped with atomic weapons, whether over Trieste, or on the broader canvas of western Europe and Greece. He also considered himself, as the author of a tract on the nationalities question, a greater expert on the management of national and ethnic issues than anyone else.

On June 28, 1948, the anniversary of the great Serb victory at the battle of Kosovo (and of the assassination that started the First World War), the Cominform denounced the "nationalism", "deviationism", and "Trotskyism" of Yugoslavia. The Yugoslav party had "taken an entirely wrong line on the principal questions of foreign and internal policy, which means a retreat from Marxism–Leninism". It had ignored the "growing class struggle" in the country, and failed to act against the power of the kulaks, "despite the precept of Lenin that a small individual economy inexorably gives birth to Capitalism and the bourgeoisie".[9]

Stalin expected that Tito would be replaced, but instead the Yugoslav party defended him and attacked the "lies" of the Cominform, from which the party was then expelled. Tito rapidly developed an alternative model to Stalinism, and placed a high emphasis on the principle of self-management. In Yugoslavia, he tried to balance nationalities, with the result that, according to his principal lieutenant, Milovan Djilas, "some Serbian nationalists see Tito as a successor to the Austro-Hungarians who sought to destroy Serbian power".[10] In international relations, he became a champion of the idea of development separate from either the American or the Soviet models, the "non-aligned movement", which Yugoslavia along with India and Indonesia led from the early 1960s.

After the break of Tito with Stalin, in each country a search for "Titoist" deviationists began. In particular, the advocates of "national communism", slight deviations from the Soviet model in the light of particular circumstances, were attacked. Since it was not clear who these deviationists were, the witch hunts often concentrated on those communist leaders who had not been in Moscow during the war, but had rather remained in underground movements, or had been in the West. Show trials on a Soviet model reflected the logic of Soviet politics, as much as any separate development in individual countries. But they produced quite different effects in individual national settings: in Hungary and Czechoslovakia they were conducted with a murderous brutality, whereas in Poland many deviationists were imprisoned but few were executed.

Rajk was moved from the Hungarian Interior Ministry to the Foreign Ministry in August 1948, and arrested in June 1949 for having engaged in a conspiracy with Tito's Yugoslavia. At a show trial, he confessed to having worked for Allen Dulles and the US intelligence organization OSS, and to conspiring to kill Rákosi. He was hanged.

In late 1948 and early 1949, one-quarter of the membership of the Czech Communist Party was purged. In 1949 and 1950 the search for nationalist deviationists concentrated mostly on Slovaks, and a number of prominent Slovaks, including the Foreign Minister, Vladimir Clementis, and the Politburo member Gustav Husák, were purged. In November 1951, Czech Stalinism reached its height when the General Secretary of the Czech Communist Party, Rudolf Slánský, who had been an associate of Zhdanov and one of the most enthusiastic Czech purgers, was arrested, together with his deputy Bedrich Geminder. They were accused of "cosmopolitanism" and "Zionism", and put on trial in November 1952. Eleven of the 14 defendants were Jewish.

In Bulgaria, in 1949 Deputy Prime Minister Traicho Kostov was arrested, accused of working with the United States, and made to confess at a well-publicized show trial. But elsewhere in eastern Europe, Stalinism was more discreet. There was an extensive purge of the East German Communist Party in 1950, without the use of much violence. In Romania, the purges came later, and took a peculiar form: it was the leadership of the Romanian Communist Party most associated with the Moscow line – Vasile Luca, Teohari Gheorghescu, and Ana Pauker – who were purged. The unusual character of the purge anticipated some later developments: the 1958 agreement on the withdrawal of Soviet troops (again quite unique in the eastern bloc), and the explicit criticism of Soviet interventionism by Nicolae Ceauşescu in 1966.

In Poland, the man identified in Moscow as the leader of "Titoism" was Władysław Gomułka, who had been Secretary of the Communist Party since 1943. In September 1948 he was forced to make a confession of his errors, and later imprisoned. In December 1948 a party congress appointed a former Comintern official, Bolesław Bierut, as General Secretary of the party, and he then became the Polish Stalin.

This tremendously brutal period was also the time in which Soviet-dominated Europe had the best economic performance. A non-communist source, the United Nations Economic Commission for Europe, estimated annual per capita growth rates over the period 1951–55 as 7.2 percent in Bulgaria, 5.7 percent in Romania, 5.3 percent in Hungary, and 4.1 percent in Poland. (The official figures were much higher.) As in 1930s Russia, the party could try to justify its brutality by its economic results.

After Stalin

In January 1953, a "doctors' plot" was discovered in the Soviet Union. A group of mostly Jewish doctors had allegedly killed and poisoned leading party officials, including Zhdanov. The repercussions included widespread arrests, and many feared that the later 1930s were about to be replayed. The death of Stalin (March 5, 1953) prevented such a replay, but also prompted a new upheaval. At first, it looked as if the most powerful figure in the post-Stalin order would be the security chief Lavrenti Beria, who appeared along with Georgi Malenkov (who became Prime Minister and was also very briefly General Secretary of the Communist Party, or CPSU) and Foreign Minister Vyacheslav Molotov at Stalin's funeral to present eulogies. Beria was clearly the dominant member of this troika, and gave the impression of being "totally cold" and indeed rather dismissive of Stalin at the funeral.[11]

At this moment, a thaw set in, perhaps because Beria and the security forces were better informed than the Communist Party about the state of public opinion. At Stalin's funeral, Beria had emphasized that the Soviet Union was a multinational state. In the mostly non-Russian west of Ukraine, he called for the use of Ukrainian and the promotion of ethnic Ukrainians in the party; he also made concessions about religious freedom. The most spectacular démarche occurred in relations with Germany, when Beria talked about abandoning the forced construction of socialism, and preparing for a united and democratic Germany.[12] On June 10, the East German Politburo announced reforms, and amnestied large numbers of prisoners. But at the same time, labor requirements were increased, and massive protests erupted on the streets of East Berlin on June 16 and 17. The demonstrations were stopped, brutally, by Soviet tanks. The East German party leader, Walter Ulbricht, whose position had been challenged by Beria and his German allies Zaisser and Herrnstadt, may have helped to set off the Berlin protests in a move to discredit his enemies. He now argued that they were the result of the mistaken liberalization course. Zaisser and Herrnstadt were purged.

The German incident had repercussions at the center of power. In Moscow, Nikita Khrushchev managed to engage some leading military figures, persuaded Malenkov that Beria was threatening to undermine socialism, and organized the arrest of Beria at a meeting of the Presidium of the Communist Party on June 26, 1953. Beria was killed, and his reputation destroyed by the circulation of stories about wild sexual excesses, rapes, and orgies.

The new Soviet leader, Khrushchev, managed his own, much more cautious, reform program. It moved inconsistently back and forth between liberalization and a new clampdown. After indicating a change in economic course, in 1955 Khrushchev emphasized that the Soviet economy would continue to concentrate on heavy industrial development. He also directed attention to the military threat against Soviet power. The creation of the military alliance of eastern Europe, the Warsaw Pact, in 1955, was largely a reply to the extension of NATO to include Germany.

In February 1956, Khrushchev launched de-Stalinization by presenting a critical address at the Twentieth Party Congress of the CPSU:

> Stalin acted not through persuasion, explanation, and patient cooperation with people, but by imposing his concepts and demanding absolute submission to his opinion. Whoever opposed this concept or tried to prove his viewpoint, and the correctness of his position, was doomed to removal from the leading collective and to subsequent moral and physical annihilation. This was especially true during the period following the Seventeenth Party Congress (1934).[13]

The idea of a new shift in Soviet ideology was enough to touch off major upheavals in eastern Europe. Immediately after the Soviet Twentieth Party Congress, the Polish leader Bierut died, probably from suicide, although he was suffering from heart problems. On June 28, 1956, workers in Poznań staged demonstrations, in which they called for an "end to communism", as well as for "bread and freedom". The army and police reacted violently, and 53 people were killed. The Polish communists responded by attempting to appease the protesters, and in particular by rehabilitating Gomułka, who had been imprisoned for most of the Stalinist period. At the party congress in October, Gomułka made a speech which (unlike Khrushchev's famous speech) was broadcast on Warsaw Radio. It denounced the errors of the industrial and agricultural policy pursued over the past seven years, announced a decollectivization (which was actually carried out, uniquely in the Soviet bloc), and promised elections in which the people would be allowed "to elect and not only to vote". A few days later, the Catholic Primate, Cardinal Wyszyński, was released from house arrest. In his speech, Gomułka had asked: "We are faced with the question of how it could happen that our party allowed so many perversions in the past."[14] Tito sent "warm and hearty congratulations" to Gomułka, while US President Eisenhower offered economic aid and also said that the United States had a mission to "expand in areas in which free men and free governments can flourish".[15] Behind the scenes, Gomułka attempted to reduce the Soviet military influence, and replace the Minister of Defense, the Polish-born Soviet Marshal Konstantin Rokossovski. The Polish Politburo had already requested that all KGB "advisers" be recalled from Poland. Khrushchev was outraged, flew to Warsaw, and mobilized Soviet troops in Poland and the fleet off the Baltic coast. Gomułka replied by attempting to deploy the Polish army around the major roads leading to Warsaw. There were also anti-Soviet demonstrations by students in Warsaw. Eventually, Gomułka worked out a compromise with Khrushchev, who stated that he did not object to the development of the Polish party as formulated in the October congress, and Gomułka said that "it is a matter for our own judgment how long and how many Soviet military experts will remain in Poland".[16] Khrushchev perhaps was scared of the consequences of a military intervention in Poland, and by late October the developments in Hungary made it quite unthinkable.

Khrushchev at an early stage had criticized Rákosi, and in 1953 Imre Nagy became Prime Minister of Hungary and proposed a "new course". It was consistently undermined by Rákosi, who remained as Party Secretary, and in 1954 tried to mobilize the party against the state. In April 1955 Nagy was expelled from the Central Committee.

In June 1956, under pressure from the Soviet Union, and as part of an attempt to shape a reconciliation between Khrushchev and Tito, Rákosi was dismissed, but he was replaced by a close ally and the architect of his economic policy, Ernő Gerő. Gerő was instructed from Moscow:

> The relaxation of international tensions and the slogan of coexistence do not presuppose but, on the contrary, exclude ideological concessions and any accommodation to hostile views. That is why you must eliminate all factors responsible for the collapse of party discipline in Hungary, restore discipline among Central Committee members and the party's rank and file, and launch a fierce struggle on the ideological front.[17]

On October 6, 1956, the rehabilitated László Rajk was reburied with substantial ceremony. On October 23, students and workers staged large-scale demonstrations in Budapest, and knocked down the gigantic statue of Stalin. (Similar statues remained standing in other eastern European countries.) The protesters demanded that Nagy lead a new government, and that Russian troops be withdrawn. On October 24, Nagy was appointed Prime Minister. He formed a new and more open administration, and the next day promised a government "on the broadest base". When Soviet tanks tried to crush the protests, they were attacked by Hungarian demonstrators. The protesters soon acquired arms and became a quite effective force. They also attacked the secret police. By October 28, the Soviet troops had withdrawn from Budapest. On October 30, Nagy announced the "discontinuation of the one-party system", and invited Hungary's first postwar leaders, including Zoltan Tildy of the Smallholders Party, to form a provisional governmental committee. At the beginning of November, new units arrived in Hungary. Nagy withdrew from the Warsaw Pact and asked the United Nations for help. It was an unfortunate moment: British and French troops had just attacked the Suez Canal.

The new Soviet units reconquered Budapest in a bloody battle, but strikes continued to paralyze Hungary for several weeks. In all, during the unrest 22,000 Hungarians and nearly 2,300 Soviet soldiers were killed or wounded (Plate 9). Nagy fled to the Yugoslav Embassy, but he was turned over to the Soviet police and deported to Romania. Two years later, he was tried and hanged. In total, 100,000 Hungarians were arrested, 26,000 were given prison sentences, and 600 were executed.[18]

The new Prime Minister was János Kádár, who had secretly left Budapest at the beginning of November, had been flown to Moscow (where at first he had warned against military intervention, which he had stated would destroy the morale of the Hungarian communists). With Soviet military support he set up a base at Szolnok, 80 kilometers southeast of Budapest, and then became Prime Minister of what he called "a government of national unity based on the ideology of the people's democracy" (i.e. eastern style). The Hungarians called this new government a "puppet regime", which it was.

The Polish and Hungarian revolts left two quite contrasting legacies. Hungary brutally showed to everyone in eastern Europe the limits imposed by the Soviet Union on change. The Polish critic Adam Michnik later wrote:

> Of course, we have to keep in mind that at that time the burning Budapest testified that there is a very narrow range of possible changes, that the most important rules of the game are fixed by Soviet presence and they are not being vetoed even by the West. Imre Nagy's appeal for aid and the silence of Western governments were much too clear a signal of the substantial validity of the Yalta agreements and of the fact that no one will help us if we do not help ourselves.[19]

Plate 9 The romance of resistance: Hungarian citizens and a captured Soviet tank, 1956. © Jack Esten/Getty Images.

On the other hand, Poland, which had been saved from closer Soviet attention and engagement by the eruption of the Hungarian revolt, learnt an internal lesson. The comparative weakness or mildness of Stalinism in Poland (imprisonment rather than hangings), the importance of the national card, the existence of the Church as a counterweight in society, and the tendency of the party to react to crises by catapulting radical critics into power, all set a precedent. In 1956, Gomułka and his supporters took over the Polish party: it was a quite unique triumph of critics, which inspired other, later critics to more radical stances. Some of them – like the journalist Jerzy Urban on the critical magazine *Po Prostu* – later moved into government as new crises produced new cooptation; some of them – like Leszek Kołakowski – did so much rethinking that they rejected the fundamental philosophical premises of the communist engagement.

There was no linear movement of reform at the center of the Soviet bloc. Khrushchev's initial attack on the cult of personality had led to profound upheavals; after 1956 he retreated quickly. Then, in 1958, Khrushchev initiated a more general thaw. His speech at the Twenty-second Party Congress in 1961 went much further than the 1956 speech. In 1962 Alexander Solzhenitsyn was allowed to publish a horrifying and vivid account of labor camps in the Stalinist era, *One Day in the Life of Ivan Denisovich*. But almost immediately Khrushchev condemned the "excesses" of avant-garde art. He tried to improve relations with the West, and to promote an early version of what was later called detente. But the superpower conflict was never as frightening as in the Khrushchev period, when the world came close to nuclear war over Cuban missiles (1962), and Berlin became a focus of international tensions in 1958 and 1961. In the economic field, an inconsistent liberalization and a botched attempt at agricultural reform discredited Khrushchev, and in part explain his overthrow in 1964.

Disillusionment

Eastern Europe achieved fast rates of growth with Soviet-style planning – indeed faster even than the contemporaneous western European "miracle". New cities were constructed in order to create new Soviet citizens. As in 1930s Russia, steel and coal were the central products. In the German Democratic Republic, a new city was constructed at Eisenhüttenstadt (Iron Foundry Town). Nowa Huta (New Foundry) near Krakow was planned as Poland's first socialist city, and aimed to correct and overwhelm the Catholic intellectuality of Krakow.

The world's first space satellite, the Sputnik, was launched in October 1957 (the term "satellite" was applied almost immediately after this ironically to describe the Soviet Union's partners in socialism). It looked like a stunning vindication of the Soviet approach to science, planning, and growth. There were also dramatic rises in living standards. In the early 1960s, surveys of opinion in the Soviet Union showed high levels of satisfaction and confidence. Most Moscow students believed that they would be able to buy a car within two or three years of graduating.[20] This optimistic view was shared not just by Soviet citizens: in 1960 the US intelligence service CIA extrapolated that Soviet GNP could reach three times the level of that of the United States by 2000.[21] The 1961 Soviet party program included a clear promise: "The party solemnly proclaims: The present generation of Soviet people shall live in communism."[22]

Leonid Brezhnev and Alexei Kosygin attempted to replace Khrushchev with a collective leadership that was calmer and less impulsive than that of their predecessors. It was also much older. The average age of the Politburo, which had been 55.4 in 1952, was 61 at the time of Khrushchev's deposition, and by 1980 was 70.1.[23] Utopianism was replaced by businesslike conduct (what the Russians called *delavitost'*). In practice, more and more this meant opportunism. By the early 1980s, a former Soviet dissident, an émigré in Paris, Alexander Zinoviev, tried to formulate what was characteristic about the new Soviet type that had emerged: *Homo sovieticus*.

I've only got a more or less stable reaction to everything I bump up against: a behavioral stereotype. Convictions are something Western man has, not Soviet man. Instead of having convictions the latter had a 'stereotype of behavior'. This doesn't presuppose any convictions, and so it's compatible with every sort of conviction. When you confuse convictions with behavioral stereotypes without convictions, you get many misunderstandings, and strange ideas arise among Westerners about Soviet behavior.[24]

Zinoviev hit the crucial point: that Soviet socialism depended upon a distinct philosophy, one that was widely believed in the immediate aftermath of the war, but that by the 1960s few shared any more – despite the fact that (in its own terms) it continued to be successful.

Consumerism went on developing quickly in the Soviet bloc. For the USSR, for instance, of the urban population, 32 percent of families had televisions in 1965 and 86 percent by 1977; 17 percent had refrigerators in 1965 and 87 percent by 1977.[25] A number of commentators have used this kind of material to explain that communism collapsed (eventually) precisely because it was so successful, an argument which of course in its simplest form looks perverse and even stupid. The West, after all, was indisputably more successful in producing consumer goods; and, despite the refrigerators, there were still many shortages of consumer goods and the refrigerators were not full.

In the 1960s, many Soviet societies experimented with economic reform, and specifically with some sort of decentralization. In 1963, the GDR launched what it called a New Economic System, but it was obliged in 1970 to restore central planning. Bulgaria loosened controls after 1964, but re-established them after 1968. The most far-ranging reforms occurred in Hungary, but even there a retreat occurred in 1972, and central supervision of large enterprises was restored. The "father of reform", Rezsö Nyers, was sacked in 1974.

From the mid-1960s, however, despite the continued increases in the provision of consumer goods, something changed, and the mood turned sour. That this was not simply a mental construct produced by intellectual disenchantment can be deduced from the demographic data, which the Soviet system kept carefully secret from this point. In the aftermath of the war, as in western Europe, as living standards rose, mortality fell and life expectancy rose. But after the mid-1960s, mortality rates began to rise again. For Poland, where these surprising results were first revealed only in the political turmoil of the early 1980s (other countries kept their secrets longer), the data for male mortality of the age range 40–44 is as follows: for 1950, a rate of 614 per 100,000; for 1965 393, a very substantial improvement; but for 1970 437 and for 1980 894. Mortality rates for all the major causes of death in this age group – cardiovascular problems, cancers, and violence – exhibit the same trend: declining until 1965, and then rising.[26]

The causes of this surprising development are complex. They lie in part in environmental degradation, which made people more vulnerable to disease; in part in increased alcohol consumption, which in the later 1980s became the first target of Mikhail Gorbachev's renewal campaign; cancers and cardiovascular disease rose with higher levels of cigarette consumption, etc. But an analogous trend reversal could not be found in western Europe. It suggests that a profound disenchantment and cynicism set in during the 1960s: as the idealism of the political elite of the *nomenklatura* waned and was replaced by a weary pragmatism, people began to look with contempt at "them" (an important book of interviews with the elite by the journalist Teresa Torańska was circulated in the Polish underground with this title, "*oni*" in Polish).

At first, the demand for change was simply expressed on a popular level in a wish to be connected to a more vibrant western culture. In 1967, there was rioting in the center of Warsaw when 3,000 young people tried to attend a Rolling Stones concert in the Palace of Culture.

The Church in Poland caught the mood of the 1960s. The reforms of the Second Vatican Council produced a more popular Church. In 1965, the Church started to move into the much more political area of German–Polish relations. For the regime, the Soviet security blanket could most easily be justified in terms of the need to protect against a revival of German militarism. The Polish bishops now published an open letter to the German bishops: "We forgive, and we ask your forgiveness." The Polish government promptly issued a counter-statement, "We do not forget, and we will not forgive." The Archbishop of Krakow then issued a statement setting the bishops' letter in a much broader context: "When we [Poles] worked together during the [German] occupation a lot of things united us, foremost a respect for the human being, for conscience, individuality, and social dignity."[27] These were, however, precisely the human virtues that were killed by communist society.

Three brackets had held eastern Europe in place: the idea of the inevitability of socialism replacing capitalism, the internal power of the communist regime, and the external framework of the German security threat and the Soviet protection. In the 1960s, all began to be weakened, and the change in German foreign policy, the gradual development of *Ostpolitik* even before Willy Brandt's tenure at the Foreign Ministry after 1966, pushed some new thinking to develop in the East. In 1965 Nicolae Ceauşescu became leader of the Romanian Communist Party after the death of Gheorghe Gheorghiu-Dej. Ceauşescu's 1966 critique of the Warsaw Pact was a response to France's departure from the military organization of NATO by a country which saw itself as the France of the eastern bloc. In the following year, he opened diplomatic relations with West Germany without asking Soviet approval.

The most far-reaching specifically political reform movement of the 1960s occurred in Czechoslovakia. In 1963 Ota Šik began a partial liberalization of the economy – in parallel with initiatives in the Soviet Union, under the direction of Yevsei Liberman, but going much further.

Youth movements, women's organizations, and Slovaks demanding greater autonomy all pushed the Czech communist leadership. In January 1968, Antonín Novotný was forced to resign as Czech Communist Party General Secretary, and was replaced by Alexander Dubček. In April 1968, the party adopted an action program; but belated concessions could not satisfy increasingly radical demands for reform. On June 27, a document, *2000 Words*, signed by 70 leading professors, intellectuals, doctors, and sportsmen (such as Colonel Emil Zátopek, the Olympic running champion), was printed in four Czech newspapers. It complained of bogus democracy: "It was with high hopes that most of the nation welcomed the socialist program. But its direction fell into the hands of the wrong people."[28]

The Soviet leader, Leonid Brezhnev, reformulated an old Marxist–Leninist thesis about the one-way inexorability of historical development in 1968. Applied to foreign policy, and in particular to Soviet control over eastern Europe, this idea became known as the "Brezhnev doctrine". It was most clearly articulated in a speech Brezhnev gave later in the year, to Polish communists in Warsaw:

> Each Communist Party cannot but take into account such a decisive fact of our time as the struggle between two opposing social systems – capitalism and socialism. [. . .] The sovereignty of each socialist country cannot be opposed to the interests of the world of socialism, of the world revolutionary movement. Lenin demanded that all Communists fight against small nation narrow-mindedness, seclusion and isolation, consider the whole and the general, subordinate the particular to the general interest.[29]

In July, a summit of the Warsaw Pact sent a joint letter from the USSR, Hungary, Poland, Bulgaria, and the GDR to the Czechoslovak communist leadership warning that reactionary forces were pushing the Czechoslovak Socialist Republic "off the road to socialism". At the end of the Second World War, the letter stated, the frontiers of the socialist world "had been moved to the center of Europe, to the Elbe and the Bohemian Forest", and the socialist countries would "never agree to these historic gains being placed in jeopardy".[30] At a meeting in Bratislava in early August, the Warsaw Pact leaders denounced US "imperialism" and West German "revanchism", and emphasized the need for the protection of the successes of socialism. There was absolutely no reference to any Czech problem, and Dubček denied that there had been any secret agreement.

On August 21, 1968, Soviet tanks tried to restore order in Czechoslovakia. They met considerable but mostly non-violent resistance. The first Soviet tank crews were so affected by the Czech protests that they were no longer reliable instruments of political control. They were replaced by other, in large part non-Russian, Soviet troops. An extraordinary party congress, which had originally been scheduled for September, met on August 22, the second day of the occupation. It voted to support the arrested leaders, demanded their release, and restated the will of the party to develop "democratic and humanistic socialism". The Soviet press now denounced Dubček and his supporters as a "minority right-wing revisionist group", and stated that the party congress was an "illegal" effort by rightists and counter-revolutionaries to subvert the party. Brezhnev summoned Dubček and President Svoboda to Moscow and systematically humiliated them (Dubček was flown out of Prague in handcuffs). Dubček now signed a statement calling for "normalization".

Czech protests continued. In January 1969 a student, Jan Palach, burnt himself in Wenceslas Square in the center of Prague. Gustav Husák, a Slovak who had been Deputy Prime Minister and had resigned from the Czech Communist Party presidium when it met in the crisis days of August 1968, replaced Dubček in April 1969 and was unremittingly loyal to Brezhnev.

The party set about a complete reversal of the post-January 1968 course of its development. Around 500,000 people were purged: university teachers, doctors, and lawyers drove trams and worked in sewers; 327,000 party members were expelled; 171,000 Czechs escaped to the West. Dubček himself was eventually set to work in the obscurity of the Forestry Commission in Bratislava.

The Czech reform movement was the most powerful expression of the spirit of '68 in eastern Europe. But there was an analogous Polish student movement. The party and the Interior Ministry (under General Mieczysław Moczar) replied with an anti-intellectual and anti-Semitic campaign. The students' movement of 1968 had almost no support from Polish workers. Conversely, workers' protests in the Baltic shipyards and ports in 1970 met little response from Polish intellectuals, although they were powerful enough to shake up the communist leadership.

At this moment, it looked as if the experiment of socialism in eastern Europe had come to a dead end. The original intellectual drive to transform society faded into a weary and corrupt cynicism. The ideology looked more and more like a prop to justify Soviet Russian political and economic dominance. The once-stunning economic growth rates faltered. The leaders got greyer (with the exception of Romania's demonically maniacal Ceauşescu).

Technology

The Czech *2000 Words* had stated, in line with standard Marxist theory, that "the source of social changes is the economy". After the dramatic political changes of 1989–91, the most usual and most powerful explanation has been a techno-materialist determinism, according to which Soviet-style social and economic engineering was appropriate to the steel- and heavy-engineering-based technologies that were central to economic life in the mid-twentieth century. The socialist countries failed to adapt, however, to the information-based electronic world of computers, and – as electronics became increasingly important – fell behind. They tried hard: when, for instance, the Eleventh Congress of the Bulgarian Communist Party set out its guidelines for the 1976–80 plan, it spoke of "raising the scientific level of social management", and the need for "objective methods of planning and cybernetics".[31] When I was a guest at the East German Economic Academy in Berlin-Karlshorst in 1981, the economists proudly pointed out that they had just installed a big computer in the area formerly occupied by the department of Marxism–Leninism. But the computers lagged consistently behind western models, and an obsession with access meant that the communist countries refused to look at micro-computers, which might have devolved power and decision-making.

The awareness of the technological lag produced an increasingly bitter debate about how to reform. When the chips were down, socialism lacked a byte. Stephen Kotkin concluded for the Soviet Union: "The very engine that had powered a peasant society to superpower status – the industrial planned economy – seemed increasingly to be exerting a severe drag."[32] Charles Maier believes that "By the end of the 1980s the Communist Party claim to political and societal leadership could no longer be sustained in view of the developmental deficit that had to be remedied."[33]

This explanation has a high degree of plausibility, but it is ultimately unsatisfactory, and does not fully explain why the crisis should have started at the fringes of the Soviet empire before it affected the heart, or the obvious demoralization that set in long before the economic crisis of communism was apparent.

Communism and its approach to technology had involved a central item of faith: that heavy industry, coal, iron, or steel would create new men or socialist men. The most striking instance of that faith was the idea that a steelworks built at Nowa Huta near Krakow could destroy Krakow as a center of intellectual Catholicism. But the steelworkers paid for and in large part themselves built a church in Nowa Huta between 1967 and 1977, when the completed Church of the Ark was dedicated by the Archbishop of Krakow, Cardinal Wojtyła. In the 1970s, 84 percent of the Nowa Huta steelworkers proclaimed their faith in God.[34]

During the 1980s, Poland became the test case for the viability of communism. The Brezhnev doctrine of the irreversibility of the social transition from capitalism, which made perfect sense in Marxist–Leninist terms, was put to the question in Poland. It became evident that socialism had not created a new type of man, and that men and women were still deeply human.

Solidarność

The legacy of the Polish unrest in 1970 was a new party leadership, with Edward Gierek as Party Secretary. Like Gomułka, Gierek picked former oppositionists as the most credible exponents of government policy. Gierek also set about modernizing Poland as quickly as he could, in order to constitute the "new man" as quickly as possible, borrowing large sums on the newly available international capital markets. He raised living standards, built fast roads and electric train lines (which the Soviet Union liked, because it offered quicker communications for Soviet forces with the "western front" in Germany). The reconstruction of the completely destroyed royal castle in the center of Warsaw was a symbol of a new national pride; the construction of an incomplete multi-lane highway between the beautiful Łazienki Park and the parliament buildings was an act of civic architectural vandalism.

He also allowed a greater degree of room for independent cultural life. The film-maker Andrzej Wajda, for instance, had had a script depicting 1950s Poland and the model worker (Stakhanovite) movement ready in 1963, but in the 1970s was allowed to actually make the movie: *Man of Marble* was released in 1977.

In 1976 price increases produced new workers' unrest, in Radom and in Warsaw (at the Ursus tractor works). Adam Michnik and Jacek Kuroń established a Committee of Workers' Defense (KOR), which for the first time linked the workers and intellectual reform movements.

By 1980 this new alliance led to Europe's first successful working-class revolution. That revolution, however, is unthinkable without one event which underlined the fundamental illegitimacy of communist rule. In October 1978 the Archbishop of Krakow, Karol Wojtyła, became Pope John Paul II. When he visited Poland for the first time as Pope, in June 1979, the government was quite helpless. The Pope celebrated a Mass with about 1 million people in Victory Square in Warsaw, and told the Polish state and party leaders that "the *raison d'être* of the State is the sovereignty of society, of the nation, of the motherland"[35] (Plate 10).

In August 1980, shipyard workers in Gdańsk went on strike. They wanted higher pay, but also some immaterial concessions, the reinstatement of two sacked leaders, Anna Walentynowicz and Lech Wałęsa, and a monument to the victims of the December 1970 protests. They occupied the Lenin shipyards and refused to settle on a limited local basis. At the end of August, they had successfully negotiated an agreement which included the recognition of the right to form independent and free trade unions, a relaxation of censorship, and the construction of the shipyard monument (in an agreed form, that of a gigantic cross). There were also many social promises: better access to child care, improved housing, more regular meat supplies, the provision of maternity leave, and the lowering of the age of retirement.

On September 5, 1980, Gierek was hospitalized, apparently with a heart attack, and was replaced by Stanisław Kania. The August upheavals had produced the sense of a new historical moment, of which 1970 had been merely an anticipation. Wajda made a film of the 1970 events, which was eventually released as *Man of Iron*; for the film, he had asked the Polish Defense Minister, General Jaruzelski, whether he could borrow army tanks for the cinematic re-enactment (the request was turned down). They also produced a remarkable fusion of working-class and intellectual opposition

Plate 10 Peaceful mass resistance to communism: Pope John Paul II's visit to Poland.
© Keystone/Getty Images.

to the government. The government treated it all as a gigantic experiment, too. In the negotiations for the August agreement in Gdańsk, the workers were assisted by young sociologists, assistants from the University of Warsaw, while the government used the professors from the same department to negotiate.

Strike committees from all over Poland elected Wałęsa as the chairman of the new organization, Solidarność, or Solidarity. For 15 months, Polish society organized itself. There was a rural trade union for the farmers.

In the August 1980 agreement, the quid pro quo for the recognition of independent trade unions was that the strikers should also acknowledge the party's monopoly on political power. But with the formation of all kinds of new organizations, this monopoly looked either irrelevant or threatened.

In September 1981, Solidarność held its first conference, in its birthplace in Gdańsk. There were now 9.5 million members, represented by 896 delegates. The new movement defined itself as a social and a moral as well as an economic protest: "What we had in mind was not only bread, butter and sausage but also justice, democracy, truth, legality, human dignity, freedom of convictions and the repair of the republic."[36] Edward Lipiński, one of the founders of the workers' self-defense committee KOR, insisted that it did not challenge the notion of state ownership: "There are no forces in Poland who struggle for the privatization of the means of production, a privatization of the Huta Katowice or Huta Lenina (Nowa Huta)." On the other hand, he did not want the regime's type of "socialism", "which meant a rotten, inefficient, wasteful economy . . . this socialism of rotten economy, this socialism of prisoners, censorship and police, has destroyed us for thirty years, as it has destroyed other nations".[37]

In September 1981, the Polish parliament (*sejm*) rejected the party's bill for workers' self-government, and adopted in its place a version very close to the Solidarność proposals. The Soviet Union was highly nervous. A general threat to socialism was more apparent than at any previous moment of unrest in the Soviet empire. On the other hand, the commitment of Soviet soldiers in the conquest and occupation of Afghanistan after 1979 meant that any further military engagement by the Soviet Union would be costly and difficult to manage; and the Soviet leaders were also aware that Soviet tanks in Budapest and Prague had damaged the idea of communism. In consequence, they rattled the saber as much as they could, and from December 1980, Soviet troops staged spectacular maneuvers near the Polish frontier. At the height of the Solidarity crisis, the East German leadership ordered the statue of Frederick the Great to be put back in Unter den Linden, facing Silesia in a martial pose. But Moscow was reluctant actually to use the saber. The Moscow leadership instead put pressure on the Polish Communist Party to remove Kania, who they thought had made too many concessions to the social movement. He was succeeded by the Prime Minister and Defense Minister, General Jaruzelski, who in Soviet eyes had rather stronger nerves. In the fall of 1981, Jaruzelski played a difficult game: on the one hand, he asked for military assistance, which the Soviet Union refused, in order to demonstrate simply that he was doing as much as he could.[38] On the other hand, he tried to build up his image with the Polish people by presenting himself as their last guarantor against Soviet invasion, who was giving in to popular demands as much as he could.

There were other ways for the Soviets to put pressure on Poland. The strikes and their settlement also helped to produce an economic crisis in Poland. The high level of indebtedness, together with much higher world interest rates after October 1979, made a debt default likely. The USSR had supplied cheap oil and gas to Poland at a time when the Iranian revolution was pushing up world prices. An economic blackmail was a much less painful and confrontational way of bringing Poland into line than an inevitably bloody military invasion.

On December 13, 1981, General Jaruzelski declared martial law. The leading figures of Solidarność were arrested, or slipped underground.

There was surprisingly little resistance, though in Silesia 1,300 coalminers occupied a mine until after Christmas. The new Archbishop of Warsaw, Józef Glemp, who had been appointed after the death of Cardinal Wysziński in May, just two weeks after a Turkish assassin had dangerously wounded Pope John Paul II, had no possibility of communicating with Rome. All the phone communications were broken by the government. On Sunday,

December 13, the day of the proclamation of martial law, he preached a sermon that was repeatedly broadcast by the state authorities:

> The authorities consider that the exceptional nature of martial law is dictated by a higher necessity, it is the choice of a lesser rather than a greater evil. Assuming the correctness of such reasoning the man in the street will subordinate himself to the new situation. . . . There is nothing of greater value than human life. Do not start a fight of Pole against Pole.[39]

The Pope later wrote to General Jaruzelski in similar terms, asking him not to use violence against the Silesian miners.

After December 13, many of Solidarność's supporters were bitterly disappointed by the absence of resistance, and concluded that that meant the end of the movement. Timothy Garton-Ash, the foremost western observer of the new social phenomenon, concluded: "The general strike, Solidarity's ultimate weapon, was broken. . . . General Jaruzelski's two-week Blitzkrieg in December 1981 was to Solidarity what the three-week Blitzkrieg of September 1939 was to the Second Polish Republic."[40]

In retrospect, it is precisely the non-violence of December 1981, largely the result of the teaching of the Catholic Church, which is so extraordinary, and which made the outcome of 1980–81 so different from that of the tragic precedents of 1956 and 1968. It was a protest against a culture of violence. At the time it was widely suspected that Soviet security agencies were involved in the papal assassination attempt, although specific confirmation of the KGB's role came only in an Italian Senate investigation in 2001. In 1984, a Solidarność priest, Father Jerzy Popiełuszko, was abducted and killed near Torun. His parish church, St Stanisław Kostka in Warsaw, almost immediately became a shrine of Catholic resistance. A Fiat Polski with its trunk open (the type of car the secret police used in the kidnapping) was placed in a side-chapel. There were pictures of Father Popiełuszko alongside a portrait of the Polish army chaplain Ignacy Skorupka, killed in the battle of Warsaw against the Red Army in 1920.

In fact, it soon became clear that nothing had really changed as a result of the banning of Solidarność. The economic stagnation remained, and the government lacked the legitimacy to impose an economic reform program which would initially be costly and painful.

In the 1980s, Poland became an equivalent of Spain in the 1930s: a European war of ideas was played out there. There were important divergences in national responses. For many French intellectuals, it was Poland that convinced them that reform socialism, or a non-authoritarian, non-Soviet Marxism (such as had been widely popular after 1968 and Czechoslovakia) was impossible. On the other hand, German intellectuals, trade union leaders, and politicians on the left distrusted the Catholicism of much of Solidarność, and were worried that the movement – indeed any movement – would "destabilize" Europe and particularly Germany. They had given up thinking about ideas and moral challenges, but they clung to the geopolitical world view of "Yalta" as a security blanket.

Notes

1   Yalta declaration, February 9, 1945, https://history.state.gov/historicaldocuments/frus1945Malta/d429.
2   Herbert Feis, *Churchill–Roosevelt–Stalin: The War They Waged and the Peace They Sought*, Princeton, NJ: Princeton University Press, 1957, p. 523.
3   Stanisław Mikołajczyk, *The Rape of Poland: Pattern of Soviet Aggression*, New York, NY: McGraw-Hill, 1948, pp. 104–5.
4   Milovan Djilas (transl. Vasilije Kojić and Richard Hayes), *Tito: The Story from Inside*, London: Weidenfeld & Nicolson, 1981, p. 60.
5   Czesław Miłosz, *The Captive Mind*, Harmondsworth: Penguin, 1980 (orig. 1953), p. 12.
6   Ibid., pp. 18–19.
7   Keesings 8761.
8   Christopher J. Zablocki, *Report of the Special Study Mission to Poland*, House Report 712, Washington, DC: US Government Printing Office, 1961; Arthur Bliss Lane, *I Saw Poland Betrayed: An American Ambassador Reports to the American People*, New York, NY: Bobbs-Merrill, 1948.
9   Keesings 9381.
10 Djilas, *Tito*, p. 62.
11 Amy Knight, *Beria: Stalin's First Lieutenant*, Princeton, NJ: Princeton University Press, 1993, p. 182.
12 Knight, *Beria*, p. 191.
13 Nikita Khrushchev, "Secret" Speech (February 1956), www.pitt.edu/~syd/khr.html.
14 Keesings 15161.
15 Keesings 15163.
16 Keesings 15163.
17 *Cold War International History Project Bulletin*, 8–9, 1996/97, p. 365.
18 *Cold War International History Project Bulletin*, 8–9, 1996/97, p. 376.
19 Quoted in Ferenc Féher and Agnes Heller, *Hungary 1956 Revisited: The Message of a Revolution – A Quarter of a Century After*, London: George Allen and Unwin, 1983, p. 52.
20 John Bushnell, "The new Soviet man turns pessimist", in Stephen F. Cohen, Alexander Rabinowitch, and Robert Sharlet (eds), *The Soviet Union since Stalin*, Bloomington, IN: Indiana University Press, 1980, p. 183.
21 Richard Reeves, *President Kennedy*, New York, NY: Simon and Schuster, 1993, p. 54.
22 Seweryn Bialer, *Stalin's Successors: Leadership, Stability, and Change in the Soviet Union*, Cambridge: Cambridge University Press, 1980, p. 55.
23 Ibid., p. 83.
24 Alexander Zinoviev, *Homo Sovieticus*, London: Victor Gollancz, 1985 (orig. French edition 1982), p. 11.
25 Bialer, *Stalin's Successors*, p. 152.
26 Marek Okolski and Beata Pukaska, *Recent Mortality Patterns and Trends in Poland*, University of Warsaw mimeograph, 1982, Table 3.
27 George Weigel, *Witness to Hope: The Biography of Pope John Paul II*, New York, NY: Cliff Street Books, 1999, p. 161.
28 Keesings 22885.
29 The Brezhnev Doctrine, 1968, https://web.viu.ca/davies/H102/brezhnev.doctrine1968.htm.

30 Keesings 22887.
31 Michael Kaser, *The Economic History of Eastern Europe*, Vol. III, Oxford: Oxford University Press, p. 221.
32 Stephen Kotkin, *Armageddon Averted: The Soviet Collapse 1970–2000*, New York, NY: Oxford University Press, 2001, p. 64.
33 Charles S. Maier, *Dissolution: The Crisis of Communism and the End of East Germany*, Princeton, NJ: Princeton University Press, 1997, p. 105.
34 Jerzy Kloczowski, *A History of Polish Christianity*, Cambridge: Cambridge University Press, 2000, p. 328.
35 Weigel, *Witness to Hope*, p. 286.
36 Cited in Timothy Garton-Ash, *The Polish Revolution: Solidarity 1980–1982*, London: Jonathan Cape, 1983, p. 223.
37 Ibid., pp. 225–6.
38 Malcolm Byrne, in "New evidence on the Polish crisis 1980–1881" (*Cold War International History Project Bulletin*, 11, 1998, p. 7), argues that Jaruzelski was consistently pushing for Soviet intervention in Poland, an argument that is undoubtedly overstated.
39 Garton-Ash, *Polish Revolution*, p. 269.
40 Ibid., p. 268.

9   A golden age
The 1960s

The 1960s was an era in which people in North America and in western Europe believed that they controlled their own destiny, and people in central Europe wanted to be the same. That is why the decade felt so distinctive, and why of all the decades surveyed here, it is the one that most clearly had its own style and remains – to many of its ageing participants – the most attractive.

The impression of the manageability of human affairs was the result of the coincidence of two moments, of two generations who both thought of themselves as uniquely creative and innovative. The first impulse came from the decision-makers of the decade, who had been junior officials or politicians in the 1940s, and drew the lesson from the wartime era and postwar reconstruction that wise decisions at the center of power could make a new and better world. Scientific and technical planning opened a way to a new future. This doctrine was the rationalism of the powerful. The second was the product of a youth culture in protest, which was convinced that it too could make its world, and detested the implications of an apparently inhuman science and technology. This philosophy became in the 1960s the irrationalism of the powerless.

The mindset of the first approach is neatly encapsulated in Roy Harrod's rather hagiographical biography of Keynes, who had been one of the most important role models for what its participants called "Our Generation". Harrod in his account left out the counter-cultural parts of Keynes's life and in particular his homosexuality: "Happy is the land where a wise man could wield power, simply because he is wise, although he has no support from any political group or any financial or trade-union interest."[1] It was this sense of benign all-knowingness that the younger generation disliked and satirized.

By the 1960s the idea of control – the "wise wielding power" – had acquired a strong technological element. Initially confined to scientific and university research laboratories, the first electronic computing devices had been developed in the Universities of Pennsylvania (ENIAC – Electronic Numerical Integrator and Computer – in 1946) and Cambridge (EDSAC – Electronic Delay Storage Automatic Calculator – in 1949) as part of the wartime mobilization of scientific resources. They operated with vacuum tubes, 19,000 in the case of ENIAC. But these cumbersome earliest models evolved rapidly: smaller transistors were developed by the end of the 1940s, and by the 1960s micro-circuits came into common use. The powerful IBM 360 generation introduced in 1964, which ended the distinction between scientific and business computing, transformed business existence. These early computers were by modern standards not very powerful or fast (the IBM 360 had 256K memory, and a transfer rate of 16 bits per cycle), but they were very expensive, and were kept and maintained in a central location. They promised at last a technical feasibility of central planning and control.

A parallel development which also seemed to herald more external control, though through a very different mechanism, was the discovery by Francis Crick and James Watson of the "double helix" of DNA, the device that genetic material used to reproduce itself. Crick dates the breakthrough to an observation in the Eagle pub in Cambridge in 1953. The precise details of DNA were still an inscrutable mystery, and were to be worked out much later in the large-scale research of the "human genome project". But it was clear that plants, animals, and of course humans were the products and the prisoners of their genes in a way that for the moment could not be changed by human action. So at the same moment as the mood of the age emphasized controllability, the most fundamental discovery showed the hopeless character of such a venture.

In economics too, an older generation of benevolent patriarchal reformers had a simple formula for management. They had learned from the economic woes of the 1930s that economic growth could resolve social tensions. The settlement of social disputes became easier when "the pie was expanding". Only a few of this generation realized that this rather simple materialism was inherently unsatisfactory. At the beginning of the 1960s, one of the most influential theorists of the German *Wirtschaftswunder* (economic miracle), Alfred Müller-Armack, warned that the "security of jobs as a result of full employment and the increase of production in a continually growing economy has not produced the expected social pacification, but has rather produced a new discontent and dissatisfaction".[2]

The major form of that dissatisfaction was a romantic utopianism, that drew principally on a mixture of Marxism and Freudianism. Herbert Marcuse's *One Dimensional Man* (1964) synthesized these traditions in an examination of consumerism as a kind of totalitarianism (because culture, the economy, and politics were all driven by the same interests). The Marxism of the protest movement wanted to differentiate itself clearly from Soviet-style doctrine, because of that doctrine's materialist or economistic quality. The central text of Marx's mature doctrine and of traditional Marxism, *Das Kapital*, was highly unattractive. One critic said that "it served to reduce critique to economic theory, to annihilate subjectivity in objectivity, to subject the subversive capacity of the proletariat to the reorganizing and repressive intelligence of capitalist power".[3] Instead, the new protest movement took up the subjectivism and romanticism of the early Marx, whose writings before the 1848 revolution (in particular the Economic–Philosophical Manuscripts of 1844, and an early draft of *Das Kapital* which was usually referred to by the German title of *Grundrisse*) were now thought to be central to the contemporary relevance of a thinker who promised not a general theory of economic and political development, but an analysis of the phenomenon of "alienation". The reason why communism was "obsolete", as the title of a book by the self-styled "cherubic Danton" of the French revolution of 1968, Daniel Cohn-Bendit, put it, was not that it bore responsibility for the crimes that had been committed in its name, but that it was too disciplined, rigorous, and inflexible. "The objections to Bolshevism," Cohn-Bendit and his brother wrote, "are not so much moral as sociological; what we attack is not the evil conduct of some of its leaders but an organizational set-up that has become its one and only justification."[4]

The new subjectivism also took up other alternative versions of Marxist doctrine – Gramscianism, Trotskyism, Maoism – and sometimes even went further in an effort to be as all-embracing as possible in its rejection of decayed materialistic culture. Some of the protest generation wanted to fuse Marxism with a radical Christianity that drew on the egalitarianism of the Sermon on the Mount, and also with non-western religions, notably Buddhism and Taoism. Easter demonstrations, often using the symbolism of the Cross, played an important part in pacifist and anti-atomic protests. Pacifist protests grew significantly during the Vietnam War, with the American anti-war and civil rights movements as models.

Generational conflict in a very acute form, in which each side accused the other of not understanding the issues at stake, was played out in almost every conceivable arena: cultural, artistic, and musical life, and the discussion of sexuality, of moral behavior, of religion. What separated the two sides of the barricades was a sharply different view of institutions: for the old generation, institutions would generate reform; for the young generation, institutions were the heart of the problem, and needed to be destroyed in order to make a world that was more spontaneous and better.

Chemicals and the youth culture

Life in the 1960s was pharmacologically transformed and enhanced. The belief that human destiny was controlled and controllable followed from the scientific application of artificial hormones. For the first time in human history, reproductive and hence demographic behavior seemed to be completely under human control. "The pill" – the use of estrogen to regulate female fertility – changed behavior and demography. It seemed a realized version of the "happiness pill" ("soma") envisaged by Aldous Huxley in the utopian fantasy *Brave New World* (1932), which would generate constant sex on demand.

The estrogen pill was developed by Min-Chueh Chang, Gregory Pincus, and John Rock, the latter a devout Catholic who saw the pill as an extension of a natural method of contraception, in which couples would choose infertile days for sex. It first became available for general use in 1960 (in doses 40 times higher than is normal today), but was prescribed quite restrictively at first. In the United Kingdom, for instance, Family Planning Clinics (the idea of planning could be ever extended) were permitted at first to prescribe contraceptive pills only to married women, or women with "printed invitations to a forthcoming wedding".[5] Philip Larkin, later to become the British Poet Laureate, claimed (perhaps rather oddly, and even incomprehensibly for non-Britons) that "sexual intercourse began in 1963".

By the mid-1960s, when the pill became more generally available to women, its widespread use was clearly evident in sharply falling birth rates. From 1960 to 1970 the birth rate (per thousand population) fell in Italy from 18.3 to 16.8, in France from 17.9 to 16.7, and in Germany from 17.8 to 13.3.

The pill and other drugs together made the youth culture of the 1960s. The ones that aroused the most interest were those that altered the mind, above all the synthetic LSD, first devised by the Swiss industrial chemist Albert Hofmann in 1940 but popularized after 1960 by the (soon to be ex-) Harvard professor Timothy Leary's Psychedelic Research Project. In 1966, LSD was featured on the cover of *Life* magazine, and was banned in the United States; the European countries soon also put it on the list of prohibited substances.

Even the less desirable consequences of this new lifestyle could seemingly be eliminated, as more licit substances were rapidly advancing the field of disease prevention. Soaring rates of sexually transmitted disease (which rose quickly in tandem with widespread use of oral contraception) could relatively easily be treated with antibiotics, another relatively recent invention. Penicillin had first been isolated by Alexander Fleming in 1928, and in an injectable form was used for treatment in 1938. The almost parallel development of streptomycin (1943) was used against tuberculosis, and together with immunization removed one of the great scourges of the nineteenth century from the developed world. Penicillin was used with great success against the wartime and postwar epidemic of sexually transmitted disease (in occupied Germany, venereal disease or VD was colloquially known as "*Veronika dankt*" – "Veronika says thank you").

The most famous expression of youth culture, the Beatles, evolved in 1960 from the Quarry Men, a Liverpool band formed by John Lennon in 1956. The band's breakthrough was made in a visit to Hamburg, and in 1963 with the song "She Loves You" and a tour of the United Kingdom, it set off a collective hysteria that was termed "Beatlemania". It was the music of self-conscious protest: the Beatles were proud of the fact that they could not read, and refused to learn, musical notation. The more sexually provocative Rolling Stones, with a mix of rhythm and blues, emerged in 1962. Both bands – the Rolling Stones (in characteristic style) more explicitly – took up the idea of mood- and mind-bending from the drug culture. When Mick Jagger was tried with possession of drugs in 1967, the establishment quickly rallied behind him and his lawyer's argument that he had nothing more than a medicine commonly used in Italy to treat travel sickness.[6] In the same year, the Beatles' manager, the Liverpool music store owner Brian Epstein, died of a drug overdose. Later the deaths of pop musicians from overdoses became a sad commonplace: Jimi Hendrix, Janis Joplin, Keith Moon, and John Entwistle.

Many of the ideas and behaviors that flourished in the 1960s counter-culture quickly became mainstream. Contraception was soon understood as a quite normal part of life. By an ironic twist, mind-altering drugs became part of the performance culture of the revived capitalism of the 1980s and 1990s: amphetamines and cocaine to increase concentration and productivity; heroin to numb the victims of society; prescription drugs such as the attractive anti-depressant Prozac to sedate and calm those people upset by the speed and pace of capitalist change. Governments continued to fight these developments, waging more or less futile "wars on drugs".

The youth revolt

Young people took themselves more importantly in part because politicians became convinced that it was worth spending more on them. The new or expanded institutions of higher education proved to be a center of the rejection of the materialist vision that lay behind the increase in educational expenditure.

One of the consequences of the academic study of growthmanship was politicians' conviction that education and especially higher education produced concrete gains in growth and prosperity. In France, the number of students in higher education expanded from 283,000 in 1960 to 622,000 in 1968; in Germany from 246,000 to 431,000; in Italy from 206,000 to 420,000; and in the United Kingdom (with poorer state funding of universities) more modestly from 271,000 to 346,000. Perhaps the relative slowness of the growth in student numbers in the latter case explains the more subdued character of the British "1968". But generally, larger student numbers, greater expectations of entry into an elite that were vulnerable to disappointment, and the inadequacy of the infrastructure (lecture halls, dormitories, and above all the professors) all contributed to an eruption of protest.

There is also a political explanation. The revolutions occurred at the same time as a general shift of practical politics to the left, a shift that the left's most idealistic supporters found almost invariably disappointing. In the United Kingdom, Harold Wilson as Labour Prime Minister proved incapable of dealing with the white rebellion (UDI) in Rhodesia, and was the most reliable ally of the United States in Europe at the time of the Vietnam War. His socialism looked more like a devotion to modern high technology (which he had referred to, in a much-derided statement, as the "white heat of technological revolution"). The Labour minister and brilliant political diarist Richard Crossman called him "a most disappointing leader for a radical left-wing government", and complained of his cynical centrism: "His main aim is to stay in office. That's the real thing and for that purpose he will use about any trick or gimmick if only he can do it."[7] The "opening to the left" in Italy produced very little real political change.

In Germany in 1966, the years of Christian Democrat government came to an end, and a Great Coalition government was formed, with the charismatic Social Democratic Party (SPD) leader Willy Brandt as Foreign Minister and Deputy Chancellor, but with a Christian Democrat with a Nazi past, Kurt Kiesinger, as Chancellor. Meanwhile, the radical right was also mobilized against the apparent consensus of establishment parties, and a new National Democratic Party managed to win seats in some *Land* parliaments. As a result, it looked as if there was a real threat of a new fascism. In France, General de Gaulle criticized the United States and particularly its engagement in Vietnam, but in a very old-fashioned way, and seemed to stifle any discussion of domestic reform, which he dismissed as "shitting in one's own bed".

Atlanticism

Atlanticism was the main alternative European foreign policy orientation to *Gaullism*. The towering figure in the development of European Atlanticism is the British wartime leader, Winston Churchill, who himself had an American mother. Churchill had a romanticism of his own about the "English-speaking peoples", which included both the United States and the British Empire, of which the United States was suspicious. The founding document of Atlanticism is the Atlantic Charter of 1941, which provided a strong set of universal claims.

After the war, Atlanticism was championed by economic modernizers, such as France's Jean Monnet and Germany's Ludwig Erhard, who saw America as a model for Europe. They learned different lessons: Monnet concentrated on American advantages of bigness, while Erhard stressed more the principle of economic freedom, but both were reacting against the particular problems of their own countries. France had suffered in the interwar period from the conservatism and reluctance to invest of its business elite, and Germany from the controlling ambitions of its governments. The UK's Atlanticists, notably Harold Wilson and Margaret Thatcher, were largely skeptical of the European integrationist drive, which they saw, in some ways correctly, as an attempt to find a European counterweight to the United States.

There was also a substantial group of Atlanticist writers and intellectuals, who helped to forge a new climate in European life: Ignazio Silone, Raymond Aron, Arthur Koestler, André Malraux. They were strongly influenced by a generation of American intellectuals, many of whom, like Melvin Lasky, Sidney Hook, and Irving Kristol, had abandoned *Marxism* or *Trotskyism*, and now propounded a blend of social democratic reformism and Cold War anti-communism. Melvin Lasky's *Der Monat*, and then the English-language *Encounter*, were central elements of this effort. Much of the initiative was lost or compromised in the 1960s, in part because these intellectuals were visibly not at the cutting edge of student politics; in part because the new thinking that came from across the Atlantic, influenced by the student movement, was critical of American power; and in part because of revelations in 1967 that the CIA had partly financed the work of Lasky's Congress for Cultural Freedom.

The student protest movement in Germany at first was focused on West Berlin, where a large number of students had congregated, in large part because the Four Power control of Berlin meant that there was no military service for men, and in part because of its increasingly agreeable atmosphere as a stage for new politics. The imbalance between the large number of male students in Berlin and the relatively small number of women (condemned to secondary positions in the student movement) created additional sexual frustrations and tensions. These could be portrayed in terms of a cosmic political struggle: if, in the eyes of the Freudianized critics, both National Socialism and Adenauer's restorationist republic originated in sexual repression, was not a struggle against sexual regulation and regimentation also a struggle against fascism?

In December 1966 radical student leader Rudi Dutschke formed an "Extraparliamentary Opposition" (APO), based around the Sozialistischer Studentenbund (SDS, the same initials as the US organization Students for a Democratic Society), in protest against the Great Coalition government. On June 2, 1967, a large demonstration against a visit of the Shah of Iran to the Berlin opera house turned violent, and a policeman shot one of the student protesters, Benno Ohnesorg. From then, confrontations developed all over Germany, and the government introduced legislation for emergency powers (which the critics saw as inherently fascist). The Interior Minister wanted to treat the relatively small (1,600-member) SDS as an illegal extremist organization. In April 1968 Dutschke was shot and seriously injured by a right-wing militant. His supporters believed that the assassin had been driven to violence by the press campaign against Dutschke mounted by the pro-American and pro-Israel publishing house of Axel Springer and Springer's populist tabloid newspaper, *Bild*.

Demonstrations then erupted over five days in many German cities (the police counted 27). The demonstrations were, by later standards, relatively small: some 4,000 in the largest, on the Kurfürstendamm in Berlin. But they were quite violent, with 280 policemen and 96 civilians injured, and there were massive police arrests. An analysis of the arrests shows how the movement had spread well beyond simply student support. Of the 827 arrested, only 286 were college students; 92 were high-school students, and 185 white-collar workers.

At this point, the left campaign focused on Kiesinger and his past. Kiesinger's own condescending statements, which seemed to imply that ex-Nazis were better people than the student protesters, were incendiary. He pronounced: "They do not know, as do we elders, how things were in Germany, and they cannot judge today's situation as we can."[8] The novelist Heinrich Böll said Kiesinger's Chancellorship was an "insult"; Journalist Beate Klarsfeld publicly slapped the Chancellor. The discussion crystallized a debate about the German past which had previously been notable through its absence. The critics now accused not just figures like Kiesinger but the whole ethos of the Adenauer era, which was condemned as restorationist and devoid of moral sensibility.

One (relatively small) wing of the student movement moved to terrorism. In April 1968, Gudrun Ensslin and Andreas Baader set fire to department stores in Frankfurt, which they described in Marcusian terms as centers of consumer terror. They termed their violence as a "project", using the language of the seminar room. The arson trial was an opportunity to set out their ideas and views. Out of these attacks there developed a terrorist movement self-styled as the Red Army Faction, or RAF (in an allusion to the wartime bombing of Germany by the Royal Air Force), or alternatively, simply as the Baader–Meinhof Gang, which attacked government figures, banks, industry, and US military installations. Baader himself was a fast-talking street criminal who terrified and fascinated the student intellectuals. He remained the driving force of the new movement, which was not halted even by his re-arrest in 1972. It was galvanized into a hard-core terror movement by the example of the murder by Palestinian terrorists of Israeli competitors during the 1972 Olympic Games in Munich, killings which Andreas Baader and Ulrike Meinhof welcomed. A new generation of urban terrorists who self-consciously modeled themselves on Latin American urban guerrillas went on to more assassinations and kidnappings, as well as a routine stream of bank robberies. The German terror movement reached its peak in 1977, when Siegfried Buback, a federal prosecutor, Jürgen Ponto, a leading banker, and Hanns Martin Schleyer, the head of the German Employers' Federation and a member of the board of Daimler-Benz, were murdered. In October 1977, terrorists hijacked a Lufthansa 737 jet and took it to Mogadishu, Somalia, in an attempt to negotiate the release of the RAF leaders from prison. The plane was stormed by a special forces unit, and three of the imprisoned leaders – Andreas Baader, Gudrun Ensslin, and Karl Raspe – then killed themselves in Stammheim Prison (October 18). Ulrike Meinhof had killed herself one year earlier. After 1977, terrorist activity receded, but did not stop completely. Sympathizers of the terrorists called October 1977 the "German autumn". Many of the terrorists escaped into the GDR and were protected by the security police there. When in 1989–90 the GDR started to disintegrate and the question of German unification became imminent, a new wave of terror began and claimed some very prominent victims: Alfred Herrhausen, the chief executive of Deutsche Bank, and Detlef Rohwedder, the head of the *Treuhand*, the management agency dealing with state property from the GDR.

The number of active terrorists was relatively small, but they were surrounded and supported by a larger number of sympathizers who protected the criminal core, and an even larger group of people who justified the actions of the terror gangs as a legitimate protest against an oppressive society that had not come to terms with its illegitimate past.

Another part of the '68 movement went into house-occupation as its major focus of political activity. In retrospect, considerable strains developed between those who interpreted the circumstances of 1967–68 as very particular ones, requiring an activist intervention to save Germany from a renewal of fascism, and the much more generalized and less specific utopias of the later protesters, who saw themselves rather as offering an alternative to the "system".

Such student movements spread across much of the continent, and the contagious and trans-continental idealism of the movement looked like an updated version of the generalized revolutions of 1848 (it also promoted a renewal of interest in the Europe-wide upheavals of 1648 among the historically minded). Like 1848, there were upheavals in very different political and economic settings. They were in both cases mildest in the reformist United Kingdom, and absent in the tsarist empire and its modern successor. Paris in the end – though not at the beginning of 1968 – proved to be an epicenter. They broke out in very liberal countries, like the Netherlands, where the violent hippy "provos" set a fierce revolutionary pace before relapsing into legalized drug-induced stupor and passivity. They also occurred in authoritarian countries. In Spain, and in particular in Catalonia, the relationship of intellectuals to the Franco regime had always been strained. In 1963 an illegal student union had been formed in Catalonia. Students at the University of Barcelona in March 1966 held a large (and also illegal) assembly at a monastery, which was raided by the police and became a famous "incident" (it was known as the Caputxinada). In 1969, one fringe of the large protest movement shifted to violence, and formed a Catalan Liberation Front (FAC), which between 1969 and 1971 committed about 100 acts of violence: these, however, unlike those by the much more radical Basque equivalent Euzkadi Ta Azkatasuna (ETA) which emerged at the same time, involved no loss of life.

In Northern Ireland, the youth rebellion drew most explicitly of all the European protests on the US civil rights movement, demanding equality of treatment of the Catholic minority. Bernadette Devlin tried to draw the Irish protest movement closer to the mainstream of European student protest, but as Irish nationalism radicalized, it remained in practice self-consciously aware of Irish differences.

In Italy, past and present interacted in a similar manner to the dynamic of the German '68. During the course of the year, there was very generalized student unrest, but it ran counter to the mood of the rest of the country. Elections at the height of the student revolt produced little change, with a slight increase in the vote for both the Christian Democrats and the Communist Party (which, unlike the German socialists, could claim to be a real opposition to the establishment), and a substantial loss for the socialists, who had been in the ruling coalition and now withdrew from government. In November 1968, a center-left government formed with Pietro Nenni as Foreign Minister. In the next year, the Socialist Party split over the question of cooperation with the communists, and Nenni resigned, leaving a Christian Democratic government which felt that it had to make broad-ranging concessions to the left. A new employment law in 1970 gave an exceptional measure of job security, making it more or less impossible to dismiss workers or even for them to move from one job to another within a factory.

The far left of the Italian student movement grew more radical after the military coup against Allende's communist government in Chile, and especially after the attempt of the Italian Communist Party (PCI) under Enrico Berlinguer to move closer to power (and in the eyes of the left, the authoritarianism of the Italian state) with a "historic compromise" with Christian Democracy on a reformist platform. In 1973, Autonomia Operaia began to work as a radical movement of shop-floor opposition to the unions and the PCI, endorsing and glorifying violence as a means to revolution. Its intellectual godfather, Antonio Negri, formulated its credo in the following terms:

> Proletarian violence, in so far as it is a positive allusion to communism, is an essential element of the dynamic of communism. To suppress the violence of this process can only deliver it – tied hand and foot – to capital. Violence is a first, immediate, and vigorous affirmation of the necessity of communism.[9]

In 1977, the autonomists began an occupation of Rome University, in which crowds fighting with the police chanted slogans about the P38 pistol, the favored weapon of radical protest. Negri himself was arrested in 1979 and sentenced to 20 years' imprisonment, but escaped to France. He returned in the 1990s to prison, where he wrote the canonical text of the anti-globalization movement of the 1990s.[10]

Red Brigades (*Brigadi Rossi*) ran a similar campaign of terror to that of the German RAF, complicated by parallel actions of right-wing fascist terrorists, and operations of the security forces designed to smear the broad left with the violence that was advocated by the extremist minority. As in Germany, terror reached a culmination in the late 1970s, in particular with the 1978 kidnapping and murder of ex-Prime Minister Aldo Moro, the Christian Democratic interlocutor of Berlinguer for the "historic compromise". The complicated story behind the Moro assassination was never fully uncovered.

The French movement was one of the last student protest movements to emerge, though there were some protests in the Sorbonne in 1964, and circulation of an influential pamphlet *On the Poverty of Student Life Considered in its Economic, Political, Psychological, Sexual and Intellectual Aspects*. A big strike in the newer Paris campus of Nanterre at the beginning of the new academic year 1967 focused primarily over the "sexual" issue of separated dormitories for male and female students. Between 10,000 and 12,000 students boycotted the campus. The Dean of Nanterre argued rather limply that all he wanted was for the university to be "one big happy family". When the Education Minister formulated a response that dealt with rather dry issues of education reform, he was told that this would not solve the students' sexual problems. Daniel Cohn-Bendit, one of the leaders of the Nanterre movement, explained why the university should be the focus of such discontent: "The mediocrity of university teaching is no accident, but reflects the lifestyle of a civilization in which culture itself has become a marketable commodity."[11]

In the spring of 1968, student unrest escalated. On May 10–11, 1968, Paris students built barricades in the Quartier Latin, which were quite brutally removed the next morning by the plastic-coated CRS riot police (Plate 11). Unlike in other European countries, the student protests and their suppression sparked a series of major industrial disputes, with almost 9 million workers on strike. Some of the workers demanded a new approach to management: self-control or *autogestion*.

Plate 11 The romance of resistance: student protesters in Paris, 1968. © Keystone/ Getty Images.

While President de Gaulle adopted a confrontational rhetoric, Prime Minister Georges Pompidou, one of de Gaulle's most loyal lieutenants (as well as being a former teacher who had played a large part in the government's failed education policies), thought that a policy of gentle moderation could defuse the conflict. He had been away in Afghanistan at the moment of the "Night of the Barricades" and had come back to Paris with a conciliatory statement that he had prepared on the plane without consulting de Gaulle. He proposed to reopen the Sorbonne, and expressed his "profound sympathy for the students".

The protests then spread to factories and businesses, especially in the Paris area. The biggest French insurance company, Assurance Générale, was taken over, as was the Atomic Energy Center at Saclay and the Rhône-Poulenc works. Gasoline became unavailable as truck drivers went on strike. Faced by the student movement and the paralyzing strike movement, de Gaulle lost his nerve. He took his family with him in a helicopter, apparently to his home at Colombey, but then ordered the pilot to fly to the French army garrisoned in Baden-Baden in Germany. The French commander, General Massu, successfully deterred de Gaulle from following the wilder possibilities suggested by memories of 1940 and 1958: using the French army in Baden to invade France, or fleeing into exile. Instead he said (as he later reported): "Mon Général, it's too bad, what can you do, you're in the shit and you must stay there. Go back to it. You can't do anything else."[12] De Gaulle followed this advice, returned and dissolved parliament.

In the ensuing elections, the right won a major victory, and the student revolution was over. But so was de Gaulle. He launched a new reform initiative in which power would be devolved from the center. Some of the technocrats – in particular de Gaulle's brilliant ex-Finance Minister, Valéry Giscard d'Estaing – publicly opposed the proposal. Most of France was simply not interested. The referendum on the reform proposal turned into a humiliation for de Gaulle, who resigned as President. He was succeeded by Georges Pompidou, in an election in which the left-wing vote was completely fragmented, with the result that Pompidou faced a run-off against a centrist candidate (Alain Poher, from the Christian Democratic MRP), and with 58 percent of the second-round votes won an even larger presidential majority than that of de Gaulle (French elections required a run-off second round if no candidate obtained an absolute majority in the first round of voting). The left was divided and defeated: there had been four leftist candidates in the first round of the elections, who all devoted considerable invective at each other. Jacques Duclos, the veteran leader of the Communist Party, won 21 percent of the vote, and was thus in third place behind Poher. Gaston Defferre, the socialist leader, who made clear his disagreements with Mitterrand (the presidential candidate of the socialists in 1965), had just over 5 percent. Michel Rocard, who called for the unity of the left ("all those who want to destroy capitalism and not merely Gaullism") had 3.6 percent; and the purest student leader of all, the Trotskyist Alain Krivine, slightly over 1 percent. The result, however, made the left feel even more strongly that the "system" was unfair, in that no leftist candidate had made it through to the second round of the elections. The abstention rate, reflecting leftist disenchantment, was 31 percent.

By the 1970s and 1980s, the aftermath of the French '68 was a movement of a substantial number of academics to the political right in the form of a revival of classical liberalism. The *nouveaux philosophes* around Bernhard-Henri Lévi distanced themselves from the New Left, which they thought had become irrational, immoral, and anti-Semitic in its repeated denunciation of Israel. The main thinker associated with hardline Marxism, Louis Althusser, killed his wife in 1980 and was interned in a psychiatric hospital. Jean-Paul Sartre's funeral in 1980 was celebrated in a grand way, with 200,000 following the casket through the streets of Paris. But after his death his reputation fell more or less continuously, while that of his liberal rival, Raymond Aron, rose sharply.

The legacy of 1968

Except in France, "1968" did not really pose a threat to the government or to political stability. In France, the threat arose more from the ageing de Gaulle's loss of nerve than from any concrete threat. The most "realistic" proposal of the French left actually looked like a return to some of the familiar faces of the Fourth (or even Third) Republic: Mitterrand as President with Pierre Mendès-France, a hero of 1940, as Prime Minister. The search for a credible alternative to de Gaulle thus looked like a return to the past. The actual left of the 1960s was hopelessly divided between the old left, the Communist Party and a large part of the strike leadership on one side, and the New Left of the students and intelligentsia on the other. But even these sides were fragmented. Curiously, some New Left historians, looking for an explanation of the "failure of 1968", attribute this to the skill with which Pompidou and de Gaulle played the strategy of good cop/bad cop, which helped to increase intra-left differences.[13]

The political side of 1968 was undoubtedly a failure, like the Europe-wide revolutions of 1848 in which some observers detected analogies. Culturally, however, 1968 left a distinct mark.

Universities in continental Europe did not become less overcrowded: on the contrary, student numbers continued to increase (by 1975 there were 811,000 students in higher education in France, 977,000 in Italy, and 1,041,000 in Germany). But they became less formal, lower-level academics played a greater role in university life, and the continuing expansion of higher education meant that the student leaders soon began to have important positions in university life. The "radical don" caricatured in Malcolm Bradbury's *History Man* or David Lodge's *Changing Places* (both 1975) influenced but also repelled subsequent generations. Universities were the site of a revolt against the concept of benign leadership by patrician luminaries.

At the time, some students had spoken of a "long march through the institutions" as an alternative path to the failed revolutionary alternative. As after 1848, many moved into business life; but they also went into culture, the media, the Church (more often into Protestant churches), and into politics. By the 1990s, they were in prominent positions. The lawyers who defended Baader–Meinhof – Horst Mahler, Otto Schily, and Hans-Christian Ströbele – all became prominent in German political life. Mahler went to the radical right, where he continued to realize the anti-Americanism inherent in almost all of the 1968 left. Ströbele, who of the three remained closest to the ideals of 1968, became an influential leader of the left wing of the new (Green) environmental party. Schily at first was a major figure in the Green Party, but then turned to the SPD and became a tough law-and-order Interior Minister after 1997 in the government led by the former Juso (Young Socialist) leader Gerhard Schröder. The Foreign Minister in the coalition government, a member of the Green Party, was Joshka Fischer, slightly younger than the '68 generation, but a veteran of the house-occupation movement. Fischer repudiated his violent past (he had been photographed attacking a Frankfurt policeman); he changed from the jeans and sneakers he had consistently worn as the first Green Environment Minister in the *Land* of Hessen into white shirts, sober ties, and dark three-piece suits. Schröder himself made a similar sartorial transformation from jeans to Armani suits, and was a feature of advertisements for another luxury Italian suit-maker, Brioni. Lionel Jospin, a Trotskyist in the 1960s, became a soberly respectable and highly moral French Prime Minister in the 1990s. In the United Kingdom, the President of the National Union of Students in the aftermath of '68, Jack Straw, became an indisputably respectable Foreign Minister.

Women's rights

The key issues that divided parties in the late 1960s and 1970s were not so much traditional distributional disputes, since it seemed as if inflation could satisfy the economic demands of a very diverse assortment of interests and provide a peaceful way of resolving conflicts over the distribution of income and wealth. Instead, quite new issues resulted from 1968. In Germany, the politics of the 1970s related to visions of the national past; and there and elsewhere, they also responded to 1968's challenge to traditional authority, and in particular its demands for women's rights.

Feminism

Feminism in the twentieth century was far from being a coherent single movement. An older version of feminism in the first half of the century concentrated on the demand for political rights (to vote, and to be elected in parliaments). These were largely realized by the midcentury in most European countries.

Afterwards, there occurred a substantial shift to the personal and the psychological. Simone de Beauvoir (1908–86) shared the *Existentialism* of Jean-Paul Sartre. In her book *The Second Sex* (1949), she examined the way in which women were defined by biology, and by their sexual organs; but at the same time, how society constructed a picture of women that then imprisoned them. The famous phrase "One is not born, but rather becomes a woman" characteristically emphasizes the process of becoming as a social one, while leaving open the idea of simple biological development.

In the 1960s, the emphasis shifted to economic rights, in large part because of the analogies made in the United States between the economics of discrimination against blacks and against women: both appeared to be ways of segmenting the labor force so that employers might find cheaper labor. The so-called second wave of feminism in the 1960s thus set out a much broader critique of the sexism and inequality inherent in modern society than had the traditional women's movement. It focused on ways in which economic and social institutions discriminated against women (most obviously by paying them less, often for equal work) and by consigning women to low-income or low-prestige positions. In 1964 the US Civil Rights Act banned employers from discriminating on grounds of sex, as well as of race. In Europe, similar results came from court decisions at the European rather than the national level, notably in the 1986 Marshall ruling of the European Court of Justice.

The second wave combined the vision of de Beauvoir with an intense concern for power relations. In the later 1960s it had a revolutionary edge: Kate Millett's *Sexual Politics* (1970) suggested that the sexual revolution would end patriarchy, and thus bring down conventional society. It was a version of *Leninist* theory, in which the role of the colonial and peripheral rebels was played by women. The Canadian Shulamith Firestone made the *Marxist* link most clearly in *The Dialectic of Sex* (1970). Gradually, and especially in Europe, feminists began to emphasize personal emancipation and fulfillment over wider social theories. The Australian Germaine Greer's work *The Female Eunuch* (1970) was deeply influential in the United Kingdom and concentrated on an argument about how repression limited the scope for the realization of personality. Many of this generation of feminists became deeply disillusioned in later years. Kate Millett, for instance, complained:

> We did not create the community necessary to support each other against the coming of age. And now we have a lacuna between one generation's understanding and that of the next, and have lost much of our sense of continuity and comradeship.
>
> (*Guardian*, June 23, 1998)

(continued)

(continued)

The new feminism had successes at a linguistic and symbolic level, so that "secretaries" became "personal assistants" and "stewardesses" were now "flight attendants" (and both jobs now opened for men as well). Women began to play a larger role in political life, especially in northern and western Europe. There were female heads of government in the 1980s and 1990s in Iceland, Norway, the United Kingdom, France, and Poland, and a female President in Ireland (and, of course, many women as titular heads of state in the surviving monarchies). Many of the most successful women politicians did not, however, view themselves as feminists: a striking case is Shirley Williams, a leading social democrat in the United Kingdom, who was the daughter of a famous feminist, Vera Brittan, and believed that feminism was no longer necessary. There were fewer prominent women in the politics of Mediterranean countries, where the only female prime ministers were in countries often not considered part of Europe (Turkey and Israel).

A "radical feminism" went much further, and argued that the status of women cannot simply be improved by social and economic change, but that women's real nature can only be realized in the exclusive company of other women.

In the wake of 1968, a culture of individualism developed, in which family units mattered less and individual lifestyle choices more. The most important of the demands for greater individual autonomy came from those who had frequently been the oppressed victims of traditional patriarchal family structures and of their revival and reassertion after the Second World War, namely women.

In socially conservative Switzerland, women were now allowed to vote in federal elections and referendums. In 1971, the all-male electorate approved the new electoral law in a referendum by a two to one majority. (There had been a similar referendum in 1959, when the proposal had been defeated by a two to one vote.)

As women became more independent, marriage patterns changed. At first, the emphasis on youth in the 1960s correlated with a slight lowering of the age of marriage. In Italy, the average age of first marriage fell from 24.8 in 1960 to 23.9 in 1980, in Germany from 23.4 to 22.9, and in France it stayed constant at 23.0. But the longer-term effect of increased independence was that women married later or not at all. More women chose to live alone, and the number of single-person households in all European countries rose. Some of the headline statistics about increases in the number of singles simply reflect increased longevity and the loneliness of elderly people (mostly women) after the death of a spouse. But there was also a new phenomenon of the "single" as an individualistic lifestyle. In the European Union in 1998, 15 percent of women aged 25–29 and 16 percent of men lived on their own, with much higher proportions in the "advanced" northern countries: for Denmark the respective figures are 36 and 20, for Finland 30 and 29, and for Germany 24 and 24.[14]

Marriage, when it did occur, was almost always preceded now by extended spells of trial marriage or cohabitation. Increased ease of divorce (see Chapter 1) also meant that couples could view their initial marriages as experimental. The divorce rate (number of divorces per thousand population) rose in Germany from 1.0 (1960) to 1.3 (1970) and 2.0 (1990); in France the corresponding figures are 0.7, 0.8, and 1.9; in the UK, 0.5, 1.1, and 2.9. In Italy, where there was almost no legal divorce in 1960, the level was 0.5 in 1990. Divorce there had been legalized in 1970, but the Catholic Alliance Movement presented a petition for a referendum, which was eventually held in 1974 and proved a heavy defeat for the Church and the anti-divorce movement, in which some leading Christian Democrats had played a very active part.

The authority of the Catholic Church was severely tested by the contraceptive pill. In 1968 Paul VI published his encyclical *Humanae Vitae*, which concluded that "Whoever deliberately renders coitus sterile attacks its meaning as an expression of mutual self-giving." By 1965, three-fifths of Catholics had been using a contraceptive, and after the encyclical, Catholic contraceptive use went up rather than down. The Church thus faced a credibility gap on one of the most sensitive areas of conduct. In practice, the Church's teaching was discreetly reformulated on a diocesan level.

Abortion was an even more contentious issue, with theories about the sanctity of life confronting the idea that women should control their own bodies. In the Scandinavian countries, there had been legalized abortions in very limited circumstances since the 1930s. Denmark had allowed abortion in order to save a woman's life since 1939; from 1956 medical and social reasons were added, and in 1973 Denmark became the first country to allow abortion on request. In 1967, the United Kingdom allowed abortion if there was a threat to a woman's life, or to her mental or physical health, circumstances which could be quite widely – or quite narrowly – interpreted by physicians. In 1975 France allowed abortion in the first ten weeks of pregnancy, provided the woman had counseling; West Germany accepted a similar provision (with a cut-off period of 12 weeks) in 1976. In the Netherlands, though abortion was widely tolerated, it was not legal until 1981, and in Belgium it was legalized only in 1990. The Italian abortion law of 1978 was – like the divorce law – bitterly contested by the Church, and a referendum was demanded. In 1981 the referendum against legalized abortion was decisively rejected.

Homosexual clashes

The reform of laws against homosexual behavior became a major priority during the 1960s. Before then, in almost all European countries (the highly repressive Catholic autocracies of Spain and Portugal were exceptions) there existed an active and sometimes, as in the case of Weimar Germany (and especially Berlin), quite visible homosexual sub-culture. But Weimar was also an exception: more usually, large numbers of people knew, but did not talk about, the sub-culture. Of the different national traditions, the best organized (characteristically) was that of Switzerland. The Swiss actor Karl "Rolf" Meier had organized a group which he named "the circle" (*Der Kreis*) from the 1930s, and in 1942 (in the inauspicious circumstances of wartime Switzerland), he started to publish a magazine. Such sub-cultures, however, quickly came under attack in the new atmosphere of the postwar years, with a restoration of conventional morality under the shadow of the big international drama of the Cold War. Some part of the backlash was also driven by a sort of moral panic after the 1948 American Kinsey Report revealed how common homosexual practice was.

The combination of active sub-cultures and a renewed interest in repression led to a quite new debate about law reform to remove legal penalties on homosexual behavior. In 1948 Axel Axgil founded a reform movement in Denmark. In 1954 Arcadie in France and in 1958 in the UK the Homosexual Law Reform Society started to press for a change to the laws that forbade homosexual acts between consenting adults. In practice, such laws had almost never been enforced in regard to private contacts, but a succession of sad figures had been ruined and discredited by the prosecution of offenses in public bathrooms (sometimes as a result of police agents provocateurs). The number of such prosecutions rose in the 1950s: in 1953, notably, the leading Shakespearian actor of his generation, Sir John Gielgud, was arrested and convicted for homosexual importuning in Chelsea. At his next stage performance, the audience vigorously applauded Gielgud on his first entrance, but there was a vicious press campaign against him. A tragic case much less well known at the time was that of Alan Turing, the discoverer of the mathematical logic of computing, who was prosecuted in 1952 for perfectly private acts: he had unwisely told the police investigating a burglary in his apartment in Manchester that he had had an "affair" with a suspect. He was not sentenced to prison, but to a therapy involving large doses of hormonal injections, and he killed himself in 1954.

In large part in response to the discussion that followed the most prominent prosecutions, in 1954 the British Conservative Home Secretary, Sir David Maxwell-Fyfe, appointed a committee under the chairmanship of Lord Wolfenden to report on law reform, and the majority of the committee recommended an end to penalties on acts between consenting adults. The British law was only reformed in 1967 with the support of the Labour Party Home Secretary, Roy Jenkins (Harold Wilson was profoundly uninterested in the reform), and through a bill introduced by a backbench parliamentarian. The government did not want to be associated too closely with such a measure. In France reform of the Vichy laws against homosexual activities (which had been strengthened in 1960) came only in 1982, under the left-wing government of President Mitterrand.

The discussion of legal reform produced in some social conservatives an even more vicious backlash against the liberalizers, as well as a radicalization of part of the homosexual movement, which for the first time became political.

The beginning of law reform in the 1960s led to a much more radical movement that picked up the term "gay" as a self-description. They mocked such old-fashioned literary and artistic homosexuals as Rolf's *Kreis* and their subdued dignity. The legality of acts between over-21s did not seem an adequate reform measure to them, and was irrelevant to some of their interests. In the 1950s, the statistics on prosecutions submitted to the British Wolfenden inquiry had shown, over the course of a decade, around 100 men convicted for having sex with men over 21. Forty of these had received prison sentences. But these 100 men constituted only 10 percent of the total number of men convicted of homosexual offenses, the overwhelming majority of which concerned young men who had not yet reached the then legal age of majority.

In 1970 London School of Economics students formed a Gay Liberation Front which wanted to use homosexual liberation as part of a large political offensive against the "system" and its cultural underpinning. For many of the new radicals, sex in any form was simply a weapon in a broad cultural struggle. The playwright Joe Orton announced in his posthumously produced play *What the Butler Saw* (1967) that "civilizations have been founded and maintained on theories which refused to obey the facts". In 1967, he noted in his diary that sex is "the only way to smash the wretched civilization".[15]

Gay liberation required a whole new theory of society. In 1972, Guy Hocquenghem tried to integrate psychoanalytic and Marxist theory in his analysis *Homosexual Desire*, and argued that it was fear of homosexuality that constituted the new phenomenon which required explanation. In comparison with the United States, however, the support for large-scale political mobilization in Europe was always rather tepid. The magazine *Gay News* complained in 1976 that only 200 had turned up for a march in the West End of London, while in San Francisco there were 90,000 protesters.

One of the demands of the older movement for law reform was the legal recognition of homosexual partnerships as a form of marriage. The first European country to allow a registered partnership equivalent to marriage was Denmark in 1989. On October 1, the day that the law came into effect, the veteran campaigners Axel and Eigil Axgil (they had already changed their names by deed poll) married, at the ages of 74 and 67, in Copenhagen along with ten other couples. They appeared at the registry office looking as respectable in their suits and ties as any conventional married couple. The first countries to follow this lead were all Scandinavian: Norway (1993), Sweden (1994), Greenland (1995), Iceland (1996). But Hungary adopted similar legislation in 1996, France in 1999, and Germany in 2001.

The Netherlands, on the avant-garde of European social liberalism, in 2001 allowed same-sex couples to marry. The Dutch stance soon influenced other countries and Spain, under a socialist government that inherited traditional Spanish republican anti-clericalism, passed a similar law in 2005. The larger countries waited longer. France (2013) and the UK both made the move under conservative or center-right governments,

314 A golden age

and British Prime Minister David Cameron's support for the measure, which appealed to an upper-income metropolitan elite, almost cost him his job as a majority of Conservative parliamentarians opposed the move. Germany followed in 2017, after the conservative Chancellor Angela Merkel decided that parliament would treat the issue as a vote of conscience. She personally voted against the measure, but then welcomed it as a step toward greater social cohesion and peace.

The clash between homosexual law reformers and gay liberationists reflects very precisely the major conflict of the 1960s: between an old style of social liberalism, that looked to piecemeal legal reform as a path to social betterment, and a new style of self-consciously provocative activism, that wanted to change by shocking. The two sides in the 1960s clash of cultures could hardly talk to each other or understand each other. In fact, the most provocative and outrageous claim that the older generation made was its specious belief that it "understood" the passion of the young, whereas in reality it did nothing of the kind – as sensitive people on both sides of the 1968 barricades realized.

Notes

1 Roy Harrod, *The Life of John Maynard Keynes*, Harmondsworth: Penguin, 1972 (orig. 1951), p. 764.
2 Cited in Arnulf Baring, *Machtwechsel: die Ära Brandt–Schmidt*, Stuttgart: Deutsche Verlags-Anstalt, 1982, p. 77.
3 Antonio Negri, *Marx beyond Marx*, South Hadley, MA: Bergin and Garvey, 1984 (orig. given as a seminar series in Paris), pp. 18–19.
4 Gabriel and Daniel Cohn-Bendit, *Obsolete Communism: The Left-Wing Alternative*, London: André Deutsch, 1968 (orig. publ. in French and German), pp. 249– 50.
5 A.D.G. Gunn, *Oral Contraception in Perspective*, Carnforth: Parthenon, 1987, p. 40.
6 *The Times*, July 1, 1967.
7 Richard Crossman (ed. Anthony Howard), *The Crossman Diaries 1964–1970*, London: Hamish Hamilton and Jonathan Cape, 1979, pp. 254–5.
8 Keesings 22932.
9 Negri, *Marx*, p. 173.
10 Antonio Negri and Michael Hardt, *Empire*, Cambridge, MA: Harvard University Press, 2000.
11 Cohn-Bendit and Cohn-Bendit, *Obsolete Communism*, p. 28.
12 Quoted in Jean Lacouture, *De Gaulle: The Ruler, 1945–1970*, New York, NY: Norton, 1992, p. 549.
13 For instance, Ingrid Gilcher-Holtey, "May 1968 in France: the rise and fall of a new social movement", in Carole Fink, Philipp Gassert, and Detlef Junker (eds), *1968: The World Transformed*, Cambridge: Cambridge University Press, 1998, pp. 253–76.
14 *The Life of Women and Men in Europe: A Statistical Portrait*, Luxembourg: Eurostat, 2002, p. 23.
15 Patrick Higgins, *Heterosexual Dictatorship: Male Homosexuality in Postwar Britain*, London: Fourth Estate, 1996, p. 153.

10 The limits to growthmanship
The 1970s

The immediate response of the establishment to '68 was to try to "manage" it, to buy off discontent, and to stimulate economic growth by the time-trusted methods of Keynesian demand management. Spending in order to create political stability might have worked better in completely closed-off economies; with greater economic openness, the money slopped out of the national buckets. The new spending created big imbalances in the external accounts (the balance of trade and the current account, which includes payment for services), and major capital flows to compensate for the trade and services imbalances. In addition, when countries tried to engage in an international version of the social experiment of paying off the disenchanted, their monetary expansion helped to produce a boom in commodity prices that raised new questions. What was at stake was no longer a debate about the best distribution of wealth and resources in the closed context of the national economy, but about international distribution; in other words, about the relationship of rich countries to poor countries.

The result of the new problems – capital flows, commodity booms, and debates about international distribution – was a growing demand to look for solutions to the big political as well as social and economic issues at the international or supranational level: through the European Community (EC), or the United Nations, or the International Monetary Fund (IMF, which played a major part in the politics of the UK and Italy in the 1970s), or new security institutions (in particular the Conference on Security and Cooperation in Europe, or CSCE).

Mediterranean instability

The most dramatic European upheavals of the 1970s occurred not in the industrial core, though the rich countries were deeply traumatized and also began to think of themselves as quite unstable. The scourges of major unrest, military coups, civil wars, and communist revolutions, which were sometimes painted on the wall as visions of the future, were actually played out in the Mediterranean world. That world reacted to the upheavals by looking for outside sources of stability, in both institutional and financial terms. Four countries, economically much less developed than northern Europe, needed to confront the traumatic legacy of military dictatorship.

When the Portuguese dictator Antonio Salazar had a stroke in 1968 (he died in 1970), power passed quite tranquilly to his disciple Marcello Caetano. But by the early 1970s, the cost of holding on to Portugal's African colonies – Angola, Guinea, and Mozambique – escalated as a consequence of a bitter war of decolonization. The African army eventually revolted (April 25, 1974), and under the leadership of a moderately conservative officer, General Antonio de Spínola, deposed Caetano and substituted him with a Junta of National Salvation. It promised to hold elections, as well as to release political prisoners and restore press and personal freedoms. The main priority, at first, was external: to find a "political solution" to the colonial wars; in other words, a quick decolonization.

It quickly looked as if Portugal were repeating the experience of Russia in 1917 or central Europe after 1945. A long and costly war had discredited the traditional elites; backwardness and impoverishment created a powerful base of social resentment; and, in the south, marginalized and landless farmers rose in revolt against large landowners who had been a bastion of the *ancien régime*. Communists now established control of much of local government. The communist leader, Alvaro Cunhal, arrived on April 30 from his exile in eastern Europe and saw himself as a Lenin arriving at the Finland Station in war-torn Petrograd. General de Spínola was quickly regarded by friends and enemies alike as a Portuguese Kerensky, who would be forced out by the radicalizing revolution. On March 11, 1975, a new military coup exiled de Spínola and imposed a Supreme Revolutionary Council.

The election to a Constituent Assembly on the anniversary of the revolution, on April 25, 1975, appeared to be a setback to the communist advance. The Communist Party had only 12.5 percent of the vote, while the center-right Popular Democrats had 26.4 percent and the Socialist Party of Mario Soares looked like an overwhelming victor, with 37.9 percent. But the Bolsheviks had also done badly in the 1917 elections to a Russian constituent assembly, and Cunhal explained: "In a revolutionary process the vote is not the only or even the most significant expression of the strength and influence of a party, much less when a stable democratic regime does not yet exist."[1] The communists still had a hold over the government, and enacted a series of changes designed to consolidate their grasp: rural land reform, as well as the nationalization of banks, heavy industry (steel), and transport, and a promise to take over mineral deposits. The communist labor union organization, Intersindical, which excluded socialists, was given a monopoly. Immediately after the elections, Soares agreed to issue a joint communiqué with Cunhal, in which both socialist and communist leaders committed themselves to "the defense of freedoms and advances made since the coup, in particular the measures taken for nationalization and agrarian reform".[2] But in August 1975, the Prime Minister, General Vasco dos Santos Gonçalves, who was close to the communists, resigned and was expelled from the Supreme Revolutionary Council, while moderate generals who had previously been excluded were readmitted. And in September the government was reconstructed, in accordance with the shares of the votes for the Constituent Assembly.

In April 1976, new parliamentary elections were held, in which the party shares of 1975 remained more or less constant, with the communists making only a small gain (14.4 percent) while Soares still obtained 34.9 percent. He now became Prime Minister, and rolled back the influence of communists at the center and then in the localities.

The revolution in Portugal coincided with the physical decline and then the death of General Franco, with the result that it looked quite probable to many observers that the revolutionary scenario in Portugal would be repeated in its larger Iberian neighbor. On May 1, 1975, there were anti-Franco demonstrations all over Spain – not only in the separatist and anti-Castilian Basque and Catalan areas. The general's nephew published an interview in which he declared himself to be "against fascism and in favor of peaceful, egalitarian and democratic coexistence among Spaniards, without privileges for any class".[3] The general's chosen successor, Prince Juan Carlos, started discussions with the opposition.

But in fact, after Franco's death was announced (November 20: he had probably died the previous day), it soon became clear that Spain was not Portugal. There was no colonial war; Spain in the 1960s had modernized quite quickly and was no longer a very poor transitional society; and there was a Spanish monarchy. Juan Carlos had already been appointed acting head of state on October 30, and on November 22 he took an oath as King. His father later renounced his claim to the throne. The Nationalist Movement was disbanded. Parties and labor unions could form. Juan Carlos initially appointed a moderate conservative, Adolfo Suárez González, as Prime Minister.

Elections to replace the largely appointed parliament (*cortes*) of the Franco era were held not until June 1977, when the Prime Minister's party of the center-right won 165 out of 350 seats, and the socialists of Felipe González 118. The communists had only 20. For all the interest in the Republic and Civil War figure of Dolores Ibarruri (*La Pasionarid*), who was easily the most effective orator of the new democratic politics, she and her party were quickly becoming as historical as the dead *Caudillo*.

The revolution in Spain was as much social as political. Restaurants, café culture, nightlife, pornography, all of which had been repressed under Franco, blossomed. The spirit of the new Spain was portrayed in Pedro Almodóvar's commercially successful films celebrating a fast-paced and multivariate sexuality: *Women on the Edge of a Nervous Breakdown* and *Tie Me Up! Tie Me Down!*

Politics in both Spain and Portugal remained quite unstable for some time. The socialists won the Spanish election and Felipe González formed a government. On February 23, 1981, an army coup under Colonel Tejero quickly failed, not least because of the determined action of the King. In the following year, a general election produced a massive victory (48.7 percent of the popular vote) for the Socialist Party of González, against a divided right. He remained in power for the next 14 years.

A crucial stabilizer was the external framework. In 1977 the Spanish government applied for membership in the EC. Portugal soon followed the Spanish example. When both countries were actually admitted to the EC in 1986, the power of externally induced stability, as a complement to an internal evolution of democracy, became apparent. The model for this action was Greece, which had negotiated an accession treaty in 1979, and which had joined the EC at the beginning of 1981. For the EC, this was a novel experiment. In 1973, when the Community had been enlarged from six to nine members, Denmark and the United Kingdom were quite prosperous and comparable to other EC members, and Ireland, though relatively poor, was very small, with a population of only 6 million. Greece, with almost 10 million, was substantially larger, and Portugal was a similar size. Spain had almost 40 million inhabitants. The new members of the 1980s, however, were also very poor: while Germany in 1986 had a per capita GDP of $14,500, that of Spain was $6,000, and those of Greece and Portugal were much lower ($4,000 and $3,000 respectively).[4]

Greece had been ruled by a military dictatorship following a coup in April 1967, conducted after the military had been traumatized by details of a planned coup by left-wing officers, associated in the Aspida group, and after fears that an imminent election would bring a strong socialist vote. The mid-level officers (the regime soon became known as the "Colonels") who seized power wanted to turn their backs on democracy and modernity. They canceled the election, arrested the socialist leader George Papandreou as well as his centrist father Andreas Papandreou, banned the EDA (the democratic left party, which was in effect the successor to the already banned Communist Party), and forbade miniskirts, long hair, and bearded "unclean" foreign tourists. The inexperienced King, who attempted a counter-coup, was exiled. The regime disintegrated in 1974, like that of Portugal, because of a military adventure: it had tried to annex the contested island of Cyprus and instead merely sparked off a Turkish invasion. After the collapse of the Colonels, a democratic coalition government under the moderate Constantine Karamanlis tried to stabilize the new order by Europeanizing. In its broadest objectives, this was a successful strategy, though Greece continued to appear as the least congruous member of the EC. In 1990, with an inflation rate four times higher than the other members of the EC, and a budget deficit running at an alarming 12 percent of GDP, it was even threatened with expulsion from the European club.

Turkey was even poorer than Greece or Portugal: its 1986 per capita GDP was only $1,000. It also descended into very bloody domestic violence in the 1970s, with large numbers of political murders carried out by the extreme right and the left, some of which were connived at by the security forces. In the end – but much later – Turkey also followed a path quite similar to that taken by Spain and Portugal. Of four northern Mediterranean countries recovering from the impact of military dictatorship, the three countries with Christian traditions and inheritances managed to secure the institutional embrace of a (very secular) northern and western Europe very quickly. Islamic Turkey waited. But it grew significantly more quickly over the next period than did the initially more prosperous more westerly countries: average real GDP growth for 1980–2000 was 1.5 percent for Greece, 2.7 percent for Spain, 2.9 percent for Portugal, and 4.4 percent for Turkey.

In contrast to Portugal, where the army became the driving dynamic of the revolution, and also to Spain, where much of the army leadership was frankly reactionary, the Turkish army saw itself as the guardian of the centrist (non-communist, non-capitalist) and secular legacy of Kemal Atatürk. Soldiers were forbidden to wear facial hair. The short-lived incursion of the military into Turkish politics in 1961 was not the last military intervention. In March 1971 the army sent a memorandum to the conservative Prime Minister, Süleyman Demirel (Justice Party), saying that he had not solved the problems of student and urban unrest, and that his economic course was failing. The center-left under Bülent Ecevit won elections in 1973, and in 1977 his party was still the largest, but did not have an absolute majority and was replaced by a coalition government of the rightist opposition led by the Justice Party. Through the 1970s, violence from both the far left and the far right increased; and the economic difficulties were exacerbated by the oil price shocks. By the end of 1978, martial law was in force in 13 of the 67 provinces of Turkey. On September 10–11, 1980, the army removed another Demirel government, although one of the most able technocrats of the Demirel administration, Turgut Özal, was retained as Economics Minister.

The military now applied its secular and apolitical appearance on all areas of public life. All public servants, as well as university faculty and students, were forbidden to wear mustaches, as these were read as signs of political affiliation. Leftists had voluminously bushy mustaches, like Stalin; rightists had narrow toothbrush-style ones, like Hitler. Jeans, miniskirts, headscarves (Islamic), and green "parka" jackets (interpreted as signs of extreme left tendencies) were also banned.

Özal recast the politics of the right with a new party, the Motherland Party (ANAP), in 1983, and was Prime Minister from 1983 to 1989 and then President until his death in 1993. His political heir, Tansu Çiller, became the first female Prime Minister of Turkey (1993–96), and made European integration and membership of the European Union (EU) key planks in her political program. In 1995, Turkey concluded a free trade agreement with the EU. But she developed her own party (the True Path Party), and by the 1990s the party landscape was parceled into small groupings around major personalities (Demirel, Ecevit, Özal, Çiller), with the result that parliamentary politics remained highly unstable.

There existed a political course, consistently applied from the 1950s to the 1990s by the secular center-right, of using international arrangements and institutions as a way of levering greater economic aid from the outside, and facilitating economic modernization and liberalization. Membership of NATO had been part of the strategy of the Democratic Party in the 1950s. In the late 1970s, the strategic dependence of the United States and the EC on a reliable and secular Islamic state in the eastern Mediterranean in the aftermath of the Iranian Revolution played a similar role: it allowed favorable treatment by international financial institutions, notably the World Bank and the IMF. In 1990–91 and 2002–03, this pattern was replayed when crises in Iraq made Turkey an essential strategic partner. Turkey followed the Spanish and Portuguese strategy of applying for membership in the EC. The first formal application was made in 1987, and rejected in 1989, largely as a result of vigorous opposition from Greece. In 1997, a new application was rejected. Turkey then tried again, hoping that (like the United Kingdom) its attempt to join the European norm would be successful the third time.

The downside of this strategy – which helped produce the military interventions – was that the expectations raised by foreign assistance and foreign inflows were greater than the reality of economic performance. Turkey grew quite rapidly, but at the price of high levels of inflation, and of volatile inflows of private foreign capital followed by episodes of investor panic.

In 1995, 21 percent of the vote in parliamentary elections went to the Islamic Welfare Party, which had developed out of predecessor parties: the National Order Party of the early 1970s, and then the National Salvation Party. It developed into the Virtue Party, which was banned as a threat to secularism, and split in 2001. A moderate wing renamed itself as the Justice and Development Party (AKP), which scored a spectacular triumph in parliamentary elections in November 2002 on a platform opposed to the corruption and inefficiency of the previous fragmented and factionalized political establishment. With 34 percent of the vote, it obtained a majority in parliament. Its language initially resembled that of the mainstream center-right in its European orientation: it explicitly saw itself as an equivalent to the moderate Christian Democratic Party of Germany, and as a way of articulating a voice of Islamic moderation and rejecting the fundamentalism that paralyzed large parts of the Moslem world. Europe – the old Kemalist idea of westernization – again provided a key to Turkish political development. In the course of the 2000s, and especially as Europe looked less stable and attractive in the aftermath of the 2008 financial crisis, the AKP's powerful leader, Recep Tayyip Erdoğan, became more authoritarian, and more corrupt. He began to see himself, along with Russia's Vladimir Putin, as a proponent of illiberal democracy. In particular, after 2016 in the aftermath of an apparent coup by supporters of a former ally turned critic, the preacher Fethullah Gülen, he began to impose a brutal repression domestically that went hand in hand with a more assertive role in international relations. Now the model appeared to be the Ottoman sultan rather than Kemal Atatürk, and Erdoğan's mindset became increasingly neo-Ottoman.

The Keynesian boom and its discontents

If the broad political situation in industrial and northern Europe stabilized quite quickly after 1968, it was most immediately and most directly because government used the techniques of economic management of the "golden age" in order to increase demand. Keynesianism provided the quintessential managerial tool for ensuring continued growth and the return of stability. Keynes himself in the 1920s and again in the Second World War had worried about the socially calamitous effects of inflation, but his disciples in the late 1960s and early 1970s regarded a moderate level of inflation as desirable. It made for an easier solution of distributional disputes, encouraged investment (in an age which believed in a strong correlation between investment today and growth tomorrow), and discouraged saving. Labor movements could meanwhile be lulled into acquiescence by higher (nominal) wages, even though the gains might quickly be lost because of further price increases.

One explanation of the surge in labor unrest of 1967–69 was that the student protests came after a slight economic downturn in the major European economies. The first signs of recovery then provided an opportunity for trade unions to flex their muscles, and industrial unrest soared. In Italy in 1965, 7 million working days were lost in strikes, in 1966 14.5 million, in 1967 8.6 million, in 1968 9.2 million, and in 1969 37.8 million days. Germany, with a much less militant labor tradition, lost 27,000 days in 1966 but 390,000 in 1967 and 249,000 in 1969.

Through the 1960s, both fiscal stimulation and the monetary accommodation of the consequences of pay rises were limited by the commitment to fixed exchange rates. France before 1969 and the United Kingdom before 1967 both suffered because their governments refused, largely for prestige reasons, to undertake a devaluation that might have allowed budgetary discipline to be relaxed. But in the later 1960s, the discipline of the international fixed exchange regime was an ever weaker limitation, as the central player in the world economy, the United States, engaged in monetary expansion in order to pay for the Vietnam War and the Great Society reform program. In August 1971, the United States abandoned its commitment to convert the dollar into gold at $35 an ounce, and national economic policy in practice no longer faced any external constraints. In all the major industrial countries at this time, monetary and fiscal policy became very expansive, and the world entered an inflationary boom that could be comfortably ridden by center-right or center-left governments.

The Bretton Woods system and its collapse

The postwar monetary order was negotiated at a conference of the United Nations in the Mount Washington Hotel, Bretton Woods, New Hampshire, in July 1944, just after the Allied landings in Normandy. The major feature of the new system, which was largely designed by John Maynard Keynes and the US Treasury official Harry Dexter White as a replacement for the discredited gold standard, was fixed but adjustable exchange rates relative to the US dollar (which was itself fixed against gold at the rate of $35 per ounce); liberalization of the current but not the capital account (i.e. to pay for goods and services, but not for capital movements); and an institution (the IMF) that would provide temporary support for countries in balance-of-payments difficulties. Critics of the new monetary order at the time feared that it could not function well, since there would be a permanent dollar shortage because of the high productivity gains of the US economy during the Second World War. In practice, the "Bretton Woods system" remained largely on paper until after 1959, when the major European countries (with Japan following somewhat later) were strong enough to go over to current account convertibility.

Quite soon, however, in the 1960s the international monetary order began to look quite vulnerable and crisis-prone. In part this was due to the increased capital movements of the late 1960s as uncontrolled offshore markets developed (the so-called Euromarkets, in dollars that were escaping the control of US monetary authorities). In part it was due to the US policy that involved an expansive domestic program as well as high military spending abroad because of the escalation of fighting in Vietnam. In part it was the consequence of the reluctance of countries to change their exchange rate parities: countries with surpluses (such as Germany and Japan) were fearful that an upward movement – revaluation – would hit the competitiveness of their export industries; while countries with deficits (such as the United Kingdom) thought that a downward adjustment (devaluation) would raise import prices and lead to inflation, and would also constitute a political humiliation. The system thus looked more and more rigid – thus replicating the problems of *the Gold Standard*. Governments began to dislike the way that it constrained their room for policy maneuver: too much spending would lead to current account deficits and a recommendation by the IMF that the budget deficit be corrected, as a price for assistance ("IMF conditionality").

The biggest adjustment problem was that facing the United States, which alone of all countries could not change its currency rate (since the fixing of currencies was relative to the US dollar). When the United States saw large capital movements to Germany and Japan in 1970 and 1971, it pressed them to act to revalue: Germany in the end abandoned the parity, and let the Deutschemark float. Japan refused, and Americans complained of unfair competition from a flood of Japanese imports. The US inability to adjust exchange rates then led to a crisis in the system as a whole. On August 15, 1971, President Nixon announced the suspension of the gold convertibility of the US dollar, and also imposed an import surcharge of 10 percent.

A new system of parities calculated at a conference at the Smithsonian Institution (December 1971) held for only just over a year. The renewed collapse is best explained in terms of an expansive US monetary policy, leading to larger US trade deficits and thus the reemergence of the same problems that had led to the breakdown of August 1971 in the first place. Letting the international monetary system break was thus widely seen as the alternative to a vicious decline into protectionism and trade wars. As it was, the 1970s witnessed a dramatic expansion in the "new protectionism" of voluntary export restraints, dubious consumer safety standards, and similar devices to overcome General Agreement on Tariffs and Trade rules. It also seemed to free countries of the constraints that Bretton Woods had placed on monetary and fiscal policy, and there was a surge of inflation.

France in the aftermath of the great student revolt went quite consistently to the right, with the 1968 elections, the presidential victory of Pompidou, and the success of Giscard d'Estaing after the death of Pompidou (1974). Giscard stood for a modern style, which he translated into symbolic gestures such as the speeding up of the revolutionary national anthem, the *Marseillaise*.

In the United Kingdom, the Conservatives won a surprise election victory in 1970 (46 percent to Labour's 43 percent, the opposite of the predictions of the opinion polls). The new Prime Minister, Edward Heath, was neither charming like Macmillan nor cheeky like Wilson. At first, he experimented with a kind of economic liberalism. It was caricatured by Harold Wilson as the rediscovery of "Selsdon man", since on the eve of the election the Conservatives had held a strategic planning group meeting in a hotel called Selsdon Park, at which they had criticized "big government", and called for lower taxes and for the control of inflation.

Was there much substantial difference between the parties – besides the contrast in governing styles? The leading contemporary British historian, Peter Clarke, calls Heath and Wilson Tweedledum and Tweedledee. In power, the Conservatives embraced corporatism, as had Labour, and public expenditure and inflation rose. Wilson and Heath shared a fundamentally technocratic and managerial approach to policy-making. Both parties in the 1970 general election had argued in favor of a British application for membership in the European Economic Community, and Heath's government carried out that promise. The Europeanization of the United Kingdom was part of a much larger strategy, in which Europe would replace the lost Empire as a source of economic challenges and possibilities. Exposure to European competition might deliver a salutary shock to the sluggish British economy. Already in the 1960s, British trade with the EC countries had increased, and Heath aimed to extend the trade connection.

Like Wilson, Heath modernized. His government decimalized the British currency (previously denominated as 12 pennies in a shilling, and 20 shillings in a pound) in 1971. It restructured and rearranged the counties of England and Wales and replaced those of Scotland with a regional local government system.

Even more than Wilson, who had been limited by the external constraint of the pound–dollar rate, Heath pushed for growth as fast as possible. His Chancellor of the Exchequer, Anthony Barber, justified the most expansionary of the Heath budgets, that of 1972, explicitly in these terms:

> the high growth of output which I intend to sustain with this Budget will entail a growth of money supply that is high by the standards of past years, in order that adequate finance is available for the extra output.

In June 1972, a wave of speculation against the pound broke out, but the United Kingdom could now quite easily disengage itself from the rest of Europe's efforts to find exchange rate stability. Barber simply responded to the new crisis by saying: "It would be quite wrong to restrict the rate of growth of the money supply in a way which would hinder the rate of economic growth at which we are aiming."

The boom was accompanied by inflation, and the politicians naïvely thought that if they could hold down inflation, the extra money they were creating would go straight into higher output. Heath, who had previously dismissed incomes policies as ineffective, dangerous, and inflationary, at the end of 1972, when faced by the dangers of a new surge of inflation, adopted a rather dramatic incomes policy. An initial 90-day pay freeze was to be followed by an extensive system of controls, with allowances for exceptions of the lower paid, and in November 1973 as "Stage Three" a limitation of pay rises to 7 percent (again with exceptions). This reversal of policy was promptly termed Heath's "U-turn".

Other symptoms of inflation were also to be held down by government fiat. In December 1972 a development tax was introduced, taxing unfair profits made by property speculators in a gigantic boom of house prices (the average price of a new house in England rose by over 50 percent from June 1972 to June 1973).

Heath's boom and the way he tackled it did more to discredit British capitalism than any Labour politician could have managed. Cheap money fueled the real-estate boom, as well as a parallel asset inflation in share prices.

The new banks ("fringe banks", permitted to act as banks by the 1967 Companies Act) which expanded rapidly were vulnerable to a collapse of the asset bubble. In 1973 and especially 1974 property prices collapsed. The *Financial Times* 30 Index in January 1975 stood at 146, a fall of 73 percent from its 1972 peak. Many of the fringe banks collapsed in 1973 and the subsequent years. The collapse discredited the government which had fueled the boom, and which also managed a political system that seemed closely tied to the suddenly dynamic world of City speculation. The most prominent of the new banks, Slater Walker Securities, had been founded by Peter Walker, who in 1970 became a minister in the Heath government. Keyser Ullmann Holdings, another eventually doomed enterprise, was headed by Edward du Cann, the chairman of the backbench 1922 Committee of Conservative parliamentarians. To be complete: the key economic policy adviser of the Labour Party, Harold Lever, held a large stake (and his family a larger one) in the Northern Commercial Trust. The leader of the Liberal Party, Jeremy Thorpe, was linked to Eagle Star. Most bizarrely, the government's own property management agency, the Crown Agents, engaged in highly dubious speculative lending and investments. By the mid-1970s, it was hard to avoid the conclusion that Keynesian expansionism not only had painful side effects (inflation), but also concealed and made possible a deeply corrupt system.

Morality and politics

Germany too in the second half of the 1960s moved into an experiment with an extended version of managerial capitalism. The Great Coalition government of Christian Democrats and Social Democrats was the first moment when German economic policy-makers really took up the tools of Keynesian macro-economic management. The new philosophy was embodied in the 1967 Law on Stability and Growth, which set out the four targets that government policy would aim at: external balance, full employment, price stability, and "stable and adequate" growth. These goals were preached by the Economics Minister in the 1966–69 coalition government, Karl Schiller, who tried to escape from the fixed exchange rate system of Bretton Woods, which in his view led to unnecessary inflation in Germany. The aura of confidence and credibility around Schiller was also the leading attraction of the Social Democratic Party (SPD) in the 1969 election, which the SPD won, leaving it free to end its participation in the Great Coalition and instead form a coalition with the small liberal Free Democratic Party, which it could dominate.

Willy Brandt, the new Chancellor, had in fact been less prominent in the campaign than Schiller. His priorities were largely non-economic, and he himself had little sympathy for the economy or for technocratic fixes. He wanted to come to terms with and atone for the German past, and sought a more moral Germany.

Brandt's new moralism most immediately transformed relations with eastern Europe, which had obviously been the victim of Nazi aggression but where because of the Cold War there had been no reconciliation process analogous to the Franco-German initiatives of the 1950s. The major triumphs of Brandt's government were in foreign policy, where Brandt continued the *Ostpolitik* he had already initiated as Foreign Minister of the Great Coalition government. In 1970, Brandt signed a treaty with the Soviet Union in which both sides renounced the use of force against each other (the Moscow Treaty). In December 1970, he signed the Warsaw Treaty with Poland, which recognized the previously bitterly contested western frontier of Poland. The Treaty stipulated "the inviolability of their [German and Polish] existing frontiers now and in the future". In 1972, even more strikingly, he signed a Basic Treaty with the German Democratic Republic, establishing "normal good neighborly relations", and declaring that the "sovereign power of each of these two states is confined to its own state territory". The Treaty was accompanied by a letter from the German Foreign Minister to his Soviet opposite number stating that the treaties (Moscow, Warsaw, and the Basic Treaty) did "not conflict with the political objectives of the Federal Republic of Germany to work for a state of peace in Europe in which the German nation will recover its unity in free self-determination". These treaties were bitterly contested in parliament, Brandt's majority was eroded, and he needed to call new elections prematurely (in 1972).

The reason why is surprising: after all, no one would argue that the Federal Republic should want non-peaceful or military conflict with the nuclear Soviet Union; there was no practical possibility of changing the Oder–Neisse line; and it was inconceivable to think of overthrowing the GDR, protected as it was by Soviet military power. So why not accept the obvious? The right-wing (Christian Democrat, or CDU) opposition argued that the treaties violated the 1949 Basic Law, according to which only the entire German people could decide the borders of Germany. Though this was the doctrine that the Foreign Minister's letter clearly stated, letters by foreign ministers, the opposition argued, are not internationally binding treaties. In practice, there is no doubt that the CDU's very moderate leader, Rainer Barzel, was pleased when his parliamentary opposition to the treaties failed. Realistically, there was little alternative; and subsequently the CDU accepted a consensus about *Ostpolitik* just as surely as the SPD had over a decade earlier accepted a consensus about western integration.

Brandt's contribution was the way in which he explained his policy: not in pragmatic terms, but as a result of the consequences of the German past. Accepting the Oder–Neisse line was thus not the result of a "sacrifice today, but rather long ago as a consequence of Hitler's crimes". His spontaneous gesture of kneeling at the monument to the Warsaw ghetto made him into an entirely new kind of German statesman, who introduced a strong element of morality and moral responsibility into the making of foreign policy.

Upholding morality is exhausting, and in the end it is not clear quite how much morality is compatible with politics. Brandt was visibly exhausted by the exercise of power. He fell because of the chance emergence of an espionage scandal (an East German spy, Gunther Guillaume, had risen to a prominent position in the Federal Chancellery). But even without the scandal it is difficult to imagine him in power for much longer. His successor, Helmut Schmidt, was much more in the tradition of practical and pragmatic politics.

In Germany, center-left politics of a technocratic kind, similar to that of contemporary France and the United Kingdom (where the same stance was represented by the political right, by Giscard and Heath) prevailed over Brandt's focus on morality. Schmidt had first proved himself as an Atlanticist Defense Minister, and then achieved an ascendancy as a "Super Minister" for Finance and the Economy in the Brandt government. Here he won a battle with Schiller in which he had defended the fixed exchange rate arrangements of the Bretton Woods system: Schmidt had wanted capital controls and fixed exchange rates in a European setting, and Schiller had unsuccessfully pleaded for capital account liberalization. The major economic policy choices were thus fought out within the governing party in Germany, rather than between the parties. But both the Schiller and the Schmidt alternatives were clearly based on the premise of technocratic management.

External constraints

Through much of the 1970s, Italy was on the brink of instability. By 1975 the weak Christian Democratic (DC) government was highly nervous about the obvious signs of recession, and by its poor performance in regional elections. As labor unrest soared to a peak in Italy (27 million working days lost in strikes in 1975), the government spent money on a very large scale to buy off discontent. The Director General of the Treasury allegedly told the Governor of the Bank of Italy to open his window on the via Milano and throw out packets of 10,000 lire notes. Parliamentary elections were due to be held in June 1976, and both the United States and Germany intervened very heavy-handedly and almost certainly counter-productively to warn the Italians of the dangers of communism. The US Ambassador in Italy had said in 1975 that the participation of communists in the government of a NATO country would be a "basic contradiction". Secretary of State Henry Kissinger warned that if communist parties came to power "there would be a shocking change in the established patterns of American policy", and added that "a Communist western Europe would be a headache for us and a headache for the Russians as well".[5] The Communist Party then staged its strongest ever electoral performance in 1976, winning over 34 percent of the vote. The DC was still the largest party (38.7 percent), but was in a vulnerable minority in parliament and vulnerable to pressure from small groups, such as the German Nationalist Party from South Tyrol.

In order to get external assistance from the IMF, Prime Minister Giulio Andreotti tried to blackmail the United States with the threat of a general collapse: "were Italy to collapse both politically and economically, Italy would not be the only loser".

At the same time, the Italian Communist Party under Enrico Berlinguer started to argue that a "historic compromise" was needed, in which it could accept a reformist alliance with the left wing of the DC. In 1978, the DC politician who had been the most outspoken advocate for some communist participation in government, Aldo Moro, was kidnapped on the street in Rome by the Red Brigades. His captors demanded an exchange with convicted prisoners, which the government (supported by the Communist Party) refused. Moro was killed, and rumors flew that his enemies within the DC had been behind the kidnapping and murder.

By the middle of the 1970s, what had become traditional ways of doing postwar European politics – the Keynesian approach to growthmanship – faced an apparently impossible situation. The easiest way of describing this is as a response to the oil price shock. The price of Europe's single most important import had been more or less constant throughout the great 1960s boom. Saudi light crude was $1.93 a barrel at the beginning of 1955, and only $2.18 in January 1971. In the meantime, the dollar had lost a great deal of its purchasing power, and with the end of the gold convertibility of the dollar in August 1971, large oil producers worried in public about the wisdom of selling their product for an unguaranteed paper currency. By 1973, the oil producers wanted to use their market power in the application of "oil nationalism". After the Yom Kippur War, when Egypt and Syria staged a sudden and spectacularly unsuccessful attack on Israel (October 1973), the price of Saudi light crude shot up to $11.65 a barrel (December). The oil issue became very heavily politicized: the Arab Organization of the Petroleum Exporting Countries (OPEC) producers threatened countries they felt to be too sympathetic to Israel with a boycott, while pro-Arab countries such as France were given favored access.

But the oil issue was part of a more general problem: the dramatic and coordinated growth of the major industrial countries in the early 1970s, fueled by a lax attitude to inflation, pushed most commodity prices higher. At the same time, extrapolating from the developments of a few years, there were warnings about the limits to industrial development – most dramatically put in the Club of Rome's 1972 report, *The Limits to Growth*. The increase in pollution and the inadequacy of petroleum and food reserves, it argued, would lead rapidly (in the 1970s) to widespread famine and starvation. Even the implementation of what the report termed "perfect birth control" could only postpone the food crisis for another ten years.

The figures for growth projected by the Club of Rome (Table 10.1) were actually not hugely wrong (with the exception of the wildly over-optimistic figure for the Soviet Union), but in practice they would be achieved without any major crisis in the supply of natural resources.

Table 10.1 Club of Rome: predictions for GDP per capita in 2000, and actual figures (1968 US dollars)

	Predicted GDP per capita in 2000	Actual GDP per capita in 1968 dollars
United States	11,000	7,980
Soviet Union	6,330	580
Germany	5,850	6,570
China	100	200

Source: Club of Rome, *The Limits to Growth*, New York: Universe Books, 1972, p. 43; World Bank data.

In the mid-1970s, European labor unrest increased again, as a response to the unpleasant combination of rising unemployment and rising inflation ("stagflation"). The United Kingdom lost 13.6 million days in strikes in 1971, 23.9 million in 1972, and 14.8 million in 1974.

The Heath government had introduced an Industrial Relations Act in 1971, which enshrined the principle of collective bargaining but also instituted an elaborate system to control and regulate such bargaining. A National Industrial Relations Court could require ballots among workers in the case of industrial disputes, impose compensation requirements on employers or trade unions acting illegally, and lay down "cooling-off periods" in industrial disputes. The 1971 Act was bitterly resented by the trade unions, who feared that they could not control their members as effectively as they had done in the past; and in fact it did nothing to reduce labor unrest.

After the oil shock had pushed up energy prices, the most powerful British union was undoubtedly the National Union of Mineworkers. Eventually, a bitter industrial dispute in the coalmines brought down the Conservative government. The successful blockading of power stations led to power cut-offs, obliging the government to reduce work to a three-day week. When Heath dissolved parliament and called an election based on the question "Who governs Britain?" he won slightly fewer seats in the House of Commons than the opposition Labour Party (297 to 301), but had a slightly higher share of the popular vote (37.8 to 37.1 percent). Neither side had enough seats in parliament to form a new government, and Heath tried to make a coalition government with the small Liberal Party, which refused. The new minority government, once more with Harold Wilson as Prime Minister, immediately repealed the Industrial Relations Act, but in the course of the passage of the bill through the lower (Commons) and upper (Lords) houses of parliament, the Liberal and Conservative opposition added clauses which protected workers' rights to join alternative independent trade unions. The Labour government, increasingly vulnerable in parliament, then called a new election (November 1974), which it won convincingly, and in 1976 a new Industrial Relations Act eliminated those clauses inserted by the Liberals and Conservatives in 1974.

In power, Labour set about restoring growth but rapidly ran into a bad payments crisis. The agreement reached in 1976 by the United Kingdom with the IMF was a turning point in British politics. In what became the most widely cited expression of the rejection of the economic philosophy of the past 20 years, Prime Minister Callaghan told the Labour Party Congress in September 1976, one day before the United Kingdom sent the formal application for IMF assistance:

> We used to think that you could just spend your way out of a recession . . . I tell you, in all candour, that that option no longer exists and that in so far as it ever did, it only worked . . . by injecting higher doses of inflation into the economy, followed by higher levels of unemployment.[6]

In setting the terms of the IMF agreement, Chancellor of the Exchequer Denis Healey also appeared to adopt a new theory – that inflation was primarily a result of monetary policy (and not of greed, trade union demands, or bad management by business leaders, as was widely believed in popular discussions): "I am satisfied that the resultant course of sterling M3 will be consistent with reduction of inflation."[7] This very sober statement, much less obviously confrontational than Callaghan's address, indicated a new way of thinking – one so strange that it would actually make the old politics irrelevant. But at the time, the major players in British politics, in particular the labor unions, did not recognize what had happened. Labor unrest, which had largely faded in 1975 and 1976, returned on a big scale in 1977 (10.1 million days lost) and 1979 (12.0 million days lost), when an industrial "winter of discontent" destroyed the credibility of the Labour government and opened the way for a completely different approach to economic management under Margaret Thatcher.

Monetarism

Monetarism in the 1970s came to be viewed as an alternative to the philosophy of *Keynesian* demand management. Its central insight, derived largely from the Chicago school of economics, from Frank Knight and especially Milton Friedman, was a quite technical one: a tight correspondence between the money supply and price levels. Expansion of the quantity of money would produce higher levels of output in monetary terms; but this would be the result only of higher price levels (or inflation), with all the undesirable effects of distorting investment decisions, and not of real increases in output.

It discredited macro-economic demand management, which had mostly taken the form of fiscal "fine-tuning", in an attempt to remove business cycle fluctuations. Its implication was that the only way in which governments could really contribute to economic growth was by micro-economic policy: in other words, by ensuring that product and labor markets worked efficiently.

As a macro-economic approach in Europe, the legacy of monetarism is mixed. This is in part because of difficulties identifying the appropriate policy target, and in part because Europeans long neglected the international aspects and implications of monetarist theory, related to exchange rate management. The initial attempts of the German Bundesbank, the Federal Reserve System, and other central banks to target money supply had only partial success. Such experiments led to the formulation of Goodhart's Law (after the British economist Charles Goodhart): that as soon as a monetary aggregate is targeted, its behavior ceases to maintain a stable link with monetary performance. In consequence, in the 1990s, most central banks (except the new European Central Bank, which saw itself as the heir of the Bundesbank) went over to inflation targeting, rather than gearing policy around a desirable growth rate of the money supply.

Monetarism also had an international implication: that fixed exchange rate regimes (see *the gold standard*) were dangerous, because they could lead to externally induced variations of the money stock and produce bad consequences: international deflation in the 1930s, and international inflation in the 1960s and early 1970s. Milton Friedman was an advocate at a very early stage of the principle of flexible or floating exchange rates because they alone allowed monetary authorities to maintain a consistently stable monetary policy. Because of the interplay of monetary and trade policies, European governments were unwilling to follow Friedmanian monetarism to this conclusion, and instead embarked on a fixed exchange rate regime on a European level, the European Monetary System (1979–98). With the transition from this to a monetary union in 1999, the debate about flexible exchange rates could be moved to the level of the appropriate relationship between the euro and other major international currencies.

Can events be controlled after all?

The British situation, the breakdown of order in Northern Ireland, the political instability in Italy, and the recessions in France and Germany, were all interpreted as the end of the stable and secure world of postwar politics. The ignominious collapse of the Nixon presidency looked as if democracy in the world's largest industrial country was discredited. Of west European politicians, Helmut Schmidt was probably the most anxious in a rational way. He feared that Bonn was following in the steps of Weimar. The situation in the United Kingdom was also very bleak. Labor unions had shown that they could shut down the country and bring down the government. In Northern Ireland, the government abandoned its monopoly of power and designated "no go areas" where the police and army would stay away. Harold Wilson was increasingly paranoid, and thought that the secret service was plotting to overthrow him, and that the portrait of Gladstone in the Cabinet Room contained a listening device. Soon after, a French political scientist, Jean-François Revel, published a best-seller account of the collapse of liberal democracy, *How Democracies Perish*. In Germany and Italy, terrorism posed a major threat to the political and business elites. Further afield, the Turkish political system appeared to be disintegrating under the pressure of a violent left and right. If revolution and military adventurism could spread from Portugal to Greece, why not to northern Europe as well?

In 1975, the major government leaders met for the first of what later became rather routinized and generally rather unproductive summit meetings. The first of these meetings, in November 1975 at Rambouillet, 50 kilometers outside Paris, occurred at the moment of greatest self-doubt. New York City, the richest city in the world, had just gone bankrupt. President Gerald Ford lacked credibility, and the French and German technocratic leaders, Giscard and Schmidt, believed they needed to build a new politics to save their world of liberal democracy. The meeting was designed to be very informal and intimate, restricted to a very limited number of participants. Even finance and foreign ministers were to attend only selected discussions, and were not to stay in the château. The very powerful US Secretary of State, Henry Kissinger, who wanted to stay with the leaders, was put off with the offer of a room without a bathroom (which he refused). Ford began the meeting with a strong statement about the crisis of the mid-1970s and its implications:

> This summit is designed to deal with economic questions but in a more fundamental sense it springs from the enormous interdependence of our societies and the common values which we share. . . . We must ensure that the current world economic situation is not seen as a crisis in the democratic or capitalist system.[8]

The European leaders were terrified that the United States was proposing to use force to deal with the situation in the Middle East, which could (in a simplified view) be regarded as the source of the threat to the world market economy. Kissinger here provided a clear and – for the economically focused Europeans – very attractive answer. His strategy aimed at breaking up the oil producers' cartel, OPEC. In particular, he guessed that Iran (under the Shah's leadership) could not afford to allow oil production to drop. If Iran – and other oil producers – were encouraged to spend their new gains as quickly and as enthusiastically as possible, they would become dependent on a high level of petroleum exports, and this would in the long run lead to a weakening of the price. A short-term response was needed to deal with the immediate effects of the oil crisis; after that, consumerism on the western model would destroy the cartel. The Shah in particular, with his commitment to the high-speed modernization of Iran and the creation of a new middle class with a taste for luxuries, was the ideal target. In general, then, markets would undermine the power of the cartels: consumer markets would bring customers in new geographic areas, and awaken new demands; and financial markets would make funds available for these purchases. A world political crisis would be managed by monetary and economic means, and not by guns.

Schmidt and Giscard were also convinced that the post-Watergate political crises of the United States and the monetary chaos that followed the breakdown of the Bretton Woods system of more or less fixed exchange rates required a European response. The global response, as agreed at Rambouillet, which allowed the IMF to accept floating as well as fixed exchange rate regimes, seemed to them unsatisfactory at the continental level. In 1978 they agreed on the principles for a European Monetary System (EMS), whose fixed but adjustable parities would replicate those of the Bretton Woods regime (which both Schmidt and Giscard greatly admired). At first some of the discussions were trilateral, since the British pound was a major (if weak) international currency. When the United Kingdom dropped out of the plans, it was much easier to reach an agreement. In practice, the plan eventually accepted was much closer to the German than to the French conception; and from beginning to end, the EMS was a currency system built around the Deutschemark. In March 1979 the new European exchange rate regime began to operate.

Money was thus solved on a European and not a national level. The crisis of heavy industry that followed from the oil shock, which reduced demand for heavy cars and for big steel-based construction projects, was also dealt with through a European approach. In 1979 Etienne Davignon designed a steel plan for the European Commission, which was followed up in 1980 by a more extensive proposal for running down steel production over a five-year period. Employment in the steel industry in Germany declined from 213,000 in 1975 to 197,000 in 1980, and 151,000 in 1985. In the UK it fell much more drastically from 184,000 to 112,000 to 59,000, and provided the prime example of the deindustrialization of the world's first industrial nation. In France, steel employment fell from 156,000 to 105,000 and then to 75,000. Angry steelworkers protested. In Lorraine, in the desolate steel town of Joeuf, they pulled down the statue of the patriarch of France's premier iron and steel dynasty, François de Wendel. Italy still boosted employment in the steel industry in the later 1970s, but from 1980 to 1985 it fell also, from 100,000 to 67,000.

Europe's highly precarious stability required some sort of institutional anchoring: hence the drive to the institutionalization of more stable monetary arrangements, and the attempt to tackle overcapacity in basic industries on a European level. Could the same multilateralization and internationalization of problems be used to defuse and de-escalate Europe's security dilemmas? Europe no longer needed steel as the prime defense good; and the debates changed to concentrate both on nuclear weapons and their stationing, and on the social and political philosophies which might guide their use or non-use.

The improved international and geopolitical perspective in the wake of detente also meant a stabilization for Europe. In particular the treaties of the early 1970s, the Moscow and Warsaw treaties, the Basic Treaty, and the Four Power Agreement on Berlin, made the Federal Republic more secure. What concessions could the West offer in return?

In 1975, the Final Act of the CSCE was signed in Helsinki. It looked like a guarantee of the Potsdam settlement, with a strong recognition of the inviolability of existing frontiers and existing state sovereignty:

> The participating States will respect each other's sovereign equality and individuality as well as all the rights inherent in and encompassed by its sovereignty, including in particular the right of every State to juridical equality, to territorial integrity and to freedom and political independence. They will also respect each other's right freely to choose and develop its political, social, economic and cultural systems as well as its right to determine its laws and regulations. . . . The participating States will refrain from any intervention, direct or indirect, individual or collective, in the internal or external affairs falling within the domestic jurisdiction of another participating State, regardless of their mutual relations.

But this was hardly a concession, as no one in the West since the 1940s had thought seriously about pushing back the frontiers of the Soviet sphere. From the point of view of the United States, the Helsinki agreements were thus largely meaningless. The *New York Times* concluded that "Never have so many struggled for so long over so little."[9] The Nixon administration had seen the long talks as a way of encouraging Soviet moderation in other areas, because the guarantee of borders would remove some of the threat that the Soviet leadership constantly feared. Henry Kissinger later concluded that "this monster diplomatic process grew out of Moscow's deep-rooted sense of insecurity and unquestionable thirst for legitimacy". Kissinger's own guru, the State Department Counsellor Helmut Sonnenfeldt, explained very candidly at the time: "We sold it for the German–Soviet treaty, we sold it for the Berlin agreement, and we sold it again for the opening of the MBFR [Mutual and Balanced Forces Reductions]."[10]

From the Soviet perspective, the territorial clauses endorsed their view of history and in particular guaranteed the permanence of the Yalta–Potsdam division of Europe. In retrospect, however, the most important parts of the agreement related to human rights. The preamble to Helsinki also stated that

The participating States will respect human rights and fundamental freedoms, including the freedom of thought, conscience, religion or belief,
for all without distinction as to race, sex, language or religion. They
will promote and encourage the effective exercise of civil, political, economic, social, cultural and other rights and freedoms all of which derive
from the inherent dignity of the human person and are essential for his
free and full development.

The obvious discrepancies between words and reality led Timothy Garton-
Ash to conclude that "like the Bible, the prayer-book, and even canon law,
Helsinki was susceptible to very different interpretations".[11] But these interpretations were not static: this part of the Treaty in practice acted as a lever
which encouraged the voicing of opposition and the organization of dissent,
and eventually prised open the closed Soviet systems. The human rights
language contained in the Helsinki agreement thus in the end overpowered
the defense and justification of national sovereignty, that the Soviet elite had
believed to be the most enticing part of the Helsinki apparatus.

The 1970s were traumatic because they suggested that big forces – so
large that they overwhelmed the nation-state – could paralyze politics and
decision-making. It was hard for the successful technocrats of the 1960s,
who had emphasized the controllability of the social process, to come to
terms with the actual limitations on their power. Harold Lever, a gifted
economist whom Harold Wilson had seen as the force behind his government's approach to policy-making, put the point very succinctly. In a review
of a fellow cabinet member's published diary, he wondered how such a
collection of brilliant individuals in government could produce such disappointing results:

These governments, like most other modern governments, overesti-
mated their ability to shape and manage the complex drives of a mature
economy. They wrongly assumed that they understood all the reasons
for its shortcomings and so, not surprisingly, were all too ready to lay
hands on superficial remedies for overcoming them. And all this without any attempt to understand the economics of an increasingly interdependent world. It is significant that the National Plans, which were no
more than a summary of Labour Party rhetoric, ultimately enjoyed the
derision even of the Cabinet itself.[12]

The most obvious response to the problem of politicians' increasingly evident
inability to manage politics in the 1970s lay in a shift to a more technocratic
approach: that of Schmidt or Heath or Giscard, which then came to char-
acterize the whole venture of European integration. But those approaches
seemed unsatisfactory unless they were buttressed by some stronger construction. Italy and the United Kingdom relied at crucial moments of their
1970s trajectory from belief in governments' capacities to a more timid

acceptance of inadequacy on the IMF as a source of external discipline, a bogeyman that could be appealed to in order to tell disenchanted voters why it was that politicians could not keep their promises.

Behind the scenes, however, appealing to the IMF was quite political. Both the United Kingdom and Italy tried to use other European countries (Schmidt was an intermediary) and their own influence with the US administration in order to get better terms. At the moment of humiliation, however, the United States was quite unsympathetic to this approach. So, it looked like a better option to tackle the issue on a European level, and to find in Europe and European integration a rationale for technocratic politics. The CSCE was a by-product of this new tone, and actually constituted in the longer run the most convincing example of the force of international commitments to change domestic political realities. The national order was giving way to internationalism.

Notes

1 Keesings 27156.
2 Keesings 27157.
3 Keesings 27179.
4 IMF figures, rounded.
5 Keesings 22796, 22797.
6 Peter Jenkins, *Mrs. Thatcher's Revolution: The Ending of the Socialist Era*, London: Jonathan Cape, 2987, p. 18.
7 Kathleen Burk and Alec Cairncross, *"Goodbye, Great Britain": The 1976 IMF Crisis*, New Haven: Yale University Press, 1992, p. 235.
8 Harold James, *International Monetary Cooperation Since Bretton Woods*, New York: Oxford University Press, 1995, p. 269.
9 "European security", *New York Times*, July 21, 1975.
10 Both quotes from Henry Kissinger, *Diplomacy*, New York, NY: Simon and Schuster, 1994, pp. 758–9.
11 Timothy Garton-Ash, *In Europe's Name: Germany and the Divided Continent*, New York, NY: Random House, 1993, p. 259.
12 Quoted in Peter Hennessy, *The Prime Minister: The Office and its Holders since 1945*, London: Penguin, 2000, p. 361.

11 Right step
The 1980s

In the 1980s, European politics moved in a largely synchronous shift to the right. There were different variants of the shift – at one extreme, Margaret Thatcher's very ideological drive; at the other, the socialist President François Mitterrand's abandonment of his original program and his reluctant engagement with reality after 1983. All of them, however, owed a great deal to external circumstances: the big increase in oil prices, the second oil shock, after the Iranian revolution; the change in US monetary policy toward anti-inflationism after October 1979; the harsh global recession of 1980–81, which was the first and quite painful synchronized downturn of the world economy since the interwar Depression; and the new security problems following the Soviet deployment of intermediate nuclear missiles (the SS-20s), the US response to that threat, and the Reagan Strategic Defense Initiative. Most people at the time looked for the explanation of political developments in primarily national terms: how parties and politicians interreacted with each other; how the press treated politics; and most dramatically the impact of strong personalities such as Thatcher, Ronald Reagan, and Helmut Kohl. They did not pay so much attention to the global forces, which through trade and the capital markets increasingly linked both national economies and the political responses to economic shocks.

In 1979 Margaret Thatcher's government moved promptly to remove exchange controls. In 1981, Germany greatly facilitated capital movements by ending the restrictions which had limited the purchase of domestic securities by non-residents. In 1984, the United States, the United Kingdom, France, and Germany abolished the withholding tax on interest and dividend payments. The Single European Act of 1986 provided for the removal of remaining capital controls in the European Community (EC). As a result of these measures, economic issues became globalized – in other words, it was ever harder for national authorities to control them.

The Thatcher model

Margaret Thatcher became Prime Minister after the Labour government of James Callaghan, whose *raison d'être* was the maintenance of industrial harmony, fell apart during a strike wave in 1978–79 (the "winter of discontent"). British Prime Ministers can choose the timing of elections, and often dissolve parliaments prematurely. Callaghan was too nervous to risk an election in the unpropitious circumstances of the autumn of 1978, with the result that he faced worse circumstances in June 1979.

Margaret Thatcher had little sympathy with the main operating features (they can hardly be called principles) of the post-1945 political world, which appear in the United Kingdom under the name "Butskellism": the quest for the center and the appeal to the median voter. She saw herself as a campaigner, with a mission to reform a creaking, cynical, corrupt system. As a young lawyer, she had found the male-dominated Bar an almost insuperable obstacle to advance. As leader of the opposition, and then as Prime Minister, she disliked establishment ways of doing business: whether the establishment was the Foreign Office, with its proclivity to compromise with foreign interests (a tendency which could easily be labeled as "appeasement"); the Department of Industry, which appeased trade unionists; or academia (especially humanistic academia), which sneered as condescendingly at her (the grocer's daughter who studied chemistry at university) as did the Tory toffs. When she had just become leader of the opposition in 1975, Harold Macmillan commented on her simply as a sign of interminable British decay: "You can't imagine a woman as Prime Minister if we were a first-class power." An old-style red-faced Tory politician, Julian Critchley, wrote of her, accurately enough: "She cannot see an institution without hitting it with her handbag."[1]

In the United Kingdom, the 1970s in general were a time of quite fierce polarization, in which politicians, at least the more imaginative ones, wanted to move away from the "Butskellite" bipartisan but rancorous consensus of the Wilson–Heath era. On the left, Anthony Wedgwood Benn, who had been a very Wilsonian technology-driven minister, responsible for the Anglo-French supersonic Concorde project which was intended to challenge the American grip over commercial aviation, now remade himself as Tony Benn, the radical critic of capitalism, high technology, and European cooperation. He complained that the British ruling class had abandoned its mission of the defense of British interests, and had "defected to Brussels". He warned that this would destroy the democratic and parliamentary tradition that constituted the British heritage (for the left, as well as the right): "If you say to nation-states that there is nothing you can do, you will end up with the withdrawal of consent from elected governments."[2] After the election defeat of 1979, the Labour Party moved sharply leftwards, though not completely in a Bennite direction. Its new leader, an old-style socialist intellectual and advocate of unilateral disarmament, Michael Foot, further polarized the party, with the result that it split. Pro-European, modernizing Labourites followed what their critics called the "Gang of Four" (Roy Jenkins, David Owen, Bill Rodgers, Shirley Williams) to form a Social Democratic Party (SDP), which was intended as an analogue to the modern German SPD. The split in the

Labour Party, combined with the British electoral system, helped to keep Mrs Thatcher in power.

Thatcherism

Margaret Thatcher was leader of the British Conservative Party from 1975 to 1990, and Prime Minister from 1979 to 1990. Her leadership broke with the tradition of postwar consensus politics, and soon became known as an "ism". It involved a break with *Keynesianism*, and the adoption of *monetarism*.

Some observers see an inconsistency between the strong economic liberalism of Thatcherism, and its emphasis on a strong state with high law-and-order priorities together with a defense of traditional social morality and values. First, it seems to these critics as odd to emphasize the weakness of the state in economic policy areas and the strength of the state as a guardian of society. Secondly, they say, wild capitalism unleashes a social dynamic that produces a demand for ostentatious excess, drugs, sex, and pornography, that Thatcherites should and generally do dislike. The logical consequence of economic liberalism should be social libertarianism, and indeed some libertarians supported large parts of the Thatcher agenda.

Defenders of Thatcherism do not find these inconsistencies problematic. They see the strengthening of the state as an important objective of every part of the policy, but a state could not be strong if it tried to do ridiculous things (like King Canute's ordering of the tide not to advance). Abandoning Keynesianism, and especially renouncing an incomes policy, was a way of shaking off unworkable policies. A more sophisticated version of the same view holds that the task of governments in a modern democracy is to set conditions that apply to all. It was the *ancien régime* that had privileges and particular justice. Thus, it makes no sense for the state to decide that some groups of workers deserve pay rises and others do not. The only legitimate activity of governments in this approach is the setting of a system of generally applicable rules, i.e. law making.

The wildness of capitalism is a harder problem, and social developments of the twentieth century have indeed generated a new society. But it is probably Canute-like to expect political leaders to be *able* to repress it, and many will feel that they *should* not attempt such repression.

In foreign policy, Thatcherism drew on the traditions of *Gaullism* in a vigorous defense of the idea of the nation-state, especially as regards British participation on European integration. She was a convinced *Atlanticist*, without subscribing to the social-democratic reformist program that accompanied mainstream Atlanticism in the postwar era.

She was confrontational and frequently strident. In continental Europe, dominated by proportional representation systems, her style of politics would have had little success, as it would have united the other parties in coalition against it. At most she could have been a de Gaulle, waiting in the wings for the call to power – as one British conservative proto-Thatcher, Enoch Powell, a great admirer of the French leader, actually did when he established his own version of Colombey in Northern Ireland. But Thatcher could succeed because of the first-past-the-post constituency electoral system, which allowed the Conservatives to control 339 out of 634 seats in the House of Commons with 43.9 percent of the vote after 1979.

The secure majorities produced by the British election system generated one new issue for Thatcher's leadership: the major opposition to Thatcherism came from within the Conservative Party, from figures who thought that she was shaking the postwar consensus too much, rather than from the parties that called themselves the opposition.

Thatcher, for all her confrontationalism, had quite strongly developed political instincts of a more conventional type. She knew that she must not alienate a core element of her support: so when it came to ending tax benefits for company cars, she blocked the proposal once she was told that every businessman in England would vote against her; and, on similar grounds, she rejected any idea of ending tax relief on mortgage payments, which the middle class regarded as essential to its house-possession-fixated lifestyle. Yet both of these steps would have been in the spirit of the belief system that she very firmly espoused.

Her most controversial but successful reforms came at the beginning of her long Prime Ministership (the longest in the twentieth-century United Kingdom); at the end, she made equally controversial but quite unsuccessful reforms (in local government finance). At the beginning, she broke decisively not only with the legacy of the Labour governments of the 1970s, but of post-1945 Keynesianism. The key concept was a multi-year approach to budgeting, the Medium-Term Financial Strategy (MTFS), that moved away from the "fine tuning" previously practiced, in which the budgetary stance was altered to fit the stage of the economic cycle. At the beginning, however, it was not clear that the government had the new style of enhanced credibility that might come from taking really unpopular measures. In 1981, in the middle of a worldwide recession that followed from the overthrow of the Shah of Iran and a second dramatic surge in petroleum prices, her government increased taxes. Because of the recession, government revenue was higher and receipts lower than planned under the MTFS. The Chancellor of the Exchequer, Geoffrey Howe, proposed tax increases amounting to 2 percent of GNP. The 1981 budget was widely condemned by an establishment – the British economics profession; 364 economists, including five former chief economic advisers to the government, wrote a letter to *The Times*:

There is no basis in economic theory or supporting evidence for the Government's belief that by deflating demand they will bring inflation permanently under control and thereby induce an automatic recovery in output and unemployment. Present policies will deepen the depression, erode the industrial base of our economy and threaten its social and political stability.[3]

Thatcher herself hesitated. She knew that any rise in the basic rate of tax would be held to be a betrayal of her promise to reduce the scope of the state, and would alienate a major part of her core constituency. In the end, she accepted instead the non-indexation of tax brackets, which in effect amounted to a tax raise. Unemployment continued at very high levels. In April 1981, street riots broke out in largely black Brixton (South London), and then in other poor and mixed-ethnic inner city areas such as Southall (London) and Toxteth (Liverpool).

The 1981 budget came into practice near the bottom of the recession. It still might have cost Thatcher the next election, had it not been for the inept opposition of the Labour Party and its radicalization under Michael Foot. In addition, a patriotic tide around another political gamble, the decision to seize the Falkland Islands (Malvinas) back from Argentina, won her a British-style landslide in June 1983, with 46 percent of the vote and 397 out of 650 House of Commons seats.

Industrial relations formed a core part of the postwar UK's economic malaise, which Thatcher intended to correct. She also had to contend with the legacy of the previous Conservative administration's collapse in the wake of a miners' strike in 1973. The strike had been accompanied by widespread blocking of industrial plants and facilities to stop coal transport ("secondary picketing"), and had brought the country to a halt. In December 1980, the coalminers' union had accepted a 20 percent wage settlement, and the government temporarily escaped from a confrontation with the coalminers. But in 1983, Thatcher appointed Ian MacGregor, an American of Scottish origins who had previously restructured and shrunk British Steel, as chairman of the National Coal Board (NCB). He prepared a plan to end the coal industry's losses by 1988, by cutting capacity by 25 million tons and the workforce by 64,000 miners. In March 1984, the NCB announced that it would close the Yorkshire pit of Cortonwood, and the National Union of Mineworkers encouraged individual mining areas to go on strike (thus avoiding the need for a national ballot, which would not have supported a general coal stoppage). Where there were votes, in Nottinghamshire, the Midlands, the North-East, and the North-West, there were majorities against striking. Faced by a prolonged miners' strike, and heavy and violent picketing, the government launched national police cooperation to stop the practice of secondary picketing. The timing of the 1984 strike, which began in spring after the peak winter demand for coal, was also bad for the miners, as was the substantial number of power-generating plants that had been converted to dual oil and coal firing. In the autumn, with no clear victory, the miners were desperate for funds: one union official visited Libya to appeal for funds from Colonel Ghaddafi; there were reports that Soviet miners were paying for the British strike; and public sympathy for the miners fell quickly. By the beginning of 1985, larger numbers of striking miners returned to work, and in March the National Union of Mineworkers' Delegates Conference voted to go back. The long strike and its outcome definitely destroyed the idea that militant trade unions could dictate economic and political events. After 1985, union membership in the United Kingdom collapsed, in part because of disenchantment with unions' capacity to represent workers effectively after the new legal changes, and in part because of the rapidity of the shift in employment away from heavily unionized industrial activity.

Behind the confrontational appearance, however, Thatcher had a keen political sense of how to build a basis of support and reach beyond the traditional core of Conservative voters. She thought she needed, and she received, the allegiance of a group equivalent to the "Reagan democrats", blue-collar Americans who felt at odds with the ascendancy of a liberal counter-culture that imposed high taxes. In particular, in the United Kingdom the sale of council houses, which began very early in the Thatcher years, was massively popular with a part of the skilled working class.

Reducing the role of the state could also be made into popular politics. The privatization of state-owned companies – British Aerospace, Cable and Wireless, British Petroleum, British Airways, British Telecom, Rolls-Royce, British Gas, British Airports Authority – raised money (thus lowering the need to tax), increased efficiency, and created stakeholders in the new rebalancing of the boundary between private and public. The mass-shareholding that was encouraged with the privatization of British Telecom in particular, when 2.3 million individuals bought shares, made capitalism popular in a way that it had never previously been. By 1990, a quarter of the British population owned shares.

The effect of privatization on this scale, and especially mass privatization of the kind associated with the British Telecom sale, was to make it practically irreversible. Previous Conservative governments had attempted smaller-scale denationalizations: the iron and steel industry had been taken over by the Labour government in 1951, but was slowly sold off between 1953 and 1963, and was then renationalized by a new Labour government in 1967. One of the many disastrous features of Labour's 1983 manifesto was its commitment to "return to public ownership the public assets and rights hived off by the Tories, with compensation of no more than that received when the assets were denationalized". The 1987 Labour Party manifesto was much vaguer, and merely said that private shares in British Telecom and British Gas would be converted into special securities with a guaranteed rate of return or a link to the growth of the company, and that could be traded on a secondary market. In 1992, the Labour manifesto even promised explicitly that there would be no rolling back of privatization, as did the manifesto for the 1997 election. Privatization thus became a way of shaping a new politics, in which Labour was driven to accept of necessity a decision that created an inherently Conservative clientele.[4]

The liberalization of capital markets, which was also vigorously encouraged by the Thatcher governments, had an analogous effect: it restricted what future governments could do, because they would be prisoners of the opinion not just of their own electors, but of traders on trading floors all over the world. In 1979 the Banking Act began the deregulation of the City that culminated in the "Big Bang" of the 1988 Financial Services Act. Most importantly, in 1979, capital controls – which had been an essential feature of postwar British monetary policy management – were lifted. This could be justified in terms of an immediate response to the UK's enhanced revenue from North Sea oil, which would otherwise produce a surge in the value of the currency (and a deterioration of the competitive position of manufacturing). The strengthening of the pound indeed occurred, but it was partially offset by an outflow of capital which, it was reasoned, would produce revenues when North Sea oil was exhausted. The concept actually had a back-to-the-nineteenth-century flavor: a return to the era when British rentiers lived off the proceeds of overseas investment. But the British liberalization was a crucial move in a general, worldwide movement toward much higher levels of capital mobility.

Thatcher's big victories over Argentina and the miners, and the successful spread of privatization, gave way to growing vulnerability in the late 1980s. In 1985 the government began to discuss, and in 1990 introduced, an ill-judged flat rate capitation tax for local government (the community charge, popularly known as the "poll tax"), which was designed to deal with the problem of a cycle of poverty and decline in major urban centers. Since there was a strong incentive for councils in predominantly poor cities, elected by predominantly poor voters, to raise business taxes and property taxes higher still, leading to a flight of business and devastated city centers, an obvious remedy would be a system which ensured that every resident bore part of the cost of local services. But when the community charge was actually applied, at much higher levels than originally envisioned, it was met with protests and non-payment. Conservative candidates were defeated in by-elections and in local elections. In March 1991, the government abandoned the community charge, but then Margaret Thatcher was no longer Prime Minister.

She was also vulnerable because of a growing dispute over the UK's relations with Europe. In the early 1980s, she had scored a major domestic triumph with her successful campaign to reduce the level of British contributions to the EC budget (which went largely on the agricultural policy, and rewarded French farmers in particular). The debate of the later 1980s centered on what was apparently a quite technical point about the best guide to monetary policy in a medium-sized open economy. After the control of money supply which had been the basis of policy in the first half of the 1980s, there were substantial pressures on the international stage to look more at exchange rates and their stabilization. The economics of globalization intruded. On a global level, at meetings at the Plaza Hotel in New York (1985) and the Louvre (1987), the Group of Five finance ministers tried to work out appropriate exchange rates between the big world currencies: the yen, the German mark, and the US dollar. In 1985, Thatcher herself was worried about the decline of the pound, and asked the major central banks to defend the British currency and drive down the high dollar rate.[5] The United Kingdom looked increasingly to the mark, and the exchange rate remained quite stable at three marks to the pound, with the Treasury fueling the expectation that the United Kingdom would one day join the exchange rate mechanism (ERM) established in the European Monetary System (EMS).

On the world level, however, the idea that governments might find and fix the correct exchange rate, which had been so persuasively attractive in the 1980s, lost credibility, and the experience of the Louvre meeting of finance ministers of 1987 was not repeated. In 1989, Thatcher appointed as her part-time independent economic adviser one of the foremost critics of the EMS and of British membership, Alan Walters. His advice that fixed exchange systems were an inherently unstable compromise between flexible rates and a true currency union ("half-baked" was the term he used) ran diametrically counter to the policy followed by the Chancellor of the Exchequer, Nigel Lawson, which depended on a claim that a fixed rate was a viable and satisfying alternative to monetary union. The Foreign Minister, Geoffrey Howe, also pushed heavily for Thatcher to agree at the European Council in Madrid (June 1989) to a date for the UK's membership of the ERM.

These issues became even more contentious after the collapse of East German communism in November 1989 and Germany's rapid move to political union. The insistence of both Germany and France that this be done as much as possible in a European context, and Thatcher's well-publicized but futile opposition to German unification, created a new strain within the Conservative Party. Both the Chancellor and the Foreign Secretary resigned, making bitterly critical speeches, and a leading ex-minister, Michael Heseltine, stood for the leadership of the Conservative Party against Thatcher. In an initial vote, she won a majority of the votes of Conservative MPs, but not sufficient (according to the rules of the process) to avoid a second round. She resigned as Prime Minister, and in a new ballot, Conservative MPs elected the man she favored as her replacement, John Major (1990).

Major, to the surprise of his supporters, won a general election in 1992, perhaps because the Labour leader, Neil Kinnock, seemed too sure of victory and celebrated in a rather premature victory rally in Sheffield. But almost immediately, Major's careful *via media* on Europe – looking for membership of the EMS but expressing skepticism about European monetary union – fell apart in a dramatic currency crisis in September 1992. The power of the markets, which Margaret Thatcher had initiated through the ending of capital controls in 1979, asserted itself in an obvious and brutal way. The Prime Minister and his Chancellor of the Exchequer, Norman Lamont, looked at the computer screens on "Black Wednesday" (September 16, 1992) to see whether an increase in British interest rates would halt the speculative attack on sterling. When within seconds it was clear that the announcement had no effect, the two politicians realized that they were quite helpless, and that the United Kingdom would be driven out of the ERM as the reserves of the Bank of England were insufficient to go against speculators who were taking a one-way bet on sterling sinking. Lamont, who had to take responsibility for the Prime Minister's policy, retired into a sulking resentment; and the government, despite a substantial economic recovery driven not least by the depreciation of the currency, looked incredible and accident-prone.

Despite these difficulties, John Major's overall brand of economic policy was uncontroversial (except for some of his supporters), and there was no longer any ideological challenge to capitalism. His government managed one more big privatization, of the railroad system; but the privatization of this public service was poorly conceived, with a separation of track and trains, and generated many complaints.

Stuck with the legacy of Mrs Thatcher (who turned into a vociferous backseat critic of the government), and with the UK's odd relationship to Europe, Major retreated into a verbal and sentimental conservatism, a demand for a return to basic values, and – at his most ridiculous – an evocation of a United Kingdom (he really meant England) "unamendable in all essentials" which would in 50 years' time "still be the country of long shadows on county cricket grounds, warm beer, invincible green suburbs and pools fillers".[6]

Major's failure was the result of the astonishing success of Margaret Thatcher in building a new politics in place of the old postwar consensus. She used ideas (as supplied by Milton Friedman and Friedrich von Hayek) to shift politics, while other politicians in Europe did the same act, but through institutional management via the constraints of the European political order. When these ideas were so obviously triumphant, she lost her political distinctiveness and with it her *raison d'être*. Her logical heir was not so much the unfortunate Major, but Tony Blair, the Labour leader who won a resounding victory in 1997 on an explicitly pro-market platform. As in the Thatcher years, the only credible opposition to this course came from within the ruling party (in this case Labour), and not from the notional parliamentary opposition. Thatcher made the market the central place in politics, and Blair announced that he intended to rule "from the center". That meant the market, and in practice meant a large measure of "Thatcherism".

France's two-year experiment with socialist policies

Valéry Giscard d'Estaing became President of France in 1974 on the death of Georges Pompidou, with an explicit commitment to modernization. The first years of his presidency were overshadowed by the problems created by the oil price shock, and in 1975–76 his Prime Minister, the Gaullist leader Jacques Chirac, tried a Keynesian strategy for growth out of the crisis. A devaluation crisis produced an abrupt change of government and an abandonment of the Keynesian growth approach, together with a shift to the right. Giscard appointed the very orthodox Raymond Barre as Prime Minister, stating that he was choosing "the best economist of France". The new "Barre Plan" looked like a classically liberal stabilization program: a key objective was to keep the exchange rate stable against the German mark, and this was accompanied by tax rises and a more restrictive monetary policy, as well as by a version of an incomes policy that included sanctions against unauthorized wage increases.

The new approach was locked in by the parallel discussions on the establishment of the EMS. Since capital mobility, fixed exchange rates, and an autonomous monetary policy are technically incompatible with each other (they form what economists term an "inconsistent triad"), the effect of combining the external constraint on the exchange rate with capital market liberalization was to make choices very limited for the French government (and its successors). In this sense, it is fair to say, as Philip Gordon and Sophie Meunier conclude, that "the Barre Plan was the precursor to the economic model that after 1983 would form the basic paradigm for all French government, of the Right or the Left, and would help ready the French economy to deal with globalization".[7] But while Thatcher had created a permanent shift through a government that was in place for a long time (and ran through phases in which it was massively unpopular), Giscard and Barre were not in office long enough to make their revolution quite permanent.

In the lead-up to the presidential elections of 1981, the government relaxed the Barre Plan, and inflation increased; but it was not enough to temper the massive unpopularity of austerity. Giscard d'Estaing's bid for a second term of the French presidency failed in May 1981 when he was defeated by François Mitterrand, the socialist candidate, by a relatively narrow margin (51.8 percent to 48.2 percent). The new President called new elections for the National Assembly, which confirmed the shift to the left, with the socialists winning 37.5 percent and the communists 16.2 percent of the vote in the first round. The socialists had an absolute majority of seats in the Assembly, but it had been achieved by an electoral pact with the communists. The new government under Pierre Mauroy included four communist ministers, the first time since 1947 that the Communist Party had participated in government. The US State Department promptly issued a statement in which it said that "the tone and content of our relationship as allies" was affected by the composition of the new French government.

The government began with bold declarations about the reduction of inequality in France. Major industries and banks were nationalized, the minimum wage was increased, social benefits were raised, the working week was reduced, and a fifth week of paid holidays was added. But unemployment continued to rise, and financial markets reacted nervously. The government was obliged to make large payments in compensation for the nationalized assets. Fear of higher and more rigorously enforced taxation prompted a wave of capital flight, which the government responded to with draconian exchange controls. As the external trade balance deteriorated, the franc was devalued within the European ERM in October 1981, in June 1982, and again in March 1983.

The latter crisis was decisive. At this point, the government faced a stark choice between the continuation of expansionary measures and an abandonment of the EMS/ERM membership, and some form of stabilization. On the left of the government, the Minister for Industry and Research, Jean-Pierre Chevènement, wanted to have a flexible exchange rate and ignore Europe. He presented himself as a left-wing Gaullist, committed to the defense of France's national way and thus the principle of the sovereignty of the French people. On the right wing of the government, the Minister of Economy and Finance, Jacques Delors, wanted to solve the French crisis within a European context. Mitterrand himself intervened increasingly on the side of Delors, criticized government bureaucratism and interventionism, and eventually dismissed Chevènement. Together with the third franc devaluation, an austerity package with a forced loan, and increases in taxes on alcohol and tobacco, Delors negotiated a substantial stabilization package not from the International Monetary Fund but from the EC. Mitterrand saw the crisis weeks of March 1983 as a chance to deal with the political uncertainty that had followed 1981, and to end his dependence on communist votes in parliament. He explained what he called "just social rigor" in the following way: "We can profit from all of this to recover. Sometimes one even needs to manufacture a crisis to deal with the situation: think of de Gaulle at Baden-Baden." "To be unpopular," he concluded, "can even be an instrument of popularity."[8] By 1984, the political part of the Mitterrand program had been achieved: the communist ministers left government, and the party rapidly dwindled into an irrelevance in French public life.

For Mitterrand, European linkages were the best way for France to deal with the challenges posed by globalization. The most obvious form of the challenge was a cultural one: in language, and in popular music and films. From 1985 to 1999, the American share of the European market for cinema ticket sales increased from 56 to 70 percent. In 1986, France led the establishment of the Organisation Internationale de la Francophonie to promote the use of the French language and stem the spread of Anglo-American speech. In 1994 the Toubon Law (after Jacques Toubon, Minister of Culture) banned a range of English words, and set quotas on films and radio music: before the passage of the law, four-fifths of the popular music on French radio had been "Anglo-Saxon". Trade law – if it were to be applied against the American cultural challenge – required action at a European level. Resistance to cultural globalization appealed to the French left, but also to the Gaullist right.

In the parliamentary elections of March 1986, the French shift to the right was complete. The two major conservative groupings, the Gaullists and the Giscardien right, won 55 percent of the vote and dominated the National Assembly. This result clearly posed a problem for the Fifth Republic's constitutionally quite vague distribution of power between President and Prime Minister, since Mitterrand had to choose a Prime Minister who could have a parliamentary majority (he appointed the Gaullist leader Jacques Chirac). The "cohabitation" of opposite political tendencies inevitably produced strains. Chirac tried to look as different from the President as possible, and took up "Thatcherite" issues, including the flexibilization of labor laws, tougher anti-crime laws, and privatization. The nationalizations of 1981–83, and some of those of the immediate postwar period, were reversed in a 200-billion-franc privatization drive that was planned for five years, but mostly realized over the course of just two years. Sixty-five companies were listed that had a majority public ownership, which were to be transferred into private hands before 1991. The initial sales included Saint Gobain (glass); the banks Paribas and Crédit National de France, which had been nationalized in 1982; the Compagnie Générale d'Électricité; and a television channel. They were acutely controversial: the socialist leader called them a "scandal", while Raymond Barre claimed the government was establishing a "political–financial oligarchy".[9] But by the end of the process, the number of share owners in France had risen from 1.5 million to 6.5 million.[10]

When Mitterrand won a second term as President (1988) in a run-off election, he called legislative elections, in which the left had a very small lead. The new government under the Prime Ministership of the reformist socialist Michel Rocard halted the privatization program, but also promised not to carry out new nationalizations.

German conservatism

The social–liberal coalition in Germany, which had been led since 1974 by Helmut Schmidt, was torn apart by the world recession at the beginning of the 1980s, at the same time as Giscard and Barre's grip on power softened. The Shah's recession thus shaped not only the initial years of Thatcherism, but also the decisive political shifts of Germany and France. The largest coalition partner in the German government, the social democrats, were divided about economic and security issues; on the right of the coalition, the much smaller liberal party (FDP) pressed for less Keynesianism and a more orthodox approach to budgetary policy.

On the left, the SPD was divided about security policy. Schmidt had been influential in formulating NATO's "twin-track strategy" of negotiating with Moscow about an arms agreement while modernizing NATO's own missile system. In the late 1970s, during the Carter presidency, he had been worried about the depth and durability of the US commitment to European defense, and saw the stationing of upgraded missiles as a way of locking the United States to the European countries. When the US Cruise and Pershing missiles were actually stationed, however, many Germans were worried that shorter-range missiles might present a security threat rather than a security enhancement. They apparently undermined the credibility of "Mutually Assured Destruction", since their use might make a limited nuclear exchange in Europe possible in which neither the Soviet nor the American homeland would be affected.

The counter-cultural protest movement of '68 had been profoundly shaken by what it saw as the "German autumn" of 1977, which ended its hopes for emancipatory revolution. The grey Bonn Republic was there to stay. But the missile issue and the parallel increase in environmental consciousness in the wake of the oil crises, which demonstrated the fragility of dependence on finite natural resources, produced a new political movement. The Greens thus developed out of one part of the legacy of '68. They created a federal Green Party in January 1980 and managed to achieve sizable votes in regional and local elections. Initially the Greens were both radical and eclectic: they allowed simultaneous membership of other political parties in large part in order not to exclude communists. A major feature of their platform was security policy, in which they demanded an immediate withdrawal from NATO.

Economic policy was also highly contested. Could Germany afford another round of an oil price shock? The left wanted to attack unemployment by higher public spending. At the SPD congress in April 1982, the party demanded more workers' participation, more economic planning, reduced working hours (in order to distribute employment more widely), and a wealth tax to pay for job creation. The FDP, however, saw in high levels of government taxation and spending a threat to Germany's internationally competitive position. The FDP Economics Minister Count Otto Lambsdorff prepared, at Schmidt's insistence, a formal paper in which he set out the basis for a recovery program which included big cuts in spending. The SPD attacked the proposal as "Manchesterite liberalism".

Schmidt demanded that the FDP ministers support the government or be dismissed. They resigned in September 1982. In the Bundestag the FDP, together with the Christian Democrats, proposed a "constructive vote of no confidence" in which the Christian Democratic leader, Helmut Kohl, was elected Chancellor. The shift in government from left to right thus took place without an election, although Kohl dissolved the Bundestag prematurely and won a striking victory in March 1983. The CDU/CSU (Christian Social Union, the Bavarian sister party of the CDU) had 48.8 percent of the vote, and the SPD 38.2 percent. The Greens entered the Bundestag with 5.6 percent of the vote. The FDP remained in the government, with Hans-Dietrich Genscher as Deputy Chancellor and Foreign Minister providing for a broad continuity in foreign and security policy.

Kohl at this time was speaking openly of a German "psychological crisis", in which the Greens and the media were being used in a Soviet campaign to separate Germany from the West.[11] He wanted to roll back the legacy of the 1960s, and started to speak about a "spiritual and moral turnaround" (*geistig– moralische Wende*). To him, the situation resembled the first half of the 1950s, when the international situation had been tense and the SPD had resisted western integration. He based his style very self-consciously on that of Adenauer, whom he thought of as a political model. References to him as "Adenauer's grandson" he found largely flattering.

But Kohl's leadership until 1989 was largely understated: he found it easiest to preserve his position by letting his political opponents, many of whom were in his own party, underestimate him. This made the first part of what later became known as the "Kohl era" appear rather unimpressive. Indeed, its most conspicuous feature was a run of foreign policy gaffes that followed from Kohl's only very gradual appreciation of the extent to which international responses to the Federal Republic were largely shaped by the way in which it was perceived to be handling its problematic historical legacy. The most striking misjudgment of the center-right government involved the staging of a Second World War remembrance ceremony to which Ronald Reagan had been invited at Bitburg, where members of the SS as well as German Wehrmacht soldiers were buried.

There was also a more general problem in the 1980s about the German perception of what could happen in the present, and a deliberate self-limitation that followed from the logic of Genscherist foreign policy. The legacy of the post-1945 division was almost universally interpreted as a complete freezing of the Cold War frontiers, since any move would raise the national issue in an uncomfortable way and would disrupt the consensus culture of the German political establishment. Kohl underestimated the radicalism of the new foreign policy approach in Moscow (and initially insulted Gorbachev by comparing him to the Nazi propagandist Joseph Goebbels). In the autumn of 1989 he was taken by surprise by the very rapid development of events in the GDR.

Genscherism

Hans-Dietrich Genscher (born 1927) was a member of the German liberal party (FDP), and Foreign Minister from 1974 to 1992. He managed to transcend the rather sterile debate in German foreign policy making between exponents of *Gaullist* and *Atlanticist* principles. His central insight was a development of a key element of post-1949 German foreign policy, that the legacy of the Nazi era meant that Germany could not assert power in the conventional way that political *realists* would like.

Instead, Germany could and should be influential through multilateral institutions. These afforded opportunities for influence that were especially great given Germany's economic strength. This meant chiefly the EC, to which as a result Germany was willing to be by far the largest net contributor. It also meant not making particular German initiatives with regard to Russia or eastern Europe, but working in the multilateral framework set by the Helsinki process and the Organization for Security and Cooperation in Europe. Other institutions were also used as a way of trying to achieve Germany's objectives: for instance, during the economic problems of the late 1970s, in the wake of the second oil price shock, Germany wanted to reduce the flow of Turkish guest workers to Germany and to stabilize the Turkish government. It did this chiefly by intense pressure through the Paris-based Organisation for Economic Co-operation and Development and through the International Monetary Fund.

The Genscherite vision bound Germany very firmly to Europe, and had major implications in the reordering of the geopolitical map in 1989–90. Helmut Kohl, the Chancellor, sometimes doubted that Genscherite measures would provide quick successes, and kept some initiatives (notably the Ten-Point Plan for German Confederation in November 1989) to himself. The vision that German unification was best handled in a European context, which Kohl eventually shared, led to German willingness to surrender its monetary sovereignty and subordinate the Bundesbank to a European Central Bank. It also made Germany the most consistent advocate in the 1990s of the eastern enlargement of the European Union, in large part to build a stable environment around Germany and to ensure that Germany would not have the problematical position of defending the eastern frontier of a rich Europe against a poor Europe. The two critical moves in European politics in the post-Cold War era, monetary union and eastern enlargement, are thus the outcome of the orientation of German policy on Genscherist lines.

At the same time, Kohl mastered the art of compromises in domestic policy, built up an extensive "system", and used his ordinariness quite successfully to maintain Germany's consensus-driven political order. Schmidt had alienated many by being too clever and sharp. Kohl had a boa constrictor quality of soothing the opposition into inaction and sloth. His most conspicuous political achievement was the consolidation of the budget, achieved by exactly the opposite of the methods of Margaret Thatcher: a persistent and non-confrontational search for compromise. This ensured that Germany was fiscally quite well prepared to meet the initial strain of German unification in 1990, but the legacy of the approach frustrated a deeper or more structural reform in the 1990s.

In 1987, the government coalition was re-elected. By the end of the 1980s, West Germany had become a very stable country. When George Bush became President in 1989, he made his first European trip to Germany rather than to a United Kingdom still intensely proud of its "special relationship". Bush's speech in Mainz referred to the changing geopolitical system and to Gorbachev's discussion of the "common European home": "There cannot be," Bush said, "a common European home until all within it are free to move from room to room." Europe would then be "whole and free". By this stage, many policymakers in Washington detected ways in which changes in the Soviet Union would alter European political affairs, while their counterparts in Bonn continued to believe unshakably in the continued solidity of the status quo.

The European framework

By the first half of the 1980s, the project of European integration looked as if it had run out of steam. Many commentators referred to "Eurosclerosis". It was "relaunched" in 1985–86 by the Single European Act.

A European Commission White Paper of 1985, largely the result of an initiative by the British Commissioner Lord Cockfield, set out 279 specific proposals which would create "an area without internal frontiers in which the free movement of goods, persons, services and capital is ensured". Institutionally, this was the most important step in promoting a general process of liberalization. It rested on the recognition that a rigorous Europe-wide standardization would provoke resentment and nationalist backlashes. There was in every member country a press eager to circulate stories about Brussels absurdities: attempts to regulate the normal size of apples, to restrict the use of traditional names, and so forth. These could be largely avoided by the application of the principle of a mutual recognition of standards. The resulting Single European Act extended the implications of a decision made by the European Court of Justice in 1979 relating to Cassis de Dijon. This dealt with a French liqueur, which was not allowed to be offered for sale in Germany on the grounds that it contained too low an alcohol content to be classed as a liqueur. The court argued that the principle of an economic community involved the possibility of exporting to other countries a product that conformed to quality and safety standards in the country in which it was produced. Thus, in probably the best known and most controversial example, Germany could not exclude British or Belgian beer because it did not conform to the Bavarian "purity law" (of 1516) banning additives, since the United Kingdom and Belgium had different standards on beer production. Similarly, Italy could not ban German-made spaghetti made from grains that would have been impermissible in Italy. The 1986 Act thus systematized the practice of the toleration of different standards systems. After 1986, many patterns of consumption changed quite dramatically: "Irish" pubs became the rage in France, Germany, and Italy; the British began to consume Stella Artois and also non-EC beers like the American Budweiser (treated as a luxury in Europe). Such a procedure greatly reduced the amount of new legislation required to liberalize trade within the EC.

The Single European Act was also accompanied by institutional measures intended to shift some of the power from nation-states to the European institutions. The 1966 Luxembourg Compromise had created a practice by which any one state could block proposals by saying that important or vital national interests were at stake, with the result that major issues could be held to ransom. With the further enlargement of the EC, such a process threatened to create a block on legislation. Indeed, the Single European Act was itself held up for a time, while Greece extracted a substantial package of Community aid in return for Greek agreement. After the implementation of the Single European Act, issues connected to the realization of an internal market (which could be interpreted quite expansively) could be determined by qualified majority voting, and could no longer be vetoed.

The new single market, which was given a concrete timetable, was widely interpreted (not least by the Commission) as a result of a new dynamism that came when Jacques Delors moved from French politics to chair the Commission as a successor to the Luxembourgeois Gaston Thorne. Delors was indeed exceptionally active and skillful; but, as the political scientist Andrew Moravcsik has pointed out, the new move also corresponded closely to the national interests of the major participants.[12] Thatcher and British business liked the liberalization agenda, and were even prepared to swallow the majority voting as a necessary price to pay; Kohl took on the Adenauer mantle of European solutions to German problems, and Germany would be a major beneficiary of a wider market for its powerful export industries; while Mitterrand could use Europe as a way of extricating himself from the apparent abandonment of socialist principles in the traumatic crisis of 1983. Economics and politics were here closely intertwined.

A new high-technology Europe held – especially for Mitterrand – the attraction of being a counterweight to the United States, which had tried to use its dominance over technology to dictate foreign policy to the Europeans. Europe looked like an instrument that could stem cultural globalization and Americanization: for instance, by trade measures such as the application of quotas for music, films, or other cultural products. Especially in France, the European dynamic was explained in terms of a need to stand up to US hegemony. For instance, after the imposition of martial law in Poland (December 1981), the United States wanted to apply trade sanctions on the Soviet Union, and in particular urged European states not to offer subsidized credits for the construction of a gas pipeline in the Soviet Union that would eventually be paid off by the export of Soviet natural gas. The gas pipeline raised what seemed for Washington a crucial issue of energy dependence: it offered a permanent way, in a world in which energy was subject to politicized control, for Moscow to control Western European policy. On the other hand, for Europe in the short term the orders looked attractive as a way out of the recession of the early 1980s; and they also seemed to solve the issue of energy dependence on the Middle East. By the mid-1980s, Mitterrand began to reflect on his political legacy. "I will have been," he said,

> the President of France's entry into modern economic competition. People won't touch my social achievement. The gains of the left will survive me. I will have transformed fundamental facts about our life in society. France will have contributed greatly to give back élan to Europe and will have retaken its role as a defender of the Third World.[13]

Europe and European integration were driven by an increased concern of European politicians to play a new role in world politics and to move away from the too-powerful embrace of American interests. That new self-assertion was the part of the "European idea" of which they were proudest. At the same time, the push to European integration was also driven in equal measure by a growing sense of the helplessness of politicians and politics in the face of big global forces (such as the oil crises and the oil-induced recession of the early 1980s). The politicians were not so proud of this, but they knew quite well that the European dynamic was born out of the bankruptcy of the conventional and accustomed politics of the postwar world. That was uncomfortable.

Notes

1 Peter Hennessy, *The Prime Minister: The Office and its Holders since 1945*, London: Allen Lane, 2000, pp. 252, 401.
2 Quoted in Peter Jenkins, *Mrs. Thatcher's Revolution: The Ending of the Socialist Era*, London: Jonathan Cape, 1987, p. 57.
3 *The Times*, March 30, 1981.
4 For instance, Oliver Letwin, with a Foreword by John Redwood, *Privatising the World: A Study of International Privatisation in Theory and Practice*, London: Cassell, 1988, p. 14.
5 Jacques Attali, *Verbatim, Vol. I, Chronique des Années 1981–1986*, Paris: Fayard, 1993, p. 763.
6 *The Independent*, April 25, 1993, p. 24.
7 Philip H. Gordon and Sophie Meunier, *The French Challenge: Adapting to Globalization*, Washington, DC: Brookings Institution, 2001, p. 18.
8 Attali, *Verbatim*, pp. 413, 416.
9 Letwin, *Privatising*, p. 62.
10 Gordon and Meunier, *French Challenge*, p. 23.
11 For instance, Attali, *Verbatim*, p. 720.
12 See Andrew Moravcsik, *The Choice for Europe: Social Purpose and State Power from Messina to Maastricht*, Ithaca, NY: Cornell University Press, 1998, p. 317.
13 Attali, *Verbatim*, p. 771 (February 21, 1985 entry).

12 Malta and communism
1989 and the restoration of Europe

In the 1980s, in the aftermath of the Solidarność movement and its crushing through General Jaruzelski's imposition of martial law, Poland had been the center of a wide-ranging debate, about the stability of communism, but also about the stability of European geopolitics. Was a division between East and West inevitable? Poles, Czechs, and Hungarians now vigorously protested about the label "East European" and insisted that they were "Europeans" or at least central Europeans. Oddly, few people connected the discussions about ideas and about geography. Even many sympathizers decided that central Europe was different, that Poland would not generate a landslide or a seismic shock for the whole of the East, and that Polish affairs could not easily be translated into Russian politics.

The Soviet system looked quite secure, bolstered by the country's large natural resources (especially oil and gas) in an age in which global attention focused on energy reserves and the politics of energy. In the event, however, there clearly was a seismic connection between the central European glacis and the Soviet heartland. It was perceived quite directly by those Soviet leaders – in particular Andropov and Gorbachev – who had some personal experience of the central European debate (a later Russian leader, Vladimir Putin, also spent a formative phase as a KGB officer in East Germany). The connection between Russia and central Europe lay in the intellectual challenge to the doctrine about the irreversibility of history, communism, and Soviet control (the Brezhnev doctrine), as well as through the way in which any change to the status of East Germany raised the German question and with it the issue of the old division of the continent. Mikhail Gorbachev repeatedly insisted on the idea that both East and West lived in "our common European house".

Gorbachev

While Solidarność grew, the Soviet position looked quite strong. The large oil and gas resources, and the contracts with west European firms to build pipelines in return for access to Soviet fuel, appeared as a great advantage in the wake of the two oil price hikes of the 1970s. The new power of petroleum, *the* major geopolitical fact of the 1970s, clearly benefited the Soviet

Union. It could also use that power in its relations with the satellite empire, since the delivery of energy at below-world-market prices created a dependency. But the high energy consumption characteristic of Soviet production that formed the basis for the central European dependency was hardly an economic advantage. Even official Soviet figures show the extent of the stagnation of the Soviet economy. While growth in the eighth Five-Year Plan period (1966–70) had been recorded at 7.5 percent, in the ninth (1971–75) it was 5.8 percent, and by the early 1980s 2.5 percent. A prominent Soviet sociologist, Tatiana Zaslavskaia of the Novosibirsk Institute of Sociology, produced a devastating account of the hollowing out of the Soviet industrial economy in the early 1980s. As industrial production became more complex, it became impossible to manage by conventional means. She wrote: "The structure of the national economy long ago crossed the threshold of complexity when it was still possible to regulate it from one common center." Perverse incentives abounded. "There often arises a paradoxical situation whereby the opportunity for a positive show of initiative by the workers is reduced by multiple administrative restrictions to naught, while the spectrum of anti-social modes of behavior remains rather broad."[1] Zaslavskaia later became a key figure in attempts at reform in the later 1980s.

The full catastrophe of the Soviet gerontocracy became apparent in the 1980s. Brezhnev died in November 1982. He was replaced as General Secretary of the Communist Party by Yuri Andropov, a reformist KGB boss in the Beria mold. Andropov began, but did not complete, a purge of Brezhnev's protégés, dismissing 19 of 84 ministers and a fifth of the regional party bosses. He had been Soviet ambassador in Budapest at the time of the 1956 uprising. On reaching the highest position in Soviet politics, he needed kidney dialysis, then quickly had a heart attack, and died in 1984. His successor, Konstantin Chernenko, was 73 when appointed; already very sick with emphysema, he wheezed heavily as he spoke. On his death in 1985, the Politburo chose Mikhail Gorbachev, who had been groomed by Andropov, and whom Andropov had tried to appoint as his immediate successor. Like Andropov, he knew something about central Europe. As a student in Moscow University, he had been a close friend of a devout Czech communist, Zdeněk Mlynář, who later became a leading figure in the Prague Spring. In 1967 Mlynář went to the Soviet Union again and visited Gorbachev. In 1971, Gorbachev had been the youngest official to be elected to the Central Committee, had become known as a protégé of the reforming secret police head Andropov, and in the 1970s had already installed modern Scandinavian furniture in his Central Committee office. In March 1985, Gorbachev stated in his acceptance speech as General Secretary: "One of the basic tasks of the internal policy of the party is the further perfecting and development of democracy."[2] But it was unclear what this meant, in that "democracy" understood as the rule of the working class was at the heart of the Soviet theory anyway. In the past – especially in the 1930s – "democracy" had been the slogan under which party purges were carried out. Later, Gorbachev tried to explain how he had evolved a plan for multi-party democracy as early as 1988; but again, it was not clear what this might mean in actual constitutional practice. Some East European states, notably the GDR and Hungary, had always had non-communist parties affiliated with the ruling party in a national alliance.[3]

The first act of economic reform was an anti-alcohol campaign, launched in 1985, which involved the punishment of officials who drank on the job, and the limitation of the sale of spirits to between 2 p.m. and 7 p.m. It was designed to deal with the increasingly obvious costs of alcoholism: absenteeism, poor-quality work, and a deterioration of public health. In practice, like Prohibition in interwar America, it produced an expansion of the criminal class, as well as shortages of sugar and anti-freeze (both used in home distilling).

The impulse to innovate more came from the mishandling of the explosion at the nuclear power reactor at Chernobyl in Ukraine in April 1986. The first information about the catastrophe came to the USSR from foreign radio transmitters, the BBC and Radio Free Europe. The Soviet media gave no information about the extent of the contamination and the spread of a radioactive cloud. The war in Afghanistan, in which 11,897 Soviet troops died as a result of military action (there were another 2,556 non-combat losses), was also veiled in secrecy, and was the cause of increasing resentment among Russian conscripts and their families. Soviet Asian and Moslem troops were on the whole not deployed in Afghanistan, an indication of doubts about their reliability.

In July 1986, Gorbachev promised "a real revolution in all relationships in society, in the minds and hearts of the people, in their psychology and understanding of the contemporary periods, and, first of all, in solving all the tasks set by technical–economic progress".[4] He initiated a dramatic reform program, built around two principles: glasnost (openness), and perestroika (restructuring). He released the dissident scientist Andrei Sakharov from exile in Gorkii (previously, and again after 1990 Nizhny Novgorod).

Apparently, he wanted to spread his reform principles to central Europe, where the old hardliners were skeptical. One German Politburo member, Kurt Hager, is reported to have said that "we don't need to repaint our house just because our neighbor has new wallpaper". The GDR security apparatus now banned Soviet publications such as the reformist *Sputnik*. In Berlin in October 1989, to commemorate the fortieth anniversary of the founding of the GDR, Gorbachev administered a very public rebuke to the East German leadership, saying that "he who comes too late is punished by history".

Jaruzelski

Of all the central European leaders, General Jaruzelski was most in agreement with Gorbachev's thinking, and believed that it created more room in which a new social consensus could be established. Martial law was gradually relaxed, and in 1986 the Polish government declared an amnesty and released all the 225 remaining political prisoners. Throughout 1987, the government wrestled with the problem of how to make economic reform acceptable with the population. It launched opinion surveys and even a referendum, which were designed to show that some price increases (i.e. economic pain) were necessary as part of a reform process. In late 1988, the government lifted some restrictions on private firms. But price rises generated new waves of labor unrest, and in April 1989 the government relegalized Solidarność. Its representatives now sat round a "Round Table", already instituted in February 1989, and Solidarność was allowed to contest a limited number of seats in a parliamentary election. The main Solidarność election poster showed a transformed picture of the American Western movie actor Gary Cooper with the text "High Noon June 4, 1989" (the date of the election). When the showdown came, the government lost all the seats that were contested. At the meeting of the Communist Party Central Committee the following day, the youthful Chairman of the social–political committee, Aleksander Kwaśniewski, asked: "Is it a passive resistance? It's well known that also party members were crossing out our candidates."[5] The party had to surrender its grip on power. A Solidarność-led government with Tadeusz Mazowiecki as Prime Minister was installed in power. Quite bloodlessly, as a product of a long stalemate about the management of economic reform, communist rule had ended.

1989

Hungarian reform moved closely in step with Poland, and for similar reasons. Hungary had adopted a gradual economic liberalization from the 1970s, allowed the establishment of small-scale private enterprises, and encouraged the inflow of foreign capital; and, like Poland, ran into a debt crisis in the early 1980s. It tried to tackle the crisis by joining the IMF, and was acutely worried that the Soviet Union might try to restrict this assertion of economic independence of the Comecon countries. One of the subsequent post-communist Prime Ministers of Hungary, Péter Medgyessy, was employed in the secret service with the task of stopping "foreign powers" (i.e. the Soviet Union) from interfering with Hungary's application for membership. But as in Poland in the late 1980s, the reforms reached a stalling point, where further economic change could not take place without some fundamental political concessions. So the Hungarian government began with some acts of political symbolism: an announcement in early 1989 that it would no longer celebrate the anniversary of the Bolshevik Revolution, but would rather commemorate the national uprising of 1848–49; the solemn reburial of Imre Nagy on Heroes' Square in a ceremony designed by the architect László Rajk, the son of the communist leader martyred in a Stalinist show trial; and the dismantling of the barbed wire at the "Iron Curtain", the frontier with Austria. This was probably intended more as a gesture of a new humanitarianism than as an act which would profoundly reshape communist politics. President George Bush was presented with a souvenir piece of frontier wire when he visited in July 1989.

Discussions of reform were also evidently tolerated by Moscow. In March 1989, in discussions in Moscow, Gorbachev demonstrated his abandonment of the Brezhnev doctrine by telling the Hungarian Communist Party General Secretary, Károly Grósz, that "today we have to preclude the possibility of repeated foreign intervention in the internal affairs of socialist countries".[6] In September and October, the Hungarian reforms went further: the Communist Party changed its name, and the government promised genuine multi-party elections, paid reparation to the victims of the 1956 revolution, disbanded the Workers' Guard, and legalized strikes.

The elections were held in March and April 1990, and in May the new National Assembly elected a veteran dissident, the writer Árpád Göncz, as interim President. The first session of parliament stressed the historical legitimacy of Hungarian parliamentarism and the Hungarian nation. The Speaker of the 1946–47 parliament gave an address; Otto Habsburg, the son of the last King of Hungary, attended. József Antall, the leader of the previous opposition movement the Hungarian Democratic Forum, was appointed as Prime Minister of a government with ministers from the Christian Democratic People's Party and the Smallholders' Party.

The end of the Hungarian barbed wire, though a primarily symbolic gesture, had quite unintended consequences, as at first a handful and then increasingly large numbers of East German vacationers in Hungary (a popular tourist spot) abandoned their cars and other possessions, and walked across the fields – avoiding border patrols – to the West. In August 1989, around 5,000 in all crossed the frontier. This movement attracted a great deal of attention, and the Hungarian government for humanitarian reasons (but also thinking that it would facilitate credits from West Germany) on September 11 allowed East Germans to cross the frontier legally. In the first three days with no travel restrictions, 15,000 Germans left. The GDR responded by canceling permission for its citizens to visit Hungary, but they began to detect new opportunities and crowded into the buildings and grounds of the West German embassies in Warsaw and Prague.

There already existed widespread discontent in the GDR after local elections in May, in which the official reports indicated a vote of 98.95 percent and a turnout of 98.77 percent. But independent civil rights groups, mostly affiliated with the Protestant Church, produced larger figures for abstentions in major cities. After the Hungarian exodus, East Germans went onto the streets, at first in relatively small numbers. On October 2, 15,000 participated in a Monday evening procession in Leipzig, and one week later there were 70,000, protesting for reform ("We want to stay in the GDR") and in support of Gorbachev and his rebuke to the regime of Erich Honecker. Honecker was quickly replaced by Egon Krenz, who had previously been the head of the party's youth movement. By November 4, there were 1 million people in East Berlin on the streets demanding free elections. For a time, some feared that East German security forces would use violence, on the model of the brutal suppression of the Chinese pro-democracy movement in June in Tiananmen Square. But the more protesters went on the street, the less likely such an outcome became (and the greater the emphasis of the Soviet military in East Germany on the need for a non-violent solution). As in the early 1950s, the East German security forces tried to devise an innovative solution, and the intelligence chief Marcus Wolf addressed the crowd in Berlin on November 4, and asked – like other intellectuals who had been protected by the regime – for a reformed socialism as a mid-way alternative between communism and capitalism. The novelist Christa Wolf (no relation to Marcus) asked, in a variant of an old anti-war slogan: "Imagine there was socialism and nobody ran away." But Marcus Wolf was booed and whistled down by the crowd.

On November 9, in a press conference announcing the lifting of travel restrictions, as an afterthought the Politburo member replied to a question by a British journalist and said yes, East Germans could cross the Berlin Wall. The surprised border guards were overwhelmed by the spontaneous surge of people through the crossing points. In the subsequent days and weeks, millions of East Germans went to the West, mostly to visit and to collect token "reception money" provided by the West German government. But 340,000 went permanently to the West. Despite all the talk of West German Chancellor Helmut Kohl of a move to confederative structures (in a Ten-Point Program he devised as a response to the crisis), and the attempt of the East German regime to present a different face, it looked as if East Germany would gradually be emptied out.

These central European political transformations were not independent, but interacted with each other. The German events, themselves a product of the slow move to change in Hungary and the slightly quicker move in Poland, touched off another peaceful revolution, in Prague (dubbed quickly the "Velvet Revolution"). Street protests initially led to the dismissal of the General Secretary of the Communist Party, Miloš Jakeš, who had succeeded the veteran Gustáv Husák in 1987 (Husák had remained as President). A new wave of street protests began in early 1989. On November 24, 1989, Dubček, the symbol of the Czech '68, appeared at a rally of 250,000 people in Wenceslas Square in Prague. On November 27, Czech workers began a general strike. At the beginning of December, a reformist communist government was put in place, but the opposition movement wanted to go beyond reformism: after more street demonstrations, an all-party government with a non-communist majority was established on December 10. Husák resigned, and in his place the dissident playwright – and the best-known opposition leader – Václav Havel was elected as President. In his New Year's address he declared that "The state, which calls itself a state of the working people, is humiliating and exploiting the workers." The new Foreign Minister, Jilí Dienstbier, had been condemned to work as a stoker in the aftermath of 1968.

Time seemed to be accelerating as one regime collapse followed another. The journalist Timothy Garton-Ash summed it up with a widely repeated line: "In Poland it took ten years, in Hungary ten months, in East Germany ten weeks; perhaps in Czechoslovakia it will take ten days."[7]

The day after the fall of the Berlin Wall, the Bulgarian Communist Party deposed the veteran leader Todor Zhivkov, who had been at the helm since 1954, and one month later the Central Committee announced that it would renounce its automatic right to take the "leading role" in state and society. Zhivkov's successor criticized the "feudal dictatorship" of nepotism and corruption. Zhivkov had at one time promoted his energetic and intelligent daughter as Minister of Culture, but after being heartbroken by her death at the age of 38, had in 1989 tried to promote his much less gifted son as a successor. On December 14, 50,000 demonstrators in Sofia demanded immediate elections.

Zhivkov was the only eastern European leader to face a regular trial in the aftermath of the collapse of communism. The main charge was corruption and embezzlement. The 14-month trial did not touch on his role in the Stalinist terror, or on the ethnic persecution of Turks in the 1980s. Zhivkov was sentenced to a seven-year prison term, but never actually went to prison.

In only one country was the revolution violent, and it is in fact doubtful how genuine a revolution that was. In Budapest, Warsaw, Leipzig, Berlin, and Prague good-natured and cheerful crowd scenes accompanied, and pushed forward, political change. In Bucharest, such scenes resembled more a melodramatic opera (in fact, there are parallels to Wagner's *Rienzi*, in which the tribune of the people, encircled in his palace by a hostile crowd, tried to escape in concealment but was recognized by the crowd by his bejeweled fingers). To use Garton-Ash's time-collapse notion, the collapse of the Romanian regime took ten minutes in a dramatic scene staged on December 21, 1989, in front of the gigantesque Palace of the People.

The Romanian revolution began with ethnic unrest in the western city of Timişoara, where the large Hungarian population – inspired by political change in Hungary – began to organize. The secret police (Securitate) mistreated and deported a Hungarian pastor, Laszlo Tokes, and in the unrest that followed, killed a substantial number of people (December 16–17). In the end, 73 were identified as having been killed in the unrest in Timişoara, but the initial press reports were much higher. The East German news agency AND immediately reported the death of "up to 4,000 people" in Timişoara, and the enormous exaggerations later led some commentators (such as the French postmodern philosopher Jean Baudrillard) to the incorrect conclusion that this was a "virtual" massacre, made by television, which had never existed in reality. Nicolae Ceauşescu gave a reassuring television interview to the government-run station on December 20, saying that the Securitate had behaved with "great patience and restraint" in their defense of "the homeland, the people, and socialist achievements". The next day, he addressed a large crowd, mostly assembled in the usual way (the Securitate closing a factory and instructing the workers to demonstrate for the government), and carrying the usual slogans: "Ceauşescu and Romania, our pride and respect!"; "Long live the Romanian Communist Party!" In the course of his address, Ceauşescu was handed a note stating that the Minister of Defense, General Vasile Milea, had committed suicide. Parts of the crowd started to jeer at the Ceauşescus (he was accompanied on the balcony by his wife, Elena, who was also Deputy Prime Minister). They looked surprised and confused. Elena tried to deal with the protest by "economic concessions", a pay rise of 100 lei. But the unrest continued, and the Ceauşescus fled by helicopter and car, both of which broke down. They were tried at the military base at Tirgoviste on December 25 in a preposterous show trial, parts of which were televised subsequently. The prosecutor, General Gica Popa, who killed himself (or was "suicided") in March 1990, read out a list of accusations: "acts that are incompatible with human dignity and social thinking . . . genocide . . . the destruction of buildings and state institutions, undermining the national economy". The trial looked like an update for the television age of the trials of the Stalinist era. Ceauşescu refused to answer the questions and said: "I will not answer you putschists." When the prosecutor talked about 34 casualties in the Palace Square, Elena Ceauşescu said, "Look, and they are calling that genocide." The couple were shot immediately afterwards, and the picture released to the media. Immediately after the drama of the Palace Square, figures from the old regime – Ion Iliescu, Petre Roman, Dumitru Mazilu, Silviu Brucan, and General Nicolae Militaru – appeared on the state television and called themselves the Front of National Salvation.

The events in Romania focused Europe-wide attention on the secret police, and in January Berlin crowds invaded the secret police (Stasi) headquarters in the Normannenstraße, where the last security agents were still busily shredding documentation. The failure of the Communist Party to deal with the secret police cost it its last shred of legitimacy. But the issue continued to fester as a sore on even the new politics of the last days of the GDR. In December a provisional all-party grouping, called the Round Table after the Polish precedent, promised free elections, which were held in March 1990. They produced a victory for those parties supporting a speedy union with West Germany. The first SPD leader of the East, Ibrahim Böhme, had to resign before the elections after revelations of his past as an agent. The CDU, which won the elections largely because it seemed the surest way to quick unification with the West, was led by Lothar de Maizière, who became the first elected Minister-President of the GDR, but was also soon discredited by revelations about his Stasi contacts. The Minister-President of Brandenburg, Manfred Stolpe, also faced very serious accusations, but continued as Minister-President for ten years.

The West German Chancellor, Helmut Kohl, who had been the major feature of the eastern CDU's election campaign, moved very quickly on the unification issue. He promised a monetary union at the rate of one western mark to each eastern mark, rather than the lower rate that the economic experts in the central bank preferred. The monetary union came into effect on July 1, and immediately made East Germans better off but in the longer term condemned many to unemployment because eastern industry was uncompetitive at the exchange level chosen.

The move to German union raised all kinds of problems at the international level. An obvious problem was that there was now a European Community country in a monetary and economic union with a non-member. The two German states were members of different alliance systems, NATO and the Warsaw Pact, both of which had originally, at least in part, been conceived to contain German expansionism. But it was increasingly clear that German unity was being made on the ground, by the protests in the East, by the vote of the East German people, and by the stampede to the West. International politics would have to react to those facts.

The unification of Germany was the major geopolitical change that followed the collapse of communism. It became a possibility (or even, some thought, an inevitability) in November 1989, and immediately produced a great deal of worry internationally as well as domestically. Both the French and British leaders tried actively to block German integration. Margaret Thatcher held a seminar with distinguished British and American historians in which her adviser minuted all the dangers that flowed from Germany's alleged national characteristics: "angst, aggressiveness, assertiveness, bullying, egotism, inferiority complex, sentimentality".[8] It was not just a question of the Nazi past: "The way in which the Germans currently used their elbows and threw their weight around in the European Community suggested that a lot had still not changed."

One of the points made at this seminar was that Kohl had given the "wrong signals" in handling the Polish issue. He had repeatedly insisted that a united Germany could constitutionally not be bound by the 1970 Warsaw Treaty (in which Willy Brandt had accepted the Oder–Neisse line). Such a stance inevitably generated uncertainty and hostility. To critics, he explained that he did not want the theme of frontier revision to be used by the radical right in Germany; but the studied ambiguities of Kohl made Germany and the German position look potentially threatening.

In these circumstances, the idea of NATO as "dual containment" looked increasingly attractive. A decoupled and unbound Germany would be more threatening than a Germany that was still locked into the western security alliance. But this might be interpreted as a humiliation of the Soviet Union, and for a long time it appeared unlikely that the Soviet Union would accept it. The German Foreign Minister prepared plans in which only part of Germany would be in NATO. In discussions in the White House in Washington on May 31, 1990, Gorbachev agreed – to the consternation of his staff, who were briefed to push for a non-NATO Germany, and to the surprise of the American delegation also – when President George Bush said: "You and I seem to agree that nations can choose their own alliances."[9] Many Russians interpreted Gorbachev's concession as a national humiliation.

French President François Mitterrand was outraged by Helmut Kohl's Ten-Point Plan for German unity, and told the Germans that there was a risk of falling back to the world of 1913 – in other words to the Great Power conflicts that had led to the First World War. Kohl gave in to French pressure and agreed at a meeting in Strasbourg on December 5, 1989, to concrete plans to hold an inter-governmental conference that would prepare for a European Union (Kohl would initially have preferred to defer the conference). France wanted to be sure that German unity was embedded firmly in a European process. Three days later, at one of the critical meetings to discuss the shape of the post-Cold War world, Kohl told US Secretary of State James Baker that Germany would be obliged, as a condition for French consent to unification, to give up its currency, and that the move was opposed by the powerful Bundesbank and would "hurt German interests". Nevertheless, Kohl saw the move as necessary since "Germany needs friends" in Europe. In consequence, and referring to this conversation, many Germans – especially German conservatives – have seen the Euro as from the beginning a concession to France, ceding monetary control from a powerful Bundesbank that in practice in the EMS dictated the conditions of European monetary policy, to a European central bank, in which the German influence would be watered down, and the German vote equal to that of very small member states such as Malta (later, with the expansion of the monetary union, a rotating voting mechanism meant that at some moments the German representative did not even have a vote). Some interpreters have seen this incident as a new version of the betrayal theory that poisoned German democracy in the 1920s with the view that Germany had not been legitimately defeated in the First World War, but that German interests had been "stabbed in the back" by domestic politicians. Kohl was responsible in this view for a key abdication of German interests.

Interpreting Kohl's statement is not easy, and it should probably not be taken at face value. Kohl wanted to impress on the US administration the sacrifice that Germany was undertaking. Some influential Germans, including the President of the Bundesbank Helmut Schlesinger, believed that the independence of the Bundesbank, which they regarded as central to Germany's political economy, could always be revoked by the German parliament, and that embodying the "German" features of central bank independence in a treaty would give a much more secure guarantee that policy would be set in the right way.

On July 16, 1990, Kohl visited Gorbachev, and secured Soviet agreement that Germany could stay in NATO. In September, the four victorious powers of the Second World War, France, the United Kingdom, the Soviet Union, and the United States, could then conclude with the two German states a treaty making German unity possible (and representing in legal fact the treaty to end the Second World War). It was generally referred to as the Two Plus Four Treaty (and *not* Four Plus Two) in order to show the German recovery of statehood. On October 3, as a result, the two states were united: from the legal perspective of the Federal Republic through the same article of the Basic Law (Article 146) that had been used in 1955 to take the Saar back to Germany. The consequence was that the new Germany from a constitutional perspective was an extension of the former western state, the Federal Republic of Germany, and not a completely new construct.

The Soviet collapse

The same western geopolitical logic that wanted to maintain Germany in NATO, a concern with stability, also critically influenced western thinking on the break-up of the federations of Yugoslavia and the Soviet Union itself. The appeal of stability was, however, much stronger in the West than in those countries whose populations had suffered from the oppressive consequences of too much stability. The Yugoslav question, which became the central issue for European security policy during the 1990s, will be dealt with in a later chapter. November 9, 1989, jolted the Soviet leadership quite profoundly. Gorbachev's foreign policy assistant, Anatoly Chernayev, noted the next day:

> The Berlin Wall has collapsed. This entire era in the history of the socialist system is over. After the PUWP [Polish Communist Party] and the HSWP [Hungarian Communist Party] went Honecker. Today we received messages about the 'retirement' of Deng Xiaoping and [Bulgarian leader Todor] Zhivkov. Only our 'best friends' Castro, Ceaușescu, [and] Kim Il-sung are still around – people who hate our guts.[10]

On December 2, 1989, US President George Bush and Gorbachev met on the Russian ship *Maxim Gorky*, in stormy seas off the coast of Malta (Plate 12). This was the meeting which its participants believed ended the Cold War. Bush emphasized how non-triumphalist his administration had been, and how he was looking for agreements on weapons reduction. He promised an agreement on the reduction of conventional forces in Europe in 1990. Gorbachev tried to explain the shift by stating boldly that the methods of the Cold War and of superpower confrontation had failed, and that the world was moving from a bipolar world to a multipolar one, in which the former superpowers would be confronted by the enormous new power of Europe.

The philosophies laid out on the ship at Malta were worked into the declaration of a CSCE meeting in November 1990 in Paris, which presented the end of the Cold War as the logical result of Helsinki, and stated that "Europe is liberating itself from the legacy of the past". The signatories in Paris pledged "to build, consolidate and strengthen democracy as the only system of government of nations".

Plate 12 The handshake that ended the Cold War: President Bush and President
Gorbachev at Malta, December 1989. © Wally McNamee/CORBIS/
Corbis via Getty Images.

The surprise of 1990 was how quickly the movement to realize Helsinki
promises about human rights shook the Soviet grip over its immediate
empire (as opposed to the central European glacis). In 1988 the Popular
Front in Estonia had begun to raise constitutional issues when it declared
that "sovereignty", which was enshrined in the Soviet constitution, is
only "possible when the priority of the Union Republic over the Union
as a whole is clearly established".[11] In March 1990, the parliament of
Lithuania voted for secession, and the parliaments of Estonia and Latvia
(all previously merely token institutions) also asserted that they were
making a transition to independence. These steps were at first not
taken very seriously outside the Soviet Union, but the KGB worried
about an "East German scenario". Soviet troops under General Dzhokhar
Dudayev (later the leader of the Chechen independence movement)
refused Gorbachev's orders to use force against Estonian separatists. A
small-scale massacre, of 13 civilians in Lithuania in January 1991, radicalized the Lithuanian situation, but also exacerbated the more general

Soviet crisis. The Caucasus began to see similar opportunities. Armenia also declared its independence.

Through this period, Gorbachev was trying to devise a reform of the "Union Treaty" which in 1922 had established the Soviet Union. This game with constitutional experiments that looked ever more unrealistic recalled Kohl's deployment of a "confederal structure" in the November 1989 Ten-Point Plan as a way of slowing down a great popular movement. Gorbachev seems to have started thinking seriously about constitutional reform in the early months of 1990.

A putsch against Gorbachev, led by old-timers frightened of Soviet disintegration, began on August 18, 1991, two days before a new Union Treaty which abandoned a commitment to "socialism" and whose membership was supposed to be "voluntary" was due to be signed. Like Khrushchev, Gorbachev was in the Crimea. Unlike with Khrushchev, the conspirators believed they had to take their enemy seriously. At first, they wanted him to impose martial law; then they proposed that he should say that he was sick. When he refused both suggestions, they announced his "illness", but had no serious program and discredited themselves in a ludicrous television performance, in which the new leader, former Vice-President Yanaev, was evidently drunk. General Dmitri Yazov, the Defense Minister and the key to effective power, did not show up. This was a group of old men, who clearly had not the slightest conviction that history was on their side. In this sort of situation, the opportunists who constituted the leadership of the party and the state would scarcely be inclined to risk anything for such a cause. As in Poland, communism collapsed because for several decades it had been run by opportunists rather than believers, and because a shock external event (in this case the central European revolutions) suddenly opened up a world of previously unthought-of possibilities.

In 1964, Brezhnev's supporters had changed the phone numbers in the Kremlin, so that Khrushchev loyalists could not mobilize. In 1991, the telephones worked, the western media reported everything, and the charismatic Boris Yeltsin, who had been elected as President of Russia on a fairly clear anti-Gorbachev platform, mounted his own defense of democracy and Russia. He climbed on a putschist tank in Moscow, was surrounded by cheering crowds, and brought something of the mystique that Lenin had had (in Eisenstein films, if not in reality). On August 20–21, the military could and – if they wanted to be successful – should have ordered the storming of the White House, the residence of the Russian President. But the commander of the crack Taman division which was brought to Moscow on August 19, General Alexander Lebed, never had any orders, and instead busied himself advising General Yazov to start the attack and at the same time advising President Yeltsin to transfer the command of the troops from the Soviet Union to Russia. The military leadership under General Yazov, which had initially apparently firmly backed the coup against Gorbachev, was quite confused, wanted to avoid massive bloodshed, and ordered its soldiers to return to their barracks.

368 Malta and communism

After this, Yeltsin effectively seized for Russia (and for his supporters) the assets of the Soviet Union on Russian territory: the soldiers and, just as importantly, the energy resources.

In Ukraine, President Leonid Kravchuk called for independence on August 24, immediately after the failure of the putsch. Within a month, seven other Soviet republics followed the Russian and Ukrainian lead: Belarus, Moldavia, Azerbaijan, Kyrgyzstan, Uzbekistan, Tadzhikistan, and finally Armenia. Kravchuk had done his best to promote the central Asian collapse: he had forbidden the export of food from Ukraine to Russia, and stated that he wished to buy energy not from Russia but from the new central Asian states. On December 1, 1991, a Ukrainian referendum approved independence. On December 8, the leaders of Russia and Ukraine, joined by the much more orthodox leader of Belarus, reached the conclusion that the Union was disintegrating. They did not take seriously any new institutions designed to replace the old Union. On December 25, 1991, precisely two years after the execution of Ceaușescu, the Russian flag replaced the Soviet flag over the Kremlin, and Gorbachev was cast out. Communism and "Yalta", the two defining features of post-1945 central and eastern Europe, thus died at the same time.

The center of the system had been destroyed by shocks emanating from the periphery of the eastern world (Poland, Hungary, the GDR), that had then affected the periphery of the Soviet Union (the Baltic states, Ukraine, and the Caucasus region), and finally produced chaos at the center. This collapse was a bizarre and deeply ironic version of the model Lenin had evolved in 1916 to explain the collapse of capitalism. Capitalism had depended economically and psychologically on imperialism, and the revolt of the subjects of imperialism would make the system unsustainable in the great metropolises of capitalism. The Soviet empire as made by Stalin during and after the Second World War had also generated an economic system of its own, and made the Soviet center proud of its world historical role. When imperialism collapsed, so did Soviet rule.

Notes

1 "The Novosibirsk Report", *Survey*, 28/1, 1984, pp. 91, 95.
2 Cited in Jerry F. Hough, *Democratization and Revolution in the USSR, 1985–1991*, Washington, DC: Brookings Institution, 1997, p. 148.
3 Hough, *Democratization*, p. 150.
4 Hough, *Democratization*, p. 109.
5 Minutes No. 64 from an expanded meeting of the PZPR CC Secretariat held on June 5, 1989, www.gwu.edu/~nsarchiv/news/19991105/Doc-57.htm.
6 Memorandum of conversation between M.S. Gorbachev and Károly Grósz, General Secretary of the Hungarian Socialist Workers Party, Moscow, 23–24 March 1989, www.gwu.edu/~nsarchiv/news/19991105/29mar89.htm.
7 Timothy Garton-Ash, *The Magic Lantern: The Revolution of '89 Witnessed in Warsaw, Budapest, Berlin and Prague*, New York, NY: Random House, 1990, p. 78.

8 Margaret Thatcher Foundation, Large Scale Document Archive, "Cold War: Chequers seminar on Germany ('Summary record')", March 24, 1990, www.margaretthatcher.org/document/111047.

9 Philip Zelikow and Condoleeza Rice, *Germany Unified and Europe Transformed: A Study in Statecraft*, Cambridge, MA: Harvard University Press, 1995, p. 278.

10 Diary of Anatoly Chernayev (Archive of the Gorbachev Foundation), November 10, 1989. www.gwu.edu/~nsarchiv/news/19991105/891110.htm.

11 Hough, *Democratization*, p. 386.

13 The return to Europe
The new politics and the end of the Cold War

In the great upheavals of 1989 two major ideas stood out: a return of the formerly communist countries to "Europe", and a return to "civil society". Both turned out to be quite problematical concepts when applied in practice. They were interdependent, in that European values were supposed to be about tolerance, reconciliation, civility, and more particularly about the rule of law, the restoration of property rights, and representative government. But were these concepts European, "western", or universal? Between 1914 and 1956 Europe and its values had been anything but civilized. In December 1989 at the superpower summit at sea off the coast of Malta that definitively ended the Cold War, when US Secretary of State James Baker talked about Germany and "western values", the General Secretary of the Communist Party of the Soviet Union asked why democracy and the market were "western" and whether they were not values which "belonged to the whole of humanity".[1]

Civil society was a beautiful goal, and it was hard to attain in the East: but it was also pretty difficult in the West. Yet despite all the difficulties of the so-called "transformation process" in the formerly communist countries, which will be examined in this chapter, the former East and the West converged at a surprisingly quick pace: the problems they had in the 1990s, and the answers they sought, were quite similar. They were fundamentally the inevitable and inescapable problems of states and peoples faced by the challenges of a globalizing world.

But post-Cold War normality was not easy. The difficulties of normalization were perhaps most evident in the largest member country of the European Community (EC; European Union, or EU, after 1992): Germany. Many German politicians, particularly those in government, liked to think that the process of unification and the diplomacy of the Two Plus Four process had ended the abnormal situation of postwar Germany. They longed to be normal. In fact, in domestic political terms, the inclusion of the former East made the country – as the only elected Minister-President of the GDR, Lothar de Maizière, predicted in 1990 – more eastern (i.e. socialist or suspicious of the market economy) and more Protestant (in a largely secularized sense, i.e. moral).[2] The population remained frightened of potential disturbances to the status quo, profoundly worried by war, and skeptical of foreign military action (at least until the problems of the Balkans raised new moral challenges: see "The new politics 2: morality and general policy" later in this chapter). In international politics, some of the institutional legacies of the war remained: in particular the absence of a former empire, the absence of nuclear weapons, and the absence of a permanent seat on the UN Security Council. There was for Germany a much reduced international leverage. Consequently, Germany repeatedly emphasized that it sought normalization only in a European setting and through multilateral organizations and institutions. That in fact was the European way of the 1990s.

Nation-states do not obviously represent the best institutional form for dealing with the new problems and issues, which are sometimes better tackled on a supranational or international level, by new institutions and codes, and sometimes better handled by local or regional political processes. For most of Europe, the most important and powerful of the international institutions was the EC/EU. Even apart from its influence on its own members, its presence and the ideas that it embodied provided a powerful attraction for many ex-communist countries, and an incentive to stay on the course of democratic and market-oriented reform. For other less developed or geographically more remote ex-communist countries, in southeast Europe and in the Soviet Union, a more important role was played by global international institutions, in particular the Bretton Woods twins: the International Monetary Fund (IMF) and the World Bank. But their part in the reform process often polarized the domestic debate much more than did the European-level institutions. Both European and global multilateralism were responses to the challenges of a process that was taking place on a global rather than merely a continental level. That process created new divisions, as an elite seemed to benefit from the new chances presented by mobility, whereas a substantial part of the population felt left behind or marginalized.

Normalized demographics

By the end of the twentieth century, western and central Europeans lived substantially longer. Life expectancy at birth for French males, which had been 63.7 years in 1950, rose by over a decade by the end of the century (74.6 in 1998). The corresponding female rates are 69.4 and 82.6. In the UK, the male expectation rose from 66.2 years to 74.8 years, and the female from 71.1 to 80.1. Age-specific mortality, which in many ways gives a better indication of the experience of the adult population (since the more widely cited life expectancy figures are highly sensitive to changes in infant mortality), shows the same development: Europeans lived for longer, and adult mortality dropped (see Figure 13.1).

They also ate more, and were taller, bigger, and heavier. A leading British mass clothing retailer, Marks & Spencer, reported that over the century, the average British woman's bust measurement rose from 81.3 to 92.7 cm, the waist from 55.9 to 76.2 cm, and the hips from 85.1 to 100.3 cm.[3]

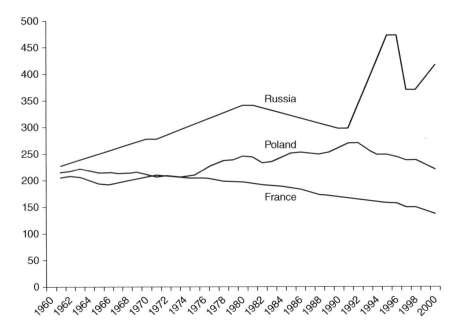

Figure 13.1 Adult male mortality (15–60) per thousand populations, 1960–2000.
(Source: World Bank Online. Adapted under the Creative Commons Attribution 4.0 International license, CC-BY 4.0.)

This success story needs some relativizing in regard to central and eastern Europe. After German unification, East German recruits to the new all-German army were on average 1.2 cm shorter than their western counterparts.[4] In communist central Europe, as noted previously, adult female and particularly male mortality rose from the 1960s; it fell again with the transformation process, quite dramatically in the case of the most successful conversions to the market economy (Hungary, Poland, Slovenia). Even in the case of less rapid adjustments to capitalism, as in Romania, the rise in mortality of the communist era stopped, and by the mid-1990s showed some signs of a slight improvement. On the other hand, further east, in the former Soviet Union, where the transformation was less immediately successful and was associated with big income falls, mortality rates rose. Traditional causes of death, such as cancers, cardiovascular disease, and violence, were now also accompanied by rises in drug- and AIDS-related mortality. But even here, the rate of the rise in mortality slowed down in comparison with the communist era, and the often-politicized attempt to blame increases in death rates on the transition to capitalism was misleading, given the longer-term demographic perspective.

A common and trans-continental phenomenon that looked more worrying than the fall in mortality was the decline in the birth rate. Together with the behavior of the death rate, it resulted in increasingly aged societies. This was a general process in the industrial world, with one of the most extreme examples appearing in Japan. To a large extent it can be explained by the changing economics of family life in rich industrial societies. It was costlier to have children, as expectations about longer education processes increased (even if the education was free to the parents, it represented a loss of potential income from children working). More importantly, the increased and quite novel availability of interesting and high-status work for women made stay-at-home motherhood a less attractive option, and one that had a high opportunity cost. Finally, with higher incomes and a welfare state, children (that is, one's own children) were no longer needed to secure living standards in old age.

The general decline in natality did, however, demonstrate striking national differences (see Figure 13.2). The lowest levels in western Europe occurred – whether or not by coincidence – in countries which had faced the greatest traumas and national humiliations in the 1930s and 1940s: Germany, Italy, and Spain. The birth rate in Germany declined from 17.3 per thousand population in 1960 to 11.0 in 1980 and 9.2 in 2000; in Italy from 18.1 to 11.3 to 9.1 in the same years; and in Spain from 21.7 to 15.2 to 9.9. Sweden had a consistently low level, but a much less radical decline: the birth rate was still 10.2 in 2000, while in the UK it was 11.5 and in France 13.2. How can these national peculiarities be explained? Especially in the 1960s and later, there were ideological or philosophical as well as economic and social reasons given for not having children. Many Germans, in particular, cited the threat of nuclear war and environmental degradation as arguments that the world was becoming so unpleasant that it would be unkind and unfair to bring new humans into existence. It is this kind of argument that constitutes the strongest link between national trauma in the 1940s, and the demographic behavior of the generation born into that trauma.

This demographic attitude, however, was also normalized between East and West in the course of the last decades of the twentieth century. High levels of Catholic religious practice in Poland did not stop a decline in the birth rate from 22.6 in 1960 to 19.5 in 1980 and then a very sharp drop in the 1980s and 1990s to 10.2 in 2000. (The drop in the 1990s may also have been caused to some extent by a one-time effect as the age of first female marriage increased and child-bearing was postponed into the thirties.) The drop in birth rates in the former Soviet Union was even more pronounced: for Russia, 15.9 in 1980 and 8.8 in 2000, and in Ukraine a decline over the same time from 14.7 to 8.7. Here there is also a link between demographic problems and national trauma.

Low birth rates produced an ageing of the population, and predictions of much greater age imbalances in the future that would subvert the ability of welfare states to produce adequate security in old age. Pensions had been at the heart of the development of the welfare state, and it now appeared

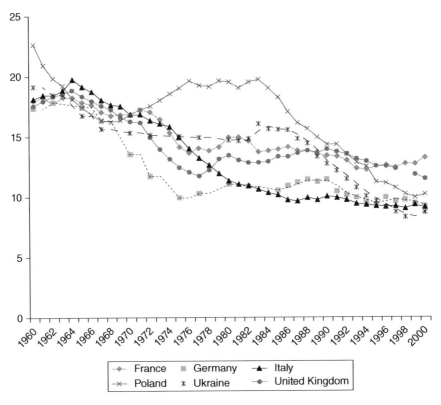

Figure 13.2 Birth rates, 1960–2000.

(Source: World Bank Online. Adapted under the Creative Commons Attribution 4.0 International license, CC-BY 4.0.)

increasingly likely that automatic pension entitlements would have to be cut. In 2000, there were 61 million people over 65 living in the EU, compared with 34 million in the same area in 1960. The EU average size of this population relative to the working age population (15–64) was 24 percent, with some national variations that are forecast to grow greater: the United Kingdom, France, and Germany were all at 24, Italy at 27, and Ireland at only 17. The ratio for the EU as a whole for 2010 was forecast as 27, with Germany at 30, Italy 31, and Spain 28. The only obvious solution to this problem lay in the toleration of higher levels of immigration, in order to increase the share of the population that was of working age, and this answer presented its own political and social challenges. By 1999, net immigration accounted for three-quarters of the EU's population growth, and without immigration there would have been population decline in Germany, Greece, Italy, and Sweden.

Sometimes politicians in the West tried to take credit for the western successes in reducing mortality levels; usually they did not like to blame their own policies for low reproduction rates. In a humorous reference to the demographic data which showed how much longer Frenchmen lived, Jacques Chirac told his audience in the presidential campaign of 1995 (which he won) that just by listening to him talk for one hour, they would live 15 minutes longer. But in reality, these changes have little to do with politics, and there is little (short of staging disasters) that politicians can do to affect them.

Normalized politics

In commenting on the Czech "Velvet Revolution", Timothy Garton-Ash said:

> Take a more or less representative sample of politically aware persons. Stir under pressure for two days. And what do you get? The same fundamental Western, European model: parliamentary democracy, the rule of law, market economy. And if you made the same experiment in Warsaw or Budapest I wager you would get the same basic result. This is no Third Way. It is not 'socialism with a human face'. It is the idea of 'normality' that seems to be sweeping triumphantly across the world.[5]

That liberal idea of normality might have been deceptive. Quite soon, a bout of post-totalitarian hangovers hit the reform countries. They began to look abnormal again, and to think of themselves once more as special cases. But the perception of abnormality was actually more deceptive than the normality, for the problems that gripped post-communist societies were actually those common to all post-Cold War (some might term this post-modern) societies.

During the era of the Cold War, European politics had been relatively stable for several reasons:

- The external ideological constraints of the Cold War;
- The security blanket created by nuclear weapons on both sides of the Iron Curtain;
- A party political dynamic (in the West) in which a left and a right played against each other in a battle to redistribute more (the left) or less (the right), in a framework set by Keynesian macro-economic demand management. In this framework, each side needed to moderate its position and appeal to the political middle in order to secure election victories. If the left appeared radically redistributionist, it would deter middle-income voters; so would the right if it resisted any form of redistribution or the many aspects of the welfare state that had a largely middle-class clientele.

In the 1990s, however, the environment changed. The big ideological battles were over. The security alliances no longer did their old jobs. The Warsaw Pact simply came to an end. The unified military command was formally dissolved on March 31, 1991. NATO had a new and initially controversial task, of providing security coverage for states struggling to join the new Europe. In 1999, the politically most advanced former communist countries – the Czech Republic, Hungary, and Poland – joined NATO. These were the countries who had most openly revolted against Soviet rule. They were also the countries where the sense of historical betrayal by the western powers was greatest: Hungary because of its treatment in 1919 in the Treaty of Trianon, and because of the western response to 1956; the Czechs because of Munich (1938); and the Poles because of Yalta (1945). NATO membership would give a firm security commitment. At a NATO summit in 2002, a much more ambitious round of expansion was agreed, to include Bulgaria, Estonia, Latvia, Lithuania, Romania, Slovakia, and Slovenia. Central Europe was thus becoming normalized as a result of the same multilateral security framework which had stabilized the West for five decades.

The domestic political game in European countries also changed, in that the extent of embeddedness in an international economy, in which factors of production were highly mobile, limited the possibilities for direct redistribution. In addition, with state shares in GNP lying between 40 and 50 percent in almost all European countries, the scope for further expansion of the share controlled by the state was minimal. The old political game thus no longer made any sense. Social democratic parties still aimed at the political middle, but now had to de-emphasize the promise of income or wealth redistribution. There was thus more convergence and consensus about the idea of the market economy than at any previous time in the twentieth century. A joint paper by German Chancellor Gerhard Schröder and British Prime Minister Tony Blair[6] in 1999, "The Way Forward for Europe's Social Democrats", set out the new politics of what they called a "new middle". It was strongly market oriented: "The weaknesses of markets have been overstated and their strengths underestimated." It pleaded for an economic deregulation and liberalization that had to a great extent already taken place in the UK, but not in Germany: "Product, capital, and labour markets must all be flexible." And it admitted that the old left–right dichotomy no longer made much sense: "Most people have long since abandoned the world view represented by the dogmas of left and right. Social democrats must be able to speak to those people."

Indeed they did. At the British general election of 1997, 36 percent of the professional and managerial classes voted Labour (in 1992 the share had been 16 percent), and 36 percent voted Conservative (1992: 59 percent).[7]

One response to this new consensus was the emergence or strengthening of radical parties on the political extremes, who collected protest votes against the "system". Both right and left protested against internationalization and globalization, and its bureaucratized institutions, the IMF and the

EU. There were some powerful voices on the right who tried to raise national issues and national myths as a challenge to globalization, and who attracted cross-national attention (and usually disapprobation): Jean-Marie Le Pen, Jörg Haider, Christoph Blocher, the German "Republican" movement, the Northern League in Italy. The left rejectionists found it hard to mobilize behind charisma, and tended to form fractious and fissiparous parties. A provisional highpoint of both tendencies (the right search for rejectionist charisma, and the left descent into rejectionist cantankerousness) came in the French presidential elections of 2002, where it was fostered by the system of two-round voting, with a final run-off election. In the first round, the two leading candidates who thus went into the final ballot were the incumbent President, Jacques Chirac (82.1 percent of the second-round vote), and Jean-Marie Le Pen (17.9 percent). The left was divided among a large number of candidates who thought that the mainstream-left presidential candidate, the incumbent Prime Minister Lionel Jospin, had made too many concessions to the system.

These trends – the convergence of the center and the radicalization of the extremes – affected the formerly communist countries, too. In the majority of countries, former communist parties quickly adapted to become centrist social democratic reformists, who accepted and embraced the idea of private property. Some of the old *nomenklatura* elite did extremely well out of the privatization of state enterprises, and supported policies that would allow continuing social benefits and economic profits. In Poland, after an initial burst of "shock therapy reform", the former Communist Party, the SLD, returned to power from 1995 to 1997 and then again after 2001. In Hungary, the left similarly returned in 1994 to 1998, and after 2002. In both cases, the left governments kept strictly to market-oriented economically liberal programs. All the responsible parties wanted to join the EU as quickly as possible, and saw it as a guarantee of political decency.

Meanwhile the disaffected and the poor moved to extreme parties: in some cases, notably in Russia, to old-style communist movements which thrived on whatever nostalgia for a communist past existed. They also turned to right-wing, nationalistic, xenophobic, and anti-European parties.

Instead of concentrating on the battle for redistribution, which had been the political theme of the world after the Depression and after the Second World War, societies in the East and West looked for new political issues. This was in part because many people became convinced of the hopelessness of conventional politics, which seemed to offer no real choice. It was also because conventional politics were straightforwardly about redistribution, whereas the redistributionist aspects of the new politics became quite carefully concealed. When capital flows undermined the capacity and the efficacy of national redistributionist politics, old-style politicians looked quite helpless.

These new issues include the discussion about the security of property rights (which replaced a discussion about redistribution of property); the debate about morality in foreign policy (a debate which replaced the traditional realist emphasis of much policy-making); the attack on corruption; and the politics of food and the environment. Finally, there is a much older theme, of local or regional identities and patriotisms in conflict with national politics (which appeared to become devoid of content), and of a consequent demand for the regionalization or devolution of power. The remainder of this chapter takes up these new issues, analyzing them in a systematic way across national frontiers and across the old East–West divide. The simple fact that such an exercise makes sense indicates the rapidity of the change: how quickly it was that central and eastern Europeans cast off their definitions as being special cases outside the European norm.

Non-national business

One manifestation of the new internationalism, and a reason for the increased concern with property rights, was a new economic and business logic. Wealth accumulated more rapidly in Europe, and in industrial countries in general. Communications became easier and faster, and produced a universalized culture in which individual national developments closely paralleled each other. Indeed, the shift in the economy produced a shift away from the older industries of the Industrial Revolution, which had been yoked to the cause of state enhancement and state extension (railroads, steel), and in the direction of an internationalized communications- and information-based economy, in which states had much less say. The logic of information and money, operating together, produced a sort of star culture, described by critics such as Naomi Klein as the ascendancy of the brand.[8]

In the 1980s and especially in the 1990s, the European business environment was restructured. At the beginning of the 1980s, the largest European corporations were still the giants of the classic producer goods industries of the Industrial Revolution, and petroleum: by sales Exxon (US) was the world's largest corporation, the Anglo-Dutch Royal Dutch Shell Group second, and Mobil (US) third. Big automobile corporations dominated the lists: General Motors and Ford, both US-based, were in fourth and eighth place; Fiat of Italy at place 13, Renault of France at 19, and German Volkswagen at 24. Thyssen Steel (Germany) was at place 32, US Steel at place 46. The historical German chemical firms Hoechst, Bayer, and BASF were at places 29, 30, and 31. These were pretty anonymous products that did not require sophisticated consumer branding: there is little obvious difference between plates of steel made by different companies, or petrol, or even between the increasingly similar automobiles of the last third of the twentieth century.

Most of the big European and American corporations of the 1980s had been in existence before the First World War, and they preserved themselves well through the course of the "short twentieth century" to 1990. But a few years later there was a completely different corporate picture, and the industrial landscape had changed. The new firms, unlike the old, needed to create elaborate images to persuade consumers to buy their products. By 2002, large telecommunications companies figured prominently in lists of the biggest companies by revenues: these were the newly privatized success stories of the 1990s, Deutsche Telekom and France Télécom. Electronics were prominent, with completely new companies such as SAP; a few years earlier they would have been even more dominant. Large retailers also came increasingly onto the scene: Wal-Mart (US) was the largest global corporation by revenue, Carrefour (France) the thirteenth largest European corporation (thirty-fifth in the world), and Metro (Germany) twenty-seventh in Europe and seventy-second in the world. They dwarfed the remnants of the old economy: the largest steel company, Thyssen Krupp (the product of the merger of two of the most famous names in German industrial history) was only the forty-third largest company in Europe, and 116th in the world.[9] The new industries tried to individualize themselves and present sharply defined images that would establish a hold over consumers.

In order to do that effectively, they needed to look big, and it helped actually to be big. The worldwide boom in mergers and acquisitions in the second half of the 1990s, together with the integration of the European capital market with the advent of the single currency, produced cross-border mergers on an unprecedented scale. Business was internationalized. The German automobile producer Daimler-Benz took over the third largest American automobile maker, Chrysler, in 1998. In 2000 Vivendi in France acquired the US–Canadian beverages and entertainment firm Seagram. In 1996, the large Swiss chemical and pharmaceutical firms Sandoz and Ciba-Geigy joined to make Novartis; two years later the Swiss Bank Corporation and Union Bank of Switzerland merged as UBS. The British new technology company Vodafone took over Mannesmann, previously known as a leading German engineering firm.

English became the language of corporate communication and corporate appeal. (The technique was imitated by politicians. When Gregor Gysi in 1990 wanted to modernize the appeal of the old East German Communist Party he used the slogan, in English, "Take it easy, vote for Gysi.") Where German and French firms joined, such as the fusion of Hoechst and Rhône-Poulenc to form Aventis, the language of corporate communication was English. This was also true of firms that still seemed anchored in a national setting, but which wanted to underline their internationalism: SAP, or Deutsche Telekom, or Deutsche Bank in Germany. The Dutch multinationals Philips and Unilever had long used English as a means of communicating.

The rise of the new, and very big, genuinely transnational corporation as a result of mergers (rather than through the establishment of subsidiaries, in the manner of US multinationals in the 1950s and 1960s) sometimes produced cultural problems that went well beyond the need to adopt a common language. The old world seemed to be one of corporate stability; the new one was marked by continual reorganization, streamlining, and downsizing (euphemisms for labor dismissals).

The new generation of chief executives, whose remuneration rose in disproportionately large steps, marketed themselves as global leaders, spoke in public frequently, promoted themselves as a brand in books, and advertised their devotion to American culture. Thomas Middelhoff of the German publishing house Bertelsmann (which acquired Random House in New York) spoke about how he felt more American than German. Jean-Marie Messier of Vivendi in France immodestly marketed himself as "the master of the world" and talked about the end of French cultural exceptionalism.

The new personal icons of a global culture of capitalism reflected very clearly a world in which major gains went to the very prominent and the large, and firms consequently stretched themselves financially in order to expand and acquire. Financial services providers, in particular investment banks, corporate lawyers, and management consultants, pushed this process. Some Europeans thought of McKinseys (management consultancy) and McDonald's (hamburgers, which became a symbol of global culture) as diabolical Scottish or Anglo-Saxon twins set on a course of cultural conquest.

Just how widely the winner-take-all mentality reached is evident from the world of competitive sport, in which brand names such as Michael Schumacher (motor racing) or Boris Becker (tennis) scored repeated successes and elevated themselves to an international superstar league. Europe's most popular sport, football (soccer), became overshadowed by just a few highly celebrated teams which dominated national championship competitions. Bayern München won the German championship once in the 1960s, but four times in the 1970s, six times in the 1980s, and four times in the 1990s. AC Milan won in Italy twice in the 1960s, and once each in the 1970s and 1980s, but five times in the 1990s. In England, Manchester United won the championship twice in the 1960s and seven times in the 1990s, while Liverpool won five times in the 1970s and six times in the 1980s.

The business world, popular culture, and sport all produced marketable and recognizable "stars", who easily eclipsed the feeble light shed by Europe's increasingly tired political elite. The astute, like Italy's Silvio Berlusconi, actually used the ownership of media and football clubs (AC Milan, of course) to remake a political brand.

The politics of TINA

In the 1980s, as cross-border economic integration ("globalization") had increased, the room for political choice had been reduced, and politicians themselves wished to reduce it. Margaret Thatcher followed Geoffrey Howe in responding to the Conservatives' unusual and unpopular 1981 budget with the phrase "There Is No Alternative" (TINA). European politicians replied more often to the same problem by looking for a non-national, non-political solution from the European process of integration. It had been the genius of Jacques Delors, as France's Economy and Budget Minister in 1983, to see this way out of the impasse of French domestic politics.

As President of the EC Commission (after 1985), he was well placed to realize the political potential in "Europe" as a way of restricting domestic politics.

The clearest example of this came in the 1990s, with the Treaty of Maastricht, concluded on December 11, 1991, which amended the Treaty of Rome to create the EU, and severely limited national monetary and fiscal policies. Maastricht firmly endorsed the principle of "subsidiarity", that decisions should be made at the most local level feasible. There was also to be a common European citizenship, so that EU citizens could vote in local and EU elections in other member countries where they resided. The Treaty also created a Council of the Regions and a blueprint for the elaboration of a common foreign and security policy. In practice, this was the least satisfactory part of European integration in the 1990s, as countries continued to view foreign policy priorities largely in national terms.

The most obvious and controversial innovation of Maastricht was the timetable it established for a move to European monetary union (EMU). At the latest the new currency (which was eventually named the "euro") was to be introduced in 1999. This timetable was actually realized, and a new money as an accounting unit was established at that time, superseding national currencies in 12 member countries of the EU. The introduction of the new currency in a physical form took place three years later, on January 1, 2002.

At the time of the negotiations, the Maastricht Treaty was frequently viewed as the product of a political compromise: a German concession to a French demand for a greater institutionalized influence on monetary policy in Europe, which under the European Monetary System (EMS) had fundamentally been set by the German Bundesbank in Frankfurt, in return for French agreement to German political unification. Germany insisted throughout the unification process that it wanted to overcome its national trauma only in the context of greater European integration. But the basis of monetary union had already been laid in the later 1980s, before anyone thought of the German question, and it corresponded to doubts about the long-term sustainability of a simple fixed exchange rate regime (that would be vulnerable to speculative attacks).

In large part Maastricht was a response to a simple and immediate question: how could national governments be restrained from fiscal irresponsibility, from creating debt that the European Central Bank would be obliged to monetize? The Maastricht Treaty laid down the criteria for a stability pact, according to which public sector deficits were limited to 3 percent of GNP, and public sector debt to 60 percent of GNP. A non-bailout clause restricted the ability of the new European Central Bank to monetize the budget deficits of member countries. Inflation and interest rates had to move into line before the monetary union for countries to qualify to participate, and exchange rates were not to move by more than the normal 2 percent margins that existed in the EMS. The convergence criteria then became the underlying basis for the operation of a currency union after 1999 (with new banknotes and coins circulating after 2001).

In practice, public controversy about Maastricht and its budgetary implications soon rocked the EMS. Denmark narrowly voted in a referendum not to participate in EMU; a similar referendum in France looked uncertain; and at the same time, Germany set high interest rates because of the surge of demand created in the wake of political unification. In September 1992, speculative attacks forced Italy, Spain, and the United Kingdom out of the narrow exchange rate bands of the EMS. The UK left the system altogether, while Italy and Spain worked with new parities and larger bands of fluctuation. France was subject to a similar speculative attack in 1993, but withstood it because of large German intervention in support of the French franc on the foreign currency markets.

The new vulnerabilities of a globalized world were demonstrated spectacularly in the early 1990s. The currency crises rocked the British government and produced a nervous paralysis. The currency fluctuations also provoked fears of a trade backlash against the market opening provided by the Single European Act, since the Italian and Spanish devaluations made the products of those countries (in particular agricultural products, but also important industrial goods such as automobiles) cheaper in the other EU members. In France in particular, the idea was raised of an import tariff to compensate for the competitive effects of devaluations: such a move would clearly have completely destroyed the process of trade liberalization which constituted the *raison d'être* of the European process since 1958. At the same time, a surge in immigration followed the end of the Cold War and the dismantling of boundaries against movement, and this too produced populist backlashes.

The external limitations imposed by the Stability and Growth Pact were used most conspicuously in Italy as the basis of a stabilization program, and were endorsed with great enthusiasm by center-left governments in the mid-1990s. The result was to bring down Italian inflation and interest rates spectacularly (and the interest rate reduction produced fiscal savings). For Italy, the EU's most important role lay in the way in which it created objective and unmovable constraints on policy-making. This role appealed not just to member countries, but also to the many former communist countries that wanted to join and applied for membership. In this way the Pact did a great deal to create stability. It also affected formerly communist countries which wanted to join the EU, and started to accept its stability criteria in advance of membership. At the Copenhagen Summit of the EU (2002) the EU governments agreed to the accession of Cyprus, the Czech Republic, Estonia, Latvia, Lithuania, Hungary, Malta, Slovakia, and Slovenia in 2004 and of Bulgaria and Romania in 2007. They also agreed to hold membership talks with Turkey in December 2004, but there was little progress and many Europeans increasingly feared the inclusion of a large Islamic country in the EU.

But the externally induced stability came at a price. One of the main methods that the EU used was to create an impression of complete necessity. A veteran EU politician, the Prime Minister of Luxembourg, Jean-Claude Juncker, put the point very neatly:

We decide on something, leave it lying around and wait and see what happens. If no one kicks up a fuss, because most people don't know what has been decided, we continue step by step until there is no turning back.[10]

This obvious strategy clearly poses a challenge to political activity as conventionally understood as a process of debating and reaching informed decisions. If politics is no longer about choices, what is it about? In 1991, former UK Chancellor Nigel Lawson explained: "I think it was Pierre Mendès-France who said that to govern was to choose. To appear to be unable to choose is to appear to be unable to govern."[11] The technocratic approach produced a discussion of the "democratic deficit" at the heart of modern European politics, and a demand for a more political instance to control the European dynamic and to offer real choices. By 2002, the President of the European Commission, Romano Prodi, could publicly state that he considered the stability pact to be "stupid". The euro would be at the center of debates about the European order after the 2008 global financial crisis.

The following sections examine aspects of the new politics of the 1990s: how fundamental questions about political morality arose that were quite unlike the old discussions of the Cold War era. Sometimes the new politics was described as neo-liberalism, and as the European part of a general movement of integration and globalization.

The new politics 1: property

A major element in the attempt to restore civil society in formerly socialist countries was the reintroduction of private property and the market economy, but this was also a political priority that was taken very seriously in western countries. It belonged to the new consensus that underlay the political reorientation of Europe during the 1990s.

The most dramatic and effective post-communist reform program was that implemented in Poland. It was described as "shock therapy" since the Finance Minister in the first non-communist government, Leszek Balcerowicz, liberalized prices very extensively, and then set about imposing budgetary stability. He had worked out the program in its broadest outlines long before 1989, and drew explicitly on much older western models of reform, above all Ludwig Erhard's 1948 currency reform in Germany and the stabilization programs of South Korea in the early 1960s. Balcerowicz had studied both these historical episodes in some detail. The key insight behind "shock therapy" was that removing the overwhelmingly inefficient parts of the socialist economy would be painful, that it could only be undertaken by a government that possessed a considerable stock of democratic legitimacy, and that the stock of legitimacy would not last very long. Hence the program needed to be implemented very quickly. A long drawn-out restructuring process, on the other hand, would only alienate those who would inevitably lose, while producing few obvious winners. Poland, like Hungary, had experimented extensively with piecemeal reforms in the 1970s and 1980s, and had found them disappointing. The Polish circumstances were uniquely auspicious, and opinion polls in early 1990 showed 90 percent approval ratings for the government, and over half the population supporting shock therapy.

As elsewhere in east-central Europe, Polish restructuring was accompanied by a fall in output, which official figures put at around a fifth of GNP (but they almost certainly overstate the extent of the collapse, by comparing output to exaggerated production statistics for the communist era). Other elements of reform – settling the large foreign debt issues that remained from the communist era, and selling off (privatizing) state enterprise – took much longer. Inequality increased. Discontent about reform and disillusion that there had been no overnight creation of a capitalist paradise ineluctably meant that the government became gradually less popular.

In Poland, the former Communist Party, renamed as a social democratic party, obtained 21 percent of a highly fragmented vote in elections in September 1993 and became the largest party in parliament. The election produced a change in government, but no fundamental change in course about economic policy. As in the other highly successful transformation economies (Hungary, the Czech Republic, Slovenia), the Communist Party accepted the market economy fully and unambiguously.

The Czech reforms, supervised by Vaclav Klaus, a rhetorically gifted market radical who admired Margaret Thatcher but had no background in the dissident movement, looked immediately more dramatic than the Polish reforms. This was because privatization, in the form of an issue of tradable vouchers in former state property, came right at the outset of reform, instead of several years into the process. Almost half of the privatization took the form of vouchers. But the government – worried about the legitimacy of its reforms – made corporate restructuring and the dismissal of workers rather hard. As a result, notionally privatized Czech enterprises continued to behave rather like old-style state enterprises. They borrowed from banks, which cultivated political contacts in order to secure their investments. The result was a major banking crisis and a slowdown of growth in 1997–98.

At the other end of the spectrum of reform success, the post-1989 Romanian government, born in the peculiar circumstances of the coup against Ceauşescu, had very little popular legitimacy, and was too frightened to undertake any large-scale reform program at the beginning. The privatization law, Law 51 of 1990, purported to transfer 30 percent of the equity of Romanian companies into private hands, but in practice generated only confusion and uncertainty. The new government was worried about the elections scheduled for May 1990 and how to bribe its way to winning them, so it awarded big pay rises, which it paid for through inflation. The exchange rate was held at an artificial level, and encouraged capital to leak out through inadequately policed capital controls. This bad start led to a number of large-scale economic and financial crises in the course of the 1990s, requiring the intervention of the IMF. In 1994 the government devalued, and tried to promote exports; but inflation recurred, and a new set of reform measures were needed in 1997.

A substantial number of formerly communist countries thus introduced an effective market economy, and went over fully to the politics of western Europe, with a center-left and center-right agreeing over most of the major aspects of economic policy, but disagreeing over important areas of social policy (divorce, abortion). The countries that missed the original reform impetus had a much harder task.

Russia at the beginning looked like one of the most enthusiastic reform countries, with a handful of very energetic democrats surrounding President Boris Yeltsin, and radical (and young) economic reformers, such as Yegor Gaidar and Anatoly Chubais in government. A basis had been laid through an extended debate in the Gorbachev period about economic reform, and the sequencing of price liberalization and privatization.

Gaidar became President Yeltsin's chief economic adviser in the last days of the Soviet Union, in November 1991, and deregulated the price system with astonishing speed at the beginning of 1992 (as with the Erhard reforms in 1948 Germany, some prices, notably in energy and transport, were still controlled). The government quickly introduced a voucher-based privatization program, and between 1992 and 1996 122,000 enterprises were privatized – the most extensive privatization program anywhere in the world. In practice, however, many of the enterprises had already been informally privatized at the initiative of their managers ("red capitalists"). The new Russian constitution of 1993 also envisaged the extension of the principle of private property to land-holding, but this was blocked by parliamentary opposition until June 2002.

Privatization quickly acquired a terrible reputation in Russia. Its proponents were apologetic. Gaidar later said that the *nomenklatura* elite "exchanged power for property".[12] He identified a

> *nomenklatura* sector . . . run by authoritative representatives of the old economic elite. The distinguishing feature of these enterprises is that even after the collapse of socialism they still perceive the state as their own and consider their problems to be the state's problems.[13]

But this problem was already deeply built into Russia's political and economic system from the last days of the Soviet empire. Yeltsin himself had made the point very clearly in his programmatic speech of October 1991:

> for impermissibly long, we have discussed whether private property is necessary. In the meantime, the party–state elite have actively engaged in their personal privatization. The scale, the enterprise, and the hypocrisy are staggering. The privatization of Russia has gone on [for a long time], and often on a criminal basis.[14]

The 1992 measures constituted a revolution from above: a reform package that came entirely from the government, and from the very young men around Gaidar. It was wholeheartedly opposed by the parliament, the Congress of People's Deputies, which had been elected in March 1990 and reflected the mentality of Soviet-era apparatchiks. Even in 1992, the pace of reform was consequently uneven. In April 1992, Gaidar was dismissed as Finance Minister, but in June he became Acting Prime Minister, only to resign in December 1992. The mass of the civil service – a substantial mass, with 1.5 million federal bureaucrats – was almost entirely ex-Soviet and very old-fashioned in outlook. So were the judges and the KGB, which remained in the new Russian state.

One of the impediments to more effective reform in 1992 was a large credit expansion, in part the consequence of enterprises piling up mutual debts which they believed the central bank would monetize, and in part the result of the same process at the governmental level as various parts of the public sector tried to free themselves from any budgetary control. Partly under international pressure, Russia had retained a monetary union with other ex-Soviet republics: these now spent as much as they could, like (as one acidic commentator put it) 14 ex-wives going crazy with their husband's credit card.

In this reform process, which tried to build consent by generous spending, Yeltsin struggled with a parliament which wanted even substantially larger budget deficits. But that would have meant the failure of the IMF program, and an end to the inflow of foreign assistance. In July 1993, the government tried an idiosyncratic anti-inflationary policy and introduced an abrupt monetary reform (all the Soviet-era banknotes were called in over a weekend). It then tried to restrict new credit. Parliament was outraged because it was thereby being blocked from voting for new funds and new projects. In early September 1993, Yeltsin suspended Vice-President Aleksandr Rutskoi, who had emerged as the leader of a parliamentary (ex-Soviet) opposition, and parliament then voted that the suspension was illegal. Gaidar was reappointed to the government as Deputy Prime Minister, and Yeltsin dissolved parliament. When the parliament resisted, and appointed Rutskoi as Acting President, Yeltsin besieged and then occupied the Moscow White House occupied by Rutskoi and parliament. At least 187 people were killed in the fighting in Moscow.

Parliamentary (duma) elections in December 1993, at the same time as a referendum approving Yeltsin's new constitution, proved a dismal setback for democratization. By far the largest party was the inappropriately named Liberal Democratic Party, formed by an eccentric nationalist, Vladimir Zhirinovsky, who had come to prominence when he did unexpectedly well in the 1991 Russian presidential elections. In 1993 his party had 22.8 percent of the vote, and took 59 of the 225 seats in the new parliament. The pro-government party, Russia's Choice, had 15.4 percent and 40 seats, while the unreconstructed Communist Party had 12.4 percent and 32 seats. A smaller pro-reform party, Yabloko, had 20 seats. The majority of the new parliament, expressing the widespread sentiment of disillusioned Russians, was thus set against capitalism and democracy, and quite hostile to the Yeltsin regime, which it blamed for the destruction of the Soviet Union and of Russian greatness. Looking at the support for the extreme left (communist) and the right (Zhirinovsky) recalled the electoral predicaments of doomed democracies in interwar Europe, in particular the Weimar Republic (also founded on the basis of a collapsed empire). Commentators in and outside Russia began to speak of "Weimar Russia".

Yeltsin and his entourage now began to see economic reform depending not on democracy but on an enlightened authoritarianism that would eventually produce a better sort of democracy: a Singapore or (in a bleaker interpretation) General Pinochet's authoritarian and repressive Chilean model for social regulation. The peculiar constitutional structure of post-1993 Russia, though, was not that of an autocracy. Its closest parallel is to the regime of General de Gaulle in the early years of the Fifth Republic, in which the power of the president was not well defined but was interpreted in a quite extensive and expansive manner. Commentators from the West loved to assert that Russia had no democratic tradition, and that there were no democrats in Russia: this was a position taken both by some old-style Cold Warriors, who had in part argued that Russia's characteristics stemmed from national character as much as from Marxist theory; but more forthrightly by western leftist critics, who derided shock therapy and its advocates as naïve and misguided. But it might as well have been argued that France before 1958 had had chronic instability and a democratic deficit; yet over the course of a decade and a half a remarkable and successful stability emerged. This was about the same length of time that the Russian transformation took.

But unlike de Gaulle, who had a quite obedient Gaullist movement in a majority in the Chamber of Deputies, under Yeltsin presidential support never really developed in Russia because of the scale and extent of the economic shock. Production collapsed as the Soviet-era factories closed down. Living standards fell, and all mortality indicators rose.

It is actually surprising how relatively peaceful Russia was, with violence exploding only at the fringes, in particular in the North Caucasus. The first Chechen President, Dzhokhar Dudayev, argued that he needed the wars "more than Russia does . . . I've got 300,000 men, homeless, jobless, embittered and with nothing to do. All they can do is fight. I need a little war and an enemy to send them to battle against."[15] The miracle is that this mood, which was widespread in Russia, did not translate into action, with the exception of the two Chechen wars (which were opposed by Russia's liberal-democratic reforming elite).

In part, the explanation lies in the way in which discontent among the Russian elites was bought off, successfully for the most part. The government got an IMF agreement to release funds ($1.5 billion in March 1994), and pressed ahead with mass privatization in order to build some support.

But popular capitalism in action proved a disappointing farce. There were numerous scams and frauds: in the most painful, around 1 million people lost their savings when the MMM investment pyramid collapsed in 1994.

A new set of parliamentary elections in December 1995 did not change much, and produced little support for the President. Already in August 1995 in the first direct election for the head of a regional government, a separatist who in 1993 had declared his own "Urals Republic" was elected to run what had once been Yeltsin's own power base, the Sverdlovsk *oblast* (district). In the Duma elections, the Communists were the largest party, with 22.3 percent of the vote and 157 of the 450 seats; and the Liberal Democrats (Zhirinovsky) the second largest, with 11.2 percent and 51 seats. (The reason why the proportion of seats was so much higher than the share of the vote is that almost half the voters chose parties that fell under a 5 percent minimum representation guillotine.)

It looked overwhelmingly probable that the leader of the Communist Party, Gennady Zyuganov, would win the presidential elections, scheduled for June 1996. Russia's leading business leaders were alarmed, especially when Zyuganov put himself across to western politicians and businessmen at the January 1996 Davos World Economic Forum meeting as a likeable and trustworthy character. On the fringes of the meeting of world movers and shakers, they concluded the "Davos pact" to pay for the re-election of Yeltsin as Russian President. They later claimed that the election of Yeltsin had cost them $3 billion, though in fact Yeltsin's campaign was paid through the state budget, and the six or seven (the number is given variously) businessmen of the *semibankivshchina* paid themselves out of state and enterprise funds.[16] The most prominent of the Six, Vladimir Potanin and Boris Berezovsky, entered government after the presidential election, which Yeltsin won in the second-round run-off against Zyuganov (53.8 to 40.3 percent; the rest of the votes were protest votes).

The new political compromise involved two new innovations for Yeltsin: buying off the "oligarchs", and a more populist tone. The main means of conscripting money behind the Tsar was a new variant of privatization known as "loans for shares". It had been proposed in 1994 and 1995 as a budget revenue-raising device: businesses would give loans to the state on the security of shares of the large companies that owned Russia's substantial natural resources. The device allowed Potanin's holding company to get control of Norilsk Nikkel in return for a $1.8 billion loan, and Berezovsky to run the former state airline Aeroflot (and its foreign currency revenue). Yeltsin in fact held the proxy for Berezovsky's shares, and in March 1997 Yeltsin's son-in-law became head of Aeroflot. This was now more the Indonesian (Suharto) than the Singapore model of capitalism.

The government was also aware that it needed to look more active and more populist. Since Yeltsin was continually unwell, had had a heart attack in July 1995, and found even a brief television appearance at the end of the 1996 presidential election campaign visibly exhausting, this was quite hard. The easiest way was to resurrect some of the Great Power rhetoric of the Soviet era. At the beginning of 1996, Andrei Kozyrev, who had been a skilled and sensitive Russian Foreign Minister since 1990, resigned and was replaced by Yevgeny Primakov, the former head of the Soviet external intelligence service. He quickly began a campaign against the US position in Bosnia, and against NATO enlargement, and eventually also (1999) against the NATO war in Kosovo.

Yeltsin himself preferred reminders of the tsarist period than of the communist dictatorship. In September 1997 he developed simultaneous plans to transfer Lenin's embalmed body from the mausoleum in the Kremlin wall (to "give him a Christian burial", as Yeltsin rather curiously put it), and to rebury Tsar Nicholas II, martyred by the communists for Russia.

He also liked to see the bankers who had arranged 1996 fall out among themselves. The occasion was another part of the sell-off of state assets, this time of Sviazinvest, which had a crucial role since it regulated the use of radio waves for TV, computers, and cellphones. Not only was it tremendously lucrative as an investment (cellphones were booming in Russia, and had become a status symbol for the new Russians); it could also control the media and their manipulation of opinion. When Potanin's Oneximbank, backed by the foreign financier George Soros, secured the deal, other "oligarchs" – in particular Vladimir Gusinsky (who controlled a media empire, Mediamost) and Berezovsky – attacked the government. Yeltsin's dismissed security chief, Aleksandr Korzhakov, spread wild stories about Yeltsin and threatened to reveal even more. In particular, he claimed that Berezovsky was blackmailing Yeltsin with the threat to reveal the financial (and perhaps also sexual) affairs of his family, and in particular of Yeltsin's daughter, Tatiana Dashchenko, who had become increasingly significant as Yeltsin's major contact with the outside world.

Meanwhile the Russian central bank chairman Sergei Dubinin alleged that $500 million of government funds had been misappropriated to pay state employees in Moscow and finance the purchase of MiG fighter planes from a favored company, and that the transfer of funds had been managed through Potanin's business empire. In an attempt to fight corruption, government officials were now obliged to list their income and assets, with ludicrous results. Berezovsky listed his total assets at $39,000.

Moscow was getting wilder and ever more scandal-ridden, and had the air of a boom town as foreign capital flowed in. The peak of the inflows occurred in the second and third quarters of 1997, when $8 billion streamed in. The government financed itself by issuing short-term treasury certificates (GKOs) which were sold, for an initial period directly, and then indirectly, to foreign investors. In March 1998 Yeltsin sacked the veteran Prime Minister, Victor Chernomyrdin. He was replaced by a young man, Sergei Kiriyenko, who could pose no possible threat to Yeltsin or his extended circle ("family"). The GKO-financed boom might have lasted longer, but it certainly would not have gone on for ever. As it was, the world financial markets were shaken from the summer of 1997 by a contagious panic originating in Asia. The problems of the Asian countries lay in part in nervous foreign investors, but in part also in chronic corruption and nepotism. Especially in the case of Indonesia, the financial and economic business of the Suharto family attracted a great deal of self-righteous opprobrium from the United States. In the middle of the Asia crisis, the IMF's managing director publicly pointed out that such problems were not unique to the Asian case, and specifically mentioned Russian "crony capitalism".

The markets became very nervous about Russian prospects, and capital outflows (mostly by Russian citizens) began. In July 1998 the IMF responded, as it had in Asia, by organizing a large rescue package. In the Russian case, this involved $17.1 billion, of which the IMF contributed $11.6 billion. On August 17, the ruble collapsed, and Russia announced a simultaneous devaluation and debt default. The move stunned foreign investors in Russia, who rather naïvely had assumed a permanent IMF guarantee of their loans since Russia was thought to be too dangerous to be exposed to a long economic crisis (a doctrine which was known as "too nuclear to fail").

Kiriyenko, thoroughly discredited, resigned, and Yeltsin tried to reappoint the experienced Chernomyrdin, who had always had good relations with the IMF. But the Russian Duma vetoed this appointment twice, and rather than dissolving it, Yeltsin appointed the apparently anti-western Primakov as Prime Minister, as the only figure who could attract parliamentary support.

Only a few weeks after the default and devaluation, Chubais said: "Today in the international financial institutions, despite everything we've done to them – and we cheated them out of $20 billion – there is an understanding that we had no alternative."[17] In a curious way, he was right, and the aftermath of the big 1998 crisis restored economic growth to Russia. The devaluation made Russian goods more competitive, and shops that had previously stocked only imported goods now carried home products.

In 1999, the Duma turned against Yeltsin even more radically, and drew up articles of impeachment for

> illegally conspiring to destroy the Soviet Union in 1991; violently dispersing the elected legislature in 1993 in contravention of the constitution; launching the war in Chechnya; undermining national defense by destroying the armed forces; and committing 'genocide' against Russian people through economic reforms which lowered the birth-rate and life-expectancy.

Yeltsin's main concern now was to find a pliable figure to succeed him as President. He dismissed Primakov as Prime Minister and appointed Sergei Stepashin in his place, but dismissed him when he appeared to be behaving too presidentially. In August 1999 Yeltsin chose another relatively young man, Vladimir Putin, as Prime Minister. New Duma elections were preceded by allegations of corruption and bribery, details of the Swiss company Mabetex that had paid Yeltsin's and his daughters' credit card bills, and claims that the President's men had paid opposition candidates to stand down; and on Putin's side, by a nationalist mobilization for a new and (for Russia) much more successful war in Chechnya. The result of an enormous media presence was that for the first time since Russia had emerged from the Soviet Union, a parliament fundamentally supported the administration, and the specter of Weimar Russia was finally banished. The Communist Party still had a substantial (24.3 percent) party list vote, but Zhirinovsky's movement had sunk to under 6 percent, and pro-government and pro-reform deputies formed a clear majority. Assured that the great struggles with the Duma were over, Yeltsin had lost his presidential *raison d'être* and announced his immediate retirement as President on the last day of the twentieth century. Putin was appointed as interim President, and in March won the presidential elections with an absolute majority in the first round. The Communist candidate, Zyuganov, had 29.2 percent, but Zhirinovsky faded into historical oblivion with only 2.7 percent of the vote.

Putin moved decisively once elected. The presidential administration soon issued warrants for the arrest of two of the great media and property oligarchs of the 1990s, Boris Berezovsky and Vladimir Gusinsky. The property rights revolution was completed with the privatization of agricultural land. Putin changed the Russian national anthem back to the Soviet music, and abandoned the melody from Glinka's opera *A Life for the Tsar* that Yeltsin had chosen in 1993. Putin initially represented the politics of normalization, and of technocratic modernization. But there was one decisive miscalculation: Putin laid a bet on Russia as a major energy producer, rather than pushing for a more general opening and modernization. Russia was in consequence highly vulnerable to developments on international oil and gas markets. From 2007–08, with the onset of the global financial crisis, he turned in an increasingly authoritarian and nationalist direction.

Privatization and the restoration of property rights by former leftists were, however, not a drama unique to the formerly communist countries. No government in the West pursued a faster program of privatization than the center-left government of Lionel Jospin in France, which extended the initiatives of the preceding center-right regime under Alain Juppé. Juppé had failed to privatize France Télécom, while Jospin succeeded; Jospin also sold the biggest French steelmaker, Usinor, the aluminum group Pechiney, and much of the nationalized banking sector including CIC and Crédit Lyonnais. The privatization of Deutsche Telekom to millions of small investors in November 1996 created a shareholder capitalism that had previously not existed in Germany. But these privatizations built potential problems, especially when share prices tumbled at the same time as extravagant payouts to failed managers were revealed. By September 2002 France Télécom had lost half of its issue price, and Deutsche Telekom two-fifths.

One of the most striking ways in which the politics of property returned in the 1990s was the completely novel and intense concern with property rights that had been violated in the era of the Second World War, by the Nazis and their allies. The most publicized of all these discussions related to assets deposited in Swiss banks by those persecuted by the Nazis. A large portion of these assets were not claimed by their immediate owners or their heirs after the war, because the owners had been killed and the heirs lacked information. Banks did not communicate with clients or their heirs, especially if these were on the other side of the Iron Curtain (for understandable reasons, since the clients would have been unlikely to welcome such communications). With the end of communism such restraints disappeared, and it became possible to address the problem of those who had been the "double victims" of Nazism and communism. In addition, East European archives opened to reveal hitherto unknown details of the Nazi spoliations. Finally, the revolution against communism made the connection between property owning and human dignity a much more evident part of the stability and legitimacy of a regime. Banks that insisted on secrecy above every other claim stood in the way of a political and moral order based on the security of property rights. The Swiss issue was solved in part by court proceedings in the United States, which led to a settlement in 1999 between the Swiss banks and largely Jewish victims of Nazism. In part, it was also solved through the nomination and appointment of commissions to supervise auditing work, and an independent historical commission. But the publicity about the Swiss bank issue raised wider problems relating to the economic legacy of the Second World War, concerning the looting of gold, and the behavior of banks and businesses in other occupied countries, and in other neutrals, as well as in the United Kingdom and the United States, and of course also in Germany; and about the appropriate compensation for forced and slave laborers in Germany, who if they lived in eastern Europe had been largely uncompensated for their mistreatment.

Part of the problem for Germany and the German government arose from the fact that the German government had made very extensive payments in the early 1990s as part of the process of stabilizing the immediate post-communist situation (and also of buying consent for German unity). German politicians had privately thought that such payments constituted an erasing of the financial legacy of German exploitation and brutality in the Second World War, but they never made this linkage in the form of any clear public statement.

Since the restoration of property rights was part of the assertion of a much broader new understanding of international morality and legality, it was, however, vital that the reasons for making payments should be transparently stated. This was in practice one of the grounds for the widespread practice of establishing historical commissions in the second half of the 1990s (when such commissions were operating in 24 countries). The new international political order and its legitimacy depended much more on morality and legality, and much less on the balancing of power relations, than did the Europe of 1945 to 1989. "Yalta" (which had also meant a large-scale violation of property rights) was definitively a thing of the past. On a global level, a consensus emerged that political and economic reform went hand in hand, that ownership and good governance required each other. Politics became more explicitly about morality than it had been in preceding decades.

The new politics 2: morality and foreign policy

The case about morality and politics was raised in a most acute way by the experience of one region in the aftermath of the collapse of communism: that of former Yugoslavia. If Poland had been the country around which a wide-ranging international debate about society and politics centered during the 1980s, that role was taken in the 1990s by the successor states of Yugoslavia. Yugoslavia created a moral challenge for Europe. It revived a discussion about human rights in international politics that had been raised already in the 1970s, notably by US President Jimmy Carter, and which had played a major element in the establishment of the Helsinki Conference on Security and Cooperation in Europe (CSCE) process. Through much of the 1980s, however, this discussion had been obscured by the focus on military and economic competition in the confrontation of the superpowers.

Before the 1990s, it was Yugoslav geopolitics that had made the country special. The idea of Yugoslavia had been kept alive in the 1970s and 1980s in large part by the conflict of the superpowers: ideologically, by the opposition of the Soviet Union, which made the Yugoslav leadership attempt to formulate a non-Soviet Marxism; and economically, by the United States, which was prepared to spend resources (its own, and through international institutions, those of other countries) in support of dissident members of the Eastern Bloc. The same logic led it to channel financial aid to the increasingly idiosyncratic Nicolae Ceauşescu in Romania.

The thaw of the later 1980s, together with the aftermath of the international debt crisis, in which borrowing by middle-income countries became much harder, coincided in Yugoslavia with the problematic legacy of a single charismatic leader. Postwar Yugoslavia had been Tito's creation, and became ever more vulnerable after his death in 1980.

Yet even in the 1980s, increasing strains on the country showed. An ill-conceived economic reform, in which factories and government-controlled institutions were subject to no controls, produced inflation and eventually hyperinflation, as debt was simply monetized at the central bank. In 1987 prices rose 120 percent, in 1988 195 percent, and in 1999 1,240 percent. In 1990, the federal republics set their own policies, and contributed to the monetary chaos. In the disintegrating federalism of Yugoslavia, the republics also started to state their mission in terms of nationalism, rather than communism.

Two major political leaders drove this nationalist radicalization: Slobodan Milošević in Serbia and Franjo Tudjman in Croatia. In April 1987, Milošević, then the secretary of the Serbian Communist Party, told Serbs in

Kosovo, "You shall not be beaten." He controlled radio and television in Belgrade and built the ecstatic and highly charged nationalist reaction (the crowd chanted "Slobo, Slobo") into a platform on which he rapidly became President of Serbia (1989), and the strongman of Yugoslav politics. On June 28, 1989, Milošević spoke to as many as 1 million Serbs in Kosovo, and told them: "After six centuries, we are again engaged in battles and quarrels. They are not yet armed battles, but this cannot be excluded yet."[18]

After the east European revolutions of 1989, the Yugoslav authorities agreed to abolish the monopoly on power of the Communist Party (but not the principle of democratic centralism within the party), and to hold multi-party elections in April 1990. At this time, a precarious political balance existed between the six republics of federal Yugoslavia: Bosnia–Herzegovina, Croatia, Macedonia, Montenegro, Serbia, and Slovenia. (The constitution of 1974 also established two "autonomous socialist provinces" in Serbia: Vojvodina and Kosovo.) The new post-1989 leadership in Montenegro supported Milošević, as did Macedonia, so that he could control half of the six votes in the federal government, but there was some counterweight to his ascendancy.

In early 1989, an opposition group, the Slovene League of Social Democrats, had started to attack the Slovenian communists. Under pressure from this new challenge to their legitimacy, in January 1990, the Slovenian communists left the general Yugoslav Communist Party. In elections in April, they were defeated, and a non-communist government under Lojze Peterle as Prime Minister formed which adopted a "declaration of sovereignty". The new President, Milan Kučan, was a former communist, but now supported independence. In December 1990, 88.5 percent of the voters in a referendum voted for independence.

In March 1991, Milošević and the Croat leader, Tudjman, responded to the Slovene challenge by discussing carving up Yugoslavia between Serbia and Croatia. In May, a referendum was held in Croatia in which 94 percent of the voters supported becoming an independent sovereign state with a later option of joining a future Yugoslav confederation (as opposed to the existing Yugoslav Federation). Such a choice posed an uncomfortable problem for those who thought that the CSCE held the key to the future development of Europe, since the Helsinki agreements very emphatically emphasized the principle of the territorial integrity of states. One month after the Slovene referendum, the US Secretary of State tried to warn Croatia and Slovenia against "independent unilateral actions". The same warning came from the EC, and Jacques Delors, the President of the European Commission, visited Yugoslavia together with the President of the European Council, who happened at that time to be the Prime Minister of the EU's smallest member, Luxembourg. They offered a $4 billion package to Yugoslavia if the conflict could be solved, and stated that the Community would "refuse to recognize breakaway republics or offer them benefits". The Luxembourg Foreign Minister, who had proudly announced that this was the "hour of Europe", looked – as Timothy Garton-Ash acerbically pointed out – rather peculiar telling Yugoslav republics that they were too small for self-determination. Slovenia and Croatia promptly did just what everyone said they should not do (but then suspended independence pending talks with the EC). On December 23, 1991, Germany recognized both states, and on January 15, 1992, under considerable pressure from Germany, the EU recognized the statehood of Slovenia and Croatia.

The recognitions discussion provoked a great deal of dissent among the major west European countries. France and the United Kingdom were skeptical about the German push to rapid recognition. They thought it was motivated partly by practical considerations, in that most of the Yugoslav guest workers in Germany were Croats, and partly by an alarming historical sense of Germany's commitment to the Croats that revived memories of the atrocities of the Second World War. The German historical argument was based, Paris and London believed, on a view of Europe that saw the East–West divide in new terms after 1989, as a division between Orthodox (Serbian) Christianity and Catholicism (the Croats). François Mitterrand burst out at an early stage of the discussion: "What a mess! Only the Serbs are serious in this country. Kohl is going to tell me about his friends, the Croats!"[19]

The Yugoslav army fought a brief war against Slovenia in June 1991, but rapidly withdrew. Slovenia lived prosperously ever after, and became by almost every measure the most economically successful of the former communist states of eastern Europe during the 1990s. In Croatia, however, the war went on much longer, and was centered around areas in which the predominant population was ethnically Serb. In December 1991 Serb shelling destroyed Vukovar completely and severely damaged the ancient port city of Dubrovnik.

The recognition of Slovenia and Croatia created a great problem in Bosnia (as the US government, and many commentators, had pointed out in advance). Power in the Yugoslav Federation shifted heavily in favor of the Serbs and Milošević after the defection of the two republics, which could thus no longer form a counterweight at the federal level. Already in September 1992, Serbs had set up "autonomous areas" in Bosnia–Herzegovina. Bosnia promptly also asked for EU recognition, and was immediately told by an EU Arbitration Commission that "the popular will for an independent state had not been clearly established". In March 1993, however, in a referendum on Bosnian independence that the Serbs boycotted, 99 percent voted for independence. When a Serb was killed at a wedding party, Serb violence erupted. At this point, Serbs started the "ethnic cleansing" of eastern and northern Bosnia, while Croats drove out Serbs from western Herzegovina. This involved intimidation, killing, and mass rape as an instrument of humiliation.

The EU recognized the two new independent ex-Yugoslav states, but now would do nothing more. In 1991 the UN imposed an arms embargo, which in practice helped Serbs who controlled most of the resources of the former Yugoslav army. In February 1992 a United Nations Protection Force was established to monitor the Croatian war, rather oddly with its base in Sarajevo. This was the second largest city in former Yugoslavia, with a population of 500,000. But Sarajevo was soon surrounded by Serb heavy artillery and subjected to a relentless bombardment that continued, with only brief interruptions, until 1995. Its population starved or fled or was killed by sniping and shell fire. Even spectacular outrages, such as the February 1994 mortar explosion in Sarajevo market, which killed 68 people, failed to produce any effective action from the EU or the UN.

Throughout the agony of Sarajevo, the rest of the world insisted that negotiations would solve the problem, while the Serb and Croat armies on the ground were creating new realities by expelling or killing other ethnic groups. The Secretary General of the UN, Boutros Boutros-Ghali, explained that "the United Nations cannot impose peace; the role of the United Nations is to monitor peace".[20] In January 1993, former American and British foreign ministers Cyrus Vance and David Owen proposed a plan under which Bosnia would be divided into ten provinces, which was accepted in March by the Bosnian government, and in May by the Bosnian Serb leader, Radovan Karadžić, but not by the Bosnian Serb Assembly. A UN resolution created six "safe areas" including Gorazde and Srebrenica, and the UN commander gave a strong personal pledge to the defense of Srebrenica, the most vulnerable of the Moslem enclaves in Serb-held territory.

The Croats established a network of concentration camps near Mostar. The largest and most infamous at Dretelj held 2,000 to 2,500 prisoners. Prisoners said they had been tortured, beaten, and forced to sing fascist songs, and that some had been released under fire into battlefield areas. There were Serb concentration camps that inflicted equal or greater brutalities at Keraterm, Omarska, Manjaca, and Trnopolje.

In 1992–93, as the major powers began to agonize about the consequences of their inaction, human rights groups suggested the creation of a war crimes tribunal on the Nuremberg model. During the 1992 presidential campaign, Bill Clinton attacked President Bush for being soft on tyrants, and called for "steps to bring [the perpetrators] to justice for these crimes against humanity."[21] Eventually, in 1993 the UN Security Council passed a resolution which established the "International Tribunal for the Prosecution of Persons Responsible for Serious Violations of International Humanitarian Law Committed in the Territory of Former Yugoslavia since 1991".

In 1995, Croatia began to win the long drawn-out war with Serbia, and very large numbers of Serb refugees from Croatia fled into Bosnia, looking for new homes. By August, the Serbs had been driven out of the Krajina. In Bosnia the level of violence increased dramatically. In July, the Serb armies in Bosnia began an offensive against Srebrenica, which was protected by a small force of Dutch soldiers. Some of the Dutch peacekeepers were taken hostage by the Serbs; but the Dutch developed an increasingly disdainful attitude to the Moslem population of Srebrenica, whose security was their responsibility. Victims who have been systematically attacked and humiliated can begin to look unappealing and even no longer fully human – their clothes are in tatters, they smell, they complain – and the Dutch soldiers seem to have treated the Srebrenica Moslems with increasing contempt. Their Serb oppressors, on the contrary, had smart uniforms, were often courteous with foreigners, and might sit down to a friendly drink. The commander of the Dutch forces admired greatly the dash and charm of the brutal Serb military commander, General Mladić, and thought the Moslem population to be difficult, whining, and idle. He still referred to Mladić as a "good guy" in a press conference after the fall of Srebrenica. The pro-Serbian attitude of the Dutch forces ("Dutchbat" in the lingo of the UN operations) was strengthened when Bosnian soldiers killed a Dutchman retreating from Srebrenica. Between 7,500 and 8,000 Moslems were massacred when Srebrenica fell, atrocities which were in part witnessed (and even filmed) by Dutch soldiers but against which the Dutch took no action.

The mechanism by which people were marginalized, made to appear inhuman, and then persecuted and killed resembled closely that of the genocide of the Second World War. The Dutch saw how Moslem men were separated from women and children, and mishandled. The fall-out from the scandal of how UN peacekeepers could watch genocide, and the official Dutch inquiry into it, eventually – seven years later – produced the resignation of the Dutch government.

The massacre of Srebrenica and the continuous and deliberate strategy of "ethnic cleansing" raised issues about the defense of human rights that had not been seriously debated since the Second World War. The Europeans had talked about talks, while postponing any action, for much too long. After Srebrenica, many influential European politicians believed that their soldiers had been bystanders to a new holocaust.

To justify their inaction, both Yugoslav and world leaders at first used and abused history in outrageous ways. Milošević repeatedly told his interlocutors that the history of the Second World War showed that the Croats were Nazis. President Mitterrand at one point told a German reporter that history showed that the Serbs could not have concentration camps. The most common line of analysis was that everyone was at fault, and that the problem had arisen from "ancient hatreds", a position which no serious historian ever endorsed or could endorse. Even if it were true that some hatreds continue over long periods of time, any serious analysis would have to explain the mechanisms by which such behavior was transmitted to new generations, which is not at all self-evident or self-explanatory. President Clinton in early 1994 spoke about how Bosnia–Herzegovina

> basically degenerated back to the conflict which had been there for hundreds of years. And you can – there is no perfect solution for life's problems, you know. But in this case, the truth is, people there keep killing each other.

John Major told the British House of Commons in 1993:

> The biggest single element behind what has happened in Bosnia is the collapse of the Soviet Union and of the discipline that that exerted over the ancient hatreds in the old Yugoslavia. Once that discipline had disappeared, those ancient hatreds reappeared.

Some of the most powerful books on the Bosnian crisis start off with an examination of the astonishing popularity of such facile so-called historical analysis. Noel Malcolm correctly pointed out that there had been no Soviet discipline since the expulsion of Yugoslavia from the Cominform in 1948.[22]

Only in August 1995 did NATO forces begin a significant aerial bombardment of the Serbian forces in Bosnia. It was a relatively small-scale operation: 3,515 air sorties in all were flown, the equivalent of one day's fighting in the Gulf War. The Croatian forces attacked the key Serbian defensive point in the Krajina, Knin, and another wave of 150,000 Serb refugees fled to Bosnia. Through all of this fighting, Milošević in Belgrade had always disclaimed any responsibility or control over the "irregular" Serb forces that were in fact being financed from Belgrade.

After the new military approach, the United States brought the leaders of Croatia, Bosnia, and Serbia – Tudjman, Milošević, and Alija Izethegović – together at the Dayton Air Force Base in Ohio. Here they agreed (November 21, 1995) to a settlement in which two "entities" would be established in the Bosnian Republic, a Moslem–Croat federation (with 51 percent of the territory), and Republika Srbska (49 percent). Each of the main three ethnic groups would keep its own army. Order would be kept by a 60,000-strong NATO force, with US troops committed initially only for one year.

In all, in the first stage of the Yugoslav wars, around 200,000 people were killed.

In May 1996, Dusan Tadić, a relatively low-rank soldier accused of mistreating and killing Moslem inmates of the Bosnian Serb concentration camps at Omarska and Keraterm, became the first war criminal to appear before the UN Tribunal in The Hague. The first indictments looked relatively unpromising, the equivalent of the border guards who had been tried in Germany for shootings at the Berlin Wall. During the Dayton negotiations, the western powers were worried that the arrest of leading Bosnian Serbs – Mladić, or Karadžić, who would be the first President of Republika Srbska – would threaten the negotiation of peace. After that, NATO troops and their commanders worried about the casualties that might follow from attempts to arrest war criminals. The existence of the Tribunal, nevertheless, gave a signal.

In 1996–97, morality became explicitly a major element in making policy with regard to former Yugoslav territories. This was in large part the result of changes in administration: in the second Clinton presidential term, Madeleine Albright became the new Secretary of State, and maintained the determined stance on human rights she had shown as US Ambassador to the UN. Albright, the daughter of a Czech refugee from the Nazis and Soviets, liked to use historical analogies in the plea for a more active foreign policy, explaining that her "mindset is Munich". She explained that "the violence is an affront to universal standards of human rights we are pledged to uphold". In 1994, she had stated that: "We believe that establishing the truth about what happened in Bosnia is essential to – not an obstacle to – national reconciliation."[23]

The "New Labour" government in the United Kingdom after 1997, with Tony Blair as Prime Minister and Robin Cook as Foreign Secretary, took a very similar line and claimed to be staking out a new morality in foreign policy (it also, for the same reason, took a leading role in the debate over the "Nazi gold" issue). Blair explained in a newspaper interview that he believed in a natural law order of the world, and that he felt that the more normal utilitarian stance of politicians was dangerous. "There used to be an idea that you just looked after your national interest, and of course it's true that you have to look after your national interest. I also think that there is a moral dimension to it." The moral dimension became a critical part of the German acceptance, for the first time in the country's postwar history, of a duty of military intervention. It was defended by politicians who came out of the student protest movement of the 1960s, Chancellor Schröder and his Foreign Minister Joschka Fischer, as being part of the responsibility created by the legacy and burden of the German past. In 1998 and 1999, NATO soldiers began to make arrests of suspected war criminals, and most of Mladić's immediate subordinates were seized and sent to The Hague. By 1999 Milošević himself was indicted.

Bosnia absorbed the attention of the world, even before the new phase of commitment in 1995, with the result that another Yugoslav issue was barely discussed at this time. Kosovo had always been the cornerstone of Milošević's concept of Serb nationalism. In March 1989, he had ended the autonomy of Kosovo (granted in 1963 by Tito, and consolidated by the provision of the 1976 constitution for autonomous provinces), and he then disbanded Kosovo's mostly Albanian police force and installed Serb security forces. Ibrahim Rugova, an Albanian leader, tried Solidarność-style non-violent tactics: organization abroad, peaceful protest, and the establishment of underground schools and universities. After Dayton, an alternative and very violent Albanian group established a Kosovo Liberation Army, which in February 1998 carried out an ambush, killing four Serbian policemen.

In 1998, Serbs in Kosovo – both locals and army and police forces sent from Belgrade – attacked Albanians and drove them out of their homes. Over a thousand Organization for Security and Co-operation in Europe (the successor to the CSCE) monitors on the ground could do nothing to prevent the Serbian violence. The Albanians fled to the hillsides, where they froze and starved, and to Macedonia, Albania, and Montenegro. In February 1999, NATO organized a meeting of Serbs and Albanians from Kosovo in Rambouillet near Paris and proposed a postponement of Kosovar independence and ground control by NATO. The Albanians eventually accepted the proposed agreement, while the Serbs refused. When NATO started to bomb not only Belgrade and the industrial and energy infrastructure of Serbia but also Serbian military positions and villages in Kosovo (March 24, 1999), even more Albanians fled. Milošević and his supporters later claimed that the mass flight was a response to NATO bombing, and not to Serb terror, and that those killed were the victims of bombs dropped by high-flying planes (the NATO aircraft were instructed to fly above 15,000 feet in order to escape ground fire). At first it looked as if Russia was supporting Milošević, and the war took place just as President Yeltsin's struggle with the Duma was escalating, but the Russian government abandoned its initial protests, and even participated in a military intervention.

Estimates of deaths in the Kosovo war are still highly disputed. In December 1999, the US State Department claimed that between March and June 1999, 10,000 ethnic Albanians were killed. One more recent German estimate suggests 30,000 Albanians killed, while the investigators for the Hague tribunal found only just over 2,000 murdered bodies by the end of 1999. But there were nearly 1 million refugees.[24]

Soon after the Serb defeat, Milošević's hold on power crumbled. In August 1999, over 100,000 anti-Milošević protesters held a rally in Belgrade. In September 2000, elections for the Presidency of Yugoslavia (the remaining federation of Montenegro and Serbia) and for the legislature were held, in which Milošević's security apparatus intimidated voters and opponents. Milošević's major opponent, Vojislav Koštunica of the Democratic Party of Serbia, claimed victory and refused to participate in run-off elections. The loyalist Yugoslav constitutional court at first annulled the election results and ruled that Milošević should serve out his term of office, which was due to end in June 2001. In early October coalminers and others went on strike, calling on Milošević to resign. On October 5, in scenes reminiscent of 1989, protesters in Belgrade stormed parliament, and the state television announced that Koštunica had won the September elections. Milošević finally congratulated Koštunica and explained (in the manner of discredited western chief executives) that he would step down in order to "spend more time with his family". The EU immediately lifted sanctions on Yugoslavia, while the United States announced a $100 million aid package if the new Yugoslav government cooperated in handing over suspected war criminals (including Milošević) to the Hague International Criminal Tribunal. In fact, in June 2001 the new government extradited him to face charges in The Hague.

An after-effect of Kosovo was that fighting spread in 2001 to Macedonia, where Albanian National Liberation Army (NLA) irregulars fought government troops, and again caused major exoduses of refugees. In August 2001 the EU and the United States imposed a cease-fire. The NLA agreed to hand its weapons over to NATO troops, and the government made concessions to Albanians: the constitution's reference to Macedonian Slavs as the only "constitutional people" was deleted. Education in Albanian was to be supported, and Albanian was made a second official language in areas where Albanians constituted more than a fifth of the population.

In the 1990s conflicts elsewhere in the world also directly raised human rights issues: in the Middle East, in the long struggle of East Timor for independence from Indonesia, and above all in the genocidal civil war in Rwanda (where the United Nations also demonstrated a remarkable passivity). Unlike these conflicts, the Yugoslav drama was very close to some of the world's richest industrial countries. Throughout the Yugoslav wars, trains in the Vienna South Station with Cyrillic lettering took passengers to the Serb capital Belgrade. Many West Europeans knew coastal Yugoslavia from vacations. Many Yugoslavs worked in Germany, and elsewhere in the EU, as "guest workers". Most obviously, refugees from the conflict areas fled into the EU and Switzerland. The human dimensions of the tragedy were thus brought home in a direct way, while Europe's elites went on with "business as usual" in the face of mass murder. The governments did not act until they were pushed by the United States; and it took a long time to make the link between morality and foreign policy.

The new politics 3: corruption

Moral politics and the fight against political corruption were at the beginning of modern political life. The French Revolution was a protest against the particular law or "privilege" that treated individuals in markedly different ways. In early-nineteenth-century England, modernizers mobilized against what they called "old corruption". Such struggles also marked European politics in the immediate postwar era. In 1950s Italy and France there had been plenty of courageous denunciations of corruption.

The alternation of parties limited the scope for corruption, because it takes time to establish well-functioning private channels of influence, and because at a change of government, a successor regime has a strong motive to investigate the peccadilloes and abuses of its predecessor. Where there were no or few changes in government, on the other hand, as in Italy under the long period of Christian Democratic rule, or in Austria under the *Proporz*, or in the long-lived communist regimes of central and eastern Europe, greater opportunities for corruption were revealed.

In the 1990s, corruption emerged again as a very large new political issue. This was in large part because the one-party or multi-party coalition systems that had been held in place by the Cold War now disintegrated. The new interest in political morality also played a role. Finally, the speed of the economic transformation made for new opportunities for gain.

The greatest political landslide of the 1990s occurred in Italy. There had been a precursor in the revelations about bribes paid by Lockheed in the early 1970s. The new scandal began when a Socialist Party official, Mario Chiesa, was arrested for having accepted bribes at an old people's home, the Pio Albergo Trivulzio, which he managed in Milan. He had been denounced by his former wife, Laura Sala. This relatively commonplace scandal escalated when it became clear that Chiesa had large sums of money on account of the Socialist leader, Bettino Craxi. A team of magistrates under the direction of Antonio de Pietro started a clean-hands (*mani pulite*) campaign to purge Milan (which was now often referred to as Bribesville or Tangentopoli). Most of the reforming investigative magistrates came from southern Italy, and had absorbed the activist political culture of the late 1960s. They developed a close relationship with the media. As the implications of the affair widened, leading Christian Democratic politicians were implicated as well (Arnaldo Forlani and the veteran Prime Minister, Giulio Andreotti), and also Umberto Bossi, the leader of the populist right-wing party the Northern League. Craxi was eventually sentenced to nine and a half years in prison, but fled to Tunis, where he died. Andreotti, who was accused of Mafia connections and involvement with a murder case, was tried but initially acquitted. He was later sentenced to a prison term. In the course of the investigations, the magistrates demanded 3,165 trials and there were 582 convictions. On the eve of the 1994 parliamentary elections, 6,000 Italian businessmen, civil servants, and politicians were under investigation, including 438 out of the 945 deputies and senators.

In the 1994 elections the Christian Democrats disintegrated, as "outsiders" campaigned against the *partitocrazia* (party rule). The new Prime Minister Silvio Berlusconi, who had in the 1980s been close to Craxi's now discredited party machine, was charged with bribery while attending a UN conference in Naples on criminality. This accusation was carefully timed to create the maximum sensation, and Berlusconi complained that the justice system was staging a "Marxist *coup d'état*". His government disintegrated, and he was replaced by a center-left and rather technocratic government committed to an anti-corruption platform, as well as to the finalization of the European Monetary Union. In 1996, parliament was dissolved, and the left parties won slightly more seats that did the right. The new Justice Minister, Giovanni Maria Flick, in 1996 proposed a "political solution" to end the process of political disintegration. The right had complained bitterly that the Milan magistrates were politically one-sided, that they never investigated communist officials, and called the *mani pulite* teams "red gowns" (*toghe rosse*). After the reforms of the judiciary, panels of judges and lawyers would examine the backlog of an estimated 1.5–2.5 million civil cases; justices of the peace, with extended competence, were appointed; and the geographical distribution of magistrates was altered.

The center-left governments managed the political stabilization of Italy quite effectively, in large part because they were expert at using the European environment and the imperatives created by the monetary union timetable. Many of the leading figures were not politicians at all, but rather officials from the Bank of Italy: Carlo Azeglio Ciampi, the Governor of the Bank until 1993, who became President of the Republic; and Lamberto Dini, the General Manager, who became Treasury Minister, Prime Minister, and later Foreign Minister. Some of the anti-corruption lawyers entered politics. De Pietro founded an "Italy of Values" party, and briefly became Minister of Public Works (a ministry that had been heavily involved in corrupt contracting). In the course of restoring order to political life, however, the left lost almost everything that had been characteristically left: they now became the party of sound administration, balanced budgets, and commitment to the European technocracy.

In general elections in May 2001, the right under Silvio Berlusconi won a convincing victory. He controlled the Italian private television stations through his company Mediainvest (and, as Prime Minister, could supervise the public sector as well). He was more in touch with Italian popular culture than was the old government: as owner of AC Milan, Italy's most powerful football club, he looked more at ease with the mood of the streets than did the left-wing–technocratic alliance that he replaced. He saw politics as much in terms of entertainment and gimmicks as of old-style political influence.

In Spain, Felipe González's long-lived socialist government disintegrated. He had been re-elected to a fourth term in office in 1993, but by 1995 the government was mired in a series of scandals, partly concerning the way in which the war against Basque terrorism was fought, but also in large part financial. The director of the Civil Guard, Luis Rolda, fled abroad after accusations of taking bribes and stealing from a fund in aid of the victims of terrorism. The Bank of Spain's takeover of a large Spanish bank with bad debts, Banesto, was highly criticized. González himself stated: "After so many years in government I have lost credibility."[25] In May 1996, his party was defeated in general elections by José María Aznar's center-right Popular Party. The most active of the anti-corruption Spanish magistrates, Judge Garzon, tried to extend the scope of the activist judiciary internationally by indicting the Chilean ex-dictator Pinochet of human rights abuses and murder.

In the United Kingdom, at the same time as John Major's government announced a "Back to Basics" campaign, two Members of Parliament admitted to taking money from corporations in return for asking questions in the House of Commons. Jonathan Aitken, the Chief Secretary of the Treasury (a cabinet position), in 1993 stayed in the Ritz Hotel in Paris on the account of a Saudi Arabian businessman, and perjured himself in court as to who had paid the bill. He was eventually sentenced to prison. The Chairman of the Conservative Party, Lord Archer, a successful popular novelist and fund-raiser, was also imprisoned for perjury. Major's predecessor, Margaret Thatcher, complained that "it's a terrible time in the political history of the West, with most of its leaders being crooks".[26] Back to Basics, with its emphasis on traditional morality, also came to look ridiculous in the light of a series of revelations about the sexual behavior of Conservative ministers.

In 1997, despite a strong economic record, John Major's Conservative Party was crushingly defeated. It had projected an image of incompetence in handling economic affairs (in the long wake of the pound's departure from the European Exchange Rate Mechanism in 1992) but above all of "sleaze". The "New Labour" administration of Tony Blair distanced itself very quickly from traditional socialism. It also introduced a major administrative and political reform, with Scottish and Welsh assemblies and a devolution of power from Westminster.

But New Labour quickly had its own "sleaze" issues. The Lord Chancellor, Lord Irvine, solicited contributions to the Labour Party from lawyers whose career he could influence. Peter Mandelson, one of the Prime Minister's closest confidants, organized contributions of £1 million to the party from successful Indian businessmen, the Hinduja brothers, who wanted to get British passports. There was permanent tension at the heart of the government between Blair and the powerful Chancellor of the Exchequer, Gordon Brown, who had been promised the succession to the Prime Ministership. Blair was discredited by his passionate advocacy of intervention in the 2003 invasion of Iraq alongside US President George W. Bush, and by the scandal of the "sexed up" dossier of September 2002 on Iraqi biological, chemical, and nuclear weapons of mass destruction that had been used to justify the intervention. Newspapers reported erroneously that the Iraqi leader could launch a chemical attack on Europe within 45 minutes.

On the other side of the Channel, both the Gaullists and the French socialists had major scandals. The affairs of Mitterrand and the left centered around the state-owned oil company, Elf-Aquitaine, which was described as the "milk cow of the republic" by the former Socialist Foreign Minister, Roland Dumas:

> It was useful in maintaining good relations with certain African heads of state, and these had good relations with certain French politicians, and all of this alloyed the irrigation of certain networks and the financing of certain people. It's well known. The system was in place for a long time.[27]

Elf-Aquitaine employed Dumas' mistress in order to get better access to orders in France and abroad (specifically six frigates which were to be sold to Taiwan), and provided her with an apartment costing 17 million francs in the chic Seventh Arrondissement of Paris. She bought her lover a variety of gifts, including antique statues and Berlutti shoes costing 11,000 francs, on her corporate credit card. Later she described her activities in a book with the title *The Whore of the Republic*.

In 1992, President Mitterrand told the President of Elf-Aquitaine, and chief manager of the "Système Elf", Loïk Le Floch-Prigent, to help Helmut Kohl by buying the East German chemical combine Leuna. Le Floch-Prigent later testified that all his bribes had been directly authorized by Mitterrand.[28] Elf would get control of the Minol chain of gas stations in eastern Germany, and commit itself to build a modern refinery near the Leuna works. In itself, of course, such a deal is not necessarily reprehensible: the problem lay in the 100 million Deutschemarks that were to flow into the party accounts of the German Christian Democratic Union (CDU), and in the excessively high price that Elf paid for its acquisition. Senior German politicians, such as the Economics Minister Hans Friedrichs, were paid directly.

The large French state-owned bank, Crédit Lyonnais, which had run an advertising campaign on the slogan "The power to say yes", was ridiculed as "the bank that could not say no". It too conducted big-scale political loan operations: loans of over 1 billion francs to companies associated with the British socialist publisher, Robert Maxwell, and loans of over 1 billion francs to Bernard Tapie, a French socialist businessman and president of the football club Olympique Marseille as well as a friend of President Mitterrand. By 1991 it was clear that the bank's bad loans amounted to 9.6 billion francs; the next year it had to make a new loss provision of 14.4 billion francs. Its director was dismissed by the center-right government in 1993.

On Mitterrand's death in 1995, the Gaullist leader Jacques Chirac was elected President. The Maastricht-induced austerity measures of the rightist government (under Alain Juppé) were bitterly unpopular, and, faced with an unstable parliamentary majority, Chirac dissolved the Chamber and called new elections. These produced a collapse of the right vote (15.7 percent for the Gaullists, 14.2 percent for the independent right), and a high level of support for the ultra-right (and politically unacceptable) National Front (14.9 percent). The surprisingly strong support for the left condemned Chirac to a new spell of "cohabitation", with a government headed by an austere and rather incorruptible former teacher, Lionel Jospin, as Prime Minister.

Chirac himself came under judicial investigation for cash payments of 2.4 million francs made for air travel and hotel accommodation between 1992 and 1995, when he had been Mayor of Paris, but paid out of funds accumulated in 1986–88 while he had been Prime Minister. In 2001, the Assembly passed a bill limiting the President's right to immunity from the next presidential tenure.

Germany clearly had its major scandals as well. In connection with the thin majority of the Brandt government in the early 1970s and the Bundestag votes on the Eastern Treaties, there had been allegations (justified, as it turned out) of the buying of parliamentary votes. In the 1980s, the large Thyssen steel and engineering concern had bought tax advantages through party donations. In business circles, there was a concept of "political horticulture", *politische Landschaftspflege*, that corresponded to Dumas's sense of *irrigation*. At the end of the 1990s, many details of previous scandals came out, and for a time it looked as if the CDU might follow the Italian Democrazia Christiana in auto-destruction. Ex-Chancellor Helmut Kohl refused to reveal a list of donors who had given in all 2.2 million marks to the CDU. The party admitted receiving a total of 50 million Deutschemarks in illegal donations. One donor had given, and had at almost the same time been allowed to purchase state-owned railway employees' housing at apparently below-market prices.

Just as the SPD was benefiting politically from the revelations about the CDU, its own dirty linen was aired. In the *Land* of Nordrhein-Westphalia, which had long been controlled by the SPD, leading figures had taken money to award local construction contracts.

Anti-corruption politics had long been one of the strongest cards of the Turkish military against the fragmented center-right parties, whose pursuit of privatization and economic liberalization seemed to open many doors to personal gain. In 1998 the coalition government of Mesut Yilmaz collapsed when the Prime Minister was accused of corruption in the case of the $800 million privatization of a bank to a property developer with Mafia links. At the same time, a former Prime Minister, Tansu Çiller, who had been driven out of office on corruption charges, was cleared by a parliamentary investigating committee.

On a European level, in March 1999 the 20-member European Commission was obliged to resign in its entirety after a report by an independent inquiry attacked its corruption, incompetence, and nepotism. The report stated that

> Protestations of ignorance on the part of the commissioners concerning problems which were often common knowledge in their services – even up to the highest official levels – were tantamount of an admission of a loss of control by the political authorities over the administration which they were supposedly running.[29]

The Research Commissioner, Edith Cresson, a former Prime Minister of France, had employed a friend of hers, a dentist, to write a scientific report, a task for which he was incompetent and which he never carried out, but for which he was paid 5.5 million Belgian francs. A new Commission, under Romano Prodi, eventually instituted a "whistleblowers' charter", in the hope that new corruption might be avoided.

Most observers rate the level of corruption in formerly communist countries at much higher levels than in western Europe. In 2002, the rankings provided by Transparency International, a non-governmental organization devoted to the study of this issue, gave its highest (i.e. cleanest) scores to Scandinavian countries (Finland and Denmark were scored as the world's two least corrupt countries, with respective scores of 9.7 and 9.5); the west European countries were slightly worse (Netherlands 9.0; the UK 8.7; Germany 7.3); the Mediterranean countries (including France) below that (Spain 7.1; France 6.3; Italy 5.2; Greece 4.2); and the ex-communist countries even lower (Slovenia, the best, scored 6.0; Estonia 5.6; Poland 4.0; the Czech Republic and the Slovak Republic both 3.7; Russia 2.7; Romania 2.6).[30]

The initial attacks on communist leaders had frequently focused – at least as far as popular protest was concerned – on their corruption rather than their tyranny. People detested Ceauşescu's and Zhivkov's nepotism, the thousands of suits accumulated by Ceauşescu, the specially protected enclave of the East German elite at Wandlitz, the revelations about Gierek's extensive film-watching habits. A decisive moment in Gorbachev's discrediting among Russians came when his opponents leaked details about his wife Raisa's alleged purchases on an American Express card account. For western observers, used to far greater disparities of income and wealth (and more ostentatious expenditure), these "extravagances" seemed merely quaint. For eastern public opinion, they were devastatingly corrupt.

Later the discussion shifted to the much larger issues generated by the dismantling of state property and the phenomenon of *nomenklatura* privatization. The first major mass privatization effort was a coupon-based initiative in the Czech Republic. Its director, Jaroslav Lizner, was arrested in 1994 for taking a bribe of around $300,000 for letting a private investor take a majority stake in a dairy farm. He was sentenced to seven years in prison. In Russia, allegations of corruption and criminality became the foundation of political life during the Yeltsin presidency. Viktor Orbán in Hungary sold off the elegant headquarters of his new party Fidesz that had been provided by the state, and used it to build up a series of large-scale construction and media enterprises. His childhood home at Feksút became the site of one of the world's most elegant football stadia, opened in 2014. Critics accused him of building a "mafia state".[31]

Corruption was not necessarily a simply financial concept. In some countries, there were also scandals that arose out of revelations about the past political activities of leading political figures. In the GDR and in the Czech Republic, systematic processes were designed to eliminate people with a secret service past from political life. In Germany, an office under a former dissident pastor, Joachim Gauck, administered the files of the Stasi, and permitted access to victims of the secret police, who could thus identify their persecutors. Gauck built a tremendous moral authority, and in 2012 was elected President of the Federal Republic (a largely honorific post).

Corruption undermined trust in institutions. One of the most remarkable dissipations of popular acceptance occurred in the case of churches, especially but not only in Catholic countries. From the 1990s, a series of television documentaries and press reports revealed the extent of child abuse by the Irish Catholic Church. Numerically the most terrible part of the Irish scandal involved the Magdalene laundries, institutions established for so-called "fallen women" – prostitutes, but also pregnant single women and mothers. The women were systematically abused, and children were taken away and killed and then buried in mass graves. A government report in 2009 established that some 30,000 women had been through these fearful establishments in the nineteenth and twentieth centuries. The last was closed only in 1996. Taoiseach (Prime Minister) Enda Kenny issued a formal state apology, describing the laundries as "the nation's shame". The issue helped to fuel a very rapid de-Catholicization of Irish life. Poland, which with Ireland was the most Catholic country in Europe in the late twentieth century, only began to see a widespread documentation of clerical abuse in

2013. Before that, critics had focused on identifying real, but also in many instances simply alleged, instances in which Catholic priests and bishops had collaborated with the communist authorities in pre-1989 Poland. In Germany the discussion had taken off slightly earlier, after 2010; and went in parallel with an older examination of secular boarding schools devoted to progressive education that had also been the scene of massive abuse. In particular the Odenwaldschule, which was dedicated to the idea that teachers should be friends and fathers rather than authority figures, was at the center of the discussion. Its director between 1972 and 1985 had been a close friend of a leading educational reformer, Hartmut von Hentig, and was allowed to stay on as a teacher even after the first accusations surfaced. The school was closed in 2015.

The complaint that Pope John Paul II had not done enough to investigate the problem of abuse became increasingly loud. In 2009 the Vatican issued a statement admitting that between 1.5 and 5 percent of the clergy had been involved in sexual abuse over the past 50 years. Pope Benedict XVI's surprising and unprecedented decision to abdicate as Pope in 2013 was chiefly driven by an increasing physical frailty, but he also felt the burden of the church abuse revelations and was increasingly frustrated by the secretive Vatican bureaucracy. As was his successor, the Argentine Jesuit who became Pope Francis and condemned the church hierarchy as suffering from "spiritual Alzheimer's".[32]

Corruption and its elimination became major issues as political systems no longer focused on class-based redistributionist politics. The class content of politics had been heavier in the East, but it had been the basis of the calculations of western party strategists also. Another related way of making the same point is that the politics of corruption now filled the gap left by the ending of ideological clashes. In both cases, corruption supplied material to allow a class war and ideological politics back in by stealth.

The new politics 4: the threatened environment

The search for a better and cleaner way of living became greater as people became richer (cleanliness is a luxury); and like corruption politics it lent itself to concealed redistributional politics. Like corruption, the environment as a political issue flared up in periodic scares, outbreaks of panic about particular cases of environmental degradation. The first such eruptions occurred on the eve of the end of the Cold War: the "mad cow" crisis in the United Kingdom, and the radiation diffusion from the Chernobyl explosion in the Soviet Union. Chernobyl played a major part in the discrediting of the Soviet apparat, and "mad cow disease" also played a (rather smaller) part in the discrediting of the British Conservatives.

In 1980, Italy restricted veal imports from other countries, including members of the EC, where hormones had been used in animal feedstuffs, and the EC responded by banning the use of hormones. In 1987, the United

States brought a case to the General Agreement on Tariffs and Trade (GATT), and when the EC refused to agree to the creation of a technical experts' group, imposed retaliatory trade measures. In 1998, the successor to the GATT, the World Trade Organization (WTO), ruled that the EU ban did not comply with scientific standards and was political. By this stage, European consumers had been mobilized into a high state of anxiety for other unrelated reasons.

In 1986, BSE ("mad cow disease") was detected in the United Kingdom, and by May 1990 13,849 cases had been discovered. The disease resulted from the consumption of diseased tissue (most importantly brain tissue), and in 1988 the United Kingdom took an initial but inadequate step to address the problem by banning the use of sheep carcasses in animal feed. Questions about the transferability of the disease to humans were answered with bland official assurances that all was well. But as it turned out, human cases of a related disorder, Creutzfeldt-Jacob disease, began to be reported, and were apparently related to meat consumption, although with an extended and sinister delay that made it very hard to trace the route of infection. By 2002, there had been in the United Kingdom some 100 human deaths, mostly of young adults, and the number of casualties was continuing to rise. In 1990, France, Germany, and Italy imposed a ban on the import of British beef. The British government replied with a xenophobic campaign in which it made it clear that it was unpatriotic not to eat British beef, and with a legal complaint against the EC (which it lost). The Minister of Agriculture, who was responsible for ensuring the safety of food and for managing the crisis of British animal farmers (two contradictory requirements), made sure that he was photographed feeding a hamburger to his daughter at an agricultural fair.

Contaminated feed spread the disease to other European countries, in particular France, Switzerland, and Germany. They blamed the United Kingdom, in very nationalist terms. In 2000, the German government appointed an energetic environmentalist, Renate Künast of the Green Party, as Minister of Agriculture, with a specific mandate of breaking the traditional links of the Agriculture Ministry with the farm lobby and of making German food safer. In 1997, the new British Labour government banned sales of beef on the bone; farmers responded with a blockade of imported (especially Irish) beef. In 1998, the EU lifted its ban on British beef imports, while farmers and consumers in other EU countries protested.

Other countries used beef nationalism of their own. Polish farmers, who were worried about the likely implications of Polish membership in the EU, successfully pressed the Polish government in 1997 to restrict beef exports from the EU. In 1999, animal feedstuffs in Belgium were found to be contaminated by dioxin. Coca-Cola was withdrawn from stores in Belgium, France, Germany, Italy, and the Netherlands because some cans of the drink had produced symptoms of food poisoning. In 2001, the United Kingdom was hit by foot-and-mouth disease, caused by the feeding to livestock of non-treated kitchen waste from a Chinese restaurant.

The food scandals were associated with hysterical displays of "econationalism". It was always food from somewhere else that was unsafe: continental Europe blamed British beef and American (hormonally treated) beef; England blamed Chinese exports; eastern Europe blamed the EU. Europeans refused to accept genetically modified crops from the United States. Individual European countries (including Austria, France, Germany, Greece, and Italy) adopted their own rules on which genetically modified crops would be excluded from their national markets. Food became one of the major indicators of the pernicious effects of globalization. In August 1999 a French farmer, José Bové, became famous for destroying a French branch of the hamburger chain McDonald's. A year later, he was one of the stars of antiglobalization protests against the meeting of the WTO in Seattle. There was a demand for more locally sourced nutrition. In Italy, in 1986 a "slow food" movement was started by Carlo Petrini, in part as a response to the establishment of the fast food McDonald's restaurant in the iconic position of Rome's Spanish steps.

Environmentalists and antiglobalization protesters complained that globalization was making the spread of disease more frequent. It might more plausibly be argued that the crisis was the result of an over-intensive agriculture, protected for political reasons in Europe, and pushed by the availability of subsidies into using unsafe animal feed. To import food from further away, where there was more farmland and less pressure to maximize the output of limited land area, would have been a safer way of solving Europe's food neurosis. But there were large measures of nationalism and local patriotism involved in the protests against the nutritional consequences of globalized living. Like much of the new angst of the 1990s, it was a response to increased uncertainty about change.

The new politics 5: localist nationalisms

Nationalism was in fact the specter haunting the European revolutions of 1989–91: terrifying, but in most places largely harmless. Many participants in the East European reform movements were driven by a strong sense of national belonging, which they believed had been violated by the long period of Soviet or Russian domination. The nation gave a framework and a meaning to social existence, and would provide a context in which civil society might be regenerated. In the particular circumstances of the collapse of communism, national community could justify the harsh sacrifices which inevitably accompanied the restructuring of the economy from plan to market.

The rediscovery of the nation was part of the 1989 phenomenon. In November 1989, East Germans began to chant "*Wir sind ein Volk*" ("we are one people") rather than "*Wir sind das Volk*" ("we are the people", in whose name the Communist Party claimed to rule). On November 4, 1989, the West German novelist Martin Walser explained that "in the human measure of things, the nation is the mightiest historical occurrence until now. Mighty in a geological, not a political sense."[33]

While the new civic solidarity could be easily interpreted by its admirers as a positive "patriotism", there were also many manifestations of a more divisive, xenophobic nationalism, which appeared to draw from the most dangerous movements of twentieth-century life. In consequence, some intellectuals felt a great deal of nostalgia for the apparent stability of the pre-1989 world. That yearning was expressed eloquently by Eric Hobsbawm, who thought it "the great achievement of the communist regimes in multinational countries to limit the disastrous effects of nationalism within them".[34]

The threat of virulent xenophobia was heightened because of the rapidity of social and political change: in very unstable circumstances it is often psychologically attractive (in a sort of infantile regression) to hold onto traditions as a kind of comfort blanket and to reject and demonize the new and the strange. Trivially, citizens of the former GDR became nostalgic about small everyday aspects of life, such as the small hard rolls that had been wiped off bakers' shelves by big fluffy West German kaiser rolls. A much more immediate cause of the new nationalism and xenophobia was the confrontation with strange people, as well as strange events. Another consequence of modernity, which was greatly accentuated by the political changes of 1989–91, was mobility. Larger numbers of people moved as walls and barbed wire fences were removed. Immigration to the countries of the EC, which was gradually rising since the early 1960s in response to economic opportunities (and falling in times of recession, in the late 1960s and the early 1980s), surged after 1989. In particular, the numbers seeking asylum soared: 397,000 in the 15 members of the EU in 1990, 511,000 in 1991, and 672,000 in 1992. After that the annual numbers fell again to the late 1990s. In 1999, 13 million people, 3.4 percent of the EU population, were nationals of other countries, double the proportion from 1985; and the proportions were higher in Germany (6.7 percent), in Austria (9.3 percent), and in Switzerland (not a member of the EU). An estimated 1 million people a year (net) were coming into the EU by the end of the century.

The movements of people were particularly intense after large-scale disasters. The wars in former Yugoslavia produced large outflows of homeless and victimized refugees. Even an economic collapse could generate large migrations. In early 1997 a number of fraudulent pyramid investment schemes in Albania disintegrated, large numbers of Albanians rioted, the government collapsed, and many citizens tried to flee across the Adriatic to Italy (from where they were repatriated).

Even larger numbers of people expressed some wish to move, and would have moved if they could have migrated easily. Governments consequently tried to find measures to deter migrants. The compulsory repatriation of illegal immigrants is rare, but its practice increased in the 1990s, leading to ugly incidents (including some fatalities) on commercial aircraft.

Nationalist reactions, fears about immigration, and enhanced mobility were interconnected phenomena at the turn of the century. Sometimes, but not always, this pattern of response to modern living was accompanied by violence. This was not an entirely novel development of the 1990s, merely one that became much more acute and dangerous. In the very mild economic downturn of the late 1960s, Germany and Switzerland, which had imported large numbers of *Gastarbeiter* (migrant "guest" workers), were able to send them home. Where immigrants stayed, they were verbally attacked. In April 1968, the British Conservative politician Enoch Powell gave an inflammatory speech in Birmingham, in which he reported how a "quite ordinary working man" had told him: "If I had the money to go, I wouldn't stay in this country . . . In this country in fifteen or twenty years' time the black man will have the whip hand over the white man." Powell himself concluded: "As I look ahead, I am filled with foreboding. Like the Roman, I seem to see 'the River Tiber foaming with much blood'."[35] London dock workers, traditionally supporters of the Labour left, marched in support of Powell's message.

In part, Powell may have been driven to these statements by a strongly nationalist anti-Americanism, which feared the replication of American life in the United Kingdom, and viewed the race riots of the late 1960s in Newark and elsewhere as a sign of the deep American malaise. In fact, neither was Newark the beginning of a general US disintegration, nor did British race relations replicate those of the United States. Though there were outbreaks of civil unrest in which ethnic and racial tensions played a substantial part in Brixton (London) in 1981 and in a number of northern cities (Bradford, Burnley, and Oldham) in 2001, these were largely isolated episodes on the road to the creation of a multi-ethnic and multi-racial United Kingdom.

Some of the most unpleasant manifestations in the 1990s of what is sometimes called the "new nationalism" involved attacks on immigrants and ethnic minorities. The unification of Germany was followed by a wave of right-wing violence against immigrants – not just in the former East Germany, where there were attacks on asylum centers, but also in the former West. The most horrific single incident was in Schleswig-Holstein in Mölln in 1992, when a Turkish family was burned in an incendiary attack and a grandmother and two daughters died.

Roma and Sinti were attacked in many countries. When they responded to persecution by flight in large numbers, other governments tried to restrict movement. For instance, in 1999 there was an upsurge of violence in Slovakia, and many EU countries quickly responded by introducing visa requirements for Slovak nationals as a means of stopping an inflow of Roma. In 2008 and 2009 there was an upsurge of attacks on Roma in Hungary.

In some European countries, an explicitly xenophobic platform helped propel parties to political success, and even to participation in government. Jean-Marie Le Pen's Front National started to gain support in the 1980s, and survived a series of splits and personal disputes in the 1990s. Again, this was quite an old phenomenon. Le Pen had begun his political career in the 1950s, when he had become the youngest member of the French parliament (1956), with essentially the same platform as that of the nationalist right against the globalized 1980s and 1990s: a rejection of internationalism and of the foreigner. In 1988, he had won 14.4 percent of the vote in the first round of the presidential election; in 2002 he collected 16.9 percent, and with this went on to the run-off round against Jacques Chirac. In 2011 he was succeeded as president of the party by his daughter, Marine Le Pen, who modernized the party and turned against the anti-Semitism of the older generation. She renamed the party as National Rally (*rassemblement national*).

The most stunning initial example of governmental participation by an extreme right party was the Austrian Freedom Party (FPÖ), a centrist liberal party which in the immediate postwar years successfully collected ex-Nazi votes for a liberal cause, but which was taken over by Jörg Haider and converted into an instrument for demagogic populism. It received 26.9 percent of the vote in parliamentary elections in 1999 and tied for second place with the People's Party (Christian Democrats); and some of its members (but not Haider) then participated in a coalition party with the People's Party. The coalition quite quickly fell apart, however, and in new elections in 2002 the Freedom Party lost a great part of its support.

In this general climate of heightening xenophobic nationalism, the most dramatic attempts to drive out ethnically different people came in former communist countries, and were linked to a drive to reformulate boundaries and territories.

The new Croat state, initially headed by the robust nationalist Franjo Tudjman, who had been an anti-Nazi partisan during the Second World War, shocked many foreigners by the rehabilitation of symbols from the German puppet state of Ante Pavelić and the Ustaša during the war. The currency of the newly independent state was called the *kuna*, the name of the wartime currency. Under Tudjman, the state encouraged the expulsion of Serbs.

Nationalism also in the 1990s resulted in the break-up of existing states. The most violent examples of break-up occurred in Yugoslavia and the Soviet Union. But even in these two cases, violence was by no means universal. In Yugoslavia the separation of Slovenia was almost entirely peaceful (almost, because the Yugoslav army fought a brief and unsuccessful war trying to prevent it); and most of the Soviet disintegration was peaceful, despite the highly militarized nature of Soviet society and the large numbers of weapons (including atomic weapons) available to successor states.

The potentially highly explosive Baltic states had substantial Russian populations (Estonia had 30 percent and Latvia 34 percent in 1989, while there were only 9 percent Russians in Lithuania). But a third of the Russian Estonians voted for independence. After independence, many Baltic Russians were worried about the new majority nationalism but still largely did not want their countries to return to Russian rule. In 1994, Latvia passed a naturalization law requiring not only a five-year residence in Latvia but also proficiency in Latvian. The Estonian law of 1995 was even more restrictive, and over seven years only 150,000 out of 4,745,000 Russians qualified to become Estonian citizens. But there was surprisingly little Russian protest.

Ukraine had a very powerful Russian population, especially in the industrial eastern Ukraine, which frequently complained about the new use of the Ukrainian language. In 1992 an ethnic Russian, Leonid Kuchma, who argued for closer ties with Russia, formed a government, and was elected President in 1994. But as President he almost immediately rejected discussions of reunification with Russia, and began to speak Ukrainian on public occasions.

Central Asia had many small-scale ethnic conflicts, with clashes in 1989 between Kazakhs and Lezgins at Novy Uzen, and between Uzbeks and Turks in the Ferghana valley. In 1990 the Tajiks fought the Kyrgyz in Kyrgyzstan, and a bitter and prolonged civil war developed in Tajikistan. But with the exception of the Tajik war, the general situation was astonishingly peaceful. Ethnic Russians simply left; some, descendants of the "Volga Germans" deported by Stalin in the 1930s, were able to use the peculiar German nationality law that included Germans by descent in order to emigrate to Germany. Surprisingly, the only real revolt of ethnic Russians against a non-Russian successor state occurred in eastern (trans-Dniestrian) Moldova, where the Russians resented the Moldavian language law of 1989 and feared that the Moldavians were proposing to join Romania. After the August 1991 coup and its failure, and as it became clear that the Soviet Union was disintegrating, these Russians held a referendum in which they declared their independence. The Transdniestr Molodovan Republic was protected by the Russian Fourteenth Army, under the command of one of the most charismatic of ex-Soviet army generals, Alexander Lebed. This was the region where nostalgia for the Soviet Union lived on in its purest form. In 1997 the two parts of Moldova reached an agreement that the two governments would "develop relations as part of a single state".

Czechoslovakia also broke apart with no violence in the "Velvet Divorce". In 1990, the country had a new name: Czech and Slovak Republic. A great deal of power was devolved to Slovakia, which had historically been much more backward, and had been the center of Soviet-era industrialization efforts in central and eastern Slovakia: Banská Bystrica, Žilina, and Kosiče. Again, there was plenty of potential for conflict. The leading figure in post-communist politics, Vladimír Mečiar, wanted to preserve as much as possible of communist economic control, and thought Slovak nationalism a good weapon for a new political era. Mečiar was at first in the forefront of the reform movement that took power after the collapse of communism, Public Against Violence, but he left it in 1991 because he interpreted its program as inimical to Slovak interests. He started a new party, Movement for a Democratic Slovakia, that could best be interpreted as a party for absorbing former *nomenklatura* communists. His dispute with the free-market Czech Prime Minister, Vaclav

Klaus, was fundamentally about market reforms (which Mečiar opposed). When Klaus refused to allow complete independence in economic policy, Mečiar could only go ahead with complete national independence.

From 1994 to 1998, Mečiar governed with the support of a coalition of his own party, an extreme leftist party, and right-wing Slovak nationalists. It was a violent and very nationalist regime, which imposed Slovak language teaching on the substantial Hungarian minority and encouraged attacks on Roma and Sinti, whom it blamed for the post-Communist crime wave. During this period, Slovakia moved farther away from the possibility of candidacy for EU membership; and Slovakia's return to normality only began in 1998 with an electoral reversal for the Mečiar party.

Localized violence thus existed, but large-scale state-organized violence in Europe was rare, and was really confined to the wars in Yugoslavia and the wars in the Caucasus in the former Soviet Union.

Armenians in Nagorno-Karabakh in the late 1980s wanted increased autonomy for this largely Armenian enclave in Azerbaijan. Azerbaijanis mobilized against the Armenian threat, and in November 1988 millions went onto the streets of Baku. The result of the protest was the creation of the Azerbaijani Popular Front. In November 1989 Gorbachev tried to respond by returning Nagorno-Karabakh to Azerbaijan, but the street movements continued. Soviet troops in January 1990 occupied Baku, and killed at least 62 people. An open war between Armenia and Azerbaijan from 1992 to 1994 ended with a defeat of Azerbaijan, but it was still impossible to find a settlement for the Nagorno-Karabakh issue.

Russia was also involved in wars between Abkhazia and Georgia. In 1991–92 Russian soldiers supported the Abkhazians against the nationalist Georgian government of Zviad Gamsakhurdia. When he was overthrown and eventually replaced by the ex-Soviet Foreign Minister Eduard Shevardnadze, the Georgians eventually managed to get Boris Yeltsin to promote a peace settlement (1994–95) which restored Georgian "territorial integrity". The Abkhazians ignored this imposed settlement, as did the population of South Ossetia, where fighting continued.

In the North Caucasus, the Russian Federation had its own problem: a revolt by Chechens, who declared independence in November 1991, which led to a brutally fought war in 1994–96, and a second war in 1999. There was a longer-term historical problem: the Chechens had been resettled by Stalin in the 1930s, along with Balkars, Ingush and Karachai, in Central Asia, and had been allowed to return home only in the 1950s. From 1994 to 1996, Chechen armies humiliated numerically superior but demoralized Russian forces, and in August 1996 as part of a pacification, Russian troops withdrew from the capital, Grozny. Russia restarted the war in 1999, after a rising in August of radical Moslems in neighboring Dagestan, which was suppressed by Russian troops, and after a series of bomb explosions in Moscow which were attributed to Chechen criminal groups. Vladimir Putin as Prime Minister and then as President made the vigorous prosecution of the Chechen war a sign of a new tough approach to the government of Russia; 200,000 refugees fled, and some 45,000 civilians who did not were trapped in Grozny, which was systematically bombarded into the ground by Russian artillery. In February 2000, Putin was able to announce the capture of the razed city, but the war continued.

The drive to find new forms of autonomous existence below the state level, such as the divisions of Moldova, the "autonomy" of Nagorno-Karabakh, or the two "entities" into which Bosnia was divided, produced unlovely words to describe the new units, as well as profoundly unlovely politics. But it matched perfectly the new fissiparous and centripetal political realities of the 1990s, which could be seen as the accelerated development in formerly communist Europe of issues that had also developed, over a substantially longer period of time, in western Europe. In this sense, the old East was just catching up and joining a general European current.

As in the East, in many cases the western quest for particularism and localism was quite peaceful, but in a minority of situations it was extremely violent. The largest and most radical regionalist movement was that of Basque nationalism. The Basque territory had had the greatest concentrations of industrial development in Spain in the interwar and Franco years. It had the classic landscape of declining European heavy industry, with the big steel mills in Extebarri and Olaberria. Under the Republic, it had been one of the strongholds of the left, and Franco had first risen to prominence in suppressing a strike movement in nearby Asturias. As the civil war began, the Republican government tried to woo the Basques by granting a statute of autonomy. But Franco's forces, based in neighboring Navarre, quickly took the Basque lands. In 1947 there was a large strike that again was fiercely repressed. In 1959 some members of the Basque Nationalist Party (PNV) broke away because the movement was too ineffective in fighting Francoism, and created the Euzkadi Ta Azkatasuna (ETA). In the course of the 1960s, ETA adopted Marxist language and after 1968 advocated and practiced revolutionary violence. The reasoning took the same line as that of North African (and other Third World) "liberation" movements. In the late 1960s, violence escalated, and in 1970 16 ETA members were tried by a military court in Burgos. Nine were sentenced to death, but Franco commuted the sentences.

With democratization, the PNV demanded immediate autonomy and complete independence as a long-term goal. In 1978 the new Spanish constitution introduced a semi-federal regional system, and affirmed the right of Spain's "nationalities and regions" to autonomy. A statute of autonomy allowed a Basque parliament, a government, Basque control of justice and the police, economic policy-making, and the recognition of Basque as an official language. As the largest party in terms of electoral support (at least in local elections), the PNV began to be willing to condemn ETA and in 1988 reached an agreement with Madrid on the "Normalization and Pacification of Euzkadi". At the same time, ETA became increasingly violent: it killed

17 people in 1976, 67 in 1978, and 88 in 1980. Most, but not all, of its victims were in the Basque country. Its most spectacular outrages occurred in bombing campaigns in Madrid.

Catalonia, too, where there had been big demonstrations during the move to democracy, had its own statute of autonomy and in 1980 its first parliament met. But here the result of the post-Franco constitutional devolution was a pacification and a return to stability as well as vigorous economic growth. In terms of a deep historical logic, the new Spain looked like a rejection of the centralization of the Spanish Republic and of Franco's Spain, and a return to the "mixed monarchy" tradition of Spain in the golden age of the Habsburg rulers. Catalonia, under a separatist government, held a referendum on independence on October 1, 2017 (it was widely called the O-1 vote). But in this case, the Spanish Constitutional Court had declared it illegal after a request from the conservative Spanish government. The vote was 92 percent in favor, but the turnout was only 43 percent. Those in favor of remaining in Spain had not voted, but in many places the ballot had also been blocked by the Spanish National Police Corps and the Guardia Civil. After the vote, the central Spanish government took action against the political leaders of the independence movement, and the separatist Catalan Prime Minister Carles Puigdemont declared: "I assume the mandate of the people for Catalonia to become an independent state in the shape of a republic." But he left it uncertain whether he was actually declaring Catalan independence. On October 27, 2017, the Parliament of Catalonia unilaterally declared independence from Spain, and the Spanish government replied by invoking a clause in the constitution which dissolved the parliament. Puigdemont and other ministers were charged by the Spanish government with sedition, and they fled abroad. In a new election for the Catalan parliament the parties that supported independence had 47.6 percent of the vote, while 43.5 percent of voters chose the constitutionalist parties.

A radicalization similar to that of the Basque country occurred in Northern Ireland (six of the original nine counties of Ulster that remained in the United Kingdom in 1922: the other three were in the Republic, or the "South"). It had been largely peaceful since the civil war of the 1920s (in which it played only a small role), until 1967. Some of the background to violent nationalism, as in the Basque country, lay in the grim social realities of declining old industries. From the 1960s, the bases of Ulster's former prosperity, linen and shipbuilding, were in permanent crisis. Job losses fueled unemployment rates that were consistently higher than in the rest of the UK, and some of the industries that were still working limited the employment of Catholics. The (Protestant) government of Ulster tried to deal with increased tensions by starting negotiations about economic cooperation with the Republic, and thereby radicalized a substantial part of the Ulster Protestant movement, which started to fear a "sell-out". The radical Presbyterian minister Ian Paisley organized marches. On the Catholic side, a civil rights movement founded in 1967 took on some of the confrontational culture of student movements elsewhere in Europe, but also of the black movements of the United States. In 1968 Paisley was arrested and imprisoned for blocking a civil rights march.

The Protestant marches turned more and more violent. In January 1969 the Paisleyites attacked, and in August (the height of the traditional marching season of the Protestant orders), assisted by parts of the Ulster police force including the terrifying "B-Specials", attacked Catholic areas in the Belfast "Bogside". Moving British soldiers into Northern Ireland was the London government's attempt to tackle the Protestant sectarianism of the Ulster police force, but gave rise to a reorganized "Provisional" IRA (Irish Republican Army). In 1971 large numbers of suspected IRA members were interned, and on January 30, 1972, 13 civilians were killed by British troops during a banned civil rights march in Londonderry. At this point, the British government suspended the Northern Irish government and imposed direct rule from Westminster. In the course of 1972, the death toll from communitarian violence in Northern Ireland was 474. The religious communities increasingly separated: the 1991 census showed half the population of Northern Ireland living in mono-religious areas, where there were more than 90 percent Protestants or more than 95 percent Catholics.

Restoring Northern Irish government, with guarantees for the participation of Catholics and for the maintenance of peace, proved a nearly impossible task. Logic might imply that it should have been easier once both the United Kingdom and the Republic of Ireland joined the EC in 1972, but the Community institutions treated Northern Ireland and its problems as a quagmire that they should best avoid. The most successful peace-building initiatives from the outside were American and not European in origin, and culminated in the Good Friday Agreement (April 10, 1998), creating some measure of devolution and power-sharing with a Northern Ireland Assembly and Northern Ireland Executive, that would work in the context of a Ministerial Council involving both Northern Ireland and the Republic. The success of the agreement depended heavily on the removal of physical restrictions at the border, the encouragement of mobility and trade, and the membership of both the United Kingdom and the Irish Republic in the EU.

Scottish nationalism, by contrast, was entirely peaceful. It too was in some part the response to the decline of traditional industries and to the empty shipyards on the Clyde. It was always stronger in robust (and partly Catholic) Glasgow than in the gentrified and rather Anglophile environment of Edinburgh. A National Party of Scotland had been founded in 1928. The major nationalist revival of the 1970s was helped greatly by two circumstances. First, the development of British oil and gas in the North Sea in the 1970s at the time of the big increase in oil prices brought prosperity to parts of eastern and northern Scotland (the oil development industry had its base in Aberdeen), but also a demand that Scotland should derive more economic benefits from oil. The commentator Tom Nairn pointed out that "even a share of the oil revenues would be enough to transform this small land into another Norway".[36] Second, the Conservative Party largely collapsed in Scotland. Its voters went to a party that in social terms embraced a broad range of interests, the Scottish National Party (SNP): like the PNV, it could loosely be described as social democratic. Labour, which remained reasonably strong in Scotland, and began its general move to the political center and voter viability under a Scottish (Edinburgh) leader, John Smith, eventually pledged itself to a substantial measure of devolution. The promise was realized, along with a less extensive devolution for Wales, in 1997–98 by the Labour government of Tony Blair. After the global financial crisis of 2007–08 raised questions about the distribution of the tax burden, and of government spending, separatism surged again. Scotland, under a SNP First Minister, held a referendum in 2014, in accordance with the terms of an agreement with the UK parliament. The outcome was a 55 percent vote against the proposal, thus confirming the union with England and Wales. But the UK-wide Brexit referendum of 2016, in which Scotland (and Northern Ireland) voted against Brexit but a majority in the whole of the United Kingdom voted in favor, ensured that the issue of Scottish independence remained alive.

The devolution that took place directly under the nose of the EC was a solution to Flemish–Walloon antagonism in Belgium that had erupted into spectacular confrontation in and after the two world wars. In 1970, Belgium was split into three regions (Flemish, Walloon, and Brussels as a divided city), with two separate cultural councils. The 1974 Law on Preparatory Regionalization gave each council advisory competence "in matters in which a regional policy is wholly or partially justified". The councils' power was further enhanced in 1980.

In Switzerland, after a long and occasionally violent campaign, the largely French-speaking Jurassiens seceded from the German-dominated canton of Bern in 1978 after a national referendum approved of the creation of the new canton of Jura.

The new particularist nationalisms of western Europe had one feature in common. They developed in classic industrial areas where the problem of the restructuring of old industries provoked major discontent. Local awareness of difference grew more acute because of the problems of iron and steel in Catalonia, shipbuilding and textiles in Northern Ireland, steel and coal in Scotland, steel in Slovakia and Ukraine, and watch-making in the Jura.

Breaking up, in more or less peaceful circumstances, was thus by no means a phenomenon confined to the former Soviet sphere of influence. In very many cases, ethnic and national differences were resolved peacefully. Where they were not, the irresolvable character of the conflict was due more to peculiar deep-seated constitutional arrangements (the division of the USSR into republics; the separate status of Northern Ireland in the British Union) than to any simple fact of difference between varied groups of human beings.

Isms and wasms

The twentieth century depended heavily on the "isms" which have in part been summarized in previous boxes. By the end of the century, there was a widespread sense that utopian ideologies, the anti-modern politics of modernism, and ideological cleavages had contributed to the European disasters of the mid-century. In the 1960s, an influential book by Daniel Bell announced *The End of Ideology: On the Exhaustion of Political Ideas in the Fifties* (1960), in essence prematurely but correctly. One way of popularizing this message was to claim that the "isms" had become, or were becoming, "wasms".

The new defining ideas of the twentieth-century *fin de siècle* in Europe were more concrete than the "isms": civil society, governance, and subsidiarity. "Civil society" was a term taken from Hegel and Marx (*bürgerliche Gesellschaft*) to refer to a sphere of social organization and institution-building that was not centrally directed or political or dependent on law. Hegel believed that it was incomplete without the state. Marx used the term in the same sense, as an incomplete social world. Oppositionists in central Europe before 1989 used the demand for civil society as a way of demanding freedom to organize voluntary associations. At the same time, in advanced industrial societies the demand for more civil society was founded on the idea that modern life had become increasingly atomized. After the end of communism, *civil society* became widely used as a way of describing a network of pressure and advocacy groups (Amnesty International, Greenpeace, Oxfam, Médecins Sans Frontières, to list only a few of the most influential and productive of them) that had quite strong political aims. Such organizations became much more powerful in the course of the last years of the century.

"Governance" is a clearer term, and became widely used in the 1990s as a way of expressing the demand for an end to the politics of corruption (see above). Good governance required rules about the conduct of political and business life, many of which were quite specific (such as the application of auditing principles). The controversial aspect related to who should bear the responsibility for improving governance: would it come as a result of the initiative of civil society, or did it need to be imposed as part of the conditionality applied by international or supranational institutions such as the EU or the IMF?

Finally, the doctrine of *subsidiarity* came from Catholic social theory, and had been used in 1931 by Pius XI to explain the organization of the Church hierarchy. The principle was that decisions should be made at the lowest administrative level possible and consistent with general principles of good governance. For the EU,

subsidiarity meant trying to dispel the idea of a centralized dictatorship in the Brussels administration. Powers and decisions – such
as on standards and trade descriptions – should be left to national
authorities as far as was consistent with the internal market. Further
down, subsidiarity meant that federal states such as Germany would
leave powers with their component states; and subsidiarity should
promote a greater move to regionalism. In this way, it is at the center
of the erosion of the powers of the nation-state – toward the center in
some areas, and toward regions in other. Since the nation-state was
the area in which most twentieth-century "isms" were played out,
this too is part of the movement away from ideology.

The EC/EU should be an ideal mechanism for solving this kind of issue,
since it involves broad and high-level economic cooperation, and at the
same time a principle of "subsidiarity" (which was rediscovered as a guide
to good governance during the 1990s): leaving as many decisions as possible
to the lowest administrative and political unit at which they can be taken.
A "Europe of regions" could well complement a "Europe of nations". But
in fact, paradoxically some of the best examples of cross-border regional
cooperation and identity formation are on the external boundaries of the
EU (where incentives to cooperate from the poorer regions are greater):
the development of the Alsace–Baden–Basel area at the corner of Germany,
France, and Switzerland, around the city of Basel; the cooperation across
the Slovenian–Italian boundary around Trieste; and a new region at the
corner of Germany, Poland, and the Czech Republic. In contrast, some of
the more recalcitrant and non-cooperative areas are wholly in the EU: most
spectacularly in the case of Northern Ireland/Ireland, but also in the Alto
Adige, in Italy across the border from Austria.

In practice, however, at the national level, at least until the 2008 global
financial crisis, the EU very effectively limits the scope for the expression of
a radical nationalist or separatist agenda, while at the same time offering a
framework for more peaceful expressions of local identity. The EU limited
political expression, but it also limited incivility and the politics of defamation
and destruction. At this point the reader may rethink the historical thought
experiment with which Chapter 4, on the crisis of interwar German democracy, began. If Hitler had taken part in a coalition government in 1932 in a
political environment which was internationally constrained (i.e. before the
Lausanne conference lifted the reparations clauses of the Versailles Treaty) he
would have quickly seen his political impotence demonstrated very clearly,
and the Nazi movement would have failed. The fall of the FPÖ coalition
in Austria in 2002 is a trivial version of such an experiment. The taming of
Spanish and Portuguese radicalism in the 1970s is a much more dramatic

example. In the EU as currently operating, it is impossible to be a successful radical populist and be in government.

The constitutional challenges and uncertainties that Europe faced at the beginning of the twenty-first century were an indication of a new development. The leaders of the EU became polarized between those in the United Kingdom, France, and Spain, who saw the driving force as being an inter-governmental process, and those (especially in Germany, and in some of the smaller countries) who wanted to see an increased role for the EU Commission. The European leaders were also uncertain as to whether the EU was a rational and logical construct that developed step by step from the economic logic of the common market, or whether it was the deeper expression of a common cultural identity. Many were aware that their thought owed much to Europe's Christian tradition, but were unwilling to state this publicly, for two reasons. First, late-twentieth-century Europe had become largely de-Christianized, and electors were highly secular. Secondly, any definition of Europe in terms of a Judeo-Christian tradition stood at odds with the economic and demographic need for greater immigration, and the already dramatic presence of large Moslem communities: mostly Turkish in Germany; North African in France, Italy, and Spain; and from the Indian subcontinent in the United Kingdom. These problems were heightened by the discussion of the threat of fundamentalist terrorism in the wake of the September 11, 2001, attacks on New York and Washington.

Thus Europe, and especially its leaders, were almost wholly opposed to making any cultural claims about their new political order. The renunciation of an idea of European culture was reflected in the design of the new European currency issued in 2002: there were no cultural icons, such as Goethe, Michelangelo, Molière, Rembrandt, or Shakespeare, since each was identified with primarily national cultures; and no portraits of great European political figures, say Charles V or Napoleon. Instead the notes showed deliberately abstracted versions of architecture and bridges, as well as a map which showed North Africa and Asian (but not European, i.e. west of the Bosporus) Turkey colored in such a way as to show that it was different from Europe. In 2002, a convention chaired by former French President Valéry Giscard d'Estaing began to discuss a new constitutional design for Europe. Giscard publicly dismissed Turkish membership of the EU as dangerous to the European mission; but his effort to give a specifically Judeo-Christian interpretation was blocked by the French government. The attempt to design a new constitution for Europe failed when it was rejected by referenda in France and the Netherlands in 2005. In its place, many of the provisions of the proposed constitution, such as easier decision-making through qualified majority voting, were handled by changing the original treaties in a new Lisbon Treaty (2007), which came into force in 2009.

The political map and design of Europe became complicated as the EU developed, like the former Soviet Union, the Russian Federation, and the other successor states, more and more into a patchwork quilt, in which there are different levels of sub-state existence and regional autonomy. The status of Kosovo and the "entities" created in the Bosnian settlement is still unclear. In the seventeenth century, the German political philosopher Samuel Pufendorf, who followed Thomas Hobbes in looking for hard sovereignty, found sovereignty so dispersed in his own homeland that he described the Holy Roman Empire, with its tiers of mediate and immediate principalities, bishoprics, abbeys, towns, and statelets as being "like a monster", i.e. impossible to classify with neat scientific precision. He would have found some aspects of early-twenty-first-century constitutional complexity quite familiar. The "new politics" of constitutional complexity was in fact very old.

The replacement of politics by morality is also, as the Oxford philosopher Isaiah Berlin pointed out in a remarkable essay, "European Unity and its Vicissitudes", in 1959, a historical return. Isaiah Berlin saw a reversion to a Europe that was universal in that it rejected the celebration of the particular and the different in late-eighteenth-century Romanticism. Before that era, the world was "a single, intelligible whole. It consisted of certain stable ingredients, material and spiritual; if they were not stable they were not real." After the catastrophes of the mid-twentieth century, which could not as easily be overcome politically or psychologically as they were materially (in the age of the Marshall Plan), there was a need for a new vision: "there is a return to the ancient notion of natural law, but for some of us, in empiricist dress – no longer necessarily based on theological or metaphysical foundations."[37]

By the end of the twentieth century, a historical reversal of institutional and political forms set in, in the manner predicted by Berlin. The end of the twentieth century brought an unraveling of the threads that had constituted what older analysts had once believed to be a one-way process of modernization in the form of the building of a strong state. 1989 immediately and obviously undid 1917 and the legacy of the Bolshevik revolution, but the business of undoing historically formed ideas and institutions did not stop there. Already in 1928, Leon Trotsky, deported by Stalin to Alma Ata, had noted that "the film of revolution is running backwards".[38] In the 1990s, Europe went back before 1789, i.e. before the era of ideological politics. By 2003, it was going back before 1648, when the Peace of Westphalia that ended the Thirty Years' War effectively introduced the concept of an international order based on a community of sovereign states. Fissiparous pressures dismantled the political institutions of the nation-state that most Europeans for most of the twentieth century had assumed to be eternally durable, even when they generated problems and disasters.

In terms of basic expectations about life – sickness and health, old age, welfare – Europe looked more certain and stable than at the beginning of the twentieth century. But when people thought about a broader world, their impressions were different and much less secure. Politics no longer assured control of economic, social, or cultural forces. Part of the problem stemmed from the sense of a need for natural law as a guide to conduct, but without any of the theological and metaphysical foundations on which it had previously been based. A part of the confusion at the beginning of the twenty-first century came from the impression that time no longer ran unambiguously forwards.

In the 1980s, Mikhail Gorbachev referred very frequently to "our common European house" that included both East and West. It would end the division of Europe, the competition of systems, the security threat, and the Cold War of the superpowers. Gorbachev indeed frequently used the idea of Europe to suggest that the bipolar world dominated by the superpowers was at an end. But many commentators in both East and West remarked in the 1980s on how vague the details of the "common European house" were in reality. In his speech to the Council of Europe on July 6, 1989, Gorbachev admitted to uncertainty about "the architecture of our common house, or how it should be built and even how it should be furnished".[39] President George H.W. Bush jibed that if it were really a common European house, people should be free to wander from one room into another.

One decade after the collapse of communism, it was clear that there was a substantial amount of convergence: in the democratic form of politics, in the rise of new political issues, the redundancy of *right* and *left* as previously understood, but also in a commitment to economic reform, the acceptance of the market and the principle of private property, and improvement of mortality rates. But the uncertainty about the architecture remained just as real as when Gorbachev was using the rhetoric of Europe in the politics of the fading Cold War. The EU had embarked on a transformatory expansion. French and Germans saw their remarkable act of national reconciliation in the 1950s as being extended to the whole continent (under their leadership). Americans unsympathetic to the EU talked about a "new Europe", driven by the more recent members, the United Kingdom and the Mediterranean and above all the central European states, replacing the "old Europe" centered around France and Germany. And the jibe about many Europeans not being able to move all around the rooms of the common European house still applied.

Notes

1 Mikhail Gorbachev, *Gipfelgespräche: Geheime Protokolle aus meiner Amtszeit*, Berlin: Rowohlt, 1993, pp. 128–9.
2 Julian Bullard, "Time to feed the country's western roots", *Financial Times*, October 29, 1990.
3 *Der Spiegel*, 17/2002, 22 April 2002, p. 196.
4 Ibid., p. 198.
5 Timothy Garton-Ash, *The Magic Lantern: The Revolution of '89 Witnessed in Warsaw, Budapest, Berlin, and Prague*, New York, NY: Random House, 1990, p. 105.
6 And in practice worked out by Bodo Hombach and Peter Mandelson.
7 Hywel Williams, *Guilty Men: Conservative Decline and Fall*, London: Aurum Press, 1998, p. 183.

8 Naomi Klein, *No Logo: Taking Aim at the Brand Bullies*, New York, NY: Picador, 1999.

9 *Fortune World Business Directory 1980*, Trenton, 1981; www.fortune.com/lists/G500.

10 Quoted in *The Economist*, September 14, 2002, p. 55.

11 Nigel Lawson, *The View from No. 11: Memoirs of a Tory Radical*, London: Bantam Press, 1992, p. 1005.

12 Peter Reddaway and Dmitri Glinski, *The Tragedy of Russia's Reforms: Market Bolshevism against Democracy*, Washington, DC: United States Institute of Peace Press, 2001, p. 254.

13 Yegor Gaidar, "The legacy of the Socialist economy: the macro- and microeconomic consequences of soft budget contraints", in Mario I. Blejer and Marko Škreb (eds), *Transition: The First Decade*, Cambridge, MA: MIT Press, 2001, p. 311.

14 Cited in Christopher Granville, "The political and societal environment of economic policy", in Brigitte Granville and Peter Oppenheimer (eds), *Russia's Post-Communist Economy*, Oxford: Oxford University Press, 2001, p. 33.

15 Quoted by Stephen Kotkin, "Trashcanistan: a tour through the wreckage of the Soviet empire", *New Republic*, April 15, 2002, p. 26.

16 David E. Hoffman, *The Oligarchs: Wealth and Power in the New Russia*, New York, NY: Public Affairs, 2002, pp. 348–9.

17 Reddaway and Glinski, *Tragedy*, p. 600.

18 Noel Malcolm, *Bosnia: A Short History*, London: Macmillan, 1994, p. 213.

19 Jacques Attali, *Verbatim, Vol. III, Chronique des Années 1988–1991*, Paris: Fayard, 1995, p. 401.

20 Quoted in Richard H. Ullman (ed.), *The World and Yugoslavia's Wars*, New York, NY: Council on Foreign Relations, 1996, p. 81.

21 Gary Jonathan Bass, *Stay the Hand of Vengeance: The Politics of War Crimes Tribunals*, Princeton, NJ: Princeton University Press, 2000, p. 214.

22 Malcolm, *Bosnia*, p. xx. Roger Cohen, *Hearts Grown Brutal: Sagas of Sarajevo*, New York: Random House, 1998, p. 244.

23 Philip E. Auerswald and David P. Auerswald, *The Kosovo Conflict: A Diplomatic History through Documents*, The Hague: Kluwer, 2000, p. 104. Bass, *Stay the Hand*, pp. 262–3.

24 Keesings December 1999. Norman M. Naimark, *Fires of Hatred: Ethnic Cleansing in Twentieth-Century Europe*, Cambridge, MA: Harvard University Press, 2001, p. 182.

25 Quoted in *Los Angeles Times*, April 18, 1995.

26 Williams, *Guilty Men*, p. 9.

27 *Le Figaro*, June 18, 2001, interview with Roland Dumas: "L'affaire des Frégates".

28 *Le Monde*, September 20, 2000: "Un ex-ministre allemande au bout de la piste des commissions d'Elf".

29 Committee of Independent Experts: First report on allegations regarding fraud, mismanagement and nepotism in the European Commission, 15 March 1999.

30 From www.transparency.org.

31 Bálint Magyar, *Post-Communist Mafia State: The Case of Hungary*, Budapest: Central European University Press, 2016.

32 Cindy Wooden, "Pope tells bishops: 'Don't suffer spiritual Alzheimer's, remember mercy'", *Catholic Herald*, August 30, 2016, https://catholicherald.co.uk/news/2016/08/30/pope-francis-mercy/.

33 Quoted in Harold James and Marla Stone (eds), *When the Wall Came Down: Reactions to German Unification*, New York, NY: Routledge, 1992, p. 78.

34 Eric Hobsbawm, *Nations and Nationalism since 1780: Programme, Myth, Reality*, Cambridge: Cambridge University Press, 1990, p. 78.

35 Speech in Birmingham, April 20, 1968, www.enochpowell.net/fr-79.html.

36 Tom Nairn, *The Break-Up of Britain: Crisis and Neo-Nationalism*, London: NLB, 1977, p. 192.
37 Isaiah Berlin, "European Unity and its Vicissitudes", in *The Crooked Timber of Humanity: Chapters in the History of Ideas*, London: John Murray, 1990, pp. 175, 204.
38 Isaac Deutscher, *The Prophet Unarmed: Trotsky 1921–1929*, London: Oxford University Press, 1959, p. 460.
39 "Address given by Mikhail Gorbachev to the Council of Europe (6 July 1989)", CVCE, www.cvce.eu/content/publication/2002/9/20/4c021687-98f9-4727-9e8b-836e0bc1f6fb/publishable_en.pdf.

14 Europe in a new world order

The financial crisis that erupted in 2007–08 changed politics globally, but also in Europe. It highlighted some long-standing European weaknesses, but initially the most obvious feature of the new global order was the reduced role of the United States. The financial meltdown appeared as an indictment of American capitalism; and the legitimacy of the US role in international affairs had already been undermined by the aftermath of the 2003 Iraq War. Politics internationally and domestically were recast along new lines, with a fading of both the Cold War division of international politics and the domestic left-right divide on distribution and the welfare state. Instead, the major axis of division between Europeans now concerned the degree of openness to migration, capital, and trade, and was often viewed as a debate about globalization and globalism. Generations confronted each other as classes had previously done. New conflicts appeared between as well as within countries, and East–West relations in Europe again became controversial and strained. The European convergence process described in Chapter 13 seemed to have ended. The new politics became possible because the old geo-politics, in which the United States had dominated and secured a multilateral political and economic order, eroded with considerable rapidity. Hungarian Prime Minister Viktor Orbán, who became the European incarnation of a new style of politics, concluded that "the strength of American soft power is in decline and liberal values today embody corruption, sex and violence, and as such discredit America and American modernization".[1] Critiques of globalism often merged easily into challenges to the process of European integration. Europe depends on a global framework within which it exists, thinks, and thrives – and whose defects produce specifically European deformations.

A critical and unresolved issue at the heart of the globalization debate was how much policy leeway there was in the interconnected world, or by how much voters could influence or change policy. Margaret Thatcher had sometimes referred to TINA: "There is no alternative." The major anti-European opposition group in Germany styled itself the Alternative for Germany (AFD), and its title was a program, a pushback against Chancellor Angela Merkel's declaration in March 2010 that there was no alternative to European financial support for Greece. But the two most simple and controversial statements that changed Europe's politics were actually demonstrations of exactly the contrary, of the need for extraordinary action. In July 2012, Mario Draghi, President of the European Central Bank (ECB), explained that he and his institution would do "whatever it takes" to save the single currency, Euro. In the late summer of 2015, in the face of a European refugee crisis, Merkel repeatedly said "*Wir schaffen das*" – "We can do it." Do it? Europe had to respond to a radically changing world order.

Financial crisis and the end of testosterone-driven American capitalism?

After 1945, European order had been built – in the west of the continent – on the transatlantic relationship (and in the east, in opposition to it). The magnetism of that American pole for politics weakened. The US 2008 National Intelligence Council report Global Trends 2025 predicted that: "The United States will remain the single most powerful country but will be less dominant." Its 2012 successor Global Trends 2030 was much more modest about American prospects:

> By 2030, no country – whether the U.S., China, or any other large country – will be a hegemonic power. The empowerment of individuals and diffusion of power among states and from states to informal networks will have a dramatic impact, largely reversing the historic rise of the West since 1750.

Both reports focus on the growth of powerful and internationally active non-state actors (businesses, tribes, religious organizations, and criminal networks). Conventional states no longer seemed to be in control of events: or if they wanted to maintain control, they needed to think of new ways of influencing and shaping a much wider debate, conducted through new technologies. In the early twenty-first century, the US failed to master this challenge, and other countries and other ideas pushed to fill the space left by the American vacuum. The result was a political and intellectual vacuum that recalled the dismal moments of the interwar epoch.

In the midst of the most intense phase of the financial crisis, in November 2008 Barack Obama was elected as President of the United States, with a mandate to play a more restrained role in the world. At first it looked as if Obama would "pivot" the emphasis of US foreign policy toward Asia, and especially toward China. Old Europe would be marginalized. But there was also in Europe an initial burst of European sympathy for Obama, who combined rhetorical depth and brilliance with a new political type (as the first African-American President). In 2009 Obama was awarded the Nobel Peace Prize. In 2012 the European Union (EU) received the same award. In neither case did the award enhance the long-run credibility of the recipient.

   The financial crisis was a crisis of a manner of existence. At the beginning of the financial crisis, German Finance Minister Peer Steinbrück explained that: "The U.S. will lose its status as the superpower of the global financial system."[2] The crisis was widely seen as a quintessentially American affair, emanating from a combination of testosterone-driven finance and a political penchant for promoting real estate as part of the American way of life even for those who could not really afford it.

   The financial crisis also spurred a debate about the effect of hormones on market behavior and willingness to take risk, with some research showing that higher levels of testosterone and cortisol led to riskier behavior.[3] Problematic banks had exclusively male management teams (see Plate 13). A popular version of this discussion held that "Lehman Sisters" would not have failed in 2008, and that a more stable financial and economic system would result if women played a greater role in business life.

   With the rise of the modern joint stock company women had largely been driven out of European management. In the early twentieth century, some women in business families even took up the mantra of Thomas Mann's fictional Tony Buddenbrook, "I'm only a goose." By the end of the century, some iconic women emerged as business leaders, above all in the countries where there was a tradition of "family capitalism" and again, many primarily because of a dynastic connection. Miuccia Prada was a rebellious former communist when she took over

Plate 13 CEO Dr. Josef Ackermann at the Annual General Meeting of Deutsche Bank. © Adam Berry/Bloomberg via Getty Images.

the company established by her grandfather in 1978. Donatella Versace in 1997 succeeded her brother as head of the family fashion company. Liz Mohn followed her husband at the head of the giant publishing group Bertelsmann. Marina Berlusconi owed her position at the Italian media holding company Fininvest to her family. Ana Patricia Botín in 2014 as a member of the fourth generation became executive chairman at the Spanish banking group Santander. Otherwise it was still hard for women to break the glass ceiling, and it remained harder than in the United States. In 2014, when *Fortune* magazine produced a list of the world's 50 most powerful women, 15 in the top 20 were working in the United States, and not one in the continental EU (there was one Briton: Alison Cooper at Imperial Tobacco).[4] The economist Ann-Kristin Achleitner explained that the problem in her eyes was the interrupted career paths of women: "To get into influential positions at big companies you have to have been working for 10 to 15 years – and there are few women over here who have really done that."[5] In the new millennium some prominent women emerged in start-ups and new technology: Joelle Frijters and Janneke Niessen in a Dutch advertising technology provider, Improve Digital; or Martha Lane-Fox, co-creator of Lastminute.com in 1998.

As a consequence, many European countries, and then the EU as a whole, experimented with legislative requirements on the representation of women at the top levels of business life. Norway was the first country to introduce a quota for women on company boards, in 2003. Spain adopted a similar measure in 2007. Belgium, France, Italy, and the Netherlands did so in 2011, with Germany following 2016. In 2015, women accounted for over 30 percent of company directors in France, and for 25 percent in Denmark and Germany, but for less than 10 percent in Greece. But the figures are partially deceptive. Germany has a two-level board system, and the regulation applied to the higher board which did not have management functions, the so-called Supervisory Board. For the top management of the 200 firms with the highest sales, the proportion remained at 8 percent.[6] The glass ceiling remained strong, despite the lessons of the financial crisis.

If the financial crisis indicated that traditional masculinity was toxic, Europe struggled to find alternatives. "Toxic masculinity" took over from an earlier discussion of "testosterone poisoning" as a diagnosis of contemporary ills. The aftermath of accusations against the American film producer Harvey Weinstein produced a global "Me Too" movement, in which large numbers of women empowered themselves and revealed previously hidden episodes of sexual harassment and abuse. The razor company Gillette in 2019 started a campaign, "The Best Men Can Be", suggesting that nice men should stop bullies and bad men should become good. The American Psychological Association guidelines declared the traits of traditional masculinity – stoicism, dominance, and aggression – as harmful. No less a figure than Queen Elizabeth II's grandson, the second in line to the British crown, took that theme up when he declared that his grandmother's generation with its insistence on the stiff upper lip had done great psychic damage to the insecure millennial generation. The financial revolution produced a revolution that was psychological, but it was obviously also political.

The financial crisis and American power

At the beginning, European politicians thought that they might play a central role in preventing the financial shock from escalating into a new version of the Great Depression. In particular the London Group of 20 (G20) summit meeting in April 2009 looked as if it was a turning point, and British Prime Minister Gordon Brown boasted about saving the world. Brown pressed for a greater role for international and multilateral institutions in crisis-fighting, and for a coordinated fiscal expansion; in short, a characteristically Keynesian approach. The determined multilateral approach reversed the precipitate decline in world trade, and many observers in consequence concluded that global and European institutions were successful, and that "the system worked".[7]

The most obviously effective large-scale immediate response to the crisis came from emerging markets, and notably from China, which launched a 4 trillion yuan stimulus program. President Hu Jintao and his successor Xi Jinping could present themselves as the champions of a new kind of globalization. The One Belt, One Road project launched in 2013 aimed at linking the Eurasian landmass with the sea but also new land links, and China sponsored railroad investment that brought Europe and Asia closer together. China also embarked on a quite aggressive strategy of purchasing European companies that might offer new technologies and markets. Some of the most controversial purchases were the Zhejiang Geely Group's acquisition of Volvo (Sweden) in 2010, Lenovo's of Medion (Germany) in 2011, Sany's of Putzmeister (Germany) in 2012, Wolong's of ATB Drive Technology (Austria) in 2011, and the Weichei Power Group's of the Kion Group AG (Germany) in 2012. The Chinese group Medea took over the German robotics producer Kuka in 2017. Most of the purchases were by private Chinese firms, although there were also some public stakes built up, such as China Investment Corporation's buying of a 10 percent stake in Heathrow Airport, and the 2011 sale of a 20 percent stake in Energias de Portugal to China's Three Gorges. The political relationship of both the United States and Europe with China deteriorated, as a Chinese bid for global leadership in technology and industry, but also in security, became increasingly apparent.

While emerging markets in Asia and Latin America – but also Turkey – did very well in the first years of the financial crisis, Europe seemed increasingly to be a burden on the entire global economy. In the winter of 2009–10 the focus of the international crisis shifted to Europe, and a dramatic European financial crisis threatened the global recovery. On October 4, 2009, the Socialist Party of George Papandreou (PASOK) won a landslide victory in Greek elections. Soon after, as the government contemplated the implementation of its program, it estimated that the fiscal deficit for the year would be likely to be 12.8 percent of GDP, over three times the previous forecast. Capital markets started to charge higher premia on Greek debt, and by the beginning of the next year, Greece looked to the EU for a rescue package. At the insistence of Angela Merkel, and in face of opposition from the French government in particular, the rescue involved the International Monetary Fund (IMF) as well. In a series of crisis negotiations, Europe created new intervention mechanisms, the European Financial Stability Facility (EFSF) and the European Financial Stabilization Mechanism, with a combined volume of up to €500 billion. In 2011 the initially temporary EFSF was transformed into a permanent European Stability Mechanism (ESM), that was eventually to morph into a European Monetary Fund.

Behind these measures was the fear that a failure to tackle the Greek crisis would produce a domino-effect contagion, with one European country after another being subject to speculative attacks. The possible disintegration of the currency union threatened the whole process of European integration. A round of devaluations for new national currencies would be very likely to provoke trade and tariff restrictions as countries feared that they were open to other countries' exports at dumping prices. In the middle of the tense discussions of May 2010 Merkel warned: "if the euro collapses, then Europe and the idea of European union will fail".[8] A few days later, she told the German Bundestag: "the rules must not be oriented toward the weak, but toward the strong. That is a hard message. But it is an economic necessity. That must have consequences for the European Union."[9] Such statements may have been over-interpreted as a move toward the imposition of a German Europe, especially by Merkel's critics inside as well as outside Germany.

A failure would have destroyed Europe; but the rescue effort itself did great damage and left a bitter legacy. The crisis brought out differences between the way Germany and much of northern Europe viewed the character of economic policy. Germans wanted a rule-based approach, with little scope for Keynesian reflation. They believed their resilience and relative success in the face of global turbulence depended on the legacy of difficult and domestically unpopular labor market reforms and the restriction of welfare, initiated in 2003 by a left-wing coalition government under Gerhard Schröder under the slogan "Agenda 2010". Merkel and her coalition partners were scarred by the initial experience of the 2008 financial crisis, and the need to support German banks. They concluded that the best way of preventing future crises and thus of building a more stable Europe was to punish speculators, by cutting their claims in a forcible "haircut". France, by contrast, along with many southern European countries, also saw the crisis as driven by speculators on financial markets, but thought that the best response was to show that governments and the ECB had the resources to fight off any challenge. Governments should spend more flexibly, and the ECB should give large amounts of liquidity support.

Europe was diverging rather than converging. The initial attempt to bridge the two divergent positions made matters much worse. On October 10, 2010, France's President Nicolas Sarkozy and Merkel met bilaterally in the faded Norman seaside resort of Deauville (Plate 14). No other European governments were present, and indeed the other Europeans began to resent the way policy was driven by the French–German couple. After an initial moment in Deauville in which it looked as if contrasting German and French visions of the world were bound for a head-on collision, the two leaders reached a dramatic compromise: Germany would loosen its approach to rules and make concessions to France, if France would in return agree to "an adequate participation of private creditors." This purely bilateral meeting is often seen as a watershed, in which risks were heightened because of market fears that other European debt besides that of Greece would be subject to a haircut. ECB President Jean-Claude Trichet was deeply angered by the move, and complained: "You're going to destroy the Euro."[10]

Deauville indeed increased rather than reduced the potential for contagion. The cost of borrowing in Portugal, Ireland, and Spain rose sharply. Ireland was the next country pushed into an international rescue program. In December 2010, an Irish rescue program was negotiated with the EU and the IMF. From a very early moment, the ECB and the IMF pulled in different directions. The IMF wanted to show that debt restructuring was a vital component of a recovery strategy, and proposed to impose a haircut

Plate 14 Chancellor Angela Merkel and President Nicolas Sarkozy in Deauville, October 2010. © PHILIPPE WOJAZER/AFP/Getty Images.

on senior bondholders who held claims on Irish banks. The ECB and the European Commission blocked that approach.

In May 2011, a similar package was agreed in Portugal, in the middle of an election campaign. The Socialist government of José Sócrates had fallen after it failed to pass an austerity budget. The election that followed the dissolution of the parliament produced a decisive defeat for the governing Socialist Party, and strong support for the center-right Social Democratic Party of Pedro Passos Coelho, who led the new government. The election looked as if it was heavily influenced by outside interventions and by national interests: Olli Rehn, the European Commissioner for Economic and Monetary Affairs, explained that an adjustment program more severe than the one that Sócrates had failed to pass was needed. That point was powerfully made by Finnish Finance Minister Jyrki Katainen, who was also facing an election, and who explained that Finland would block a package that was not augmented. Rehn was also Finnish. The President of the European Commission was a former Social Democratic Portuguese Prime Minister, José Manuel Barroso, and many Portuguese believed that he was likely to be more sympathetic to a government formed by his own party. The shape of the eventual deal was heavily shaped by European politics.

The Passos Coelho government successfully exited the troika program in 2014, but failed to be reelected in 2015. An anti-austerity post-electoral left-wing coalition had 62 percent of the vote and also a small majority of seats in the chamber. But President Aníbal Cavaco Silva at first blocked the left-wing coalition from governing on the grounds that it threatened the European treaties, and invited a minority right-wing coalition under the incumbent prime minister to form a government, which was soon brought down by a no-confidence motion. The new government (of the Socialist Party under Antonio Costa and independents) took office in November 2015 with a parliamentary majority thanks to the support of some fringe parties.

In the summer of 2011, the focus shifted to a much larger European country. It was not even clear that the IMF had the resources needed to deal with such a major economy. Tensions rose between the Italian Prime Minister, Silvio Berlusconi, who saw tax rises as threats to his popularity, and the Finance Minister, Giulio Tremonti, who insisted on the need for budget cuts and budget balancing. The spat was overshadowed by a backdrop of judicial inquiries: Italian magistrates had charged Berlusconi with tax offenses as well as with involvement with underage prostitutes, and Tremonti was investigated for living in a rent-free apartment. But the clash between the two men also indicated the problems of running democratic regimes in a Europe of austerity and budgetary orthodoxy. Berlusconi seemed to reject Tremonti's plans and stated that he needed to think about winning elections. As the crisis escalated, Tremonti raised the stakes by asserting: "If I fall, Italy falls. And if Italy falls, then the Euro falls."[11]

On November 4, 2011 Berlusconi went to the G20 Summit in Cannes, and had a private joint meeting with Merkel and Sarkozy, during which he was strongly urged to act decisively. Berlusconi saw the meeting as a public humiliation, especially since Merkel and Sarkozy seemed to grin or smirk at a press reference about him. In parliament, Berlusconi had lost its majority and would not survive a vote of confidence. But the manner and mechanism of his fall gave rise to the suspicion that Germany was imposing its demands and its choices on Italy. Chancellor Merkel talked on the telephone with the President of the Republic, Giorgio Napolitano (whose office was mainly symbolic, but played a considerable role at moments of governmental instability) on November 7, 2011. The next day, November 8, Berlusconi announced his resignation, just days after the fall of Greek Prime Minister Papandreou in Greece, who had suggested a referendum on the bailout package and was then told by the European leaders to withdraw that exercise in direct democracy. Papandreou was replaced by an interim "technocratic" caretaker Prime Minister, Lukas Papademos, who had previously been Vice-President of the ECB. In Italy, Berlusconi's successor, Mario Monti, was an academic and a devout Catholic with a personally blameless life that contrasted with the morass of fiscal and sexual scandal that emanated from Berlusconi; but he was also someone who as a highly successful former EU Commissioner with responsibility for competition policy had the confidence of Europe's elites.

The Italian events, and the parallel with the Greek change in government, gave rise to conspiracy theories about how Europe, in other words the European officials in Brussels, but above all Germany, was imposing outside preferences over the democratically expressed will of the people. Berlusconi started to talk about a "coup," but that interpretation was also taken up by many of his critics.

In the summer of 2012, the euro was close to collapse. The programs in Greece, Ireland, and Portugal had not established confidence and credibility. There were regular meetings of high-level European politicians that issued reassuring communiques and that produced a brief respite in market pressure; but those respites did not last long. The tide was turned by an agreement in June 2012 of the European leaders to move toward a "banking union". The agreement opened the door to possible direct bank recapitalizations by the ESM after the creation of an effective single supervisory mechanism. That agreement was interpreted as a triumph in Italy (by chance, it also coincided with a victory of the Italian team over Germany in the European Football Championship). It formed the backdrop against which on July 26, in a speech to investors in London, ECB President Mario Draghi could promise to do "whatever it takes" to save the euro. His unscripted and unprepared remarks had a dramatic and stabilizing effect on financial markets. The yield premia for peripheral debt came down. In subsequent months, the ECB fleshed out the details of its approach to euro rescue: an Outright Monetary Transactions program, in which the ECB would buy bonds of countries that had a program with European institutions and the IMF; and then long-term refinancing operations (LTROs), central bank lending to banks against collateral.

A test of the contagion hypothesis came in January 2013, when Cyprus needed a rescue program. The German discussion of the case was dominated by the perception that a great deal of the liabilities of the Cyprus banking system consisted of assets of Russian oligarchs, which constituted a possible criminal or even security threat, and hence required no special protection by European governments. For Berlin, there was little that constituted systemic risk in the Cyprus situation, and German officials complained that "if Cyprus is systemic, then everything is systemic". By contrast, many policymakers in France, but also in Italy and Spain, feared that penalization of Cypriot depositors might lead to a bank run in other countries (including their own). In the end, the holders of deposits as well as bondholders were bailed in. The Cyprus crisis changed European's attitude toward debt restructuring as part of rescue packages. The new chair of the Eurogroup, Netherlands Finance Minister Jeroen Dijselbloom, spoke of the Cyprus approach as offering a "template".

In the first half of 2015, Greece emerged again as an epicenter of the European financial crisis. In December 2014, the Greek parliament failed to elect a new President of the Republic (a largely symbolic office), but constitutionally that failure led to dissolution of parliament and new elections, which were won by Syriza (an abbreviation for the Greek words for "Coalition of the Radical Left"). There was no overall majority, however, and thus the government headed by Syriza leader Alexis Tsipras formed a coalition with a nationalist right-wing populist party, the Independent Greeks. The main platform of the party was a rejection of the "austerity" imposed by the troika, but the leaders were also frightened of the potential fallout from a break with Europe and a disorderly exit. The government consequently accepted on February 20, 2015, a four-month extension of the existing program, with some cosmetic changes but also a requirement that the Greek government submit an extensive reform agenda. During the Grexit discussion in summer 2015, France openly went against Germany, fearing contagion risk. French Prime Minister Manuel Valls stated that "we can't take the risk of Greece leaving the Euro area".

As the new program was negotiated, Tsipras called a referendum on the terms of the agreement; in that referendum, on July 5, the bailout proposal was rejected by a majority of 61 percent. But the fear of disorderly exit remained, and three days after the vote Tsipras asked for a new negotiation. He eventually agreed to a package whose terms were, if anything, slightly more unfavorable than the deal which the people had voted on. The Finance Minister of the Syriza administration, Yanis Varoufakis, a powerful and articulate advocate of the "No" position, resigned. When the ESM program came to an end, in August 2018, the

EU Currency Commissioner, a former French finance minister, called the whole program "delayed and suboptimal".

The threat of global contagion from the euro area had diminished by 2015. The question of Greek sovereign debt was largely an issue of who in Europe would absorb the losses, since most had been transferred to euro-area governments and EU institutions, including the ECB. European private sector financial institutions had largely succeeded in disengaging themselves. Only a few American and other hedge funds had engaged in high-yielding Greek debt as a speculative play on European solidarity. But the issue of leadership in Europe remained acute. In particular, after the election of the populist Donald Trump as US President in 2016, the American as well as European media called on Germany to replace the United States. In May 2017, Angela Merkel explained that: "We Europeans must really take our destiny into our own hands. The times in which we can fully count on others – they are somewhat over." But for many reasons – largely historical, and many concerned with the legacy of National Socialism – Germany could not really take on that leadership role, and instead appeared as what a political scientist called a "semi-hegemon".

The refugee crisis

As the debt crisis looked as if it was fading in the summer of 2015, a new issue emerged, in which – by bad geographical luck – Greece, Italy, and Spain, the central players in the European debt crisis, were also on the forefront. And again, Germany appeared as the decider. One of the indirect consequences of the global financial crisis had been an undermining of political stability in the Middle East. There had been an extensive drought in Syria and elsewhere from 2006. In 2008 food prices surged as biofuel production increased. A wave of discontent and anti-government protests began in December 2010 with the overthrow of the autocratic Tunisian government of Zine El Abidine Ben Ali, and then swept over the Middle East. One government after another fell, including the well-established autocratic regime of Hosni Mubarak in Egypt. It looked as if the circumstances of 1918–19, described at the time as the "Arab awakening", were being repeated. "The Arab Spring" was initially interpreted, notably in powerful western countries, as a victory of democracy – a final endorsement of the Fukuyama thesis that the historical conflict that characterized former eras had now come to an end – that was this time additionally pushed by new social media, in particular Facebook and Twitter. An uprising in Syria in the spring of 2011 led to an extended civil war. At first it looked as if the autocracy of Bashar al-Assad would be toppled also, and he lost control of almost all of Syria by the summer of 2013. Fighting in Iraq and Syria, and the disintegration of Libya after the overthrow of the autocrat Muammar Gaddafi, produced a surge of refugees, initially across Turkey to EU countries but also increasingly in small boats from Libya to Italy. Most of the refugees wanted to settle in northern Europe – especially in just three countries: Sweden, the United Kingdom, and Germany.

As refugees surged in, but were trapped in Hungary, Angela Merkel reacted on the night of September 4–5, 2015. On August 19, German officials had made a prediction that 800,000 refugees would move to Germany in the course of the year (the final figure was around 1 million). On August 25, the Federal Office for Migration and Refugees tweeted that Germany was now accepting unregistered refugees from Syria, and after that refugees in Hungary started to refuse to register with the Hungarian authorities, explaining that they would rather be in Germany. Hungary's Prime Minister Orbán explained that the refugee crisis was not a European problem, but rather a German one. Merkel's actions on the night of September 4 only highlighted that interpretation: pressed by the Austrian Chancellor, who was frightened by the number of refugees on their way from Hungary and into Austria, Merkel agreed to let them go on into Germany. She defended her approach by referring to Germany's especial obligations, in the light of the terrible history of the mid-twentieth century, to help the victims of conflict: if Germany were not to be open and friendly it "would not be my country". Repeatedly she stated, "We can do it." She also emphasized European responsibilities. Moreover, she explained that her party, the Christian Democrats, had a special Christian obligation to help the displaced.[12] Indeed, the churches strongly supported her position, and many volunteers also assisted refugees as they arrived in Germany (see Plate 15). But a great deal of opposition also came from her party and its Bavarian

Plate 15 Munich train station 2015 as Syrian refugees arrive. © Sonja Novak/Alamy Stock Photo.

sister party. Grotesquely, Merkel's response to the humanitarian crisis was presented by nationalist critics as an "invitation".

Other European countries reacted skeptically. President François Hollande explained that France would accept 1,000 refugees, and that France had "never raised unrealistic hopes".[13] The radical-right National Front would build a great deal of its 2017 election platform on an anti-Merkel campaign, with its leader sometimes suggesting that Merkel wanted cheap workers in order to consolidate the German economic dominance over Europe. In the UK, then United Kingdom Independence Party (UKIP) leader Nigel Farage made a similar case. Hungary's Foreign Minister Peter Szijjarto called Merkel's policy a "form of ritual suicide". These were odd reactions, in that almost all the refugees went to three countries: Austria, Germany, and Sweden. Vladimir Putin in 2015 mobilized sentiment about particular cases, such as when an Austrian (immigrant) child was raped in a swimming pool by an Iraqi immigrant: "A society that cannot defend its children has no future." Donald Trump in the United States, when he was trying to be polite about Merkel, called the September 2015 choice "a very tragic mistake". Before that he had tweeted that Merkel was "ruining Germany".

The discussion of immigration and diversity intensified in the wake of violent attacks by Islamicist terrorists: some of the most deadly were the invasion of the offices of a satirical magazine, *Charlie Hebdo*, in Paris on January 7, 2015, when 12 journalists were killed; simultaneous attacks in Paris on the night of November 13–14, 2015, with 130 deaths; bomb attacks at Brussels Airport and in the city on March 22, 2016, with 32 killed; a bomb at Istanbul Airport on June 28, 2016, with 43 deaths; a truck attack on the seaside promenade in Nice on the French national holiday, July 14, 2016, with 86 killed; an attack on a Christmas market in Berlin with 12 dead; a car attack on Westminster Bridge, London, on March 22, 2017, with five killed; and an attack on the St Petersburg metro on April 3, 2017, with 15 dead. Other violent confrontations hardened attitudes: notably cases of sexual violence or rape or murder committed by migrants. The largest of these events, the harassment of women on New Year's Eve 2015–16 in Cologne, Germany, was additionally controversial as the police and the conventional news media initially suppressed reports out of fear of escalating nationalist critiques. For right-wing critics, such as the French writer Éric Zemmour, Europe was committing suicide (he wrote a book in 2014, *The French Suicide*). Already, in 2010 a German politician and former member of the board of the central bank had written an analogous book, titled *Germany Abolishes Itself*.

On the day of the attack on *Charlie Hebdo*, the controversial French novelist Michel Houellebecq published a novel, *Submission*, which envisaged a France of the future with an Islamic president and the legalization of polygamy. The central figure of the novel, a disillusioned academic, welcomed the move as ending the era of female emancipation, and saw a new order (or a reversion to an old order) in which women would submit to men and men to God. Houellebecq, a splendidly unattractive man with blotched skin and rotting teeth, seemed to have a knack of capturing the zeitgeist. The issue of *Charlie Hebdo* that was just being published when the terrorist attack took place had a caricature of Houellebecq on the front cover with the words, "The predictions of the sorcerer Houellebecq: In 2015, I lose my teeth. In 2022, I observe Ramadan."

It was the refugee crisis that also turned a new party, the AFD, from a rather wonkish anti-euro party led by professors of law and economics into a populist anti-migration party. The refugee crisis also transformed East–West relations, as a substantial number of central European countries refused to take non-Christian migrants. The Visegrad Group of the Czech Republic, Hungary, Poland, and Slovakia, which in the 1990s had constituted a group that enacted quick and effective economic reform, now reconstituted itself as a block to resist attempts by western European countries to "Europeanize" the refugee crisis.

Security

Until 2008, President Putin appeared to much of the world as a rather pro-western, modernizing leader who sought an engagement with the international community and the global economy – that included access to capital markets in order to allow Russia to develop. Before 2008, a logic of global capitalism received Russian acquiescence. Russia needed to cooperate with global multinational companies in order to build up an economy based on raw material and energy production, but also on technologies that developed the raw materials.

But in 2007–08, Russia's strategy changed. On the eve of the financial crisis, Putin had presented a new front to the world when he spoke to the annual Munich Security Conference about the new power potential of the BRICs (the emerging economies of Brazil, Russia, India, China – later South Africa was added to the informal grouping) as an alternative to what he dismissed as an arbitrary "unipolarity". His audience was shocked and surprised, and many at the time took the speech as evidence of an insecurity or irrationality. In contrast, as the financial crisis spiraled out of control, Putin reached the conclusion that he had been prophetic. After the crisis, if one follows power logic instead of the logic of economic growth, there was no longer so much to be gained from global markets. Instead, the best game in town was to cooperate with other countries with a more state-centered capitalism, notably China. After the 2008 crisis, Putin saw a disintegrating global governance framework. The global financial crisis looked first like the end of American capitalism, and then a demonstration of European ineffectiveness and division. As an immediate response to the financial crisis, President Putin, speaking in Sochi in September 2008, conspicuously revived de Gaulle's language: "Regarding the global financial crisis, we should pause and think up ways to change the architecture of international finance and to diversify risks. The world economy cannot be supplied 'from one currency-printing press'."[14]

In August 2008, Russia invaded Georgia after Georgian troops had moved into the border region of South Ossetia to fight pro-Russian separatists. The move was widely interpreted as a warning against Georgia's ambitions to join NATO, and US encouragement of NATO expansion. The response to the Russian attack divided other countries: while the United States, the United Kingdom, Sweden, Poland, and Ukraine issued condemnations of the Russian action, France and Germany were much more ambivalent, and Italy under Silvio Berlusconi seemed to endorse the Russian action.

Russian leaders increasingly saw Ukraine as a test tube of political ideas as much as a struggle place for conventional power. Putin worried that the celebratory US interpretation of the Arab Spring meant support for a "color revolution" that would also sweep Russia. There had been a precedent for such regime change in the 2003 Rose Revolution in Georgia, as well as the 2004–05 Orange Revolution in Ukraine that followed protests against vote-rigging in the run-off presidential election between the pro-western Viktor Yushchenko and the pro-Russian Viktor Yanukovych. On March 5, 2012, in Moscow, there were around 25,000 protesters on the streets contesting the manipulation of the presidential elections. A successful, prosperous, and democratic Ukraine would look like a beacon of political reform. Obscuring the beacon required not just making Ukraine unstable, but also fighting the liberal political idea at the heart of European and American success.

Ukraine's President Yanukovych initially negotiated an association agreement with the EU, but then refused to sign the pact. Protests erupted, especially in Kiev, where the demonstrators flocked to the Maidan Square that had been at the center of the movement for the Orange Revolution. The new incarnation of anti-government protest became known as "Euromaidan". Attempts to end the protests produced a substantial number of casualties, with around 100 demonstrators killed. The clashes led to the collapse of the regime and the flight of Yanukovych on February 22, and to the calling of new elections.

On March 1, the Russian parliament authorized the deployment of Russian troops in Ukraine, and Russian special forces seized Crimea and installed a new Supreme Council of Crimea. The new authority quickly called a referendum, which was held on March 16 and led to a 96.77 percent vote in favor of joining the Russian Federation. Russian forces also moved into eastern Ukraine, and heavy fighting continued despite EU and US attempts at mediation, and the imposition of economic sanctions by both the EU and the United States. The sanctions, in combination with a sharp fall in the oil price in 2014, made Russia appear very vulnerable; but at the same time Russian political and military leaders turned to "hybrid warfare", a mixture of conventional military deployment, fighting by informal operatives, and cyberwarfare. Previously, in Georgia in 2008, the Russian attack had coincided with substantial computer attacks on Georgian government websites.

Hybrid war

In the Cold War era, strategy relied on a clearly defined notion of conflict and escalation, in which the decisions were made by centralized states with clearly organized military commands, whose continued existence in the event of conflict needed to be guaranteed. The 2001 terrorist attacks on the United States, and subsequent attacks on western Europe, raised the possibility of a different kind of conflict, with loosely organized networks of non-state actors. They would combine propaganda, attempts to influence through social media, with acts of violence designed to mobilize and escalate opinion. The term "hybrid warfare" appeared around 2005, and was used to describe the strategy used by Hezbollah in the 2006 Lebanon War. Alternative terms include "full spectrum" and "non-linear" war. In 2011 the US army defined the term as "the diverse and dynamic combination of regular forces, irregular forces, criminal elements".[15] The aspect that came to the fore, especially after Russia's 2014 occupation of Crimea and the continued fighting in eastern Ukraine, in which combatants wore non-marked and non-identifying uniforms and appeared as "green men", and in which social media were used to influence behavior behind the front. Soldiers were sent pictures of their families to indicate that they might be vulnerable. Hybrid war also involved the use of social media to discredit the other side: Russian "trolls" identified Ukrainians as fascists, and the United States and EU as aggressors. The best known "troll factory" was the Internet Research Agency established in St Petersburg by Yevgeny Prigozhin. Economic methods, in particular the control of energy supply, constituted another element of the approach. Other countries might be lured into a long-term dependency, which would involve the conversion of economic and political elites to a supportive stance. Hybrid war also included old-fashioned financing of political activity in other parties: anti-EU parties, such as the Front National in France, the Liga Nord in Italy, or UKIP in the UK. In early 2016, Russian news media but also senior political figures including the Foreign Minister gave details of a 13-year-old Russian girl in Germany who had been gang-raped by Moslem immigrants. The aim of the fictitious account was to mobilize opinion against the German government in the aftermath of a large-scale wave of migration. When German media failed to report on real or alleged crimes of Moslems, they were denounced as "lying press" (*Lügenpresse*), a term originally widely used in Nazi propaganda during the Weimar Republic. Donald Trump in the United States used a similar term, "fake news", to discredit mainstream media.

The new information war included western as well as eastern Europe. Russian media presented the EU as "hypocritical, multicultural, and decadent". The new Russian world view presented three main narratives as a challenge to the old "West": that the EU is aggressive and interventionist, and had launched a propaganda war against Russia and against traditional values; that the EU was on the point of collapse; and that it promoted bizarre behaviors incompatible with a traditional understanding of Christianity, including homosexuality, pedophilia, and even zoophilia (copulation with animals). At the Valdai forum, in which Putin liked to present and debate his world view, he linked gay rights with a western model that "opens a direct path to degradation and primitivism, resulting in a profound demographic and moral crisis".[16] At the same time he began to present himself as the embodiment of unapologetic traditional masculinity (Plate 16).

This message was then channeled through traditional media – in particular an international broadcasting service that provide entertaining and visually attractive television, Russia Today (later rebranded as RT). But Russia also used many other channels, including donations and loans to anti-EU parties. The most successful vehicle of influence was the aggressive use of new social media – Twitter and Facebook. The financial crisis coincided with the launching of Apple's iPhone (June 2007), which allowed users to communicate in completely new ways with broader groups of contacts among like-minded people. The "i" was intended to stand for

Plate 16 Russian President Vladimir Putin hunting. © DMITRY ASTAKHOV/AFP/ Getty Images.

"internet", but also for "individual", "instruct", "inform", and "inspire".[17] The longer-term consequences of a completely changed style of communications, where face-to-face personal connections were replaced by "virtual" friendships and linkages, "likes" and "tweets" and "retweets", are likely to prove much more transformative than the shorter-term economic effects of the financial crisis. The communications could be more and more focused to like-minded people with similar preferences, so that the new technology made a general and genuine social dialogue harder rather than easier. It amplified existing prejudices, in what was sometimes referred to as a "filter bubble", and could in this way easily provide disinformation rather than information, and revulsion rather than inspiration. For conventional politicians, the new world proved confusing. Angela Merkel complained in 2013 that the internet was "Neuland", unexplored territory.

Many conservatives in the US but also in Europe embraced the bleak vision generated through the new social media as a promising alternative to a crumbling American-centered unilateralism. But it also was a vehicle for promoting a more radical left-wing agenda in place of the "third way" visions that had flourished in the 1990s. The new social media were thus politically transformative, and radicalizing.

Energy

Energy discussions had always been linked to security thinking. The oil crisis of the 1970s had been a major channel to western European democracy. The Iraq wars of 1991 and 2003 appeared driven by worries about energy dependence. Russian Ukrainian policy used Russia's grip on energy supplies, and in 2014 gas became a major weapon of Russian policy.

Russia exerted such powerful influence because of its role as a major oil and gas supplier, as well as a provider of nuclear technology to countries in east-central Europe that had constructed nuclear reactors in the Soviet era. The share of gas imports in the EU rose steadily from around 40 percent in the mid-1990s to approximately 70 percent in the mid-2000s. In 2013, 39 percent of extra-EU imports (in volume) came from Russia, followed by Norway (34 percent), Algeria (13 percent) and Qatar (7 percent). Almost all of this gas came through pipelines, with Nord Stream, which opened in 2011–12, supplying Finland and Germany, and the older Yamal–Europe line supplying Poland and Germany. Nord Stream was highly controversial, with the Polish government in particular seeing it as a threatening German–Russian cooperation project: Foreign Minister Radek Sikorski compared it to the notorious 1939 Molotov–Ribbentrop Pact. The follow-up project for a second pipeline, Nord Stream 2, unleashed similar controversies, exacerbated in the wake of the Ukraine conflict, as it looked like a way that Russian could send energy to Europe without being dependent on transit pipelines through Ukraine.

Gas played a larger role because of European ambivalence about nuclear energy. While some countries – notably France – saw nuclear energy as a safe and clean alternative form to the burning of carbon fuels, Germans had long worried about nuclear energy. After the 2011 catastrophe in Fukushima, when an earthquake and tsunami destroyed a nuclear reactor and led to widespread radioactive contamination, German Chancellor Merkel announced quite abruptly that her country would phase out nuclear power by 2022: the decision became widely known as the turning point in energy (*Energiewende*). A large budget was devoted to the promotion of renewable energy sources. Merkel seemed to pick up both an older romanticism about energy, and the long-established environmentalist critique of the risks of modern technology. In 2017, for instance, she explained that: "we should look at the *Energiewende* in a rational way, and of course always take into account the basic economic possibilities. But we should also develop a certain passion and joy for it."[18]

The prominence of very different energy debates in different national cultures meant that Europe found it hard to formulate a coherent energy policy. Energy coordination in respect to coal, the primary fuel and basis of industrial prosperity at the time, had been at the heart of the first major push for postwar integration and the institutional forerunner of the EU, the European Coal and Steel Community (1953). Energy issues were highlighted in the 2007 Lisbon Treaty, where Article 194(1) recognized the reality that national states were primarily in charge of determining energy policy, but set out the four principal overall aims of EU energy policy as: ensuring the functioning of the energy market, ensuring the security of supply in the Union, promoting energy efficiency and energy saving, and promoting the interconnection of energy networks. Subsequent European responses to the challenges of meeting different threats to continuing energy supply – whether geopolitical, environmental, or just in terms of limited grid capacity – remained limited by national calculations and realities. The Paris climate agreement concluded in 2015 called for national plans to limit temperature increases to 2° C, but the actual implementation was sporadic and spotty. France committed to banning diesel and petrol automobiles by 2040, and Germany thought of phasing out coal and lignite power by 2038, but these deadlines seemed very distant, and emissions of carbon gases continued to rise. Proposals for higher carbon taxes, especially fuel taxes, in fact set off immediate large-scale protests.

Populism

As in the case of the Great Depression, the economic turmoil discredited incumbent governments and produced a wave of new political movements that were generally termed "populist". But the phenomenon was rather older, and the term was first used in a contemporary setting to describe left-wing nationalist movements in Latin America, with an agenda that was economically and financially unsustainable, and which regularly ended in large government deficits as a result of over-spending, and in inflation or hyper-inflation. European populist movements sometimes emerged within older parties: thus Jörg Haider modernized and radicalized the Austrian Freedom Party (FPÖ) and eventually brought it into a coalition government that lasted from 2000 to 2007. Fidesz in Hungary began as a liberal anti-communist party and then moved right and became much more radically nationalist. In Slovakia, Robert Fico came from the Communist Party and then the post-communist Party of the Democratic Left to create Direction – Social Democracy (SMER), which he described as a "third way", i.e. looking for an alternative to communism and free-market individualism. After winning the 2006 election, Fico formed a coalition government with another populist party and with an ultranationalist party. Aleksandar Vučić in Serbia emerged from the populist and nationalist movement of Slobodan Milošević but tempered that legacy with a pragmatic pro-European stance.

The most remarkable populist was Italy's Silvio Berlusconi, a property developer originally affiliated with the Socialist Party. When corruption charges destroyed the Socialist Party, Berlusconi struck out on his own, and established Forza Italia in December 1993; it went on to win the 1993 election and Berlusconi was Prime Minister from 1994 to 1995, and then again from 2001 to 2006 and from 2008 to 2011. Berlusconi's contribution to politics was to build up a vast media empire. His television channels, along with the state television when he controlled the government, brought a mixture of low-grade entertainment with political propaganda. Within a day he compared himself both to Napoleon and to Jesus Christ: "I am the Jesus Christ of politics. I am a patient victim. I put up with everyone. I sacrifice myself for everyone."[19]

Political scientists worried about how to define populism. The phenomenon represents the claim to speak for a single people and a popular will against a corrupt elite that was globalized and betrayed deep underlying national interests. Populists also, like their Latin American equivalents, promised more in social services and in low taxation. They were also happy to ignore conventional constitutional and legal constraints. Strikingly, almost all populists in government ended up with much deeper and more sustained and also personalized corruption than their predecessors.

Populism

"Populism" as a historical and political term was mainly used to describe political movements in the United States and Latin America. Its widespread use as a tool of analysis of European politics in the twenty-first century is an indication of the extent to which political vocabulary has been globalized. Populists begin with an anti-liberal concept of democracy, and often end by subverting democratic principles as well and pushing for an autocracy that articulates their values. They reject pluralism, elites, and experts, and claim that they and they alone represent the real people and their true interests. It is helpful to distinguish socio-cultural populism, where the term originated, from a cultural populism that took up very old nineteenth-century ideas about national character and the danger of cosmopolitanism and what in the twenty-first century was referred to as "globalism".

The origins of the term lie in a debate about economic policy, and about who benefits from conventional or orthodox economics. US populism referred originally to a late-nineteenth-century movement of farmers and others against the East Coast money elite, which also pushed for "soft money" or a more inflationary monetary policy and a departure from the gold standard on the grounds that mild inflation would help indebted businesses and farmers. It preached: "Get rid of 'the plutocrats, the aristocrats, and all the other rats', install the people in power, and all would be well."[20] The highpoint of the movement was the failed 1896 presidential campaign of William Jennings Bryan. Latin American populism in the later twentieth century similarly describes an "approach to economics that emphasizes growth and income redistribution and deemphasizes the risks of inflation and deficit finance, external constraints, and the reaction of economic agents to aggressive nonmarket policies".[21] European populism in the early twenty-first century similarly involved an attack on economic orthodoxy and on what it characterized as "austerity". In a right-wing variant, it also emphasized national tradition, and opposed supranationalism, above all in the form of the EU, and migration. It blamed emigration for the brain drain that afflicted eastern and southern Europe, and immigration, especially Islamic immigration, for undermining Christianity and traditional European culture. Socio-economic populism was fueled by the global financial crisis, but since 2012 receded while a cultural populism continued to advance.

In Greece, the conventional political parties of the center-right and center-left failed in the face of the most severe and long-lasting of the European crises. PASOK, the socialist party, had a substantial populist element, but it was discredited by its handling of the early stages of the financial crisis. Syriza built in substantial part on disaffected PASOK supporters, as well as on radicals from the autonomous left. In Spain, Podemos ("We Can") was founded by a political scientist in the wake of widespread anti-government and anti-austerity protests, when Indignados ("the outraged") staged protests from 2011 on against austerity, and linked up to a worldwide protest movement (the US equivalent was the Occupy Wall

Street campaign). The most prominent actions involved long occupations of prominent public places: the center of the protests was in Madrid's Puerto del Sol. Podemos surged to spectacular success in the December 20, 2015, parliamentary elections, when it became the third party with 20.65 percent of the vote, but it did not succeed in entering the government, and its support slipped as Syriza in Greece adopted more conventional policies. Podemos was also hit by revelations of its financial dependence on Venezuela's populist regime of Hugo Chávez and then Nicolás Maduro. An alternative anti-corruption party of the pro-European center-right, Ciudadanos ("Citizens"), looked more durable.

North European populism, by contrast, generally took a right-wing nationalist line. A central component was anti-Europeanism, but also hostility to Islam. The main driver of electoral supporter was fear of the consequences of large-scale Moslem immigration. Geert Wilders in the Netherlands had worked with the main center-right party before he created a new movement, the Freedom Party, in 2006. He took on a large part of the support that a charismatic gay anti-Islamic crusader, Pim Fortuyn, had built up; Fortuyn had been assassinated in 2002. Fortuyn and initially Wilders were opposed to the conventional neo-fascist right, but Wilders gradually moved closer. In 2017, Wilders attended a meeting in Koblenz, Germany, with Marine Le Pen, the leader of France's Front National; Frauke Petry, of the AFD; and Matteo Salvini, of Italy's Lega (Northern League). In 2017, it looked as if a pan-European radical populist right was forming.

A corresponding movement grew stronger in central Europe. Poland's Law and Justice Party (PiS), founded in 2001 by Jarosław and Lech Kaczyñski, won power in 2015 and immediately launched a radical program. It bought votes by reducing the pension age, and paying large child supplements. It presented itself as the defender of a Catholic and nationalist vision of Polish identity, and worked with the support of much of the Church hierarchy. It weakened the Constitutional Tribunal, tightened control of the media, attacked opposition journalists, launched new presidential decree powers, clamped down on immigrants, and banned demonstrations of supporters of gay rights. Its voters were largely in rural and small town Poland, the so-called "Polska B" that had been left behind in the process of European integration.

These movements cannot be explained in terms of economic malaise alone. Poland was the only member of the EU not to experience a recession after the Lehman financial crisis. A better explanation of the revival of national thinking lies in a pushback against the politics of the 1990s and 2000s when politicians repeatedly claimed to be following a path of economic and political liberalization to which there was said to be no alternative in an increasingly globally interconnected world. Loss of population as a consequence of outward migration threatened national identity. By 2016, the number of migrants from east-central and southeastern Europe was estimated at 9.6 million, or 8 percent of the population. Around

4.7 million Poles and 3.6 million Romanians were living abroad.[22] Before 1989, travel out of the communist countries had been difficult – impossible in many cases. The revolution of 1989–90 meant that there was more mobility, and the EU enlargements of 2004 and 2007 made movement much simpler. And as politics in central-eastern Europe became more nationalist, many of the liberal winners of the revolution moved out, leaving populations behind that felt they were missing the tide of history.

One of the models for the PiS government was the experience of Hungary after 2010. Viktor Orbán had launched Fidesz as a pro-market liberal party. After 2008 he was deeply disenchanted by what he called "the great Western financial collapse in 2008", and saw that he might mount a highly effective attack on the governing post-socialist party MZSP. The socialist Prime Minister, Ferenc Gyurcsány, was discredited and deeply unpopular. He had boasted about how he had been "lying" in an originally secret speech in May 2006 in Balatonőszöd whose sensational contents were soon leaked:

> There is not much choice. There is not, because we have fucked it up. Not a little but a lot. No European country has done something as boneheaded as we have. It can be explained. We have obviously lied throughout the past one and a half–two years. It was perfectly clear that what we were saying was not true.

In 2011 Orbán won the parliamentary elections, and immediately set about revising the constitution.

Populism was also associated with a push for "illiberal democracy" – a term first used by Fareed Zakaria in a *Foreign Affairs* article in 1997.[23] From 2010, Orbán made this new form of government a central plank in his critique of existing conditions:

> The determinative moment in today's world can perhaps be described by saying that there is a race underway to find the method of community organisation, the state, which is most capable of making a nation and a community internationally competitive. [. . .] The stars of the international analysts today are Singapore, China, India, Russia and Turkey.[24]

Recep Tayyip Erdoğan was a successful football player and mayor of Istanbul before he was dismissed for reciting a religious poem. He founded the Turkish Justice and Development Party (AKP) in 2001 as a way of promoting a moderate pro-Islamic agenda. The party won a spectacular election victory in 2002, and the next year – after a ban on him serving in public office was removed – Erdoğan became Prime Minister. He started to negotiate for Turkish membership of the EU, but the negotiations stalled. At first, the Turkish development looked like a convincing demonstration of how a modern Islamic political movement might work.

Outside commentators made analogies with the way Christian democracy in western Europe had reversed the Catholic Church's traditional hostility to the modern world. But with the financial crisis, and the weakness of the EU, and the increasing centrality of Turkey as a recipient of the largest number of refugees from Syria and Iraq, Turkey moved in a clearly autocratic direction. It also built up its claims to regional preeminence, in a move described as "neo-Ottomanian" foreign policy. In 2016, Erdoğan appeared to claim back the territories in the west (and the islands) that Turkey had lost to Greece after the First World War. In domestic politics, he had already built a powerful autocracy. In 2007 and 2010 Erdoğan used referenda to change the constitution, and to strengthen the role of the presidency – the position that he took on after an election in 2014. In 2016 a coup against Erdoğan was blamed on a widespread network of supporters of his former collaborator, Fethullah Gülen, and was followed by mass arrests and a consolidation of Erdoğan's power. By 2018, the regime confronted a large-scale financial crisis, analogous to that of 2001 which had originally shaped the conditions for the rise of the AKP.

The most dramatic challenge to the EU came with a referendum called in 2016 by the UK government, which was under pressure from a populist and anti-European party, UKIP. By a narrow majority, on June 23 UK voters opted to leave the EU. The outcome looked from the outset problematical, in that the participation rate was low, many young people in particular had not voted, and two parts of the United Kingdom – Scotland and Northern Ireland – voted to remain.

The decision to use a referendum reflected both a deep failure of the British political class, and the depth of the breakdown of its relationship with Europe. With no party commanding an overall majority in parliament, the United Kingdom in 2010 formed a surprisingly stable coalition government between the Liberal Democrats (the most clearly pro-European of the three major British parties) and the Conservatives, whose party was dominated by a powerful and articulate Eurosceptic wing. But the Conservatives had the upper hand, with the Prime Minister (David Cameron), the Chancellor of the Exchequer (George Osborne), and the Foreign Minister (William Hague). Cameron had deeply internalized the lesson of Margaret Thatcher – that the United Kingdom needed to defend itself against budgetary claims from Europe. He and Osborne were also impressed by American economists who told them that a monetary union without a full fiscal union was inherently unstable, and that as a consequence Europe could only save itself by going ahead quickly with a real fiscal union.

On November 18, 2011, David Cameron went on what he believed was a successful trip to Berlin to negotiate a special deal for the United Kingdom. He had picked up from the United States the idea that a "big bazooka" was needed to deal with a big financial crisis, but was left out in the cold when Merkel and Sarkozy struck a separate deal.

The drama reached a new highpoint in the December 2012 negotiations for a treaty-based fiscal compact. Cameron started with an optimistic spin that the proposed banking union will "lead to opportunities for the UK to make changes in our relationship with the EU". But for the first time he raised the possibility of a British exit:

> I believe the choice we should make is to stay in the European Union, to be members of the single market, to maximise our impact in Europe, but where we are unhappy with parts of the relationship we shouldn't be frightened of standing up and saying so.[25]

Then Cameron gave a big "Europe speech":

> There is a growing frustration that the EU is seen as something that is done to people rather than acting on their behalf. And this is being intensified by the very solutions required to resolve the economic problems . . . People are increasingly frustrated that decisions taken further and further away from them mean their living standards are slashed through enforced austerity or their taxes are used to bail out governments on the other side of the continent.[26]

The major message was that there would be negotiations to improve the UK's position in Europe, followed by a referendum in which Cameron would put the results to a popular test; but nobody could really say what results or "benefits" the British negotiators could possibly achieve. Cameron in private said he wanted to avoid the referendum. The British initiative could certainly be given a positive twist, and there were certainly some people on the continent who shared these sentiments. Unease about the development of the EU, and its dubious anchoring in democratic legitimacy, is not uniquely a product of British peculiarity or insularity. In smaller north European countries, but also in Germany, there seemed to be plenty of support, mostly for recasting the EU along more economically liberal lines. Cameron imagined that his speech was a helpful nudge to rethinking a more viable mix of liberal economics and a European fiscal regime that is in need of reform.

In fact, the negotiations between the United Kingdom and the EU before the referendum produced little of substance that could be held up as an illustration of British success. Anti-immigration sentiment drove a substantial popular vote turning against the EU, with older people voting disproportionately to leave the EU, and younger people choosing *Remain* – or in many cases not voting. In the aftermath of the June 2016 referendum, the British political system tore itself apart. Cameron, who had pledged to stay in his position as Prime Minister, almost immediately resigned and was replaced by the Home Secretary, Theresa May, who had campaigned, rather unenthusiastically, to remain in the EU, and now promised to deliver on the narrow majority and repeated as a mantra that "Brexit means Brexit." The outcome of the vote reflected the outcome of a long history of semi-engagement in Europe. The main original political economy of the European Community and EU, protection of a large rural population in order to forestall political radicalization, made little sense to a country that had already lost most of its farmers. The political psychology of European integration had lain in overcoming the legacy of defeat and occupation in the Second World War; but that had no appeal to a country that had not been vanquished. In the constant political tension that resulted, many British – and particularly English – politicians and intellectuals tried to look back to old English traditions, and particularly to the foundation story of England in the break with Rome in the 1530s. May also took up some of the populist critique of globalization. In her first major policy speech as Prime Minister, she devoted little attention to how precisely the United Kingdom might leave the EU. Instead she denounced globalists: "If you believe you are a citizen of the world, you are a citizen of nowhere – you don't understand what citizenship means."

The election of Donald Trump on November 8, 2016, also looked like a confirmation of European populism. Orbán and Le Pen were exultant. Merkel commented after the election that she looked forward to cooperation with the United States on the basis of shared values: "democracy, freedom, the respect for the law and the dignity of human beings, independent of their origin, skin color, religion, gender, sexual orientation or political position". The message was intended as a rebuke to Trump, and also interpreted by the recipient in this way.

The populist wave was interrupted by the French elections of 2017. The candidates of both the populist right – Marine Le Pen, the daughter of the founder of the National Front – and the populist left – Jean-Luc Mélenchon – did surprisingly well, and Le Pen reached the second round of the presidential election. Both populists made opposition to Germany a central part of their platform. Le Pen explained that Chancellor Merkel was bringing refugees into Europe to work as slave labor for the German economy. Mélenchon, who won 19.6 percent of the votes in the first round of the election (Le Pen had 21.3), had written a book entitled *Bismarck's Herring (The German Poison)*, in which he argued that the way Germany was treating Greece was just an anticipation of the way Angela Merkel would deal with France.

But the election was won by an outsider, Emmanuel Macron, a former investment banker who had briefly been Minister for the Economy in the Socialist government under President Hollande. Macron, who had founded a new political movement, En Marche, secured a surprising victory, helped by disunion among the socialists and criticisms of corruption directed against the official candidate of the center-right, a former French prime minister. In the second run-off round, facing Marine Le Pen from the National Front, Macron won with a dramatic 66 percent of the vote.

He then called new legislative elections, which produced an equally striking victory for En Marche, which together with another centrist party won 350 of the 577 seats in the French assembly. The socialists, the previous governing party, were reduced to 30 seats. Populism of the center looked, briefly, as if it might be a winner. But Macron faced a major problem: he understood that his modernizing concept could only be applied on a European level, and that European politics as a whole needed a remake. But there was no obvious mechanism to do that. Domestically, an inchoate opposition from both the left and the right started a yellow-vest (*gillet jaune*) movement, wearing the high-visibility yellow jackets that French motorists were obliged to carry as a security provision, and initially protesting against fuel tax increases, speeding fines, and the abolition of the wealth tax. Illiberal states – in particular Hungary, Italy, and Poland – were trying to create a new "axis" (the word had sinister overtones from the 1930s) on the basis of resistance to immigration, but also on the basis of a new ideal of "strong men" making politics. If in 2008 the major threat to European stability had come from macho finance, in 2019 it came from macho politics.

The aftermath of the UK's Brexit referendum provided a sharp warning to anti-system parties in other European countries. As the British government invoked Article 50 of the Lisbon Treaty, with a two-year path to leaving the EU, it became increasingly clear that the exit process involved a vast number of technically complicated issues, and that the outcome presented economic and financial risks that were almost impossible to calculate. A regulatory framework that had been constructed for more than 40 years needed to be reworked. The question of the land border in Ireland with the Republic raised an almost insuperable issue of how controls could be carried out without interfering with movements of people. Negotiating new trade agreements with external countries was complicated, and the size of the United Kingdom made it a less attractive counterpart than the much larger EU. Trade in goods occupied the majority of the economic discussion, but the more problematic issue of trade in services – which require very high levels of coordinated regulation – was almost entirely neglected.

The economic risks of exit paled in comparison to the political disintegration that appeared to follow the Brexit vote. Both the large political parties were split, and the rhetoric of dissension escalated. Prime Minister Theresa May called an election in June 2017 in order to strengthen her hand in negotiations by creating a "strong and stable government", but failed to achieve a parliamentary majority and became dependent for support on the regional (Northern Irish) Democratic Unionist Party. The incapacity of the government and of parliament to produce an acceptable solution within the timeframe provided by Article 50 made the United Kingdom into an icon of dysfunctionality and incompetence. Ministers resigned; those that remained, like the Transport Secretary Chris Grayling, were spectacularly incompetent, negotiating contracts for ferry operations to deal with post-Brexit chaos to a company with no ships. May attacked parliament as the source of the problem, telling the British public: "You're tired of the infighting, you're tired of the political games and the arcane procedural rows, tired of MPs talking about nothing else but Brexit."[27] Almost all parliamentarians by contrast believed that May had not a shred of credibility. May's successor as prime minister, Boris Johnson, saw his majority disappear, and tried to take a more confrontational stance in dealing with the EU. Three years of tumultuous debate over the terms of Brexit appeared as only the beginning of a more complicated and fissiparous process of negotiation, one that might threaten the integrity of the UK as it pushed Scotland and Northern Ireland away from the union.

The EU came in consequence of the Brexit chaos to look essential and unavoidable for the rest of the EU, even to Euro-skeptic and Euro-critical parties. It was not just a question of holding what had become highly intertwined economies together, but also of rescuing the possibility of a stable framework for political debate. Any alternative raised too many questions to be really or practically thinkable. But sustainability based on the very high cost of exit creates its own continuing and substantial vulnerabilities.

An aging, graying Europe

Nation-states in Europe were running up against their limits in that they were institutionally incapable of handling the demographic imbalances that were accelerated and aggravated by large-scale migration. They were increasingly torn apart by generational conflict. The clashes between generations underlay a great deal of the populist wave.

The first chapter of this book examined modernization without thinking of politics. The crisis of modernization became a story of personal life and experience as mediated by a political system that was geared to produce increasingly large transfers, between social groups and also between generations.

Society began to fragment, in some part because more people lived as individuals: young people who enjoyed urban existence as "singles", and older people whose spouses had died. In 2018, after a report established that 9 million Britons suffered from loneliness, the government even appointed a junior minister to be responsible for the problem. Marriage rates fell in all European countries, and the age of marriage increased progressively. From 1990 the average age of first marriage rose for men in Germany from 28.2 to 33.8, and for women from 25.5 to 31.1; in Italy the figure for men rose from 28.9 to 34.7 and for women from 25.9 to 31.9. The number of children steadily fell. Divorce rates soared from the 1970s, but after the millennium stabilized and fell in most countries, largely because the marriage rates had fallen so dramatically. But there was an increasingly obvious "marriage gap", as society polarized into two sections. Richer households, and more educated households, had much higher rates of marriage, whereas marriage dwindled among the poorer and less educated. In Denmark, at the most extreme, 81 percent of the highest income quintile were married, but only 21 percent of the poorest. The equivalent figures in the United Kingdom were 84 and 40, and for France, where the movement away from marriage was most generalized, and the class aspect least pronounced, 68 and 37. The marriage gap increasingly became a reinforcer of income and wealth inequality, which also increased in the last decades of the twentieth century.[28]

With individualization, there was also an increasing emphasis on the short term. Three-fifths of the world's clothing was thrown away within a year of production. Only a few countries tried to combat this development by recycling, with Germany collecting almost three-quarters of all used clothing, and reusing half and recycling one-quarter.[29]

Modern Europe was aging rapidly. The changing demographic pyramid gave incentives to politicians to cater for the demands of the elderly, since they had become numerically ever more dominant, and to overlook the concerns of young people. They focused more on the payout of savings than in the investment for the future. In many European countries, a majority of voters were either retired or expected to retire within the next legislative period of the elected parliaments: they were thus focused very much on the provision of payouts. In addition, younger citizens had lower voting rates. As a consequence, the political structure appeared as a gerontocracy, and that perception may feed into the sense of younger potential voters that they are disenfranchised. Voting ratios and electoral participation thus fell even further, indicating that young people wish to opt out of the political system, and that its character as a gerontocracy becomes further solidified. Pensions and old age care became more salient politically than education provision, which in some (not all) European countries was quite neglected. Speaking to the European Parliament, Pope Francis memorably described Europe as producing the "general impression of weariness and aging, of a Europe that is now a 'grandmother', no longer fertile and vibrant".[30] These effects – the marginalization of the young and the assertion of the self-interest of the old – interacted.

It might be said that a rational middle-aged voter – even a late-middle-aged or early retired voter – could have a far-seeing motive in pushing for more investment in the education of the young in order to guarantee higher returns, and thus facilitate existence in their high old age – in the future. That incentive is reduced, however, by the time gap between the decision and the expected outcome: the rational voter might either hope that technical change could produce unexpected windfalls that make old age more supportable, even on reduced incomes compared to present levels, or fear that investments are no longer generating the returns that were available in the past. Prominent economists began to talk about the prospects of secular stagnation.

The extent to which the balance is shifted in favor of the older cohorts varies from country to country, and is driven by demography and changes in fertility and mortality, but also by migration. One of the most striking developments of postwar Europe has been the increase in life expectancy, with the result that most Europeans look forward to a long period after their retirement or after they cease to be economically active. By living longer, people have placed themselves in the position of extracting more resources from the contractual pool. Since labor mobility is a key feature of the EU, it might be anticipated that the young will use the exit option from the most gerontocratic societies, making their already problematic social imbalance even more lop-sided and ultimately unsustainable. Gerontocracies thus create a vicious feedback loop, through which they constrain the only sources that could provide a basis for continuation.

By the early twenty-first century, a questioning of the way that the current contract has been constructed translated into a new mood of intergenerational conflict. The class conflict of previous centuries reasserted itself in a new way. Since it is the well-educated and affluent, the major gainers of the state's expenditure in the early life phase, that follow healthier lifestyles, they also live longer. So they are the beneficiaries of the transfer payments in old age. Education and longer life expectancy have become in general the levers that the privileged use to secure and perpetuate their advantages. They live longer, extract greater resources in pensions and medical care, and then expect to leave larger legacies to their children. A prediction might be that it is precisely where the gerontocracy is strongest that the most powerful protest movements arise, involving above all a mobilization of younger-generation voters, and that it is there that the old-established parties will be unable to mobilize the young.

A powerful mechanism making for intergenerational stability in the twentieth century derived from productivity increases. Economic growth could assure that each generation would realize that it was better off than previous generations, and thus could easily and unproblematically afford to pay for the old. At the height of this confidence, it was easy to agree on a principle of dynamic pensions, in which pensions were regularly adjusted not just to cost of living increases, but also to productivity increases. They were spectacularly popular politically: the West German election of 1957, that followed immediately after the introduction of the dynamic pension principle, is the only one in German history where a party (the ruling party) received an absolute majority of votes. As productivity growth faded, however, the promises incurred at this time began to look as if they were too much of a burden. Falling productivity growth reduces both market returns (real interest rates) and the implicit return in pay-as-you-go pension provision (PAYG). But even in absence of the productivity slowdown, changing demographic composition of the population would have adverse effects – the implicit returns in PAYG schemes fall when fertility goes down (longevity goes up).

Perhaps the most obvious and politically explosive breach in the principle of the modern social contract is that large numbers of expensively trained or educated young people were excluded from the labor market, and in the course of unemployment or underemployment or engagement in low-productivity occupations suffered a deskilling that reduces their long-term chances of productive employment, and hence their capacity to repay as part of the contract. They had received expensive training (perhaps not enough of it), but they are in no position to repay into the social contract. Relatively high rates of youth and younger-generation unemployment have been a phenomenon of crisis economics, but the phenomenon of high rates of exclusion in some parts of Europe preceded the crisis. Even in high-pre-crisis-employment countries such as Spain, the employment growth was concentrated in low-skilled sectors (such as construction) in which there was little stability or potential for skill enhancement.

The conjunction of employment guarantees for established employees together with poorly developed social security systems is a feature of southern European labor markets, while northern Europe has moved to greater overall flexibility in labor contracts while maintaining security (protecting people rather than jobs). The difficulty of dismissing established employees can mean that poorly motivated workers are trapped in low-productivity jobs, and that employers are reluctant or unwilling to hire new workers. Both effects depress the possibility of economic growth, and thus the capacity of society to create and open new opportunities for a next generation. Younger workers are excluded from the regular or protected market, are frequently unemployed, and when they do find employment move rapidly through a succession of short-term contracts, in which it is harder to accumulate skills.

But this development is not only characteristic of southern Europe. Throughout the industrial world, the development among young people of a culture of short-term "gigs" fosters the development of what is often termed the "precariat". Changes in economic structure and the advent of new technologies have produced a corporate instability, which means that the old assumptions of secure lifetime employment with one employer are no longer realistic. In some cases, "gigs" are presented as lowly paid, or unpaid internships, in which the sole motivating goal for the young worker is supposed to be a valuable work experience, but where the intern then requires financial support, usually from parents.

The problem of excessive job security as a source of inflexibility has been recognized for a long time, and in most southern European countries during the 1990s and 2000s there was a vigorous debate about reform that would make for more flexible labor markets. But it remained a largely theoretical debate. Tackling the issue required real courage: indeed in Italy, just as anti-Mafia judges and prosecutors were assassinated, there were two notorious cases in which economists were killed because of their identification with the cause of labor market reform. In May 1999, during the Romano Prodi administration, Massimo D'Antona, a center-left law professor who advised the Minister of Labor on reform, was killed in Rome. In 2002, under the center-right Berlusconi government, Marco Biagi was killed as he cycled to work in Bologna. He had been calling publicly for a reform of the pensions system, but also for a reform of Article 18 of the 1970 Labor Statute, which required the reinstatement of dismissed workers if the dismissal was judged unfair by an adjudication panel. The Biagi case in particular highlighted the variety of the opposition to reform. Biagi, like D'Antona, was killed by left-wing terrorists, the so-called New Red Brigades; but Biagi had received multiple threats, and the Minister of the Interior withdrew his police protection a few months before the killing.

The failure to reform before the crisis is one explanation for the striking rise in youth unemployment during the global financial crisis, which was most characteristic of southern European crisis countries, but is also evident in central and eastern Europe. In both areas, it has produced a widespread sentiment that political process is failing younger people. By contrast, the Scandinavian countries, the Baltics, and Germany did much better, and they looked like more of a magnet for the young. Statistics on youth unemployment tell a similar story to the measured ratio of those not in employment or education; in other words, those who are so discouraged that they opt out altogether of the formal labor market and training. But even the continued education of many young people may not be an altogether positive sign, as it may simply represent a way of escaping the dismal realities of the labor market. The cyclical response of youth unemployment (relative to aggregate unemployment) generally has not been that different during the Great Recession than in past business cycles – but clearly the large number makes the problem more visible. The Great Recession has thus highlighted a fundamental preexisting weakness (and perhaps spurred reform initiatives).

The stasis and rigidity of labor markets also interacted with a deficiency in human capital in Europe. It is difficult to establish which is cause and effect: it could be either that poor employment prospects act as a deterrent to obtain better qualifications, or that the absence of qualifications makes young people less attractive on the labor market. Improving education might be a way round the problem of the gerontocratic society and polity, but it obviously needs to be the right education and not simply a diversionary substitute in the absence of employment.

Many of the most skilled young people emigrated from the societies with high levels of youth unemployment. The outflow of the young is driven in part by very high rates of youth unemployment, but also by a sense that society is organized to marginalize them. The high rates of outflow are also characteristic of central and eastern Europe, where the "brain overflow" affects even economically dynamic countries such as Poland. The phenomenon of youth exit as a response to gerontocracy was evident even before the euro crisis. In a widely discussed public letter to his son published in 2009 in the newspaper *La Repubblica*, the head of Rome's LUISS university Pier Luigi Celli wrote:

> This country, your country, is no longer a place where it's possible to stay with pride . . . That's why, with my heart suffering more than ever, my advice is that you, having finished your studies, take the road abroad. Choose to go where they still value loyalty, respect and the recognition of merit and results.[31]

After the outbreak of the crisis, the exodus increased. The result is a stunning demographic collapse. Bulgaria, the country in the world currently experiencing the fastest depopulation, had a fall from 8.77 million in 1990 to 7.08 million in 2017, and neighboring Romania fell at an almost parallel rate, from 23.23 million to 19.68 million. Latvia's decline was even more stunning, from 2.67 million to 1.95 million. Around two-thirds of the demographic decline of eastern and southeastern Europe was due to emigration. The United Nations estimated in 2017 that Bulgaria, Latvia, Moldova, Ukraine, Croatia, Lithuania, Romania, Serbia, Poland, and Hungary will experience population decline of 15 per cent or more by 2050.[32] The gerontocratic politics of southern and eastern Europe protect vested (middle-aged) interests, and have been counterproductive and endanger long-term stability.

The redistributive effects were augmented by the debt crisis, which had an important intergenerational dimension. Public debt represents a commitment by taxpayers in the future to make payments for goods and services that have been supplied in the present. As a consequence, an argument is often made that debt-financed activity should be confined to investments – for instance, in infrastructure –that will produce substantial returns for future citizens. Debt-financed growth can pay down debt; but in the absence of that growth, a vicious cycle sets in. If debt produces a promise of larger future burdens, it will prompt those who are bound to shoulder those burdens to try to escape. But that choice will make the predicament worse. When productive and innovative (young) people abandon their country, they leave behind a highly indebted country. Now the debt has to be paid off by a smaller, less productive, aging population. In a sense, individual citizens have an option to "walk away" from their government debt obligation by leaving the country. Emigration can be seen as an individual's "private default option" on government debt.

Emigrants also walk away from infrastructure financed by previous generations. If that infrastructure is extensive and well-designed, would-be emigrants have incentives not to move and to stay with a free gift from the past. Where, however, mistaken investments in inadequate infrastructure in uneconomic areas predominate, the incentives are with movement. The extensive debt-financed infrastructure investments for Greece's Olympic Games in 2004, crumbling stadia and swimming pools, do not constitute a strong argument for young people to stay in Greece.

Individualized education and the accretion of human capital – another important investment by the welfare state – are movable, however. Some European countries with education systems that are generally recognized as superior – such as Finland – suffer from the problem that highly educated young people take the exit option and withdraw their accumulated human capital, without contributing in taxes to financing the education of the next generation.

Emigration has strained welfare provision within national states. Germany's eastern *Länder* and the Italian *Mezzogiorno* are also predominantly areas where the young move and the old remain. Medical resources for the remainers became strained and inadequate. In the case of nation-states, social and medical services are provided by budget transfers, so that taxpayers in the more prosperous and dynamic areas shoulder the financial burden. This burden-sharing currently does not take place in the case of cross-border or international migration.

The ability to exit debt in an economic area constituted by high labor mobility provides one of the clearest arguments for the partial mutualization of debt in Europe. The alternative would be to move to a contributions-based insurance system of old age pensions on a cross-national or European basis.

The phenomena of advantages for the old at the expense of the young exist at the national level and are a consequence of national choices about education, pension, medical, and tax regimes. But there is also a global sense in which today's middle-aged population is living at the expense of subsequent generations. The build-up of environmental damage is often interpreted as a burden that today's generation is imposing on its successors without that cost having been unambiguously calculated. The current generations do not internalize the costs. Processes such as global warming will require costly adjustments by subsequent generations. Some argue that these high costs could be avoided by relatively small investments today. The failure to make these present-day investments is in effect a tax on tomorrow's generation – a generation that is already being starved of life opportunities because of the way in which incentives are currently structured. The landmark 2006 report of Nicholas Stern suggested that the eventual costs of global warming would amount to around 5 percent, and perhaps – in a catastrophic scenario – up to 20 percent of world GDP, while tackling the problem today would have a much lower present price tag (1 percent of GDP).[33] But there are major difficulties in devising programs that will really lead to environmental sustainability. The discussion of long-term sustainability highlights the urgency of current measures to reduce the sources of global threats, in particular in the area of carbon dioxide emissions and global warming. Europe's institutional features, the legacy of the history of the nineteenth-century nation-state, made it peculiarly ill-adapted in the twenty-first century to confront genuinely global challenges.

The twentieth century is over: long and short centuries

Historians sometimes like to think of centuries as chronological brackets that define a certain type of society, and that do not in consequence necessarily coincide with the simple arithmetic of numbers. Thus a "long sixteenth century" lasted from the 1490s, the French invasion of Italy that shook the balance of power, and the Spanish voyages to the New World, until the 1640s, where the ending of the Thirty Years' War came together with a wave of revolutions. Or the "long nineteenth century", the era of industrial revolution and liberal political revolution, lasted from 1789, when the French Revolution broke out, to 1914 and the First World War. If that is the case, then there might be a "short twentieth century". As identified by Eric Hobsbawm, it lasted from 1914 to 1989–90, the fall of the communist systems that had originated in the First World War. On the other hand, there might also be a case for a longer twentieth century. The First World War began a process of a shift of economic and political power away from Europe, and at first principally toward the United States. On February 17, 1941, *Life* magazine identified the beginning of a "great American century". The American ideals of democracy and freedom would "do their mysterious work of lifting the life of mankind from the level of the beasts to what the Psalmist called a little lower than the angels". Henry Luce, the China-born owner and editor of the magazine, called for an "internationalism of the people, by the people and for the people". That concept took a severe political knock in 2001 with the terrorist attacks, and in 2003, with the launching of a war that no longer appeared as a "good" American war. In 2007–08 there followed an economic shock with the outbreak of the global financial crisis. So the American century lasted from 1917 (when the United States entered the First World War) to 2008.

Or perhaps there is an oil-based century, that followed the coal century of the 1800s, which also began with the First World War and which ended with 2018, the year of the peak global production of automobiles. Or a demographic century: the dominant demographic features of the twentieth century in Europe were decreasing fertility and increasing life expectancy. In demographics too, the twenty-first century brought a radical change. A large number of high-income countries experienced a decline in life expectancy in 2014–15. In the United States, the decline can be explained largely in terms of the casualties of an epidemic of opioid abuse. The European cases saw an even more dramatic reversal of the previous trend, but they cannot be explained quite so simply. The causes were increases in cardiovascular diseases, Alzheimer's and similar diseases of the nervous system, and mental disorders. The effect was greatest in some of the largest countries, with Italy experiencing the most dramatic decline followed by Belgium, Germany, France, and the UK.[34]

The dream of a better future seemed to be shattering. The mood of pessimism was caught by a Bulgarian intellectual, Ivan Krastev, who concluded that "People no longer dream of the future. They dream of other places."[35] Europeans had become polarized between nostalgia for an irrecoverable past and half-hearted optimism about an uncertain and unknowable future. To neither group did Europe seem attractive. Europe had given up. Europe in its most important twentieth-century meaning had been a cultural space within which ideas flowed and ripened, and that Europe could no longer be reconciled with the twenty-first century's nervous glances backward and forward. The narrative of successful modernization had now collapsed. Was Europe now relapsing into its own dark history?

Notes

1 Orbán 2014 speech, at www.kormany.hu/en/the-prime-minister/the-prime-minister-s-speeches/prime-minister-viktor-orban-s-speech-at-the-25th-balvanyos-summer-free-university-and-student-camp.

2 Peer Steinbrück quoted in David Leonhardt, "A power that may not stay so super", *New York Times*, October 12, 2008, Weekend, p.1.

3 Carlos Cueva, R. Edward Roberts, Tom Spencer, Nisha Rani, Michelle Tempest, Philippe N. Tobler, Joe Herbert, and Aldo Rustichini, "Cortisol and testosterone increase financial risk taking and may destabilize markets", *Scientific Reports*, Volume 5, Article 11206, www.nature.com/articles/srep11206; see Irene van Staveren, "The Lehman Sisters hypothesis", *Cambridge Journal of Economics*, Volume 38, Issue 5, 1 September 2014, pp. 995–1014.

4 Rupali Arora, Catherine Dunn, Beth Kowitt, Colleen Leahey, Patricia Sellers, and Anne VanderMey, "The 50 most powerful women in business: Global edition", *Fortune*, February 6, 2014, http://fortune.com/2014/02/06/the-50-most-powerful-women-in-business-global-edition-fortunes-most-powerful-women/.

5 Konstantin Richter, "Women in business: Strategies for success", *Wall Street Journal Europe*, March 1, 2001.

6 *Zeit Online*, "Mehr weibliche Aufsichträte", January 10, 2018, www.zeit.de/wirtschaft/unternehmen/2018-01/frauenquote-aufsichtsraete-gleichberechtigung-deutsches-institut-wirtschaftsforschung.

7 Daniel Drezner, *The System Worked: How the World Stopped Another Great Depression*, New York, NY: Oxford University Press, 2014.

8 *Spiegel Online*, "Merkel warns of Europe's collapse: 'If euro fails, so will the idea of European Union'", May 13, 2010, www.spiegel.de/international/germany/merkel-warns-of-europe-s-collapse-if-euro-fails-so-will-the-idea-of-european-union-a-694696.html.

9 Deutscher Bundestag, Stenografischer Bericht, 17/42. Sitzung, Berlin, Mittwoch, den 19. Mai 2010.

10 Carlo Bastasin, *Saving Europe: Anatomy of a Dream*, Washington, DC: Brookings Institution, p. 225.

11 See for instance "Press Review Tuesday 12 July 2011", RNW Archive, www.rnw.org/archive/press-review-tuesday-12-july-2011

12 On October 7, 2015, she told an interviewer, Anne Will, on German television that "I am the chair of a Christian party."

13 *Spiegel Online*, "Merkel's refugee policy divides Europe", September 21, 2015, www.spiegel.de/international/germany/refugee-policy-of-chancellor-merkel-divides-europe-a-1053603.html.

14 Press conference at Sochi, September 20, 2008. Vladimir Putin and François Fillon, http://archive.government.ru/eng/docs/1961/.

15 Brian P. Fleming, "The hybrid threat concept: Contemporary war, military planning and the advent of unrestricted operational art", https://www.researchgate.net/publication/235168761_Hybrid_Threat_Concept_Contemporary_War_Military_Planning_and_the_Advent_of_Unrestricted_Operational_Art.

16 Meeting of the Valdai International Discussion Club, September 19, 2012, http://en.kremlin.ru/events/president/news/19243; see also Tim Snyder, *The Road to Unfreedom: Russia, Europe, America*, New York, NY: Penguin, 2018.

17 Will Wei, "The meaning of the 'i' in 'iPhone' – as explained by Steve Jobs", *Business Insider*, September 7, 2016.

18 Sven Egenter and Julian Wettengel, "Merkel: Need to develop a certain passion and joy for the Energiewende", Clean Energy Wire, April 24, 2017, www.cleanenergywire.org/news/merkel-need-develop-certain-passion-and-joy-energiewende.

19 Oliver Burkeman, "Silvio Berlusconi is not Jesus Christ", *The Guardian*, February 14, 2006, www.theguardian.com/world/2006/feb/14/italy.religion.

20 Canovan, M. (1999). "Trust the people! Populism and the two faces of democracy". *Political Studies*, 47(1), 2–16.

21 Rudiger Dornbusch and Sebastian Edwards (eds.), *The Macroeconomics of Populism in Latin America*, Chicago: University of Chicago Press, 1991, p. 9.

22 Pew Research Center, "Origins and destinations of the world's migrants, 1990–2017", February 28, 2016, www.pewglobal.org/2018/02/28/global-migrant-stocks/?country =RO&date=2017.

23 Fareed Zakaria, "The rise of illiberal democracy", *Foreign Affairs*, November/ December 1997, 22–43.

24 Website of the Hungarian Government, "Prime Minister Viktor Orbán's speech at the 25th Bálványos summer free university and student camp", July 26, 2014, www.kormany.hu/en/the-prime-minister/the-prime-minister-s-speeches/prime-minister-viktor-orban-s-speech-at-the-25th-balvanyos-summer-free-university-and-student-camp.

25 James Kirkup, "David Cameron: I can imagine Britain leaving EU", *Daily Telegraph*, December 17, 2012, www.telegraph.co.uk/news/worldnews/europe/ eu/9751026/David-Cameron-I-can-imagine-Britain-leaving-EU.html.

26 Nicholas Watt and Juliette Jowit, "Cameron postpones big speech on Europe", *The Guardian*, January 18, 2013, www.theguardian.com/politics/2013/jan/18/ cameron-europe-speech-postponed.

27 Hatty Collier, "Theresa May speech in full: PM makes Brexit statement blaming MPs for failing to make a choice", *Evening Standard*, March 20, 2019, www. standard.co.uk/news/politics/theresa-mays-brexit-statement-in-full-prime-minister-blames-mps-for-failing-to-make-a-choice-on-eu-a4097126.html.

28 From Eurostat.

29 Nathalie Remy, Eveline Speelman, and Steven Swartz, "Style that's sustainable: A new fast-fashion formula", McKinsey & Company, October 2016, www.mckinsey. com/business-functions/sustainability-and-resource-productivity/our-insights/style-thats-sustainable-a-new-fast-fashion-formula.

30 "Pope describes Europe as 'Elderly and Haggard'", *Wall Street Journal*, November 25, 2014.

31 Stephan Faris, "Arrivederci, Italia: Why young Italians are leaving", *Time*, October 18, 2010.

32 UN 2017 Revision of World Population Prospects, https://population.un.org/wpp/.

33 UK Treasury, *The Stern Review on the Economics of Climate Change*, 2006.

34 Jessica Y. Ho and Arun S. Hendi, "Recent trends in life expectancy across high income countries: Retrospective observational study", *British Medical Journal*, August 15, 2018, BMJ 2018;362:k2562, http://dx.doi.org/10.1136/bmj.k2562.

35 Ivan Krastev, "The unraveling of the post-1989 order", *Journal of Democracy*, October 2016, 27/4, p. 14.

Appendix 1
Populations of major European countries

Populations of major European countries (thousands)

	1900/01	*1930/35*	*1950/54*	*2000*
France	38,451	41,228	42,741	58,892
Germany[1]	56,347	66,030	50,747	82,150
Italy	32,475	41,177	47,516	57,690
Poland		32,107	25,008	38,650
Russia[2]	155,433	165,000	193,200	145,555
Spain	18,594	23,564	27,977	39,465
Turkey[3]	24,814	17,821	20,947	65,293
United Kingdom[4]	41,977	46,216	50,320	59,738
Yugoslavia[5]	2,493	13,934	16,937	10,637

[1]German Empire 1900, 1933; Federal Republic of Germany 1950, 2000.

[2]Russian Empire; Soviet Union 1930; Russian Federation 2000.

[3]Ottoman Empire immediate possessions (i.e. not including Egypt), 1900; subsequently Turkish Republic.

[4]Great Britain and Ireland 1901; subsequently Great Britain and Northern Ireland.

[5]Kingdom of Serbia 1900; Yugoslavia; Yugoslav Federation 1950; Yugoslav Federation (Serbia and Montenegro) 2000.

Sources: B.R. Mitchell, *European Historical Statistics 1750–1970*, London: Macmillan, 1975; *Statesman's Yearbook*, various issues; World Bank database (2000).

Appendix 2
Short biographies

Adenauer, Konrad, 1876–1967. Mayor of Cologne 1917–33; Christian Democrat, and Chancellor of the Federal Republic of Germany 1949– 63.

Albright, Madeleine, 1937–. US Ambassador to the UN 1993–97; Secretary of State 1997–2001.

Andreotti, Giulio, 1919–2013. Christian Democrat, Prime Minister of Italy 1972–73, 1976–79, and 1989–92.

Andropov, Yuri, 1914–84. Head of the KGB 1967–82; General Secretary of CPSU 1982–84.

Anouilh, Jean, 1910–87. French dramatist.

Antonescu, Ion, 1882–1946. Romanian general and dictator. After King Carol appointed him as Prime Minister in 1940, Antonescu forced Carol's abdication and joined Germany. Carol's son Michael instigated a coup in 1944 that overthrew Antonescu. He was executed for war crimes.

Atatürk, originally Mustafa Kemal, 1881–1938. A Turkish general who won the Gallipoli campaign of 1915–16. As inspector of the army, he led Turkish forces in Anatolia in 1919. He rejected the Treaty of Sèvres, was elected President by the Grand National Assembly in 1920, and led the campaign against the Greeks. In 1923 he founded the Republican People's Party, and in 1924 abolished the Caliphate and made Turkey a republic.

Attlee, Clement, 1883–1967. Labour Party leader 1935–55; Deputy Prime Minister 1942–45 in the wartime coalition under Winston Churchill; Prime Minister of the United Kingdom 1945–51.

Azaña y Diaz, Manuel, 1880–1940. Prime Minister of Spain 1931–33 and 1936; President 1936–39. He resigned and fled the country shortly before the final Republican defeat.

Baader, Andreas, 1947–77. German terrorist in Red Army Faction (RAF); he was caught in 1972, and committed suicide in prison, though German leftist activists claim he was murdered by the state.

Baldwin, Stanley, 1867–1947. Prime Minister of the United Kingdom 1923–24, 1924–29, and 1935–37.

Barber, Anthony, 1920–2005. Conservative politician, UK Chancellor of the Exchequer 1970–74.

Barre, Raymond, 1924–2007. Economist and center-right politician, Prime Minister of France 1976–81.

Barzel, Rainer, 1924–2006. German Christian Democrat Party chairman 1971–73.

Benedict XVI (Joseph Ratzinger), 1927. Pope 2005–13, and the first Pope to abdicate.

Beneš, Edvard, 1884–1948. President of Czechoslovakia 1935–38, 1940–45 (government-in-exile), and 1946–48. Resigned after the 1948 coup.

Beria, Lavrenti, 1899–1953. Head of the secret police (NKVD) after November 1938; executed without a trial in the struggle for power after Stalin's death.

Berlinguer, Enrico, 1922–84. Secretary General of Italian Communist Party 1972–84.

Berlusconi, Silvio, 1936–. Media magnate; owner of AC Milan 1986–2017, when the team was sold to a Chinese investment company; founder and leader of center-right Forza Italia party; Prime Minister of Italy 1994, 2001–06, and 2008–11; convicted of tax fraud 2013.

Bierut, Bolesław, 1892–1956. Polish Communist (Stalinist), who was in exile in the USSR during the Second World War; President of Poland 1945–52, he deposed and replaced Gomułka as Party Secretary; also Prime Minister 1952–54.

Blair, Tony, 1953–. Leader of Labour Party, Prime Minister of the United Kingdom 1997–2007.

Blum, Léon, 1872–1950. Prime Minister of France 1936–37, 1938, and 1946–47. Architect of the Popular Front coalition of socialists, communists, and radicals. Blum opposed the Munich agreement and was tried and imprisoned in Vichy France.

Bonomi, Ivanoe, 1873–1952. Center-left Italian politician, who had been expelled from the Socialist Party in 1912. Prime Minister of Italy 1921–22, and again after the liberation as interim Prime Minister 1944–45. Bonomi led the Italian resistance movement during the Second World War.

Brandt, Willy (originally Herbert Frahm), 1913–92. Mayor of Berlin 1957–66; German Foreign Minister and Vice-Chancellor 1966–69; Chancellor 1969–74. A socialist politician who fled to Norway and then to Sweden under the Nazis, he became the first postwar socialist chancellor of Germany but resigned after an East German spy was discovered in his office.

Brasillach, Robert, 1909–45. A French anti-Semite and collaborationist writer and intellectual, and editor of the tabloid *Je Suis Partout*. He was executed in 1945.

Brezhnev, Leonid, 1906–82. Prime Minister of the USSR 1960–64; First Secretary of Central Committee of CPSU 1964–82; President of the USSR 1977–82.

Briand, Aristide, 1862–1932. Prime Minister of France 11 times; Foreign Minister 1925–32. He concluded the Locarno Pact of 1925 and the Kellogg–Briand Pact of 1928, and shared the Nobel Peace Prize with Stresemann for his efforts. He was a passionate advocate of European integration, and was hated by the French nationalist right.

Brown, Gordon, 1951–. Labour Party politician, Chancellor of the Exchequer 1997–2007; Prime Minister of the United Kingdom 2007–10.

Brüning, Heinrich, 1885–1970. German Catholic politician and Chancellor of Germany 1930–32. In his memoirs, he revealed that he would have liked to restore the German monarchy.

Bukharin, Nikolai Ivanovich, 1888–1938. Russian revolutionary leader and main inspiration of 1920s New Economic Policy. Chairman of Comintern 1926–29. He was then denounced by Stalin, partly recovered his position in the mid-1930s and was influential in formulating the 1936 constitution, but was attacked by Stalin again and eventually executed after a show trial.

Bush, George H.W., 1924–2018. President of the United States 1989–93.

Butler, Richard Austen, 1902–82. British Conservative politician, who had important positions in the MacDonald, Baldwin, Chamberlain, and Churchill governments, but never became Prime Minister.

Callaghan, James, 1912–2005. Labour Party Chancellor of the Exchequer of the United Kingdom 1964–67; Prime Minister 1976–79.

Cameron, David, 1966–. Conservative politician, Prime Minister of the United Kingdom 2010–16; called referendum on "Brexit" 2016 and stepped down after defeat of proposal.

Ceauşescu, Nicolae, 1918–89. First Secretary of Romanian Communist Party 1965–89; President 1967–89. With his wife, he was deposed and executed in December 1989.

Chamberlain, Austen, 1863–1937. Conservative politician, son of tariff reformer Joseph Chamberlain; UK Foreign Secretary 1924–29 and one of the principal authors of the Locarno Pact (1925).

Chamberlain, Neville, 1869–1940. Conservative politician, younger half-brother of Austen; UK Chancellor of the Exchequer 1923–24, 1931–37; Prime Minister 1937–40 and architect of "appeasement".

Chernenko, Konstantin, 1911–85. Elected General Secretary of CPSU on Andropov's death in 1984 when already very sick.

Chernomyrdin, Victor, 1938–2010. Prime Minister of Russia 1992–98.

Chirac, Jacques, 1932–. Gaullist politician, Prime Minister of France 1974–76 and 1986–88; President 1995–2007. Cut France's deficit in preparation for European common currency and has advocated greater European military independence from the United States.

Churchill, Winston, 1874–1965. First Lord of the Admiralty of the United Kingdom 1911–15 and 1939–40; Chancellor of the Exchequer 1924–29; Prime Minister 1940–45 and 1951–55.

Ciano, Count Galeazzo, 1903–44. Son-in-law of Mussolini, Foreign Minister of Italy 1936–43; captured, tried, and executed by the Fascist Party.

Clemenceau, Georges, 1841–1929. Prime Minister of France 1906–09 and 1917–20. A French patriot who began his political life on the left, but later became a fierce anti-socialist.

Clinton, Bill, 1946–. President of the United States 1993–2001.

Codreanu, Corneliu Zelea, 1899–1938. Founder and leader of the Romanian Iron Guard, a fascist, anti-Semitic, and Romanian nationalist terrorist organization. Allegedly killed while trying to escape prison.

Craxi, Bettino, 1934–99. Prime Minister of Italy 1983–87; General Secretary of the Italian Socialist Party (PSI) 1976–93. Charged with corruption, he lived in exile in Libya until his death.

Daladier, Édouard, 1884–1970. Prime Minister of France 1933, 1934, and 1938–40. Daladier signed the Munich Pact of 1938.

Darlan, Admiral Jean François, 1881–1942. Commander of the French navy 1936–42. During Laval's temporary eclipse from power, Darlan was appointed Vice Prime Minister, but was dismissed at German insistence. He was assassinated in Algiers by a member of the resistance.

de Gasperi, Alcide, 1881–1954. Elected by the Trentino as a deputy to the Austrian parliament in 1911. After the First World War, he was a founder of the Partito Popolare Italiano, was active in the wartime resistance, and founded the postwar

Democrazia Cristiana. Prime Minister of Italy 1945–53, and a successful advocate of Italian participation in European integration.

de Gaulle, General Charles, 1890–1970. Minister of War in 1940; leader of "Free France"; head of provisional government 1944 to January 1946; President of France 1959–69.

de Valera, Éamon, 1882–1975. President of Ireland 1932–48, 1951–54, and 1957–59. Born in the United States, de Valera led Irish resistance to Britain before and during the establishment of the Irish Free State.

Delors, Jacques, 1925–. French Socialist politician, Minister of Economy and Finance 1981–84; President of the European Commission 1985–94.

Demirel, Süleyman, 1924–2015. Turkish center-right politician, Prime Minister 1965–71, 1977–78, 1979–80 (overthrown by coup), 1991–93; President 1993–2000.

Djilas, Milovan, 1911–95. A critic of Soviet power in Eastern Europe, Djilas was cultivated by Tito as a political heir, but was dismissed from office in 1954.

Dollfuss, Engelbert, 1892–1934. Chancellor-dictator of Austria 1932–34. An Austro-fascist (corporatist), assassinated by Austrian Nazis.

Dubček, Alexander, 1921–92. First Secretary of the Czechoslovak Communist Party 1968–69. After replacing Novotný, Dubček instituted numerous reforms (the "Prague Spring"), which provoked the Soviet invasion of 1968.

Dzerzhinsky, Feliks Edmundovich, 1877–1926. Son of a Polish nobleman, founder and first head of the Leninist secret police (Cheka) in 1917.

Ebert, Friedrich, 1871–1925. President of Germany 1919–25. A German socialist leader, he proclaimed the German Republic on November 9, 1919, and became a member of the Council of People's Commissars and then the first President of republican Germany.

Ecevit, Bülent, 1925–2006. Center-left Turkish politician, Secretary General of Republican People's Party 1966; Prime Minister 1974, 1977, 1978–79, 1999–2002.

Eden, Anthony, 1897–1977. Foreign Minister of the United Kingdom 1935–38, 1940– 45, and 1951–55; Prime Minister 1955–57. Eden resigned in protest against Chamberlain's appeasement policies, but was reappointed by Churchill. He succeeded Churchill as Prime Minister, but resigned after the mishandled Suez crisis.

Eisenstein, Sergei Mikhailovich, 1898–1948. Russian film director.

Erhard, Ludwig, 1897–1977. Federal Republic of Germany Minister of Economics 1949–63; Vice-Chancellor 1957–63; Chancellor 1963–66. He was appointed economic advisor in Nuremberg to US occupation authorities in 1945, and was a major figure in the 1948 currency reform. As Minister of Economics he presided over the German economic recovery or "miracle" (*Wirtschaftswunder*), though he proved to be a rather unsuccessful chancellor.

Ezhov, Nikolai, 1895–1939. Director of Soviet secret police (NKVD) from September 1936 to November 1938, during the Stalinist terror, which was also known as the *Ezbovshchina*.

Facta, Luigi, 1861–1930. Prime Minister of Italy, February–October 1922. He resigned because of the fascist threat.

Fischer, Joschka, 1948–. Green politician. German Foreign Minister 1998–2005.

Francis (Jorge Mario Bergoglio), 1936–. Elected Pope 2013.

Franco, Francisco, 1892–1975. Spanish general, leader of the army revolt against the Republic, and dictator of Spain 1939–75.

Funk, Walther, 1890–1960. Deputy Minister (State Secretary) in the German Propaganda Ministry 1933–37; Economics Minister 1937–45. A journalist who joined the Nazi Party, Funk put forward plans for European economic and monetary integration during the war. At Nuremberg he was sentenced to life imprisonment, but was released in 1957 because of age and poor health.

Gaidar, Yegor, 1956–2009. Vice Prime Minister of Russia 1991–92; acting Prime Minister 1992; Economics Minister under Yeltsin 1993–94; informal advisor to the President through much of the 1990s.

Genscher, Hans Dietrich, 1927–2016. Liberal Party (FDP) leader and Foreign Minister of Federal Republic of Germany 1974–92.

Gheorghiu-Dej, Gheorghe, 1901–65. Secretary General/First Secretary of Romanian Communist Party 1944–54 and 1955–65; Prime Minister 1952–55; President 1961–65.

Gierek, Edward, 1913–2001. First Secretary of the Polish United Workers' Party 1970–80.

Giolitti, Giovanni, 1842–1928. Italian liberal politician, and Prime Minister of Italy five times between 1892 and 1921. In his last period in office, June 1920 to June 1921, he cultivated the support of Mussolini's fascists.

Giscard d'Estaing, Valéry, 1926–. Center-right politician, Minister of Finance 1962–64 and 1969–74; President of France 1974–81. Chairman of EU constitutional convention 2002.

Goebbels, Joseph, 1897–1945. Nazi politician who became Minister for Propaganda and Popular Enlightenment in 1933. He killed himself in a Berlin bunker with his family after Hitler's death on May 1, 1945.

Gömbös, Gyula, 1886–1936. Leader of the fascist Arrow Cross; Prime Minister of Hungary 1932–36. He died suddenly in 1936.

Gomułka, Władysław, 1905–82. Polish communist leader who fought in the underground in the Second World War in occupied Poland against the German occupation, and was resented by "Moscow communists" such as Bierut. He opposed the creation of the Cominform in 1947 and was purged by Bierut but returned as part of the process of destalinization. First Secretary of the Polish United Workers' Party 1943–47, 1956–70.

Gorbachev, Mikhail, 1931–. First Secretary of Stavropol Communist Party 1970–78; General Secretary of CPSU 1985–91; President of USSR 1989–91.

Göring, Hermann, 1893–1946. An air ace in the First World War, Göring became Commissar for Aviation for Germany and Minister-President of Prussia in 1933, and in 1936 Commissar for the Four-Year Plan, which administered German rearmament. In 1940 Hitler gave him the title of *Reichsmarschall*. He was condemned to death at the Nuremberg trial, but committed suicide.

Gorky, Maxim, pseudonym of Aleksey Maximovich Pyeshkov, 1868–1936. Russian writer.

Gottwald, Klement, 1896–1953. Communist, and major architect of the 1948 coup in Czechoslovakia; Prime Minister of Czechoslovakia 1946–48; President 1948–53.

Gramsci, Antonio, 1891–1937. Major theoretician of Italian Communist Party; imprisoned by Mussolini 1926–37.

Grósz, Károly, 1930–96. Prime Minister of Hungary 1987–88; First Secretary of Socialist Workers' Party 1988–89.

Guisan, Henri, 1874–1960. Commander-in-Chief of Switzerland's armed forces during the Second World War.

Havel, Václav, 1936–2011. Dissident playwright, founder of Charter 77; imprisoned 1979–83; President of Czechoslovakia 1989–92, and the Czech Republic 1993–2002.

Heath, Edward, 1916–2005. Conservative politician, Prime Minister of the United Kingdom 1970–74.

Herriot, Édouard, 1872–1957. Radical (center-left) politician, Prime Minister of France 1924–25, 1926, and 1932. His first government evacuated the Ruhr and negotiated the Dawes Plan.

Heydrich, Reinhard, 1904–42. Major figure in the SS. In 1939 he was appointed chief of the Reich Security Main Office (*Reichssicherheitshauptamt*); in 1941 he planned the killing of Jews, and was appointed Reich Protector of Bohemia and Moravia. He was killed by Czech patriots.

Himmler, Heinrich, 1900–45. "*Reichsführer*" of the Nazi *Schutzstaffel* (SS) or "protective corps" 1929–45. Chief architect of the Nazi killing of Jews.

Hindenburg, Paul von, 1847–1934. Chief of German general staff 1916–18; President of republican Germany 1925–34. Retired from military service in 1911, in August 1914 he was appointed commander of German armies in East Prussia and became "victor of Tannenberg"; the resulting prestige sent him to presidency following the death of Ebert. A victim of Alzheimer's disease, in 1933 he capitulated to advisors and appointed Hitler chancellor.

Hitler, Adolf, 1889–1945. Leader of National Socialist German Workers' Party 1920–45; Chancellor and dictator (*Führer*) 1933–45.

Hollande, François, 1954–. President of France 2012–17.

Hoover, Herbert, 1874–1964. President of the United States 1929–33.

Horthy de Nagybanya, Admiral Miklós, 1868–1957. Admiral of Austro-Hungarian fleet during First World War; regent and head of state of Hungary 1920–44. Horthy was forced to resign by Hitler after surrendering German-occupied Hungary to Soviet forces in 1944.

Howe, Geoffrey, 1926–2015. Conservative politician, UK Chancellor of the Exchequer 1979–83; Foreign Secretary 1983–89; Deputy Prime Minister 1989–90. Architect of the original Thatcher economic policy, but quarreled with her over her increasingly hostile attitude to European integration.

Hull, Cordell, 1871–1955. US Secretary of State 1933–44.

Husák, Gustáv, 1913–91. A Slovak communist who led the 1944 revolt against the Tiso regime and the Germans. He was purged in 1951 and imprisoned from 1954–60, but then was rehabilitated and became Deputy Prime Minister in April 1968 during the Czech liberalization. After the 1968 invasion, he became a Soviet puppet: First Secretary of the Czechoslovak Communist Party 1969–87; President of Czechoslovakia 1975–89.

Inönü, Ismet, 1884–1973. Foreign Minister of Turkish Grand National Assembly 1922–23; negotiated Treaty of Lausanne; Prime Minister of Turkey 1923–37, President 1938–50, and again Prime Minister 1961– 65, following the military coup of 1960.

Izethegović, Alija, 1925–2003. President of Bosnia–Herzegovina 1990–96; member of collective presidency 1996–2000.

Jaruzelski, General Wojciech, 1923–2014. First Secretary of Polish United Workers' Party 1981–85; President 1985–90. Declared martial law 1981–83.

Jenkins, Roy, 1920–2003. Home Secretary of the United Kingdom 1965–67 and 1974–76; Chancellor of the Exchequer 1967–70; President of European Commission 1977–81; co-founder of British Social Democratic Party 1981.

John XXIII (Angelo Roncalli), 1881–1963. Appointed Nuncio to France 1944; Pope 1958–63, and architect of the Second Vatican Council.

John Paul II (Karol Wojtyła), 1920–2005. Became Archbishop of Cracow in 1963 and Cardinal in 1967; Pope 1978–2005.

Jospin, Lionel, 1937–. Graduate of *École nationale d'administration* and French Socialist politician who had been a member of the International Communist Organization (Trotskyist); Prime Minister of France 1997–2002.

Kaas, Monsignor Ludwig, 1881–1952. Leader of German Catholic Center Party 1928–33; advocate of a positive vote for Hitler's enabling act in 1933.

Kádár, János,1912–89. Prime Minister of Hungary 1956–58 and 1961–65; First Secretary of Socialist Workers' Party 1956–88. Kádár supported the suppression of the 1956 rising, but eventually allowed a cautious economic and then also an even more cautious political liberalization.

Kamenev (originally Rosenfeld), Lev Borisovich, 1883–1936. Russian revolutionary leader, closely associated with Zinoviev. With Stalin and Zinoviev, he was in a triumvirate after Lenin's death. Expelled from the party by Stalin in 1927, he was executed after the first show trial in 1936.

Kania, Stanisław, 1927–. First Secretary of Polish United Workers' Party 1980–81.

Kerensky, Aleksandr Feodorovich, 1881–1970. Russian revolutionary who succeeded Prince Lvov as head of provisional government in July 1917; removed by the Bolshevik revolution in the October Revolution and fled to Paris.

Keynes, John Maynard, 1883–1946. British economist, critic of Versailles and of deflationary policies in the 1930s; major architect (with Harry Dexter White) of the Bretton Woods conference of 1944.

Khrushchev, Nikita, 1894–1971. Prime Minister of the USSR 1958–64; First Secretary of Central Committee of CPSU 1953–64. Deposed but died of natural causes.

Kiesinger, Kurt, 1904–88. Christian Democrat Minister-President of the state of Baden-Württemberg 1958–66; Chancellor of the Federal Republic of Germany 1966–69. Kiesinger joined the Nazi Party in 1933 and from 1933–45 worked in the radio department of the German Foreign Ministry. After the war, he joined the Christian Democrat Party, eventually becoming Chancellor of a coalition government.

Kirov, Sergei Mironovich, 1888–1934. Leader of the Leningrad Communist Party from 1930; assassinated in mysterious circumstances in 1934.

Kissinger, Henry, 1923–. Historian and political scientist who became US Secretary of State 1973–77.

Kohl, Helmut, 1930–2017. Christian Democrat politician, Minister-President of Rhineland-Palatinate 1969–76; Chancellor of the Federal Republic of Germany 1982–97; a major architect of German unification 1990.

Kołakowski, Leszek, 1927–2009. Polish philosopher, expelled from the Polish United Workers' Party in 1968.

Kwaśniewski, Aleksander, 1954–. Communist and then founder of Social Democratic Party in Poland; President of Poland 1995–2005.

Lambsdorff, Count Otto, 1926–2009. German liberal (FDP) Minister of Economics 1977–84.

Largo Caballero, Francisco, 1869–1946. Socialist leader, Prime Minister of Spain 1936–37. Was removed from office by pressure from the communists.

Laval, Pierre, 1883–1945. Prime Minister of France 1931–32 and 1935–36, as well as Foreign Minister 1934–35, and architect of the Franco-Soviet Pact as well as of the Hoare–Laval Pact, which promised African territory to Italy. Under Vichy, Laval served first as Vice Prime Minister, but was sacked by Pétain in December 1940 and was reinstated as Prime Minister with dictatorial powers by Hitler in 1942. He was tried for treason and executed in 1945.

Le Pen, Jean-Marie, 1928–. Founder of the French Front National party.

Lemkin, Raphael, 1901–59. A Polish lawyer and Second World War resistance fighter, Lemkin fled to Sweden and then to the United States after six months of hiding in occupied Poland. Lemkin invented the term "genocide".

Lenin (originally Ulyanov), Vladimir Ilyich, 1870–1924. Russian revolutionary leader of Bolshevik Party.

Lipiński, Edward, 1888–1986. Polish economist and a member of the Committee for Workers' Defense, a group of intellectuals who in 1976 asked for the release of imprisoned strikers.

Litvinov, Maxim Maximovich, 1876–1951. Soviet Commissar for Foreign Affairs 1930–39; Ambassador to the United States 1941–43.

Lloyd George, David, 1863–1945. UK Chancellor of the Exchequer 1908–15; Prime Minister 1916–22.

Ludendorff, Erich, 1865–1937. Chief of General Staff of German army in East Prussia 1914; First Quartermaster General of army command (*Oberste Heeresleitung*) 1916–18; leader (with Hitler) of attempted putsch in Munich, November 1923.

Lvov, Prince Georgi Yevgenyevich, 1861–1925. Head of provisional government in Russia, March–July 1917.

Lysenko, Trofim Denisovich, 1898–1976. Russian agronomist who opposed Mendelian genetics.

MacDonald, Ramsay, 1866–1937. Labour Party politician and Prime Minister of the United Kingdom 1924 (the first Labour government) and 1929–35.

Macmillan, Harold, 1894–1986. Prime Minister of the United Kingdom 1957–63.

Macron, Emmanuel, 1977–. French politician, Minister of the Economy 2014–16; President of France 2017– .

Major, John, 1943–. Conservative politician, UK Foreign Secretary 1989; Chancellor of the Exchequer 1989–90; Prime Minister 1990–97. He succeeded Margaret Thatcher, and played an influential role in the negotiation of the Maastricht Treaty; also negotiated a cease-fire in Northern Ireland.

Malenkov, Georgi, 1902–88. Prime Minister of the USSR 1953–55. After succeeding Stalin as Prime Minister, he was forced to resign in February 1955 and was expelled from the party in 1961.

Márquez González, Felipe, 1942–. Socialist Workers' Party leader 1974–97; member of parliament for Madrid since 1977; Prime Minister of Spain 1982–96.

Marshall, George, 1880–1959. US Army Chief of Staff 1939–49, US Secretary of State 1947–49. He devised the European Recovery Program ("Marshall Plan") to promote European economic recovery after the Second World War.

Masaryk, Jan, 1886–1948. Foreign Minister of Czechoslovakia 1940–45 (government-in-exile) and 1945–48, when he died after falling out of a window in the Czernin Palace (Foreign Ministry). The son of the first Czech President Tomáš Masaryk.

Masaryk, Tomáš, 1850–1937. Professor of philosophy and proponent of Czech independence. First President of Czechoslovakia 1918–35.

Maurras, Charles, 1868–1952. French political theorist and monarchist, who supported Pétain and admired Mussolini and Franco.

May, Theresa, 1956–. Conservative politician, Prime Minister of the United Kingdom 2016–19.

Mazowiecki, Tadeusz, 1927–2013. Catholic politician, Prime Minister of Poland 1989–90.

Meinhof, Ulrike, 1934–76. Journalist who in 1968 joined the terrorist RAF movement. She was arrested in 1972 and died in prison, probably as a suicide.

Mendès-France, Pierre, 1907–82. Prime Minister and Foreign Minister of France 1954–55.

Merkel, Angela, 1954–. Chair of CDU 2000–18; Chancellor of Germany since 2006.

Metaxas, Ioannis, 1871–1941. Greek general, who was appointed Prime Minister in 1935 and given dictatorial powers 1936–41.

Mikołajczyk, Stanisław, 1901–66. Vice Prime Minister of Poland's government-in-exile 1941–43; Prime Minister 1943–44. After the Yalta conference, he became Deputy Prime Minister in a communist-dominated coalition government, but fled to the United States after the rigged election of 1947.

Milošević, Slobodan, 1941–2006. President of Serbia 1989–97; President of Yugoslavia 1997–2000.

Miłosz, Czesław, 1911–2004. Polish poet, left Polish diplomatic service in 1951 and moved first to France. 1980 Nobel Prize in literature.

Mitterrand, François, 1916–96. French socialist leader, PoW in Germany in 1940; escaped and worked as civil servant in Vichy France 1941–43; joined resistance 1943; independent socialist in the Fourth Republic, and a cabinet member in 11 administrations, including Minister of the Interior 1954–55 and Minister of Justice 1956–57; President of France for two terms in the Fifth Republic 1981–95.

Molotov, Vyacheslav, 1890–1986. Prime Minister of USSR 1930–41; Commissar of Foreign Affairs (later Foreign Minister) 1939–49 and 1953–56. He was expelled from the Central Committee of the Communist Party in 1957 for opposing Khrushchev.

Monnet, Jean, 1888–1979. French economist; Deputy Secretary General of the League of Nations 1919–23; President of the European Coal and Steel Community 1952–55.

Moro, Aldo, 1916–78. Christian Democrat, Prime Minister of Italy 1963–68 and 1974–76. Architect of the "historical compromise" with the Communist Party. Assassinated by the Red Brigades.

Mosley, Sir Oswald, 1896–1980. British politician who left the Labour Party and after 1932 organized the British Union of Fascists.

Mountbatten, Lord Louis, 1900–79. Last British Viceroy of India 1947; Chief of Defence Staff of Great Britain 1959–65. He was assassinated by the Irish Republican Army.

Müller, Hermann, 1876–1931. Chancellor of Germany 1920 and 1928–30. A socialist politician, Müller first became Chancellor in the aftermath of the Kapp putsch.

Mussolini, Benito, 1883–1945. Socialist leader and journalist, editor of *Avanti* (the party newspaper), before being expelled from the party for supporting Italy's entry into the First World War. He then founded his own newspaper, *Il Popolo d'Italia*, and the Italian Fascist Party. Prime Minister of Italy 1922–43, and then leader of a puppet state in the Republic of Salò. With his mistress, Clara Petacci, he was shot near Como by Italian partisans on April 28, 1945.

Nagy, Imre, 1896–1958. Prime Minister of Hungary 1953–55 and 1956. He was dismissed from his first Prime Ministership for reformism, but regained power in the Hungarian uprising of 1956. After the uprising was put down, he was executed.

Negri, Antonio, 1936–. Italian political philosopher and theorist of violent revolution in the 1970s; anti-globalization thinker in the 1990s.

Negrín, Juan, 1891–1956. Prime Minister of Republican Spain 1937–39.

Nitti, Francesco, 1868–1953. Politician of the center-left and Prime Minister of Italy June 1919 to June 1920.

Novotný, Antonín, 1904–75. First Secretary of the Czechoslovak Communist Party 1953–68; President of Czechoslovakia 1957–68.

Orwell, George, pseudonym for Eric Arthur Blair, 1903–50. British writer. The author of *Animal Farm* and *Nineteen Eighty-Four*.

Özal, Turgut, 1927–93. Economist and liberal (center-right) Turkish politician, Deputy Prime Minister 1980–82, after a military coup; founded Motherland Party (ANP) 1983; Prime Minister 1983–89; President 1989–93.

Papandreou, Andreas, 1919–98. A leading opponent of the Colonels in Greece, and founder of Panhellenic Socialist Movement (Pasok); Prime Minister of Greece 1981–89 and 1993–96.

Papandreou, Georgios, 1888–1968. Head of Greek coalition government 1944, and later founder of Center Union; Prime Minister 1963–65, he was dismissed by the King, and his probable election victory in 1967 prompted the coup of the Colonels.

Papen, Franz von, 1879–1969. German military attaché in Washington 1914–15, where he planned acts of sabotage; Chancellor 1932; Vice-Chancellor 1933. A Catholic Center party politician, in January 1933 von Papen negotiated with Hitler about the formation of a government in which he became Vice-Chancellor. In April 1933 he resigned, and narrowly escaped being killed in June 1934. He then became an ambassador, first in Vienna and then in Turkey. He was tried but acquitted at Nuremberg.

Pétain, Philippe, 1856–1951. Prime Minister of Vichy France 1940–45. Fled in 1945 but returned voluntarily to France to face treason charges; he was found guilty, but de Gaulle commuted his death sentence to life imprisonment.

Piaf, Edith (originally Edith Gassion), 1915–63. French *chansonnière*.

Pilet-Golaz, Marcel, 1889–1958. Swiss Foreign Minister, 1940–45.

Piłsudski, Józef, 1867–1935. Member of Polish Socialist Party who organized a Polish army to fight against Russia in the First World War, and became head of the military in the Polish Council of State after Germany and Austria agreed to Polish independence in 1916. From 1918 to 1922 he was the head of state of a fully independent Poland. In May 1926 he staged a coup and seized effective power (though formally he was Defense Minister).

Pius XI (Achille Ratti), 1857–1939. Prefect of the Vatican library, then Papal Nuncio in Warsaw 1919–21; Archbishop of Milan 1921–22; Pope 1922–39. In 1929 he concluded the Lateran Treaty with Mussolini, which brought the Vatican State into independent existence and established its neutrality, but also recognized the legality of the Kingdom of Italy.

Pius XII (Eugenio Pacelli), 1876–1958. Papal Nuncio in Bavaria 1917–25, in Berlin 1925–29; Cardinal Secretary of State 1929–39; Pope 1939–58.

Pleven, René, 1901–93. French Minister of Defense 1949–50 and 1952–54; Prime Minister 1950–51 and 1951–52.

Pompidou, Georges, 1911–74. Gaullist politician, Prime Minister of France 1962–68; President 1969–74.

Powell, Enoch, 1912–98. UK Minister of Health 1960–63; shadow Minister of Defence 1964–68. In 1968 he made an inflammatory speech against the level of non-white immigration to the United Kingdom, and came to see himself as a British Gaullist.

Primo de Rivera, José Antonio, 1903–36. Son of Miguel Primo de Rivera. Organized the Spanish Falange fascist party which sought a Spain modeled after Mussolini's Italy. He was executed during the Spanish Civil War by loyalists, and became a martyr figure for the right. His body is buried beside Franco's in the grotesque basilica of the Valley of the Fallen.

Primo de Rivera, Miguel, 1870–1930. Spanish dictator 1923–30. Abrogated the Spanish constitution and imposed martial law, but eventually resigned after losing public support.

Prodi, Romano, 1939–. Academic economist; Prime Minister of Italy 1996–98; President of European Commission 1999–2008.

Putin, Vladimir, 1952–. Acting President of Russia after Yeltsin's resignation in December 1999; President 2000–2008, 2012–.

Rajk, László, 1909–49. First Secretary of the Hungarian Communist Party 1941–49. He was accused of Titoism by Rákosi and executed.

Rákosi, Mátyás, 1892–1971. First Secretary of Hungarian Communist Party 1944–48, and of United Workers' Party 1948–53; Prime Minister 1952–53 and 1955–56. A convinced Stalinist, who in 1956 fled to the USSR.

Rathenau, Walther, 1867–1922. Foreign Minister of Germany 1922. Son of the founder of a major German electrical company, AEG, and a visionary intellectual, Rathenau became Director of the Office for Raw Materials during the First World War and Foreign Minister in 1922, where he negotiated with the Soviet Union at Rapallo. He was killed by nationalist terrorists on June 24, 1922.

Reynaud, Paul, 1878–1966. Anti-appeasement and anti-deflation politician of the moderate right; Prime Minister of France 1940.

Roosevelt, Franklin Delano, 1882–1945. President of the United States 1933–45.

Salazar, António, 1889–1970. Prime Minister of Portugal 1932–68.

Sarkozy, Nicolas, 1955–. French politician, Minister of Finance 2005; Minister of Interior 2005–07; President of France, 2007–12.

Sartre, Jean-Paul, 1905–80. French existentialist philosopher.

Sauckel, Fritz, 1894–1946. Nazi Gauleiter (regional boss) of Thuringia 1927–45; German General Plenipotentiary for the Use of Labor 1942–45. During the Second World War he directed the Nazi slave labor program. He was sentenced to death at Nuremberg, and executed.

Schacht, Hjalmar, 1877–1970. President of the Central Bank of Germany (Reichsbank) 1923–30 and 1933–39. From 1934 to 1937 he was also Acting Minister of Economics, and remained in the cabinet as Minister without Portfolio until 1943. He was acquitted at Nuremberg.

Schiller, Karl, 1911–94. German Economics Minister 1966–72. Schiller favored free capital movements.

Schily, Otto, 1932–. Interior Minister of Germany 1997–2005. A German lawyer who acted in defense of the RAF in the 1970s, Schily helped to found the Green Party, but later joined the SPD.

Schleicher, Kurt von, 1882–1934. Chancellor of Germany, December 1932 to January 1933. In 1929 he served as chief of the ministerial office for the press and politics in the German Army Ministry. After his intrigues helped to bring down Chancellors Brüning and von Papen, in December 1932, he became Chancellor himself for 57 days. On June 30, 1934, he was killed by the SS in the so-called Night of the Long Knives.

Schmidt, Helmut, 1918–2015. SPD politician, German Defense Minister 1969–72; Economics and Finance Minister 1972–74; Chancellor 1974–1982.

Schmitt, Carl, 1888–1985. German political theorist. Arrested for war crimes in 1947 but acquitted.

Schröder, Gerhard, 1944–. SPD politician, chairman of Jusos (Young Socialists) 1978–80; Minister-President of Lower Saxony 1990–98; Chancellor of Germany 1998–2005.

Schumacher, Kurt, 1895–1952. Chairman of the SPD in Germany 1946–52. After suffering 10 years as a political internee in Dachau, became the first postwar leader of the German SPD.

Schuman, Robert, 1886–1963. Prime Minister of France 1947–48; Foreign Minister 1948–53. Architect of the European Coal and Steel Community.

Snowden, Philip, 1864–1937. UK Chancellor of the Exchequer 1924 and 1929–31.

Soares, Mario, 1924–2017. Portuguese socialist leader, imprisoned and then exiled under dictatorship; Prime Minister of Portugal three times between 1976 and 1985.

Speer, Albert, 1905–81. After joining the Nazi Party in 1931, Speer became Hitler's personal architect and was later appointed as Armaments Minister, 1942–45, where he mobilized the German war economy. He was sentenced to 20 years' imprisonment at Nuremberg, and died in London the morning after an interview with the British historian Norman Stone.

Stalin (originally Dzhugashvili), Joseph, 1879–1953. Russian revolutionary; General Secretary of the Central Committee of the Communist Party of the Soviet Union 1922–53, Prime Minister of the USSR 1941–53.

Stamboliski, Aleksandr, 1879–1923. Prime Minister and dictator of Bulgaria 1919–23. Launched dramatic agrarian reforms, but was assassinated in a fascist–nationalist coup.

Stresemann, Gustav, 1878–1929. Chancellor of Germany 1923; Foreign Minister 1924–29. A liberal politician, he became a member of the Reichstag in 1907, and in 1917 became leader of the National Liberal Party group in the Reichstag. Chancellor briefly in 1923; Foreign Minister and architect of reconciliation with France until his death in October 1929.

Suárez González, Adolfo, 1932–2014. Founded Unión Centro del Democrático; Prime Minister of Spain 1976–81.

Szálasi, Ferenc, 1897–1946. Hungarian fascist and pro-German politician, Prime Minister of Hungary 1944–45.

Thatcher, Margaret, 1925–2013. Conservative politician, Secretary of State for Education 1970–74; Prime Minister of the United Kingdom 1979–90.

Tiso, Father Jozef (originally Velká Bytča), 1887–1947. President-dictator of Slovakia 1939–45; executed for treason and war crimes in 1947.

Tito, Josip Broz, 1892–1980. Secretary-General of Yugoslav Communist Party 1939–80; leader of partisans 1941–45; Prime Minister of Yugoslavia 1945–53; President 1953–80.

Todt, Fritz, 1891–1942. German engineer who organized the building of divided highways (*Autobahnen*) under Hitler. He created the "Organization Todt" to employ foreign and slave labor in vast building projects, and in 1940 became Armaments Minister. He was killed in a plane crash.

Trotsky, Leon (originally Lev Davidovich Bronstein), 1879–1940. Russian revolutionary, originally a Menshevik, who was first Minister for Foreign Affairs and then for War in the revolutionary government after the October Revolution.

Tudjman, Franjo, 1922–99. President of Croatia 1990–99; Leader of Croatian independence forces during the 1991–92 civil war.

Vishinsky, Andrei Yanuarievich, 1883–1954. Soviet diplomat and lawyer; chief prosecutor at Moscow show trials of 1936–38.

von Hindenburg, Paul: see Hindenburg.

von Papen, Franz: see Papen.

von Schleicher, Kurt: see Schleicher.

Wajda, Andrzei, 1926–2016. Polish filmmaker and social critic.

Wałęsa, Lech, 1943–. Electrician in Gdańsk shipyards, and later Chairman of the Solidarność movement, he was imprisoned when General Jaruzelski imposed martial law in 1981 but released in 1982. He became the first freely elected President of Poland 1990–95.

Weber, Max, 1864–1920. German sociologist.

Wilson, Harold, 1916–95. UK Labour Party leader, and modernizing Prime Minister 1964–70 and 1974–76.

Wilson, Woodrow, 1856–1924. Political scientist and university president; President of the United States 1913–21.

Yeltsin, Boris, 1931–2007. First Secretary of Moscow Communist Party Committee 1985–87; President of Russia 1991–99.

Zhdanov, Andrei Aleksandrovich, 1896–1948. Soviet Communist theorist and loyal supporter of Stalin.

Zhivkov, Todor, 1911–98. First Secretary of Bulgarian Communist Party 1954–89; Prime Minister 1962–71; President 1971–89.

Zinoviev (originally Radomyslsky), Grigori Evseyevich, 1883–1936. Russian revolutionary leader, who had advised against seizure of power in the October Revolution; Chairman of Comintern 1920–26; formed a triumvirate with Lev Kamenev and Joseph Stalin after Lenin's death, but was expelled from the party by Stalin in 1927 and executed after the first show trial in 1936.

Zogu, Ahmet (King Zog), 1895–1961. Prime Minister of Albania 1922–24; President 1925–28; King 1928–39.

Zyuganov, Gennady, 1944–. Russian Communist, who ran unsuccessfully against Yeltsin in presidential elections 1996 and against Putin in 2000.

Appendix 3
Further reading

A very detailed and very helpful overall history is C.E. Black and E.C. Helmreich, *Twentieth Century Europe: A History* (4th edn, New York, NY: Knopf, 1972), though unfortunately it has not been updated adequately; C.E. Black (with others), *Rebirth: A History of Europe since World War II* (Boulder, CO: Westview Press, 1992) contains an overview and some national chapters. Eric Hobsbawm, *Age of Extremes: The Short Twentieth Century 1914–1991* (London: Michael Joseph, 1994) is highly interesting, if tendentiously nostalgic about the legacy of the Bolshevik revolution. Mark Mazower, *Dark Continent: Europe's Twentieth Century* (New York, NY: Random House, 1998) has tremendous insights, in particular into the story of racism and ethnic conflicts. Richard Vinen, *A History in Fragments: Europe in the Twentieth Century* (London: Little, Brown, 2000) is insightful and partial. Other overviews include Konrad Jarausch, *Out of Ashes: A New History of Europe in the Twentieth Century* (Princeton, NJ: Princeton University Press, 2015) is cautiously optimistic. On interwar Europe, Ian Kershaw's brilliant survey is the best guide: *To Hell and Back: Europe, 1914–1949* (London: Allen Lane, 2015). There is also from a critical perspective, focusing on violence, Enzo Traverso (transl. David Fernbach), *Fire and Blood: The European Civil War, 1914–1945* (London: Verso, 2016). On the second half of the twentieth century, see Tony Judt, *Postwar: A History of Europe Since 1945* (New York, NY: Penguin, 2005), and also his fine essay, *A Grand Illusion? An Essay on Europe* (New York, NY: Hill and Wang, 1996); and William Hitchcock, *The Struggle for Europe: The Turbulent History of a Divided Continent* (New York, NY: Doubleday, 2003).

Some fine historical atlases are Georges Duby, *Atlas historique mondial* (Paris: Larousse, 2000); Michael L. Dockrill, *Collins Atlas of Twentieth Century World History* (Glasgow: HarperCollins, 1991); and *Westermanns Atlas zur Weltgeschichte* (Braunschweig: George Westermann Verlag, 1956). Martin Gilbert, *Atlas of the Holocaust* (Oxford: Pergamon Press, 1988) is very useful.

The First World War

On the origins of the First World War, see the studies of individual countries and their foreign policies: V.R. Berghahn, *Germany and the Approach of War in 1914* (New York, NY: St Martin's Press, 1973); Fritz Fischer (transl. Marian Jackson), *War of Illusions: German Policies from 1911 to 1914* (New York, NY: Norton, 1975); D.C.B. Lieven, *Russia and the Origins of the First World War* (New York, NY: St Martin's Press, 1983); and Zara S. Steiner, *Britain and the Origins of the First World War* (New York, NY: St Martin's Press, 1977). On the course of the war, there are several overall histories: Hew Strachan, *The First World War* (Oxford: Oxford University Press, 2001); John Keegan, *The First World War* (London: Hutchinson, 1998); and Niall Ferguson, *The Pity of War* (New York, NY: Basic Books, 1999). The centenary of the Great War produced a flood of literature, notably the epochal Christopher Clark, *The Sleepwalkers: How Europe Went to War in 1914* (London: Allen Lane, 2012); Hew Strachan (ed.), *The Oxford Illustrated History of the First World War* (Oxford: Oxford University Press, 2014); and Jörn Leonhard (transl. Patrick Camiller), *Pandora's Box: A History of the First World War* (Cambridge, MA: Harvard University Press, 2018). Robert Gerwarth extends the study of the war into civil war and peacemaking in the important *The Vanquished: Why the First World War Failed to End* (New York, NY: Farrar, Straus and Giroux, 2016). There is also an older, and brief, history that lays out the social history of the war: Marc Ferro (transl. Nicole Stone), *The Great War, 1914–1918* (London: Routledge, 1973). On the social history of the war, see also Gerald D. Feldman, *Army, Industry, and Labor in Germany, 1914–1918* (Princeton, NJ: Princeton University Press, 1966); and Jürgen Kocka, *Facing Total War: German Society, 1914–1918* (Cambridge, MA: Harvard University Press, 1985). On the important issue of the eastern war, see Norman Stone, *The Eastern Front, 1914–1917* (London: Hodder and Stoughton, 1975); and Vejas Gabriel Liulevicius, *War Land on the Eastern Front: Culture, National Identity and German Occupation in World War I* (Cambridge: Cambridge University Press, 2000). On memory: J.M. Winter, *The Experience of World War I* (London: Macmillan, 1988); Jay Winter and Emmanuel Sivan (eds), *War and Remembrance in the Twentieth Century* (Cambridge: Cambridge University Press, 1999); and Stéphane Audoin-Rouzeau and Annette Becker (transl. Catherine Temerson), *14–18: Understanding the Great War* (New York, NY: Hill and Wang, 2002).

On peacemaking, see the two older books by Arno J. Mayer, *Political Origins of the New Diplomacy, 1917–1918* (New Haven, CT: Yale University Press, 1959) and *Politics and Diplomacy of Peacemaking: Containment and Counterrevolution at Versailles, 1918–1919* (New York, NY: Knopf, 1967); and the recent accounts in Erez Manela, *The Wilsonian Moment: Self-Determination and the International Origins of Anticolonial Nationalism* (Oxford: Oxford University Press, 2007); and Adam Tooze, *The Deluge: The Great War, America and the Remaking of the Global Order, 1916–1931* (London: Penguin, 2014).

The Russian Revolution

A standard work which provides a Kremlin's eye view is E.H. Carr, *The Bolshevik Revolution* (Harmondsworth: Penguin, 1966). Marc Ferro deals brilliantly with a view from below: (transl. L. Richards) *The Russian Revolution of February 1917* (Englewood Cliffs, NJ: Prentice-Hall, 1972) and (transl. Norman Stone) *October 1917: A Social History of the Russian Revolution* (London: Routledge, 1980). There are superb narrative histories by Richard Pipes, *The Russian Revolution* (New York, NY: Knopf, 1990); and Orlando Figes, *A People's Tragedy: The Russian Revolution, 1891–1924* (London: Cape, 1996). Figes has also written an illuminating monograph on the peasant question: *Peasant Russia, Civil War: the Volga Countryside in Revolution, 1917–1921* (Oxford: Oxford University Press, 1989). Again the centenary of the revolution produced some important new accounts, including Dominic Lieven, *Towards the Flame: Empire, War and the End of Tsarist Russia* (London: Penguin, 2016); Sean McMeekin, *The Russian Revolution: A New History* (New York, NY: Basic Books, 2017); Steve Smith, *Russia in Revolution: An Empire in Crisis 1890 to 1928* (Oxford: Oxford University Press, 2017); and Laura Engelstein, *Russia in Flames: War, Revolution, Civil War, 1914–1921* (New York, NY: Oxford University Press, 2018).

The interwar radical right

On the general history of fascism, the best introduction is Stanley Payne, *A History of Fascism 1914–1945* (Madison, WI: University of Wisconsin Press, 1995); Walter Laqueur (ed.), *Fascism: A Reader's Guide: Analyses, Interpretations* (Berkeley, CA: University of California Press, 1976) is helpful, as is Richard Bessel (ed.), *Fascist Italy and Nazi Germany: Comparisons and Contrasts* (Cambridge: Cambridge University Press, 1996), which contains some very fine essays. Important contributions to the literature include Ruth Ben-Ghiat's *Fascist Modernities: Italy 1922–1945* (Berkeley, CA: University of California Press, 2001); and Zeev Sternhell's (transl. David Maisel) *Neither Right nor Left: Fascist Ideology in France* (Princeton, NJ: Princeton University Press, 1995). Martin Conway sets a context in *Catholic Politics in Europe 1918–1945* (New York, NY: Routledge, 1997). See also Renzo de Felice (transl. Brenda Huff Everett), *Interpretations of Fascism* (Cambridge, MA: Harvard University Press, 1977). On fascist and Nazi ideas, see Pierre Aycoberry, *The Nazi Question: An Essay on the Interpretation of National Socialism* (New York, NY: Pantheon, 1981). One of the most interesting contemporary accounts is in a book of extracts from political tracts edited by Michael Oakeshott, *The Social and Political Doctrines of Contemporary Europe* (Cambridge: Cambridge University Press, 1940): Oakeshott was unable to obtain copyright permission to reprint passages from Adolf Hitler's *Mein Kampf*, so he paraphrased them, with a remarkable result as a finely trained philosophical mind grappled with the banalities and confused logic of Hitler's thought.

Ian Kershaw's two-volume biography of Hitler is a modern classic, a superb study integrating social history with the study of the psychology of dictatorship: *Hitler: 1889–1936: Hubris* (London: Allen Lane, 1998) and *Hitler, 1936–45: Nemesis* (New York, NY: Norton, 2000). Thomas Weber has recently added an important element to our understanding of Hitler's political and intellectual background, *Becoming Hitler: The Making of a Nazi* (New York, NY: Basic Books, 2017). Karl Dietrich Bracher's *The German Dictatorship: The Origins, Structure, and Effects of National Socialism* (New York, NY: Holt, Reinhart & Winston, 1970) is a broad survey. On the problems of Weimar democracy, a useful guide to the debate is in Ian Kershaw (ed.), *Weimar: Why did German Democracy Fail?* (London: Weidenfeld & Nicolson, 1990). A good survey is given by Hans Mommsen (transl. Elborg Forster and Larry Eugene Jones), *The Rise and Fall of Weimar Democracy* (Chapel Hill, NC: University of North Carolina Press, 1996). On the Nazi rise to power, see William Sheridan Allen, dealing with a case study of a small town: *The Nazi Seizure of Power: The Experience of a Single German Town, 1922–1945*, rev. ed. (New York, NY: F. Watts, 1984); Thomas Childers, *The Nazi Voter: The Social Foundations of Fascism in Germany, 1919–1933* (Chapel Hill, NC: University of North Carolina Press, 1983); and Richard Hamilton, *Who Voted for Hitler?* (Princeton, NJ: Princeton University Press, 1982). The most modern and complete study of voting for the Nazis is by Jürgen Falter, *Hitlers Wähler* (Munich: Beck, 1991).

On the Nazi regime, see Richard J. Evans, *The Third Reich in Power*, 2005, and *The Third Reich at War*, 2008 (both New York, NY: Penguin). David Welch, *Propaganda and the German Cinema, 1933–1945* (Oxford: Clarendon Press, 1983) is a subtle study of Nazi propaganda; there is also a large study of the major German film company: Klaus Kreimeier (transl. Robert and Rita Kimber), *The Ufa Story: a History of German's Greatest Film Company, 1918–1945* (New York, NY: Hill & Wang, 1996). The best biography of the Propaganda Minister Joseph Goebbels is Peter Longerich (transl. Alan Bance, Jeremy Noakes, and Lesley Sharpe) *Goebbels: A Biography* (New York, NY: Random House, 2015), which replaces Ralf Georg Reuth's still interesting *Joseph Goebbels* (New York, NY: Harcourt Brace, 1993). There is also a fine biography of Himmler: Peter Longerich, *Heinrich Himmler: A Life* (Oxford: Oxford University Press, 2011); and of Reinhard Heydrich by Robert Gerwarth, *Hitler's Hangman: The Life of Heydrich* (New Haven, CT: Yale University Press, 2011).

On the German economy, the standard work is Adam Tooze, *The Wages of Destruction: The Making and Breaking of the Nazi Economy* (London: Allen Lane, 2006). Albert Speer is the subject of a biography by Martin Kitchen, *Speer: Hitler's Architect* (New Haven, CT: Yale University Press, 2015), as well as the author of an interesting but mendacious account of Nazi Germany and his role in it, (transl. Richard and

Clara Winston), *Inside the Third Reich*, New York, NY: Macmillan, 1970). Tim Mason's *Social Policy in the Third Reich* (Oxford: Oxford University Press, 1993) is a classic study. Peter Hayes, *Industry and Ideology: IG Farben in the Nazi Era* (Cambridge: Cambridge University Press, 1987); and Gerald D. Feldman, *Allianz* (Cambridge: Cambridge University Press, 2002) are model studies of the complexity of German business life. Neil Gregor makes an interesting case about the continuity of business plans from the war to the postwar world: *Daimler-Benz in the Third Reich* (New Haven, CT: Yale University Press, 1998). On Nazism and economic expansion, see Stephen G. Gross, *Export Empire: German Soft Power in Southeastern Europe, 1890–1945* (Cambridge: Cambridge University Press, 2015).

There are several good biographies of Mussolini, in particular Denis Mack Smith, *Mussolini* (New York: Knopf, 1982); and R.J.B. Bosworth, *Mussolini* (New York, NY: Hodder Arnold, 2002). Renzo de Felice's epochal multi-volume biography has never been translated from Italian. On Italian cultural life, see Victoria de Grazia, *The Culture of Consent: Leisure in Fascist Italy* (Cambridge: Cambridge University Press, 1981); and Marla Stone, *The Patron State: Culture and Politics in Fascist Italy* (Princeton, NJ: Princeton University Press, 1998).

On the Spanish Civil War, begin with the epic history by Hugh Thomas, *The Spanish Civil War*, 3rd edn (London: Hamish Hamilton, 1986). Paul Preston has written a masterly *Franco: A Biography* (London: HarperCollins, 1993). See also his *The Coming of the Spanish Civil War: Reform, Reaction, and Revolution in the Second Republic* (London: Routledge, 1994). Shlomo Ben-Ami, *The Origins of the Second Republic in Spain* (Oxford: Oxford University Press, 1978) presents the story of the Republic.

Interwar democracies

On France in the Third Republic, there are some classic essays in Stanley Hoffman's *Decline or Renewal? France since the 1930s* (New York, NY: Viking Press, 1974). See also the very interesting book by Julian Jackson, *The Popular Front in France: Defending Democracy, 1934–1938* (Cambridge: Cambridge University Press, 1987). Philip Nord gives a beautiful account of the debate about the end of the Republic: *France 1940: Defending the Republic* (New Haven, CT: Yale University Press, 2015).

The United Kingdom is very well analyzed in A.J.P. Taylor's classic *English History: 1914– 1945* (Oxford: Oxford University Press, 1965), and in two wonderful biographies: David Marquand, *Ramsay MacDonald* (London: Jonathan Cape, 1977); and Philip Williamson, *Stanley Baldwin: Conservative Leadership and National Values* (Cambridge: Cambridge University Press, 1999). On the links between domestic and foreign policy, see Maurice Cowling, *The Impact of Hitler: British Politics and British Policy, 1933–1940* (Cambridge: Cambridge University Press, 1975).

Sheri Berman's *The Social Democratic Moment: Ideas and Politics in the Making of Interwar Europe* (Cambridge, MA: Harvard University Press, 1998) is illuminating on Sweden and the welfare state, and on the reasons why similar German initiatives failed.

Eastern Europe

For interwar eastern Europe, see Antony Polonsky, *The Little Dictators: The History of Eastern Europe since 1918* (London: Routledge and Kegan Paul, 1975). The issue of minorities is dealt with unsympathetically by C.A. Macartney, *National States and National Minorities* (London: Oxford University Press, 1934). See also Carol Fink, "Defender of minorities: Germany in the League of Nations 1926–1930", *Central European History*, 1972, pp. 330– 57; and Inis L. Claude, Jr, *National Minorities: An International Problem* (Cambridge, MA: Harvard University Press, 1955). On the Soviet Union, the most important work is Hélène Carrère d'Encausse (transl. Nancy Festinger), *The Great Challenge: Nationalities and the Bolshevik State, 1917–1930* (New York, NY: Holmes & Meier, 1992).

Stalinism

Of the many biographies of Stalin, Isaac Deutscher's *Stalin: A Political Biography* (London and New York, NY: Oxford University Press, 1949) is the most accessible, Robert Tucker's *Stalin in Power: The Revolution from Above, 1928–1941* (New York, NY: Norton, 1990) the most balanced, Adam Ulam's *Stalin: The Man and his Era* (New York, NY: Viking Press, 1973) the clearest, and Roy Medvedev's (transl. Colleen Taylor) *Let History Judge: The Origins and Consequences of Stalinism* (New York, NY: Vintage Books, 1971) the most passionate, and Dmitri Volkogonov's (ed. and transl. Harold Shukman), *Stalin: Triumph and Tragedy* (London: Weidenfeld & Nicolson, 1991) is interesting in its archival revelations. All are superseded by the superb work of Stephen Kotkin, *Stalin: Paradoxes of Power, 1878–1928* (New York, NY: Penguin, 2015); and *Stalin: Waiting for Hitler, 1929–1941* (New York, NY: Penguin, 2017). The ruling party is best approached through the work of Leonard Schapiro, *The Communist Party of the Soviet Union*, 2nd edn (London: Eyre & Spottiswoode, 1970). The work of Moshe Lewin has been tremendously important in understanding the social history of the 1930s: *The Making of the Soviet System: Essays in the Social History of Interwar Russia* (New York, NY: Pantheon Books, 1985). See also the classic regional study by Merle Fainsod, *Smolensk under Soviet Rule* (Cambridge, MA: Harvard University Press, 1958); and Olga A. Narkiewicz, *The Making of the Soviet State Apparatus*

484 Further reading

(Manchester: Manchester University Press, 1970). Anne Applebaum, *Red Famine: Stalin's War on Ukraine* (New York, NY: Penguin, 2017) deals with the great Ukrainian famine, sometimes called the Holodomor. A peculiar, and largely failed, attempt to show that the purges were driven from below is J. Arch Getty, *Origins of the Great Purges: The Soviet Communist Party Reconsidered, 1933–1938* (Cambridge: Cambridge University Press, 1985). Sheila Fitzpatrick offers a more nuanced version of the same thesis: *Everyday Stalinism: Ordinary Life in Extraordinary Times: Soviet Russia in the 1930s* (New York, NY: Oxford University Press, 1999). Stephen Kotkin's *Magnetic Mountain: Stalinism as a Civilization* (Berkeley, CA: University of California Press, 1995) is a superb example of applied social history. Robert Conquest's *The Great Terror: Stalin's Purge of the Thirties* (New York, NY: Macmillan, 1968) is still the best account of the descent of Stalinist rule into terror in the 1930s, though the numbers of victims are too high: see the essay by Nicholas Werth in Stéphane Courtois (ed.) (transl. Jonathan Murphy and Mark Kramer), *The Black Book of Communism: Crimes, Terror, Repression* (Cambridge, MA: Harvard University Press, 1999). Victoria Bonnell, *Iconography of Power: Soviet Political Posters under Lenin and Stalin* (Berkeley, CA: University of California Press, 1997) is a superb study of propaganda.

Interwar economics

On the interwar depression, there are two classic histories: W. Arthur Lewis, *Economic Survey 1919–1939* (London: Methuen, 1949); and Charles P. Kindleberger, *The World in Depression*, 2nd edn (Berkeley, CA: University of California Press, 1986). The argument of the latter is actually more clearly put in the original 1973 edition. More recent works are the authoritative Barry Eichengreen, *Golden Fetters: the Gold Standard and the Great Depression* (New York, NY: Oxford University Press, 1992); Harold James, *The End of Globalization: Lessons from the Great Depression* (Cambridge, MA: Harvard University Press, 2001); and Patricia Clavin, *The Great Depression in Europe, 1929–1939* (New York, NY: St Martin's Press, 2000). National studies include Knut Borchardt (transl. Peter Lambert), *Perspectives on Modern German Economic History and Policy* (Cambridge: Cambridge University Press, 1991); Harold James, *The German Slump: Politics and Economics 1924–1936* (Oxford: Oxford University Press, 1986); and Julian Jackson, *The Politics of Depression in France, 1932–1936* (Cambridge: Cambridge University Press, 1985). Gianni Toniolo's *L'economia dell'Italia fascista* (Rome: Laterza, 1980) is alas not available in an English translation. An excellent way of considering the problems of economic policy is through the biography of the world's leading economist in the interwar period: Robert Skidelsky's three-volume *John Maynard Keynes* (London: Macmillan, 1983–2000).

Interwar international relations

The best-surviving but controversial survey of international relations in the interwar period is the two-volume survey by Zara Steiner, *The Lights that Failed: European International History 1919–1933* (Oxford: Oxford University Press, 2005); and *The Triumph of the Dark: European International History 1933–1939* (Oxford: Oxford University Press, 2010). E.H. Carr, *International Relations between the Two World Wars, 1919–1939* (London: Macmillan, 1948) is still important. For a further development of Carr's realist thought, see his *The Twenty Years Crisis 1919–1939* (London: Macmillan, 1939); and Hans Morgenthau, *Politics among Nations: The Struggle for Power and Peace* (New York, NY: Knopf, 1948). On the League of Nations, see F.S. Northedge, *The League of Nations: Its Life and Times, 1920–1946* (New York, NY: Holmes and Meier, 1986); Patricia Clavin, *Securing the World Economy: The Reinvention of the League of Nations, 1920–1946* (Oxford: Oxford University Press, 2013); and Susan Pedersen, *The Guardians: The League of Nations and the Crisis of Empire* (New York, NY: Oxford University Press, 2015). Henry Kissinger's *Diplomacy* (New York, NY: Simon & Schuster, 1994) is masterly and consistently thought-provoking. On the origins of war, A.J.P. Taylor's *The Origins of the Second World War* (London: Hamilton, 1961) was the subject of a vigorous demolition by Hugh Trevor-Roper, originally in the journal *Encounter*. The debate between the two, one of the most sheerly enjoyable scholarly polemics on this period, is reproduced in Esmonde M. Robertson (ed.), *The Origins of the Second World War: Historical Interpretations* (London: Macmillan, 1971). Taylor is himself the subject of an interesting biography by Kathleen Burk, *Troublemaker: The Life and History of A.J.P. Taylor* (New Haven, CT: Yale University Press, 2000), which shows that Taylor had not bothered to read *Mein Kampf* before writing about German foreign policy in the 1930s. A more recent book, by Donald Cameron Watt, *How War Came: The Immediate Origins of the Second World War* (London: Heinemann, 1989) is interesting but as detailed diplomatic history suffers from some rather embarrassing mistakes. To understand the folly of British diplomacy at the time, it is revealing to read Nevile Henderson's *Failure of a Mission* (New York, NY: Putnam, 1940). Hitler's interpreter, Paul Schmidt, provided a fascinating glimpse into the way the dictator conducted foreign policy: (ed. R.H.C. Steed), *Hitler's Interpreter* (New York, NY: Macmillan, 1951).

The Second World War

The best general overview of the war is Gerhard L. Weinberg, *A World at Arms: A Global History of World War II* (Cambridge: Cambridge University Press, 1994). There is a useful guide in the form of annotated maps in Richard Overy, *The Penguin Historical Atlas of the Third Reich* (London: Penguin Books, 1996).

On the Second World War economy, see Alan S. Milward's *German Economy at War* (London: Athlone Press, 1965) and *War, Economy and Society 1939–1945* (London: Allen Lane, 1977). More recent is Mark Harrison, *Economics of World War II: Six Great Powers in International Comparison* (Cambridge: Cambridge University Press, 1998); and Richard Overy, *Why the Allies Won* (London: Jonathan Cape, 1995), which helps to put economics in a broader setting. Recently, there have been many historical commissions investigating the contributions of the neutrals to the continuation of the war. The discussion can be seen in Stuart E. Eizenstat, *U.S. and Allied Effort to Recover and Restore Gold and Other Assets Stolen or Hidden by Germany During World War II* (Washington, DC: US State Department, 1997); and Independent Commission of Experts, *Switzerland, National Socialism and the Second World War* (Zurich: Pendo, 2002). On the question of the compensation of historical injustices, see Elazar Barkan, *The Guilt of Nations: Restitution and Negotiating Historical Injustices* (New York, NY: Norton, 2000).

On the controversial issue of Pope Pius XII, see the classic works of Saul Friedländer (transl. Charles Fullman), *Pius XII and the Third Reich; a Documentation* (New York, NY: Knopf, 1966); and Owen Chadwick, *Britain and the Vatican during the Second World War* (Cambridge: Cambridge University Press, 1986). John Conway has provided a sober assessment: "The Vatican, Germany and the Holocaust", in P. Kent and J.F. Pollard, *Papal Diplomacy in the Modern Age* (Westport, CT: Praeger, 1994). John Cornwell, *Hitler's Pope: The Secret History of Pius XII* (London: Viking, 1999) promises much, but is less revolutionary than its title. See also Susan Zuccotti, *Under His Very Windows: The Vatican and the Holocaust in Italy* (New Haven, CT: Yale University Press, 2000); Giovanni Miccoli, *I Dilemmi e i Silenzi di Pio XII* (Milan: Rizzoli, 2000); Alessandro Duce, *Pio XII e la Polonia: 1939–1945* (Rome: Edizioni Studium, 1997); Carol Rittner and John K. Roth, *Pope Pius XII and the Holocaust* (London: Leicester University Press, 2002); and David Kertzer, *The Pope and Mussolini: The Secret History of Pius XI and the Rise of Fascism in Europe* (New York, NY: Random House, 2014).

The history of the Holocaust is best approached through Raoul Hilberg, *Destruction of the European Jews* (New York, NY: Holmes & Meier, 1985); and Saul Friedländer, *Nazi Germany and the Jews: the Years of Persecution 1933–1939*, 1997, and *The Years of Extermination: Nazi Germany and the Jews, 1939–1945*, 2006 (both New York, NY: HarperCollins). There is a provocative and controversial book by Arno Mayer, *Why Did the Heavens Not Darken?* (New York, NY: Pantheon, 1989), which when it appeared was viciously reviewed by Daniel Jonah Goldhagen, who went on to write a really simplistic account: *Hitler's Willing Executioners: Ordinary Germans and the Holocaust* (New York, NY: Knopf, 1996). Christopher Browning, *Path to Genocide: Essays on Launching the Final Solution* (Cambridge: Cambridge University Press, 1992) is lucid and balanced. Henry Friedländer,

The Origins of Nazi Genocide: From Euthanasia to Final Solution (Chapel Hill, NC: University of North Carolina Press, 1995) shows the links between the killing of the disabled and the Holocaust.

Occupied and Vichy France has produced some superb historical analysis, starting with the classic by Robert Paxton, *Vichy France: Old Guard and New Order, 1940–1944* (New York, NY: Knopf, 1972); and Michael Marrus and Robert Paxton, *Vichy France and the Jews* (New York, NY: Basic Books, 1981). More recently there have been three superb overviews: Philippe Burrin (transl. Janet Lloyd), *France under the Germans: Collaboration and Compromise* (New York, NY: New Press, 1996); Robert Gildea, *Marianne in Chains: In Search of the German Occupation, 1940–1945* (London: Macmillan, 2002); and Julian Jackson, *France: The Dark Years, 1940–1944* (Oxford: Oxford University Press, 2001). Edward Spears, *Two Men who Saved France* (London: Eyre and Spottiswoode, 1966) contrasts Pétain and de Gaulle. On other occupied countries, see Jan Gross, *Polish Society under German Occupation: The Generalgouvernement, 1939–1944* (Princeton, NJ: Princeton University Press, 1979); Jan M. Ciechanowski, *The Warsaw Rising of 1944* (Cambridge: Cambridge University Press, 1974); and Jan Gross, *Neighbors: The Destruction of the Jewish Community in Jedwabne, Poland* (Princeton, NJ: Princeton University Press, 2001). See also Alex Alexiev, *Soviet Nationalities in German Wartime Strategy 1941–1945* (Santa Monica, CA: Rand, 1982); Christopher Browning, "Wehrmacht reprisal policy and the murder of male Jews in Serbia", in his book *Fateful Months: Essays on the Emergence of the Final Solution* (New York, NY: Holmes & Meier, 1985); and Alexander Dallin, *German Rule in Russia: A Study of Occupation Policies* (New York, NY: St Martin's Press, 1957). For a contrast, see Mark Harrison and John Barber, *The Soviet Home Front 1941–45* (London: Longman, 1991).

The postwar world and European integration

On postwar planning and the European Recovery Program, see Barry Eichengreen (ed.), *Europe's Post-War Recovery* (Cambridge: Cambridge University Press, 1995); Charles Maier and Günter Bischof, *The Marshall Plan and Germany* (Providence, RI: Berg, 1991); and Michael Hogan, *The Marshall Plan: America, Britain, and the Reconstruction of Western Europe 1947–1952* (Cambridge: Cambridge University Press, 1987). Charles Maier wrote an important interpretative essay: "The two postwar eras and the conditions for stability in twentieth-century western Europe", *American Historical Review* 86 (1981). Alec Cairncross, *The Price of War* (Oxford: Blackwell, 1986) gives a good account of British dilemmas.

On general economic history, see Bart van Ark and Nicholas Crafts (eds), *Quantitative Aspects of Post-War European Economic Growth* (Cambridge: Cambridge University Press, 1996); and Angus Maddison, *Phases of Capitalist Development* (Oxford: Oxford University Press, 1982).

The evolution of the European idea and of European integration is best approached through the hagiographical Walter Lipgens (transl. P.S. Falla and A.J. Ryder), *A History of European Integration* (Oxford: Clarendon Press, 1982), and the skeptical Alan Milward, *The Reconstruction of Western Europe, 1945–1951* (Berkeley, CA: University of California Press, 1984); see also Alan Milward (with George Brennan and Federico Romero), *The European Rescue of the Nation State* (London: Routledge, 1992). Timothy Garton-Ash, *In Europe's Name: Germany and the Divided Continent* (New York, NY: Vintage Press, 1994) has produced an interesting account of both how western Europe worked, and how it affected the communist bloc. Wolfram Kaiser, *Christian Democracy and the Origins of the European Union* (Cambridge: Cambridge University Press, 2007) sets a context. Andrew Moravcsik, *The Choice for Europe: Social Purpose and State Power from Messina to Maastricht* (Ithaca, NY: Cornell University Press, 1998) is a very stimulating recent study of the connection between domestic politics and European integration. For some recent interpretations, see also Larry Siedentop, *Democracy in Europe* (New York, NY: Columbia University Press, 2001). A good recent account is Luuk van Middelaar, *The Passage to Europe: How a Continent Became a Union* (New Haven, CT: Yale University Press, 2013).

The Cold War context is best approached through John Lewis Gaddis, *The United States and the Origins of the Cold War, 1941–1947* (New York, NY: Columbia University Press, 1972) and *We Now Know: Rethinking Cold War History* (Oxford: Clarendon Press, 1997). Some older books, such as Herbert Feis, *Churchill, Roosevelt, Stalin: The War They Waged and the Peace They Sought* (Princeton, NJ: Princeton University Press, 1957) and *From Trust to Terror: The Onset of the Cold War, 1945–1950* (New York, NY: Norton, 1970) are still revealing. David Reynolds (ed.), *The Origins of the Cold War in Europe: International Perspectives* (New Haven, CT: Yale University Press, 1994) contains important essays on the different national settings of the Cold War.

Individual postwar national histories

France of the Fourth Republic is well dealt with in Philip M. Williams, *Crisis and Compromise: Politics in the Fourth Republic* (London: Longmans, 1964); and by Philip Nord, *France's New Deal: From the Thirties to the Postwar Era* (Princeton, NJ: Princeton University Press, 2010); and Herrick Chapman, *France's Long Reconstruction: In Search of the Modern Republic* (Cambridge, MA: Harvard University Press, 2018). See also Ronald Tiersky, *French Communism, 1920–1972* (New York, NY: Columbia University Press, 1974). On the end of empire, see Miles Kahler, *Decolonization in Britain and France: the Domestic Consequences of International Relations* (Princeton, NJ: Princeton University Press, 1984); and more recently Matthew Connelly, *A Diplomatic Revolution: Algeria's Fight for Independence and the Origins of the Post-Cold War Era* (New York, NY: Oxford University Press, 2003); and Todd Shepard, *The Invention of Decolonization: The Algerian War and the Remaking of France* (Ithaca, NY: Cornell University Press, 2006) (both about the Algerian War). On the issue of Americanization and consumer culture, see Richard Kuisel, *Seducing the French* (Cambridge: Cambridge University Press, 1993). The Algerian War is covered vividly in Alastair Horne, *A Savage War of Peace, Algeria, 1954–1962* (London: Macmillan, 1977). De Gaulle is the subject of a wonderful biography by Robert Lacouture, alas abbreviated in the English translation (by Patrick O'Brian and Alan Sheridan): *De Gaulle the Rebel 1890–1944* (New York, NY: Norton, 1990), and *De Gaulle the Ruler 1945–1970* (New York, NY: Norton, 1992). Most recently, there is a biography by Julian Jackson, *De Gaulle* (Cambridge, MA: Harvard University Press, 2018). See also Alain Peyrefitte, *C'était de Gaulle* (Paris: Editions de Fallois, Fayard, 1994–96). But de Gaulle's own memoirs are a masterpiece of literature: *War Memoirs I: Call to Honor 1940–42* (London: Collins, 1955), and *War Memoirs II: Unity 1942–44* (London: Weidenfeld & Nicolson, 1959). A good start to the Fifth Republic is William G. Andrews and Stanley Hoffmann, *The Fifth Republic at Twenty* (Albany, NY: State University of New York Press, 1981). There are several studies of Gaullism, including Anthony Hartley, *Gaullism: The Rise and Fall of a Political Movement* (London: Routledge, 1972). Jean-Jacques Servan-Schreiber (transl. Ronald Steel), *The American Challenge* (New York, NY: Atheneum, 1968) is essential to understanding how France viewed Europe and the United States. Ronald Tiersky, *François Mitterrand: The Last French President* (New York, NY: St Martin's Press, 2000) is helpful; but the best sources on the Mitterrand period are the compelling diaries and notebooks of Jacques Attali (*Verbatim*, 3 vols, Paris: Fayard, 1993–95). See also Philip Gordon and Sophie Meunier's *The French Challenge: Adapting to Globalization* (Washington, DC: Brookings Institution Press, 2001).

On Italy, see above all two books by Paul Ginsborg, *A History of Contemporary Italy: Society and Politics, 1943–1988* (London: Penguin, 1990) and *Italy and its Discontents: Family, Civil Society, State, 1980–2001* (London: Allen Lane, 2001).

Two important works on the Iberian transformations of the 1970s are Paul Preston, *The Triumph of Democracy in Spain* (London: Routledge, 1996); and Nancy Bermeo, *The Revolution Within the Revolution: Workers' Control in Rural Portugal* (Princeton, NJ: Princeton University Press, 1986).

There are some good overall studies of British politics, above all Peter Clarke's *Hope and Glory: Britain 1900–1990* (London: Allen Lane, 1996); and Peter Hennessy's *The Prime Ministers: the Office and its Holders since 1945* (New York, NY: Palgrave, 2001); Andrew Roberts, *Eminent Churchillians* (London: Weidenfeld & Nicolson, 1994); a series of colorful and convincing studies by David Kynaston (*Austerity Britain, 1945–51*, 2007, *Family Britain, 1951–57*, 2009, and *Modernity Britain, 1957–62*, 2014, all London: Bloomsbury); and some quite wonderful political biographies. This indeed emerged as the best genre for the study of British politics. Among the best are Alan Bullock's *Ernest Bevin, Foreign Secretary, 1945–1951* (New York, NY: Norton, 1983); Alastair Horne's two-volume *Harold Macmillan* (London: Macmillan, 1988–1989); Ben Pimlott, *Harold Wilson* (London: HarperCollins, 1992); Philip Ziegler, *Wilson: The Authorised Life of Lord Wilson of Rievaulx* (London: Weidenfeld & Nicolson, 1993); and John Campbell, *Edward Heath: A Biography* (London: Jonathan Cape, 1993). The finest account of the sensibilities of the mid-twentieth-century United Kingdom is a biography of a man who never made it quite to the top: Anthony Howard, *RAB: The Life of R.A. Butler* (London: Jonathan Cape, 1987). Wilson is best viewed through the eyes of his ministers who kept diaries, of whom the most interesting are Richard Crossman (ed. Anthony Howard), *The Crossman Diaries: Selections from the Diaries of a Cabinet Minister, 1964–1970* (London: Hamish Hamilton and Jonathan Cape, 1979); Barbara Castle, *The Castle Diaries, 1964–70* (London: Weidenfeld & Nicolson, 1984); and Tony Benn, *Out of the Wilderness: Diaries 1963–67*, 1987, and *Office without Power: Diaries 1968–72*, 1988 (both London: Hutchinson). John Major was given a rather unflattering profile by his brother, Terry Major-Ball, *Major: Memories of an Older Brother* (London: Duckworth, 1994).

Margaret Thatcher elicited many volumes of vitriolic denunciation, most of which have worn rather badly over time. The most interesting is a novel, Iris Murdoch's *The Book and the Brotherhood* (London: Chatto & Windus, 1987), which is deeply revealing about the intelligentsia who derided Thatcher. See also the fine studies by Hugo Young, *One of Us: A Biography of Margaret Thatcher* (London: Macmillan, 1989); and Peter Jenkins, *Mrs. Thatcher's Revolution: The Ending of the Socialist Era* (London: Jonathan Cape, 1987), who is informative and critical, as are William Keegan, *Mrs Thatcher's Economic Experiment* (London: Allen Lane, 1984) and Philip Stephens, *Politics and the Pound: The Conservatives' Struggle with Sterling* (London: Macmillan, 1996). The definitive biography is by Charles Moore, *Margaret Thatcher: The Authorized Biography: Volume One: From Grantham to the Falklands* (New York: Knopf, 2013) and *The Authorized Biography, Volume Two: Everything She Wants* (London: Allen Lane, 2015). Nigel Lawson, *The View from No. 11: Memoirs of a Tory Radical* (London and New York, NY: Bantam Press, 1992) is a superb account by a key maker of economic policy. Patrick Higgins gives a new dimension to the understanding of British developments: *Heterosexual Dictatorship: Male Homosexuality in Postwar Britain* (London: Fourth Estate, 1996).

For Germany, the best overall surveys are Mary Fulbrook (ed.), *Twentieth-Century Germany: Politics, Culture and Society 1918–1990* (London: Arnold, 2001); and Klaus Larres, *Germany since World War II: From Occupation to Unification and Beyond (Short Oxford History of Germany)* (Oxford: Oxford University Press, 2012). Two good books which examine the legacy of the past for postwar Germany are Jeffrey Herf, *Divided Memory: The Nazi Past in the Two Germanys* (Cambridge, MA: Harvard University Press, 1997); and Norbert Frei (transl. Joel Golb), *Adenauer's Germany and the Nazi Past: The Politics of Amnesty and Integration* (New York, NY: Columbia University Press, 2002). The fine two-volume biography of Adenauer by Hans Peter Schwarz unfortunately is not available in an English translation: *Die Ära Adenauer: Gründerjahre der Republik, 1949–1957*, 1981, and *Die Ära Adenauer: Epochenwechsel, 1957–1963*, 1983 (both Stuttgart: Deutsche Verlags-Anstalt). On the Willy Brandt years, the best source is Arnulf Baring, *Machtwechsel: die Ära Brandt-Scheel* (Stuttgart: Deutsche Verlags-Anstalt, 1982). On East Germany, see Mary Fulbrook, *Anatomy of a Dictatorship: Inside the GDR, 1949–1989* (New York, NY: Oxford University Press, 1995). Economic slowdown and the end of the economic miracle are analyzed in Herbert Giersch, Karl-Heinz Paqué, and Holger Schmieding, *The Fading Miracle: Four Decades of Market Economy in Germany* (Cambridge: Cambridge University Press, 1992).

1968

On the phenomenon of 1968 see Carole Fink, Philip Gassert, and Detlef Junker (eds), *1968: The World Transformed* (Cambridge: Cambridge University Press, 1998); also Diane Kunz (ed.), *The Diplomacy of the Crucial Decade: American Foreign Relations during the 1960s* (New York, NY: Columbia University Press, 1994); and the account of a participant, Tariq Ali: *1968 and After: Inside the Revolution* (London: Blond & Briggs, 1978). See also Ronald Fraser, *1968: A Student Generation in Revolt* (London: Chatto & Windus, 1988). Jillian Becker provides an unsympathetic and chillingly accurate account of the development of German terrorism: *Hitler's Children: The Story of the Baader–Meinhof Terrorist Gang* (Philadelphia, PA: Lippincott, 1977). An interesting text in the spirit of 1968, which refuses to say that the RAF leaders killed themselves, is Geoff Eley, *Forging Democracy: The History of the Left in Europe 1850–2000* (New York, NY: Oxford University Press, 2002).

The welfare state and domestic politics

For an introduction to the welfare state, see Gosta Esping-Andersen, *Politics Against Markets: the Social Democratic Road to Power*, 1985, and *Three Worlds of Welfare Capitalism*, 1990 (both Princeton, NJ: Princeton University Press). Edmund Dell, *A Strange Eventful History: Democratic Socialism in Britain* (London: HarperCollins, 2000) is a fine history in the British setting. David Marquand and Anthony Seldon examine *Ideas that Shaped Post-War Britain* (London: Fontana Press, 1996); and Peter Hall (ed.) extends the study internationally: *The Political Power of Economic Ideas: Keynesianism Across Nations* (Princeton, NJ: Princeton University

Press, 1989). For a general account, see also Herman Van der Wee, *Prosperity and Upheaval: The World Economy 1945–1980* (Berkeley, CA: University of California Press, 1986).

A good introduction to the literature on corruption is given in Stephen Kotkin and András Sajó (eds), *Political Corruption in Transition: A Sceptic's Handbook* (Budapest: Central European University Press, 2000).

Eastern Europe

On communism and eastern Europe, Czesław Miłosz (transl. Jane Zielonko), *The Captive Mind* (New York, NY: Knopf, 1953) is deeply revealing. So is the penitential of Arthur Koestler (ed. Richard Crossman), *The God That Failed* (New York, NY: Harper, 1949). The best account of Marxist thought is Leszek Kołakowski's three-volume *Main Currents of Marxism* (Oxford: Oxford University Press, 1978). On eastern Europe in general, see Hugh Seton-Watson, *The East European Revolution* (New York, NY: Praeger, 1956); and Olga A. Narkiewicz, *Petrification and Progress: Communist Leaders in Eastern Europe, 1956–1988* (London: Harvester Wheatsheaf, 1990). The Yugoslav communist dissident, Milovan Djilas, provided some powerful insights, especially in *The New Class: An Analysis of the Communist System* (New York, NY: Praeger, 1957) and (transl. Michael B. Petrovich) *Conversations with Stalin* (New York, NY: Harcourt, Brace & World, 1962). For Yugoslavia specifically, see Milovan Djilas, *Tito: The Story from the Inside* (London: Weidenfeld & Nicolson, 1981); and Ivo Banac, *With Stalin against Tito: Cominformist Splits in Yugoslav Communism* (Ithaca, NY: Cornell University Press, 1988).

On Soviet politics after the Second World War, there is great insight into alternative paths to post-Stalinism in Amy Knight, *Beria: Stalin's First Lieutenant* (Princeton, NJ: Princeton University Press, 1993). See also Giuseppe Boffa (transl. Carl Marzani), *Inside the Khrushchev Era* (New York, NY: Marzani & Munsell, 1959); Robert Tucker, *Political Culture and Leadership in Soviet-Russia* (New York, NY: Norton, 1987); and Stephen F. Cohen (ed.), *The Soviet Union since Stalin* (Bloomington, IN: Indiana University Press, 1980). A way of understanding the motivation of the Stalinist elite is offered in Teresa Toranska (transl. Agnieszka Kolakowska), *Oni: Stalin's Polish Puppets* (London: Collins, 1987). The important revolts in Hungary are discussed in Ferenc Fehér and Agnes Heller, *Hungary 1956 Revisited: The Message of a Revolution, a Quarter of a Century After* (London: Allen & Unwin, 1983). The year 1968 in Czechoslovakia is covered extensively by H. Gordon Skilling, *Czechoslovakia's Interrupted Revolution* (Princeton, NJ: Princeton University Press, 1976). On Poland after 1989, see the eyewitness account of Timothy Garton-Ash, *The Polish Revolution: Solidarity* (London: Granta Books, 1991); and a complex and insightful account by a Polish sociologist involved in the Solidarity struggles, Jadwiga Staniszkis (ed. Jan T. Gross), *Poland's Self-Limiting Revolution*

(Princeton, NJ: Princeton University Press, 1984). On the role of the Stasi in the collapse of East Germany, see David Childs and Richard Popplewell, *The Stasi: The East German Intelligence and Security Service* (Basingstoke: Macmillan, 1996).

Timothy Garton-Ash, *The Magic Lantern: The Revolution of '89 Witnessed in Warsaw, Budapest, Berlin and Prague* (New York, NY: Random House, 1990) is superb eyewitness journalism of the final round of revolutions against communism. A preliminary historical account is provided by Padraic Kenney, *A Carnival of Revolution: Central Europe 1989* (Princeton, NJ: Princeton University Press, 2002).

The wars in Yugoslavia have also produced some wonderful eyewitness accounts, of which the best is Roger Cohen, *Hearts Grown Brutal: Sagas of Sarajevo* (New York, NY: Random House, 1998). For a profound historical setting, see Noel Malcolm, *Bosnia: A Short History*, 1994, and *Kosovo: A Short History*, 1998 (both New York, NY: New York University Press). Some works which put former Yugoslavia in the context of other twentieth-century developments are Michael Ignatieff, *Blood and Belonging: Journeys into the New Nationalism* (New York, NY: Farrar Strauss Giroux, 1993); Gary Jonathan Bass, *Stay the Hand of Vengeance: The Politics of War Crimes Tribunals* (Princeton, NJ: Princeton University Press, 2000); and Norman M. Naimark, *Fires of Hatred: Ethnic Cleansing in Twentieth-Century Europe* (Cambridge, MA: Harvard University Press, 2001). On the international aspects of the Yugoslav wars, see Richard Ullman (ed.), *The World and Yugoslavia's Wars* (New York, NY: Council on Foreign Relations, 1996).

Russia in the 1990s has produced some fine near-instant accounts. The best are highly polemical. Jerry F. Hough, *Democratization and Revolution in the U.S.S.R. 1985–1991* (Washington, DC: Brookings Institution, 1997) is critical of Gorbachev's reforms. For an overall survey, see Stephen Kotkin, *Armageddon Averted: The Soviet-Collapse, 1970–2000* (Oxford: Oxford University Press, 2001). Chrystia Freeland shows how free-booting capitalism was established: *Sale of the Century: Russia's Wild Ride from Communism to Capitalism* (New York, NY: Crown Business, 2000). Janine Wedel, *Collision and Collusion: The Strange Case of Western Aid to Eastern Europe, 1989–1998* (New York, NY: St Martin's Press, 1998) shows what went wrong with foreign aid to Russia. Peter Reddaway and Dmitri Glinski denounce the IMF: *The Tragedy of Russia's Reforms: Market Bolshevism against Democracy* (Washington, DC: US Institute of Peace Press, 2001). The most sober assessment of Russia's economic reforms is given by Brigitte Granville and Peter Oppenheimer (eds), *Russia's Post-Communist Economy* (Oxford: Oxford University Press, 2001); and by Ånders Åslund, *Building Capitalism: The Transformation of the Former Soviet Bloc* (Cambridge: Cambridge University Press, 2002). More recently, see Ånders Åslund, *Ukraine: What Went Wrong and How to Fix It* (Washington, DC: Peterson Institute for International Economics, 2015).

On more recent developments in Russia's "near abroad": Andrew Wilson, *Ukraine Crisis, What It Means for the West* (New Haven, CT: Yale University Press, 2014). Hélène Carrère d'Encausse (transl. Franklin Philip), *The End of the Soviet Empire: The Triumph of the Nations* (New York, NY: Basic Books, 1993) looks at nationalities conflicts. On the Chechen wars, see John B. Dunlop, *Russia Confronts Chechnya: Roots of a Separatist Conflict* (Cambridge: Cambridge University Press, 1998); and Anatol Lieven, *Chechnya: Tombstone of Russian Power* (New Haven, CT: Yale University Press, 1998). Lieven has also written a fine study of the re-emergence of the Baltic republics: *The Baltic Revolution: Estonia, Latvia, Lithuania, and the Path to Independence* (New Haven, CT: Yale University Press, 1993).

Mikhail Gorbachev has a biography by William Taubman, *Gorbachev: His Life and Times* (New York, NY: Simon and Schuster, 2017). For Putin, see Masha Gessen, *The Man Without a Face: The Unlikely Rise of Vladimir Putin* (New York, NY: Riverhead Books 2012); and Simon Ostrovsky, *The Invention of Russia: The Rise of Putin and the Age of Fake News* (London: Penguin, 2017).

There are several biographies of the most commanding and profound figure of Europe's late twentieth century, of which the best are Tad Szulc, *Pope John Paul II: The Biography* (New York, NY: Scribner, 1995); and George Weigel, *Witness to Hope: The Biography of Pope John Paul II* (New York, NY: Cliff Street Books, 1999), which is more detailed about theological issues.

The crisis of Europe

Most accounts of the European crisis that coincided with or followed the financial crisis are gloomy; for instance, Jan Zielonka, *Is the EU Doomed?* (Cambridge: Polity, 2014); William Drozdiak, *Fractured Continent: Europe's Crises and the Fate of the West* (New York, NY: Norton, 2017); Ivan Krastev, *After Europe* (Philadelphia, PA: University of Pennsylvania Press, 2017). For an only slightly more upbeat assessment there is Jean-Claude Piris, *The Future of Europe: Towards a Two-Speed EU?* (Cambridge: Cambridge University Press, 2012).

For a discussion of populism in Europe, see Jan-Werner Müller's *What Is Populism?* (Philadelphia, PA: University Of Pennsylvania Press, 2016); Yascha Mounck, *The People vs. Democracy: Why Our Freedom is in Danger and How to Save It* (Cambridge, MA: Harvard University Press, 2018); Tim Snyder's illuminating *The Road to Unfreedom: Russia, Europe, America* (New York, NY: Crown, 2018); and Peter Pomerantsev's *Nothing Is True and Everything Is Possible: The Surreal Heart of the New Russia* (New York, NY: Public Affairs, 2014).

Like many epochal events in history, the Brexit vote has already produced a masterpiece of instant history: Tim Shipman's *All Out War:*

The Full Story of How Brexit Sank Britain's Political Class, 2016, and a follow up volume, *Fall Out: A Year of Political Mayhem*, 2017 (both London: William Collins). A more sociological treatment is Harold Clarke, Matthew Goodwin, and Paul Whiteley, *Brexit: Why Britain Voted to Leave the European Union* (Cambridge: Cambridge University Press, 2017). Kevin O'Rourke puts Brexit elegantly in a long-term historical context: *A Short History of Brexit: From Brentry to the Backstop* (London: Pelican, 2019); another account from an Irish perspective is the bitter-sweet and illuminating Fintan O'Toole, *Heroic Failure: Brexit and the Politics of Pain* (London: Head of Zeus, 2019).

The financial crisis is dealt with by many books. The most recent comprehensive accounts are Ashoka Mody, *EuroTragedy: A Drama in Nine Acts* (New York, NY: Oxford University Press, 2018); and Markus Brunnermeier, Harold James, and Jean-Pierre Landau, *The Euro and the Battle of Ideas* (Princeton, NJ: Princeton University Press, 2016). See also the authoritative chronology of the early years of the crisis by Carlo Bastasin, *Saving Europe: Anatomy of a Dream* (Washington, DC: Brookings, 2015). For a German perspective on the issue, see Hans-Werner Sinn, *The Euro Trap: On Bursting Bubbles, Budgets, and Beliefs* (New York, NY: Oxford University Press, 2014).

Index

Page numbers in **bold** refer to information in tables. Those in *italics* refer to figures and plates.